Frontiers in Economic History

Economic historians have contributed to the development of economics in a variety of ways, combining theory with quantitative methods, constructing new databases, promoting interdisciplinary approaches to historical topics, and using history as a lens to examine the long-term development of the economy. Frontiers in Economic History publishes manuscripts that push the frontiers of research in economic history in order to better explain past economic experiences and to understand how, why and when economic change occurs. Books in this series will highlight the value of economic history in shedding light on the ways in which economic factors influence growth as well as social and political developments. This series aims to establish a new standard of quality in the field while offering a global discussion forum toward a unified approach in the social sciences.

Leandro Prados de la Escosura

A Millennial View of Spain's Development

Essays in Economic History

OPEN ACCESS

Springer

Leandro Prados de la Escosura
Department of Social Sciences
Carlos III University of Madrid
Getafe, Spain

ISSN 2662-9771 ISSN 2662-978X (electronic)
Frontiers in Economic History
ISBN 978-3-031-60791-2 ISBN 978-3-031-60792-9 (eBook)
https://doi.org/10.1007/978-3-031-60792-9

This work was supported by Fundación Rafael del Pino

This Springer imprint is published by the registered company Springer Nature Switzerland AG
The registered company address is: Gewerbestrasse 11, 6330 Cham, Switzerland

"This book by one of Europe's leading economic historians provides major insights into Spain's economic growth and development since before the era of the Black Death. Based on painstaking quantitative research, it establishes, for the first time, the long-term trends as well as fluctuations in GDP per capita growth, capital accumulation, productivity, inequalities in income and other key measures. These results will help us better understand the great diversity of economic structures and trajectories across Western Europe since the late medieval era."

—*Şevket Pamuk,* Professor of Economics and Economic History, Bogaziçi University, Istanbul

"During several decades of intensive and fruitful activity, Leandro has produced a large amount of important contributions to the economic history of Spain, Latin America and the international economy as a whole. It is therefore very good news that we have now available in a single volume a revised and updated version of this valuable work."

—*Luis Bértola,* Professor of History, Economics and Social Development, Universidad de la República, Uruguay

"This book draws on a huge research effort to offer a quantitative outline of development of Spain. It deals with long-run growth and its determinants and also with its international dimension and its consequences on distribution. As such, model for any modern, data-based, country economic history."

—*Giovanni Federico,* Professor of Economic History at New York University Abu Dhabi

"For those with a serious interest in Spanish (and indeed European) economic history, A Millenial View is a must. In this impressive work, Leandro Prados ranges over a multitude of the most important issues and presents all we need to know in order to keep up-to-date in this rapidly changing field."

—*Jaime Reis,* Senior Research Fellow, Instituto de Ciências Sociais at University of Lisbon

To Ignacio

Preface

One autumn evening at Oxford in 1978, the late economic historian Gianni Toniolo told me that in our countries, Italy and Spain, too many historical interpretations are published (usually under the title of "essays"), but too few research monographs. I was then a graduate student and I took good note of my senior friend's words, promising myself to bear them in mind for my future work. I believe I have been faithful to that promise, and have always tried to provide solid empirical grounds for any interpretation I dared to put forward. Moreover, I have always insisted to my students that it is crucial to make explicit and transparent the construction of historical data and the hypotheses to be tested. This explains, or perhaps simply provides a convoluted excuse for my decision to assemble a collection of (research) essays on topics I have worked on over the past three and a half decades rather than produce a concise interpretative text.

By then I had published a research monograph on growth and backwardness in Spain between the 1780s and the 1930s, in which I proposed a revisionist quantitative interpretation to challenge the pessimistic *dependentist* view which prevailed at the time.[1]

From then on, I broadened the scope of my research on Spanish economic history both forwards, to include the last 100 years, and backwards, to the *de facto* end of the *Reconquista* (Reconquest) in the late thirteenth century. A selection of this research output provides the content of this volume, which is millennial in scope, although not all eras are covered in the same detail, as I emphasise the major developments, and thus the modern era receives disproportionate attention.

Thus, rather than a chronological narrative of Spain's historical development, this volume offers a mosaic of papers in which I address two issues: economic growth and its distribution (Part I), and the economic consequences of Spain's integration into the global economy (Part II). In order to place the chapters in historical context,

[1] Prados de la Escosura, L. (1988), *De imperio a nación. Crecimiento y atraso económico en España (1780 1930)*, Madrid: Alianza.

the volume opens with an overview of Spain's economic development from a millennial perspective.

In all but one case, the chapters in this volume draw on work that has previously appeared as journal articles or book chapters, which, in a few cases, I have co-authored, although they often depart from the latter, as I have carried out a thorough revision of the data and the narrative.

What are the main topics covered and what is the takeaway from it? In Part I, Chap. 2 addresses Spain's performance over the half a millennium between the end of the *Reconquista* and the beginnings of modern economic growth. It rejects an interpretation of the successive growing and shrinking phases that take place and account for the absence of a significant net improvement in average income over the long run in the conventional Malthusian framework, and stresses the synchronised evolution of per capita income and population, which grow and shrink simultaneously, consistent with a frontier economy such as pre industrial Spain's. Growth and decline and long-term stagnation are explained by individual and collective economic decisions under institutional constraints. Chapters 3 and 4 address distinctive features of modern economic growth: capital accumulation and labour productivity growth in which the latter depends on both capital deepening and efficiency gains in the use of broadly defined capital (human and physical). The main findings are that the net capital (wealth) stock-GDP ratio rose steadily since 1850, doubling in the last half century. Labour productivity accounted for all per capita GDP growth over time, with half of its growth resulting from capital deepening (that is, capital services per hour worked) and one-third from efficiency gains (total factor productivity). Labour productivity proceeded steadily, accelerating during the 1920s and from the mid-1950s to the late 1980s, but decelerating thereafter due to the fact that expanding sectors attracted less investment-specific technological progress, largely as a result of institutional constraints. Part I closes with an assessment of how the fruits of sustained economic growth were distributed over time (Chap. 5). Although growth and inequality do not move together over time, in the last century, the main phases of economic growth went hand-in-hand with a decline in inequality. The substantial fall in absolute poverty resulted from growth but also from a reduction in inequality during the interwar period and the late 1950s, and was eradicated by 1975.

In Part II, a defining event, the loss of the mainland American empire (Chap. 6) is assessed together with the impact of two global episodes, that of the industrial revolution on the terms of trade between Spain and Britain, and subsequently on Spanish well-being (Chap. 7) and the effects of opening-up and closing down during the first globalisation (Chap. 8). Although the loss of the colonies impacted negatively on the metropole in the short run, with a contraction of international trade and domestic investment and the Monarchy's revenues, its aggregate economic effects were narrower and less deep than conventionally assumed, and contributed to the demise of the Ancien Régime, paving the way for the liberal society (Chap. 6). The evolution of the terms of trade between Spain and Britain had a positive effect on Spain's welfare, as productive factors embodied in exportables improved in absolute and relative terms, supporting the view that Spain's relative decline in the nineteenth century cannot be blamed on specialization along lines of comparative advantage (Chap. 7). During the first globalization, opening up until 1890 allowed a net capital inflow that made it possible to meet the demand for investment boosting economic performance. Conversely, current account reversals in a context of macroeconomic domestic imperfections help explain the economic slowdown at the turn of the century (Chap. 8).

A research project spanning more than three decades incurs many academic and personal debts. The list of names below is surely incomplete, but even so, those who appear in it deserve my sincere thanks. Let me begin by expressing my gratitude to those who inspired me by their own work and example and often encouraged me to focus on particular issues. Patrick O'Brien's research provided inspiration for Chaps. 6 and 7 specifically, but also for the book as a whole. The influence of the late Angus Maddison is apparent in Chaps. 2–4. He persuaded me to devote a decade of my academic life to reconstructing Spain's historical national accounts, and insisted that I should take my research back to Roman times—although I stopped earlier and only returned as far as the Reconquista in my joint work with Carlos Álvarez-Nogal and Carlos Santiago-Caballero (see Chap. 2), from whom I have profited so much. Angus also provided an example of how to construct historical capital series and investigate the sources of long-run growth. However, it was the late Nick Crafts who most profoundly influenced my approach to labour productivity growth and its determinants. Needless to say, collaborating with Joan Rosés in Chap. 4 was an extraordinary experience from which I learnt much. Chapter 5 would not have been possible without the advice and example provided by Branko Milanovic and Jeff Williamson. Chapter 8 owes a great deal to Gabriel Tortella, the late Piero Tedde de Lorca, and the late Pablo Martín Aceña. It is also inspired by the work of Sebastián Edwards and Luis Catão and, it goes without saying, by the seminal contribution made by Joan Sardà Dexeus, a forerunner of modern Spanish economic history.

I would also like to acknowledge the most helpful comments and suggestions offered by Luis Ayala, Eva Benages, Luis Bértola, Juan Carmona Pidal, Luis Catão, Francisco Comín, Javier Cuenca Esteban, Joan Esteban, Pedro Fraile Balbín[+], Francisco Goerlich, María Gómez León, Alfonso Herranz-Loncán, Stefan Houpt, Santos Juliá[+], Humberto López, Agustín Llona, Enrique Llopis Agelán, Matilde Mas, César Molinas, Christian Morrisson[+], Alfonso Novales, Jordi Palafox, Francisco Pérez, M. Ángeles Pons, David Reher, Fernando del Rey, Juan Carlos Robledo, Carlos Rodríguez Braun, Richard Salvucci, Blanca Sánchez-Alonso, Pedro Schwartz, Lorenzo Serrano, Luis Servén, Javier Silvestre, James Simpson, Cecilio Tamarit, Antonio Tena Junguito, Ezequiel Uriel, Giovanni Vecchi, and Ilya Voskoboynikov.

Over the years, financial support was provided by the Spanish Ministry of Science and Innovation (Research Project 'Consolidating Economics', Consolider-Ingenio 2010 Programme) and the HI-POD Project, Seventh Research Framework Programme Contract no. 225342. I would also like to acknowledge Fundación Rafael del Pino's generous support through a research grant (Rafael del Pino Chair) without which this volume would not have been possible. In particular, I would like to express my appreciation to its director, Vicente Montes Gan, its head of research, Carlota Taboada, and its former director and member of the board of trustees, Amadeo Petitbò. Last but not least, Universidad Carlos III deserves my gratitude for providing the right research environment for more than three decades.

I am very grateful to Claude Diebolt and Mike Haupert, the academic editors of the Springer collection in which this book is published, for their generous invitation to contribute to it, and to Niko Chtouris, its publishing editor, for his help. I also thank Mark Hounsell for his excellent editing job.

On a personal note, I would like to express my deepest gratitude to Blanca Sánchez-Alonso for her encouragement, support and patience over almost four decades. The book is dedicated to Ignacio, my millennial son.

Madrid, Spain
December 2023

Leandro Prados-de-la-Escosura

About the Book

How much economic progress has Spain achieved and what impact had on living standards and income distribution over the very long run? Leandro Prados de la Escosura presents the evolution of the Spanish economy over the past seven centuries since the end of the Reconquest. Although levels of output per head in the early nineteenth century were not much different from those in the eve of the Black Death (1348), preindustrial Spain was far from stagnant. Phases of simultaneous per capita output and population expansion and shrinkage alternated, lending support to the recurring growth and frontier economy hypotheses. A long phase of sustained growth and lower inequality collapsed in the 1570s and gave way to another one of sluggish growth and higher inequality. Over of the last two centuries, real per capita income has improved substantially, driven by increased labour productivity, derived from a more intense and efficient use of physical and human capital per worker. Exposure to international competition has provided a stimulus for this. In European perspective, Spain underperformed up to 1950. Thereafter, Spain's economy caught up with advanced countries until 2007. Although the relationship between growth and inequality has not been linear, the most dynamic economic phases of the last century have been associated to an improvement in income distribution. Thus, modern economic growth is associated with an increase in the material well-being of its inhabitants.

Contents

About the Author

Leandro Prados-de-la-Escosura is Emeritus Professor at Universidad Carlos III, Madrid and a Research Fellow at the Centre for Economic Policy Research. He holds a D. Phil. (Oxford) and a Ph.D. Economics (Complutense, Madrid). He has served as President of the European Historical Economics Society (EHES) (2001–2003). He is an editor of the *Economic History Review* and belongs to different academic journals' editorial boards. He has taught at Georgetown University (Prince of Asturias Professor) and University of California, San Diego. He is currently Fundación Rafael del Pino Chair, and has been Honorary Maddison Chair (Groningen), Leverhulme Professorial Fellow (LSE), Visiting Fellow, All Souls College, Oxford, and Jean Monnet Fellow at the European University Institute (Florence). He is the author of *Spanish Economic Growth, 1850–2015* (Palgrave Macmillan, 2017) and *Human Development and the Path to Freedom* (Cambridge University Press, 2022). His current research interests are economic freedom and well-being in historical perspective and Spain's economic development in the very long run.

List of Figures

List of Tables

Chapter 1
Introduction: *A Millennial View of Spain's Development*

1.1 Introduction

The hockey stick is a popular depiction of economic evolution over the very long run, portraying a picture of persistent stagnation, interrupted only by the Industrial Revolution, which triggered widespread modern economic growth in the last two centuries.[1] The conventional explanation for the stagnation of average incomes prior to 1820 is the Malthusian view, in which land is in fixed supply, capital accumulation and technological change proceed, if at all, very slowly, and any increase in output per head prompts a direct response of population that cancels said increase.[2]

Does the historical evidence for the case of Spain support such a dichotomy between stagnation and growth? Let us take a look at Fig. 1.1. It represents the evolution of absolute and per capita GDP[3] from the *de facto* end of the *Reconquest* in the late thirteenth century to 2020.[4] Absolute GDP improved over time (220-fold up the present) but exhibited strong fluctuations until the nineteenth century, and only trebled up to 1820. The crucial issue however, is what happened to the evolution of GDP per person. Average income multiplied by more than 20 times over the last 750 years, but most of this gain was achieved in the last 200 years, and per capita

---

[1] Such a view has led some economists to model the transition from a society with stagnant living standards before 1820 to another in which they increase irreversibly. See, for example, Hansen and Prescott, 2002).

[2] See, for example, Clark (2008), and Galor and Weil (2000), who present strict and mild versions of the Malthusian interpretation, respectively.

[3] Their evolution is represented in semi-log scale which implies that changes in level are proportional and that the slope of the curve at any point corresponds to its growth rate.

[4] The Reconquest (*Reconquista*) is the name of a long process by which the Christian polities recaptured the territory occupied by the Muslims since the eighth century. It was practically ended by the late thirteenth century when only the Nazri kingdom of Granada remained independent and became a sort of protectorate of the kingdom of Castile until it was conquered by the Catholic Monarchs in 1492. See https://www.britannica.com/event/Reconquista

L. Prados de la Escosura, *A Millennial View of Spain's Development*, Frontiers in Economic History, https://doi.org/10.1007/978-3-031-60792-9_1

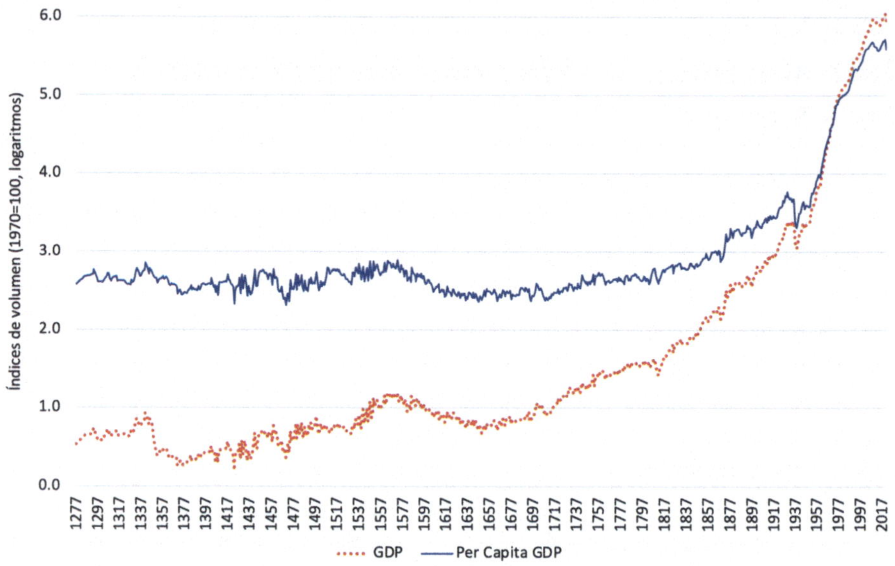

Fig. 1.1 Absolute and per capita real GDP, 1277–2020 (1970=100, natural logs). Sources: https://frdelpino.es/investigacion/en/category/01_social-sciences/01_spanish-economy/02_historical-perspective-spanish-economy/

GDP increase was about one-fifth from the 1270s to 1820. Such a small gain over half a millennium seems, at first sight, to provide support for the stagnation hypothesis. However, closer examination reveals that far from having a flat performance, per capita GDP exhibited growing and shrinking phases until the early nineteenth century. Could it be argued, then, that preindustrial Spain conformed to a Malthusian pattern?

A related issue in the historical literature is Spain's poor performance relative to north-western European countries. A glance at Fig. 1.2 shows that Spain currently belongs to the lower part of the OECD ranking, below most western European countries.[5] When did such unexceptional position originate? Historians concur that Spain's backwardness has deep roots, but do not agree as to when it originated. Was it in the autarchic early Francoism? Was it during the nineteenth century transition to a liberal society? Or did it, perhaps, result from the decline of Imperial Spain in the seventeenth century or, even further back, from the Black Death (1348)?

Answering these questions requires a very long-term view. For the sake of simplicity, I will distinguish two epochs, with 1850, as the dividing line. The first one, a period of long and deep fluctuations in average incomes and, the second, of

[5]These are the most recent direct estimates of comparative (purchasing-power parity adjusted) average income levels. Any more recent figures only represent projections of the basis of the 2017 benchmark.

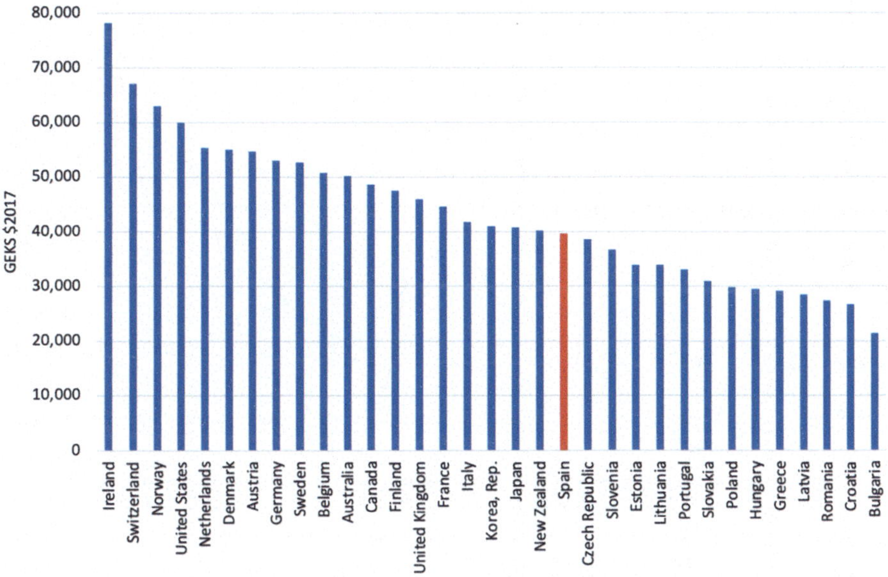

Fig. 1.2 Spain's relative per capita in 2017 (GEKS $2017) (World Bank, ICP, 2017)

sustained improvement in per capita GDP that resulted in the current level of affluence.

1.2 Economic Change over Half a Millennium[6]

A glance at Fig. 1.3 shows three phases of economic expansion as measured by GDP: (1) from the *de facto* end of the Reconquest (mid-1260s) and, perhaps, earlier from its push forward in the late eleventh century, until the Black Death (1348); (2) from the second quarter of the fifteenth century, accelerating between the 1520s and 1560s, to a peak by 1570; and (3) from the late seventeenth century recovery that gave way to an expansionary phase in the eighteenth century that resumed after the Peninsular War interlude. Population followed suit but at slower pace, except from 1570 to the early 1620s, when it continued expanding while GDP shrank.

GDP per capita shadowed GDP evolution, although at slower pace during the growing phases, and moved hand-in-hand with population, but for short episodes (i.e., the first quarter of the seventeenth century). However, unlike absolute GDP, the gains achieved in per capita GDP during each growing phase were reverted during the next shrinking phase, so no net gains resulted over the long run. This was the case

[6]This section draws on Álvarez-Nogal and Prados de la Escosura (2013) and Chap. 2.

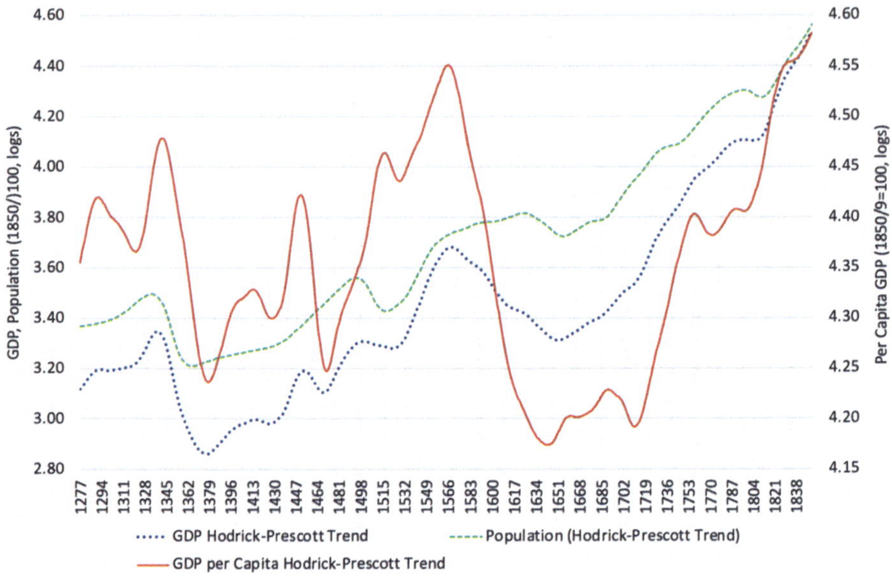

Fig. 1.3 Real absolute and per capita GDP and population, 1277–1850 (Hodrick-Prescott Trend) (1850/1859=100, natural logs). Source: See the text and Table 2.3

after the Black Death and during the post-1570 decline, and that is why per capita income levels reached by the early 1340s and 1570 were only superseded in the early nineteenth century.

In this recurrent growing and shrinking process over half a millennium, two distinctive epochs could be distinguished. The first one, up to 1570, corresponds to a high land–labour ratio, pastoral, trade-oriented economy, led by towns, and helped by the relatively abundance of specie, in which real wages and consumption were relatively high. Economic expansion was largely based on a commodity (wool) whose production was well suited to the relative abundance of land and was helped by the spread of transhumance s grazing land was won from the Muslims. A vibrant commercial sector supplied international markets and, as rising living standards stimulated urban industry, domestic markets as well.

After the collapse of the 1570s, a new equilibrium was reached in the mid-seventeenth century, which lasted until 1820. Crops then played a central role, while wool, trade and urban activity ceased to be the engines of growth in a poorer and gradually more densely populated society.

Did these changes affect income distribution? The long-term evolution of income inequality can be estimated using two measures: the ratio between nominal land rent and wage rates, which captures the returns to land and labour, respectively, and the ratio between nominal output per capita and wage rates (the so-called Williamson index), which compares the returns to all factors of production per capita with the returns to labour per worker. An increase in the Williamson Index means that

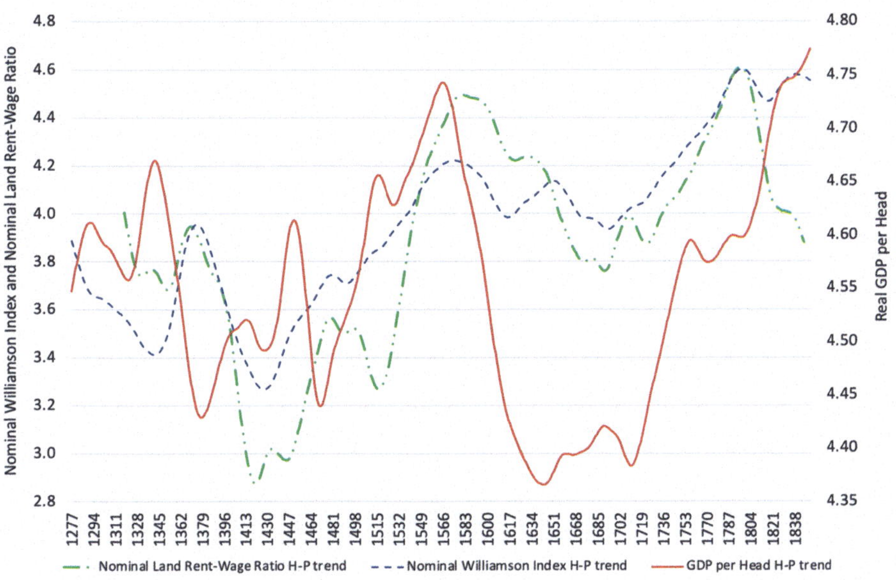

Fig. 1.4 Real per capita GDP and inequality, 1277–1850 (Hodrick-Prescott Trend) (1790/1799=100, natural logs). Source: See the text and Table 2.3

average individual returns improve relative to those at the bottom of the distribution. An improvement in either of these two indices signifies an increase in inequality.

Figure 1.4 reveals that inequality moves with per capita income. However, until the early sixteenth century, income was more evenly distributed; but as Spain became a more rural society, inequality increased.

How does Spain's performance compare with that of Western European economies? At the time of the Black Death, average income levels in Spain were above those of the North Sea Area (Netherlands and the United Kingdom) and France (Fig. 1.5). By 1570, at the height of its imperial expansion, Spain's GDP per capita was still higher than that of the United Kingdom and France, but much lower than that of the Netherlands or northern Italy. As a result of the economic collapse from the 1570s to mid-seventeenth century, Spain fell behind. In the early eighteenth century and, later, after the Napoleonic Wars, Spain's growth was not strong enough for it to catch-up. It is worth noting, though, that average income in preindustrial Spain, was, but for exceptional periods, always more than twice the World Bank's absolute poverty line.[7]

In the attainment of a relatively high living standard before the Black Death, a high land/labour ratio was undoubtedly an important element. Nevertheless, openness to foreign goods and ideas was crucial for Spain to take advantage of its

[7] The absolute poverty line was set by the World Bank at 1985 $1 a day per person, that is, $1.05 expressed in 1990 Geary-Khamis dollars or $2.15 in GEKS $2017. That is, $383 in the commonly used international 1990 prices.

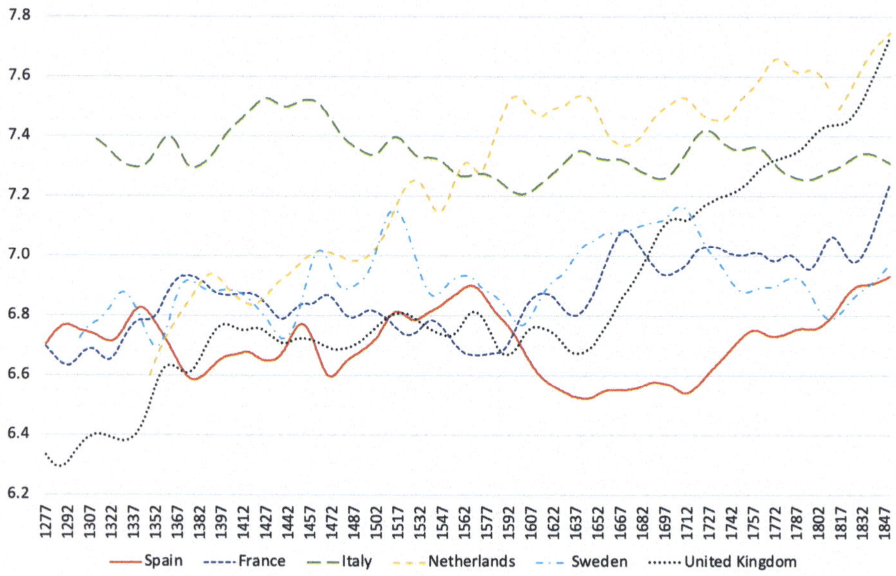

Fig. 1.5 Comparative real per capita GDP, 1277–1850 (Hodrick-Prescott Trend) (Geary-Khamis $1990, natural logs). Source: See the text and Table 2.3

privileged position at the crossroads of the European and Muslim economies. It was the combination of the two factors that enabled Spain to achieve a relatively prosperous position in Europe before its expansion into the Americas.

A question remains unanswered, however. Why did Spain, a frontier economy that did not obey Malthusian forces, alternate phases of growing and shrinking, so no significant long-run net gains in living standards were achieved? In order to provide explanatory hypotheses, let us focus on three episodes that proved decisive: the Black Death, the decline of Imperial Spain, and the Napoleonic Wars.

1.2.1 The Black Death[8]

The Black Death was the deadliest pandemic in recorded history. It differs from other epidemic experiences in terms of the extent and severity of the shock over a very short period of time, and the recurrent reappearance of the disease.

A widely held view of the economic impact of the Black Death is based on the Malthusian interpretation. The demographic expansion of the High Middle Ages (1000–1340s) would have brought Europe's population close to its maximum potential, given capital endowment and technological constraints, increasing

[8]This sub-section draws on Álvarez-Nogal et al. (2020) and Chap. 2.

pressure on natural resources. This fragile equilibrium was broken when deteriorating climatic conditions reduced harvests and led to subsistence crises that facilitated the spread of disease (Postan, 1973).[9]

In spite of the widespread acceptance of the Malthusian interpretation in Spanish historiography, this was far from being the case.[10] Indeed, while the demographic impact in Spain was comparatively moderate—between a third and a half of the population was wiped out in Western Europe compared to a quarter in Spain (Álvarez-Nogal et al., 2020)—the economic effects were more severe and per capita income fell sharply.

As Fig. 1.3 shows, per capita GDP was higher before than after the plague. The Black Death (1348) resulted in a sharp decline in per capita GDP until the 1370s, which continued at slower pace thereafter until reaching a trough in the early fifteenth century. A recovery phase followed, although it reversed during the late 1460s to early 1470s, as civil war and social unrest spread across Castile and, by 1500, average income levels were still well below pre-Plague ones. In the case of population, the contraction was milder (Chap. 2, Fig. 2.12).

The intense recovery in north-western European countries after the Plague contrasts with Spain's decline (Fig. 1.5). The European behaviour appears to be in line with the Malthusian prediction: as population fell due to the Plague, the survivors' average income rose. The Black Death led to a change of demographic regime in Europe that set the grounds for the Great Divergence between western Europe and Asia (Broadberry, 2013; de Pleijt and van Zanden, 2016), while their different responses to the Plague initiated the 'Little Divergence' between European countries (Pamuk, 2007; Jedwab et al., 2022; Prados de la Escosura and Rodríguez-Caballero, 2022).

Spain's exceptional behaviour in the European context was a consequence of being a frontier economy. A frontier economy is defined by an abundance of natural resources and a shortage of labour, where economic activity is organised around the exploitation of the abundant resource. The frontier in Spain was literal and originated during the Reconquest. The instability of borders and the high land-labour ratio favoured the development of a pastoral system that was intensive in land use and low in labour use (MacKay, 1977). The territories incorporated to the Christian kingdoms (mainly Castile) from the eleventh century onwards relieved any potential demographic pressure in the north (Rodriguez, 2011), and the increase in the land/peasant ratio helps explain the rise in output per worker (Oliva Herrer, 2007).

Spain had one of the lowest population densities and one of the highest urbanisation rates in Europe. This means that the amount of land available per worker was much higher than in the rest of Europe. Far from living at subsistence levels,

---

[9]Cf. Campbell (2016) for an alternative explanation that stresses the exogenous character of the Black Death.

[10]A conventional view for the case of Spain is presented by Valdeón Baruque (1969), who stressed the relative scarcity of land, increasing use of marginal land as population expanded, and growing fiscal pressure that triggered famines, facilitating the spread of the plague.

peasants in pre-Black Death Spain were part of a highly integrated and relatively wealthy economy in which commercial links between towns and the countryside were very intense.

The frontier economy helps explain why the Black Death, despite its comparatively milder demographic impact in Spain, had devastating effects on an economy organised around a fragile system that was highly sensitive to changes in the scarce resource, labour. The demographic shock destroyed trade networks and isolated an already sparse population, with the consequence of reducing the ability to maintain per capita production levels.

Meanwhile, in north-western Europe, the Black Death reduced demographic pressure on resources, raised land- and capital-labour ratios, and led to higher returns to labour vis-à-vis land or capital and higher relative prices for non-agricultural goods. Cheaper capital and labour scarcity led to lower interest rates and higher wages that incentivised physical and human capital accumulation and stimulated labour-saving technical innovation, and female participation (Pamuk, 2007). The fact that factor proportions (high land-labour ratios, and, hence, high non-agricultural relative prices) in post-Plague Western Europe (Pamuk, 2007) were similar to those existing in pre-Plague Spain helps explain why the Black Death had such negative consequences in Spain.

The years following the Black Death in Spain witnessed an increase in inequality, as the remuneration of labour decreased more rapidly than proprietors' gains. Figure 1.4 shows that inequality experienced a substantial increase, reaching a peak, while conversely per capita income shrank. This finding is at odds with the experience in most of Western Europe, in which the effects of the Plague produced an intense reduction in economic inequality (Scheidel, 2017; Alfani, 2021). Nonetheless, inequality fell sharply again in Spain between the late 1370s and the 1420s and remained at lower levels for the rest of the fifteenth century.

1.2.2 The Rise and Decline of Early Modern Spain[11]

Why Spain fell behind after 1570 remains unclear. Explanations tend to be highly speculative, stressing the insecurity of property rights and the impact of absolutism on trade and colonial extractive institutions (Acemoglu and Robinson, 2012; North, 1989), the fragmentation into different urban and regional political and fiscal institutions that would have hindered market integration (Grafe, 2012), and the negative impact on the most dynamic (tradable) sectors of the Dutch Disease caused by American silver (Forsyth and Nicholas, 1983; Delichman, 2005). The resulting image is one of a weak government subject to powerful local elites, insecure property rights, trade barriers, and distortions in resource allocation.

[11] This sub-section draws on Álvarez-Nogal et al. (2016) and Chap. 2.

However, before addressing these grand interpretations, an assessment of the immediate drivers of Spain's decline—agricultural performance, urban activities, public finance, trade and credit—is a prerequisite.

One possible explanation for Spain's decline in the late sixteenth and early seventeenth centuries could be the unintended consequences of its efforts to maintain its European empire (Álvarez-Nogal and Chamley, 2016). As of 1570, fiscal pressure on urban activities, the driver of the commercial and industrial expansion earlier in the century, rose, in order to finance increasingly expensive wars in Europe (the Low Countries rebellion of 1567 and open war after 1573 and the Lepanto battle in 1571) plus domestic conflict (the Moorish uprising in the Alpujarras in 1569).

A specific event merits consideration. The main taxes were not collected directly by the king but via cities and, in 1574, the king's proposed increase of consumption taxes (*alcabalas*) was rejected by the Castilian cities. This led the king to stop payments to the Genoese bankers between 1575 and 1577, a decision that had a trickle-down effect, driving local banks into bankruptcy and impacting negatively upon small traders and merchants. Fiscal conflict between cities and the king led to the destruction of local markets from 1570 onwards. Eventually, the cities accepted the doubling of the *alcabalas*, opening the way to successive tax increases, including additional taxes on consumption goods, wine, meat, oil and vinegar, the so-called *millones*. Thus, the Monarchy's success in defeating the cities' resistance led to subsequent increases in consumption tax until the 1660s.

In addition, monetary alterations, especially the devaluation of the vellón—a copper currency that up to 1602 included a lower proportion of silver—also contributed to preventing recovery (Álvarez Nogal, 2005). Monetary instability and military conflict in the central decades of the seventeenth century—war with France (1635–1659) and Portuguese (1640–1668) and Catalan (1640–1652) rebellions—heightened the pressure on the economy. Over time, all this placed an unbearable burden on the most dynamic sectors, triggering de-urbanisation and the collapse of average real incomes from which early modern Spain never fully recovered.

The case of agriculture helps to confirm that a Malthusian narrative is not appropriate in the case of early modern Spain. Trends in agricultural output per worker and the labour force evolved hand in hand, rather than in opposite directions, as postulated by the neo-Malthusian model, so when population and labour declined or grew, labour productivity did so too, and this pattern lasted until mid-nineteenth century. Moreover, land rent and labour productivity in agriculture also moved together.

Increasing ruralisation resulting from higher taxation on urban activities between 1570 and 1650 did not lead to greater agricultural efficiency. On the contrary, as the tax burden increased, incentives to cultivate the land were reduced and agricultural activities and crops stymied.

How does the experience of Spanish agriculture compare with those of Western Europe? In the early sixteenth century, output levels per worker in Spain and Italy were significantly higher than in Britain and Holland, but they declined late in the century and throughout the seventeenth century (Table 1.1). Meanwhile, labour productivity experienced a remarkable improvement in Britain and, especially, in

Table 1.1 Comparative agricultural labour productivity (1910 £ per worker, British relative prices)

	Spain	Italy		Holland		Britain
1510/1519	24.8	25.0	1510	20.7	1522	17.9
1580/1589	19.8	21.4				
1700/1709	21.9	21.9	1700	29.1	1700	22.6
1750/1759	24.1	22.8			1759	31.6
1790/1799	23.1	19.9	1807	34.7	1801	37.5

Sources: Álvarez-Nogal et al. (2016)

Holland, as output increased and the share of the labour force in agriculture declined. During the eighteenth century, in spite of Spain's partial recovery, the North-Sea countries forged ahead. The divergence between Spain and the North Sea Area (England and the Low Countries) after the 1570s can be explained by the fact that, while in the North Sea area urban progress increased the incentives for peasants to demand new urban goods and services and thus stimulated an agricultural revolution, in Spain, lack of urban stimulus led to a decline in labour productivity and labour force in agriculture.

1.2.3 The Napoleonic Wars[12]

The Napoleonic Wars (1793–1815) are usually depicted as a major juncture in European history. For Spain, the wars with France and Great Britain, the Napoleonic invasion of the Peninsula, and the loss of the colonial empire coincided in time. Moreover, the transition to the liberal regime triggered by these events appears longer and more costly in Spain than in other European societies.

The Peninsular War had very negative short-run economic consequences in Spain. The demographic impact represented a fall in population to 1 million short of its potential and its direct effects were half a million casualties, around 5% of the population, the bloodiest conflict in Spain's modern history. The effects upon agriculture were ambiguous. On the one hand, lack of enforcement of Ancien Régime institutions allowed producers to increase cultivation and pay lower land rents. On the other, war confiscations hit livestock reducing the stock of capital as well as calorific consumption. The war afflicted the industrial sector by reducing consumption, increasing transport costs and input prices, and diverting productive investment. Services were also disrupted and international trade collapsed, as did Government revenues. The monetary system was also disrupted and became unstable. As a consequence, GDP per head fell, with an uneven impact across regions, and income inequality increased.

The Peninsular War also sparked the fight for independence in Spanish America. The empire reinforced the absolutist monarchy, as colonial revenues (a substantial

[12]This sub-section draws on Prados de la Escosura and Santiago-Caballero (2022) and Chap. 6.

share of total income) reduced the need to raise taxes in the metropole, and allowed for a concentration of power without the need to negotiate extensively with its subjects and institutions.

The loss of the colonies had negative effects on trade, manufacturing and government revenues, but the upper bound impact on GDP (around 5%), industrial employment (below 7%) and capital accumulation (around 13%) was much smaller than assumed and unevenly distributed, mainly restricted to specific regions and economic sectors. However, by facilitating the fall of absolutism, the loss of the colonial empire may have contributed significantly to the transition to liberalism in Spain.

The institutional changes that started with and followed the Peninsular War were part of the liberal revolution which brought with it a redefinition of property rights that changed the population status from subjects to citizens equal before the law, the liberalization of commodity and factor markets, and the Parliamentary control of public revenues and expenditure. It was, nonetheless, a long process fraught with difficulties and partial reversals.

The empirical evidence on the post–war era suggests that the Napoleonic Wars constituted a defining moment in Spanish history. However, the relevant question seems to be whether in the absence of war, the Enlightenment elite would have carried out the reform of the absolutist state, initiating a gradual transition towards a liberal society. Sound public finance and international integration into the commercial and financial world, plus the spread of liberal ideas prior to the war suggest a positive answer, while the connections between absolutism and the colonial empire and the difficulties and reversals faced by liberal reformers endorse a negative response. The statistical analysis of macroeconomic series suggests that had pre-war trends persisted in the early nineteenth century, the important gains achieved would not have been possible.

A glance at the post-Napoleonic Wars era reveals a discontinuity in any dimension of social and economic activity. Population expansion accelerated, nearly doubling its pace in the late eighteenth century, while the rate of urbanization increased remarkably. Agriculture became more efficient, gradually oriented towards expanding Western European markets, and consumption per head improved. As for manufacturing, while traditional industries collapsed, modern industries continued to adopt new technologies. The more competitive and flexible sectors adapted to new circumstances with the economy expanding steadily, except during the Carlist War (1833–1839), and population growth was accompanied by a sustained increase in GDP per head and a reduction in income inequality (Fig. 1.4). Nonetheless, despite faster growth and higher levels of per capita income than ever before, Spain gradually fell behind north-western European countries (Fig. 1.5).

To sum up, although the economic consequences of the Peninsular War in Spain were clearly negative in the short term, the Napoleonic Wars triggered a complex transition from an absolutist empire to a modern nation. The liberal reforms redefined property rights and gradually shifted the control of the executive to the parliament. The long-term consequences were a more efficient allocation of resources and sustained economic growth, despite serious obstacles (civil wars and military takeovers) that deferred the transition.

1.3 Modern Economic Growth and Its Distribution[13]

If we accept Simon Kuznets's (1966: 1) definition of modern economic growth as a sustained increase in output per head and worked hour, accompanied by population expansion and structural change, its beginnings in Spain can be traced back to the mid-nineteenth century (Fig. 1.6).

Let us first consider the evolution of Gross Domestic Product. Absolute GDP has increased over 50-fold since 1850, which implies a cumulative rate of growth of 2.3% per year. As its progress was far from steady, four different phases may be distinguished: from the mid-nineteenth to the mid-twentieth century; the 'Golden Age' (early 1950s to 1974); from the end of General Franco's rule (1975) to the eve of the Great Recession (2007); and from then to the present. In the phase of fastest growth, the Golden Age, GDP grew nearly 5 times faster than in the previous 100 years and almost twice as much as from 1975 to 2007. From 2008 onwards, GDP stagnated as a result of the Great Recession (2008–2013) and Covid pandemics.

This sustained increase in the production of goods and services over 170 years was the result of a profound transformation in the way resources were allocated. On the demand side, the share of total consumption (private and government) declined

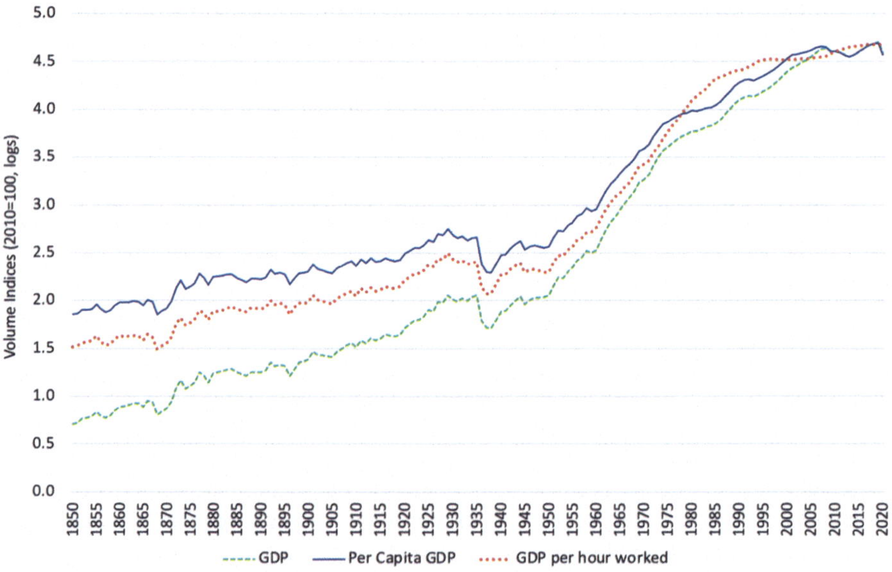

Fig. 1.6 Absolute, per capita and per hour worked GDP, 1850–2020: volume indices (2010=100, natural logs). Sources: Table 4.8

[13]This section draws on Prados de la Escosura (2017) and Chaps. 3–5.

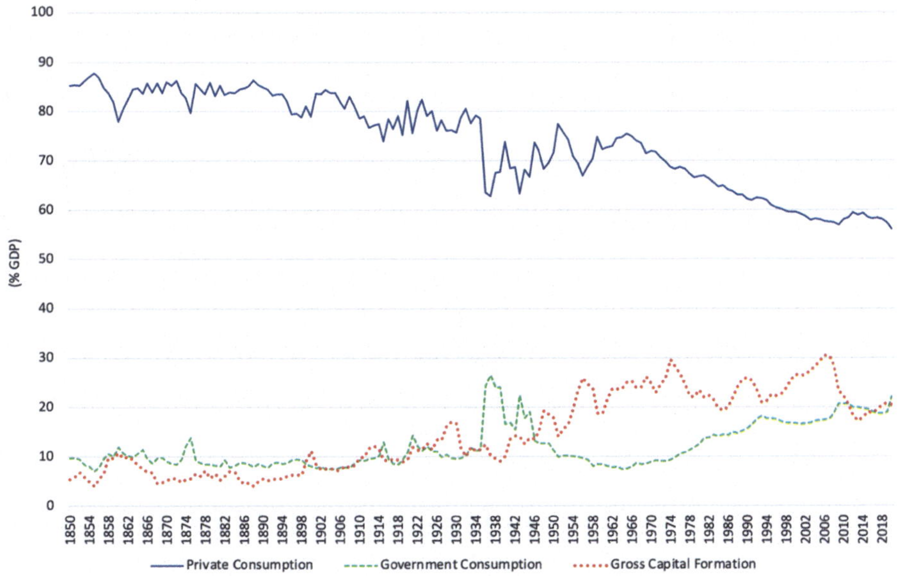

Fig. 1.7 Consumption and investment (% GDP) 1850–2020 (current prices). Source: Prados de la Escosura (2017), updated dataset https://frdelpino.es/investigacion/en/category/01_social-sciences/01_spanish-economy/02_historical-perspective-spanish-economy/

slowly from a high level and only fell below 80% of GDP in the late 1950s, dropping to three-quarters in the 2000s. Behind the gradual decline of the late twentieth century lies a sustained fall in private consumption offset by a rise in government consumption that intensified from the 1980s onwards, as the welfare state expanded and a centralized state gave way to a regional state (Fig. 1.7).

Investment fluctuated at around 5% of GDP through the nineteenth century, except during the railway construction boom from the late 1850s to the mid-1860s, when it nearly doubled (Fig. 1.8). From the turn of the twentieth century, a long-term rise brought investment to a peak in the mid-2000s (30%), falling below one-fifth after the Great Recession. As a result, the net capital (wealth) stock-GDP ratio reached a peak value of four by 2013, multiplying 2.7 times from the 1850s to the 2010s and doubling in the last half a century (Chap. 3, Fig. 3.17).

Spain's integration into global markets increased over time. A gradual rise in openness (exports and imports of goods and services as a share of GDP) stabilised in the early twentieth century, followed by a gradual decline as of the 1920s that deepened in the late 1930s and 1940s. A cautious exposure to international competition started in the mid-1950s, accelerating after the reforms associated with the 1959 Stabilization and Liberalization Plan and, again, after the end of Franco's regime, reaching two-thirds of GDP in the late 2010s. Moreover, imports and investment appear to be correlated, suggesting an association between international trade and capital formation that stimulated economic growth.

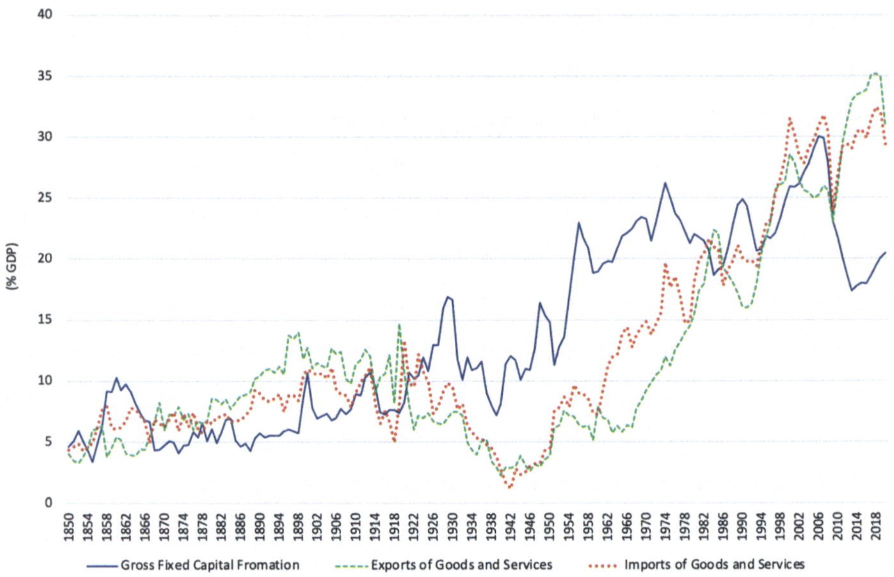

Fig. 1.8 Gross fixed capital formation and trade (% GDP), 1850–2020 (current prices). Source: Prados de la Escosura (2017), updated dataset https://frdelpino.es/investigacion/en/category/01_social-sciences/01_spanish-economy/02_historical-perspective-spanish-economy/

On the supply side, changes in the composition of GDP and employment followed the same patterns but differed in intensity over time, reflecting relative labour productivity differences across economic sectors. In a first stage, the share of agriculture contracted, especially in the 1920s and from 1950 to 1980, and industry expanded to reach 30% of GDP around 1960 (Fig. 1.9). In a second stage, from 1980 onwards, the relative decline continued in agriculture and extended to industry, while the service sector, whose share of GDP and employment had remained relatively stable until the mid-twentieth century, accelerated to represent nowadays about three quarters of both GDP and employment (Fig. 1.10).

But to what extent did a larger amount of goods and services impact on individuals' living conditions? Changes in GDP can be decomposed into those of GDP per capita and population. Since the population trebled, real GDP per capita experienced a 16-fold increase (at a yearly rate of 1.6%) and drove the expansion of absolute GDP from 1850 (Fig. 1.6). Per capita GDP doubled its initial level in the first 100 years, growing at 0.7% per year. Its pace then accelerated to 5.3% per year during the Golden Age, so by 1975 per capita income was 3.6 times higher than in 1950. Although the economy decelerated, down to 2.5% per year over 1975–2007, per capita GDP in 2007 more than doubled its level in 1975. Then, it shrank during the Great Recession (2008–2013) and the Covid pandemics, so per capita GDP is nowadays back to mid-2000s levels.

Albeit following an evolution similar to that of western European countries, Spanish per capita GDP grew at different pace (Fig. 1.11) Growth was slower

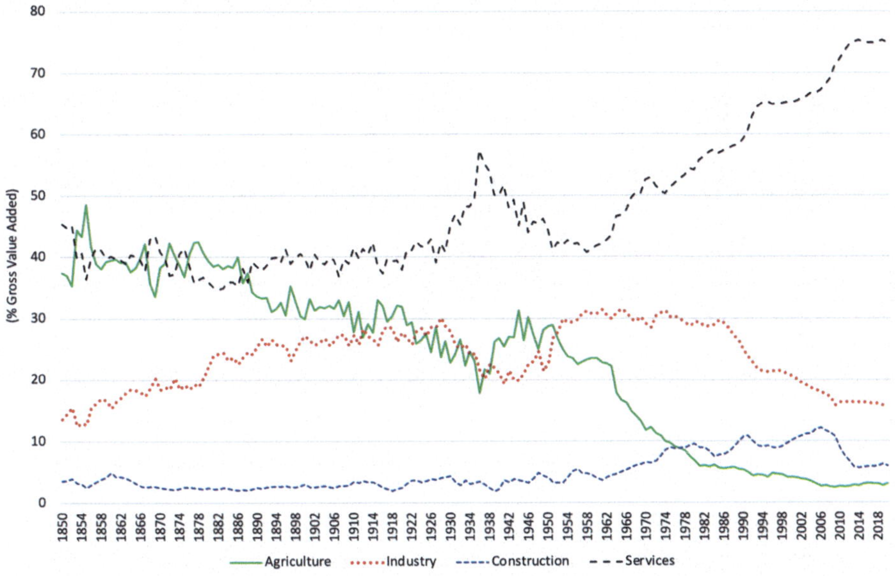

Fig. 1.9 Gross value added by economic activity (% GDP), 1850–2020 (current prices). Source: Prados de la Escosura (2017), updated dataset https://frdelpino.es/investigacion/en/category/01_social-sciences/01_spanish-economy/02_historical-perspective-spanish-economy/

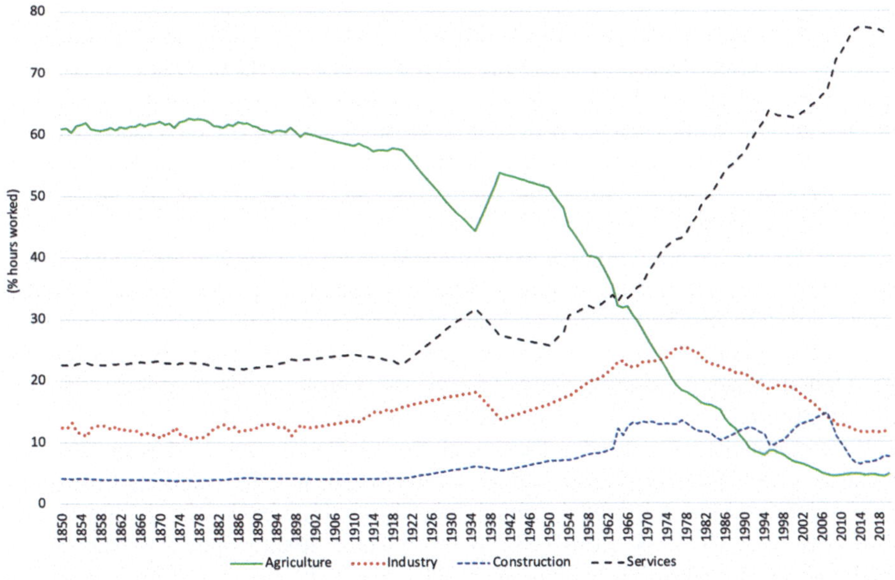

Fig. 1.10 Employment by economic activity (%), 1850–2020 (hours worked). Source: Prados de la Escosura (2017), updated dataset https://frdelpino.es/investigacion/en/category/01_social-sciences/01_spanish-economy/02_historical-perspective-spanish-economy/

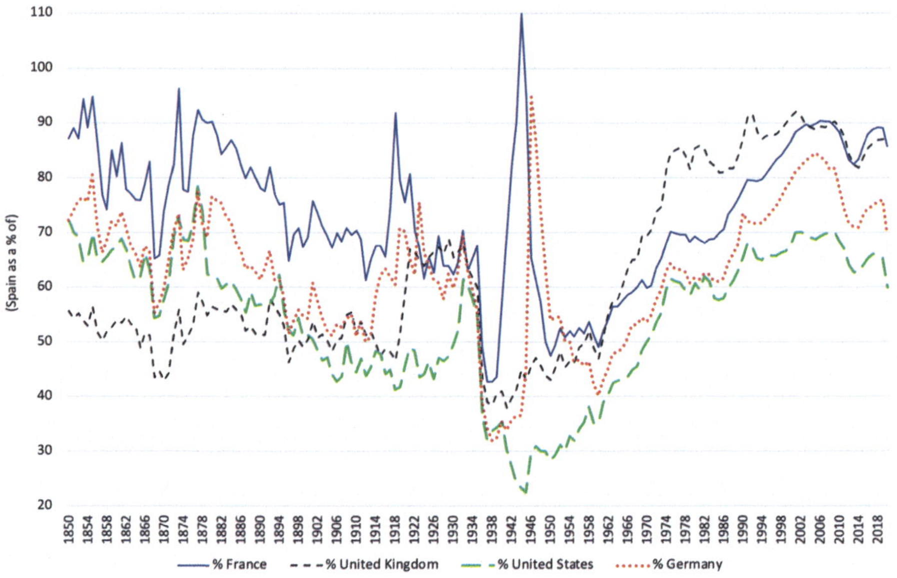

Fig. 1.11 Spain's relative* real per capita GDP, 1850–2020: Main countries (GEKS $2017) (%) *Spain as a % of each country's per capita GDP. Sources: https://frdelpino.es/investigacion/en/category/01_social-sciences/01_spanish-economy/02_historical-perspective-spanish-economy/

from 1880 to 1920 and during the World Wars, while the 1920s acceleration was offset by the Great Depression and the Civil War (1936–1939), failing to recover during the autarchic 1940s. Hence, the sustained long growth since the mid-nineteenth century fell short of that of Western countries. Conversely, growth was faster in Spain in the late twentieth century, with particular intensity in 1960–1974 and again since the late 1980s. Per capita GDP growth has come to a halt in the twenty-first century.

Thus, Spain's position relative to the main Western countries evolved as a broad U-shaped curve, falling behind until 1950 before catching-up until the early 2000s, except for 1976–1985, the years of Spain's transition from dictatorship to democracy, and lagging behind in the new century. Nowadays Spain's position vis-à-vis the United States, Germany and France is similar to what it was in the mid-nineteenth century, only narrowing the gap with Great Britain.

If the comparison is carried out now with the population-weighted average of the countries which today belong to the OECD, the European Union, and the Eurozone, respectively over the last half a century, two distinctive phases of catching up are observed: up to 1975 and from 1986 to 1992. Thus, Spain stopped converging in 1992 and has been lagging behind since 2001. By 2020, Spain had returned to its relative position in 1975 (Fig. 1.12).

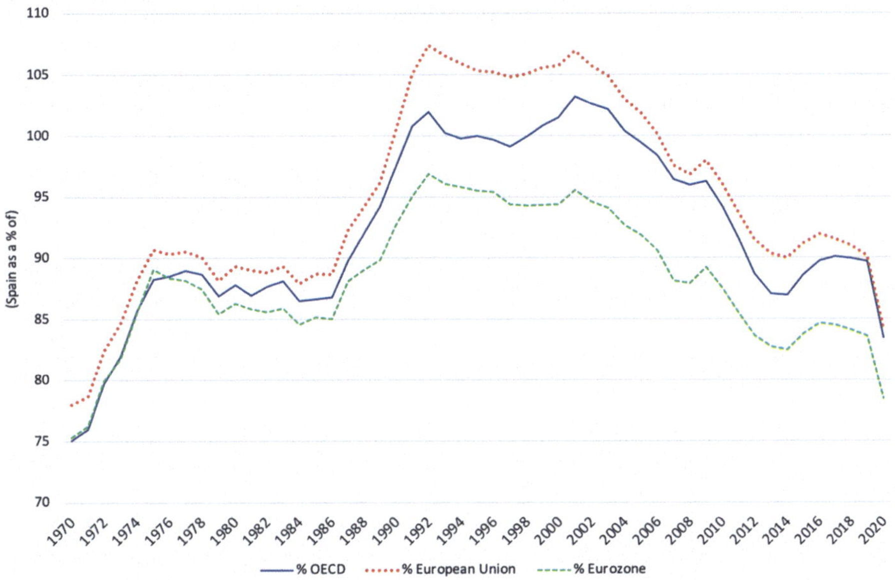

Fig. 1.12 Spain's relative* real per capita GDP, 1970–2020: Main clubs (GEKS $2017) (%) * Spain as a % of each Club's per capita GDP. Source: World Bank, ICP (2017); Conference Board (2023). Spain, as Fig. 1.11

1.3.1 Accounting for Per Capita GDP Growth[14]

GDP per capita depends on the output obtained per hour worked (labour productivity) and the number of hours worked per person. GDP per hour worked and per capita increased over time, while the number of hours worked per person shrank and is largely accounted for by the reduction in hours worked per full time equivalent worker. This means that GDP increased more per hour worked than per capita and that long-term gains in output per capita result exclusively from improvements in labour productivity. Moreover, acceleration phases of GDP per capita and per hour worked match each other, i.e. the 1920s or the Golden Age (1950–1974).

The long-run synchronised behaviour of GDP per hour worked and per person was interrupted, however, after 1975. Thus, in periods of sluggish (1975–1985) or negative (2008–2020) per capita GDP growth, labour productivity accelerated; and from 1986 to 2007, when per capita GDP growth intensified, labour productivity slowed down. The Spanish economy would have been unable to combine job creation and improved productivity, which suggests that sectors which created new jobs in expansionary phases (construction and services, in particular) failed to attract productive investment and technological innovation.

[14] This sub-section draws on Chap. 4.

But what drives the rise of labour productivity? In the long run, capital deepening (that is, capital services per hour worked) accounted for up to one-half of labour productivity growth, while efficiency gains (total factor productivity [TFP]) accounted for one-third, with human capital contributing the rest (Chap. 4, Table 4.6). Thus, more and better use of capital per hour appear to be complementary. Furthermore, the main spurts in capital deepening and total factor productivity tend to coincide, i.e. railway construction (1850–1880), electrification (1920s and 1950s), or the adoption of new technologies (1950–1974).

A closer examination reveals that from 1850 to 1950 (except for the 1920s) and from the late 1980s to the present, capital deepening drove labour productivity growth, while in the 1920s and from the early 1950s to the late 1980s, efficiency gains in the use of available resources represented the main force behind labour productivity growth.

How can one explain, then, the counterintuitive result that since Spain's accession to the European Union the main source of labour productivity growth has been physical capital deepening rather than TFP?

One might think that as the economy approached the technological frontier, achieving higher levels of efficiency became more difficult. Moreover, structural change, i.e. the shift of resources from sectors with low labour productivity to sectors where it was higher (e.g. from agriculture to industry) that contributed to rising labour productivity until the late 1980s, had already taken place. Thus, Spain would have exhausted its potential to close the productivity gap with advanced countries and efficiency gains would have slowed to match their pace.

However, the fact that TFP growth from 1990 to 2019 has been systematically lower in Spain than in OECD countries with higher labour productivity levels in 1990 challenges this hypothesis. Low R&D spending and under-investment in intangible capital (intellectual property) and in specific-technical change and human capital, together with restrictions on competition through regulation in product and factor markets, appear as more promising research hypotheses.

1.3.2 Growth and Distribution[15]

How have the fruits of modern economic growth been distributed? Let us start by comparing the evolution of the share of property income (which includes returns to capital and land) in GDP and the Gini, that is, functional and personal distribution, respectively.[16] We observe their parallel evolution until the early 1950s, when they started diverging, and while the property share shows an upward trend, the Gini index falls and, then, stabilises (Fig. 1.13).

---

[15] This sub-section draws on Chap. 5.

[16] The share of property provides an inequality measure somehow comparable to the Williamson Index and also partially to the land rent-wage ratio used for medieval and early modern Spain (Fig. 1.4).

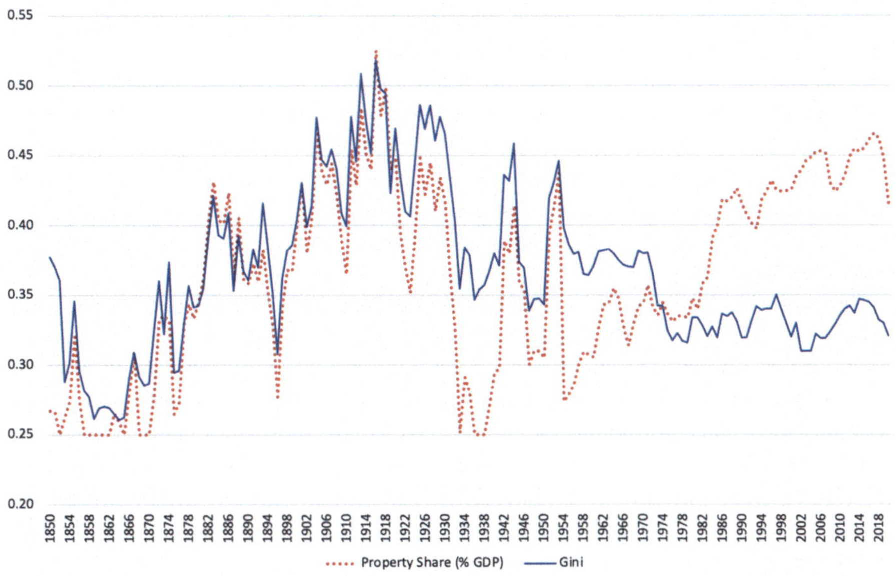

Fig. 1.13 Property share (% GDP) and the Gini, 1850–2021. Source: Property share, Table 4.11; Gini, Table 5.1

How can this discrepancy be explained? Let us consider a simple model in which there are only two social groups, owners (recipients of capital and natural resource returns) and workers, with no overlap between their components (i.e. no worker is an owner and vice versa). In this context, the increase (decrease) in inequality would come either from greater (lesser) dispersion within each of these two groups or from the increase (decrease) in the distance between the average incomes of the two groups. The share of property (capital and land) in GDP would provide information about the inequality derived from the gap between the average incomes of the two groups, owners and workers.

In early stages of economic development, inequality would stem from the gap between the average incomes of owners and workers, most of whom would be unskilled and living near subsistence—which is why David Ricardo (1817) associated the personal distribution of income with its functional distribution. However, as the economy develops and the labour force moves from rural to urban centres and from agriculture and traditional services into industry and modern services, the number of skilled workers increases, as does the dispersion of labour incomes; however, in a later stage, most workers will be skilled and, therefore, the dispersion of their incomes reduced. This evolution would correspond to the one described by Kuznets (1955), who included the role of social security, that is, the welfare state, as an additional driver of the decline in income dispersion.

The close evolution of the property share and the Gini (Fig. 1.13) suggests that, until the 1950s, the property share would have been the main force behind the evolution of personal income distribution (the Gini). However, this was no longer the case from the mid-twentieth century onwards.

Economic growth since the mid-1950s led, on the one hand, to a larger share of capital income, as capitalisation of the economy increased, and, on the other, as labour became largely skilled, to a lower dispersion of labour income, which became the driving force of income distribution. This helps explain the reduction of the Gini coefficient, in which redistribution also plays a part, as the Gini reflects inequality of disposable income, that is, after taxes and transfers (post-fisc), unlike the pre-fisc property share.

The evolution of personal income distribution, measured by the Gini coefficient, presents the shape of a wide inverted U with a peak in 1916 (Fig. 1.13). Different phases can be observed in the evolution of inequality. A long-term rise took place between the mid-nineteenth century and World War I. Then, a sustained reduction in inequality took place during the 1920s and early 1930s, stabilising in the years of the Civil War (1936–1939). The decline in inequality was reversed during the 1940s and early 1950s. Inequality fell in the late 1950s and again in the early 1970s. From the mid-1970s onwards, inequality stabilised, fluctuating within a narrow 0.31–0.35 Gini range.

In a comparative perspective, Spain matched the evolution of OECD countries during the last century and a half, with an intermediate level of inequality, but within the European Union, Spain currently belongs to the upper inequality quartile (Chap. 5, Fig. 5.10).

How can we account then for the alarm generated in recent times by a perceived rise in inequality? Is this perception adjusted to reality, or does it simply derive from the fact that our tolerance threshold to inequality is now much lower than in the past?[17] One explanatory hypothesis would be the deterioration of the welfare state due to public spending cuts during the Great Recession. This interpretation expands the view that democracy has failed to reduce inequality in Spain (Torregrosa Hetland, 2015). One way to test this proposition is to compare the evolution of inequality (the Gini) before and after taxes. The difference between the two measures provides an idea of whether there has been progressive redistribution, i.e. whether the 'market' Gini has been reduced as a result of progressive taxation and social transfers. It can be shown (Chap. 5, Fig. 5.9) that the trend has been towards progressive redistribution and that the Great Recession did not interrupt this. In fact, the increase in progressive redistribution from 2007 to 2013 shows how the automatic mechanisms of the welfare state provide for greater redistribution in times of crisis.

---

[17] That is, an effect of Peter Lindert's (2004: I, 15) 'Robin Hood' paradox, 'in which redistribution from the rich to the poor is least present when and where it seems most needed'.

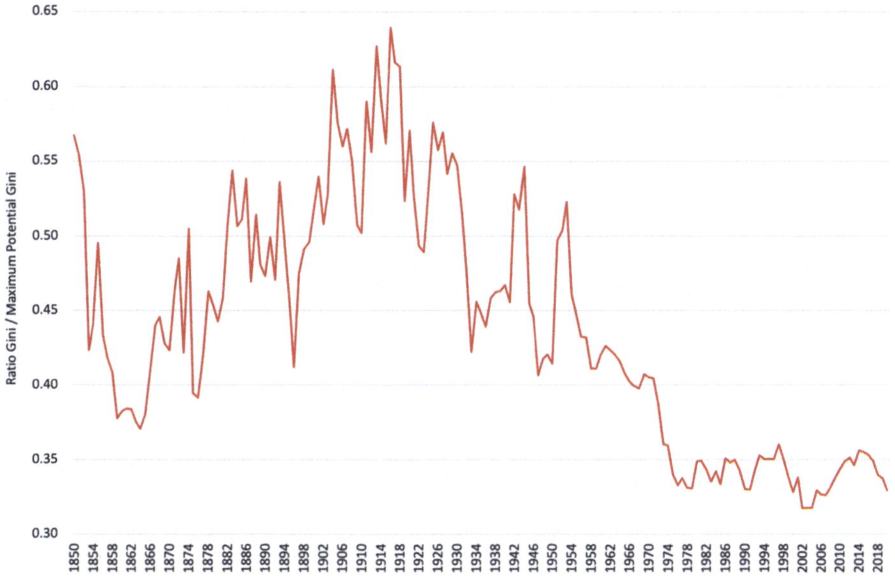

Fig. 1.14 Actual/maximum potential inequality ratio, 1850–2021. Sources: See the text

It could be argued, however, that the impact of an increase in inequality on well-being is not the same when the average income rises and when it falls. Thus, a fall in real net national disposable income per person of 13%, coupled with a rise of three percentage points in the Gini, as was the case during the Great Recession, could have represented a very negative effect on welfare.

The comparison between the actual and the maximum potential inequality (i.e. Milanovic's (2016) 'inequality extraction ratio' [IER]), provides a measure of the impact of inequality on well-being.[18] The higher the ratio, the more negative the impact on well-being. It can be observed that the IER has fluctuated around one-third since the mid-1970s, far lower than the 0.5 value of the late nineteenth century or the early 1950s (Fig. 1.14). Hence, the impact of inequality on well-being would have been lower in recent decades and would not support the claim of the Great Recession's negative effect.

A more detailed impact of distribution changes on well-being is offered by the so-called 'growth incidence curve', which instead of only considering average inequality, as the Gini does, measures how, in a given period, the different percentiles of the distribution evolved. In Fig. 1.15, we observe that, from 2007 to 2016, the fall in real income between percentiles 50th to 25th, that is, for the lower middle class (defining the middle class as the population between the 25th and 75th

[18] Thus, IER $= G / G^*$, being G, the actual Gini, and G* the maximum feasible Gini. $G^* = (\alpha - 1) / \alpha$, where α equals average income expressed in terms of subsistence (1990 $1.05 per day per person).

Fig. 1.15 Inequality: growth incidence curve, 2007–2016. Real per capita household income change across percentiles of the income distribution (%). Source: LIS, kindly provided by Branko Milanovic

percentiles) ranges from −0.5 to −8.7% with −3.2% average (s.d. 2.8) while below the 25th percentile income contraction ranges between −8.8 and 49.3% with –20.4% average (s.d. 12.3). Therefore, a closer look at disaggregated evidence supports the widespread perception of a negative impact on welfare.

What is the reason for such a strong effect on well-being, when in aggregate terms inequality increased moderately? Although a precise answer requires further research, labour market rigidities, with adjustments via quantity, in times of crisis do not seem unrelated to such a dramatic situation.

1.4 Concluding Remarks

Over the last 170 years, real income per person has improved remarkably in Spain, driven by increases in labour productivity, derived from a more intensive and efficient use of physical and human capital per worker. In this process, exposure to international competition has been a stimulus, associated with increases in investment and convergence with more developed countries.

Moreover, the most dynamic phases of the last 100 years have been accompanied by a reduction in economic disparities in Spanish society, so modern economic growth can be associated with an improvement in the material well-being of its population.

References

Acemoglu, D. and J.A. Robinson (2012), *Why Nations Fail. The Origins of Power, Prosperity and Poverty*, London: Profile Books.

Alfani, G. (2021), "Economic Inequality in Preindustrial Times: Europe and Beyond", *Journal of Economic Literature* 59(1): 3-44.

Álvarez Nogal, C. (2005). Incentivos económicos y derechos de propiedad en la Castilla del siglo XVI. *Cuadernos de ICE* **70**, 77-96

Álvarez-Nogal, C. and C. Chamley (2016), "Philip II against the Cortes and the Credit Freeze of 1575-1577", *Revista de Historia Económica/Journal of Iberain and latin American Economic History* 16(3): 351-382.

Álvarez-Nogal, C. and L. Prados de la Escosura (2013), "The Rise and Decline of Spain, 1270-1850", *Economic History Review* 66 (1): 1-37

Álvarez-Nogal, C. L. Prados de la Escosura, and C. Santiago-Caballero (2016), "Spanish Agriculture in the Little Divergence" (2016), *European Review of Economic History* 20 (4): 452-477.

Álvarez-Nogal, C. L. Prados de la Escosura, and C. Santiago-Caballero (2020), "Economic Effects of the Black Death: Spain in European Perspective", *Investigaciones de Historia Económica-Economic History Research* 16 (4): 35-48

Broadberry, S.N. (2013), Accounting for the Great Divergence. LSE Economic History Working Papers 184.

Campbell, B.M.S. (2016), *The Great Transition. Climate, Disease, and Society in the Late Medieval World*, Cambridge: Cambridge University Press,.

Clark, G.,(2008), "In Defense of the Malthusian Interpretation of History", *European Review of Economic History* 12: 175–199

Conference Board (2023), Total Economy Database Growth. TED 1. Output, Labor, and Labor Productivity, 1950–2023 https://www.conference-board.org/data/economydatabase/total-economy-database-productivity

Drelichman, M. (2005), "The Curse of Moctezuma: American Silver and the Dutch Disease", *Explorations in Economic History* 42: 349–380.

Forsyth, P.J. and S.J. Nicholas (1983), "The Decline of Spanish Industry and the Price Revolution: A Neoclassical Analysis", *Journal of European Economic History* 12 (3): 601-610

Galor, O. and D.N. Weil (2000), "Population, Technology, and Growth: From Malthusian Stagnation to the Demographic Transition and Beyond", *American Economic Review* 90 (4): 806-828.

Grafe, R. (2012), *Distant Tyranny. Markets, Power, and Backwardness in Spain, 1650-1800*. Princeton: Princeton University Press

Hansen, G.D. and E.C. Prescott (2002), "Malthus to Solow", *American Economic Review* 92 (4): 1205–1217.

Jedwab, R. N.D. Johnson, and M. Koyama (2022), "The Economic Impact of the Black Death", *Journal of Economic Literature* 60(1): 132-178.

Kuznets, S. (1955), "Economic Growth and Income Inequality", *American Economic Review* 45(1): 1–28.

Kuznets, S. (1966), *Modern Economic Growth: Rate, Structure, Spread*, New Haven: Yale University Press.

Lindert, P.H. (2004), *Growing Public. Social Spending and Economic Growth Since the Eighteenth Century*, 2 vols. Cambridge: Cambridge University Press.

MacKay, A. (1977), *Spain in the Middle Ages. From Frontier to Empire, 1000-1500*, Houndsmill, Basingstoke: Palgrave Macmillan

Milanovic, B. (2016), *Global Inequality: A New Approach for the Age of Globalization*, Cambridge, MA: Harvard University Press.

North, D.C. (1989), "Institutions and Economic Growth: An Historical Introduction," *World Development* 17(9): 1319-1332.

Oliva Herrer, H.E. (2007), "El mundo rural en la Corona de Castilla en la Baja Edad Media", *Edad Media. Revista de Historia* 8: 295-328

Pamuk, S. (2007), "The Black Death and the Origins of the 'Great Divergence' across Europe, 1300-1600", *European Review of Economic History* 11 (3): 289-317.

Postan, M. (1973), *Essays on Medieval Agriculture and General Problems of the Medieval Economy,* Cambridge: Cambridge University Press.

de Pleijt, A.M. and J.L. van Zanden (2016), "Accounting for the "Little Divergence": What Drove Economic Growth in Pre-industrial Europe, 1300-1800?, *European Review of Economic History* 20: 387-409.

Prados de la Escosura, L. (2017), *Spanish Economic Growth, 1850-2015*, London: Palgrave Macmillan.

Prados de la Escosura, L. and C. Santiago-Caballero (2022), "The Napoleonic Wars: a Watershed in Spanish History", in P.K. O'Brien (ed.), *The Crucible of Revolutionary and Napoleonic Warfare and European Transitions to Modern Economic Growth*, Leiden: Brill, pp. 171-204.

Prados de la Escosura, L. and C.V. Rodríguez-Caballero (2022), "War, Pandemics, and Modern Economic Growth in Europe", *Explorations in Economic History* 86, 101467.

Ricardo, D. (1817), *Principles of Political Economy and Taxation*, London: John Murray.

Rodríguez, A. (2011), "Spain", in H. Kitsikopoulos (ed.), *Agrarian Change and Crisis in Europe, 1200-1500*, London: Routledge, pp. 167-203.

Scheidel, W. (2017), *The Great Leveller: Violence and the Global History of Inequality from the Stone Age to the Present*, Oxford: Oxford University Press.

Torregrosa Hetland, S. (2015), "Did Democracy Bring Redistribution? Insights from the Spanish Tax System, 1960-90", *European Review of Economic History* 19 (3): 294-315.

Valdeón Baruque, J. (1969), "Aspectos de la crisis castellana en la primera mitad del siglo XIV", *Hispania* 29: 5-24.

World Bank (2017), *Purchasing Power Parities and the Size of World Economies. Results from the 2017 International Comparison Program*, Washington D.C.: The World Bank

Part I
Growth and Well-Being

Chapter 2
Growth Recurring in a Preindustrial Economy

2.1 Introduction

'Prior to 1800, living standards in world economies were roughly constant over the very long run: per capita wage income, output, and consumption did not grow' asserted Gary Hansen and Edward Prescott two decades ago.[1] This stylised fact has spread among economists in more simplified terms: income per person remained stagnant in human societies until the Industrial Revolution heralded the beginning of modern economic growth. The Unified Growth Theory's depiction of preindustrial societies as Malthusian has reinforced this perception (Galor and Weil, 2000).[2]

Although the Malthusian depiction of preindustrial economies enjoys the support of distinguished scholars (cf. Clark, 2007, 2008; Madsen et al., 2019), it has recently been challenged by research in economic history. Historians are now more prone to accept a transcending of the Malthusian constraint in preindustrial Western Europe, as capital accumulation and productivity gains permitted, simultaneously, higher population and income levels, but with the caveat that such achievements were limited in scope and time (i.e. after the Black Death), and only had long term effects in the North Sea Area (Pamuk, 2007). Broadberry et al.'s (2015) ground-breaking

---

Co-authored with Carlos Álvarez-Nogal and Carlos Santiago-Caballero. An earlier version appeared as L. Prados de la Escosura, C. Álvarez-Nogal and C. Santiago-Caballero (2022), "Growth Recurring in Preindustrial Spain?", *Cliometrica* 16(2): 215–241. This chapter includes a revision of the estimates for population, GDP and its components, and per capita GDP.

---

[1]Hansen and Prescott (2002: 1205) aimed to model "the transition from stagnant to growing living standards".

[2]That is, assuming a fixed supply of land and population growth as a response to an increase in living standards. It is worth noting that the use of the term 'Malthusian' in the growth literature is an oversimplified version of the interpretation Malthus offered in his works, in which he distinguished between the (Malthusian) trap of stagnant productivity, as a result of the operation of an unrestricted principle of population, and the classical principle of population (Lueger, 2018).

L. Prados de la Escosura, *A Millennial View of Spain's Development*, Frontiers in Economic History, https://doi.org/10.1007/978-3-031-60792-9_2

research, for example, rejects the use of the term Malthusian to portray the early modern British economy. However, Voigtländer and Voth (2013) claim that, in north-western Europe, the Black Death brought with it an increase in the endowment of land and capital per survivor, which resulted in higher output per head within a Malthusian framework.

In an attempt to break the growth-stagnation dichotomy in preindustrial societies, historians have highlighted 'efflorescences' (Goldstone, 2002: 333) and 'growth recurring' episodes (Jones, 1988; Jerven, 2011) that feature a succession of phases of growing and shrinking output per head and only give way to modern economic growth when shrinking phases become less intense and frequent (Broadberry and Wallis, 2017). Growth driven by gains from specialisation resulting from the expansion of international and domestic markets (the so-called Smithian growth) may explain these episodes of sustained but reversible per capita income gains.

Did Smithian growth episodes take place in preindustrial Europe beyond the North Sea Area? New research suggests that they did in Iberia (Palma and Reis, 2019; Álvarez-Nogal and Prados de la Escosura, 2013), although qualitative perceptions of early modern Spain as a stagnant economy are deeply rooted (Kamen, 1978: 49; Cipolla, 1980: 250).

In this chapter, new yearly estimates of Spanish output and population for more than half a millennium are provided, which revise and improve on previous estimates. The new evidence offers empirical grounds to discuss the extent to which Malthusian efflorescences, recurring growth, or Smithian growth are defining elements of preindustrial Spain.

The chapter makes some methodological contributions to the literature on historical national accounts. It includes controlled conjectures on population and sectoral and aggregate output estimates. More specifically, it provides the first agricultural output estimates from the supply side, on the basis of a religious tax, the tithe, incurred by total production, for over 400 years, which are compared to estimates derived with a demand function for the entire time span considered by Álvarez-Nogal and Prados de la Escosura (2013). Their levels and long-run trends are rather similar, even though some significant discrepancies emerge at specific junctures. This result supports the use of the indirect demand approach to deduce trends in agricultural output.

The chapter is structured as follows. In Sect. 2.2, we construct quantitative conjectures about the population. Agricultural output is estimated, and output per head compared to earlier estimates derived with a demand approach in Sect. 2.3. Urban population estimates, adjusted to exclude those living from agriculture, are used in Sect. 2.4 to proxy trends in economic activity outside agriculture. Section 2.5 constructs aggregate output (total and per capita) estimates on the basis of the results obtained in previous sections and draws their long-run trends. In Sect. 2.6, these findings are discussed in the context of the historical debate and some conclusions extracted with regard to secular stagnation, the Malthusian model, and income distribution in preindustrial societies. Section 2.7 provides a long view of Spain's performance in European perspective. Section 2.8 concludes.

The findings can be summarised as follows: (1) The peak average income levels reached in the late 1330s and the 1560s were only surpassed in the early nineteenth century. (2) However, preindustrial Spain's economy was far from stagnant, exhibiting long phases of output per head growth and contraction. (3) Population and output per head moved together, at odds with the Malthusian narrative and supporting the hypothesis of Spain as a frontier economy. (4) Spain's performance suggests Smithian growth episodes during distinctive phases: the long rise up to the Black Death, the century-long expansion up to 1570, and the sustained expansion of the eighteenth century, as larger markets favoured specialization and urbanisation. (5) Income appears less unequally distributed until the early sixteenth century and increasingly more unequally thereafter, as the relative importance of crops increased.

From these results, a puzzling question emerges: why were no significant long-run gains in living standards achieved in Spain's frontier economy? In the absence of a persuasive Malthusian interpretation, an institutional explanation merits exploration.

2.2 Quantitative Conjectures on Population

Aggregate population figures for late medieval and early modern Spain consist of scattered benchmark estimates from household population surveys usually collected for taxation purposes—the so-called *vecindarios* (literally, neighbourhoods), that present the challenge of converting households into inhabitants-, national censuses for the late eighteenth century, and sporadic assessments for the early nineteenth century.[3] Available benchmark estimates allow us to derive long run population trends, and historians have relied on baptism records to represent population dynamics.[4]

Baptism data are available from 1580 to the Peninsular War, and most regions are covered from 1700 onwards. Thus, total Spanish population can be derived by weighting each regional index by the regions' population in a benchmark year (See Appendix A.1, Population, Estimate 1, and Fig. 2.14). However, inferring population trends from baptisms implies assuming that deaths rates maintained a

[3] Pre-1850 population estimates from household surveys and censuses are available for 1530, 1591, 1646, 1712–1717, 1752, 1768, 1787, 1797, 1821, 1833, and 1842. Cf. Nadal (1984), Bustelo (1972, 1973, 1974), Pérez Moreda (1988) For the conversion of households into inhabitants, cf. Martín Galán (1985).

[4] Cf. Nadal (1988), Reher (1991), Llopis Agelán (2004), and Llopis Agelán and Sebastián Amarillas (2007).

stable short-term relationship with birth rates[5] and that net migration flows were negligible over time.[6]

Álvarez-Nogal et al. (2016) attempted to reconcile population benchmarks with decadal estimates of baptisms, available since the 1520s, so the resulting estimates capture migration (forced or voluntary) and over time variations in the proportion between birth and death rates (and between births and baptised children) (Appendix, A.1 Population, Estimate 1). Unfortunately, projecting a population benchmark with baptism indices is misleading, since population is a stock variable while baptism series, as a proxy for births, represent a flow. In fact, using baptisms as measure of population amounts to proxy capital stock by investment.

Ideally, to reconstruct annual population figures we require a reliable population figure at the beginning of a benchmark year (N_t) annually adding the natural increase in population, that is, births (b_t) less deaths (d_t), less net emigration (m_t). Thus,

$$N_{t+1} = N_t + b_t - d_t - m_t \tag{2.1}$$

As there are population estimates available at various benchmarks (see Appendix, A.1 Population), all we need, then, is data on the natural increase in population (births less deaths) and net migration.

On migration, no yearly data are available and only guesstimates can be proposed. As regards emigration to the Americas, we have relied on Morner (1975: 64) who provides aggregate estimates for five periods over 1506–1670 (1506–1540, 1541–1560, 1561–1600, 1601–1625, 1626–1650) and has distributed them annually within each period.[7] We also allowed for the outflow of Moorish population after their expulsion, which Pérez Moreda (1988: 380), estimates to be, at least, 0.3 million. Thus, we have added a figure of 60,000 emigrants for each year between 1609 and 1613 inclusively. Estimates from 1670 onwards come from Martínez Shaw (1994: 151, 167, 249) for the periods 1670–1700, 1700–1800, 1800–1830, and 1830–1850, and have been distributed annually. As regards immigration, a figure around 0.2 million has been estimated for the sixteenth century, mostly French moving to Catalonia (Pérez Moreda, 1988: 374), which we have distributed, assuming a steady inflow of 2000 people per year.

---

[5]Llopis Agelán (personal communication) discusses the relationship between deaths and baptisms during the eighteenth century, showing an 11% decline in this ratio between the early and the late century, which, however, does not seem attributable to a decline in infant mortality. This author also warns us that the number of births exceeded that of baptised children and their proportion declined during the eighteenth century. He estimates a 5–6% gap for Old and New Castile.

[6]Some evidence exemplifies how misleading this assumption is. For example, the number of Moorish expelled from Spain (1609–1613) could have reached 300,000 (Pérez Moreda 1988: 380). As regards voluntary migration, flows to Spanish America have been estimated as 250,000 and 100,000 in the sixteenth and seventeenth centuries, respectively, and about 125,000 over 1700–1824 (Martínez Shaw, 1994: 152, 167, 249).

[7]Although Martínez Shaw (1994) argues that Morner's figures for the early seventeenth century are grossly overexaggerated, we have accepted them as a way to offset the population lost as a consequence of war in Europe during the second quarter of the century.

We lack yearly crude birth (*cbr*) and death (*cdr*) rates for Spain prior to the 1850s, and although baptisms would roughly amount to b in expression (2.1), that is, *cbr* times population at the beginning of the year, assuming a fixed *cdr*, or a fixed *cbr/cdr* ratio, is unacceptable, as crude birth and death rates fluctuate widely in the short run, and even more so at times of pandemics. Fortunately, David Reher (1991) computed yearly crude birth and death rates for New Castile since 1565 (Appendix, Fig. 2.15). Hence, a possible provision of plausible conjectures on annual population levels consists of constructing alternative population estimates in which each population benchmark (N_{bk}) is projected forwards by adding the annual natural increase in population derived from yearly crude birth and death rates for New Castile (cbr_{nct} and cdr_{nct}), less net emigration (m_t) guesstimates. This is the procedure to adopt when we move forward (that is, when starting from, say, 1787, we want to estimate population in 1788), while we need to subtract the natural increase in population and to add net emigration in the previous year when we project population backwards (namely, when starting from 1787 we want to compute population in 1786).[8] That is,

$$N_{t+1} = N_{bk} + (cbr_{nct} - cdr_{nct})_* N_{bk} - m_t \qquad \text{for } t > bk \tag{2.2}$$

$$N_{t-1} = N_{bk} - (cbr_{nct-1} - cdr_{nct-1})_* N_{bk} + m_{t-1} \qquad \text{for } t < bk \tag{2.3}$$

Accepting crude birth and death rates from New Castile implicitly assumes that they are representative for the whole of Spain. Nonetheless, the crude death rate for New Castile matches the main famine mortality episodes not only for inland Spain, but for Spain as a whole.[9] However, such an arbitrary and unrealistic assumption is largely relaxed by the procedure we propose to reconcile the resulting series. In fact, the exercise suggested by expressions (2.2) and (2.3) provides a set of population series, one for each benchmark, that do not match each other for the years in which they overlap (Appendix, Fig. 2.16). Therefore, we need to carry out a reconciliation between these alternative estimates.

A solution is to interpolate the series, accepting the levels for each benchmark-year as the *best* possible estimates and distributing the gap or difference between adjacent benchmark series (say, series obtained by projecting the 1752 benchmark forward, N_{1752t}, and the 1787 benchmark backwards, N_{1787t}) in the overlapping year T at a constant rate over the time span in between the two benchmark years.

[8] This crude approach is inspired by the inverse and back projection (Lee, 1985).

[9] Specifically, the dates of famine mortality in Spain indicated by Pérez Moreda (2017: 54) are matched by the rise of the crude death rate (in brackets): 1591–1595 (1591), 1599–1600 (1599), 1605–1607 (1606), 1630–1631 (1631–1632), 1647–1652 (1647), 1678–1685 (1684), 1706–1710 (1707), 1730 (1735), 1741–1742 (1740), 1786–1787 (1786), 1803–1804 (1804), 1809 (1809), 1812 (1812), and 1834 (1834).

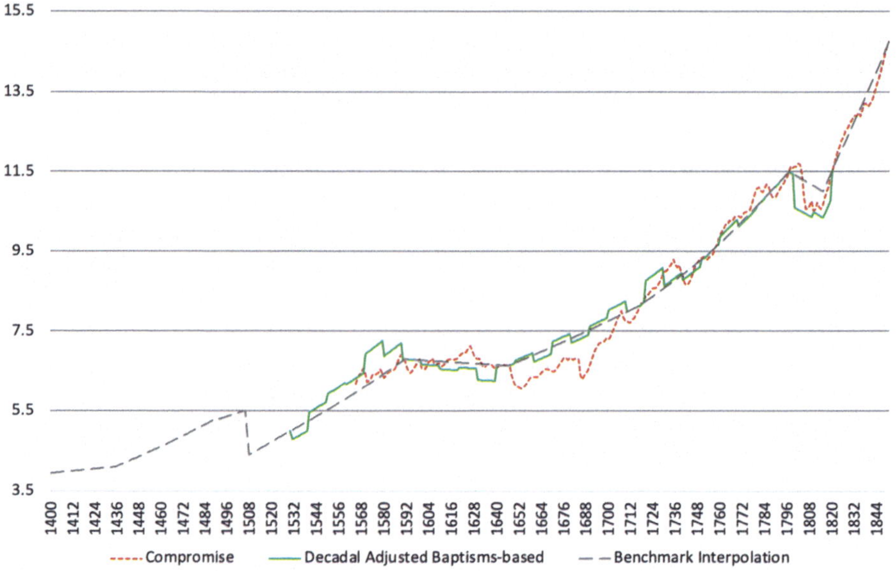

Fig. 2.1 Population: Benchmarks interpolation, decadal adjusted baptisms-based, and compromise estimates, 1400–1850 (million)

$$N^I{}_{t=} N_{1752t*}\left[\left(N_{1787T}/N_{1752T}\right)^{1/n}\right]^t \qquad \text{for } 0 \leq t \leq T. \qquad (2.4)$$

N^I being the linearly *interpolated* new series, N_{1787t} and N_{1752t} the series pertaining to population obtained by projecting two adjacent population benchmarks (i.e. 1752 and 1787) with expressions (2.2) and (2.3), respectively; *t*, the year considered; *T*, the overlapping year between the two benchmarks series (say, 1787); and *n*, the number of years in between the two benchmark dates (that is, 35 years, 1787 less 1752, in our example).[10]

Figure 2.1 presents the compromise estimate along the decadal-adjusted series and the benchmarks interpolation. The comparison reveals that the main discrepancies correspond to the pre-1700 period, and while the decadal-adjusted series peaks in the 1580, the compromise series continues expanding during the first quarter of the seventeenth century, and declines thereafter, especially, in the second half of the seventeenth century, with deep contractions in the late 1640s-early 1650s and in the mid-1680s. Furthermore, the compromise series departs from the other two in the early nineteenth century as it captures the impact of the demographic crisis in the early 1800s and during the Peninsular War.

[10]Alternatively, a variable-weighted geometric average for each pair of estimates derived using adjacent benchmarks, in which the closest benchmark series is given a larger weight, can be used (expression 2.14). We have used both approaches with identical results, but have retained from the linear interpolation, as this is the splicing procedure used in modern national accounts.

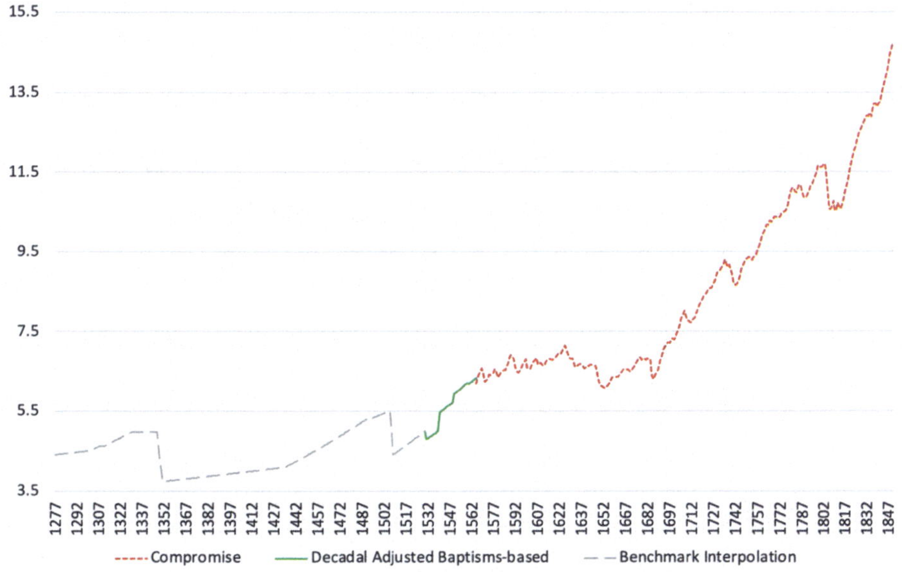

Fig. 2.2 Population conjectures, 1277–1850 (million) (natural logs)

In Fig. 2.2, we present our conjectures with regard to the evolution of Spanish population that combines the compromise series since 1565 with the annual population figures obtained through the decadal adjustment (with baptism data) of the benchmarks interpolated series for the period 1520–1565, and the benchmarks interpolated series for the pre-1520 period.

2.3 Agricultural Output

In pre-industrial Europe, lack of data has led to indirect estimation of agricultural output (Wrigley, 1985; Malanima, 2011; van Zanden and van Leeuwen, 2012). Using a demand function approach, Álvarez-Nogal and Prados de la Escosura (2013) computed agricultural consumption per head over 1277–1850, and assuming the net imports of foodstuffs were negligible, they used it to proxy output per head.[11] As this approach relies on proxies for per capita income and assumptions about income and price elasticities, it is worth exploring alternatives.

Early modern economic historians have used indirect information on a religious tax, the tithe, to draw trends in agricultural output and Álvarez-Nogal et al. (2016)

[11] Real consumption per head of agricultural goods (***C***) can be expressed as $C = a\, P^{\varepsilon}\, Y^{\mu}\, M^{\gamma}$ in which P and M denote agricultural and non-agricultural prices relative to the consumer price index, respectively; Y stands for real disposable income per head; ε, μ, and γ are the values of own price, income and cross price elasticities, respectively; and a represents a constant.

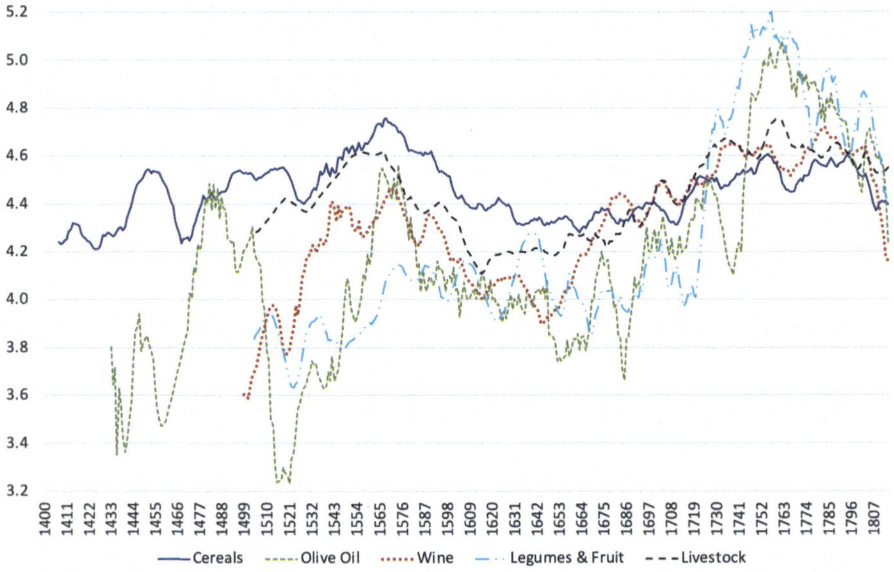

Fig. 2.3 Output by main produce, 1407–1814 (1790/1799=100). 11-year centred moving average (logs)

we adopted this approach to infer the evolution of agricultural output in Spain between 1500 and 1800. In this section we start from this work but extend the coverage of produce and regions as well as the time span back to 1400 and forward to 1835 (See Appendix, A.2 Computing Agricultural Output Indices from Tithes).

Figure 2.3 presents output for the main crops on the basis of tithes. Cereals show a long-run expansion up to the 1570s. Wine and livestock produce, especially, shadow cereal tendencies. Wine and olive production expanded remarkably during the central decades of the sixteenth century, remaining at high output levels until 1590. Most crops fell during the early seventeenth century, recovering at a different pace between the mid-seventeenth and the mid-eighteenth centuries. In the late eighteenth century, opposite trends are found: fruits and legumes and olive oil production declined, while cereals, must, and livestock produce expanded. A fall is observed across the board in the early nineteenth century.

The share of each major crop in agriculture output at current prices is presented in Fig. 2.4. Cereal and animal produce are seen to be the main contributors to agricultural output, and show opposite trends, with the share of animal produce increasing and that of cereals declining up to the 1570s and in the late seventeenth and early eighteenth century, and cereals' share expanding at the expense of animal produce in the early seventeenth and late eighteenth century.

We have constructed a Törnqvist index of agricultural output by weighting yearly variations in each crop's output by the average shares in adjacent years of each crop in agriculture output, at current prices, and, then, obtaining its exponential. That is,

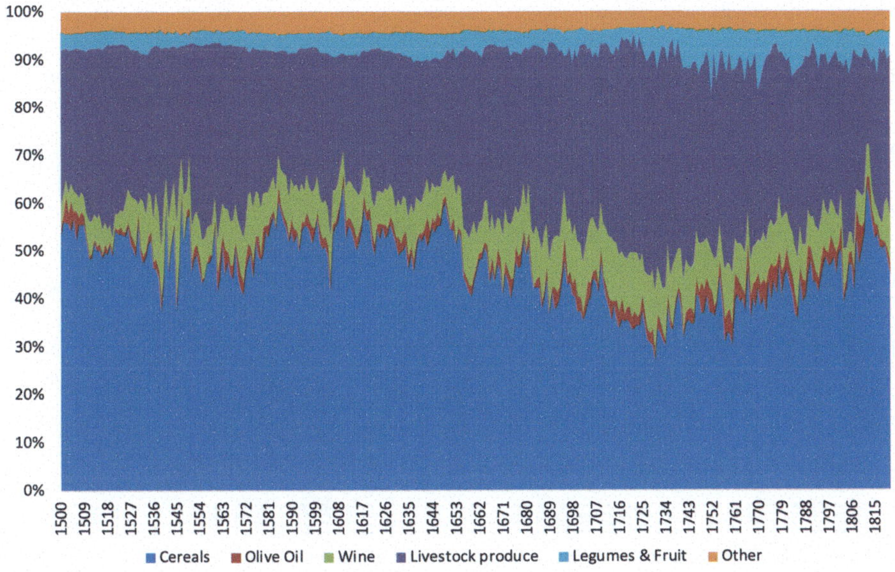

Fig. 2.4 Output composition, 1500–1820 (%) (current prices)

$$\mathrm{lnQ_{at}\text{–}lnQ_{at-1}} = \Sigma_{\mathrm{i}}[\theta_{\mathrm{Qit}}(\mathrm{lnQ_{it}} - \mathrm{lnQ_{it-1}})] \tag{2.5}$$

with share values computed:

$$\theta_{\mathrm{Qit}} = ½[\theta_{\mathrm{it}} + \theta_{\mathrm{it-1}})] \tag{2.6}$$

Previously, current values, *V*, for each crop *i* at year *t* can be derived by projecting the value of each crop in 1799, V_{i1799}, backwards with the quantity index built on the basis of tithes, *Q*, and a price index, *P* (expressed as 1790/1799 = 1) and then, added up in order to obtain the value of total agricultural output, Va_j.

$$Va_{\mathrm{t}} = \Sigma V_{\mathrm{it}} = \Sigma V_{\mathrm{i1799}}{}^{*}\mathrm{Q_{it}}{}^{*}\mathrm{P_{ijt}} \tag{2.7}$$

Later, the share of each crop, V_{it}/Va_t, needs to be obtained.[12]

In the evolution of agricultural output, distinctive phases can be found (Fig. 2.5). The first one was of sustained expansion that peaked in the early 1560s. A contraction between the mid-1570s and the early 1610s was followed by stagnation until 1650. A long-run expansion from the mid-seventeenth to the mid-eighteenth century, punctuated by the War of Spanish Succession (1701–1714), peaked in the 1750s, when the highest output level in four centuries was reached. Output

[12] See the sources of agricultural prices in the Appendix, A.3 Commodity and Factor Price Indices.

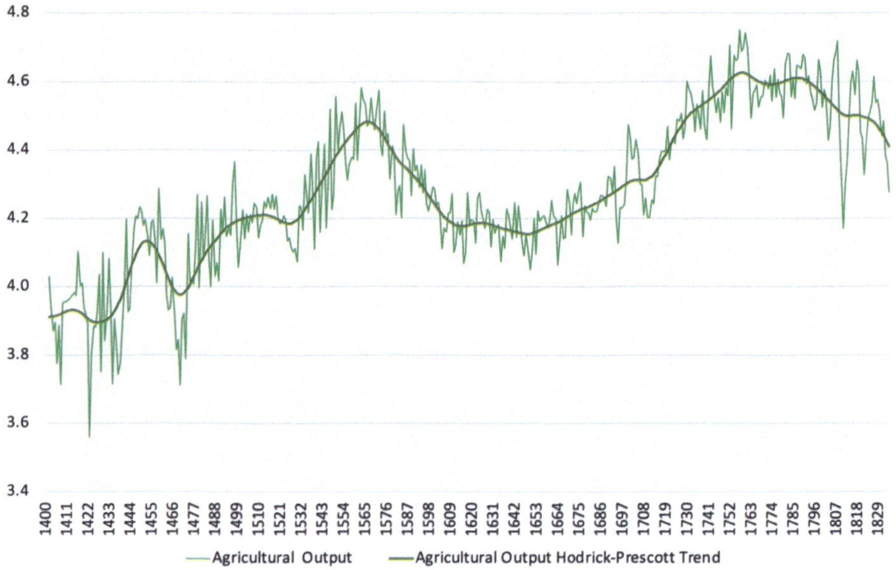

Fig. 2.5 Agricultural Output Törnqvist Index, 1402–1835: Level and Hodrick-Prescott Trend. (1790/1799=100) (natural logs). Sources: See the text

stabilised, then, until 1790, when a decline initiated that reached a trough during the Peninsular War.

If we now focus on agricultural output per person (Fig. 2.6, continuous line), two main phases can be identified: a high plateau covering the fifteenth century and up to early 1570s, and a low plateau spanning between the early seventeenth century and the 1750s, with a transitional phase of decline, between the late 1570s and the 1620s, in between, in which output per person shrank by one-third. A new phase of severe contraction is apparent from the 1750s to the Peninsular War, representing one-fourth of the initial level.

How does the new tithes-based agricultural output per head compare to the consumption per head estimates derived with the demand approach? Both series present roughly the same trends since the early sixteenth century (Fig. 2.6). However, some differences emerge. While the demand approach series were already on high plateau since 1400, the tithes-based series show lower levels and higher volatility up to the 1500s. The shift from a high to a low path of output per head is also common to both estimates, reaching a trough in the early seventeenth century, but the tithes-based series present a sharper and neater decline, starting in the mid-late 1570s. Lastly, although the lower plateau covers roughly the same period in the two set of estimates, the post-1650 recovery is stronger and exhibits less volatility in the tithes-based ones.

It is worth noting that the parallel behaviour of the demand-approach and tithes-based series supports the view that crop and livestock destruction appears as the main factor behind the sharp decline in tithes collection during the Peninsular War,

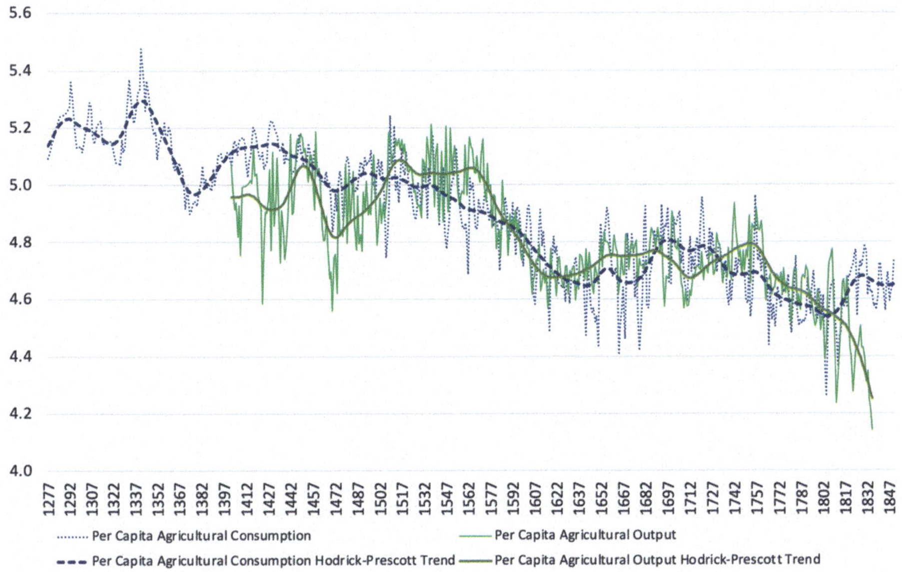

Fig. 2.6 Agricultural output and consumption per head Törnqvist Indices, 1277–1850: Levels and Hodrick-Prescott Trend (1790/1799=100) (natural logs). *Sources*: Text and Álvarez-Nogal and Prados de la Escosura (2013)

rather than peasants' lack of compliance with the religious tax. However, Fig. 2.6 also shows that the tithes-based output departs sharply from the demand approach estimates from 1819 onwards, and the fact that the years between 1820 and 1833 correspond to a period of peace, suggests that it is non-compliance with the religious tax that explains the widening gap between the two indices. The so-called Trienio Liberal (1820–1823), a phase of liberalisation, weakened Ancien Régime institutions and discouraged tithe compliance (Anes and García Sanz, 1982; Canales, 1982; Torras, 1976). The bottom line is, therefore, that the parallel trends of the tithe-based and the demand approach estimates endorse the use of tithes as a reliable indicator of agricultural output tendencies until 1818. Moreover, our findings challenge the dismissal of the demand approach as simple controlled conjectures. Lacking direct sources of agricultural production, as it is often the case in preindustrial societies, the demand approach appears to provide a reasonable procedure to infer agricultural output trends.

Since our goal here is to provide the best possible estimate for long-run agricultural output, we propose a new index that accepts the demand approach estimates for 1818–1850 and the tithe-based ones for 1402–1818, and projects its level for 1402 back to 1277 with the demand approach index (dotted and dashed lines in Fig. 2.7).[13]

[13]The average ratio between the tithe-based and the demand approach indices is 1.0018 for 1994–1818. The same ratio for 1402–1500 is 0.8776 (with a coefficient of variation of 0.13), so we applied this ratio to the demand-based estimates in order to extend our series back to 1277.

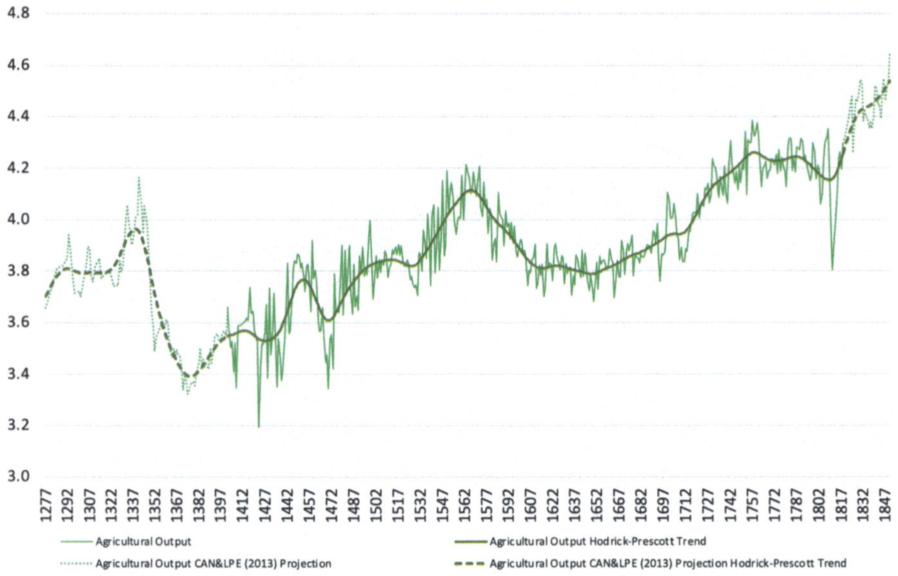

Fig. 2.7 Agricultural Output Törnqvist Index (spliced), 1277–1850: Level and Hodrick-Prescott Trend (1850/1859=100) (natural logs). *Sources*: Text

2.4 Output in Non-agricultural Activities: Urbanization as a Proxy

A reconstruction of trends in industrial and services output is beyond the scope of this chapter. It would require a thorough investigation of industrial output, sector by sector, most probably on the basis of a variety of indirect indicators among which taxes merit analysis. In the case of services, the prospects of obtaining a proper assessment of output are even bleaker. A crude short cut to proxy trends in economic activity outside agriculture is urbanization, more specifically, the use of changes in the urbanization rate (ratio between urban and total population) to infer trends in non-agricultural output per head.[14] In this section, we follow Álvarez-Nogal and Prados de la Escosura (2013) and improve on their estimates by including additional urbanization benchmarks and better population data.

We have adopted the definition of 'urban' population as dwellers in towns of 5000 inhabitants or more.[15] However, a caveat is necessary. Urban population has

[14]The association between urbanization and the expansion of modern industry and services is not new (Kuznets, 1966: 271). Economic historians have suggested parallels between changes in urbanization rates and per capita income (Acemoglu et al., 2005; Craig and Fisher, 2000; Temin, 2006; van Zanden, 2001; Wrigley, 1985).

[15]Although this is a discretional threshold (Wrigley, 1985: 124), this way, we maintain consistency with Bairoch et al.'s (1988) large database facilitating international comparisons. Alternative thresholds of 10,000 (de Vries, 1984) and 20,000 inhabitants have been used (Flora, 1981).

been accepted here as a proxy for output in non-agricultural activities after excluding those living on agriculture. The reason is that the existence of 'agro-towns' (namely, towns in which a sizable share of the population was dependent on agriculture for living) appears to be a feature of pre-industrial Spain. 'Agro-towns' have their roots in the *Reconquest*. In a frontier economy, towns provided security and lower transactions costs during the re-population following the southwards advance (Ladero Quesada, 1981; Rodríguez Molina, 1978). In the thirteenth century, Christian settlers from Aragon, Catalonia, and Southern France acquired farms but preferred to live in towns (MacKay, 1977: 69). It has been claimed that, in southern Spain, "agro-towns" were the legacy of highly concentrated landownership after the acceleration in the pace of the Reconquest and the Black Death, which increased the proportion of landless agricultural workers (Vaca Lorenzo, 1983; Valdeón Baruque, 1966), although Cabrera (1989) attributes the rise of latifundia to the generalization of the seigniorial regime during the fourteenth and fifteenth centuries. In our estimates, 'agro-towns' appear as mainly located in Andalusia, and since the late eighteenth century, also in Murcia and Valencia. Thus, we have computed trends in the rate of *adjusted* urbanization—that is, the share of non-agricultural urban population in total population—in an attempt to capture those in industry and services output per head (See Appendix, A.4 Adjusted Urban Population).[16]

Notwithstanding the existence of 'agro-towns', urban economic activity was closely associated to industry and services. In sixteenth-century Old Castile, Yun-Casalilla (2004) calculates, only 1 in 12 in the urban labour force worked in agriculture. Pérez Moreda and Reher (2003: 129) suggest, for 1787, a similar proportion of farmers in Spain's urban population.[17] Moreover, the rural population carried out non-agricultural activities (storage, transportation, domestic service, construction, light manufacturing) especially during the slack season in agriculture (Herr, 1989, López-Salazar, 1986).[18]

Bairoch et al. (1988) employed alternatively 2000, 5000, 10,000, and 20,000 inhabitants. Moreover, using a fixed threshold may provide a lower bound of the actual level of urbanization as it does not take into account the increase in the population living in larger towns and cities.

[16] In order to mitigate the inclusion of 'agro-towns', Malanima (2011) proposed for the south of Italy a limit of 10,000 inhabitants to be considered urban, as opposed to the 5000 inhabitants limit for the north and centre of Italy. Cf. Llopis Agelán and González Mariscal (2006) for a more astringent definition of 'urban' centre.

[17] However, Reher (1990) estimated that half the economically active population living in towns in Spain worked in agriculture by 1787. Nonetheless, Reher's computations are on the high side, as he artificially increased the share of urban population employed in agriculture by allocating all day labourers to this sector while excluding servants from the labour force.

[18] The number of days (and hours) worked per EAP in Spain was lower in agriculture than in industry and services, leaving extra time to work in non-agricultural activities. Cf. Santaolaya (1991), Vilar (1970: 19), and Ringrose (1983).Wool provides a case in point in early modern Spain. A mainly rural activity, it had both industrial and services (trade, transport, financial services) dimensions (García Sanz, 1986). A more rigorous option might be to measure employment composition by sector in terms of days or hours worked, rather than assigning each worker to a specific occupation (Wrigley, 1985: 137).

Table 2.1 Adjusted urbanization rates, 1277–1857: Benchmark estimates (%)

1277	(8.0)
1347	(8.3)
1400	(7.6)
1530	9.5
1561	13.7
1591	14.6
1646	8.7
1717	9.9
1752	13.8
1787	17.4
1857	22.9

Sources: Bairoch et al. (1988), Correas (1988), and Fortea (1995); see the text and Appendix A.4, Adjusted Urban Population
Note: Figures in brackets are highly conjectural

Spain's urban population, adjusted to exclude population living on agriculture, has been computed at benchmark years for the period 1530–1857 (Correas, 1988; Fortea, 1995). Total and adjusted urban population levels for 1530 were projected backwards with Bairoch et al. (1988: 15–21) estimates.[19] The urban population for Spain in 1530, 1561, and 1646 has been inferred from data for the Kingdom of Castile (Fortea, 1995). Adjusted urbanization rates, that is, urban population not living on agriculture expressed as a share of total population, are presented at benchmark years in Table 2.1. Annual figures of 'adjusted' urbanization rates have been derived via linear interpolation of the benchmark estimates.

The accelerated expansion of the early 1500s slowed down in its second half of the century and was reversed during the first half of the seventeenth century. Then, urbanization recovered slowly, accelerating after the War of Succession to surpass the late sixteenth-century peak by the second half of the eighteenth century. Interestingly, these figures are at odds with the rather stable rate of urbanization (around 20%) widely used in estimates by Bairoch et al. (1988).

2.5 Aggregate Output

The next stage is to construct an index of aggregate output (Q). Rather than estimating long-run output with fixed weights, which introduces an index number problem, as it implicitly assumes that relative prices do not change over time, we have computed a Törnqvist index in which real GDP is obtained by weighting yearly output variations in agriculture, Q_{at}, and industry and services, proxied by 'adjusted'

[19] Bairoch et al. (1988) provide benchmark estimates of urban population for 1100–1500. We have assumed Bairoch et al.'s (1988) value for 1300 as representative of the pre-Black Death peak (1347).

urban population, $N'_{urb\text{-}nonagr\ t}$, with the average, in adjacent years, of the shares of agriculture, θ_{Qat}, and non-agricultural activities, θ_{Qi+st}, in GDP at current prices.[20] That is,

$$\ln Q_t - \ln Q_{t-1} = \theta_{Qat}(\ln Q_{at} - \ln Q_{at-1}) + \theta_{Qi+st}\left(\ln N'_{urb-nonagr_t} - \ln N'_{urb-nonagr_{t-1}}\right) \quad (2.8)$$

where agricultural, θ_{Qat}, and non-agricultural, θ_{Qi+st}, share values are computed as:

$$\theta_{Qat} = ½[\theta_{at} + \theta_{at-1})] \text{and} \theta_{Qi+st} = ½[\theta_{i+st} + \theta_{i+st-1})] \quad (2.9)$$

and, then, Q_t is obtained as its exponential.

In order to get sector shares in current GDP, θ_{it}, current values, V, for each sector i at year t are derived by projecting each sector's value added average in 1850/1859, $V_{i1850/9}$, backwards with the quantity, Q, and price P, indices previously built for each sector, Q_{at} and P_{at} for agriculture, and $N'_{urb\text{-}nonagr\ t}$ ('adjusted' urban population) and P_{i+st}, for industry and services, respectively, (expressed as 1850/1859 = 1) and, then, added up to attain the value of total output, $V_{\cdot t}$

$$V_{at} = V_{a1850/9} Q_{at} P_{at} \quad (2.10)$$

$$V_{i+st} = V_{i+s1850/9} N'_{urb-nonagr_t} P_{i+st} \quad (2.11)$$

$$V_{\cdot t} = V_{at} + V_{i+st} \quad (2.12)$$

Later, the shares of agricultural and non-agricultural activities were obtained, respectively, as $\theta_{Qat} = V_{at}/V_{t\cdot}$ and $\theta_{Qi+st} = V_{i+st}/V_{t\cdot}$.

As regards price indices, the price index already built in the section on agriculture has been accepted. For non-agricultural activities, an unweighted Törnqvist index was computed with industrial goods and consumer price indices and nominal wages.[21] This amounts to allocating one-third of the weight to industry (the industrial price index) and two-thirds to services (nominal wage and consumer price indices), which represents a good approximation to these sector shares in non-agricultural output in the 1850s (Prados de la Escosura, 2017). (For the source of prices see Appendix, A.3 Commodity and Factor Price Indices.)

[20] In the case of agriculture, note, as discussed in the section on agriculture, real output estimates with the demand approach (Álvarez-Nogal and Prados de la Escosura, 2013) have been used for 1818–1850 and, then, spliced to the tithes-based index back to 1402 and, then, projected backwards to 1277 with the demand approach index. As regards non-agricultural output, the 'adjusted' index of urban population, that is, the 'adjusted' urbanization rate times population, has been accepted to represent the latter.

[21] Thus, average rates of variation for manufacturing prices, the CPI, and nominal wage rates were arithmetically averaged and the price index obtained as its exponential.

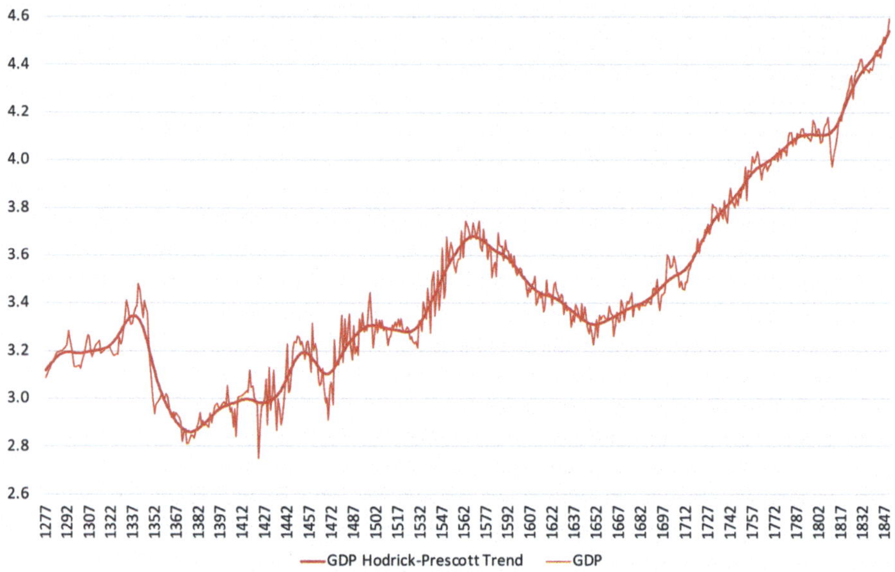

Fig. 2.8 Real GDP Törnqvist Index, 1277–1850: Level and Hodrick-Prescott Trend (1850/1859=100) (natural logs). *Sources*: See the text

What does the long run evolution of total output show? Distinctive phases can be observed (Fig. 2.8). Three phases of expansion: (1) between 1277 (the earliest date for which we have estimates) and the early 1340s, whose origins possibly go as far back as to the late eleventh century; (2) from the 1470s to 1570, disrupted in the early decades of the sixteenth century; and (3) from the mid-seventeenth to mid-nineteenth century, interrupted during the Spanish Succession (1701–1714) and Napoleonic (1793–1815) Wars. Two phases of sustained decline complete the picture: the first one, triggered by the Black Death (1348), very intense until the 1370s, followed by stagnation until the first quarter of the fifteenth century; and a second one, from the late sixteenth to the mid-seventeenth century.

If we now turn to output per head, its evolution follows a wide W shape, with phases of growth which peak in 1341, 1566, and 1850, separated by deep contractions in the late fourteenth and early seventeenth century (Fig. 2.9). Each phase of expansion up to the Napoleonic Wars (1277–1341, 1472–1566, and 1643–1850) shows similar trend growth but, as output per head declined sharply during shrinking episodes, each subsequent phase of growth started from a lower level and, hence, evolved along a lower path, with the result that, in the very long run, the trend growth rate is practically nil and per capita income levels hardly change at all (Table 2.2, Panel A).

Trend growth rates[22] for the new estimates (Table 2.2) show that in phases of economic expansion and contraction, total output responded more than

[22] Hodrick-Prescott trends derived using a smoothing parameter set at $\lambda = 1000$ for each series.

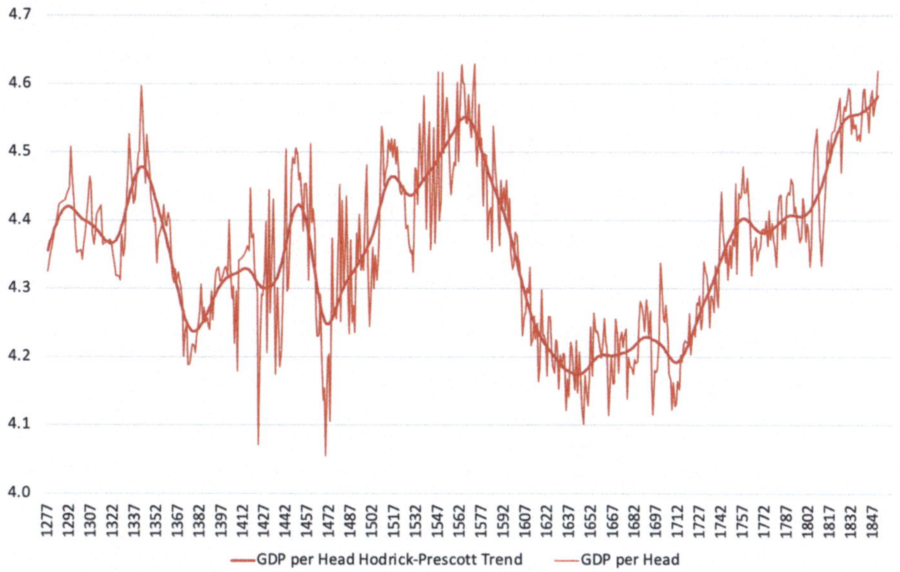

Fig. 2.9 Real GDP per head Törnqvist Index, 1277–1850: Level and Hodrick-Prescott Trend (1850/1859=100) (natural logs). *Sources*: See the text

proportionally to population and confirm the view that output per head and population trends were directly associated.

When we compare the new index of output per head to earlier estimates by Álvarez-Nogal and Prados de la Escosura (2013), it is noticeable that in the new series, the economic collapse in the late sixteenth century began earlier, in the 1570s, not in the late 1580s, and was deeper. Nonetheless, the use of supply and demand methods to assess trends in agricultural production provides similar long-term results in both levels and trends over 1402–1818 (Fig. 2.10).[23] This key methodological finding supports the use of an indirect approach such as a demand function when no sources for a direct estimation are available.[24]

[23] Álvarez-Nogal and Prados de la Escosura (2013) also computed a Törnqvist index of output per head, using the 'adjusted' urbanization rate as a proxy for non-agricultural activities per person but derived consumption per head of foodstuffs with a demand approach from which agricultural output per head was inferred.

[24] The use of tithes, a fiscal source for which good archival records are available, in the supply side estimate of agricultural production, also represents an indirect approach.

Table 2.2 Output and population trend growth, 1277–1850 (%)[a] (annual average logarithmic rates)

	Output	Population	Output per head
1277–1850	0.25	0.21	0.04
Panel A[b]			
1277–1341	0.34	0.20	0.19
1342–1471	−0.18	−0.02	−0.18
1472–1566	0.60	0.28	0.32
1567–1642	−0.45	0.06	−0.50
1643–1850	0.58	0.38	0.20
Panel B			
1342–1471			
1342–1377	−1.32	−0.73	−0.67
1378–1471	0.26	0.25	−0.01
1643–1850			
1643–1710	0.29	0.25	0.03
1711–1758	0.88	0.45	0.44
1759–1807	0.31	0.23	0.06
1808–1850	1.01	0.71	0.35

Sources: See the text

Notes:

[a]Hodrick-Prescott trends derived using a smoothing parameter set at λ = 1000 for each series

[b]The periodization corresponds to that of output per head

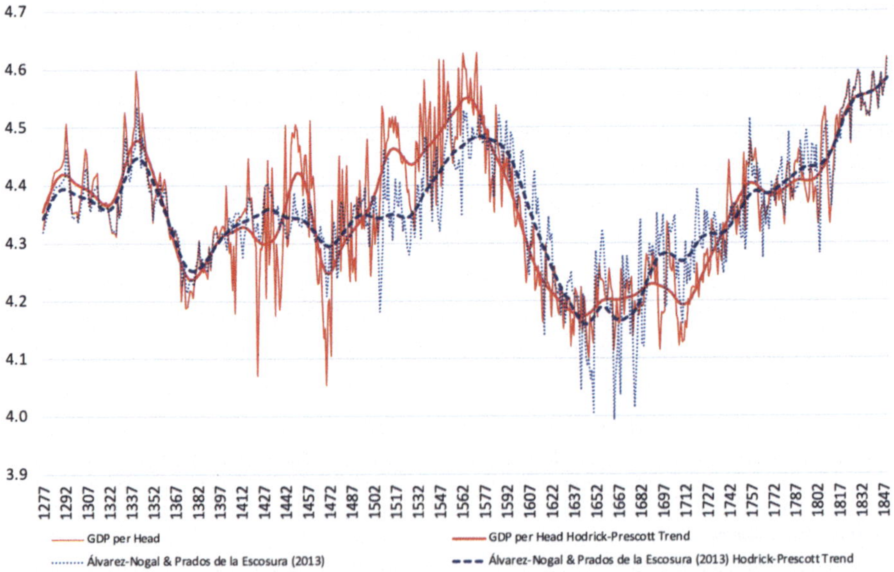

Fig. 2.10 Real GDP per head, 1277–1850: New and Álvarez-Nogal and Prados de la Escosura (2013) Törnqvist Indices: Level and Hodrick-Prescott Trend (1850/1859=100) (logs). *Sources*: See the text and Álvarez-Nogal and Prados de la Escosura (2013)

2.6 Interpreting the Results: Evidence and Hypotheses

Are there any lessons to be drawn from the new quantitative evidence on preindustrial Spain's performance? Some stylised facts about preindustrial societies can perhaps be put to the test. An initial example is that of stagnant average incomes. Although living standards did not experience a noticeable improvement over the very long run, the expansive and contracting phases in the W-shaped evolution of Spain's real output per head contradict this view (Fig. 2.9). Instead, our results lend support to the idea of growth recurring over six centuries. Moreover, Broadberry and Wallis (2017) claim that, as shrinking phases become shorter and less frequent after growing phases, modern economic growth emerges, appears to be confirmed by Spain's early nineteenth century experience.

A second stylised fact is the Malthusian nature of preindustrial economies. Trends in Spanish population and per capita income, expressed in logs, are offered in Fig. 2.11.[25] Population and real output per head expanded simultaneously up to

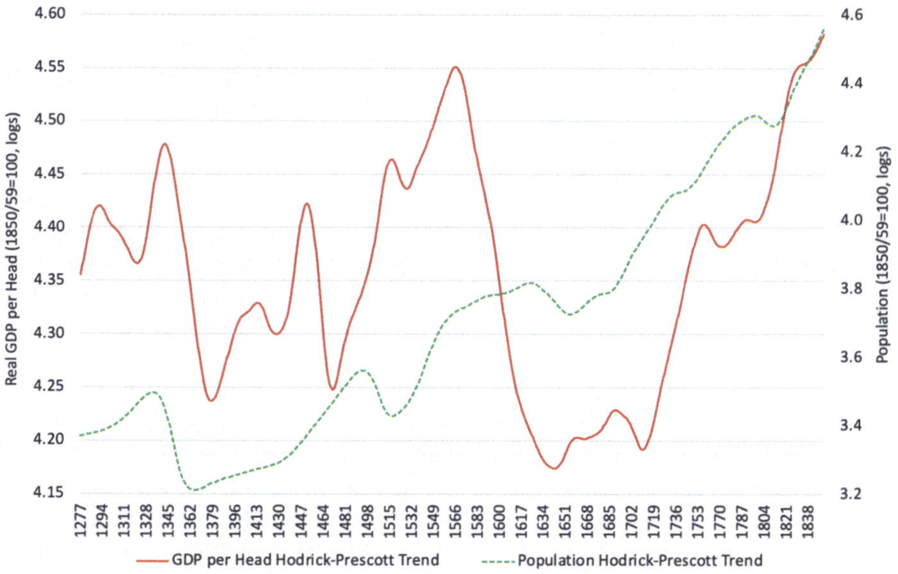

Fig. 2.11 GDP per head and population Hodrick-Prescott Trends, 1277–1850: (1850/1859=100) (logs). *Sources*: See the text

[25]The logarithmic transformation makes trends clearer as the slope of the curves provide the pace at which growth or decline occurred. Trends have been obtained with the Hodrick-Prescott filter.

the Black Death, during the late fifteenth and the sixteenth century, and from the early eighteenth to the mid-nineteenth century; conversely, population and income per person shrank in the late fourteenth and in the early seventeenth centuries. How can we explain these results, at odds with the Malthusian view? A plausible explanatory hypothesis is the existence of a frontier economy, resource abundant in preindustrial Spain, but how long did Spain remain a frontier economy? Labour productivity moved together with the labour force in agriculture, so when population and labour declined or grew, labour productivity did so too, and this pattern, which applied not only to Habsburg Spain but also to Bourbon Spain, may have lasted until the mid-nineteenth century. Furthermore, land rent and labour productivity in agriculture also moved together (Álvarez-Nogal et al., 2016: 466–467). Moreover, the fact that in Spain the Black Death was not the watershed that it constituted in central and Western Continental Europe and the British Isles may be explained by its specific traits. In Western Europe, by wiping out between one-half and one-third of the population, the Black Death reduced demographic pressure on resources, raised land- and capital-labour ratios, and led to higher returns to labour vis-à-vis land or capital and higher relative prices for non-agricultural goods. Cheaper capital and labour scarcity led to lower interest rates and higher wages that incentivised physical and human capital accumulation and stimulated labour saving technical innovation and female participation (Pamuk, 2007). The fact that factor proportions in post-Plague Western Europe were apparently similar to pre-Plague Spain's helps to explain why the negative economic consequences of the Black Death, despite its comparatively milder demographic impact, prevailed in Spain during the late fourteenth and early fifteenth century. In Spain, population density before the Plague (8.9 inhabitants per square kilometre in 1300) was much lower than in most Western European countries after the Plague in 1400 (Álvarez-Nogal et al., 2020) and the Plague destroyed a pre-existing fragile equilibrium between population and resources (Álvarez-Nogal and Prados de la Escosura, 2013).[26] Furthermore, the collapse in the late sixteenth century and its lasting effects do not adjust to the Malthusian narrative.[27] The fall in real output per head that, in its early stage (−0.65% over 1567–1610), was as sharp as the one associated with the Black Death (−0.67% from 1342 to 1377), seems crucial to Spain's falling behind. From 1570 to 1650, while population stagnated and per capita income shrank, the economy shifted from commercial and trade-oriented to inward looking and rural.

Long-run performance has been discussed, so far, in average terms, but how were the gains and losses over successive growing and shrinking phases of per capita income distributed among social groups? The Williamson Index, defined here as the nominal (that is, current price) ratio between output per head and unskilled wage rates and expressed with 1790/1799=100, makes it possible to draw trends in inequality. The rationale underlying the Williamson Index is that GDP captures

[26] There were substantial regional difference within Spain, though, as discussed in Álvarez-Nogal et al., 2020). On the case of Catalonia, cf. the survey by Catalan (2020).

[27] This discussion merits econometric testing, but this is beyond the scope of this chapter.

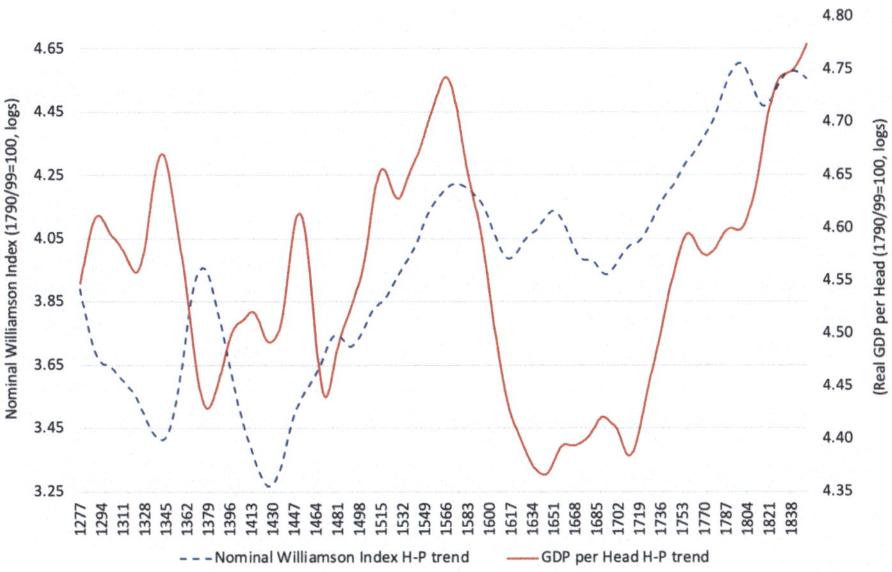

Fig. 2.12 Nominal Williamson Index and real GDP per head Hodrick-Prescott Trends, 1277–1850 (1790/1799=100) (natural logs). *Sources*: See the text

the returns to all factors of production, while the unskilled wage only captures the returns accruing to one factor, raw labour.[28] This way, average returns are compared with returns to unskilled labourers, that is, those at the middle of distribution are compared with those at the bottom. We cannot establish precisely, however, how close to the absolute poverty line unskilled wages were, although attempts to compute welfare ratios (namely, the ratio between a male labourer's yearly returns and the cost of maintaining his family) suggest that unskilled workers were living close to subsistence in early modern Spain (Allen, 2001; but see López Losa and Piquero Zarauz, 2021). The new Williamson Index improves on the one used in Álvarez-Nogal and Prados de la Escosura (2013) by employing current prices and, hence, avoiding the distortions introduced by the use of different deflators for GDP and wages (see Appendix, A.3 Commodity and Factor Price Indices, for the sources of wages), and more reliable GDP estimates.

Inequality trends followed those of GDP per head, expanding and contracting accordingly. Two phases in the evolution of income distribution can be distinguished, however. One of lower inequality, from the late thirteenth century (and probably earlier) up to the early sixteenth century, and another, of higher inequality, from the mid-sixteenth century onwards (Fig. 2.12), which presents an upward trend and matches the experience of early modern Europe (Hoffman et al., 2002; Alfani, 2021).

---

[28] Ideally, one would require GDP and wage dividing by per hour worked in order to normalise them, so our comparison of output per person and wage rates provides a crude metric that may distort inequality tendencies.

2.7 Spain in an International Perspective

How did Spain perform internationally? Angus Maddison (1995, 2006) compared average incomes across countries and over time in a common monetary unit and at constant prices. Maddison's set of international estimates of real income per head in 1990 Geary-Khamis dollars international prices resulted from projecting per capita GDP levels in 1990 dollars, expressed in purchasing power parity (PPP) terms—that is, adjusted for differences in price levels across countries-, back and forth with volume indices taken from historical national accounts. Although Maddison's approach has been widely used, it can certainly be challenged. Its main shortcoming derives from the severe index number problem it introduces in the comparisons, since the basket of goods and services produced and consumed in 1990, and their prices, become less and less representative as one moves back and forth in time.[29]

If, with all the caveats about the reliability of income levels derived with a remote benchmark, we follow Maddison's approach and express product per head in 1990 Geary-Khamis (G-K) dollars, Spain's average income ranged between G-K 1990 $600–1100 over half a millennium.[30] As the absolute poverty line was set by the World Bank at 1985 $1 a day per person, that is, 1990 $426, preindustrial Spain's average income always remained above the absolute poverty line, more than doubling it in the early fourteenth century, in the late fifteenth and the sixteenth century and, again, since the late eighteenth century (See Appendix, Table 2.3).[31]

How does Spain compare to major economies in preindustrial Western Europe? At the time of the Black Death, average income levels in Spain were above those of the North Sea Area (Netherlands and the United Kingdom) and France (Fig. 2.13). Then, in 1560s, at the peak of its expansion, Spain's per capita GDP still remained ahead the U.K and France's, but way below that of the Netherlands. The collapse from the 1570s represented a watershed and Spain fell behind during the seventeenth century. In the early eighteenth century and the post-Napoleonic Wars economic recovery, Spain partially caught up with France but not with the U.K., and its growth was not strong enough to prevent another episode of falling behind during the early nineteenth century.

[29] In a nutshell, Maddison's approach implicitly assumes that the relative prices of 1990, and therefore, 1990 technology, remained unchanged over time (Cf. Prados de la Escosura, 2000).

[30] Actually, the lowest level, 1990 $600, corresponds to 1470 and the highest, 1990 $1138, to 1341, with an average per capita income of 1990 $838 (c.v. 0.127) during 1277–1850.

[31] Converted in G-K$ 1990 with the US GDP deflator https://www.measuringworth.com/datasets/usgdp. A similar figure is derived by Allen (2013) using the welfare ratio approach.

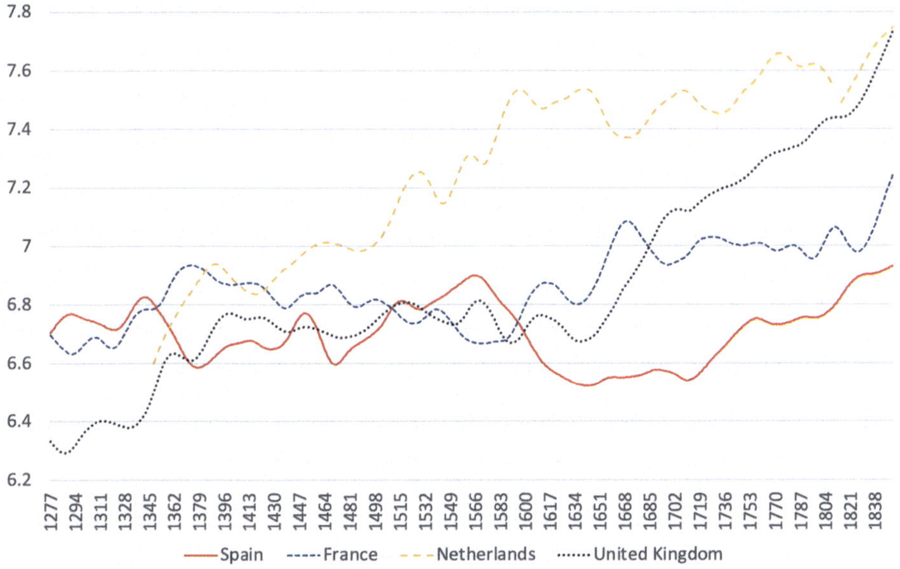

Fig. 2.13 Real GDP per head Hodrick-Prescott Trends 1270–1850: European Perspective ($1990) (logs). *Sources*: Spain, see the text; France, Ridolfi and Nuvolari (2020); Netherlands, van Zanden and van Leeuwen (2012); United Kingdom, Broadberry et al. (2015)

2.8 Concluding Remarks

In this chapter, we have attempted to make the most of scattered data. The results, conjectural as they may be, offer some preliminary conclusions and hypotheses for further research.

1. Our aggregate output estimates revise and improve on previous work by (Álvarez-Nogal and Prados de la Escosura, 2013; Álvarez-Nogal et al. 2016). In particular, our agricultural output estimates based on tithes largely confirm those previously obtained with a demand approach. This represents a relevant methodological finding for the reconstruction of historical national accounts: the use of indirect methods such as a demand function to assess trends in agricultural output is warranted in the absence of direct sources.
2. Although no significant long-term change in per capita output emerges over more than half a millennium, Spain's preindustrial economy was far from stagnant and long phases of absolute and per capita growth and decline alternated. 'Smithian' and 'growth recurring' episodes seem to be present in Spain's performance.
3. Population and output per head moved together, at odds with the conventional depiction of preindustrial societies as Malthusian. This finding is consistent with the high land-labour ratios found in a frontier economy.

4. In a frontier economy, living standards are usually relatively high and incomes not very unequally distributed. These features seem to reflect Spain's experience until the early sixteenth century.
5. If we project Spain's per capita income trend growth during 1470–1570 until the onset of the Napoleonic Wars, we obtain similar levels to the U.K.'s. Why was Spain's performance up to the 1570s cut short, giving way to a sustained falling behind? Why did Spain never return to the virtuous path initiated in the late fifteenth and consolidated during the sixteenth century? Conventional Malthusian narratives do not appear persuasive in a context of simultaneous growth or decline of population and per capita income. The answer seems to be in policymakers' economic decisions and new incentives. The long-run unintended consequences of Spain's attempt to preserve its European Empire provides an explanatory hypothesis that needs to be explored. Sustained increases in fiscal pressure on dynamic urban activities to finance imperial wars in Europe triggered de-urbanisation and led to a collapse in average real incomes, from which early modern Spain never fully recovered. Furthermore, post-1570s Spain appears to present a mirror image of the North Sea Area's experience where the pull of urban demand triggered an agricultural revolution, as peasants had an incentive to raise their purchasing power to access the new urban goods and services.

Appendix

See Table 2.3.

Table 2.3 GDP, population, and inequality, 1277–1850

	Agricultural output	Total output	Output per capita	GDP per capita	Nominal GDPmp	Population	Nominal per capita GDPmp	Nominal Williamson Index	Nominal land rent/wage
	(1850/1859=100)	(1850/1859=100)	(1850/1859=100)	(G-K $1990)	(million Reales)	(million)	(Reales)	(1790/1799=100)	(1790/1799=100)
1277	39	22	76	791	289	4.4	66	52	
1278	40	22	77	801	286	4.4	65	50	
1279	40	23	77	811	282	4.4	64	49	
1280	41	23	78	822	279	4.4	63	47	
1281	42	23	79	832	276	4.4	62	46	
1282	43	23	80	842	273	4.4	62	45	
1283	43	24	81	853	269	4.4	61	43	
1284	44	24	82	863	266	4.4	60	42	
1285	45	24	83	874	263	4.4	59	41	
1286	45	24	84	875	265	4.4	60	40	
1287	45	25	84	877	267	4.4	60	40	
1288	46	25	84	878	269	4.5	60	40	
1289	46	25	84	879	271	4.5	61	39	
1290	46	25	84	885	271	4.5	61	38	
1291	47	25	85	890	271	4.5	61	38	
1292	47	25	85	895	271	4.5	61	37	
1293	52	27	91	950	245	4.5	55	33	
1294	49	26	87	915	265	4.5	59	35	
1295	46	25	84	880	287	4.5	64	37	
1296	43	24	81	846	311	4.5	69	40	
1297	41	23	78	813	338	4.5	75	42	
1298	41	23	78	814	340	4.5	76	42	
1299	41	23	78	815	343	4.5	76	42	

(continued)

Table 2.3 (continued)

	Agricultural output	Total output	Output per capita	GDP per capita	Nominal GDPmp	Population	Nominal per capita GDPmp	Nominal Williamson Index	Nominal land rent/wage
	(1850/1859=100)	(1850/1859=100)	(1850/1859=100)	(G-K $1990)	(million Reales)	(million)	(Reales)	(1790/1799=100)	(1790/1799=100)
1300	41	23	78	816	346	4.5	77	41	
1301	40	23	77	805	358	4.5	80	42	
1302	42	23	79	822	346	4.5	77	40	
1303	43	24	80	840	335	4.5	74	39	
1304	45	25	82	859	324	4.6	71	37	
1305	47	25	84	878	314	4.6	69	36	
1306	49	26	87	910	297	4.6	65	34	
1307	49	26	86	900	302	4.6	66	34	
1308	44	24	80	838	320	4.6	69	40	
1309	43	24	79	823	336	4.6	73	41	
1310	44	24	80	838	336	4.6	73	38	
1311	46	25	82	861	345	4.6	75	35	
1312	46	25	83	866	368	4.6	79	34	
1313	47	25	83	869	391	4.7	84	33	
1314	47	26	83	872	415	4.7	89	32	
1315	43	24	79	823	415	4.7	88	37	
1316	44	24	79	824	421	4.7	89	37	
1317	44	25	79	825	426	4.7	90	37	
1318	44	25	79	827	432	4.8	91	36	69
1319	44	25	79	828	437	4.8	92	36	68
1320	45	25	79	830	443	4.8	92	36	60
1321	45	25	79	825	446	4.8	93	35	53
1322	44	25	78	812	457	4.8	95	35	47

1323	43	24	76	799	468	4.8	97	35	41
1324	42	24	75	786	480	4.9	99	35	36
1325	42	24	75	786	494	4.9	101	35	37
1326	42	24	75	786	508	4.9	104	35	38
1327	42	24	75	782	528	4.9	107	36	39
1328	46	26	80	835	480	4.9	97	32	41
1329	45	25	77	809	507	5.0	102	33	38
1330	46	26	78	819	497	5.0	100	32	38
1331	49	27	83	868	446	5.0	90	29	39
1332	53	29	87	914	408	5.0	82	27	41
1333	58	30	92	968	434	5.0	87	28	43
1334	55	29	89	934	478	5.0	96	30	41
1335	52	28	86	898	514	5.0	103	32	41
1336	50	27	84	874	545	5.0	109	35	41
1337	50	28	84	880	538	5.0	108	34	42
1338	53	29	87	914	502	5.0	101	32	42
1339	55	29	90	939	524	5.0	105	34	67
1340	56	30	90	945	487	5.0	98	32	66
1341	64	33	99	1039	403	5.0	81	27	52
1342	61	32	96	1006	419	5.0	84	27	55
1343	57	30	92	960	447	5.0	90	29	44
1344	52	28	86	901	499	5.0	100	32	45
1345	58	30	92	967	438	5.0	88	28	43
1346	55	30	90	942	457	5.0	92	29	42
1347	53	29	88	917	477	5.0	96	30	40
1348	47	26	84	881	458	4.6	99	32	40
1349	42	23	83	866	425	4.3	99	33	40

(continued)

Table 2.3 (continued)

	Agricultural output	Total output	Output per capita	GDP per capita	Nominal GDPmp	Population	Nominal per capita GDPmp	Nominal Williamson Index	Nominal land rent/wage
	(1850/1859=100)	(1850/1859=100)	(1850/1859=100)	(G-K $1990)	(million Reales)	(million)	(Reales)	(1790/1799=100)	(1790/1799=100)
1350	38	22	81	851	395	4.0	98	34	40
1351	36	20	82	856	381	3.7	102	32	34
1352	33	19	76	801	477	3.7	128	33	25
1353	35	20	79	831	399	3.7	107	34	33
1354	35	20	80	836	398	3.7	106	34	35
1355	36	20	81	844	400	3.8	107	34	37
1356	36	20	81	851	414	3.8	110	32	34
1357	37	21	83	873	460	3.8	122	29	30
1358	36	20	81	848	417	3.8	111	36	43
1359	36	20	81	846	398	3.8	106	38	55
1360	37	20	82	863	421	3.8	112	36	44
1361	37	20	81	853	408	3.8	108	39	46
1362	34	19	78	817	386	3.8	102	48	59
1363	33	19	75	788	411	3.8	109	53	59
1364	32	19	74	778	426	3.8	112	56	58
1365	33	19	76	794	441	3.8	116	54	54
1366	32	19	74	780	452	3.8	119	54	56
1367	33	19	75	791	492	3.8	130	47	45
1368	32	19	75	781	485	3.8	128	47	46
1369	32	19	74	775	587	3.8	154	48	57
1370	31	18	72	756	646	3.8	169	54	93
1371	28	17	67	699	759	3.8	199	51	46
1372	29	17	69	723	770	3.8	201	50	55

1373	30	18	70	734	744	3.8	195	48	58
1374	28	17	66	690	654	3.8	171	57	47
1375	28	17	66	691	627	3.8	164	58	49
1376	29	17	67	702	649	3.8	169	53	43
1377	29	17	68	712	665	3.8	173	51	42
1378	29	17	68	710	646	3.8	168	55	48
1379	29	17	67	702	514	3.9	133	63	69
1380	30	17	69	720	543	3.9	141	55	51
1381	31	18	70	734	529	3.9	137	51	43
1382	31	18	71	747	531	3.9	137	48	43
1383	33	19	74	777	583	3.9	151	40	30
1384	31	18	70	734	643	3.9	166	42	34
1385	32	18	72	750	573	3.9	148	42	40
1386	31	18	70	734	726	3.9	187	42	30
1387	31	18	71	739	692	3.9	178	44	35
1388	31	18	70	732	572	3.9	147	50	49
1389	31	18	69	727	581	3.9	149	50	51
1390	33	19	73	769	608	3.9	156	42	40
1391	31	18	70	737	600	3.9	154	44	45
1392	33	19	73	762	580	3.9	148	40	41
1393	35	19	75	790	565	3.9	144	39	39
1394	35	20	76	794	512	3.9	131	35	43
1395	35	20	76	796	522	3.9	133	37	43
1396	34	19	75	780	569	3.9	145	37	39
1397	34	19	75	781	628	3.9	160	39	39
1398	35	20	75	788	654	3.9	166	38	40
1399	35	20	76	796	726	3.9	184	38	43

(continued)

Table 2.3 (continued)

	Agricultural output (1850/1859=100)	Total output (1850/1859=100)	Output per capita (1850/1859=100)	GDP per capita (G-K $1990)	Nominal GDPmp (million Reales)	Population (million)	Nominal per capita GDPmp (Reales)	Nominal Williamson Index (1790/1799=100)	Nominal land rent/wage (1790/1799=100)
1400	35	20	76	797	819	3.9	208	37	40
1401	35	20	75	786	916	3.9	232	38	37
1402	39	21	82	854	1111	4.0	281	42	35
1403	36	20	76	801	955	4.0	241	33	31
1404	33	19	73	761	865	4.0	218	29	29
1405	34	19	74	774	938	4.0	237	30	26
1406	30	18	68	712	904	4.0	228	29	24
1407	34	19	73	769	945	4.0	238	29	23
1408	28	17	65	684	837	4.0	210	25	23
1409	36	20	77	805	974	4.0	245	30	24
1410	36	20	77	806	984	4.0	247	30	23
1411	36	20	77	807	1038	4.0	260	31	21
1412	36	20	77	809	1147	4.0	287	34	21
1413	37	20	78	813	1252	4.0	313	38	21
1414	37	21	78	817	1189	4.0	297	33	19
1415	37	21	78	822	1132	4.0	282	31	19
1416	37	21	78	816	1085	4.0	270	27	18
1417	42	23	85	894	1168	4.0	291	27	16
1418	38	21	79	832	1106	4.0	275	26	17
1419	38	21	80	836	1106	4.0	275	27	15
1420	36	20	76	794	1116	4.0	277	27	15
1421	35	20	75	783	1146	4.0	284	29	15
1422	34	20	73	767	1160	4.0	287	27	14

1423	24	16	59	614	871	4.0	215	20	14
1424	31	18	69	720	1128	4.1	278	28	15
1425	34	20	73	766	1121	4.1	277	29	16
1426	34	20	73	764	1134	4.1	279	29	17
1427	35	20	76	792	1024	4.1	252	25	19
1428	39	22	81	851	1011	4.1	249	26	22
1429	30	18	67	703	824	4.1	202	21	26
1430	42	23	85	892	1032	4.1	253	29	32
1431	32	19	71	745	847	4.1	208	25	30
1432	35	20	76	792	927	4.1	227	27	27
1433	41	23	84	880	1046	4.1	256	29	24
1434	36	20	76	793	1006	4.1	246	29	22
1435	28	18	65	681	846	4.1	206	24	19
1436	34	20	74	772	968	4.1	235	27	19
1437	32	19	70	735	895	4.1	216	25	20
1438	29	18	66	688	993	4.2	239	27	19
1439	30	19	67	705	994	4.2	238	26	20
1440	34	20	73	760	1098	4.2	262	29	19
1441	38	22	78	814	1166	4.2	277	31	20
1442	46	25	90	947	1456	4.2	344	39	20
1443	35	21	73	769	1184	4.3	278	32	19
1444	36	21	74	772	1181	4.3	276	32	19
1445	40	23	80	839	1256	4.3	292	35	20
1446	45	25	87	913	1263	4.3	293	35	19
1447	47	26	89	935	1209	4.3	279	33	17
1448	46	25	89	927	1096	4.4	252	28	16
1449	48	26	91	948	1203	4.4	275	34	16

(continued)

Table 2.3 (continued)

	Agricultural output	Total output	Output per capita	GDP per capita	Nominal GDPmp	Population	Nominal per capita GDPmp	Nominal Williamson Index	Nominal land rent/wage
	(1850/1859=100)	(1850/1859=100)	(1850/1859=100)	(G-K $1990)	(million Reales)	(million)	(Reales)	(1790/1799=100)	(1790/1799=100)
1450	47	26	90	938	1091	4.4	248	35	19
1451	45	25	86	905	1165	4.4	264	38	19
1452	46	26	87	914	1218	4.4	274	39	20
1453	44	25	84	880	1196	4.5	268	38	22
1454	41	24	80	840	980	4.5	219	30	22
1455	46	25	86	899	1121	4.5	249	34	24
1456	46	26	86	900	1142	4.5	253	36	25
1457	43	25	82	859	1159	4.5	255	37	26
1458	38	22	75	781	843	4.6	185	29	26
1459	50	28	91	955	1038	4.6	226	37	27
1460	43	25	81	850	1062	4.6	231	39	28
1461	45	25	83	868	1093	4.6	236	39	26
1462	43	25	80	838	1232	4.7	265	40	26
1463	37	22	71	744	995	4.7	213	36	29
1464	35	21	69	720	957	4.7	204	35	28
1465	36	21	69	721	953	4.7	202	35	28
1466	39	23	73	766	958	4.7	202	36	28
1467	35	21	67	705	965	4.8	203	36	29
1468	31	20	63	655	901	4.8	188	33	29
1469	32	20	64	666	988	4.8	206	37	29
1470	28	18	58	604	1032	4.8	214	40	23
1471	34	21	66	695	1166	4.9	240	44	26
1472	35	22	67	701	971	4.9	199	38	30

1473	31	20	61	635	1042	4.9	213	41	34
1474	44	26	79	831 .	1212	4.9	246	46	37
1475	38	23	71	743	1012	4.9	205	38	40
1476	39	23	72	751	1037	5.0	209	40	41
1477	38	23	71	738	1252	5.0	251	55	46
1478	42	25	76	800	1320	5.0	263	54	43
1479	50	28	86	899	1009	5.0	200	45	48
1480	38	23	70	736	826	5.1	163	34	43
1481	49	28	84	878	1041	5.1	205	43	40
1482	41	25	74	774	1050	5.1	206	42	36
1483	44	26	78	812	1107	5.1	216	45	33
1484	49	29	84	884	1239	5.2	240	55	34
1485	41	25	73	770	1105	5.2	213	45	29
1486	38	24	69	723	1060	5.2	204	39	27
1487	46	27	79	829	1349	5.2	258	46	26
1488	39	24	70	735	1059	5.3	202	35	26
1489	41	25	72	753	1018	5.3	193	34	27
1490	38	24	69	724	999	5.3	189	34	29
1491	47	28	80	837	1231	5.3	231	41	29
1492	44	27	76	801	1034	5.3	195	35	31
1493	49	29	82	861	1144	5.3	215	41	33
1494	44	27	76	793	1043	5.3	196	38	35
1495	45	27	77	806	1068	5.3	200	39	37
1496	44	27	76	793	1007	5.4	188	36	37
1497	51	30	84	884	1417	5.4	264	52	36
1498	55	31	88	925	1486	5.4	276	52	36
1499	46	27	77	806	1310	5.4	243	47	37

(continued)

Table 2.3 (continued)

	Agricultural output	Total output	Output per capita	GDP per capita	Nominal GDPmp	Population	Nominal per capita GDPmp	Nominal Williamson Index	Nominal land rent/wage
	(1850/1859=100)	(1850/1859=100)	(1850/1859=100)	(G-K $1990)	(million Reales)	(million)	(Reales)	(1790/1799=100)	(1790/1799=100)
1500	40	25	70	730	1065	5.4	197	39	40
1501	43	26	73	764	1125	5.4	207	42	40
1502	47	28	78	820	1226	5.4	225	42	37
1503	44	26	74	771	1160	5.5	213	38	35
1504	47	28	77	810	1210	5.5	221	41	36
1505	45	27	75	782	1206	5.5	220	39	35
1506	47	28	77	807	1472	5.5	268	49	38
1507	46	27	82	863	1433	4.9	291	50	34
1508	48	27	93	978	1429	4.4	325	56	26
1509	48	27	92	966	1391	4.4	314	54	24
1510	44	25	86	897	1312	4.5	295	48	23
1511	45	26	88	918	1210	4.5	270	45	25
1512	46	26	88	925	1213	4.5	269	45	25
1513	49	27	92	960	1284	4.5	284	46	23
1514	48	27	90	944	1273	4.6	279	46	22
1515	49	28	92	961	1312	4.6	286	47	24
1516	48	27	89	936	1275	4.6	277	46	26
1517	50	28	92	961	1300	4.6	280	46	25
1518	48	27	89	927	1281	4.7	275	44	26
1519	49	28	91	950	1332	4.7	284	46	27
1520	47	27	86	906	1267	4.7	269	42	27
1521	46	27	85	890	1486	4.7	313	49	32
1522	46	27	85	887	1514	4.8	317	49	32

1523	47	27	86	897	1529	4.8	318	50	29
1524	46	27	85	886	1521	4.8	315	49	18
1525	43	26	81	843	1466	4.9	302	47	28
1526	44	26	81	847	1674	4.9	343	54	29
1527	43	26	79	825	1659	4.9	338	52	27
1528	42	25	78	813	1650	4.9	334	51	38
1529	42	26	78	816	1690	5.0	340	53	39
1530	41	25	76	791	1660	5.0	332	54	44
1531	48	28	88	921	1747	4.8	364	57	40
1532	48	28	88	917	1735	4.8	360	55	37
1533	45	27	83	874	1657	4.8	342	52	34
1534	53	30	94	983	1875	4.9	385	58	37
1535	50	29	90	942	1782	4.9	364	55	35
1536	47	28	86	905	1667	4.9	339	50	55
1537	56	32	98	1024	1890	4.9	382	56	37
1538	50	30	90	945	1759	5.0	354	52	38
1539	42	26	80	842	1603	5.0	321	46	49
1540	55	33	91	954	1992	5.5	364	52	50
1541	58	34	94	986	2275	5.5	414	60	59
1542	44	28	78	817	1930	5.5	349	50	62
1543	50	31	85	890	2104	5.6	379	54	61
1544	57	34	93	977	2313	5.6	414	58	54
1545	45	29	79	825	1958	5.6	349	48	50
1546	52	32	87	908	2597	5.6	460	63	60
1547	64	38	101	1061	3027	5.7	534	74	57
1548	47	31	81	853	2464	5.7	432	59	60
1549	50	32	84	879	2612	5.7	456	60	59

(continued)

Table 2.3 (continued)

	Agricultural output	Total output	Output per capita	GDP per capita	Nominal GDPmp	Population	Nominal per capita GDPmp	Nominal Williamson Index	Nominal land rent/wage
	(1850/1859=100)	(1850/1859=100)	(1850/1859=100)	(G-K $1990)	(million Reales)	(million)	(Reales)	(1790/1799=100)	(1790/1799=100)
1550	66	40	101	1060	3211	5.9	541	71	57
1551	56	35	90	941	2745	6.0	460	63	67
1552	61	37	95	992	2923	6.0	488	66	68
1553	63	39	98	1021	3010	6.0	500	66	67
1554	60	37	94	980	2913	6.1	481	62	67
1555	54	35	88	919	2769	6.1	455	57	74
1556	52	34	85	886	2998	6.1	490	62	74
1557	54	35	87	915	3181	6.1	518	62	76
1558	55	36	89	928	3212	6.2	520	63	78
1559	55	36	88	924	3221	6.2	519	62	71
1560	65	41	100	1045	3705	6.2	600	69	67
1561	55	36	89	930	3444	6.2	555	64	72
1562	61	39	95	997	3697	6.2	593	69	75
1563	68	42	102	1072	4012	6.3	640	69	70
1564	66	41	100	1044	3907	6.3	620	67	72
1565	64	41	100	1043	3878	6.2	625	65	70
1566	61	39	94	985	3987	6.3	629	65	75
1567	61	40	94	983	4073	6.4	634	67	79
1568	66	42	98	1026	4309	6.5	663	70	85
1569	62	40	93	977	4096	6.6	622	67	83
1570	60	39	92	963	4001	6.5	617	65	84
1571	63	40	98	1030	4272	6.2	684	72	89
1572	67	42	102	1073	4500	6.3	718	74	89

1573	57	38	91	956	4052	6.3	642	66	78
1574	55	37	88	924	3941	6.4	613	63	77
1575	63	41	97	1012	4354	6.4	678	69	88
1576	58	39	91	957	4607	6.4	716	72	91
1577	59	39	92	962	4685	6.5	724	72	109
1578	52	36	83	871	4324	6.6	658	66	113
1579	57	38	90	941	4611	6.5	713	69	96
1580	56	38	90	938	4513	6.4	710	68	91
1581	47	33	79	829	4547	6.4	711	65	88
1582	50	35	82	861	4766	6.5	736	66	90
1583	51	36	83	869	4910	6.5	755	68	98
1584	46	34	78	815	4633	6.5	709	60	81
1585	61	40	94	979	5602	6.5	857	71	78
1586	56	38	88	923	5333	6.6	808	71	82
1587	55	38	86	900	5343	6.7	795	67	79
1588	55	38	85	886	5359	6.8	783	64	79
1589	49	36	79	822	5071	6.9	733	60	94
1590	57	39	86	905	5532	6.9	806	66	91
1591	53	37	83	873	5337	6.8	784	65	89
1592	54	37	85	895	5414	6.6	817	67	79
1593	51	35	83	866	5147	6.5	791	64	86
1594	54	37	86	905	5418	6.5	838	68	102
1595	50	35	81	850	5022	6.5	770	63	88
1596	53	37	84	881	5629	6.6	854	68	86
1597	48	34	78	814	5284	6.7	793	63	82
1598	47	34	76	794	5290	6.7	785	62	92
1599	48	34	76	800	5475	6.8	805	63	95

(continued)

Table 2.3 (continued)

	Agricultural output	Total output	Output per capita	GDP per capita	Nominal GDPmp	Population	Nominal per capita GDPmp	Nominal Williamson Index	Nominal land rent/wage
	(1850/1859=100)	(1850/1859=100)	(1850/1859=100)	(G-K $1990)	(million Reales)	(million)	(Reales)	(1790/1799=100)	(1790/1799=100)
1600	51	35	80	839	5620	6.6	853	67	98
1601	50	35	80	834	5443	6.6	828	64	87
1602	48	33	77	807	5286	6.6	806	58	77
1603	48	34	77	802	5333	6.7	802	58	74
1604	46	33	74	771	5146	6.7	763	55	78
1605	42	31	69	720	4924	6.8	726	53	88
1606	45	32	71	741	5489	6.8	802	58	94
1607	44	31	71	745	5354	6.7	800	58	96
1608	47	32	74	772	5494	6.7	823	59	88
1609	47	32	73	767	5403	6.7	805	57	70
1610	50	34	76	796	5604	6.7	837	60	65
1611	42	30	68	710	4471	6.6	672	48	58
1612	43	30	68	717	4548	6.7	681	50	64
1613	46	31	71	741	4729	6.7	701	52	62
1614	44	31	68	717	4684	6.8	689	51	65
1615	46	31	70	733	4835	6.8	709	52	69
1616	40	29	64	674	4897	6.8	718	51	71
1617	42	29	66	686	4896	6.8	720	53	87
1618	50	33	74	770	5485	6.8	805	58	70
1619	45	31	69	720	5079	6.8	744	54	65
1620	46	31	69	721	5127	6.9	745	55	59
1621	46	31	68	712	4786	6.9	691	51	61
1622	43	30	65	679	4559	7.0	655	49	63

1623	49	32	71	740	5085	7.0	731	56	70
1624	50	33	71	741	5003	7.0	713	54	69
1625	47	32	68	708	4841	7.1	683	57	69
1626	46	31	66	689	5001	7.1	699	66	69
1627	45	30	65	682	5001	7.0	711	63	68
1628	47	31	68	716	5203	6.9	753	67	76
1629	47	31	68	714	5267	6.8	769	60	71
1630	43	29	64	666	4865	6.8	713	56	71
1631	46	30	67	700	5105	6.8	748	59	81
1632	44	29	66	687	4795	6.7	713	56	72
1633	45	29	67	702	4763	6.6	721	59	67
1634	45	29	67	702	4736	6.6	714	59	68
1635	41	27	62	645	4421	6.7	662	54	68
1636	44	28	65	676	4356	6.7	651	54	70
1637	42	28	63	658	4262	6.7	637	53	65
1638	48	30	68	714	4591	6.6	692	58	66
1639	47	29	67	707	4463	6.6	677	59	65
1640	45	29	66	687	4252	6.6	645	60	62
1641	44	28	64	665	3992	6.6	601	61	69
1642	48	30	68	715	4202	6.6	632	77	69
1643	44	28	63	662	4119	6.7	617	50	65
1644	48	30	67	703	4380	6.7	657	55	61
1645	46	28	65	677	4130	6.7	620	56	70
1646	43	27	62	650	4865	6.6	733	63	62
1647	41	26	60	633	4740	6.6	714	63	79
1648	44	27	65	680	4908	6.4	765	69	73
1649	42	26	64	665	4706	6.3	752	67	70

(continued)

Table 2.3 (continued)

	Agricultural output	Total output	Output per capita	GDP per capita	Nominal GDPmp	Population	Nominal per capita GDPmp	Nominal Williamson Index	Nominal land rent/wage
	(1850/ 1859=100)	(1850/ 1859=100)	(1850/ 1859=100)	(G-K $1990)	(million Reales)	(million)	(Reales)	(1790/1799=100)	(1790/ 1799=100)
1650	40	25	62	650	4567	6.2	742	64	69
1651	42	26	65	678	4406	6.1	720	62	54
1652	46	28	70	729	4782	6.1	784	65	51
1653	42	26	65	679	4364	6.1	718	65	49
1654	47	29	71	744	4803	6.1	789	69	56
1655	46	28	69	724	4671	6.1	762	68	57
1656	47	28	69	725	4270	6.2	688	57	47
1657	47	29	69	721	4205	6.3	670	59	51
1658	46	28	67	706	4201	6.4	661	55	44
1659	45	28	67	698	4150	6.4	653	58	48
1660	46	28	68	707	4255	6.4	668	58	57
1661	49	30	71	738	4622	6.4	726	65	52
1662	47	29	68	715	4444	6.4	697	63	46
1663	46	29	68	707	4515	6.4	704	63	44
1664	40	26	61	641	4246	6.5	656	61	64
1665	43	27	64	669	4560	6.5	699	60	60
1666	47	29	67	699	4348	6.6	662	53	49
1667	44	28	64	671	4136	6.6	631	51	46
1668	44	28	64	672	4207	6.6	642	54	58
1669	50	30	70	738	4483	6.5	685	59	48
1670	48	30	69	721	4332	6.5	665	59	37
1671	44	28	65	682	3435	6.5	528	46	40
1672	48	30	68	715	3675	6.6	560	46	33

1673	50	30	69	724	3684	6.6	556	49	35
1674	48	30	68	708	3646	6.7	544	47	37
1675	50	31	69	720	3787	6.8	559	49	44
1676	51	31	69	727	4914	6.8	718	58	39
1677	44	28	63	656	4517	6.9	659	54	45
1678	48	30	67	698	4817	6.8	708	57	49
1679	47	30	66	687	4717	6.8	690	58	44
1680	47	30	66	688	4670	6.8	684	56	59
1681	46	29	65	681	4499	6.8	662	54	53
1682	48	30	66	696	4482	6.8	657	62	55
1683	47	30	66	692	4571	6.8	672	61	64
1684	47	30	66	693	4580	6.8	672	60	67
1685	48	30	70	735	4481	6.4	699	64	61
1686	50	30	72	757	3424	6.3	543	49	46
1687	50	30	72	750	3433	6.4	536	49	37
1688	49	30	71	740	3377	6.5	523	49	34
1689	48	30	69	725	3352	6.5	513	49	33
1690	52	32	73	760	3636	6.7	546	49	33
1691	52	32	71	746	3703	6.8	544	47	31
1692	50	31	69	720	3659	6.9	528	47	37
1693	54	33	71	747	3788	7.0	537	50	39
1694	46	30	64	674	3538	7.1	497	44	33
1695	43	29	61	642	3451	7.2	479	39	37
1696	48	31	65	684	4065	7.2	563	55	46
1697	48	31	65	683	4030	7.2	558	54	47
1698	48	31	65	685	4142	7.3	569	56	67
1699	52	33	69	718	4400	7.3	601	59	68

(continued)

Table 2.3 (continued)

	Agricultural output	Total output	Output per capita	GDP per capita	Nominal GDPmp	Population	Nominal per capita GDPmp	Nominal Williamson Index	Nominal land rent/wage
	(1850/1859=100)	(1850/1859=100)	(1850/1859=100)	(G-K $1990)	(million Reales)	(million)	(Reales)	(1790/1799=100)	(1790/1799=100)
1700	61	37	76	801	4920	7.3	674	65	58
1701	59	36	74	780	4375	7.4	594	54	47
1702	55	35	71	739	4099	7.5	549	50	46
1703	55	35	70	735	4080	7.6	538	49	46
1704	58	36	72	753	4156	7.7	540	51	46
1705	56	36	69	726	4049	7.8	517	49	49
1706	51	34	65	682	4331	7.9	547	57	56
1707	51	34	64	675	4324	8.0	539	59	58
1708	47	32	62	646	4022	7.9	511	58	62
1709	49	33	64	672	4180	7.8	537	61	63
1710	46	32	62	649	4125	7.8	531	59	75
1711	46	32	62	651	3770	7.7	487	56	73
1712	49	33	64	673	3900	7.7	504	57	60
1713	48	33	64	665	3924	7.8	503	59	56
1714	52	34	67	700	4121	7.8	526	61	51
1715	52	35	66	693	4155	7.9	523	64	51
1716	55	36	68	712	3676	8.0	458	52	45
1717	56	37	68	715	3612	8.2	443	51	44
1718	56	37	68	714	3657	8.2	445	53	51
1719	56	37	68	713	3744	8.3	451	54	41
1720	60	39	71	745	3880	8.4	463	56	39
1721	55	37	67	702	3628	8.4	432	54	35
1722	58	39	69	724	3811	8.5	450	56	48

1723	59	39	70	729	3953	8.5	464	57	57
1724	58	39	69	720	3965	8.6	462	58	54
1725	62	41	72	756	4099	8.6	478	60	46
1726	61	41	72	754	4145	8.6	481	59	44
1727	63	42	73	764	4256	8.7	490	60	42
1728	58	40	69	727	4084	8.8	466	59	47
1729	60	41	71	738	4210	8.9	473	59	44
1730	69	45	77	804	4658	9.0	519	66	55
1731	67	45	76	791	4630	9.0	514	64	49
1732	67	45	75	787	4644	9.1	513	64	50
1733	64	44	73	765	4539	9.1	496	62	52
1734	60	42	70	730	4485	9.2	487	61	65
1735	65	45	73	764	4764	9.3	512	63	61
1736	63	44	72	759	4748	9.2	518	65	60
1737	60	43	71	746	4750	9.1	522	65	67
1738	67	46	76	799	5149	9.2	561	71	63
1739	61	43	73	762	4741	9.0	526	67	58
1740	58	42	72	752	4704	8.9	529	67	65
1741	67	46	79	832	4776	8.7	548	69	64
1742	74	49	85	890	4981	8.7	575	72	59
1743	68	46	81	844	4641	8.7	534	67	49
1744	66	46	79	828	4595	8.8	524	66	53
1745	63	45	77	802	4459	8.9	501	63	50
1746	66	47	78	818	4606	9.0	509	63	48
1747	61	45	75	782	4489	9.2	489	61	53
1748	67	48	79	823	4846	9.2	525	65	57
1749	63	47	76	796	4758	9.3	511	63	65

(continued)

Table 2.3 (continued)

	Agricultural output	Total output	Output per capita	GDP per capita	Nominal GDPmp	Population	Nominal per capita GDPmp	Nominal Williamson Index	Nominal land rent/wage
	(1850/1859=100)	(1850/1859=100)	(1850/1859=100)	(G-K $1990)	(million Reales)	(million)	(Reales)	(1790/1799=100)	(1790/1799=100)
1750	68	49	79	830	5155	9.3	552	67	65
1751	66	48	78	822	5795	9.4	619	74	66
1752	77	53	86	901	6375	9.4	681	81	63
1753	60	46	75	789	5771	9.3	621	74	82
1754	74	52	85	888	6602	9.3	706	81	69
1755	73	52	84	882	6347	9.4	677	78	64
1756	74	52	84	884	5683	9.4	603	72	53
1757	80	55	88	924	5941	9.5	622	75	57
1758	75	54	85	888	5720	9.7	592	75	61
1759	76	55	85	890	5805	9.8	594	70	58
1760	80	57	87	908	6033	9.9	609	69	66
1761	76	56	84	882	6745	10.0	674	77	61
1762	69	53	80	836	6440	10.1	639	72	67
1763	62	50	75	787	6366	10.2	626	72	78
1764	67	52	78	818	6814	10.2	669	75	75
1765	67	53	79	822	6971	10.3	678	77	86
1766	68	54	80	833	7517	10.2	733	83	74
1767	64	52	77	804	7265	10.3	705	80	81
1768	66	53	78	817	7547	10.4	727	79	68
1769	66	54	78	820	7587	10.4	732	82	84
1770	69	55	80	842	7550	10.4	727	83	75
1771	69	55	81	843	7243	10.4	699	78	68
1772	68	55	80	837	7402	10.4	712	78	78

1773	70	56	81	853	7665	10.5	731	81	84
1774	65	54	79	822	7315	10.5	696	78	76
1775	72	57	83	866	7654	10.5	728	85	76
1776	66	55	79	830	7520	10.5	713	80	73
1777	69	57	81	850	7805	10.7	731	82	70
1778	67	57	79	829	7559	10.8	697	78	77
1779	66	57	78	822	7723	11.0	702	79	83
1780	62	56	76	797	7770	11.1	700	78	98
1781	73	60	82	863	8416	11.1	758	89	86
1782	75	61	84	884	8489	11.0	770	94	84
1783	75	61	85	886	8465	11.0	770	95	77
1784	66	58	79	830	8100	11.1	730	89	82
1785	70	60	81	850	8686	11.2	776	88	86
1786	66	58	79	831	9059	11.1	813	87	83
1787	72	61	84	883	9487	11.0	862	102	111
1788	72	61	85	889	9445	10.9	869	100	100
1789	72	61	85	886	9612	10.9	882	91	102
1790	75	62	87	907	9635	10.9	885	95	99
1791	74	62	86	900	10,014	11.0	913	102	89
1792	69	60	82	863	10,053	11.0	910	100	94
1793	70	61	83	870	10,553	11.2	946	97	104
1794	67	60	81	851	10,531	11.2	940	97	107
1795	66	60	80	842	10,508	11.3	931	93	94
1796	63	59	79	826	11,358	11.4	998	101	99
1797	65	60	80	833	11,989	11.5	1042	102	96
1798	74	65	84	881	13,026	11.6	1119	109	107
1799	71	63	83	870	12,321	11.6	1062	105	110

(continued)

Table 2.3 (continued)

	Agricultural output	Total output	Output per capita	GDP per capita	Nominal GDPmp	Population	Nominal per capita GDPmp	Nominal Williamson Index	Nominal land rent/wage
	(1850/ 1859=100)	(1850/ 1859=100)	(1850/ 1859=100)	(G-K $1990)	(million Reales)	(million)	(Reales)	(1790/1799=100)	(1790/ 1799=100)
1800	64	61	79	827	11,657	11.6	1002	94	100
1801	67	62	81	849	12,886	11.6	1107	99	98
1802	66	62	80	841	12,895	11.7	1101	98	81
1803	58	59	76	797	13,076	11.7	1120	101	113
1804	60	59	78	821	14,098	11.4	1232	122	147
1805	69	62	86	901	15,403	10.9	1415	124	102
1806	74	63	91	949	13,719	10.6	1296	104	88
1807	75	64	92	962	13,153	10.6	1244	92	75
1808	78	65	93	976	12,444	10.7	1168	90	77
1809	62	60	84	884	10,636	10.8	987	72	69
1810	52	55	80	837	11,513	10.5	1094	80	79
1811	45	53	76	799	12,562	10.6	1189	87	92
1812	51	56	80	833	14,902	10.7	1389	99	105
1813	54	57	82	860	13,352	10.6	1257	86	81
1814	61	60	87	906	13,069	10.6	1235	85	65
1815	69	64	91	952	14,076	10.7	1319	87	66
1816	71	65	92	960	13,592	10.8	1254	81	63
1817	66	64	89	930	15,319	11.0	1391	71	42
1818	73	68	92	967	14,305	11.1	1287	87	49
1819	75	69	93	972	13,788	11.3	1221	83	46
1820	76	70	93	973	13,912	11.5	1211	84	51
1821	79	72	94	986	12,946	11.7	1110	85	47
1822	81	74	95	992	12,917	11.8	1091	81	43

1823	86	77	97	1012	13,116	12.0	1091	81	47
1824	88	78	98	1021	13,903	12.1	1146	84	57
1825	71	71	87	915	11,392	12.3	928	159	154
1826	83	77	95	990	16,898	12.4	1364	96	55
1827	88	80	96	1008	15,499	12.5	1237	92	53
1828	86	79	96	1002	15,906	12.6	1264	94	45
1829	90	81	97	1020	15,245	12.7	1203	89	39
1830	94	83	99	1037	14,337	12.8	1122	83	48
1831	93	83	99	1032	14,838	12.8	1156	90	55
1832	80	79	92	968	16,779	12.9	1301	107	72
1833	84	81	95	992	15,695	12.9	1217	100	66
1834	81	80	93	976	15,919	13.0	1226	99	56
1835	81	80	94	982	15,689	12.9	1217	98	50
1836	78	79	92	959	16,759	13.1	1283	103	59
1837	80	80	92	967	16,743	13.2	1267	104	69
1838	78	80	92	958	17,262	13.2	1306	104	70
1839	81	81	94	983	16,530	13.1	1258	97	53
1840	91	86	99	1033	14,657	13.2	1111	88	46
1841	92	86	99	1035	15,134	13.3	1141	90	47
1842	85	84	96	1001	16,920	13.4	1264	97	53
1843	86	85	96	1001	17,281	13.6	1275	98	48
1844	81	84	93	971	18,593	13.7	1354	104	48
1845	90	89	97	1016	16,999	13.9	1226	95	42
1846	94	91	99	1034	17,058	14.0	1214	93	
1847	87	89	95	994	19,253	14.2	1352	103	
1848	90	92	96	1009	18,262	14.4	1264	97	
1849	94	94	98	1022	18,126	14.6	1240	94	
1850	104	99	101	1063	17,720	14.8	1201	88	

A.1 Population

Benchmarks

The benchmark levels used have been 1100, 1300, 1347, 1435, 1492, 1506, 1508, 1530, 1591, 1646, 1712–1717, 1752, 1787, 1797, 1821, 1833, and 1850. The main source are Pérez Moreda (1988, 2002). Benchmark estimates have been derived as follows.

- *1000*. We assumed that Portugal's population represented the same proportion of total Iberia's population as in 1300, and the resulting figure was subtracted from Iberia's to obtained that of Spain, 3.75 million.
- *1300*. Population figures for Aragon and Castile kingdoms, 4 million (Pérez Moreda, 2002) have been increased with Pérez Moreda (1988) conjectures on Nazri Granada and Navarre's population in 1300 (0.4 and 0.1 million, respectively) reaching a total of 4.5 million for present-day Spain.
- *1347*. Pérez Moreda (2002) assumes 0.5% population growth over 1300–1347, reaching 5.1 million. We find this assumption on the high side, as qualitative evidence suggests substantial population losses due to bad harvests and famines in the early fourteenth century (Valdeón, 1969; Ladero Quesada, 1981; Vaca, 1983). Instead, we have accepted Pérez Moreda's growth assumption but excluding years of famine (1301, 1309–1311, 1331–1347) for which no population growth was assumed. The resulting figure, 5.0 million, would imply a yearly growth rate of 0.2% over 1300–1347.
- *1351*. As the Black Death had a dramatic impact on the population within a short period of time, 1348–1350, we hypothesise a 25% contraction between 1347 and 1351, in line with the regional evidence available (Castán Lanaspa, 2020; Furiò, 2013; Pérez Moreda, 1988, 2002).
- *1435*. Population was obtained by adding up the estimate for Christian Spain in 1435, 3.8 million (Pérez Moreda, 2002), and Granada and Navarre's population, 0.3 million, c. 1420 (Pérez Moreda, 1988).
- *1492 onwards*. Pérez Moreda (2002) estimates for 1492, 1506, and 1508 include the entire population of present day Spain. Population growth between c. 1492 and 1500 was offset by the decline resulting from the Jew population expelled after 1492, that Pérez Moreda (1988: 368) estimates in 0.15 m., and Muslim emigration to North Africa during the Granada war and after the conquest of the Nazri Kingdom by the Catholic Kings (1492), that altogether could be estimated in 0.3 million. The figures for 1530 and 1591 from Pérez Moreda (2002, 1988: 372) and the one for 1646 from Reher (personal communication).
- *1712–1717*. Pérez Moreda (1988: 384), on the basis of Bustelo (1973, 1974) provides a 7.7–8.15 million range. We have been accepted the upper bound for 1717, which appears to be consistent with the available estimates for mid-eighteenth century.
- *1752–1850*. The figures for 1752 come from the Ensenada population census (Pérez Moreda, 1988: 385). Figures for 1787 (10.4 million) and 1797 (10.5 million) from Floridablanca and Godoy population censuses have been raised

to 11.0 and 11.5 million, respectively, following Bustelo's (1972) proposal. Pérez Moreda assumes zero net growth between 1797 and 1815. Estimates for 1821 and 1833, from Pérez Moreda (1988: 402). The latter has been increased by 5% to offset its underestimate. The estimate for 1850 from Prados de la Escosura (2017).

Alternative Yearly Estimates

Estimate 1

Baptism indices are yearly available for practically all regions between 1700 and 1809, although its coverage declines as one moves back to 1580 and from 1809 onwards.[32] An annual national index can be derived by weighting each regional baptism index, B_{rt}, expressed as 1790–1799=1, by the average of regional population in 1787 and 1797 censuses, $N_{r1787\text{-}97}$.[33]

$$B_{.t} = \Sigma N_{r1787-97*} B_{rt} \qquad \text{for } 0 \leq t \leq T \tag{2.13}$$

Figure 2.14 presents annual population estimates derived from baptism indices along those obtained through log-linear interpolation of each pair of adjacent benchmark estimates. It can be observed that, from the early seventeenth to the late eighteenth century, the baptism-based series shadows the interpolated series but at a lower level. It also reveals the high volatility of baptism series that precludes inferring yearly population levels from it.[34]

---

[32] From 1700 onwards we used Llopis Agelán (personal communication), who kindly provided us with an updated dataset, completed with Nadal (1988) for 1580–1700. In the case of New Castile we have preferred Reher (1991) indices. For La Rioja, Gurría (2004) indices have been used. We assumed that missing regions were represented by neighbour ones (see fn. 34).

[33] As the regional coverage of baptism series diminishes as we move back in time, we have constructed indices for each regional sample and spliced them into a single index given preference to the indices with broader regional coverage.

[34] Unless we assume an almost perpetual pandemic scenario with population varying by the hundred thousand from 1 year to another! Regional data on baptisms, expressed in index form, are available at decadal intervals for all Spanish regions since 1700, with its regional coverage narrowing down as one moves back to the 1520s. For 1580s–1790s we used Llopis Agelán (personal communication) and Llopis Agelán and Sebastián Amarilla (2007) decadal regional estimates, completed with Reher's for 1520s–1580s (personal communication). Since the coverage for earlier decades declines, we assumed that some regions' population moved with its neighbours', namely, Asturias presumably evolved as Galicia during 1610–1630; Cantabria as the average of Galicia and the Basque region, 1620–1630; and Galicia, Asturias, and Cantabria as the Basque region over 1580–1610. Also, Valencia and Murcia were assumed to move with Catalonia during 1580–1600, and with Balearics during 1580–1590. Regional coverage is restricted to the Kingdom of Castile and Navarre for the 1580s as information is available neither for Valencia, and Balearics, nor for the Canaries. Data for 1550–1580 are restricted to Castilla-León that was assumed to represent also the evolution of northern Spain (Galicia, Asturias, Cantabria, and the Basque region), Castilla-La Mancha, Madrid, and Extremadura (that was used to represent the evolution of Andalusia).

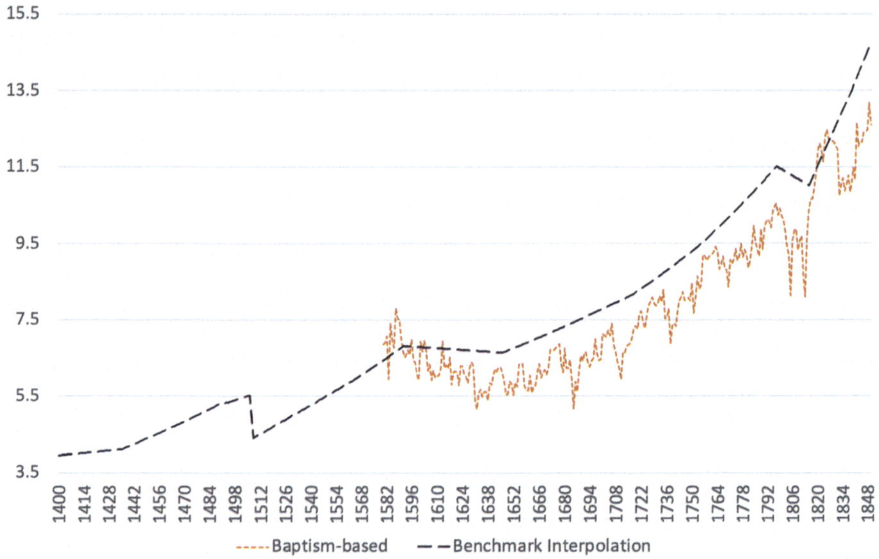

Fig. 2.14 Population: Benchmarks' interpolation and estimates derived by projecting regional 1787–1797 population average with baptism series, 1400–1850 (million)

Estimate 2

This estimate offers an alternative solution to the one used in the main text—expression (2.4)—, as a variable-weighted geometric average has been computed for each pair of estimates previously derived using adjacent benchmarks, in which the closest benchmark series gets a larger weight.

$$N_d = (X_d)^{(n-t)/n} * (Y_d)^{t/n} \qquad \text{for } 0 \le t \le T \qquad (2.14)$$

Being N the population at decadal estimates d, X and Y, the values corresponding to the projection of each adjacent benchmark (initial and final) figures (i.e., 1700 and 1750) with baptism decadal indices, respectively; and n the number of years in between 0 and T.

See Figs. 2.14, 2.15 and 2.16.

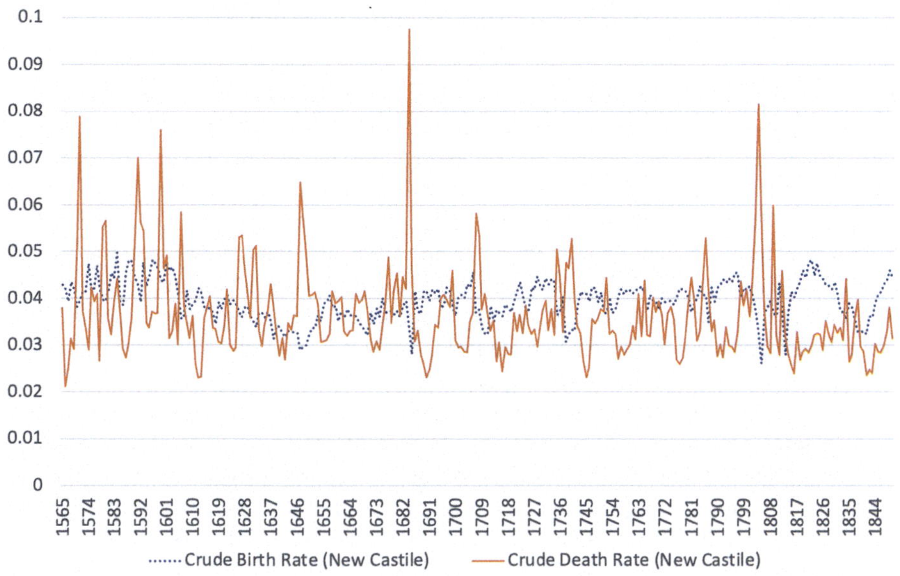

Fig. 2.15 New Castile crude birth and death rates, 1565–1850 (0/00). Source: Reher (1991)

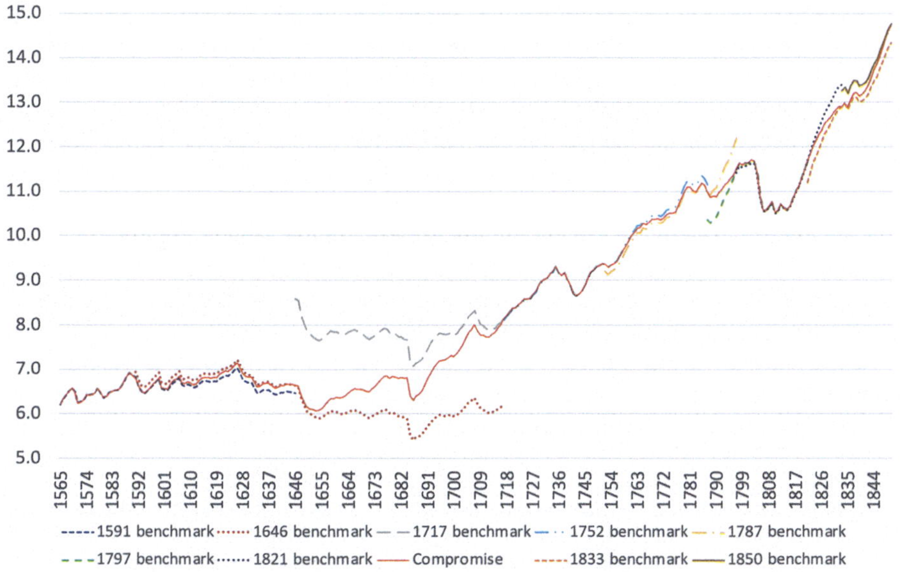

Fig. 2.16 Population, 1565–1850: Alternative Benchmarks Projected with Reher's New Castile crude birth and death rates and compromise estimates (linear interpolation) (million)

A.2 Computing Agricultural Output Indices from Tithes

Tithe records go back to the Middle Ages but the dearth of written sources reduces the time span in which they are available. In Spain, tithes can be traced back to the early fifteenth century for cereals and olive oil and to the end of the century for wine, while for fruits and vegetables and livestock tithes already exist for the sixteenth century. In Roman Catholic countries tithes did not disappear until the French Revolution and the Napoleonic Wars. In the case of Spain, tithes persisted until the 1830s (Canales, 1982), but its reliability to capture output tendencies after 1808 is hampered by lack of compliance as a result of the Peninsular War and the institutional collapse of the Ancien Régime.

The translation of tithes into output trends raises some questions. Tithes were imposed on farming and livestock production and although, nominally, represented 10% of total production, in practice, its share fluctuated and was usually smaller. Collection procedures, whether direct or rented out to private agents, and the payment system (in kind or cash) changed over time and varied across regions. Also, the resistance of peasants to pay the tax varied, as did the tax exemptions of specific producers, and the opportunities for evasion resulting from the emergence of new crops. Does all this render tithes questionable as a proxy for output tendencies?

In favour of the use of tithes it can be asserted, though, that in late medieval and early modern Spain, where different fiscal systems operated, tithes provided homogeneous information across regions. Moreover, tithes were computed on total output, with the local priest acting as supervisor and making public the names and amounts paid by each producer. The latter also found in its publicity a guarantee of property rights on the harvested land (Santiago-Caballero, 2011, 2014). Lastly, the diversity of tithe beneficiaries multiplied the accounting records available allowing a direct comparison between alternative sources. All this has led historians to depict tithes as a fixed proportion of total production from which output trends can be inferred (García Sanz, 1979).

Unlike most studies we have chosen national rather than a regional or local approach. Thus, aggregates for main crops have been constructed on the basis of an extensive dataset of tithe series at regional and local levels. We have been able to gather tithe records from as early as the fourteenth century.[35]

The choice of a procedure to aggregate multiple series into homogenous and continuous series was a key decision.[36] When the sources made it possible, our favoured approach has been working on the series at a local level. The first step has

[35] Given the lack of consistent data no adjustment has been made for crops partially or totally exempt from paying the tithe (i.e., "Excusado" and "diezmos privativos") as it would have required applying an arbitrary correction. Moreover, until 1761, "Excusado" was collected through a distribution of a yearly lump-sum payment among bishops and other ecclesiastical institutions, and such distribution was estimated using tithes.

[36] We considered that an advanced statistical manipulation of the original series would imply loosing important information about local trends that would be diluted into the aggregate figures while rendering the resulting series useless for econometric treatment.

been establishing whether the series are complete on an annual basis. In most of the cases we found gaps in the records that ranged from just 1 year to longer periods of time. The way in which we have dealt with missing values depended on the amount of information lost and on the availability of sources. If the number of missing observations was small, we derived them by extrapolating the results from series in the same region that presented a similar behaviour due to analogous climatic and soil conditions. In order to obtain the best estimation, we used as proxy the series that were geographically close to the one to be estimated. Missing years were interpolated using the available series that showed a higher correlation in the years around the missing values.[37] In our opinion, when the amount of years to be estimated was manageable, this procedure offers the most reliable way to filling the gaps in the series and provides the best possible estimations.

If the number of missing values was large or the existence of alternative local series scarce, we have relied on alternative methods. In these cases, we filled the missing values using the average weight that the local series to be estimated did represent in the aggregate provincial sample.[38] However, we were aware of the fact that the weights of the series within the sample changed over time and, therefore, that we had to make adjustments to calculate missing years in the same location that were separated by long periods of time. For that reason we decided to re-calculate the weight of the municipality around each gap. The periods used to estimate the weights therefore varied within the same municipality depending on the years that had to be estimated, a fact that adds robustness to our estimation. Once we had estimated the missing years for all the local series, we simply aggregated them in order to generate the provincial series. When local series from different authors for the same province and period were available, we used the overlapping periods in order to splice them and derive a single series. We also followed the same process in those cases in which the series came from the same source but different local series were available for different periods of time, and we spliced them through on the basis of the overlapping years.

As a result of a long and detailed process we derived series at provincial or regional level that were, then, combined in order to obtain national aggregates for the main crops: cereals, wine, olive oil, legumes, fruit, and animal produce (including wool and silk).

[37] When we found missing values, we interpolated them using other tithe series in the same region that presented a high correlation with the incomplete one. However, our experience shows that series that presented high correlations in the very long run do not have to necessarily have high correlations in the short term. For that reason we estimated the correlation of the incomplete series with the complete ones around the missing years and not for the whole sample. For instance, if for the same region we had several series between 1500 and 1800 but one of them had missing values between 1550 and 1555, we proxied those missing values using the most similar series in the region around that period (1530–1580 for example) and not for the whole 300 years.

[38] For example, if we had a study with ten local series and the one with the missing years represented a 20% of the total production, we used that percentage to estimate the gaps from the information contained in the other nine.

It is for cereals for which the availability of data is wider over space and time with different series covering Andalusia (three out of four provinces, Seville—which included also Cadiz and Huelva—, Cordoba, and Granada, which included Malaga), Extremadura, Murcia, New Castile, Old Castile-Leon (including Burgos—which also included Rioja and Santander—, Leon—which included Asturias—, Palencia, Segovia, Soria, Valladolid, and Zamora), Galicia, Basque provinces, and the Canaries, within the Kingdom of Castile; plus Aragon, Balearics, Catalonia, and Valencia, in the Kingdom of Aragon; plus the Kingdom of Navarre.

As for wine, tithes information was restricted to Andalusia (Seville, Cadiz, Huelva, and Cordoba), Murcia, Old Castile (Rioja, Segovia, and Santander), Basque, Navarre, Aragon, and Catalonia). These regions represented, nonetheless, the main producing areas.

In the case of olive oil information only related to Andalusia (Seville and Cordoba), Extremadura, Balearics, Catalonia, and Navarre. Again, these were the main producers in early modern Spain.

Information about tithes on legumes and fruit is scant and we only managed to get tithes for Balearics and Catalonia, Valencia, and Navarre. These areas represent, nonetheless, above 40% of the value of production in the 1799 Census.

In the case of animal produce, tithes for livestock and wool, are available for Old Castile (Segovia and Soria), Extremadura, Murcia, Navarre, Aragon, and Valencia.

In all cases, we had to interpolate missing values with the help of the geographically closer series. We then constructed regional series by assuming that series for missing provinces evolve alongside those for which data were available. Alternatively, missing values for odd years were log-linearly interpolated.

Weighting provincial series for each crop poses a major challenge. The 1799 *Census of Fruits and Manufactures* provides the only available estimate of quantities and values of agricultural and industrial goods for early modern Spain. It has a poor reputation largely due to Josep Fontana's (1967) severe critique. Nonetheless, Fontana largely exonerated cereal production from his criticism and suggested a correction for olive oil output. Unfortunately there is no alternative to the 1799 Census. A possibility would be to derive weights from the highly reputed Cadastre of Ensenada for the 1750s, but it only covers the Kingdom of Castile, leaving aside the Kingdom of Aragon (including Aragon, Balearics, Catalonia, and Valencia) and the Kingdom of Navarre. Furthermore, no distinction is made in the Cadastre's "respuestas generales" (aggregate results) by crops, only between crops and animal produce (Matilla Tascón, 1947; Grupo '75, 1977).

We have re-computed the value of total output for the 1799 benchmark by, firstly, correcting olive oil production, as suggested by Fontana (1967); then, valuing each crop at a single price derived as the weighted average of provincial prices. Using a single set of prices helps to correct for the risk of spurious provincial prices (as pointed out by Fontana), while provides us with consistent estimates. Furthermore, it implies a purchasing power parity adjustment across Spanish provinces. The value of agricultural output c. 1799 resulted from aggregating the value of each crop obtained by multiplying its quantity by the average national price. We used, then, provincial (regional) shares in the value of each main crop in 1799 as weights to construct national volume indices for each of them, expressed using 1790/1799 as 100.

The valuation of livestock output in the 1799 Census raises a problem as the livestock total (number of different type of cattle) is mixed with animal produce (i.e., wool). The total value of animal output should then be reduced, in principle, to offset this exaggeration. However, livestock figures are grossly underestimated in the 1799 Census. The data from the 1750s Cadastre of Ensenada for the Kingdom of Castile roughly doubles the 1799 Census figures for the Castilian provinces (García Sanz, 1994). Since there no evidence of a major decline in Castilian livestock during the late eighteenth century exists, such a discrepancy evidences under-reporting in the 1799 Census.[39]

A detailed list of the sources used can be found in L. Prados de la Escosura, C. Álvarez-Nogal and C. Santiago-Caballero (2022), "Growth Recurring in Preindustrial Spain?", *Cliometrica* 16(2): 215–241, Supplementary file1 (DOCX 402 KB).

A.3 Commodity and Factor Price Indices

Agricultural Prices

For each main crop, prices for 1276–1500 derive from Argilés (1999), for Catalonia (Lérida), Zulaica (1994) and Hamilton (1936), for Aragon, and Hamilton (1936) for Valencia and Navarre, Izquierdo Benito (1983), for Toledo, and Alonso Casado (1991, 2009), for Burgos. Prices for 1501–1800, come from Felíu (1991), for Catalonia, and from Hamilton (1934, 1947), and Hamilton's unpublished manuscript working sheets (kindly provided by Robert Allen) for Andalusia, New and Old Castile, and Valencia. From 1800, prices comes from Felíu (1991), for Catalonia, up to 1808; Morilla (1972) and Ponsot (1986) for Andalusia; and Llopis Agelán (1980) for wool in Guadalupe. Prices for each produce have been weighted by the regional shares in each main produce's production by 1799 in order to derive prices at national level.

Industrial Prices

An unweighted Törnqvist index of manufacturing prices (building materials—timber, plaster, lime, tiles, nails—, fuel—coal, wood—, paper, parchment, textiles—cloth, linen, silk—, wax) for 1276–1500 was constructed on the basis of those we had previously built on the basis of original data, for Aragon, 1276–1429 (Zulaica

[39] It is worth noting that the share of animal produce in agricultural final output was 25.3% in 1890 and 29.3% in 1909/1913 (Prados de la Escosura, 2017: 69). Given the expansion of crops, largely at the expense of livestock, throughout the nineteenth century, a share of 31% for animal produce in 1799 does seem reasonable, so we have accepted it. Agricultural historians coincide in pointing to a decline in livestock output simultaneous to a rise in crop output over the late nineteenth century. See GEHR (1978/1979).

Palacios, 1994), and 1429–1500 (Hamilton, 1936); Toledo, 1401–1475 (Izquierdo Benito, 1983); and Burgos, 1390–1500 (MacKay, 1981; Casado Alonso, 1985, 1991). For the period 1501–1860, we have used an aggregate manufacturing price index kindly supplied by Joan Rosés.

Consumer Price Index
A CPI for 1276–1501 was constructed as a weighted average of agricultural (0.75) and industrial (0.25) Törnqvist price indices, except for Valencia (Allen, 2001). For 1501–1860, a Törnqvist index was derived from regional CPIs: Catalonia, 1501–1807 (Felíu, 1991), and 1830–1860 (Maluquer de Motes, 2005); Valencia, 1501–1785 (Allen, 2001); New Castile (Reher and Ballesteros, 1993), Old Castile, 1518–1650 (Llopis Agelán et al., 2000) and 1751–1860 (Moreno Lázaro, 2002).

Wage Rates
Unweighted Törnqvist indices of nominal wage rates for masons, bricklayers, tilers, and carpenters were computed from the following sources: Aragon, 1277–1423 (Zulaica Palacios, 1994) and 1423–1497 (Hamilton, 1936); Lérida, 1361–1500 (Argilés, 1999); Valencia, 1413–1500 (Allen, 2001) in the Kingdom of Aragon; Toledo, 1401–1475 (Izquierdo Benito, 1983); and Burgos, 1390–1500 (MacKay, 1981; Casado Alonso, 1985, 1991) in the Kingdom of Castile. For 1501–1860, the sources used were: Catalonia (Felíu, 1991; Maluquer de Motes, 2005), New Castile (Reher and Ballesteros, 1993), Old Castile (Moreno Lázaro, 2002), and Valencia (Allen, 2001).

A.4 Adjusted Urban Population

In order to distinguish those in the urban population who depended on industrial and service activities, an arithmetical exercise has been carried out. Wrigley (1985) assumed that, in pre-industrial Europe, all agricultural population lived in rural areas so to derive the population related to non-agricultural activities, to those living towns, the rural population not involved in agricultural activities should be added. Therefore, the crucial distinction to make was between the agricultural and non-agricultural shares of rural population. However, in preindustrial Spain, the existence of 'agro-towns' (namely, towns in which a sizable share of the population was dependent on agriculture) is assumed. Hence, the challenge is to establish which share of rural and urban population lived on agriculture.

In order to distribute rural and urban population into agricultural and non-agricultural we start by comparing the share of the economically active population (L) occupied in agriculture (L_{ag}/L), and the share of total population (N) living in rural areas (N_{rur}/N). If the ratio between these two shares $[(L_{ag}/L):(N_{rur}/N)]$ is above one, this would mean that part of the population living in towns worked in agriculture. Conversely, a ratio below one suggests that part of those living in the countryside work for industry and services.

However, deriving the ratio between the agricultural, L_{ag}, and the rural economically active populations, L_{rur} (L_{ag}/L_{rur}) requires further adjustment which allows for urban-rural differences, firstly, in the proportion of total population (***N***) in working age, or potentially active population (***PAP***), and, then, in the share of the working age population (***PAP***), which is economically active (***L***).

Fortunately, we have information on the ***PAP/N*** ratio in both rural and urban areas by region for 1787 (Marcos Martín, 2005). This ratio (computed—due to the census distribution by age cohorts—as population ages 16–50 over total population) differs by region (***i***) between urban $(PAP/N)_{urb\ i\_1787}$ and rural $(PAP/N)_{rur\ i\_1787}$ areas, being larger in urban areas, but showing low dispersion in both cases.[40]

The implication is that using rural and urban population without previously adjusting for age composition biases the results against agricultural employment, as, on average, the rural $(PAP/N)_{rur}$ ratio is 87.5% of the urban one. Unfortunately, no yearly data on the ***PAP/N*** ratio are available for Spain, except for New Castile, for which Reher (1991) computed it from the late sixteenth century onwards.[41] Thus, we are forced to proxy long-run changes in Spain's ***PAP/N*** by those in New Castile's (***NC***) $(PAP/N)_{NC\_t}$.[42]

Thus, we derived the urban and rural working age at each benchmark year ***t*** as follows,[43]

$$PAP'_{urb_{it}} = N_{urb_{it}} {}^{*} (PAP/N)_{urb_{i\_1787}} {}^{*} \left((PAP/N)_{NC_t} / (PAP/N)_{NC\_1787}\right) \quad (2.15)$$

$$PAP'_{rur_{it}} = N_{rur_{it}} {}^{*} (PAP/N)_{rur_{i\_1787}} {}^{*} \left((PAP/N)_{NC_t} / (PAP/N)_{NC\_1787}\right) \quad (2.16)$$

Then, in order to arrive to figures for economically active urban ($L_{urb\ it}$) and rural ($L_{rur\ it}$) populations at each benchmark we needed to derive the relevant ***L/PAP*** ratios. Alas, we were only able to compute the ***L/PAP*** ratio for 1787 without being able to distinguish between urban and rural ratios. Hence, we estimated figures of urban and rural ***EAP*** for every benchmark year as

[40] They were, on average, 55.7% and 48.8% in urban and rural areas, respectively. The urban and rural coefficients of variation are 0.056 and 0.023, respectively and are computed from Marcos Martín (2005). The regional dispersion in the activity rate (EAP/PAP) is also low, 0.113.

[41] The sample used by Reher (1991) consists of 26 villages, from which only five belong to the province of Madrid.

[42] Regional dispersion was low for *PAP/N* in 1787 but we do not really know if this was the case in previous epochs. In New Castile, the *PAP/N* ratio, computed for the share of population between 15 and 50 years old, was rather stable over time, with less than a 5% variation around the 1787 ratio (Reher, 1991: 70:74).

[43] In expressions 2.15 to 2.25 ' means an approximated estimate, as opposed to the actual value, since some simplifying assumptions were needed in order to facilitate the computation.

$$\boldsymbol{L'_{urb_{it}}} = \boldsymbol{PAP'_{urb_{it}}}^* (\boldsymbol{L}/\boldsymbol{PAP})_{\mathbf{i\_1787}} \tag{2.17}$$

$$\boldsymbol{L'_{rur_{it}}} = \boldsymbol{PAP'_{rur_{it}}}^* (\boldsymbol{L}/\boldsymbol{PAP})_{\mathbf{i\_1787}} \tag{2.18}$$

Next, we compared the economically active population occupied in agriculture ($\boldsymbol{L_{ag}}$), with that living in rural areas ($\boldsymbol{L'_{rur}}$). If $\boldsymbol{L_{ag}} > \boldsymbol{L'_{rur}}$ it can be presumed that part of the population living in towns worked in agriculture. Conversely, if $\boldsymbol{L_{ag}} < \boldsymbol{L'_{rur}}$ the implication is that those living in the countryside allocated part of their working time to industry and services. This way, we distributed the rural ($\boldsymbol{L'_{rur}}$) and urban ($\boldsymbol{L'_{urb}}$) economically active populations into agricultural ($_{ag}$) and non-agricultural ($_{nonag}$) occupations and reached a figure for urban non-agricultural labour ($\boldsymbol{L'_{urb\text{-}nonag\ it}}$).

$$L'_{rur-nonag_{it}} = L'_{rur_{it}} - L_{ag_{it}} \quad \text{if } L'_{rur_{it}} > L_{ag_{it}}, 0 otherwise \tag{2.19}$$

$$\boldsymbol{L'_{rur\text{-}ag_{it}}} = \boldsymbol{L'_{rur_{it}}} - \boldsymbol{L'_{rur\text{-}nonag_{it}}} \tag{2.20}$$

$$L'_{urb-ag_{it}} = L_{ag_{it}} - L'_{rur_{it}} \quad \text{if } L_{ag_{it}} > L'_{rur_{it}}, 0 otherwise \tag{2.21}$$

$$\boldsymbol{L'_{urb\text{-}nonag_{it}}} = \boldsymbol{L'_{urb_{it}}} - \boldsymbol{L'_{urb\text{-}ag_{it}}} \tag{2.22}$$

Thus, economically active population outside agriculture is obtained as

$$\boldsymbol{L'_{nonag_{it}}} = \boldsymbol{L'_{rur\text{-}nonag_{it}}} + \boldsymbol{L'_{urb\text{-}nonag_{it}}} \tag{2.23}$$

Moreover, we can estimate the adjusted urban population in towns of 5000 or more inhabitants (excluding those living on agriculture), by re-scaling the resulting figures for urban economically active population outside agriculture with the activity rate (***L/N***),

$$\boldsymbol{N'_{urb\text{-}nonag_{it}}} = \boldsymbol{L'_{urb\text{-}nonag_{it}}} / \left(\boldsymbol{L'_{urb_{it}}} / \boldsymbol{N_{urb_{it}}} \right), \tag{2.24}$$

Thus, we can obtain an *adjusted* rate of urbanization ($\boldsymbol{Ua_{it}}$) that partly offsets at least the upward biased effect of the agro-towns:

$$\boldsymbol{Ua_{it}} = \mathbf{100}^* \boldsymbol{N_{urb\text{-}nonag_{it}}} / \boldsymbol{N_{it}} \tag{2.25}$$

Regrettably, though, we lack data to compute the share of labour in agriculture ($\boldsymbol{L_{ag}} / \boldsymbol{L}$) at each benchmark year. For $\boldsymbol{L_{ag}}$ evidence can only be obtained for 1857 and 1787, from population census and for 1752, restricted to the Kingdom of Castile, from the Cadastre of Ensenada (Grupo '75, 1977).[44] Wrigley (1985) and Allen

[44]The Kingdom of Castile covered nowadays Spain excluding the Kingdom of Aragon (Aragon, Catalonia, Valencia, and Balearics) and the Kingdom of Navarre.

(2000) also faced this shortcoming, and Wrigley assumed that, in early sixteenth century England and France, up to 80% of the rural labour force was in agriculture and reduced arbitrarily this figure over the three following centuries. Allen (2000) accepted the same percentage for most European countries *circa* 1500 and interpolated the years up to the first one (1800) for which he had estimates. In the case of Spain, we assumed a fixed 80% share of EAP in agriculture and interpolated log-linearly the shares between 1530 and 1787 and 1787 and 1857.[45]

However, efficiency changes resulting from variations in the composition of labour by economic sectors and in the dependency rate could affect our proposed measure. Thus, we have carried out a sensitivity test by estimating the intersectoral shift effect that results from changes in the shares of industry and services in non-agricultural employment and in the productivity gap between industry and services. Furthermore, we have allowed for changes in the potentially active to total population ratio (PAP/N) that could also affect our index. Fortunately trends in the proposed index of output outside agriculture do not appear to be significantly altered by either demographic or output composition changes during the early modern era.[46]

References

Acemoglu, D., S. Johnson, and J.A. Robinson (2005), "The Rise of Europe: Atlantic Trade, Institutional Change and Economic Growth", *American Economic Review* 95 (3): 546-579.

Alfani, G. (2021), "Economic Inequality in Preindustrial Times: Europe and Beyond", *Journal of Economic Literature* 59(1): 3-44.

[45] The share of EAP in agriculture in the Kingdom of Castile is systematically higher in the Floridablanca Census (1787) than in the Cadastre de Ensenada (1752). Choosing the 1787 Census provides an upper bound for our L_{agr} estimates and, hence, biases downwards the adjusted urbanization rates. We have carried out a sensitivity test assuming that the Lag/L in 1787 remained unchanged for the entire time span considered. The results exhibited the same trends for the adjusted urbanization rates but differ for the sixteenth century (12.0 rather than 9.9 in 1530 and 16.5 instead of 14.5 in 1591).

[46] Services increased relative to manufacturing in terms of output and employment in early modern Spain (García Sanz, 1994; López-Salazar, 1986; Reher, 1990) probably as a consequence of the Dutch disease provoked by the inflow of American silver (Forsyth and Nicholas, 1983; Drelichman, 2005). Given the lack of national data, we arbitrarily assumed that the evolution of the internal composition of non-agricultural employment in Spain was captured by the shares in non-agricultural economically active population (L_{i+s}) of industry (L_i/L_{i+s}) and services (L_s/L_{i+s}) in a New Castile town, Cuenca (Reher, 1990). As regards the productivity ratio between industry and services, lack of data forced us to accept a fixed ratio (1.4) derived from the Cadastre de Ensenada for the Kingdom of Castile c. 1750. The resulting intersectoral shift effect [$IS = (L_s/L_{i+s}) + (1.4^* (L_i/L_{i+s})$] shows a mild decline over time. If alternatively the productivity gap for the 1850s were used (Prados de la Escosura, 2017) the productivity index would rise slightly over 1750–1850. Changes in the potentially active to total population ratio (PAP/N) can also affect our index of output outside agriculture. Alas, we only know the evolution of the PAP/N ratio for the case of New Castile from 1586 onwards which does not exhibit major changes over time (Reher, 1991).

Allen, R. C. (2000), "Economic Structure and Agricultural Productivity in Europe, 1300–1800", *European Review of Economic History* 3(1): 1-25

Allen, R. C. (2001), "The Great Divergence in European Wages and Prices in Europe from the Middle Ages to the First World War", *Explorations in Economic History* 38 (4): 411-447.

Allen, R.C. (2013), Poverty Lines in History, Theory, and Current International Practice, Oxford Discussion Paper 685.

Álvarez-Nogal, C. and L. Prados de la Escosura (2013), "The Rise and Decline of Spain, 1270-1850", *Economic History Review* 66 (1): 1-37

Álvarez-Nogal, C. L. Prados de la Escosura, and C. Santiago-Caballero (2016), "Spanish Agriculture in the Little Divergence", *European Review of Economic History* 20 (4): 452-477.

Álvarez-Nogal, C. L. Prados de la Escosura, and C. Santiago-Caballero (2020), "Economic Effects of the Black Death: Spain in European Perspective", *Investigaciones de Historia Económica-Economic History Research* 16 (4): 35-48.

Anes and A. García Sanz (1982), "Dime et production agraire dans l'Espagne moderne, de la fin du XVIe au milieu du XIXe siècle", in J. Goy and E. Le Roy Ladurie, (eds.), *Prestations Paysannes, Dîmes, Rente Foncière et Mouvements de la Production Agricole à l'époque Préindustrielle*, Paris: Éditions de l'École des Hautes Études en Sciences Sociales, pp. 453-461.

Argilés Aluja, M. C. (1999), *Preus i salaris a la Lleida dels segles XIV i XV segons els llibres d'obra de la Seu*, Alicante: Biblioteca virtual Cervantes https://www.cervantesvirtual.com/obra/preus-i-salaris-a-la-lleida-dels-segles-xiv-i-xv-segons-els-llibres-dobra-de-la-seu%2D%2D0/

Bairoch, P., J. Batou, and P. Chève (1988), *La population des villes européennes. Banque de données et analyse sommaire des résultats, 800 à 1850*, Genève: Librairie Droz.

Broadberry, S.N. and J. Wallis (2017), Growing, Shrinking and Long Run Economic Performance: Historical Perspectives on Economic Development, CEPR Discussion Papers 11973.

Broadberry, S.N., B.M.S. Campbell, A. Klein, M. Overton, and B. van Leeuwen (2015), *British Economic Growth, 1270-1870*, Cambridge: Cambridge University Press.

Bustelo, F. (1974), "El Vecindario general de España de 1712 y 1717 o Censo de Campoflorido (y II", *Revista International de Sociología* 11-12: 7-35.

Bustelo, F. (1972), "La población española en la segunda mitad del siglo XVIII", *Moneda y Crédito* 123: 53-104.

Bustelo, F. (1973), "El Vecindario general de España de 1712 a 1717 o Censo de Campoflorido", *Revista International de Sociología* 7-8: 83-103.

Cabrera, E. (1989), "The Medieval Origins of the Great Landed Estates of the Guadalquivir Valley", *Economic History Review* 42 (4): 465-483

Canales, E. (1982), "Los diezmos en su etapa final", in G. Anes (ed.), *La economía española al final del Antiguo Régimen.* I *Agricultura*, Madrid: Alianza-Banco de España, pp. 105-187.

Casado Alonso, H. (1985), "La construction à Burgos à la fin du Moyen-Age, prix et salaires", *Cahiers de la Méditerranèe* 31: 125–149.

Casado Alonso, H. (1991), "Producción agraria, precios y coyuntura económica en las diócesis de Burgos y Palencia a fines de la Edad Media", Studia Historica. Historia Medieval 9: 67–107

Casado Alonso, H. (2009), "¿Existió la crisis del siglo XIV? Consideraciones a partir de los datos de la contabilidad de la catedral de Burgos", in M. I. del Val Valdivieso and P. Martínez Sopena (eds.), *Castilla y el mundo feudal. Homenaje al profesor Julio Valdeón*, Valladolid: Junta de Castilla y León, pp. 9–25

Castán Lanaspa, G. (2020), *La construcción de la idea de la peste negra (1348-1350) como catástrofe demográfica en la historiografía española*, Salamanca: Ediciones Universidad de Salamanca.

Catalan, J. (2020), "Del crecimiento con crisis a la crisis de crecimiento, 1315-1516. La gran depresión bajomedieval y la economía catalana", *Revista de Historia Industrial* 29(80): 13-83.

Cipolla, C.M. (1980), *Before the Industrial Revolution. European Society and Economy, 1000-1700.* New York: Norton. 2nd edition

Clark, G. (2007), *A Farewell to Alms. A Brief Economic History of the World*, Princeton: Princeton University Press.

Clark, G.,(2008), "In Defense of the Malthusian Interpretation of History", *European Review of Economic History* 12: 175–199.
Correas, P. (1988), "Poblaciones españolas de más de 5.000 habitantes entre los siglos XVII y XIX", *Boletín de la Asociación de Demografía Histórica* 6 (1): 5-23.
Craig, L.A. and D. Fisher (2000), *The European Macroeconomy. Growth, Integration and Cycles, 1500-1913*, Cheltenham, UK: Edward Elgar
Drelichman, M. (2005), "The Curse of Moctezuma: American Silver and the Dutch Disease", *Explorations in Economic History* 42: 349–380.
Feliu, G. (1991), *Precios y salarios en la Cataluña moderna*, 2 vols., Madrid: Banco de España.
Flora, P. (1981), "Historical Process of Social Mobilization: Urbanization and Literacy, 1850-1965", In S. N. Eisenstadt and S. Rokker (eds)., *Building State and Nation*, pp. 213-258.
Fontana, J. (1967), "El "Censo de frutos y manufacturas" de 1799: un análisis crítico", *Moneda y Crédito* 101: 54-68.
Fortea Pérez, J.L. (1995), "Las ciudades de la Corona de Castilla en el Antiguo Régimen: una revisión historiográfica", *Boletín de la Asociación de Demografía Histórica* 13 (3): 19-59.
Forsyth, P.J. and S.J. Nicholas (1983), "The Decline of Spanish Industry and the Price Revolution: A Neoclassical Analysis", *Journal of European Economic History* 12 (3): 601-610
Furió, A. (2013), "La primera gran depresión europea (Siglos XIV-XV)", in E. Llopis and J. Maluquer de Motes (eds.), *España en crisis. Las grandes depresiones económicas, 1348-2012*, Barcelona: Pasado & Presente, pp. 17-58.
Galor, O. and D.N. Weil (2000), "Population, Technology, and Growth: From Malthusian Stagnation to the Demographic Transition and Beyond", *American Economic Review* 90 (4): 806-828.
García Sanz, A. (1979), "La evolución de la producción de cereales y leguminosas en Castilla la Vieja de 1570 a 1800: los diezmos del obispado de Segovia", *Anales del CUNEF*, 223-246.
García Sanz, A. (1986), *Desarrollo y crisis del Antiguo Régimen en Castilla la Vieja. Economía y sociedad en tierras de Segovia, 1500-1814*, Madrid: Akal.
García Sanz, A. (1994), La ganadería española entre 1750 y 1865: Los efectos de la reforma agraria liberal", *Agricultura y Sociedad* 72: 81–119
Gurría García, P.A. (2004), "Dinámicas demográficas de La Rioja a partir de las series de bautismos, 1580-1900", *Áreas* 24: 67-82.
Goldstone, J.A. (2002), "Efflorescences and Economic Growth in World History: Rethinking 'The Rise of the West' and the Industrial Revolution", *Journal of World History* 13 (2): 323.389.
Grupo '75 (1977). *La economía del Antiguo Régimen. La "Renta Nacional" de la Corona de Castilla*, Madrid: Universidad Autónoma de Madrid
Grupo de Estudios de Historia Rural [GEHR] (1978/1979), "Contribución al análisis histórico de la ganadería española, 1865-1929", Agricultura y Sociedad 8: 129-182; 10: 105-169.
Hamilton, E.J. (1934), *American Treasure and the Price Revolution in Spain, 1501.1650*, Cambridge, Mass: Harvard University Press.
Hamilton, E. J. (1936), *Money, Prices and Wages in Valencia, Aragon, and Navarre, 1351–1500*, Cambridge, Mass.: Harvard University Press.
Hamilton, E.J. (1947), *War and Prices in Spain, 1651-1800*, Cambridge, Mass.: Harvard University Press.
Hansen, G.D. and E.C. Prescott (2002), "Malthus to Solow", *American Economic Review* 92 (4): 1205-1217.
Herr, R. (1989), *Rural Change and Royal Finances in Spain at the End of the Old Regimen*, Berkeley: University of California Press.
Hoffman, P.T., D. Jacks, P.A. Levin, and P.H. Lindert (2002), "Real Inequality in Europe since 1500", *Journal of Economic history* 62 (2): 322-355.
Izquierdo Benito, R. (1983), *Precios y salarios en Toledo durante el siglo XV (1400–1475)*, Toledo: Caja de Ahorro Provincial.
Jerven, M. (2011), "African Growth Recurring: An Economic History Perspective of African Growth Episodes, 1690-2010", *Economic History of Developing Regions* 25 (2): 125-154.

Jones, E.L. (1988), *Growth Recurring: Economic Change in World History*, Oxford: Oxford University Press.

Kamen, H. (1978), "The Decline of Spain: A Historical Myth?" *Past and Present* **81**: 24-50

Kuznets, S. (1966), *Modern Economic Growth: Rate, Structure, and Spread.* New Haven: Yale University Press.

Ladero Quesada, M.A. (1981), "Población, economía y sociedad", *in Historia General de España y América*, vol. 5, Madrid: Rialp, pp. 3-105

Lee, R.D. (1985), "Inverse projection and back projection: a critical appraisal, and comparative results for England, 1539 to 1871", *Population Studies* 39 (2): 233-248.

Llopis Agelán, E. (1980), Las economías monásticas al final del Antiguo Régimen en Extremadura, Universidad Complutense Unpublished Ph.D. Dissertation.

Llopis Agelán, E. (2004), "El crecimiento de la población española, 1700-1849: índices regionales y nacional de bautismos", *Áreas* 24: 9-24.

Llopis Agelán, E., M. Jerez, A. Álvaro, and E. Fernández (2000), "Índices de precios de la zona noroccidental de Castilla-León, 1518–1650", *Revista de Historia Económica* 18: 665–686.

Llopis Agelán, E. and González Mariscal, M. (2006), La tasa de urbanización en España a finales del siglo XVIII: el problema de las agrociudades, AEHE Documentos de Trabajo 0602.

Llopis Agelán, E. and J.A. Sebastián Amarilla (2007), "La economía española en el Antiguo Régimen: balance y legado", in R. Dobado, A. Gómez Galvarriato, and G. Márquez (eds.), *España y México. ¿Historias económicas semejantes?*, Mexico D.F., Fondo de Cultura Económica, pp. 77-135

López Losa, E. and S. Piquero Zarauz (2021), "Spanish Subsistence Wages and the Little Divergence in Europe, 1500–1800", *European Economic Review* 25(1): 59-84.

López-Salazar, J. (1986), *Estructuras agrarias y sociedad rural en la Mancha (siglos XVI-XVII)*, Ciudad Real: Instituto de Estudios Manchegos

Lueger, T. (2018), The Principle of Population vs. the Malthusian Trap. A Classical Retrospective and Resuscitation, Darmstadt Discussion Papers 232.

MacKay, A. (1977), *Spain in the Middle Ages. From Frontier to Empire, 1000-1500*, Houndsmill, Basingstoke: Palgrave Macmillan.

MacKay, A. (1981), *Money, Prices and Politics in Fifteenth-century Castile*, London:

Maddison, A. (1995), *Monitoring the World Economy 1820-1991*, Paris: OECD.

Maddison, A. (2006), *The World Economy*, Paris: OECD.

Madsen, J.B., P.E. Robertson, and L. Ye (2019), "Malthus Was Right: Explaining a Millennium of Stagnation", *European Economic Review* 118: 51-68.

Malanima, P. (2011), "The Long Decline of a Leading Economy: GDP in Central and Northern Italy, 1300–1913", *European Review of Economic History* 15 (1): 169-219.

Maluquer de Motes, J. (2005), "Consumo y precios", in A. Carreras and X. Tafunell (eds.), *Estadísticas históricas de España. Siglos XIX y XX*, Bilbao: Fundación BBVA, III, pp. 1247–96

Marcos Martín, A. (2005), "Viejos en la ciudad. La estructura de edad de la población en los núcleos urbanos españoles del Antiguo Régimen", in F. García González (ed.), *Vejez, envejecimiento y sociedad en España, siglos XVI–XXI*, Cuenca: Universidad de Castilla-La Mancha, pp. 67–100.

Martín Galán, M. (1985), "Nuevos datos sobre un viejo problema: el coeficiente de conversión de vecinos en habitantes", *Revista Internacional de Sociología* 43(4): 593-633.

Martínez Shaw, C. (1994), *La emigración española a América (1492-1824)*, Colombres: Archivo de Indianos.

Matilla Tascón, A. (1947), *La única contribución y el Catastro de Ensenada*, Madrid: Servicio de Estudios de la Inspección General del Ministerio de Hacienda.

Moreno Lázaro, J. (2002), "¿Fomentó el capitalismo agrario la desigualdad? Salarios y niveles de vida en Castilla la Vieja, 1751–1861", in J. M. Martínez Carrión (ed.), *El nivel de vida en la España rural, siglos XVIII–XX*, Alicante: Universitat d'Alacant, pp. 75–112.

Morilla Critz, J. (1972), *Introducción al estudio de las fluctuaciones de precios en Málaga. 1787-1829*, Málaga: Diputación de Málaga.

Morner, M. (1975), "La emigración española al Nuevo Mundo antes de 1810. Un informe del estado de la investigación", *Anuario de Estudios Americanos* 32: 43-131.

Nadal, J. (1984), *La población española (Siglos XVI a XX)*, Barcelona: Ariel.

Nadal, J. (1988), "La población española durante los siglos XVI, XVII y XVIII. Un balance a escala regional", in V. Pérez Moreda and D.S. Reher (eds.), *Demografía histórica española*, Madrid: El Arquero, pp. 39-54.

Palma, N. and J. Reis (2019), "From Convergence to Divergence: Portuguese Economic Growth, 1527–1850", *Journal of Economic History* 79 (2): 477-506.

Pamuk, S. (2007), "The Black Death and the Origins of the 'Great Divergence' across Europe, 1300-1600", *European Review of Economic History* 11 (3): 289-317.

Pérez Moreda, V. (1988), "La población española", in M. Artola (ed.), *Enciclopedia de Historia de España*, I. *Economía. Sociedad*, Madrid: Alianza, pp. 345-431.

Pérez Moreda, V. (2002), "La población española en tiempos de Isabel I de Castilla", in J. Valdeón Baruque (ed.), *Sociedad y Economía en tiempos de Isabel la Católica*, Valladolid: Instituto Universitario de Historia Simancas-Ámbito Ediciones, pp. 13-38.

Pérez Moreda, V. (2017), "Spain", in G. Alfani and C. Ó Gráda (eds.), *Famine in European History*, Cambridge: Cambridge University Press, pp. 48-72.

Pérez Moreda, V. and D.S. Reher (2003), "Hacia una definición de la demografía urbana: España en 1787", *Revista de Demografía Histórica* 21 (1): 113-140.

Ponsot, P. (1986),*Atlas de historia económica de la Baja Andalucia (siglos XVI–XIX)*, Sevilla: Editoriales Andaluzas Unidas.

Prados de la Escosura, L. (2000), "International comparisons of real output, 1820-1990: An Alternative Data Set", *Explorations in Economic History* 37 (1): 1-41.

Prados de la Escosura, L. (2017), *Spanish Economic Growth, 1850-2015*, London: Palgrave Macmillan.

Reher, D.S. (1991), "Dinámicas demográficas en Castilla la Nueva, 1550-1900: un ensayo de reconstrucción", in J. Nadal Oller (ed.), *La evolución demográfica bajo los Austrias*, Alicante: Instituto de Cultura Juan Gil-Albert, pp. 17-75.

Reher, D.S. (1990), *Town and Country in Pre-industrial Spain*. Cambridge: Cambridge University Press.

Reher, D. S. and E. Ballesteros Doncel, (1993), "Precios y salarios en Castilla la Nueva: la construcción de un índice de salarios reales, 1501–1991", *Revista de Historia Económica* 11: 101–151.

Ridolfi, L. and A. Nuvolari (2020), *L'Histoire Immobile?* A Reappraisal of French Economic Growth using the Demand-Side Approach, 1280-1850, CEPR Discussion Papers 14985.

Ringrose, D.R. (1983), *Madrid and the Spanish Economy, 1560-1850*, Berkeley: University of California Press.

Rodríguez Molina, J. (1978), *El Reino de Jaén en la Baja Edad Media: aspectos demográficos y económicos*, Granada: Universidad, Secretariado de Publicaciones

Santaolaya Heredero, L. (1991), *Una ciudad del Antiguo Régimen:Toledo en el siglo XVIII (Personas, propiedad y administración)*, Madrid: UNED.

Santiago-Caballero, C. (2011), "Income inequality in central Spain, 1690-1800", *Explorations in Economic History* 48: 83-96.

Santiago-Caballero, C. (2014), "Tithe series and grain production in central Spain (1700-1800)", *Rural History* 25: 15-37.

Temin, P. (2006), "The economy of the Early Roman Empire", *Journal of Economic Perspectives* 20 (1): 133-151.

Torras Elías, J. (1976), *Liberalismo y rebeldía campesina, 1820-1823*, Barcelona: Ariel.

Vaca Lorenzo, A. (1983), "Una manifestación de la crisis castellana del siglo XIV: la caída de las rentas de los señores feudales. El testimonio del monasterio de Sahagún", *Studia Historica. Historia medieval* 1: 157-166.

Valdeón Baruque, J. (1966), *Enrique II de Castilla: la guerra civil y la consolidación del régimen (1366-1371)*. Valladolid: Universidad de Valladolid.

Valdeón Baruque, J. (1969), "Aspectos de la crisis castellana en la primera mitad del siglo XIV", *Hispania* 29: 5-24

Vilar, P. (1970), "Estructures de la societat espanyola cap al 1750", *Recerques* 1: 9-32.

Voigtländer, N. and H.-J. Voth (2013), "Gifts of Mars: Warfare and Europe's Early Rise to Riches", *Journal of Economic Perspectives* 27 (4): 165-186

Vries, J. de (1984), *European Urbanization, 1500-1800*, Cambridge, Ms.: Harvard University Press.

Wrigley, E. A. (1985), "Urban growth and agricultural change: England and the Continent in the Early Modern Period", *Journal of Interdisciplinary History* 10 (4): 683-728.

Yun Casalilla, B. (2004), *Marte contra Minerva. El precio del Imperio Español, c. 1450-1600*, Barcelona: Crítica.

Zanden, J.L. van (2001), "Early modern economic growth. A survey of the European economy, 1500-1800", in M. Prak (ed.), *Early Modern Capitalism, Economic and Social Change in Europe 1400-1800*, London: Routledge, pp. 69-87.

Zanden, J.L. van and B. Van Leeuwen (2012), "Persistent but Not Consistent: the Growth of National Income in Holland 1347–1807", *Explorations in Economic History* 49: 119-130.

Zulaica Palacios, F. (1994), *Fluctuaciones económicas en un periodo de crisis. Precios y salarios en Aragón en la Baja Edad Media (1300–1430)*, Zaragoza: Diputación Provincial de Zaragoza. Institución Fernando El Católico.

Chapter 3
Capital Accumulation

3.1 Introduction

Capital is back on the economist's agenda. Thomas Piketty's (2014) defence of rising capital-output ratio over time has triggered an interest in historical research. The debate on the productivity slowdown has also stimulated the search for its historical roots and, in particular, the role played by capital accumulation.

Using 'state of the art' methodology, this chapter offers consistent and integrated estimates of net capital (wealth) stock and capital services that provide a sound basis to address welfare and growth issues.[1] For example, testing current views about increasing capital/output ratios or investigating the contribution of capital deepening to labour productivity growth (see Chap. 4).

The new set of estimates provides the longest homogeneous historical series of capital stock and services available internationally. This represents an improvement on existing capital estimates for Spain, in particular, the historical series by Prados de la Escosura and Rosés (2010) for 1850–2000, and those for later periods, such as Ivie (Mas and Pérez, 2022), Penn World Tables 10.0 (Feenstra et al., 2015, updated), and Conference Board (2022). Not only by considering a longer time span but, more importantly, by closely following the OECD's Manual (2009), which provides the latest consensus on capital stock and services estimates. Furthermore, unlike the capital estimates for recent decades, the new estimates employ gross fixed capital formation (GFCF) series obtained through splicing national accounts using the

---

An earlier version was published as L. Prados de la Escosura (2022), "Capital in Spain, 1850-2019", *Cliometrica* 16(1): 1–28. The estimates of capital stock and services have been revised and updated.

---

[1] By consistent and integrated estimates, Oulton and Wallis (2016) mean a common dataset and a common set of assumptions in the construction of long run estimates of capital stock and capital services.

L. Prados de la Escosura, *A Millennial View of Spain's Development*, Frontiers in Economic History, https://doi.org/10.1007/978-3-031-60792-9_3

interpolation, rather than backward projection method. This procedure avoids over-exaggerating investment levels and, hence, capital stock.

But why study Spain? The case of Spain is that of a middle-income country (at least, until 1970, according to the World Bank's definition) that succeeded in joining the upper income countries (Calvo-González, 2021). As most historical research on capital has focused on the pioneers of the first and second industrial revolution, providing long-run estimates of capital stock and services, for a country that carried out a transition from a poor, agricultural economy to a post-industrial advanced one, represents an addition to the research on welfare and growth.

The main findings can be summarised as follows.

1. Capital input (namely, the flow of capital services into production) grew at a 3.5% annual rate during the last 170 years, accelerating in the 1920s and especially from the mid-1950s to the onset of the Global Financial Crisis (2008). Until 1975, the acceleration of capital input growth was assisted by an increase in the 'quality' of capital, that is, a compositional shift towards more productive assets.
2. Capital deepening (that is, capital services per hour worked) grew steadily up to World War I, accelerating in the 1920s and even more so between the mid-1950s and mid-1980s, before slowing down, from 1986 to 2007 and, after a strong recovery during the Global Financial Crisis, stagnating since 2014, as expanding economic sectors attracted less investment-specific technological progress.
3. The net capital (wealth) stock-GDP ratio, at current prices, rose over time, with a fourfold increase between the early 1880s and 2020, contradicting one of Kaldor's (1957) stylised facts, and increased by four-fifths from 1970 onwards, in line with Piketty and Zucman (2014) for Western Europe's wealth-income ratio.
4. The consumption of fixed capital (CFC) in terms of GDP increased over time, shadowing the capital-output ratio but, as a proportion of the net capital stock (that is, the rate of depreciation), only rose up to the 1960s, falling from 1970 to 2007 as embodied technological change led to a decline in the relative prices of new capital goods.

The chapter is organized as follows. Section 3.2 discusses the concepts, method, and sources used and presents new estimates of net capital stock and productive capital stock derived with the Perpetual Inventory Method, testing its sensitivity and comparing the results to available series of capital stock. Section 3.3 provides a volume index of capital services, in which the user cost of capital is derived with an ex-ante exogenous rate of return. The volume index of capital services (VICS) is compared to the productive capital stock (PKS), as a growing gap between the two reveals the shift from low return and long life assets to higher return but shorter life assets, that is, an increase in the "quality" of capital. Next, trends in VICs and capital deepening are presented and weighed against available estimates. Lastly, Sect. 3.4 offers the evolution of the capital-output ratio, as well as the consumption of fixed capital (% of GDP) and the depreciation rate (% net capital stock).

3.2 Capital Stock

The publication of the *OECD Manual* in 2009 (OECD, 2009) provided a unified methodology with which to measure capital stock and services, which builds bridges between previous OECD methodology and that pioneered by Jorgenson (1963) and further developed by Jorgenson (1989, 1990) and Hulten (1990).[2] This chapter follows the OECD approach and distinguishes between net capital stock, also labelled wealth, which measures capital assets at their market price, and productive stock, an intermediate stage to derive a volume index of capital services (capital input), that is, the flow of capital services into production.

In the construction of net capital stock estimates, the Perpetual Inventory Method (PIM) is used, cumulating flows of investment, corrected for retirement and depreciation, for each asset. Implementing the PIM requires, by type of asset, (a) investment volumes and deflators; (b) average service lives; (c) depreciation rates; and (d) an initial benchmark level of capital stock.

(a) Four different types of asset have been distinguished: dwellings, other construction, transport equipment, and machinery and equipment. Biological resources and intellectual property products have been added to machinery and equipment assets because information on them is only available in national accounts beginning in 1980.[3] No distinction has been made between ICT and non-ICT assets, due to the dearth of data in national accounts and the aim of providing homogeneous long-run series of capital stock.[4]

Gross fixed capital formation (GFCF) volume series for each type of asset are obtained by deflating current values, and expressed in 2010 Euro. GFCF current value and deflator series come from Prados de la Escosura (2017, updated). GFCF series are derived from spliced national accounts for 1958–2020 (see Appendix), and via the commodity flow method (CFM), that is, production and trade data to proxy investment by asset type, for 1850–1958.[5]

It is worth noting that the GFCF deflator series have been smoothed using a Hodrick-Prescott filter in order to avoid negative values for the unit user costs.

---

[2] OECD (1993, 2001). For developments and applications of the Jorgenson approach, cf. Jorgenson and Griliches (1967), Hall and Jorgenson (1967), Christensen et al. (1980), Jorgenson et al. (1987), Elías (1978), and Young (1995).

[3] Conference Board (2022) follows the same practice. As a sensitivity test, I have replicated the estimates of net capital stock using six, rather than four types of assets (that is, considering biological resources and intellectual property products separately) from 1980 onwards. No trend discrepancies are found between the two set of estimates even though the six assets estimates exhibit a slightly lower level (See Figs. 3.24 and 3.29 in Appendix A.2).

[4] See Mas and Pérez (2022) and Conference Board (2022) for estimates for Spain, which distinguish between ICT and non-ICT of assets.

[5] The CFM approach is widely used to reconstruct GFCF series in present-day developing countries (Conference Board, 2022). Also, in the Penn World Tables 10.0, in the absence of direct estimates, investment in an asset is assumed to vary with the economy-wide supply (production + imports – exports) (Feenstra et al., 2015, updated).

The same smoothing procedure has been applied to the general price index, which in our case, is the GDP deflator.[6]

(b) The choice of average services lives, that is, the length of time that assets are retained in the capital stock, presents a challenge. Although choosing different average lives for different periods represents the usual historical practice (Feinstein, 1988; Prados de la Escosura and Rosés, 2010) a single set of average service lives is used here in order to facilitate comparisons with other estimates, as service lives for each asset type are kept constant in most country studies. Moreover, there is no concluding evidence that service lives fall over the long run, as offsetting tendencies are at work.[7] Thus, dwellings and other construction are assigned average service lives of 60 and 40 years, respectively, while transport and machinery equipment are attributed 15 years each.[8] Nonetheless, compositional changes in the capital stock imply that the average service life of total capital varies over time and, in so far as a shift towards more productive assets takes place, it declines.

(c) As regards depreciation rates, a declining balance is chosen, that is, a geometric rate, $\delta = R/T$, where T is the asset's average service life and R the selected parameter. Geometric depreciation rates differ across assets but are constant over time. Following the US Bureau of Economic Analysis (Fraumeni, 1997), Hulten and Wykoff's (1981) directly computed depreciation rates and implicit R values, 1.65 for transport equipment and machinery and 0.91 for structures, have been accepted. The resulting depreciation rates are, thus, 1.52%, 2.28%, 11.0%, and 11.0% for dwellings, other constructions, transport equipment, and machinery and equipment (plus intellectual property and biological resources since 1980), respectively.[9]

---

[6]Alternative estimates using the private consumption deflator provide similar results.

[7]On the one hand, service lives tend to fall as 'product cycles' become shorter and capital goods face higher rates of obsolescence but, on the other, some assets become more durable (OECD, 2009). Maddison (1995) used fixed average lives for his historical estimates.

[8]These service lives are in line with those used by Mas and Pérez (2022). Alternative estimates have been computed with another set of longer average service lives: 70 years (dwellings), 50 years (other construction), and 20 years (transport equipment and machinery). Although longer service lives increase the gross stock and reduce depreciation and, hence, deliver a larger net capital stock, the comparison between the two set of estimates reveals minor differences over time. A third set of estimates has been derived by combining the longer average lives set for 1850–1958 and the shorter average lives set for 1959–2020. Interestingly, the result is lower growth of aggregate capital stock than when the shorter lives set is employed for the entire time span. This finding may be attributed to the fact that the set of average assets lives for the pre-1958 period assigns larger weight to slower growing assets and, consequently, result in lower net capital stock. (See the resulting alternative Net Capital Stock/GDP ratios in Fig. 3.30 in the Appendix).

[9]Hulten and Wykoff (1981) implicit R values were also used in Prados de la Escosura and Rosés (2010). Alternative estimates have been obtained using a double declining balance (T=2) and the same average service lives, with the resulting depreciation rates of 3.3%, 5.0%, 13.3%, and 13.3% for each of the four asset types. Figure 3.31 in the Appendix compares the net capital stock derived alternatively with the double declining balance and Hulten and Wykoff's R values, revealing that

(d) In the absence of an initial stock of capital, two main approaches have been used to derive the latter. One assumes, after Harberger (1978), that the economy is at its steady-state and derives the initial stock for each asset type as,

$$W^{t0} = I^{t0}/(\delta + \theta) \tag{3.1}$$

where I is real investment; δ, the rate of depreciation; and θ, the growth rate of investment in early years.

An alternative to the steady state assumption approach is to estimate a functional relationship between real GFCF and GDP and, supposing that such a relationship is stable over time, to derive volume GFCF series for the previous period on the basis of available GDP series. Here the relationship between each asset type and GDP has been estimated for 1850–1920 and the regression coefficients applied to the available real GDP estimates to produce GFCF volume series for each type of asset between 1780 and 1850.[10]

The initial (1850) level for each capital asset type has been derived with the PIM and the average lives and depreciation rates accepted for the post-1850 period with each approach. Figure 3.1 compares the results of the two approaches. It can be observed that their difference disappears by 1890. As the alternative option to the steady state approach seems to be less stringent, it has been preferred here.

Another important issue is the sensitivity of the net capital stock series to the choice of initial level. Thus, the estimates have been replicated, adopting as initial capital both half and twice the level obtained in the favoured option. Figure 3.2 shows that differences diminish as time goes by and fade away by the 1920s. Thus, the estimates seem to be robust to alternative ways of computing the initial level for the last 100 years at least.

Next, the Net Capital Stock has been computed for 1850–2020 using the stock-flow relationship (PIM). If we define the net stock at the beginning (^{B}) of the first

the net capital stock derived with the double declining balance is lower, as the depreciation rates are larger for the same average lives of assets, and so is the consumption of fixed capital (Fig. 3.32).

[10]The OLS regression results are (with standard error in parentheses),

$$\ln(\text{Dwellings}) = -5.75 + 1.23\ \ln(\text{GDP})$$
$$(0.995)\ (0.095) \qquad \text{Adj.R}^2 = 0.70$$

$$\ln(\text{Other Construction}) = -11.23 + 1.70\ \ln(\text{GDP})$$
$$(1.271)\ (0.121) \qquad \text{Adj.R}^2 = 0.74$$

$$\ln(\text{Machinery}) = -29.07 + 3.19\ \ln(\text{GDP})$$
$$(1.062)\ (0.101) \qquad \text{Adj.R}^2 = 0.93$$

$$\ln(\text{Transport Equipment}) = -17.18 + 2.07\ \ln(\text{GDP})$$
$$(2.755)\ (0.263) \qquad \text{Adj.R}^2 = 0.47$$

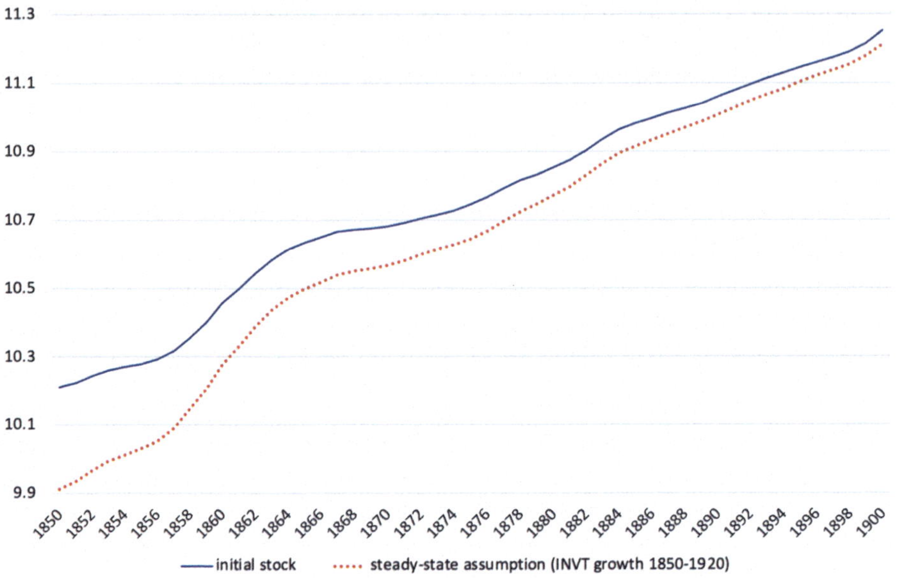

Fig. 3.1 Initial net capital stock: alternatives estimates, 1850–1900 (2010 Million Euro) (natural logs)

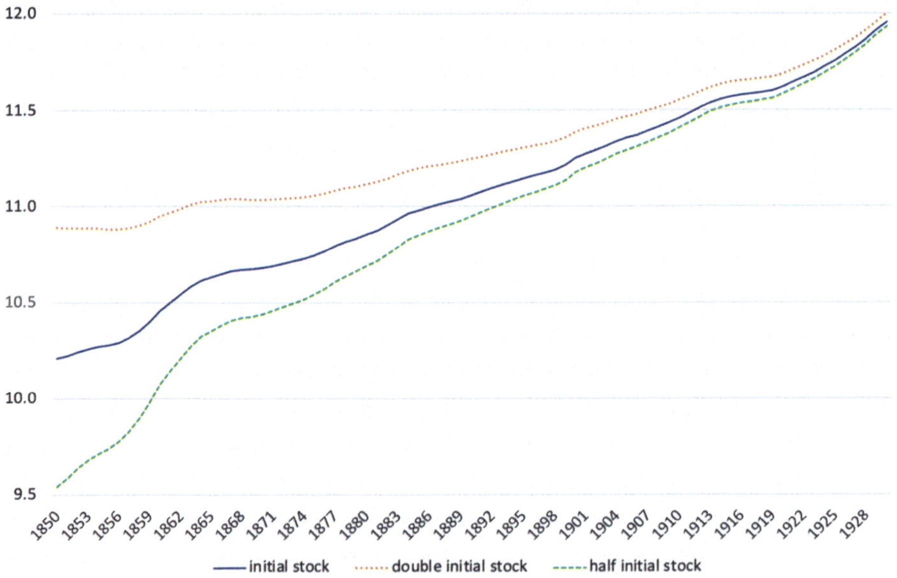

Fig. 3.2 Initial net capital stock: sensitivity to alternative options, 1850–1930 (2010 Million Euro) (natural logs)

year, 1850, as $W^{1850,B}$, end-year (^{E}) net stocks for each asset in all consecutive years are,

$$W^{tE} = W^{tB} + I^{t} - \delta\left(I^{t}/2 + W^{tB}\right) \tag{3.2}$$

where I^{t} is real yearly gross fixed capital formation and δ, the rate of depreciation. All stocks are valued at average prices of 2010 and by adding them up the Net Capital Stock in 2010 Euro is obtained.

The value of the consumption of fixed capital (depreciation) for each asset at 2010 prices, $D^{t}/P_{0}^{\,t}$, results from applying the rate of depreciation to the net stock at the beginning of the period plus half the current period's investment,

$$D^{t}/P_{0}^{\,t} = \delta\left[I^{t}/2 + W^{tB}\right]. \tag{3.3}$$

The net (wealth) capital stock at current prices, $P_{0}^{\,t}W^{t}$, is obtained by reflating the average of the net capital stock at the beginning and the end of each year with the average yearly price index for each asset, $P_{0}^{\,t}$ and, then, adding them up.

$$P_{0}^{\,t}W^{t} = P_{0}^{\,t}\left(W^{tB} + W^{tE}\right)/2 \tag{3.4}$$

Similarly, the current value of the consumption of fixed capital, D^{t}, has been derived by revaluing its constant price value with the deflator for each asset, $P_{0}^{\,t}$.

$$D^{t} = \delta\left[I^{t}/2 + W^{tB}\right]P_{0}^{\,t} \tag{3.5}$$

A final step is to consider the destruction of capital stock resulting from the Spanish Civil War (1936–1939). Although capital assets in transport equipment and dwellings derived through PIM include war damage, this does not seem to be the case for other construction and machinery, as destruction estimates in the historical literature appear to be larger than those resulting from the PIM exercise. Hence, the historical estimates of asset destruction have been accepted and distributed at constant yearly rates over 1936–1939.[11] The resulting figures imply a 4.9% contraction of the total net capital stock between 1935 and 1939 which, by asset type, represents a fall of 2.0% (dwellings), 6.8% (other construction), 13.7% (machinery and equipment), and 30.4% (transport equipment), much lower than Maddison's (1995: 138) guesstimates for World War II destruction in belligerent European countries, except the UK.

How do the new estimates compare to the recent computations of the net stock of fixed capital by the Spanish official statistical office, Instituto Nacional de

[11] The yearly rates assumed are −2.75% for other construction and −5.8% for machinery, following Prados de la Escosura and Rosés (2010). Although the destruction, as a share of net capital stock, is lower in the new estimates, 5% vs 7%, a fact that derives from the use of different asset average service lives and from methodological differences in the computation of the capital stock.

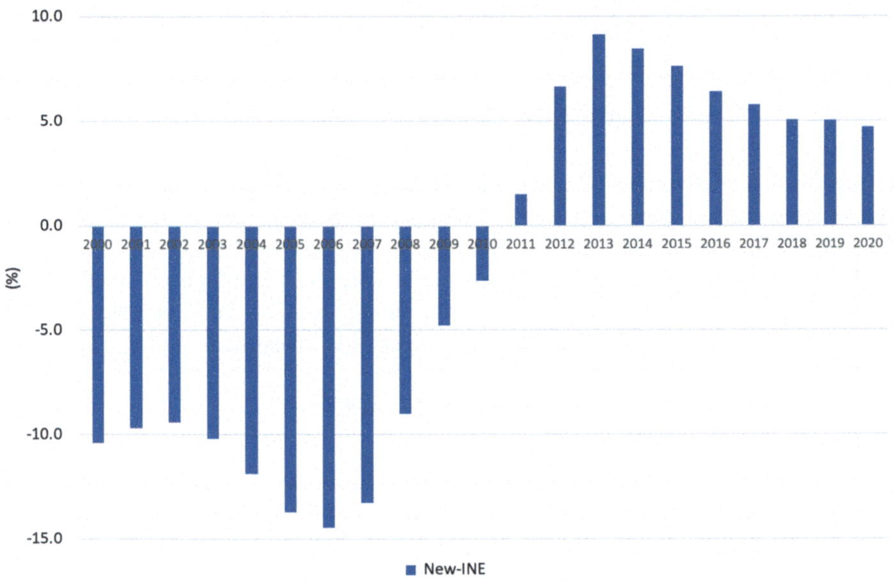

Fig. 3.3 New net capital stock: differences from INE estimates, 2000–2020 (natural logs %) (current prices) computed with Interpolated GFCF and declining balance

Estadística (INE)? Figure 3.3 presents the logarithmic deviations expressed in percentages.[12] The new estimates approximately match the INE's figures, with lower levels in the 2000s and higher ones in the 2010s, and an average absolute difference of 7.7% (standard deviation 3.9).

Moreover, the new net capital stock series are systematically lower than Ivie's figures (Mas and Pérez, 2022) between 1964 and 2011, and only slightly higher thereafter (Fig. 3.4). Why does such a discrepancy exist? A major difference is that the Ivie's GFCF series for the period 1965–1995 have been spliced using the retropolation method, not through interpolation as in our case (See Appendix, A.1 A Note on Splicing GFCF Series in Spain's National Accounts). I have replicated the comparison but the new net capital stock estimates are now computed with retropolated GFCF series. The resulting gap between the two series narrows down remarkably, with the average (absolute) difference shrinking to 6.6% (s.d. 6.6) from 20.4% (s.d. 12.6). Therefore, methodological differences explain most of the discrepancy between the two set of estimates.

An interesting contrast results from comparing the estimates obtained with the PIM and the capital stock derived from a wealth survey for 1965 (Universidad Comercial de Deusto, 1968–1972), often used to initialise capital stock series.[13] It

[12]The formula used is 100*(natural log X – natural log Y), X being the new estimates and Y, Ivie and INE figures, alternatively.

[13]For example, in Myro (1983) and Mas et al. (2000).

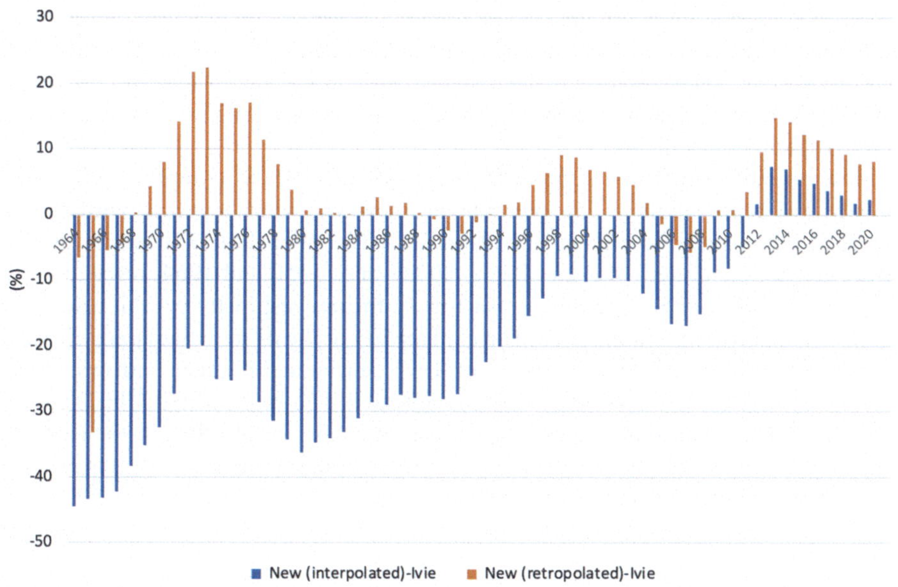

Fig. 3.4 New net capital stock differences from Ivie estimates, 1964–2020 (natural logs %) (current prices). Computed alternatively with interpolated and retropolated GFCF series

Table 3.1 Wealth survey and perpetual inventory method estimates in 1965 (000 million Peseta)

	(I) Wealth Survey	(II) PIM Estimate	(III) [(II)/(I)]
Dwellings	1166	1006	0.86
Other Structures	1236	827	0.67
Machinery and Equipment	633	352	0.56
Transport Equipment	194	146	0.75
Total Capital Stock	3229	2330	0.72

Sources: Universidad Comercial de Deusto (1968–1972), reproduced in Myro (1983) Table 3.3; PIM estimates, see the text

can be observed that the wealth survey exaggerates the size of the capital stock (Table 3.1).[14]

Lastly, productive stock, K^t, has been obtained by adding investment in the latest period to the net capital (wealth) stock,

$$K^t = I^t/2 + W^{tB} \tag{3.6}$$

It is worth noting that while in order to derive the net capital stock the cumulating flow of investment is corrected for retirement and depreciation, in the case of

[14] Cf. Young (1995: 650–1) for similar results in the cases of South Korea and Taiwan.

productive capital only efficiency losses are subtracted. In practical terms, the difference results from the fact that the net capital is valued at the end of the year and productive capital represents the average value in the year. Moreover, productive stocks for each type of asset are computed at constant prices only and used to derive capital service flows.

How do our results for the productive capital stock (PKS) compare with those already available? Figure 3.5a presents the new estimates together with those provided for Spain by the Penn World Tables 10.0 (PWT 10.01) (Feenstra et al., 2015, updated) and Ivie (Mas and Pérez, 2022) since 1950 and 1964, respectively. Although the three series present similar trends, the new estimates exhibit a steeper trend, that is, grow at a faster pace. The explanation of the differential largely lies in the use of retropolated GFCF series before 1995, since the difference narrows down sharply when the new PKS estimates are replicated with retropolated GFCF series (Fig. 3.5b). However, other elements also contribute to explain this; in the case of Ivie's figures, for example, the initial level derives from the 1965 wealth survey and uses a more detailed breakdown by asset type.

3.3 Capital Services

We can now proceed to compute the capital input, that is, the flow of capital services into production. To do so, a volume index of capital services is derived as a weighted average of productive stock indices by type of asset, in which each asset's share in total user cost of capital (that is, the current value of capital services) are the weights. This procedure implies that, for each asset, its flow of capital services is proportional to its productive stock, although the rate of variation of capital services differs across assets (Jorgenson and Griliches, 1967).

Thus, we need to compute the unit user cost of capital for each asset, which represents the marginal return an asset generates during one period of production (OECD, 2009). Once obtained, the unit use cost, F_0^t, is multiplied by the asset's productive capital stock, $K^{k,t}$, to derive the value of its capital services, $U^{k,t}$. Adding up the values of all assets we obtain the total value of capital services, U^t.

Different rates of return have been used to compute the unit user cost in empirical studies. The *ex-post* endogenous rate of return is the realised rate of return and, in principle, preferable. For example, it is used by both the Penn World Tables 10.0 (Feenstra et al., 2015, updated) and Conference Board (2022). An *ex-post endogenous* rate of return equals the value of capital services to capital compensation in national income (that is, the gross operating surplus plus the capital share in gross mixed income), which is consistent with an economy of perfect competition and

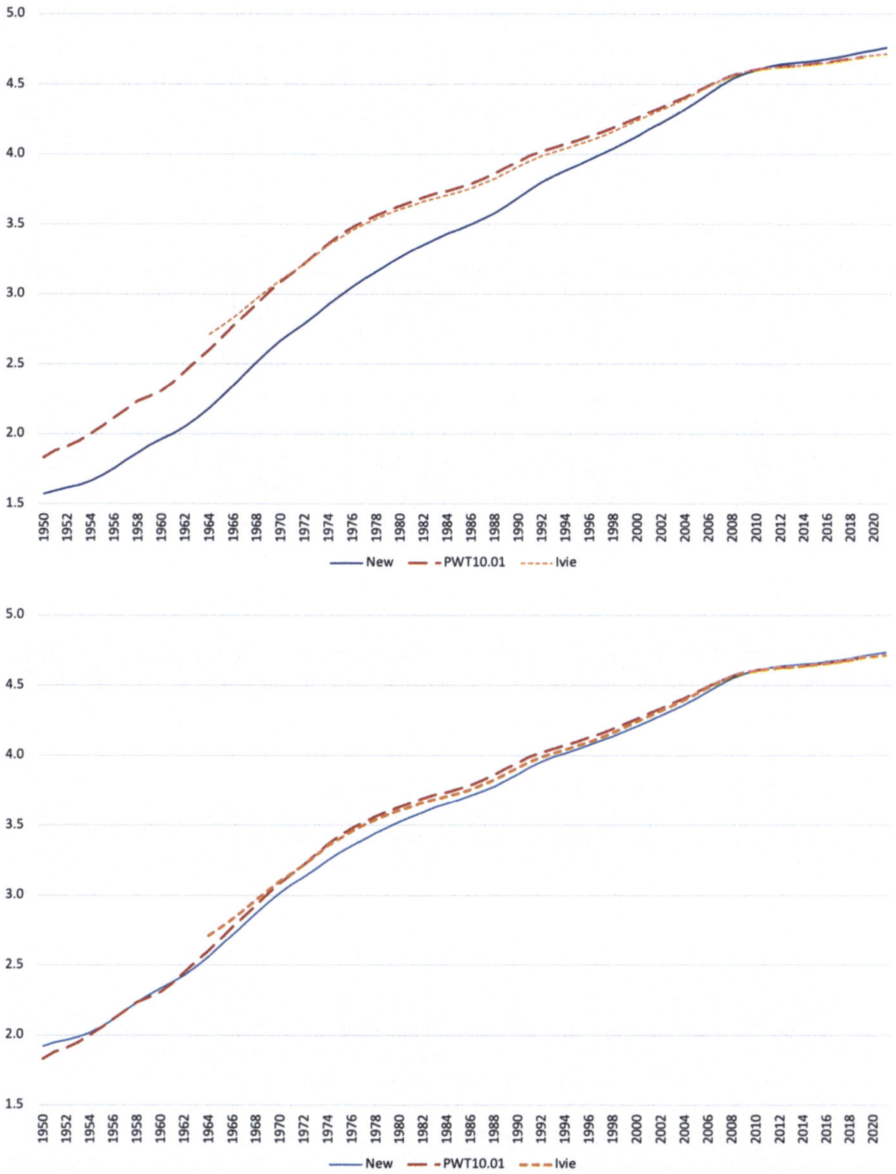

Fig. 3.5 (**a**) New productive capital stock, 1950–2020: Comparison with PWT10.01 and Ivie estimates (2010=100) (natural logs). (**b**) New productive capital stock derived with GFCF retropolated series, 1950–2020. Comparison with PWT10.01 and Ivie estimates (2010=100) (natural logs)

constant returns to scale (OECD, 2009).[15] The use of an *ex-post endogenous* rate of return requires, however, a complete coverage of all assets and a distinction between market and government sectors. Otherwise, the rate of return will be biased.[16] Unfortunately, our data do not meet such stringent requirements.

The alternative is, then, to compute an ex-ante exogenous rate of return, that is, the one expected by the investor.[17] In an ex-ante approach, the rate of return for investment on a given asset should not be higher than in an alternative investment of comparable risk. The OECD Manual (OECD, 2009) recommends working with real rates of return and real changes in asset prices, as they are independent from inflation and less volatile, and, in particular, suggests a 4% real rate of return, which is close to Spain's historical rate, and has been adopted in Ivie's estimates (Mas and Pérez, 2022).[18] In fact, assuming a fixed real rate of return on investment matches one of Kaldor's (1957) stylised facts, namely, that the rate of return on investment is roughly constant over long periods of time. The objection can be raised, however, that when an ex-ante exogenous rate of return is chosen, the resulting value of capital services may not match capital compensation in national income.

The ex-ante unit user cost, or capital service price, $F_0{}^t$, can be defined as

---

[15] Thus, the endogenous, ex-post rate of return for every period is computed by equating capital compensation G^t *plus* capital related taxes on production $T_K{}^t$ to the total user costs of capital U^t

$$G^t + T_K{}^t = U^t = \Sigma_{k=1}{}^N P_0{}^{k,tB}(1+\rho^t)\left[r^{t*} + \delta^k\left(1 + i^{k,t*}\right) - i^{k;t*}\right]K^{k,t} \quad (3.7)$$

From which the ex-post endogenous real rate of return can be derived,
$r^{t*} = \{(G^t + T_K{}^t)(1+\rho^t) - \Sigma_{k=1}{}^N P_0{}^{k,tB}[\delta_0{}^k(1 + i^{k,t*}) - i^{k;t*}]K^{k,t}\}/\{\Sigma_{k=1}{}^N P_0{}^{k,tB}K^{k,t}\}$t user cost per unit of capital services for a particular type of asset is obtained as

$$F_0{}^t = P_0{}^{k,tB}(1+\rho^t)\left[r^{t*} + \delta_0{}^k\left(1 + i^{k,t*}\right) - i^{k,t*}\right] \quad (3.9)$$

where G^t Non-labour income consists of gross operating surplus and the part of mixed income that can be attributed to capital

$T_K{}^t$ taxes on production

$P_0{}^{k,tB}$ is the purchase price of a new asset at the beginning (^{B}) of year t

ρ^t is the rate of change of the consumer price index at the beginning of period t

r^{t*} is the real rate of return that applies at the beginning of period t

δ^k is the rate of depreciation for a new asset k

$i^{k,t*}$ is the ex-post, real rate of asset price inflation for asset k during period t

$K^{k,t}$ is the productive capital stock of asset k during period t

[16] Upwards biased if coverage is incomplete, since capital income will be compared to an undervalued capital stock, and downwards biased if no clear distinction is made between market and government sectors since, probably, only market capital income will be compared to the value of the total capital stock.

[17] Nonetheless, capital services have also been derived using an ex-post endogenous rate of return in order to provide a contrast to the ex-ante exogenous estimates. See the figures in Appendix A.2.

[18] Actually, in Ivie's estimates 4% real rate of return is chosen for the market sector and 3.5% rate for the non-market sector. The average real rate of return of bank deposits in Spain since 1850 is 4.5% (computed from underlying data in Prados de la Escosura and Rosés, 2010, updated to 2020).

$$F_0{}^t = P_0{}^{k,tB}\left(1 + \rho_{(tB)}\right)\left[r_a{}^* + \delta_0\left(1 + i_{(tB)}{}^*\right) - i_{(tB)}{}^*\right] \tag{3.10}$$

The ex-ante user cost of an asset,

$$U^{k,t} = F_0{}^t K^{k,t} \tag{3.11}$$

And the total user cost of capital,

$$U^t = \Sigma_{k=1} U^{k,t.} \tag{3.12}$$

where $P_0{}^{k,tB}$ is the purchase price of a new asset at the beginning (^{B}) of year t,

$\rho_{(tB)}$ the rate of change of the price index (GDP deflator) at the beginning (^{B}) of year t,

$r_a{}^*$ the real rate of return (the nominal rate corrected for inflation), 4%, in this case,

$i_{(tB)}{}^*$ the real anticipated change in asset prices at beginning (^{B}) of year t,

δ_0 the rate of depreciation of a new asset, $K^{k,t}$ the productive capital stock of asset k during period t.

Furthermore, a simplified ex-ante exogenous rate of return can be derived by setting the anticipated real holding gains term i^{*t} equal to zero. Although this approach has the advantage that it does not require us to estimate anticipated real holding gains, it is only a reasonable alternative if asset price changes do not deviate significantly from changes in the GDP deflator. The resulting user cost, then, becomes,

$$SF_0{}^t = P_0{}^{k,tB}\left(1 + \rho_{(tB)}\right)\left[r_a{}^* + \delta_0\right] \tag{3.13}$$

Lastly, a Törnqvist index of aggregate capital services is computed as,

$$\ln\left(KS^{k,t}/KS^{k,t-1}\right) = \Sigma\overline{v}^{k,t}\ln\left(K^{k,t}/K^{k,t-1}\right) \tag{3.14}$$

where $K^{k,t}$ is the productive capital stock of asset k and $\overline{v}^{k,t} = ½\left(v^{k,t-1} + v^{k,t},\right)$ the two adjacent year average share of each asset in total user cost of capital, being $v^{k,t} = U^{k,t}/U$. Then, the volume index of capital services (VICS) is obtained as the exponential.

It is worth noting the different weighting of the capital stock (the share of assets in its total current value) and the index of capital services (the share of assets in total returns to capital). Figure 3.6 shows the composition of the net capital stock, dominated by structures (dwellings and other construction) that in spite of the long-term fall in the share of dwellings until the early 1990s and the rise of machinery and equipment up to the early 1960s, still contribute four-fifths of the net capital stock value in 2020. A different and more volatile picture results from the composition of capital returns, as assets with lower average service lives (and, hence, higher depreciation rates) are those with higher marginal returns (Fig. 3.7). Thus,

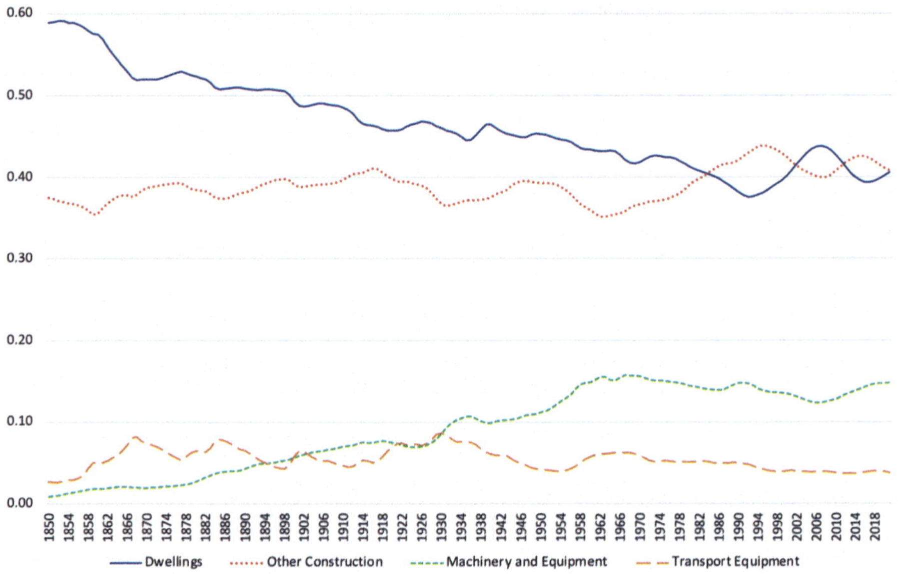

Fig. 3.6 Net capital stock composition (current prices) (%)

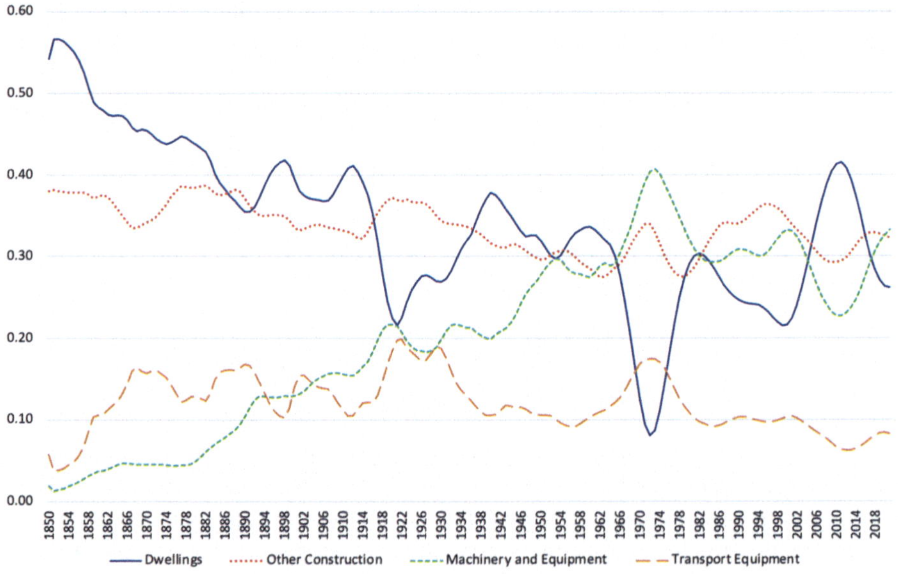

Fig. 3.7 Capital services' composition (ex-ante exogenous rate of return) (current prices) (%)

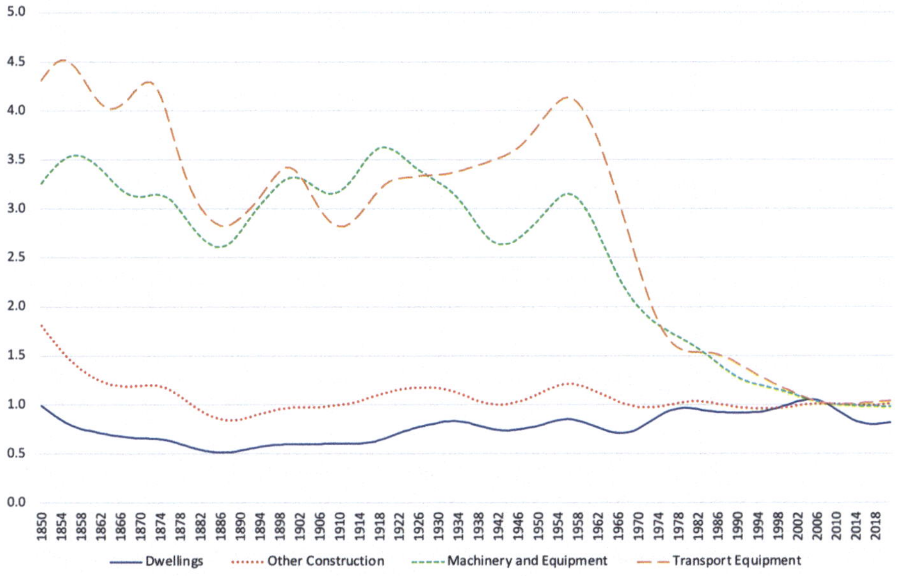

Fig. 3.8 GFCF prices relative to the GDP deflator (2010=1) (Hodrick-Prescott smoothed)

machinery and equipment matches the share of other construction since the mid-twentieth century and the share of dwellings declines more than in the net capital stock.[19]

But how different is the composition of capital services when they are obtained with the simplified ex-ante exogenous rate of return, as favoured in Ivie's estimates (Mas and Pérez, 2022)? Similar but less volatile trends appear, even though machinery and equipment's remains below the share of other construction (Fig. 3.21), but the validity of the simplified approach depends on the stability of relative GFCF prices.

Figure 3.8 offers the evolution of the price of each type of asset relative to the GDP deflator and shows how they fluctuate.[20] For example, the relative price of both machinery and transport equipment experienced a decline between the late 1850s and 1880s, which coincided with railway construction and the early stage of industrialisation, and a sustained fall from the 1950s, which was steeper until the late 1970s. Embodied technological change helps explain these assets' relative price trends. Thus, assuming that asset prices mimic the general price index is unrealistic and alters the weighting of the volume index of capital services.

The different weighting of the net capital stock and capital services is also reflected in the evolution of productive capital stock and the volume index of capital

[19] Similar trends, although less marked, and machinery and equipment never matches other construction, are observed when the ex-post endogenous rate of return is used (Fig. 3.20).

[20] Similar results are obtained using the private consumption deflator.

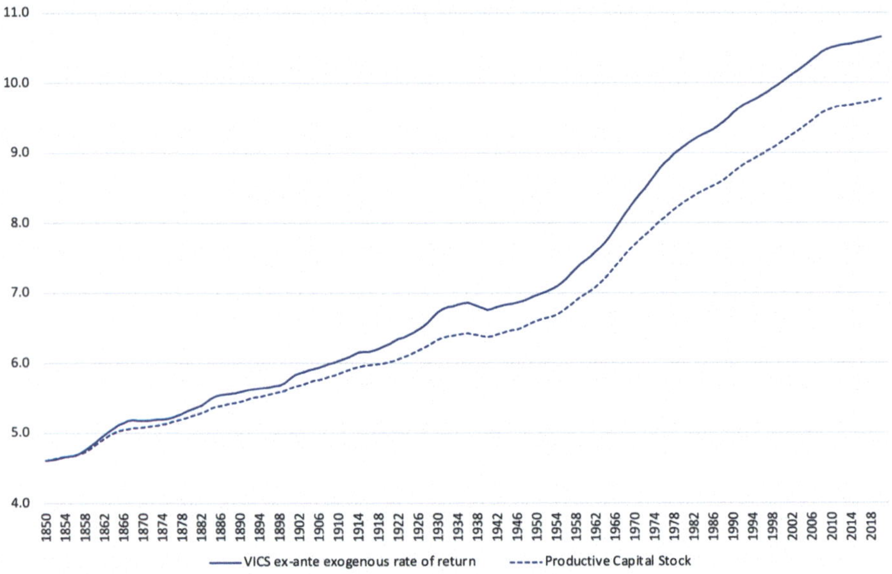

Fig. 3.9 Volume index of capital services (VICS) (ex-ante exogenous rate of return) and productive capital stock (PKS), (1850=100) (natural logs)

services, since VICS grows faster than PKS as more dynamic assets are usually those of shorter average service life but higher returns. Figure 3.9 confirms their divergent evolution, which has widened since the 1970s.[21]

An index of capital "quality" that measures the capital input's composition effect can be derived as the ratio between the volume index of capital services and that of productive capital stock,

$$KQ^{k,t} = KS^{k,t}/K^{k,t} \tag{3.15}$$

Figure 3.10 shows a long-run increase in the "quality" of capital, punctuated by reversals, in which a contraction during the Civil War (1936–1939) and its autarkic aftermath (1939–1953) and a fast increase between the mid-1950s and the late 1970s, followed by deceleration, only broken by the late 1980s spurt, stand out.[22]

[21] The gap is narrower when VICS is obtained with an ex-post endogenous, rather than an ex-ante exogenous rate of return. This finding is consistent with the presumed underestimate of capital services derived with an ex-post endogenous rate of return when information on capital assets is incomplete as in our case (Fig. 3.22). It is also worth stressing that the VICS derived with the full and simplified ex-ante exogenous rate of return are practically identical until 1970, when the 'simplified' VICS lags mildly behind the "full" VICS (Fig. 3.23).

[22] Although the evolution of "quality" of capital using alternatively ex-ante exogenous and ex-post endogenous rates of return share the same tendencies, the level of capital "quality" is lower for the latter as could be anticipated due to the possible underestimate of capital services when they are

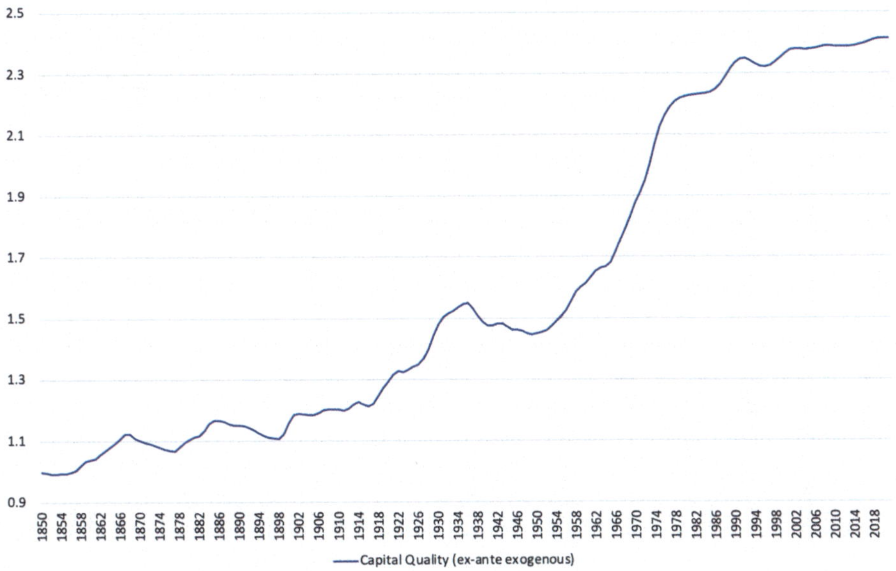

Fig. 3.10 Capital quality (ex-ante exogenous rate of return) (1850=1). Note: Capital quality = Ratio of volume index of capital services to productive capital stock

A rise in the index signals a shift towards capital goods with higher unit user costs and, hence, higher marginal productivity.

A comparison between the new volume index of capital services and earlier estimates is pertinent. In the first place, let us compare the new results with Prados de la Escosura and Rosés's (2010) estimates, under similar assumptions (namely, Hulten and Wykoff's declining balance depreciation rates and GFCF series spliced through interpolation). A common pattern is found, but the new VICS presents lower levels, although they tend to converge in the late twentieth century (Fig. 3.11). Such a difference may derive from the lower (and fixed) average service lives used here, while Prados de la Escosura and Rosés employed higher (and variable) average service lives, which, by increasing the gross stock and reducing depreciation, result in a larger net capital stock.

The comparison between the new volume index of capital services and those VICS derived by PWT10.01 and Ivie (Mas and Pérez, 2022), to which Conference Board (2022) estimates since 1990 have been added, shows slower growth for the PWT10.01 and Ivie series, but rather similar for the Conference Board series (Fig. 3.12a).[23] The main explanation for the different pace of growth is that both PWT10.01 and Ivie estimates are based on pre-1995 GFCF series spliced through

computed with incomplete information (Fig. 3.25a). The choice of a 'simplified' VICS underestimates the improvement in capital quality since the late 1960s (Fig. 3.25b).

[23] See Fig. 3.26 for a comparison that included the new estimates derived with both ex-ante exogenous and ex-post endogenous rate of return.

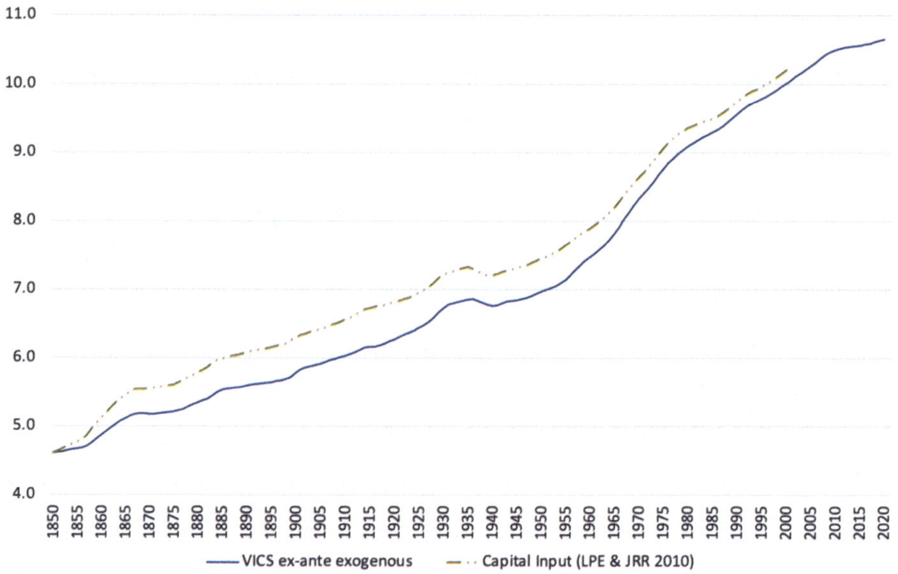

Fig. 3.11 Volume index of capital services (VICS)*: comparison with Prados de la Escosura and Rosés (2010) (1850=100) (natural logs). *Ex-ante exogenous rate of return

retropolation, unlike the new VICS, which draw on GCFC interpolated series. Figure 3.12b confirms that when VICS are derived using retropolated GFCF series, the gap with PWT10.01 and Ivie narrows sharply, especially from the late 1970s onwards. Moreover, as PWT10.01 estimates are derived with ex-post endogenous rates of return, the differential narrows further when the new VICS are computed with this rate of return (Fig. 3.27).

The comparison in terms of capital quality, that is, the ratio between capital services and productive capital indices, reveals that quality gains are much larger in the new estimates than in the PWT10.01 and Ivie's (Fig. 3.13).[24]

What are the observed trends in capital input? Capital services grew at 3.5% over the last 170 years but at an uneven pace. It is possible to distinguish a period of steady growth, slightly above 2% per year, up to 1920, in which the compositional change of capital (capital quality) represented a minor proportion (Table 3.2). In the 1920s, the growth rate doubled, with nearly a third contributed by capital quality. The slowdown of the early 1930s did not revert to the pre-1920 growth thanks to its compositional change. After shrinking during the Civil War and recovering mildly during the World War II years, capital input growth returned to its pre-1920 growth trend until the mid-1950s when it began an intense acceleration that lasted for half a century and was cut short by the onset of the Global Financial Crisis (2008). During Spain's delayed and short Golden Age (1959–1975), capital input growth was nearly

[24]Figure 3.28 adds up the new estimates of capital quality derived with ex-post endogenous rate of return that exhibits milder gains than when obtained with the ex-ante exogenous rate of return.

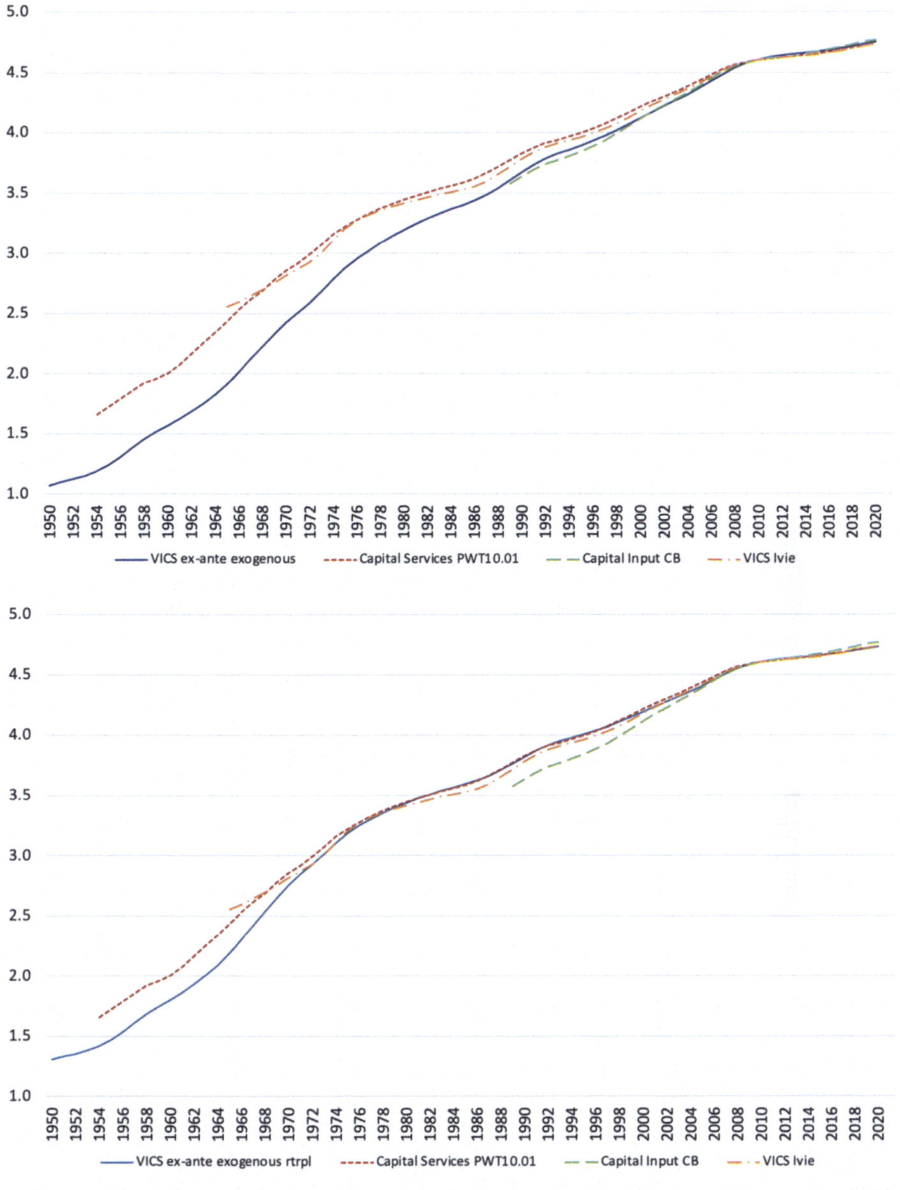

Fig. 3.12 (**a**) New volume index of capital services (VICS): Comparison with PWT10.01, Ivie, and conference board (CB) estimates, 1950–2020 (2010=100) (natural logs). (**b**) New VICS, 1950–2020. Alternative estimates derived with GFCF retropolated series. Comparison with PWT10.01, Ivie, and conference board (CB) estimates (1850=100) (logs)

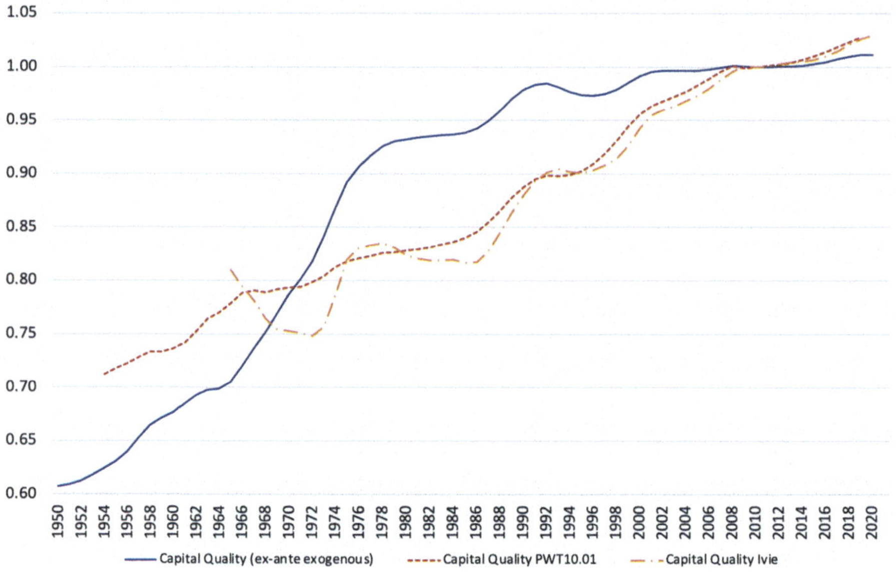

Fig. 3.13 Capital quality: comparison with PWT10.01 and Ivie estimates, 1950–2020 (2010=1)

Table 3.2 Capital input growth, 1850–2020 (%) ex-ante exogenous rate of return (annual average logarithmic rates)

	Productive capital stock	Capital quality	Capital input
1850–2020	3.0	0.5	3.6
1850–1872	2.2	0.4	2.6
1873–1892	1.9	0.2	2.2
1893–1913	2.1	0.3	2.4
1914–1919	1.2	0.7	2.0
1920–1929	3.0	1.3	4.2
1930–1935	2.0	1.1	3.1
1936–1939	-0.8	-0.9	-1.7
1940–1945	1.4	-0.3	1.1
1946–1953	2.5	0.1	2.6
1954–1958	4.6	1.5	6.1
1959–1975	6.6	1.7	8.4
1976–1985	4.7	0.5	5.2
1986–2007	4.7	0.3	4.9
2008–2013	2.7	0.0	2.7
2014–2020	1.3	0.2	1.5

Sources: See the text

Table 3.3 Capital deepening growth, 1850–2020 (%) ex-ante exogenous rate of return (annual average logarithmic rates)

	Productive capital stock/hour	Capital input/hour
1850–2020	2.6	3.1
1850–1872	1.6	2.0
1873–1892	1.9	2.1
1893–1913	1.5	1.8
1914–1919	0.8	1.6
1920–1929	2.3	3.6
1930–1935	0.4	1.6
1936–1939	−0.1	−1.1
1940–1945	0.7	0.4
1946–1953	1.2	1.3
1954–1958	3.9	5.3
1959–1975	6.4	8.2
1976–1985	7.8	8.3
1986–2007	2.2	2.4
2008–2013	5.7	5.7
2014–2020	1.2	1.4

Sources: See the text

fourfold that of the pre-1920 era, with capital quality contributing one-fifth of the total. The oil crises that coincided with the decade of 'transition to democracy' (1976–1985) represented a substantial slowdown in absolute and per capita GDP but not in terms of capital input that, with hardly any quality improvement, kept growing at 5% yearly during the 'transition' decade and after Spain's accession to the European Union. The Great Recession (2008–2013) nearly halved the post-1975 rate of capital services growth and, since 2014, capital input has been growing at the slowest pace since World War II.

If we look now at the volume of capital services per hour worked, that is, capital intensity or deepening, this grew steady up to World War I, intensified in the 1920s and, after nearly stagnating for two decades, expanded at an accelerated pace between the early-mid 1950s and mid-1980s (Table 3.3 and Fig. 3.14). Capital deepening slowed down thereafter, particularly between the mid-1990s and 2007 and, after a spurt during the Great Recession, practically stagnated. A comparison with alternative capital deepening figures for the post-1950 era shows that the new estimates grew faster than PWT10.01 estimates and similarly to the Conference Board's since 1989 (Fig. 3.15).

It is worth highlighting the inverse association between capital deepening and employment growth in post-Franco Spain (Fig. 3.16). Employment destruction during the decade of 'transition to democracy' (1976–1985) and the Global Financial Crisis (2008–2013) contribute to explain capital deepening in those years; conversely, from the accession to the EU to the onset of the Global Financial Crisis (1986–2007), and in the post-2014 recovery, employment creation underlies the

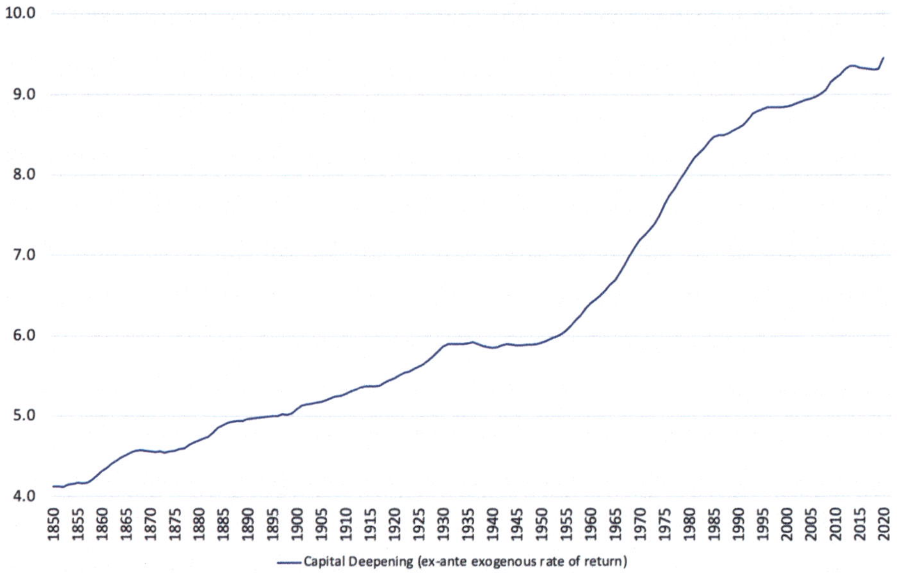

Fig. 3.14 Capital deepening* (2010=100) (natural logs of ×100 level). *Volume index of capital services (VICS) (ex-ante exogenous rate of return) per hour worked

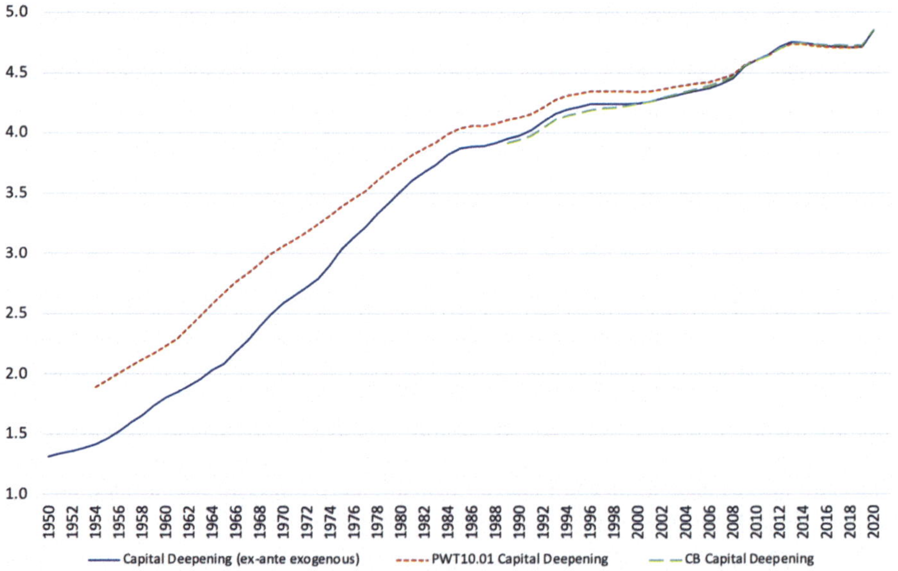

Fig. 3.15 New capital deepening* estimates, 1950–2020: comparison with PWT10.01 and conference board (CB) (2010=100) (natural logs). *VICS (ex-ante exogenous rate of return) per hour worked

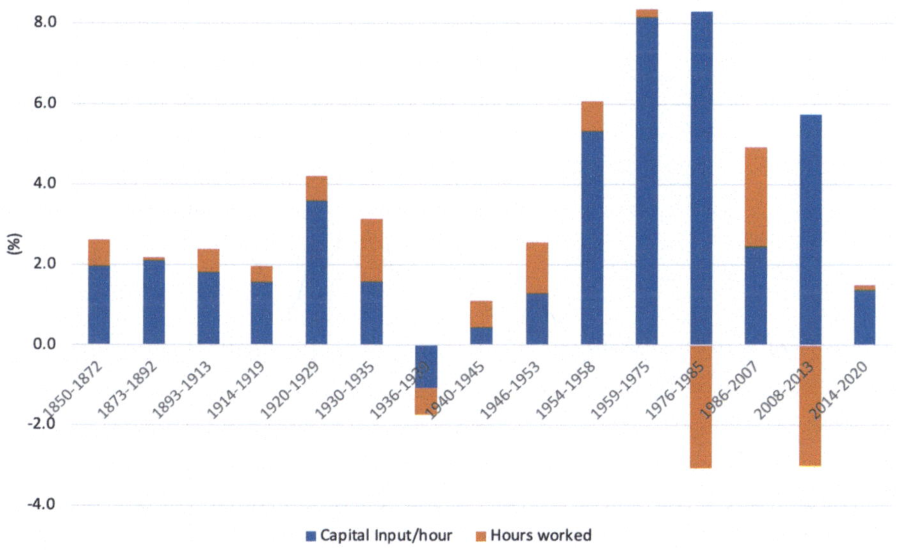

Fig. 3.16 Growth breakdown of volume index of capital services (VICS)* (ex-ante exogenous rate of return) (%). *VICS = VICS/hour × hours worked

deceleration in capital deepening. Thus, capital deepening slowdown since 1986 suggests that expanding sectors have not attracted much investment-specific technological progress.

3.4 Capital-Output Ratio and Capital Consumption

Capital has a dual nature as a storage of wealth and provider of capital services to production (OECD, 2009). So far, the focus has been on capital services. Let us now look at the evolution of wealth or net capital stock.

Piketty's (2014) identification of a fluctuating capital-output ratio going back to the eighteenth century has challenged one of Kaldor's (1957) stylised facts. Namely, the stability of the capital-output ratio. Such a claim is hardly news for economic historians, who have long been sceptical about empirical regularities. Prados de la Escosura and Rosés (2010) challenged the long-run stability of the capital-output ratio, and Gallardo-Albarrán and Inklaar (2020) have rejected it for more than 30 countries over the last 100 years.

The evolution of Net Capital Stock ratio to GDP, expressed at current prices, shows that after declining until the early 1880s, a sustained increase took place, with the capital-output ratio rising fourfold between the early 1880s and 2020 (Fig. 3.17). An initial phase of expansion, in which the ratio more than doubled, lasted until the

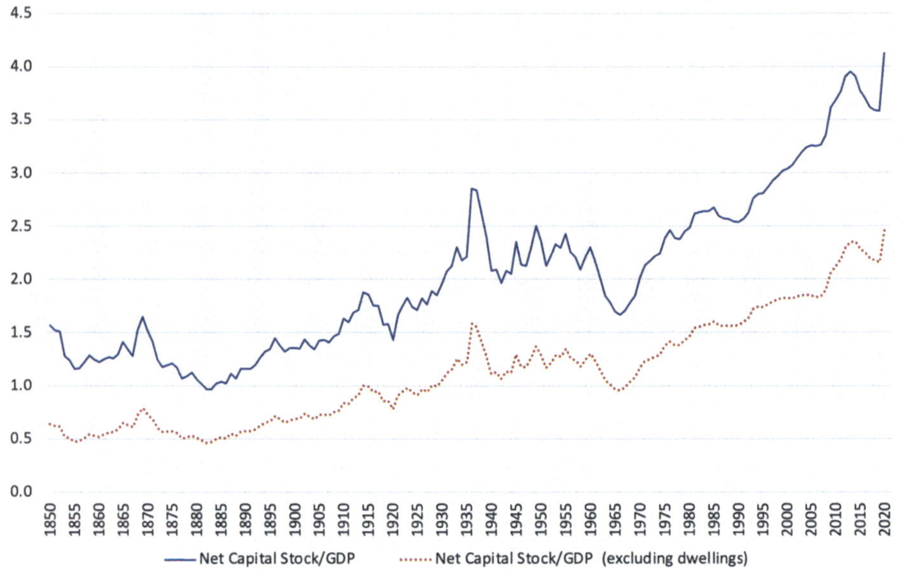

Fig. 3.17 Net capital stock/GDP ratio (current prices): with and without dwellings

early 1930s, peaking during the Civil War (1936–1939) when economic activity severely contracted. Relative stability from the late 1940s to 1960, with the ratio ranging between 2.0 and 2.5, was followed by a dramatic fall until the mid-1960s, at a time of fast economic growth, and a subsequent recovery that heralded a strong and sustained increase in the capital-output ratio, punctuated by reversals in the late 1980s and, again, in the late 2010s. The sustained rise of the capital-output ratio and capital deepening led to the decline of capital productivity (that is, real GDP per VICS) over the long run (Fig. 3.18).

From the late 1990s, low interest rates and the scarcity of urban land fuelled a boom in the price of dwellings—as the increase in the relative price of dwellings until the mid-2000s confirms (Fig. 3.8)—that contributed to the rise of the capital-output ratio. That is why the capital-output ratio excluding dwellings is also presented in Fig. 3.17. The same trends, but with less intensity, are confirmed.

The evolution of the capital-output ratio in Spain matches the experience of a large sample of countries in which the capital output ratio doubled during the last century (Gallardo-Albarrán and Inklaar, 2020), although the increase seems to have been more intense in the Spanish case, unlike the UK's, where the capital-output ratio ceased its expansion and declined during the last two decades of the past century (Oulton and Wallis, 2016). By 2013, the capital (wealth)-output ratio at current prices reached a value of 4, when it was just two in 1970, in line with the findings of Piketty and Zucman (2014) for Western European countries. However, this represents practically half the ratio of personal wealth to national income

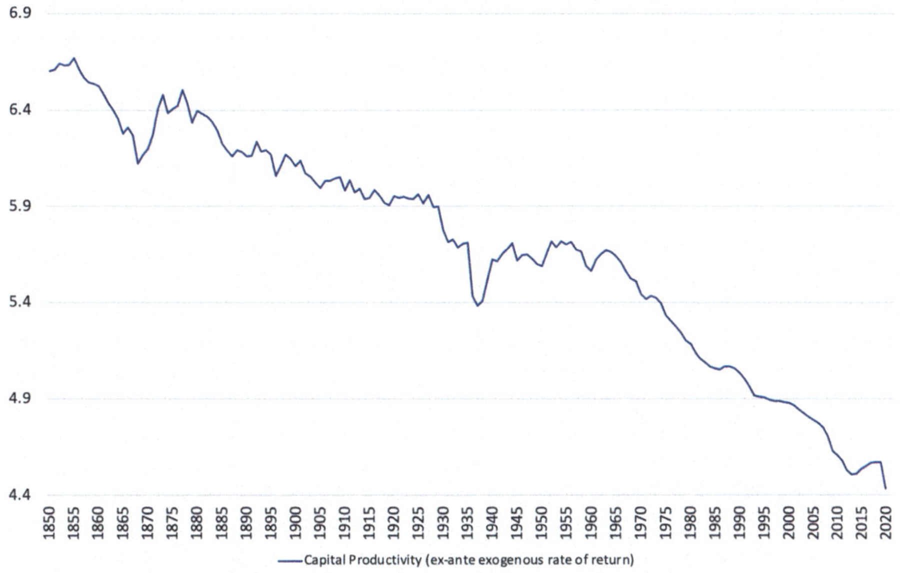

Fig. 3.18 Capital productivity* (ex-ante exogenous rate of return) (2010=100) (natural logs). *Capital productivity: ratio of real GDP to volume index of capital services (VICS)

estimated for Spain, although it also doubled over the same time span (Artola Blanco et al., 2020). A necessary caveat is that private wealth estimates add financial assets to the net capital (wealth) stock (that is, non-financial assets) and exclude financial liabilities.

The consumption of fixed capital, expressed as a proportion of GDP, follows the pattern of the capital-output ratio, jumping from 3 to nearly 15% between the 1880s and 2020 (Fig. 3.19). However, when the ratio of capital consumption to net capital stock—that is, the depreciation rate—is considered, it expanded up to the mid-1930s and, again, as of 1950, peaking in the late 1960s, before declining steadily until the mid-2000s, to rebound later. What explains this behaviour? As the composition of capital stock changes towards more productive but higher depreciation assets, one would expect a rise in the depreciation rate. However, new capital goods are more productive as they embodied new vintage technology, so a decline in their relative prices would accompany their expansion (Fig. 3.8) and helps explain the fall in the rate of depreciation between 1970 and 2006.[25]

[25] It is worth stressing that the described patterns for the capital-output ratio and the consumption of fixed capital are confirmed for alternative estimates derived using different average service lives and depreciation rates. Longer lives, by reducing depreciation, increase the level of net capital stock (Fig. 3.30).

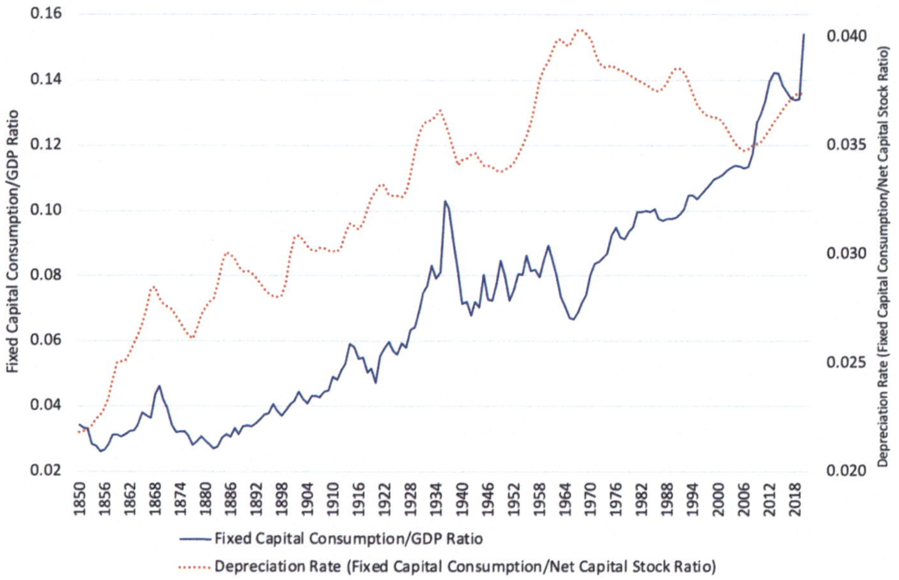

Fig. 3.19 Consumption of fixed capital/GDP ratio and depreciation rate (consumption of fixed capital/net capital stock ratio), (current prices)

3.5 Conclusions

The on-going debate on the rising trend in the capital-output ratio and the productivity slowdown requires long run, consistent, and integrated series of output and production factors. This chapter presents new estimates of net capital (wealth) stock and capital services for Spain during the last 170 years, which allow us to address welfare and growth issues.

Methodological differences matter for the resulting estimates. The new OECD methodology used here clearly differentiates between stock as wealth and capital as an input (that is the flow of services capital provides to production) and represents a major advance in the construction of capital estimates reconciling different approaches, including those previously used by the OECD and those employed by Jorgenson and his school. Most historical estimates, however, are based on outdated methodologies that are not compatible with recent capital stock and services estimates. Consistency with the latest vintage methodology used by international organizations facilitates, for example, testing current views in relation to increasing capital/output ratios or investigating the contribution of capital deepening to labour productivity growth. The chapter also rejects the option of using GFCF series derived by splicing national accounts through backwards projections, as they bias GFCF levels upward and, consequently, capital stock levels too, and adopts GFCF series derived through interpolation of national accounts. These methodological contributions can be applied elsewhere, especially to those developing countries experiencing a deep structural transformation and in the construction of historical series.

The new net capital stock estimates are not off the mark when compared to official national statistical series for the twenty-first century, and the differences over the last half a century when compared with the Penn World Tables 10.0 and Ivie's figures are largely methodological in nature, mainly splicing available GFCF series through retropolation (backward projection) rather than using interpolation as is the case here.

Capital services expanded over time, accelerating in the 1920s and between the mid-1950s and 2007, with capital 'quality' (composition effect) contributing until 1975. Capital deepening increased in the long run, especially from 1955 to 1985, slowing down after Spain's accession to the European Union, as expanding economic sectors attracted less investment-specific technological progress.

The net capital (wealth) stock-GDP ratio rose over time, contradicting Kaldor's (1957) stylised fact while confirming Piketty and Zucman (2014) results. Although the consumption of fixed capital (% GDP) shadowed the capital-output ratio, the rate of depreciation fell from 1970 to the onset of the Global Financial Crisis, as new capital goods' relative prices declined due to embodied technological change.

The inverse association between capital deepening and employment growth in post-Franco Spain mimics the behaviour of labour productivity, which rises when employment falls and declines when employment expands (Prados de la Escosura, 2017). How much did capital deepening contribute to raising labour productivity over the long run? The next chapter provides an answer.

Appendix

A.1 A Note on Splicing GFCF Series in Spain's National Accounts

Available national accounts' series are provided for different and usually short periods on the basis of different benchmark or reference years and different methodologies. In order to present a single homogeneous series, splicing is required. There is no consensus on how to do it. The most frequent splicing procedure has been retropolation in which the value provided by the latest benchmark estimate is projected backward with the rate of variation for previous benchmark series so the earlier series is re-scaled to match the new benchmark level. The practical advantage is that it preserves the rate of variation of the earlier benchmark series. On the downside, however, retropolation tends to overexaggerate past levels since new rounds of national accounts introduce new definitions and classifications and new sources and estimation procedures that usually translate into higher levels for the new benchmark series at the year in which the new and the old benchmark series overlap.

The interpolation method, instead, accepts the levels computed directly for each benchmark-year as the best possible estimates—as they are computed with 'complete' information on quantities and prices-, and distributes the gap between the 'new 'and 'old' benchmark series in the overlapping year at a constant rate over the time span in between the old and new benchmark years. By respecting the levels for the different benchmark years, the interpolation method alters the rate of variation, unlike the retropolation method. The consequence is that earlier levels are usually lower in the interpolated series than in the retropolated series.

In other words, the retropolation method presumes the error lies in the level of the 'old' series, but not in its rate of variation. The interpolation method challenges this assumption and deems the cumulative result of the emergence of new goods and services, not considered in the old benchmark series, the source of error.

The interpolation method appears provides a superior alternative, supported by the fact that recent rounds of national accounts have chosen it. In the case of Spain, for 1995–2020, national accounts provide spliced estimates in which, once adjustments are made for methodological changes, the different benchmark series are interpolated (Prados de la Escosura (2016, 2017). Thus, the dilemma about the splicing method refers only to the pre-1995 period (with the exception of 1980–86 in which national accounts were also interpolated).[26]

More specifically, since the 2000 benchmark (CNE00) the *interpolation* method was used after adjusting upwards the old benchmark series for methodological changes. Thus, the gap between, say, CNE15 and CNE10 in the year 2015, was decomposed into methodological and statistical plus other differences. Firstly, CNE10 series for 2010–2014 were adjusted upwards for methodological discrepancies with CNE15. Then, the *residual* gap, due to statistical and other differences, was distributed at a constant rate throughout the in-between benchmarks years, 2011–2014.[27] A detailed discussion of the splicing of Spanish national accounts and the available alternatives is provided in Prados de la Escosura (2017, Ch. 9) https://link.springer.com/chapter/10.1007/978-3-319-58042-5_9

See Tables 3.4, 3.5, 3.6, 3.7 and 3.8.

[26] A break in the linkage of GDP series through retropolation was introduced in CNE86, when national accounts were spliced using the interpolation approach and the GDP differential between CEN86 and CEN80 in 1985 was distributed at a constant rate over the years 1981–1984.

[27] The Spanish Statistical Institute notes, for example, "The [remaining] differences between both estimates [say, CNE00 and CNE95 in the year 2000] are due to the statistical changes, and given that information is not available regarding how and at what time they have been generated, it is assumed that this has occurred progressively over time, from the beginning of the previous base" (INE, 2007: 5).

Table 3.4 Net capital stock and consumption of fixed capital 1850–2020 (million Euro)

	Dwellings	Other construction	Machinery and equipment[a]	Transport equipment	Total net capital stock	Consumption of fixed capital
1850	24	15	0.4	1.1	40	0.9
1851	23	15	0.4	1.1	40	0.9
1852	24	15	0.4	1.1	40	0.9
1853	24	15	0.5	1.1	40	0.9
1854	23	15	0.5	1.2	40	0.9
1855	23	14	0.6	1.2	39	0.9
1856	23	14	0.6	1.3	39	0.9
1857	23	14	0.7	1.4	40	0.9
1858	23	15	0.7	1.8	41	1.0
1859	24	15	0.8	2.1	42	1.1
1860	25	16	0.8	2.2	44	1.1
1861	26	17	0.9	2.3	46	1.2
1862	27	18	0.9	2.5	48	1.2
1863	27	19	1.0	2.8	50	1.3
1864	28	19	1.0	3.1	51	1.4
1865	28	20	1.1	3.4	53	1.4
1866	28	20	1.1	3.8	53	1.5
1867	28	20	1.1	4.4	54	1.5
1868	28	21	1.1	4.5	55	1.6
1869	28	21	1.1	4.2	54	1.5
1870	28	21	1.1	4.0	54	1.5
1871	28	21	1.1	3.9	55	1.5
1872	29	21	1.1	3.9	55	1.5
1873	29	22	1.2	3.7	56	1.5
1874	29	22	1.2	3.5	56	1.5
1875	30	22	1.2	3.3	56	1.5
1876	30	22	1.3	3.2	56	1.5
1877	30	22	1.3	3.1	57	1.5
1878	30	22	1.4	3.3	57	1.5
1879	30	22	1.4	3.6	57	1.6
1880	30	22	1.6	3.7	58	1.6
1881	30	22	1.7	3.7	58	1.6
1882	30	22	1.9	3.7	58	1.6
1883	30	22	2.1	4.0	59	1.7
1884	31	23	2.2	4.6	60	1.8
1885	31	23	2.3	4.8	60	1.8
1886	31	23	2.4	4.7	60	1.8
1887	31	23	2.4	4.5	60	1.8
1888	31	23	2.4	4.3	60	1.8
1889	31	23	2.5	4.1	61	1.8
1890	31	24	2.7	4.0	62	1.8
1891	32	24	2.9	3.9	63	1.8
1892	33	25	3.1	3.7	64	1.9

(continued)

Table 3.4 (continued)

	Dwellings	Other construction	Machinery and equipment[a]	Transport equipment	Total net capital stock	Consumption of fixed capital
1893	33	26	3.2	3.5	66	1.9
1894	34	27	3.3	3.4	68	1.9
1895	35	27	3.5	3.3	70	2.0
1896	36	28	3.6	3.3	72	2.0
1897	37	29	3.8	3.2	74	2.1
1898	38	30	4.0	3.3	76	2.1
1899	40	31	4.3	3.8	79	2.3
1900	41	33	4.7	4.9	84	2.5
1901	43	34	5.2	5.7	88	2.7
1902	44	35	5.5	5.8	90	2.8
1903	45	36	5.7	5.6	92	2.8
1904	46	37	6.0	5.3	95	2.9
1905	48	38	6.2	5.2	97	2.9
1906	49	39	6.4	5.2	99	3.0
1907	50	40	6.7	5.4	102	3.1
1908	51	41	7.1	5.4	105	3.2
1909	53	43	7.5	5.3	109	3.3
1910	56	45	8.0	5.4	114	3.5
1911	59	49	8.6	5.5	121	3.7
1912	62	53	9.4	6.1	130	4.0
1913	67	57	11	7.2	142	4.4
1914	72	63	12	8.3	155	4.9
1915	78	69	13	8.9	169	5.3
1916	85	76	14	9.3	184	5.7
1917	92	82	15	10	200	6.3
1918	100	89	17	13	218	7.0
1919	108	95	18	15	236	7.7
1920	116	101	19	18	253	8.3
1921	124	107	20	20	272	9.0
1922	132	114	21	22	288	9.6
1923	140	119	21	22	302	9.9
1924	147	124	22	23	316	10
1925	153	129	23	24	329	11
1926	160	133	24	24	341	11
1927	166	137	25	26	355	12
1928	173	142	28	29	371	12
1929	181	146	31	33	392	14
1930	190	152	35	36	414	15
1931	197	157	40	36	431	16
1932	202	162	44	35	442	16
1933	207	168	47	35	457	17
1934	214	176	50	36	476	17
1935	223	186	53	38	500	18

(continued)

Table 3.4 (continued)

	Dwellings	Other construction	Machinery and equipment[a]	Transport equipment	Total net capital stock	Consumption of fixed capital
1936	234	195	56	39	524	19
1937	246	203	57	39	545	19
1938	262	213	58	38	571	20
1939	280	225	59	38	603	21
1940	302	245	64	40	651	22
1941	333	275	73	43	723	25
1942	373	312	83	49	818	28
1943	422	358	95	56	932	32
1944	480	413	109	59	1062	36
1945	546	477	126	63	1212	41
1946	624	549	147	69	1390	47
1947	722	636	174	76	1608	55
1948	848	741	204	84	1877	64
1949	993	863	240	95	2190	74
1950	1150	999	284	107	2540	86
1951	1320	1149	332	121	2923	99
1952	1502	1313	388	136	3340	114
1953	1702	1492	459	152	3806	132
1954	1935	1687	544	173	4339	152
1955	2207	1908	640	204	4959	176
1956	2522	2159	762	246	5689	206
1957	2854	2425	914	302	6495	241
1958	3184	2690	1069	370	7313	278
1959	3511	2941	1196	440	8087	312
1960	3813	3167	1304	505	8789	342
1961	4119	3388	1443	570	9519	375
1962	4469	3646	1605	631	10,351	413
1963	4887	3987	1757	695	11,325	452
1964	5410	4425	1899	775	12,509	496
1965	6045	4971	2114	876	14,006	555
1966	6790	5653	2464	995	15,901	636
1967	7687	6548	2878	1143	18,255	736
1968	8855	7708	3336	1321	21,221	855
1969	10,435	9153	3930	1525	25,043	1005
1970	12,504	10,972	4678	1761	29,915	1193
1971	15,167	13,263	5539	1999	35,968	1414
1972	18,633	16,234	6650	2308	43,823	1701
1973	23,214	20,190	8211	2812	54,427	2102
1974	29,191	25,457	10,329	3569	68,546	2650
1975	36,638	32,158	12,960	4544	86,300	3337
1976	45,567	40,281	16,051	5608	107,507	4145
1977	56,132	50,147	19,756	6862	132,897	5110
1978	68,352	62,020	24,112	8416	162,900	6258

(continued)

Table 3.4 (continued)

	Dwellings	Other construction	Machinery and equipment[a]	Transport equipment	Total net capital stock	Consumption of fixed capital
1979	82,076	75,868	28,831	10,157	196,932	7538
1980	97,209	91,851	33,987	12,143	235,190	8969
1981	113,801	109,591	39,729	14,317	277,437	10,552
1982	131,753	128,654	45,746	16,715	322,868	12,245
1983	150,494	149,317	52,133	19,254	371,199	14,046
1984	169,578	170,886	58,674	21,460	420,598	15,852
1985	188,909	193,316	65,418	23,608	471,251	17,698
1986	209,037	217,498	72,947	26,045	525,527	19,723
1987	230,843	243,664	81,960	28,983	585,450	22,049
1988	255,170	272,482	93,153	32,650	653,455	24,814
1989	282,231	305,789	106,523	36,889	731,432	28,043
1990	312,149	344,635	120,982	41,215	818,981	31,581
1991	344,609	388,169	135,119	45,155	913,053	35,183
1992	378,509	433,401	148,218	48,502	1,008,630	38,657
1993	413,742	477,303	158,818	50,756	1,100,619	41,701
1994	451,060	521,044	167,923	52,467	1,192,494	44,537
1995	492,556	567,285	178,745	54,659	1,293,244	47,750
1996	539,266	614,665	191,930	57,221	1,403,083	51,388
1997	590,424	662,901	206,894	60,557	1,520,776	55,410
1998	647,092	714,983	224,149	65,310	1,651,533	60,036
1999	711,799	773,012	243,782	71,575	1,800,169	65,375
2000	789,187	835,471	265,240	79,389	1,969,287	71,402
2001	879,013	901,677	287,168	87,458	2,155,315	77,790
2002	976,875	973,713	308,108	94,419	2,353,114	84,191
2003	1,082,507	1,050,817	329,166	101,190	2,563,681	90,819
2004	1,194,206	1,132,216	351,059	108,833	2,786,314	97,837
2005	1,309,328	1,218,246	374,674	117,650	3,019,898	105,351
2006	1,425,643	1,309,068	401,353	127,679	3,263,744	113,492
2007	1,535,390	1,401,108	431,802	138,529	3,506,829	122,094
2008	1,623,437	1,487,836	463,627	147,946	3,722,846	130,236
2009	1,673,546	1,559,566	487,777	150,670	3,871,559	135,781
2010	1,688,746	1,613,881	505,876	149,292	3,957,795	139,210
2011	1,681,535	1,654,887	523,586	149,033	4,009,042	142,074
2012	1,659,804	1,682,915	537,902	148,989	4,029,609	144,048
2013	1,633,148	1,701,414	548,771	149,369	4,032,702	145,376
2014	1,614,252	1,716,613	558,871	151,157	4,040,893	146,821
2015	1,610,257	1,734,151	571,887	154,996	4,071,290	149,125
2016	1,622,645	1,755,020	588,978	159,432	4,126,075	152,301
2017	1,654,612	1,779,620	609,148	165,110	4,208,490	156,364
2018	1,706,518	1,811,442	631,942	172,539	4,322,440	161,408
2019	1,775,794	1,852,397	656,714	179,521	4,464,425	167,105
2020	1,852,588	1,897,264	680,451	182,127	4,612,431	172,378

[a]Includes biological resources and "other" that, after 1995, incorporates intellectual property

Table 3.5 Net capital stock/GDP ratio

	Net capital stock/GDP	Net capital stock/GDP (excluding dwellings)
1850	1.6	0.6
1851	1.5	0.6
1852	1.5	0.6
1853	1.3	0.5
1854	1.2	0.5
1855	1.2	0.5
1856	1.2	0.5
1857	1.2	0.5
1858	1.3	0.5
1859	1.2	0.5
1860	1.2	0.5
1861	1.3	0.5
1862	1.3	0.6
1863	1.3	0.6
1864	1.3	0.6
1865	1.4	0.7
1866	1.3	0.6
1867	1.3	0.6
1868	1.5	0.7
1869	1.6	0.8
1870	1.5	0.7
1871	1.4	0.7
1872	1.2	0.6
1873	1.2	0.6
1874	1.2	0.6
1875	1.2	0.6
1876	1.2	0.6
1877	1.1	0.5
1878	1.1	0.5
1879	1.1	0.5
1880	1.1	0.5
1881	1.0	0.5
1882	1.0	0.5
1883	1.0	0.5
1884	1.0	0.5
1885	1.0	0.5
1886	1.0	0.5
1887	1.1	0.5
1888	1.1	0.5
1889	1.2	0.6
1890	1.2	0.6
1891	1.2	0.6
1892	1.2	0.6

(continued)

Table 3.5 (continued)

	Net capital stock/GDP	Net capital stock/GDP (excluding dwellings)
1893	1.3	0.6
1894	1.3	0.7
1895	1.3	0.7
1896	1.4	0.7
1897	1.4	0.7
1898	1.3	0.7
1899	1.4	0.7
1900	1.4	0.7
1901	1.4	0.7
1902	1.4	0.7
1903	1.4	0.7
1904	1.3	0.7
1905	1.4	0.7
1906	1.4	0.7
1907	1.4	0.7
1908	1.5	0.8
1909	1.5	0.8
1910	1.6	0.8
1911	1.6	0.8
1912	1.7	0.9
1913	1.7	0.9
1914	1.9	1.0
1915	1.9	1.0
1916	1.8	0.9
1917	1.8	0.9
1918	1.6	0.9
1919	1.6	0.9
1920	1.4	0.8
1921	1.7	0.9
1922	1.7	0.9
1923	1.8	1.0
1924	1.7	0.9
1925	1.7	0.9
1926	1.8	1.0
1927	1.8	0.9
1928	1.9	1.0
1929	1.9	1.0
1930	2.0	1.1
1931	2.1	1.1
1932	2.1	1.2
1933	2.3	1.3
1934	2.2	1.2
1935	2.2	1.2

(continued)

Table 3.5 (continued)

	Net capital stock/GDP	Net capital stock/GDP (excluding dwellings)
1936	2.9	1.6
1937	2.8	1.6
1938	2.6	1.4
1939	2.4	1.3
1940	2.1	1.1
1941	2.1	1.1
1942	2.0	1.1
1943	2.1	1.1
1944	2.1	1.1
1945	2.4	1.3
1946	2.1	1.2
1947	2.1	1.2
1948	2.3	1.3
1949	2.5	1.4
1950	2.4	1.3
1951	2.1	1.2
1952	2.2	1.2
1953	2.3	1.3
1954	2.3	1.3
1955	2.4	1.3
1956	2.3	1.3
1957	2.2	1.2
1958	2.1	1.2
1959	2.2	1.2
1960	2.3	1.3
1961	2.2	1.2
1962	2.0	1.1
1963	1.8	1.0
1964	1.8	1.0
1965	1.7	1.0
1966	1.7	1.0
1967	1.7	1.0
1968	1.8	1.0
1969	1.8	1.1
1970	2.0	1.2
1971	2.1	1.2
1972	2.2	1.2
1973	2.2	1.3
1974	2.2	1.3
1975	2.4	1.4
1976	2.5	1.4
1977	2.4	1.4
1978	2.4	1.4

(continued)

Table 3.5 (continued)

	Net capital stock/GDP	Net capital stock/GDP (excluding dwellings)
1979	2.5	1.4
1980	2.5	1.5
1981	2.6	1.5
1982	2.6	1.6
1983	2.6	1.6
1984	2.6	1.6
1985	2.7	1.6
1986	2.6	1.6
1987	2.6	1.6
1988	2.6	1.6
1989	2.5	1.6
1990	2.5	1.6
1991	2.6	1.6
1992	2.6	1.6
1993	2.8	1.7
1994	2.8	1.7
1995	2.8	1.7
1996	2.9	1.8
1997	2.9	1.8
1998	3.0	1.8
1999	3.0	1.8
2000	3.0	1.8
2001	3.1	1.8
2002	3.1	1.8
2003	3.2	1.8
2004	3.2	1.9
2005	3.3	1.8
2006	3.3	1.8
2007	3.3	1.8
2008	3.4	1.9
2009	3.6	2.1
2010	3.7	2.1
2011	3.8	2.2
2012	3.9	2.3
2013	4.0	2.4
2014	3.9	2.4
2015	3.8	2.3
2016	3.7	2.2
2017	3.6	2.2
2018	3.6	2.2
2019	3.6	2.2
2020	4.1	2.5

Table 3.6 Productive capital stock, 1850–2020 (million 2010 Euro)

	Dwellings	Other construction	Machinery and equipment[a]	Transport Equipment	Total
1850	20,013	6995	97	222	27,327
1851	20,293	7042	100	211	27,646
1852	20,680	7114	105	202	28,101
1853	21,067	7213	111	204	28,596
1854	21,354	7304	120	210	28,988
1855	21,549	7371	128	207	29,255
1856	21,757	7459	134	220	29,570
1857	22,129	7624	142	249	30,145
1858	22,745	7871	154	312	31,082
1859	23,654	8187	168	380	32,389
1860	24,822	8717	178	400	34,118
1861	25,835	9416	187	420	35,857
1862	26,672	10,101	200	464	37,437
1863	27,574	10,754	217	514	39,059
1864	28,375	11,305	233	564	40,477
1865	28,958	11,681	245	622	41,506
1866	29,372	11,928	252	698	42,249
1867	29,760	12,148	253	788	42,949
1868	30,049	12,327	253	800	43,429
1869	30,191	12,440	250	737	43,619
1870	30,340	12,513	250	701	43,803
1871	30,613	12,598	254	683	44,148
1872	31,003	12,734	263	671	44,671
1873	31,429	12,874	274	648	45,224
1874	31,848	13,011	280	632	45,771
1875	32,350	13,199	287	614	46,449
1876	32,987	13,469	298	604	47,357
1877	33,757	13,819	314	607	48,497
1878	34,513	14,151	331	683	49,679
1879	35,114	14,434	352	770	50,670
1880	35,683	14,781	387	816	51,668
1881	36,309	15,198	434	843	52,785
1882	37,052	15,684	486	849	54,072
1883	37,983	16,262	538	949	55,733
1884	38,942	16,862	585	1098	57,487
1885	39,694	17,372	620	1174	58,861
1886	40,225	17,818	641	1167	59,851
1887	40,662	18,294	654	1141	60,751
1888	41,062	18,810	660	1086	61,617
1889	41,488	19,285	677	1049	62,498
1890	42,036	19,776	718	1038	63,567
1891	42,648	20,324	765	1004	64,742
1892	43,304	20,866	812	947	65,928

(continued)

Table 3.6 (continued)

	Dwellings	Other construction	Machinery and equipment[a]	Transport Equipment	Total
1893	44,014	21,376	840	896	67,125
1894	44,743	21,813	851	851	68,258
1895	45,478	22,236	870	808	69,392
1896	46,182	22,646	893	775	70,497
1897	46,873	22,997	923	753	71,546
1898	47,611	23,356	953	740	72,660
1899	48,537	23,795	995	844	74,171
1900	49,887	24,438	1078	1086	76,490
1901	51,242	25,112	1166	1260	78,780
1902	52,263	25,622	1227	1288	80,401
1903	53,314	26,150	1287	1259	82,011
1904	54,580	26,755	1355	1239	83,928
1905	55,736	27,292	1413	1237	85,678
1906	56,578	27,756	1471	1270	87,074
1907	57,512	28,320	1544	1331	88,707
1908	58,657	28,950	1619	1341	90,568
1909	59,888	29,559	1688	1322	92,457
1910	61,176	30,336	1747	1323	94,582
1911	62,578	31,271	1798	1314	96,963
1912	64,050	32,232	1859	1379	99,521
1913	65,509	33,158	1953	1541	102,161
1914	66,895	33,947	2012	1657	104,511
1915	67,978	34,581	2003	1634	106,196
1916	68,714	35,052	2022	1577	107,364
1917	69,165	35,413	2076	1638	108,293
1918	69,425	35,692	2147	1852	109,115
1919	69,705	36,019	2205	2096	110,025
1920	70,417	36,623	2235	2321	111,597
1921	71,606	37,610	2329	2540	114,084
1922	72,987	38,861	2399	2690	116,936
1923	74,664	40,133	2446	2702	119,945
1924	76,604	41,386	2556	2827	123,373
1925	78,743	42,835	2708	2943	127,229
1926	81,095	44,499	2892	3006	131,491
1927	83,622	46,220	3120	3229	136,191
1928	86,449	47,986	3449	3618	141,503
1929	89,705	50,007	3925	4152	147,789
1930	93,183	52,293	4562	4486	154,524
1931	95,156	54,279	5178	4513	159,126
1932	95,520	55,713	5634	4338	161,205
1933	95,719	57,158	5984	4186	163,047
1934	95,828	58,698	6267	4166	164,959
1935	95,901	60,128	6530	4165	166,724

(continued)

Table 3.6 (continued)

	Dwellings	Other construction	Machinery and equipment[a]	Transport Equipment	Total
1936	95,837	61,300	6770	4041	167,947
1937	95,447	60,419	6554	3722	166,141
1938	94,893	59,386	6287	3334	163,901
1939	94,348	58,163	6033	3021	161,564
1940	93,858	57,153	5859	2830	159,700
1941	94,541	58,249	6104	2729	161,623
1942	96,390	59,732	6333	2789	165,244
1943	98,398	61,458	6521	2835	169,211
1944	100,183	63,260	6653	2691	172,787
1945	101,505	64,694	6803	2539	175,540
1946	102,891	65,802	7037	2461	178,191
1947	105,352	67,160	7309	2389	182,209
1948	109,643	68,962	7599	2333	188,537
1949	113,978	70,833	7906	2333	195,051
1950	117,374	72,580	8282	2349	200,585
1951	120,139	74,165	8629	2369	205,303
1952	122,371	75,671	9014	2387	209,442
1953	124,722	77,193	9574	2402	213,890
1954	128,345	78,942	10,250	2469	220,007
1955	133,758	81,466	11,004	2660	228,888
1956	141,124	84,957	12,067	2968	241,115
1957	149,357	88,895	13,494	3397	255,143
1958	157,660	92,895	14,940	3926	269,422
1959	166,288	96,573	16,008	4462	283,330
1960	174,151	99,659	16,913	4934	295,657
1961	182,231	102,675	18,297	5405	308,609
1962	191,971	106,726	20,034	5859	324,590
1963	203,855	112,962	21,687	6344	344,847
1964	218,750	121,443	23,235	6994	370,422
1965	235,678	132,055	25,630	7845	401,207
1966	252,720	144,757	29,470	8853	435,800
1967	269,071	160,444	33,673	10,087	473,275
1968	285,847	178,676	37,757	11,524	513,804
1969	303,692	197,782	42,404	13,061	556,939
1970	320,520	217,266	47,346	14,672	599,804
1971	335,252	236,343	51,686	16,015	639,295
1972	349,239	255,864	56,277	17,541	678,921
1973	364,951	277,259	62,132	19,992	724,335
1974	383,198	301,195	69,119	23,400	776,913
1975	402,100	325,678	76,184	27,124	831,086
1976	420,509	348,335	82,692	30,146	881,682
1977	439,445	370,823	89,336	32,923	932,527
1978	459,019	394,078	96,141	35,856	985,094

(continued)

Table 3.6 (continued)

	Dwellings	Other construction	Machinery and equipment[a]	Transport Equipment	Total
1979	478,679	417,320	102,031	38,359	1,036,389
1980	498,652	441,437	107,593	40,697	1,088,379
1981	519,654	465,080	113,516	42,718	1,140,968
1982	541,218	487,532	119,152	44,622	1,192,524
1983	561,173	510,831	125,061	46,292	1,243,358
1984	578,297	533,272	130,956	46,859	1,289,383
1985	592,758	555,382	137,107	47,285	1,332,533
1986	606,540	579,811	144,664	48,359	1,379,374
1987	622,208	606,617	154,711	50,391	1,433,928
1988	641,626	636,760	168,120	53,635	1,500,142
1989	664,795	673,663	184,419	57,703	1,580,581
1990	691,527	718,503	201,403	61,801	1,673,235
1991	720,741	768,606	216,678	65,278	1,771,303
1992	749,839	817,759	229,263	67,930	1,864,791
1993	778,320	860,646	237,243	69,162	1,945,372
1994	807,078	899,939	242,613	69,810	2,019,440
1995	838,845	940,112	250,229	71,220	2,100,406
1996	873,965	978,327	260,872	73,179	2,186,343
1997	909,769	1,013,602	273,583	76,139	2,273,092
1998	946,830	1,049,855	288,912	80,820	2,366,417
1999	987,981	1,089,263	306,816	87,241	2,471,302
2000	1,038,961	1,129,188	326,494	95,353	2,589,997
2001	1,099,054	1,169,032	346,286	103,550	2,717,922
2002	1,163,495	1,212,069	364,530	110,240	2,850,334
2003	1,234,047	1,258,038	382,652	116,555	2,991,293
2004	1,311,661	1,307,109	401,550	123,732	3,144,052
2005	1,397,223	1,361,139	422,294	132,103	3,312,760
2006	1,492,736	1,421,920	446,444	141,696	3,502,796
2007	1,594,607	1,487,150	474,796	152,069	3,708,622
2008	1,690,869	1,551,254	504,784	160,776	3,907,683
2009	1,765,852	1,605,017	526,735	162,219	4,059,823
2010	1,820,112	1,645,919	542,631	159,348	4,168,010
2011	1,861,761	1,677,505	558,622	157,762	4,255,649
2012	1,892,024	1,698,963	571,412	156,429	4,318,827
2013	1,913,210	1,712,167	580,777	155,502	4,361,656
2014	1,932,904	1,721,487	589,221	155,917	4,399,529
2015	1,955,623	1,730,715	600,278	158,236	4,444,852
2016	1,981,651	1,739,159	614,834	160,893	4,496,536
2017	2,015,023	1,746,119	631,596	164,505	4,557,243
2018	2,057,315	1,754,692	649,942	169,536	4,631,485
2019	2,107,221	1,766,804	669,138	173,807	4,716,970
2020	2,155,545	1,777,816	686,169	173,625	4,793,154

[a]Includes biological resources and "other" that, after 1995, incorporates intellectual property

Table 3.7 Capital input, productive capital stock, and capital quality, 1850–2020 (2010=100)

	Productive capital stock	Capital quality	Capital input
1850	0.7	41.9	0.3
1851	0.7	41.8	0.3
1852	0.7	41.7	0.3
1853	0.7	41.7	0.3
1854	0.7	41.7	0.3
1855	0.7	41.7	0.3
1856	0.7	41.8	0.3
1857	0.7	42.1	0.3
1858	0.7	42.8	0.3
1859	0.8	43.4	0.3
1860	0.8	43.5	0.4
1861	0.9	43.8	0.4
1862	0.9	44.3	0.4
1863	0.9	44.8	0.4
1864	1.0	45.3	0.4
1865	1.0	45.8	0.5
1866	1.0	46.4	0.5
1867	1.0	47.1	0.5
1868	1.0	47.1	0.5
1869	1.0	46.5	0.5
1870	1.1	46.1	0.5
1871	1.1	45.9	0.5
1872	1.1	45.7	0.5
1873	1.1	45.4	0.5
1874	1.1	45.2	0.5
1875	1.1	44.9	0.5
1876	1.1	44.8	0.5
1877	1.2	44.7	0.5
1878	1.2	45.3	0.5
1879	1.2	45.9	0.6
1880	1.2	46.3	0.6
1881	1.3	46.6	0.6
1882	1.3	46.8	0.6
1883	1.3	47.5	0.6
1884	1.4	48.5	0.7
1885	1.4	48.9	0.7
1886	1.4	48.9	0.7
1887	1.5	48.8	0.7
1888	1.5	48.4	0.7
1889	1.5	48.2	0.7
1890	1.5	48.3	0.7
1891	1.6	48.2	0.7
1892	1.6	47.9	0.8

(continued)

Table 3.7 (continued)

	Productive capital stock	Capital quality	Capital input
1893	1.6	47.5	0.8
1894	1.6	47.1	0.8
1895	1.7	46.8	0.8
1896	1.7	46.6	0.8
1897	1.7	46.5	0.8
1898	1.7	46.4	0.8
1899	1.8	47.1	0.8
1900	1.8	48.6	0.9
1901	1.9	49.7	0.9
1902	1.9	49.9	1.0
1903	2.0	49.7	1.0
1904	2.0	49.7	1.0
1905	2.1	49.7	1.0
1906	2.1	49.9	1.0
1907	2.1	50.3	1.1
1908	2.2	50.4	1.1
1909	2.2	50.4	1.1
1910	2.3	50.4	1.1
1911	2.3	50.3	1.2
1912	2.4	50.5	1.2
1913	2.5	51.1	1.3
1914	2.5	51.4	1.3
1915	2.5	51.1	1.3
1916	2.6	50.8	1.3
1917	2.6	51.2	1.3
1918	2.6	52.2	1.4
1919	2.6	53.4	1.4
1920	2.7	54.2	1.5
1921	2.7	55.2	1.5
1922	2.8	55.7	1.6
1923	2.9	55.5	1.6
1924	3.0	55.9	1.7
1925	3.1	56.3	1.7
1926	3.2	56.5	1.8
1927	3.3	57.3	1.9
1928	3.4	58.7	2.0
1929	3.5	60.5	2.1
1930	3.7	62.0	2.3
1931	3.8	63.1	2.4
1932	3.9	63.6	2.5
1933	3.9	63.9	2.5
1934	4.0	64.4	2.5
1935	4.0	64.8	2.6

(continued)

Table 3.7 (continued)

	Productive capital stock	Capital quality	Capital input
1936	4.0	65.0	2.6
1937	4.0	64.2	2.6
1938	3.9	63.2	2.5
1939	3.9	62.4	2.4
1940	3.8	61.8	2.4
1941	3.9	61.9	2.4
1942	4.0	62.1	2.5
1943	4.1	62.1	2.5
1944	4.1	61.7	2.6
1945	4.2	61.3	2.6
1946	4.3	61.3	2.6
1947	4.4	61.1	2.7
1948	4.5	60.8	2.7
1949	4.7	60.6	2.8
1950	4.8	60.8	2.9
1951	4.9	60.9	3.0
1952	5.0	61.2	3.1
1953	5.1	61.8	3.2
1954	5.3	62.4	3.3
1955	5.5	63.1	3.5
1956	5.8	64.0	3.7
1957	6.1	65.2	4.0
1958	6.5	66.5	4.3
1959	6.8	67.2	4.6
1960	7.1	67.6	4.8
1961	7.4	68.5	5.1
1962	7.8	69.3	5.4
1963	8.3	69.7	5.8
1964	8.9	69.9	6.2
1965	9.6	70.5	6.8
1966	10.5	72.0	7.5
1967	11.4	73.7	8.4
1968	12.3	75.2	9.3
1969	13.4	76.9	10.3
1970	14.4	78.7	11.3
1971	15.3	80.1	12.3
1972	16.3	81.8	13.3
1973	17.4	84.2	14.6
1974	18.6	86.9	16.2
1975	19.9	89.2	17.8
1976	21.2	90.6	19.2
1977	22.4	91.7	20.5
1978	23.6	92.6	21.9

(continued)

Table 3.7 (continued)

	Productive capital stock	Capital quality	Capital input
1979	24.9	93.0	23.1
1980	26.1	93.2	24.3
1981	27.4	93.4	25.6
1982	28.6	93.5	26.8
1983	29.8	93.6	27.9
1984	30.9	93.7	29.0
1985	32.0	93.9	30.0
1986	33.1	94.2	31.2
1987	34.4	94.9	32.7
1988	36.0	95.9	34.5
1989	37.9	97.0	36.8
1990	40.1	97.9	39.3
1991	42.5	98.3	41.8
1992	44.7	98.5	44.0
1993	46.7	98.2	45.8
1994	48.5	97.7	47.3
1995	50.4	97.4	49.1
1996	52.5	97.3	51.0
1997	54.5	97.5	53.2
1998	56.8	97.9	55.6
1999	59.3	98.5	58.4
2000	62.1	99.2	61.6
2001	65.2	99.6	64.9
2002	68.4	99.7	68.2
2003	71.8	99.7	71.5
2004	75.4	99.7	75.2
2005	79.5	99.7	79.2
2006	84.0	99.8	83.8
2007	89.0	99.9	88.9
2008	93.8	100.1	93.9
2009	97.4	100.1	97.5
2010	100.0	100.0	100.0
2011	102.1	100.0	102.1
2012	103.6	100.0	103.7
2013	104.6	100.1	104.7
2014	105.6	100.1	105.7
2015	106.6	100.3	106.9
2016	107.9	100.5	108.4
2017	109.3	100.7	110.1
2018	111.1	101.0	112.2
2019	113.2	101.2	114.5
2020	115.0	101.2	116.3

Table 3.8 Capital deepening[a] 1850–2020 (2010=100)

	Capital Input/hour worked
1850	0.6
1851	0.6
1852	0.6
1853	0.6
1854	0.6
1855	0.7
1856	0.6
1857	0.6
1858	0.7
1859	0.7
1860	0.8
1861	0.8
1862	0.8
1863	0.9
1864	0.9
1865	0.9
1866	0.9
1867	1.0
1868	1.0
1869	1.0
1870	1.0
1871	1.0
1872	1.0
1873	0.9
1874	1.0
1875	1.0
1876	1.0
1877	1.0
1878	1.0
1879	1.1
1880	1.1
1881	1.1
1882	1.2
1883	1.2
1884	1.3
1885	1.3
1886	1.4
1887	1.4
1888	1.4
1889	1.4
1890	1.4
1891	1.4
1892	1.5

(continued)

Table 3.8 (continued)

	Capital Input/hour worked
1893	1.5
1894	1.5
1895	1.5
1896	1.5
1897	1.5
1898	1.5
1899	1.5
1900	1.6
1901	1.7
1902	1.7
1903	1.7
1904	1.8
1905	1.8
1906	1.8
1907	1.9
1908	1.9
1909	1.9
1910	2.0
1911	2.0
1912	2.1
1913	2.1
1914	2.2
1915	2.2
1916	2.2
1917	2.2
1918	2.3
1919	2.3
1920	2.4
1921	2.5
1922	2.6
1923	2.6
1924	2.7
1925	2.8
1926	2.9
1927	3.0
1928	3.1
1929	3.3
1930	3.5
1931	3.7
1932	3.7
1933	3.7
1934	3.7
1935	3.7

(continued)

Table 3.8 (continued)

	Capital Input/hour worked
1936	3.7
1937	3.7
1938	3.6
1939	3.5
1940	3.5
1941	3.5
1942	3.6
1943	3.6
1944	3.6
1945	3.6
1946	3.6
1947	3.6
1948	3.6
1949	3.7
1950	3.7
1951	3.8
1952	3.9
1953	4.0
1954	4.1
1955	4.3
1956	4.6
1957	4.9
1958	5.2
1959	5.7
1960	6.1
1961	6.3
1962	6.7
1963	7.1
1964	7.6
1965	8.1
1966	8.9
1967	9.8
1968	11.0
1969	12.2
1970	13.3
1971	14.2
1972	15.2
1973	16.3
1974	18.2
1975	20.9
1976	23.1
1977	25.1
1978	27.9

(continued)

Table 3.8 (continued)

	Capital Input/hour worked
1979	30.6
1980	33.7
1981	36.9
1982	39.4
1983	41.9
1984	45.6
1985	47.9
1986	48.9
1987	49.1
1988	50.2
1989	52.1
1990	53.5
1991	55.9
1992	59.9
1993	64.3
1994	66.6
1995	67.8
1996	69.4
1997	69.6
1998	69.4
1999	69.5
2000	70.0
2001	71.1
2002	72.8
2003	74.4
2004	76.0
2005	77.6
2006	79.4
2007	82.1
2008	86.2
2009	95.2
2010	100.0
2011	104.5
2012	111.4
2013	115.8
2014	115.7
2015	113.6
2016	112.3
2017	111.7
2018	111.0
2019	111.7
2020	127.5

[a]Capital input per hour worked

A.2 Alternative Estimates: Figures

See Figs. 3.20, 3.21, 3.22, 3.23, 3.24, 3.25, 3.26, 3.27, 3.28, 3.29, 3.30, 3.31 and 3.32.

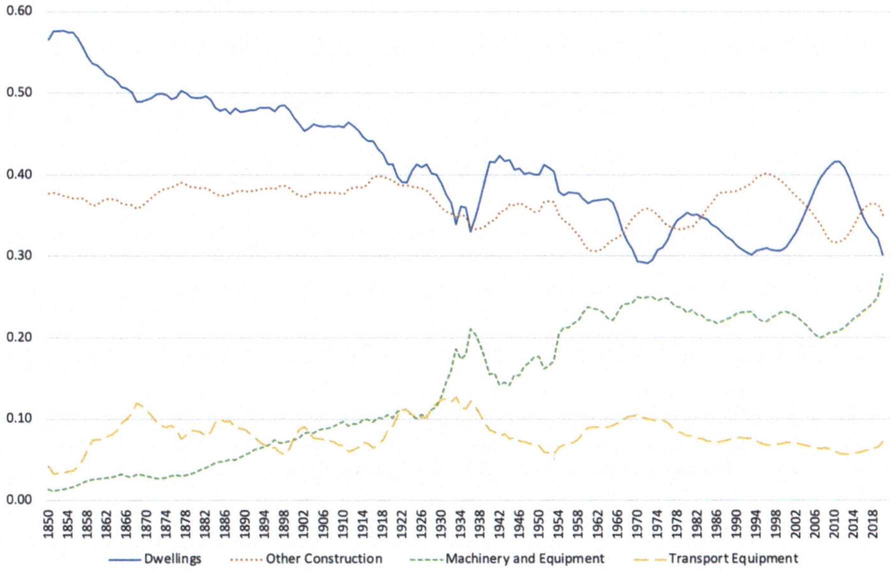

Fig. 3.20 Capital services' composition (ex-post endogenous rate of return) (current prices) (%)

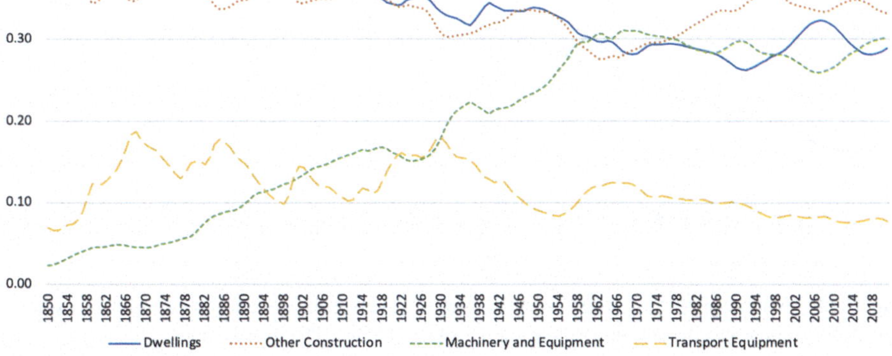

Fig. 3.21 Capital services' composition (simplified ex-ante exogenous rate of return) (current prices) (%)

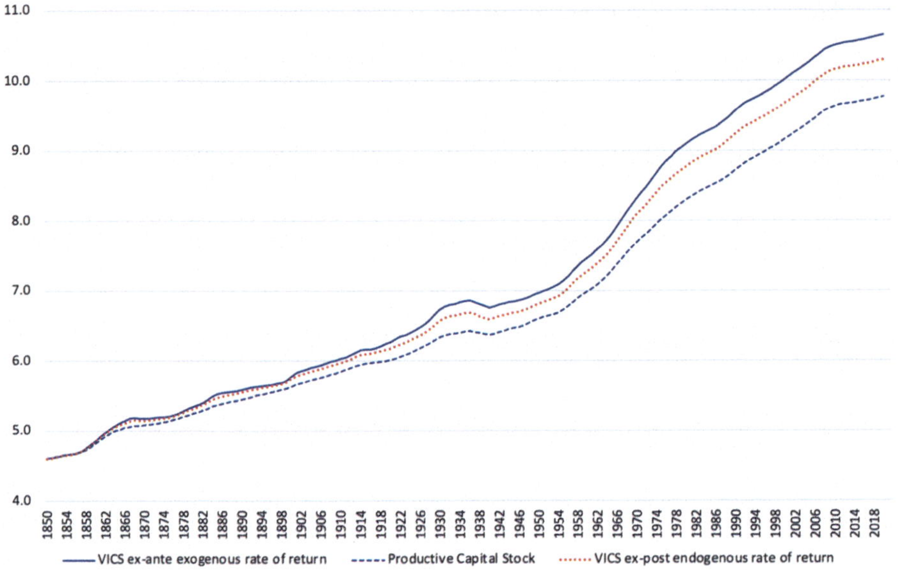

Fig. 3.22 Volume index of capital services (VICS) (ex-ante exogenous and ex-post endogenous rate of return) and productive capital stock (1850=100) (natural logs)

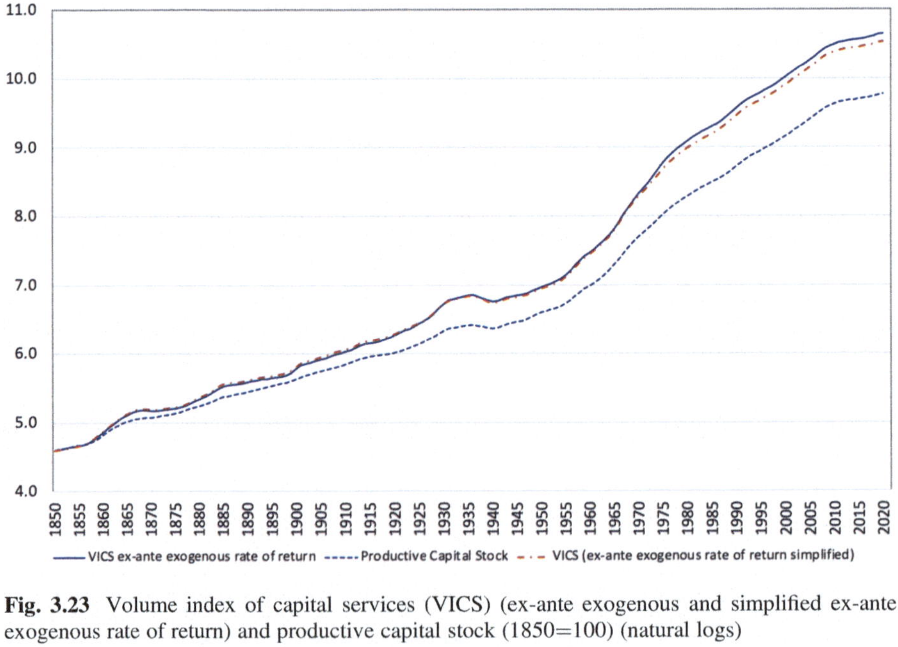

Fig. 3.23 Volume index of capital services (VICS) (ex-ante exogenous and simplified ex-ante exogenous rate of return) and productive capital stock (1850=100) (natural logs)

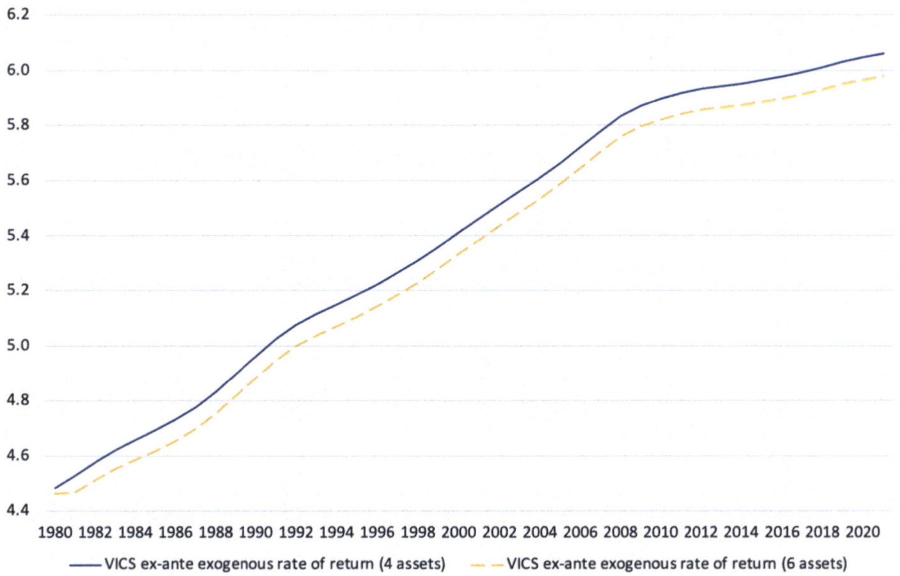

Fig. 3.24 Volume index of capital services (VICS) with four and six assets, 1980–2020 (2010=100) (natural logs) ex-ante exogenous endogenous rates of return

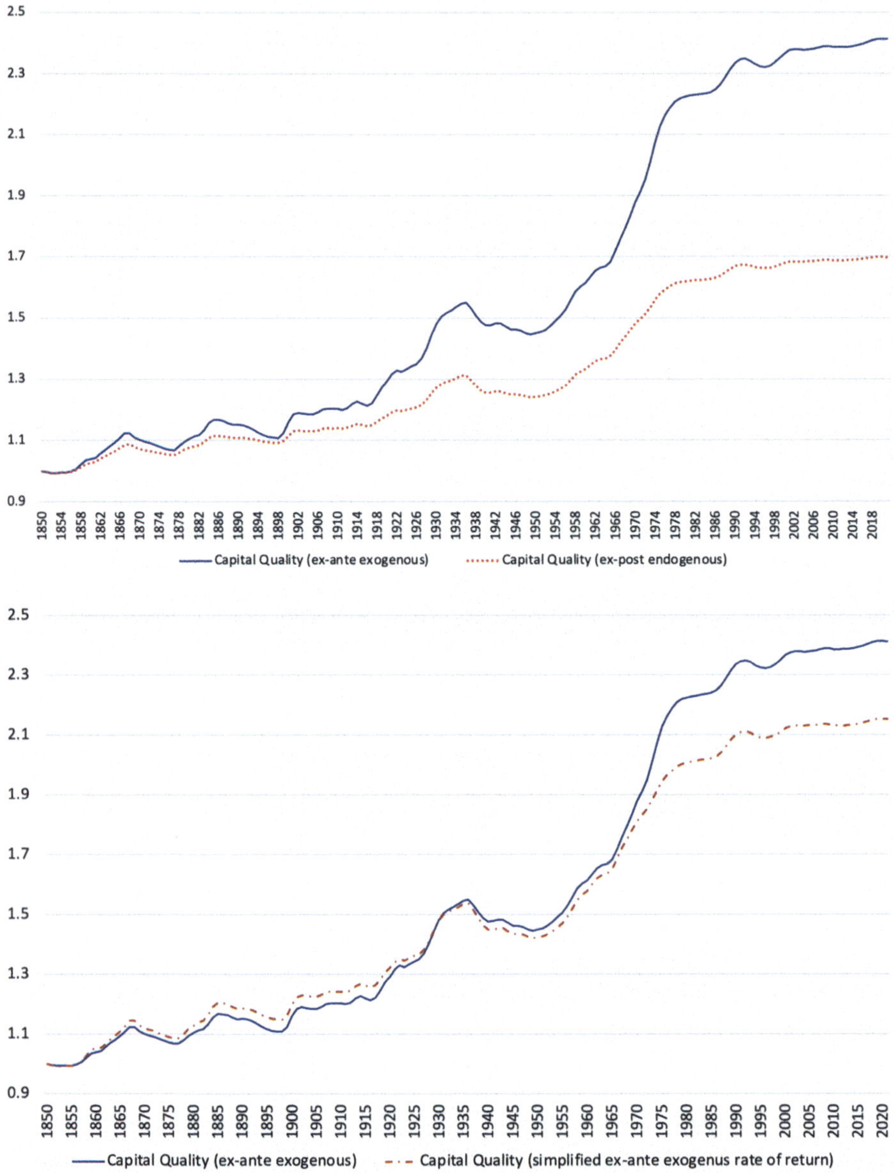

Fig. 3.25 (**a**) Capital quality* (ex-ante exogenous and ex-post endogenous rate of return) (1850=1). *Capital quality = Ratio of VICS to productive capital stock. (**b**) Capital quality* (full and simplified ex-ante exogenous rate of return) (1850=1). *Capital quality = Ratio of VICS to productive capital stock

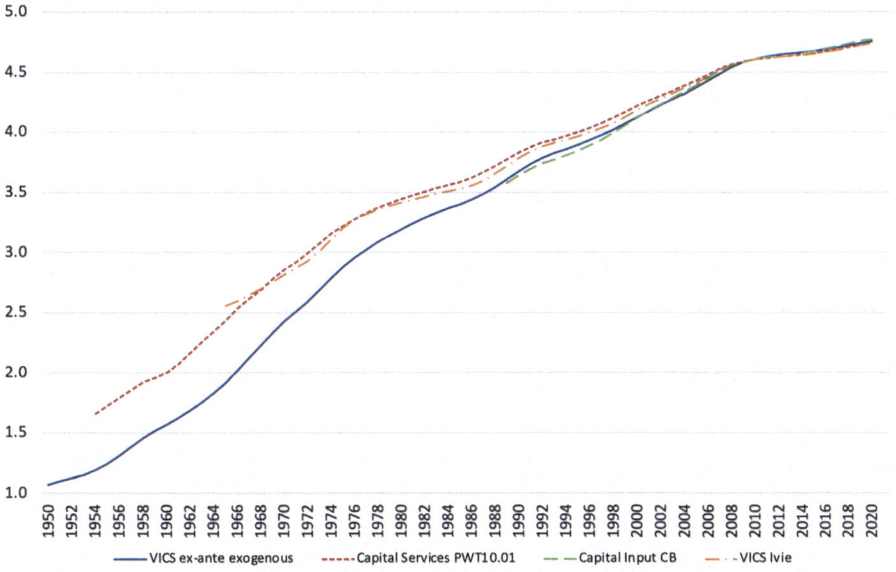

Fig. 3.26 New VICS*: comparison with PWT10.01, conference board (CB), and Ivie estimates, 1950–2020 (2010=100) (natural logs) ex-ante exogenous and ex-post endogenous rates of return

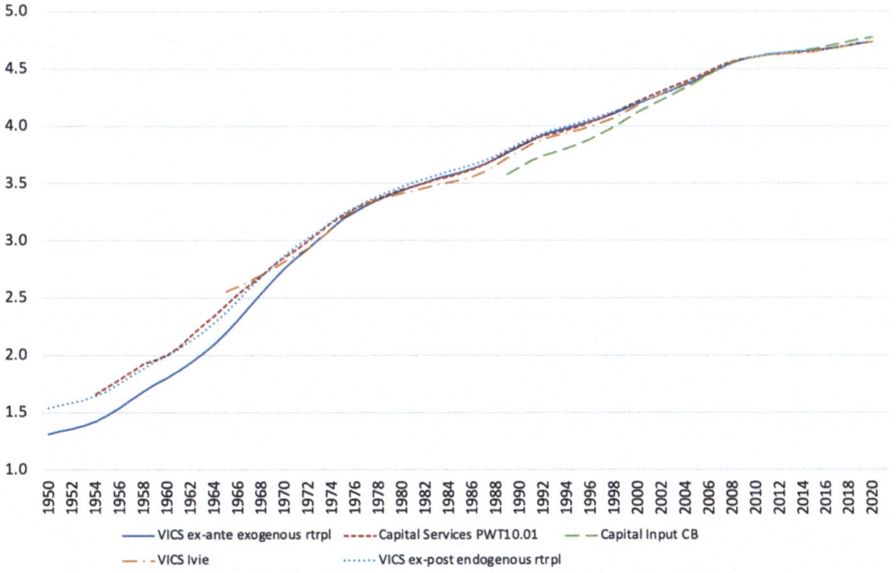

Fig. 3.27 VICS estimates with GFCF retropolated series, ex-ante exogenous and ex-post endogenous rates of return. Comparison with PWT10.01, conference board (CB), and Ivie (2010=100) (logs)

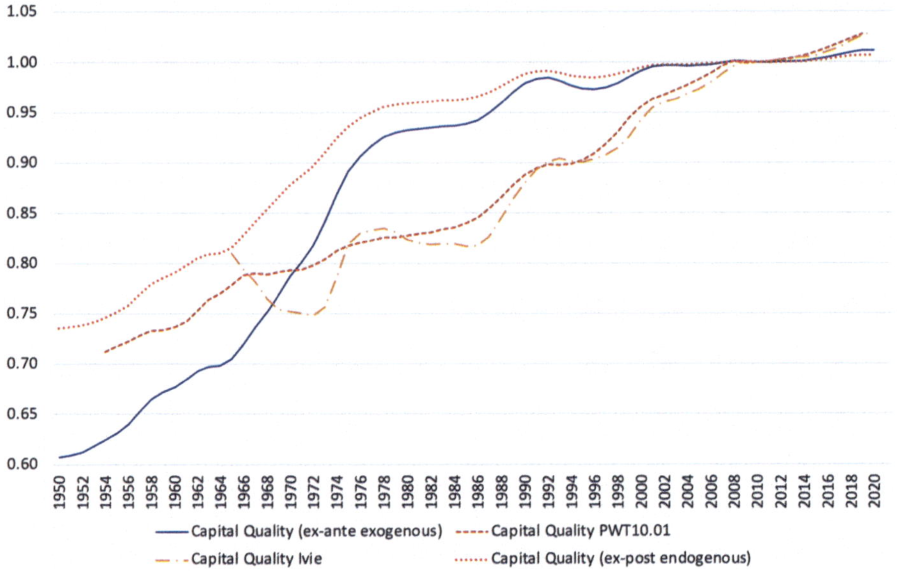

Fig. 3.28 Capital quality*: comparison with PWT10.01 and Ivie estimates, 1950–2020 (2010=1). *Derived with ex-ante exogenous and ex-post endogenous rates of return

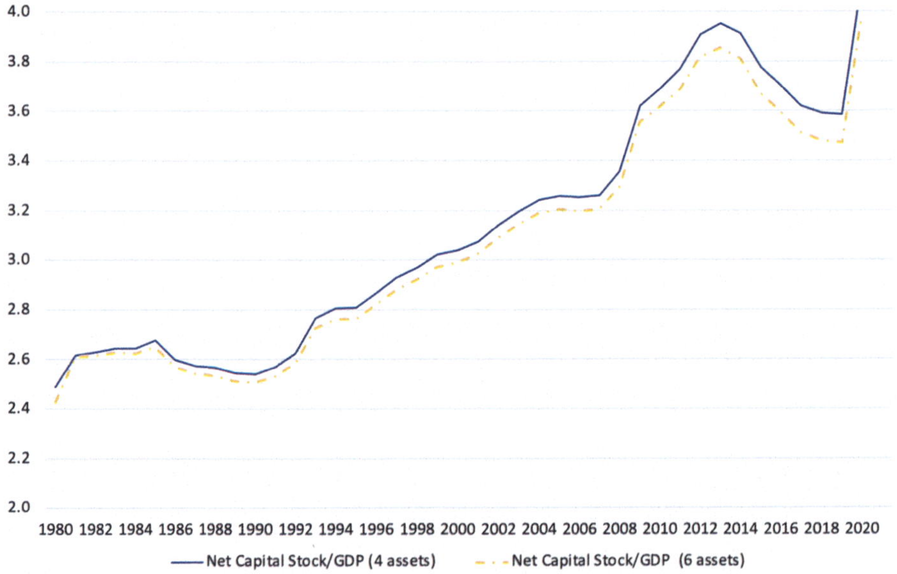

Fig. 3.29 Net capital stock/GDP ratio with four and six assets, 1980–2020 (current prices)

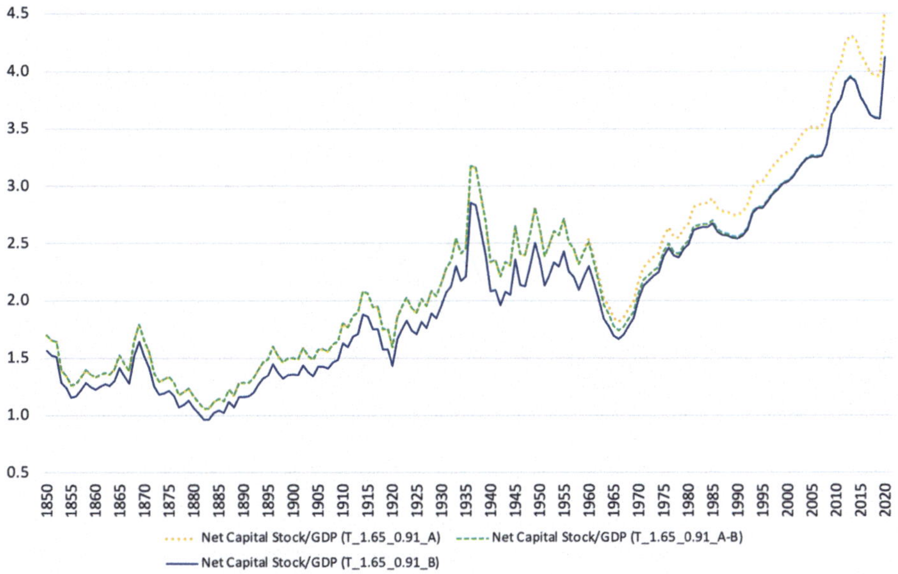

Fig. 3.30 Net capital stock/GDP ratio: estimates with alternative average service lives (current prices). Note: A, longer lives; B, shorter lives; A-B, A up to 1958 and B thereafter

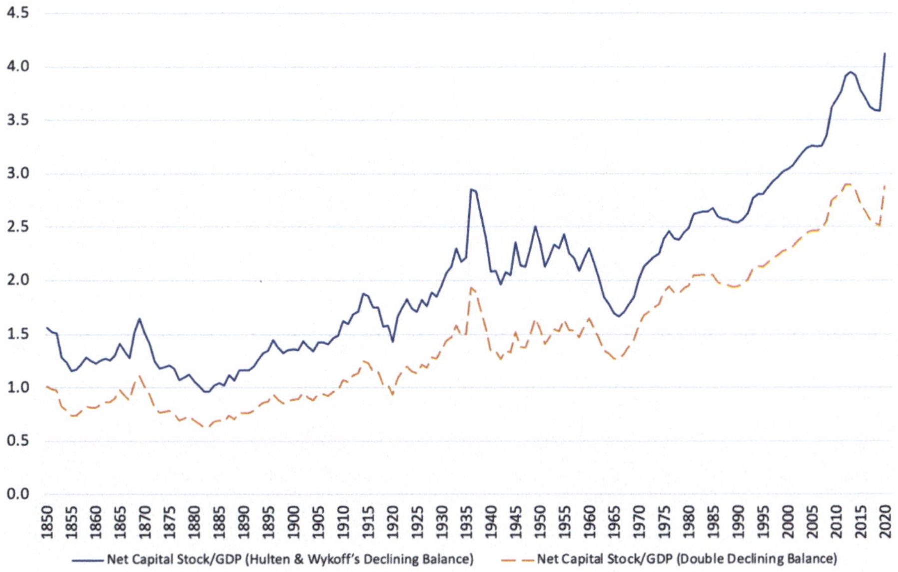

Fig. 3.31 Hulten & Wykoff and double declining balance net capital stock/GDP ratio (current prices)

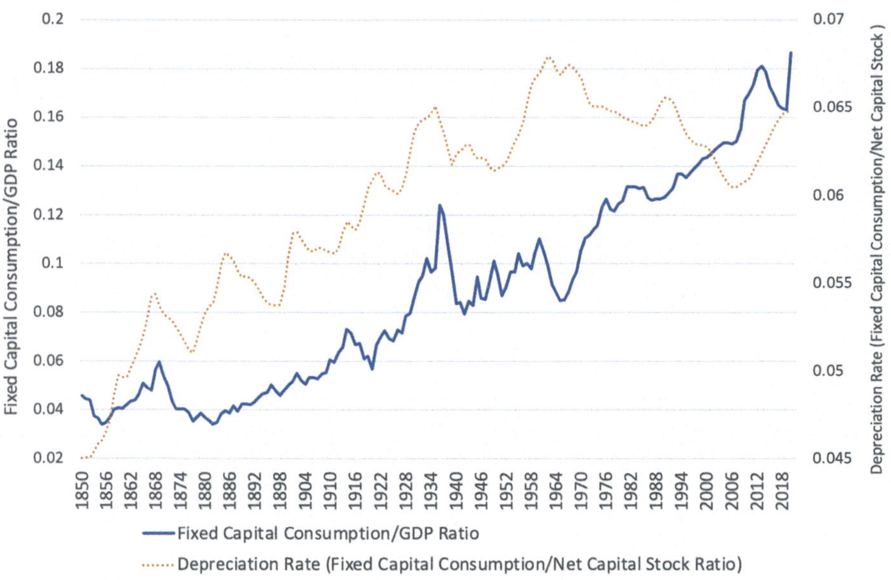

Fig. 3.32 Double declining balance consumption of fixed capital/GDP ratio and depreciation rate (consumption of fixed capital/net capital stock ratio), (current prices)

References

Artola Blanco, M., L. Estévez Bauluz, and C. Martínez-Toledano (2020), "Wealth in Spain, 1900-2014: A Country of Two Lands", *Economic Journal* 131: 129-155.

Calvo-González, O. (2021), *Unexpected Prosperity. How Spain Escaped the Middle Income Trap*, Oxford: Oxford University Press.

Christensen, L.R., D. Cummings, and D.W. Jorgenson (1980), "Economic Growth, 1947-1973: An International Comparison," in J.W. Kendrick and B.N. Vaccara (eds.) *New Developments in Productivity Measurement and Analysis*, Chicago: University of Chicago Press/NBER, pp. 595-698.

Conference Board (2022), Total Economy Database. Growth Accounting and Total Factor Productivity, 1990-2022, dataset accessible at https://www.conference-board.org/data/economydatabase/total-economy-database-productivity

Elías, V.J. (1978), "Sources of Economic Growth in Latin American Countries", *Review of Economics and Statistics* 60 (3) (Aug., 1978): 362-370.

Feinstein, C.H. (1988), "Sources and Methods of Estimation for Domestic Reproducible Fixed Assets, Stocks and Works in Progress, Overseas Assets, and Land", in C.H. Feinstein and S. Pollard, eds., *Studies in Capital Formation in the United Kingdom 1750-1920*, Oxford: Clarendon Press, pp. 257-471.

Feenstra, R. C., R. Inklaar and M.P. Timmer (2015), "The Next Generation of the Penn World Table", *American Economic Review* 105 (10): 3150-3182, Updated dataset at www.ggdc.net/pwt

Fraumeni, B.M. (1997), "The Measurement of Depreciation in the U.S. National Income and Product Accounts, *Survey of Current Business* July: 7-23

Gallardo-Albarrán, D. and R. Inklaar (2020), "The Role of Capital and Productivity in Accounting for Income Differences Since 1913", *Journal of Economic Surveys* (forthcoming).

Hall, R. and D.W. Jorgenson (1967), "Tax Policy and Investment Behavior," *American Economic Review* 57 (3): 391-414
Harberger, A. (1978), "Perspectives on Capital and Technology in Less Developed Countries", in M.J. Artis and A.R. Nobay (eds.), *Contemporary Economic Analysis*, London: Croom Helm, pp. 15-40.
Hulten, Ch. (1990), "The measurement of capital", in E. Berndt and J. Tripplett (eds), *Fifty Years of Economic Measurement. The Jubilee of the Conference on Research in Income and Wealth*, Chicago: University of Chicago Press// NBER, pp. 119-152.
Hulten, Ch. and F. Wykoff (1981), "The Estimation of Economic Depreciation Using Vintage Asset Prices", *Journal of Econometrics* 15: 367-96.
Instituto Nacional de Estadística [INE] (2007), Spanish Regional Accounts, base 2000. Homogeneous Series 1995-2006. Methodological Note, Madrid: INE:
Jorgenson, D.W. (1989), "Capital as a Factor of Production", in D.J. Jorgenson and R. Landau (eds.), *Technology and Capital Formation*, Cambridge, MA: MIT Press, pp. 1-35.
Jorgenson, D.W. (1990), "Productivity and Economic Growth", in E. Berndt and J. Tripplett (eds.), *Fifty Years of Economic Measurement. The Jubilee of the Conference on Research in Income and Wealth*, Chicago: University of Chicago Press and NBER, pp. 19-118.
Jorgenson, D. W (1963), "Capital Theory and Investment Behavior", *American Economic Review* 53 (2): 247–259.
Jorgenson, D.W. and Z. Griliches (1967), "The Explanation of Productivity Change", *Review of Economic Studies* 39 (3) 99: 249-282.
Jorgenson, D.W., F. Gollop and B. Fraumeni (1987), *Productivity and US Economic Growth*, Cambridge, MA: Harvard University Press.
Kaldor, N. (1957), "A Model of Economic Growth", *Economic Journal* 67 (268): 591–624
Maddison, A. (1995), "Standardised Estimates of Fixed Capital Stock: A Six Country Comparison", in A. Maddison, *Explaining the Economic Performance of Nations. Essays in Time and Space*. Aldershot: Edward Elgar, pp. 137-66.
Mas Ivars, M. and F. Pérez García, eds. (2022), El stock de capital en España y sus comunidades autónomas, Madrid: Fundación BBVA, Documentos de Trabajo 1.
Mas, M., F. Pérez, and E. Uriel (2000), "Estimation of the Stock of Capital in Spain", *Review of Income and Wealth* 46 (1): 103-116.
Myro, R. (1983), "La evolución de la productividad global de la economía española en el período 1965-1981", *Información Comercial Española* 594: 115-127.
OECD (1993), *Methods Used by OECD Countries to Measure Stocks of Fixed Capital*. National Accounts: Sources and Methods No. 2, Paris: OECD.
OECD (2001), *Measuring Capital: Measurement of Capital Stock, Consumption of Fixed Capital and Capital Services.*
OECD (2009), *Measuring Capital: OECD Manual*, Paris: OECD.
Oulton, N. and G. Wallis (2016), "Capital Stocks and Capital Services: Integrated and Consistent Estimates for the United Kingdom, 1950–2013", *Economic Modelling* 54: 117-125.
Piketty, T. (2014), *Capital in the Twenty-First Century*, Cambridge, MA: Harvard University Press.
Piketty, T. and G. Zucman (2014), "Capital is Back: Wealth-Income Ratios in Rich Countries 1700–2010", *Quarterly Journal of Economics* 129 (3): 1255–1310.
Prados de la Escosura, L. (2016), "Mismeasuring Long Run Growth. The Bias from Spliced National Accounts: The Case of Spain", *Cliometrica* 10 (3): 251-275
Prados de la Escosura, L. (2017), *Spanish Economic Growth, 1850-2015*, London: Palgrave Macmillan. https://www.palgrave.com/la/book/9783319580418 Updated data accessible at https://frdelpino.es/investigacion/en/category/01_social-sciences/01_spanish-economy/04_historical-perspective-1850-2018-spanish-economy/

Prados de la Escosura, L. and J.R. Rosés, (2010), "Capital Accumulation in the Long-Run: The Case of Spain, 1850-2000", *Research in Economic History* 27: 141-200.
Universidad Comercial de Deusto (1968–1972), *Riqueza nacional de España*, Bilbao: Universidad Comercial de Deusto. 5 vols.
Young, A. (1995), "The Tyranny of Numbers: Confronting the Statistical Realities of the East Asian Growth Experience", *Quarterly Journal of Economics* 90, 2: 641-80.

Chapter 4
Productivity Growth

4.1 Introduction

The current productivity slowdown in advanced economies has triggered a lively debate about its causes. The long phase of robust productivity growth initiated in the aftermath of World War II, which brought about unprecedented progress in absolute and per capita GDP, has given way to a phase of deceleration in output per hour worked. Exploring the origins and drivers of such a vigorous productivity expansion may cast some light on the causes of today's poor performance. Economic history research provides an opportunity to expand the exploration beyond the narrow time boundaries of modern national accounts.

This chapter focuses on modern economic growth in Spain, highlighting phases of fast growth and stagnation, and aims, on the one hand, to present new, consistent long-run trends in labour productivity and its drivers, including capital deepening, labour quality, and total factor productivity; and, on the other, to determine how much physical and human capital and efficiency gains have contributed to labour productivity enhancement over time and to what extent they are complementary.

The main findings are that labour productivity (measured as output per hour worked) dominated GDP long-run growth, accounting for four-fifths of the latter, while population contributed 30% and the number of hours worked per person contracted. About half of the increase in labour productivity resulted from capital deepening (that is, capital services per hour worked) and one-third from efficiency gains in the use of physical and human capital (namely, total factor productivity), while labour quality contributed the rest. The progress of labour productivity was not

---

Co-authored with Joan R. Rosés. An earlier version was published as L. Prados de la Escosura and J.R. Rosés (2021), "Accounting for Growth in Spain, 1850–2019", *Journal of Economic Surveys* 35(3): 804–832. The estimates have been thoroughly revised and updated and, subsequently, the main text. Also, in Sect. 4.3, the sub-section on capital input has been eliminated as it overlapped with Sect. 3.3 in Chap. 3.

L. Prados de la Escosura, *A Millennial View of Spain's Development*, Frontiers in Economic History, https://doi.org/10.1007/978-3-031-60792-9_4

steady. During its phases of acceleration (the 1920s and, especially, 1954–1975), total factor productivity was its driving force, complemented by capital deepening. Since Spain's accession to the European Union, labour productivity has sharply decelerated as capital deepening slowed down and TFP stagnated. Sustained GDP growth up to the Global Financial Crisis (1986–2007) largely resulted from an increase in hours worked per person (one-half) and to a less extent from labour productivity (less than one-third), the sluggish growth of which stemmed mostly from weak capital deepening. Institutional constraints help to explain the labour productivity slowdown.

The chapter opens by examining GDP growth and considering its proximate determinants: population, hours of work per person, and output per hour worked (Sect. 4.2). This is followed by a breakdown of the hours worked per person. Next, Sect. 4.3 investigates output per hour worked and its proximate sources, namely, intensity in the use of production factors and efficiency gains. To this end, long series of capital, land, and labour inputs are constructed, as well as factor shares in GDP to proxy their output elasticities. Section 4.4 includes a discussion of the main drivers of labour productivity.

4.2 GDP Growth and Its Determinants

Between 1850 and 2020, Gross Domestic Product (GDP) rose nearly 50-fold. A breakdown of GDP can be carried out using an identity,

$$Y = LP^{*} LQ/N^{*} N \tag{4.1}$$

Y being GDP; *N*, population; *LQ*, the number of hours worked; and *LP (= Y/LQ)*, GDP per hour worked. Note that GDP per head, *Y/N*, equals *LP *LQ/N.*

During the last 170 years, population multiplied over three times, hours worked per person shrank by one-third, and output per hour worked rose 24-fold. GDP per head gain was lower (16-fold) though, as we have to detract the decline in hours worked person from the gains in output per hour worked.

Logarithmic rates of variation allow us to compare the pace of growth of GDP and its components over periods of different length. Thus, *ln* being the natural logarithm,

$$\begin{aligned} ln\left(Y^{t}/Y^{t-1}\right) &= ln\left(LP^{t}/LP^{t-1}\right) + ln\left((LQ/N)^{t}/(LQ/N)^{t-1}\right) \\ &+ ln\left(N^{t}/N^{t-1}\right) \end{aligned} \tag{4.2}$$

Long-term growth in GDP (2.3% per year) appears to be largely attributable to labour productivity gains, which grew at 1.9%, compared to population, at 0.7%, and hours worked per person, which shrank at −0.3% (Table 4.1).

Table 4.1 GDP growth and its composition, 1850–2020 (annual average logarithmic rates %)

	GDP	Population	Hours worked per head	GDP per hour worked
1850–2020	2.3	0.7	−0.3	1.9
1850–1872	1.7	0.5	0.2	1.1
1873–1892	1.3	0.4	−0.3	1.2
1893–1913	1.2	0.7	−0.1	0.6
1914–1919	0.5	0.8	−0.4	0.1
1920–1929	4.1	0.9	−0.3	3.5
1930–1935	0.0	1.5	0.0	−1.6
1936–1939	−6.6	0.4	−1.0	−5.9
1940–1945	2.8	0.2	0.4	2.1
1946–1953	3.4	1.0	0.3	2.1
1954–1958	5.7	0.8	−0.1	4.9
1959–1975	6.4	1.1	−0.9	6.2
1976–1985	2.5	0.7	−3.8	5.6
1986–2007	3.5	0.7	1.8	1.0
2008–2013	−1.3	0.5	−3.5	1.7
2014–2020	0.5	0.2	−0.1	0.4

Sources: Prados de la Escosura (2017), updated data accessible at https://frdelpino.es/investigacion/en/category/01_social-sciences/01_spanish-economy/02_historical-perspective-spanish-economy/

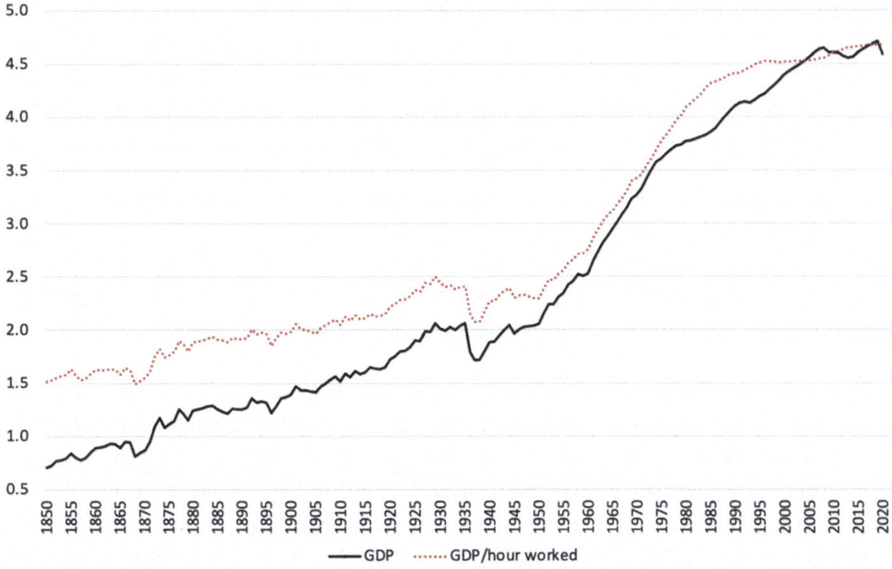

Fig. 4.1 Real GDP, absolute and per hour worked (2010=100) (logs)

Different long phases can be distinguished, in which growth deviates from its long-run trend as a result of technological change, economic policies, and access to international markets (Fig. 4.1).

Moderate growth took place between mid-nineteenth century and the Golden Age (1850–1953), with GDP growing at a yearly average rate of 1.5%, to which output per hour worked was the largest contributor (0.9%), followed by population (0.6%), while hours worked per person contracted mildly. Then, Spain's Golden Age (1954–1975), witnessed a fourfold GDP growth acceleration, almost exclusively attributable to labour productivity (5.9% of 6.2% GDP growth), as population expansion was largely offset by the reduction in hours worked per person (1% against −0.7%).

The 1970s oil crises took place at the time of the transition from General Franco's dictatorship (1939–1975) to democracy that culminated with Spain's accession to the European Union (1985). Output per hour worked continued to thrive from 1976 to 1985, as the economic crisis and stabilisation and liberalisation reforms led to the closure of inefficient industries sheltered from competition. Labour productivity growth (5.6%) more than offset the sharp decline in hours worked per person (−3.8%), allowing mild growth in absolute and per capita GDP (2.5% and 1.8%, respectively).

Fast GDP growth (3.5% yearly) prevailed from Spain's EU accession (1985) to the eve of the Great Recession (2007). Nearly half of this resulted from an increase in hours worked per head, since unemployment fell and new jobs were created, while labour productivity contributed only one-third.

During the Global Financial Crisis (2008–2013), GDP shrank with similar intensity to that experienced in the Great Depression (1929–1933) (−1.34% vs −1.50% per annum), second only to the sharp contraction (−6.6%) during the Civil War (1936–1939). The pace of employment destruction from 2008 to 2013 was similar to that of the 'transition to democracy' decade (1976–1985), with hours worked falling at −3% yearly, but labour productivity lacked the strong response of the 'transition' years (1.7% vs. 5.6% growth rate) and was unable to prevent a contraction in absolute and per capita GDP (−1.3% and −1.8%, respectively). In the post-Great Recession recovery (2014–2019), halted by the impact of the COVID pandemics, GDP and GDP per head grew similarly (2.6% and 2.4%), as the inflow of immigrants, the driver of population growth, was cut short, and per capita GDP growth mainly resulted from the increase in hours worked per person (about three-fourths).

A pattern can be observed since 1975: output per hour worked and hours worked per person exhibit opposite tendencies. Phases of (absolute and per capita) GDP growth acceleration and recovery (1986–2007 and 2014–2019) went hand-in-hand with rising hours worked per person through employment creation, while labour productivity growth slowed down. Conversely, phases of sluggish or negative (absolute and per capita) GDP growth, and employment destruction (1976–1985 and 2008–2013), coincided with those of labour productivity acceleration. Thus, it can be concluded that since the mid-1970s the Spanish economy has been unable to combine employment creation and labour productivity growth. This is consistent with the fact that expanding sectors that created more jobs (construction and services) had lower labour productivity relative to industry and experienced slower output per hour growth (Prados de la Escosura, 2017), which implies that they were less successful in attracting investment and technological innovation.

This paradox leads us to explore what underlies the behaviour of hours worked per person and output per hour worked.

We can break down the evolution of the number of hours worked per person (*LQ/N*) as follows,

$$(LQ/N) = (LQ/LF) * (LF/WN) * (WN/N) \tag{4.3}$$

(*LQ/LF*) being the hours per full-time equivalent worker; (*LF/WN*), the ratio of full-time equivalent workers to the working age population (those aged 15–64), that is, the participation rate; and (*WN/N*), the share of the working age population in total population.

Thus, in rates of variation,

$$\begin{aligned} \ln\left((LQ/N)^{t}/(LQ/N)^{t-1}\right) &= \ln\left((LQ/LF)^{t}/\left((LQ/LF)^{t-1}\right)\right. \\ &+ \ln\left((LF/WN)^{t}/(LF/WN)^{t-1}\right) + \ln\left((WN/N)^{t}/(WN/N)^{t-1}\right) \end{aligned} \tag{4.4}$$

The change in hours per full-time equivalent worker (*LQ/LF*), which fell from 2800 h by mid-nineteenth century to less than 1800 h in 2020, represents the main driver of hours worked per person in the long run (Table 4.2). Its contribution is especially noticeable during phases of industrialization and urbanization in the 1920s—in which the 8 h/day standard was gradually adopted—and 1959–1975. It also contributed to a lesser extent during phases of labour market adjustment and union activism such as the II Republic (1931–1936) and the 'transition to democracy' decade (1976–1985).

The participation rate (*LF/WN*) also made a substantial contribution to hours worked per person. During the Civil War (1936–1939), it accounted for the latter's entire decline, while in the 1950s it mitigated its fall. From 1975 onwards, the participation rate became its main driver. Thus, *LF/WN* accounts for over two-thirds of the contraction in hours worked per head during the 'transition' decade (1976–1985) and for practically all its reduction during the Great Recession (2008–2013). In both cases, the decline was due to a dramatic surge in unemployment. In the 'transition' decade, the fall in hours worked per head largely resulted from the impact of the oil shocks and the exposure to international competition in industrial sectors traditionally sheltered from competition, plus the return of migrants from Western Europe. Conversely, from Spain's EU accession (1985) up to the Global Financial Crisis (2008), the increase in the participation rate (*LF/WN*) was the main contributor to the increase in the number of hours worked per person, helped by rising female participation and, especially, the inflow of immigrants, which represented about 5 million people between 1996 and 2008 (Izquierdo et al., 2015: 25). Again, the rise in the participation rate, as unemployment gradually

Table 4.2 Growth of hours worked per head and its composition, 1850–2020 (annual average logarithmic rates %)

	Hours worked per head	Hours/FTE worker	FTE worker/ WAN	WAN/ population
1850–2020	−0.3	−0.3	0.0	0.0
1850–1872	0.2	0.0	0.1	0.1
1873–1892	−0.3	0.0	−0.1	−0.1
1893–1913	−0.1	−0.1	0.1	0.0
1914–1919	−0.4	−0.3	−0.3	0.1
1920–1929	−0.3	−0.4	0.0	0.1
1930–1935	0.0	−0.4	0.2	0.2
1936–1939	−1.0	0.0	−1.3	0.2
1940–1945	0.4	0.0	0.0	0.4
1946–1953	0.3	−0.1	0.2	0.2
1954–1958	−0.1	−0.6	0.9	−0.3
1959–1975	−0.9	−0.6	0.0	−0.2
1976–1985	−3.8	−1.6	−2.6	0.4
1986–2007	1.8	−0.1	1.5	0.3
2008–2013	−3.5	0.4	−3.4	−0.5
2014–2020	−0.1	−1.1	1.2	−0.2

Sources: Prados de la Escosura (2017), updated data accessible at https://frdelpino.es/investigacion/en/category/01_social-sciences/01_spanish-economy/02_historical-perspective-spanish-economy/

declined and immigration resumed, has been a main actor in the aftermath of the Great Recession.

Lastly, the population share of those of working age (*WN/N*) increased during the 1930s and 1940s and, again, between 1976 and 2007, as the dependency rate (the population of children and elderly over working age) fell, representing a demographic bonus, which prevented further decline in the number of hours worked per person during the 1930s and 1976–1985, and became its main driver in the 1940s.

What explains the evolution of output per hour worked? A growth accounting framework allows us to break down labour productivity between the contribution of factor (physical and human capital and land per hour worked) and multifactor intensity, total factor productivity that includes "changes in efficiency in the use of those inputs and changes in technology" (Bosworth and Collins, 2003: 114).

Labour productivity (*LP*) can be decomposed as,

$$LP^t = A(KS^t/LQ^t)^\alpha(X^t/LQ^t)^\beta(LI^t/LQ^t)^\gamma \tag{4.5}$$

LP being labour productivity; *KS*, a volume index of capital services; X^t, land input; *LI,* labour input*; and LQ*, the quantity of labour (hours worked); *A*, total factor productivity; and α, β, and γ output elasticities to each factor of production.

Thus, to disentangle the proximate determinants of labour productivity we require volume series of capital, land, and labour inputs.

4.3 Factors of Production

4.3.1 Labour Input

The labour input is the flow of services the labour force provides for production. To compute it we begin with an estimate of the labour quantity expressed as hours worked.[1] The data for the main sectors (agriculture, forestry, and fishing, industry construction, and services) come from Prados de la Escosura (2017, updated). For the period 1850–1994, the number of hours worked is derived by allocating workers and days worked per occupied in each of the main four sectors to their subsectors and, then, multiplying the number of days worked by the average hours worked per day in each subsector on the basis of Prados de la Escosura and Rosés (2010) estimates. From 1995 onwards, the national accounts (CNE10 and CNE15) supply the hours worked by subsector.

Next, we need to allow for quality of the labour force, and here we face a choice between an income-based approached, pioneered by Jorgenson (1990), and an education-based approach inspired by Mincer (1958) (See the discussion in Oxley et al., 2008).

In the income-based approach, a labour input index results from weighting the hours worked by each category of workers within each branch of economic activity according to their share in total nominal labour earnings. The rationale is that relative wages reflect the relative productivity of workers with different attributes and, thus, any returns per worker above those received by the unskilled worker represent returns to workers' skills (human capital). However, this approach assumes a fully competitive economy, and not complying with this assumption may result in upwards biased estimates.[2]

Returns to each type of worker have been taken from Prados de la Escosura and Rosés (2010) up to 1984.[3] From then onwards, national accounts provide average returns per employee at a disaggregated sector level although, unfortunately, no detailed information is provided according to age, sex, and qualification within each

---

[1]Here this chapter goes beyond the OECD convention that labour input is represented by the number of hours worked. Cf. OECD (2019: 122).

[2]This is a simplified approach that results from the lack of reliable and consistent data. See the alternative approaches to assessing human capital via cost-based (namely, evaluating human capital based on costs of education and rearing) and income-based (that is, assessing human capital as the discounted lifetime labour income) measures in Le et al. (2003) and Oxley et al. (2008).

[3]From 1954, Prados de la Escosura and Rosés (2010) distributed workers for each industry into four occupational categories (unskilled and skilled operatives, technicians, and managers).

industry.[4] This lack of differentiation within the labour force may bias the labour input index.[5]

Returns per occupied worker have been used to weight total labour (employees and self-employed) by branch. No distinction is made between employees and self-employed in the labour force estimates for the pre-national accounts period, 1850–1953. However, national accounts distinguish between compensation of employees and gross operating surplus and mixed incomes.[6] Part of the mixed incomes correspond to self-employed compensation. Thus, for the post-1954 years, we have estimated self-employed labour returns following the principle of opportunity cost and assuming that the self-employed labour cost equals that of the average employee in their specific industry.[7]

Thus, total labour compensation is obtained as

$$w^t L^t = (w^t E^t / E^t) L^t \tag{4.6}$$

$w^t L^t$ being the total labour compensation in period t; $w^t E^t$, the compensation of employees; E^t, the number of employees; and L^t, total employment (employees plus self-employed) in period t.

A Törnqvist index of labour input (LI) is then computed,

$$\ln\left(LI^{\mathrm{t}}/LI^{\mathrm{t}-1}\right) = \Sigma \bar{v}^{\mathrm{i,t}} \ln\left(LQ^{\mathrm{i,t}}/LQ^{\mathrm{i,t}-1}\right) \tag{4.7}$$

where $LQ^{\mathrm{i,t}}$ is the quantity of labour (hours worked) in branch i and $v^{\mathrm{i,\,t}} = ½(v^{\mathrm{i,\,t}-1} + v^{\mathrm{i,\,t}})$ the 2 year average share of each branch in total labour compensation ($w^t L^t$), being $v^{\mathrm{i,t}} = w^{it} L^{it} / w^t L^t$. Then, the labour input index is obtained as the exponential.

An index of labour quality (H) that measures the labour input's composition effect can be derived as the ratio between the labour input and labour quantity indices.[8]

---

[4]The number of sectors distinguished is 56 for 1985–1995 and 63 from 1995 onwards. There are no significant discrepancies between our results and those in Prados de la Escosura and Rosés (2010) for 1985–2000.

[5]This implies arbitrarily assuming homogenous quality within each sector. Fortunately, there are no significant discrepancies between our results and those in Prados de la Escosura and Rosés (2010) for 1985–2000.

[6]In order to provide a single employment series from different national accounts benchmark series, the splicing procedure (interpolation) used in Prados de la Escosura (2016, 2017) is followed here.

[7]This has been a commonly used procedure. Cf. Kuznets (1966), Jorgenson (1990), and OECD (2019). In using this procedure, the more disaggregated the set of industries for which the exercise is carried out, the more accurate the estimate.

[8]Using this approach, as in Mulligan and Sala-i-Martín (1997), we exclude the contribution of physical capital to labour income (See the discussion in Oxley et al., 2008: 301–302). It could be argued that as this index the employment shift towards sectors with higher relative wages, it actually represents an improvement in resource allocation rather than in labour quality. We owe this remark to Lorenzo Serrano. It may be argued that improving factor allocation and labour quality are not excluding consequences of the employment shift.

$$H^{t} = LI^{t}/LQ^{t.} \tag{4.8}$$

Our alternative education-based labour input combines the quantity of labour (hours worked) with an estimate of the quality of labour on the basis of school attainment. Up to 2000, data on average years of schooling for working age population (15–64 years) derive from Prados de la Escosura and Rosés (2010), who draw on Núñez's (2005) education attainment estimates, completed for 2000–2010 with Barro and Lee's (2013, updated) 5-year benchmark estimates, linearly interpolated, and UNESCO data, from 2010 onwards.

Following Bosworth and Collins (2003) and Lee and Lee (2016), labour quality is derived by combining years of schooling with the rate of return of education.[9] Rates of return tend to be higher in early phases of development, but decline as economies develop. However, since private rates of return overestimate social rates of returns, it seems reasonable to adopt low values for the rate of return over time, and 7% per year of education has been chosen.[10]

$$\text{Thus, } EDU = (1 + r)^{s} \tag{4.9}$$

r being the rate of return and s the average years of schooling.

Then, the education-based labour input index is derived as the product of the labour quantity and labour quality indices.

An important caveat is that the education approach only considers levels of quantitative achievement (number of years of schooling), without any adjustment for the quality of education received. It ignores experience, on-the-job training, and informal education, as well as differences in the rate of return between different types of education. It also neglects the fact that education can be pursued as consumption, not as investment for production. Furthermore, in early stages of economic development, labour skills are largely dependent on experience and on-the job training, while formal education contributes more to labour quality in later phases.[11]

A comparison of the alternative labour input indices derived with income- and education-based labour quality shows a similar evolution although the education-based series exhibit faster growth over time (Fig. 4.2). However, if we focus on labour quality, substantial differences emerge between the income- and education-based estimates (Fig. 4.3). Education-based labour quality accelerated in the late nineteenth century before flattening until the mid-1920s, when another spurt took

---

[9] Again, this is an over-simplified approach due to lack of homogeneous data for such a long time span. On the use of education as a proxy for human capital, see the surveys in Wössmann (2003), Fraumeni (2015), and Liu and Fraumeni (2020) and the contrast between education-based and cost- and income-based approaches in Oxley et al. (2008).

[10] This rate of return matches obtained by Montenegro and Patrinos (2014) for Spain, 2004–2008. See the discussion in Collins and Bosworth (2003) and Psacharopoulos and Patrinos (2004). Prados de la Escosura and Rosés (2010) explored alternative rates of return but there is no significant difference between the various results until the late twentieth century.

[11] Cf. Rosés (1998) for labour quality in the mid-nineteenth century Catalan textile industry.

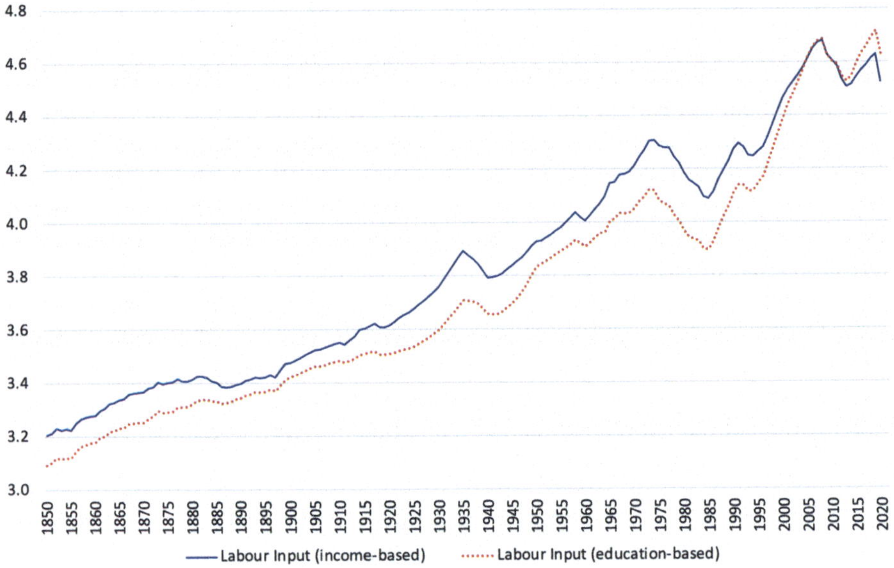

Fig. 4.2 Labour input: income- and education-based estimates (2010=100) (logs)

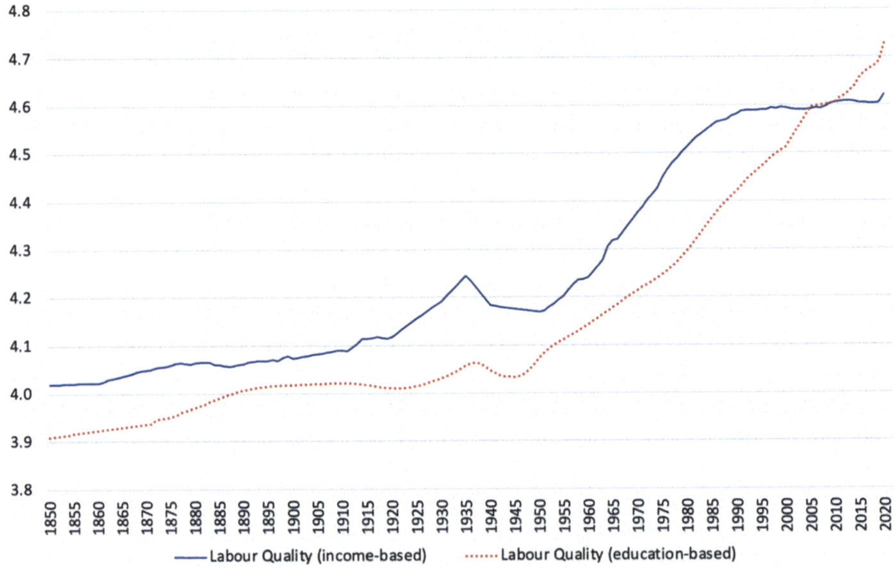

Fig. 4.3 Labour quality: income- and education-based estimates (2010=100) (logs)

place. Following the fall in the aftermath of the Civil War (1936–1939), there was steady growth that only slowed down during the Great Recession. Conversely, income-based labour quality improved moderately until 1920, when it accelerated

Table 4.3 Labour input growth, 1850–2020 (annual average logarithmic rates %)

		Income-based		Education-based	
	Labour quantity	Labour quality	Labour input	Labour quality	Labour input
1850–2020	0.4	0.4	0.8	0.5	0.9
1850–1872	0.7	0.2	0.8	0.2	0.8
1873–1892	0.1	0.1	0.1	0.3	0.4
1893–1913	0.6	0.2	0.8	0.0	0.6
1914–1919	0.4	0.2	0.6	−0.1	0.3
1920–1929	0.6	0.7	1.3	0.2	0.8
1930–1935	1.6	1.0	2.6	0.5	2.1
1936–1939	−0.7	−1.2	−1.9	−0.1	−0.8
1940–1945	0.7	−0.3	0.3	−0.4	0.3
1946–1953	1.3	0.1	1.4	0.8	2.1
1954–1958	0.7	1.0	1.7	0.6	1.3
1959–1975	0.2	1.3	1.5	0.7	0.9
1976–1985	−3.1	1.1	−2.0	1.2	−1.9
1986–2007	2.5	0.2	2.7	1.1	3.6
2008–2013	−3.0	0.3	−2.7	0.5	−2.5
2014–2020	0.1	0.2	0.3	1.4	1.5

Sources: See the text

until the eve of the Civil War. The post-1950 recovery, which only matched the pre-war level in 1960, gave way to an improvement until 1990, although it decelerated in the 1980s, and has flattened during the last three decades. In a nutshell, the main difference between the two outcomes of the two approaches is that, in the education-based labour input, labour quality has made a substantial contribution since the mid-twentieth century while, according to the income-based labour input, the contribution of labour quality was significant only during the 1920s and early 1930s and between 1950 and the mid-1980s (Table 4.3).

A challenge is posed by these opposite trends between the income- and education-based labour quality estimates. Which one better reflects the evolution of human capital? Both the income- and the education-based approaches have serious shortcomings. The fully competitive economy assumption in the income-based approach, if relaxed, would imply that labour quality is upwards biased in the resulting estimates, as part of it would simply represent the market power effect of higher income members in the labour force. In turn, ignoring experience, informal education and on-the-job training would bias upwards the growth of education-based estimates of labour quality, as compulsory and universal formal education (not just primary and secondary) has increased the number of years of schooling since the mid-twentieth century. Moreover, it could be argued that education is a high-income elastic good whose consumption demand must have increased substantially over the last 30 years as per capita income has doubled since Spain's accession to the EU

(1985), without necessarily having a significant impact on the quality of labour.[12] Therefore, although the actual evolution of labour quality might lie somewhere between the two alternative estimates, the income-based approach, though possibly downward biased, seems to provide a less distorted picture.[13]

4.3.2 Capital Input[14]

Land Input

According to the OECD Manual (OECD, 2009), only land under dwellings and other construction and cultivated land should be considered as sources of capital services. Although land under structures is assumed to evolve as structures do and is, therefore, included under capital, agricultural land—a non-produced asset that suffers no depreciation—is considered to be an independent factor of production that provides a flow of services into production, an established practice in historical studies.[15]

Assessing the actual amount of land currently in agricultural use represents a challenge, and even more difficult is the valuation of land. Lack of annual data on land used prior to 1958, has forced us to accept the data at available scattered benchmarks and derive yearly figures through interpolation. For 1850–2000, Prados de la Escosura and Rosés (2009) estimates have been accepted, but without any adjustment for the agricultural economic cycle; from 2000 onwards these estimates are completed with data taken from official surveys on dry and irrigated land by type of use (Encuesta sobre superficies y rendimientos de cultivos en España, ESYRCE, 2023). Prices of different types of land for 1931 and 1985 are taken from Prados de la Escosura and Rosés (2009), and those for 2017 come from the Encuesta de Precios de la Tierra (2023).

A land input index has been obtained, weighting hectares of land assigned to different types of cultivation over 1850–1931, 1931–2000, and 2000–2020 by their average prices in 1931, 1985, and 2017, respectively. The resulting indices were then spliced into a single Laspeyres index.

---

[12]Labour market rigidities, the quality of education, and over-qualification in terms of formal education may also help explain the limited effect of education on the quality of labour.

[13]The contrast between income- and education-based estimates in other countries shows the same pattern of lower labour quality growth when the former approach is used. Cf. Prados de la Escosura and Rosés (2010). It is worth noting that education-based labour quality is adopted by the PWT10.01 and the Conference Board. See Fig. 4.9 in the Appendix.

[14]Chapter 3, Sect. 3.3, provides the estimates.

[15]This follows Prados de la Escosura and Rosés (2009). Crafts (2018) and Antràs and Voth (2003) also consider land as an independent production factor in their studies of Britain's Industrial Revolution. In growth accounting exercises for today's developing countries, land is often included separately from capital. Cf. Bosworth and Collins (2007).

Table 4.4 Land input growth, 1850–2020 (annual average logarithmic rates %)

	Land input	Land input/hour
1850–2020	0.2	−0.2
1850–1872	0.0	−0.7
1873–1892	0.1	0.0
1893–1913	0.9	0.3
1914–1919	0.6	0.2
1920–1929	0.4	−0.2
1930–1935	0.5	−1.1
1936–1939	−1.4	−0.8
1940–1945	0.7	0.0
1946–1953	0.5	−0.8
1954–1958	0.0	−0.7
1959–1975	0.1	−0.1
1976–1985	0.0	3.0
1986–2007	−0.3	−2.7
2008–2013	0.1	3.1
2014–2020	0.5	0.3

Sources: See the text

Land input expanded in the late nineteenth and early twentieth century, and after declining during the Civil War, recovered in the 1940s. However, hardly any growth is observed thereafter and its contraction over 1986–2007 was partly reversed after the Great Recession (Table 4.4). Land input per hour worked exhibits negative growth except for 1890–1920 and during phases of employment destruction (1976–1985 and 2008–2013).

4.4 Proximate Determinants of Labour Productivity Growth

To establish the contribution of each factor of production to aggregate productivity growth, we need to weight their growth by their output elasticities. Under perfect competition and constant returns to scale, the values of these elasticities correspond to factor shares in GDP.[16] Although the Spanish economy was far from fully competitive over time, we follow the usual practice (OECD, 2019) and accept this oversimplifying assumption, although it will bias our total factor productivity estimates.[17]

[16] Assuming constant returns to scale for each factor of production we impose output elasticities to add up to 1, $\alpha + \beta + \gamma = 1$.

[17] If there were competitive monopolistic rents, TFP growth obtained under the assumption of perfect competition would be biased downwards, as the capital share in GDP—by including competitive monopoly profits—would overstate the elasticity of output with respect to capital. Conversely, had the aggregate production function increasing returns to scale, TFP growth would be over-exaggerated (Young (1995: 648).

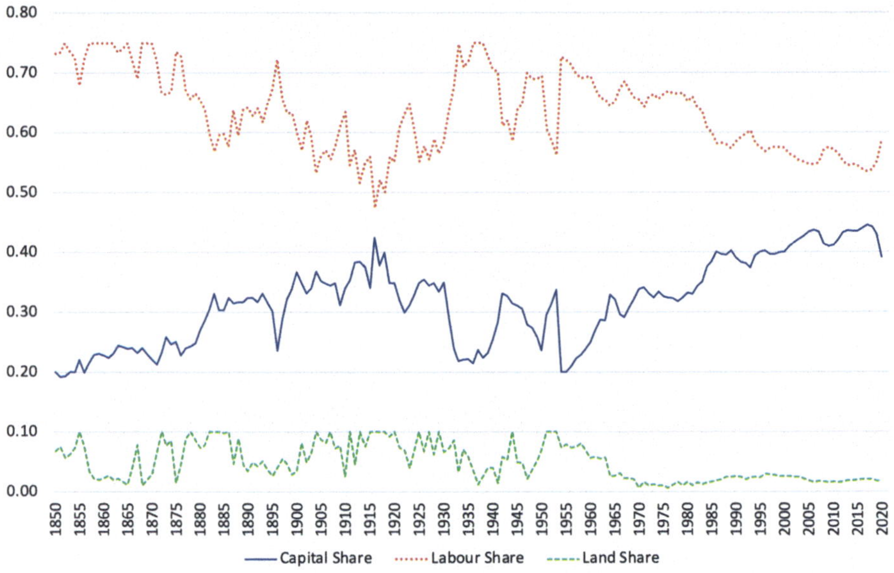

Fig. 4.4 Three factor shares (% GDP)

The labour share has been obtained by dividing total labour compensation (see the subsection on labour input above) by GDP at market prices.[18] Then, the share of other factors, that is, 1 less the labour share, needs to be distributed between capital and land. Lack of information on land rents forces us to estimate land compensation as a residual, assuming that the difference between agricultural value added and labour outlays accrued to land property. However, this estimate provides an upper bound for the land share as it assumes no returns to capital in agriculture.[19] The share of capital was, then, derived as a residual after subtracting labour and land returns from GDP.

Although, on average, factor shares conform to the stylised fact of two-thirds corresponding to labour and one-third to property owners (capital and land), factor shares are far from stable over time, contradicting Kaldor's (1957: 592) stylised fact (Fig. 4.4). Labour and capital shares evolved as mirror images. Capital compensation increased its contribution to GDP, while labour reduced it, between 1880 and World War I and from 1960 onwards, and during a short episode in the late 1940s and early 1950s. Conversely, while the capital share declined in the interwar years (1919–1935) and, again, in the late 1950s, the labour share rose.

[18] Computing the labour share in terms of GDP at market prices implies that net taxes on products and imports (taxes minus subsidies) are attributed to capital income. This procedure is used by Conference Board (2017: 32).

[19] Given the sharp drop in the relative size of agriculture in the late twentieth century, the resulting bias in our TFP growth estimates should not be large.

We can now compute the proximate sources of labour productivity growth using a Törnqvist index,

$$\begin{aligned}
&\ln\left(LP^{t}/LP^{t-1}\right)\\
&\quad \Sigma\overline{v}^{k,t}\left[\ln\left(KS^{t}/KS^{t-1}\right) - \ln\left(LQ^{t}/LQ^{t-1}\right)\right]\\
&= + \Sigma\overline{v}^{x,t}\left[\ln\left(X^{t}/X^{t-1}\right) - \ln\left(LQ^{t}/LQ^{t-1}\right)\right]\\
&\quad + \Sigma\overline{v}^{l,t}\left[\ln\left(LI^{t}/LI^{t-1}\right) - \ln\left(LQ^{t}/LQ^{t-1}\right)\right] + \ln\left(TFP^{t}/TFP^{t-1}\right)
\end{aligned} \tag{4.16}$$

where $\overline{v}^{i,t} = \frac{1}{2}\left(v^{i,t-1} + v^{i,t}\right)$ the 2 year average share of each factor of production in GDP at market prices.

Total factor productivity (*TFP*) growth is, then, derived as a residual,

$$\ln\left(TFP^{t}/TFP^{t-1}\right) = \begin{array}{l} \ln\left(LP^{t}/LP^{t-1}\right) - \left\{ \Sigma\overline{v}^{k,t}\left[\ln\left(KS^{t}/KS^{t-1}\right)\right.\right. \\ \left. - \ln\left(LQ^{t}/LQ^{t-1}\right)\right] + \Sigma\overline{v}^{x,t}\left[\ln\left(X^{t}/X^{t-1}\right)\right. \\ \left.\left. - \ln\left(LQ^{t}/LQ^{t-1}\right)\right]\right\} \end{array} \tag{4.17}$$

and the TFP index is obtained as its exponential.

Table 4.5 presents the breakdown of the average logarithmic growth rate of GDP per hour worked into the contribution of factor accumulation and efficiency gains (total factor productivity) and offers two alternative estimates of TFP growth derived with income- and education-based labour quality series, respectively. Figure 4.5 provides the yearly evolution of TFP using both indices.[20]

From 1850 to 2020, capital deepening contributed over half the growth of labour productivity and efficiency gains about one-third, with the remainder attributable to labour quality. A glance at the evolution of labour productivity makes it possible to distinguish different phases of growth, three of them with TFP significant contributions. Between the mid-nineteenth century and World War I, a phase of sustained progress from 1850 to the early 1890s gave way to another of sluggish performance until 1919. Efficiency gains account for the growth differential between the two phases. While capital contribution was steady during these 70 years, TFP only expanded from 1850 to 1892, providing half the growth of labour productivity (slightly less when education-based labour quality is used in the computation).

[20] In Fig. 4.10 in the Appendix, the evolution of TFP computed with VICS ex-ante exogenous and ex-post-endogenous (and income-based labour quality in both cases) is compared. It can be observed that they evolve hand-in-hand, but the one derived with VICS ex-post endogenous has a lower level (relative to 2010=100) until 1970 and, especially until 1930. This implies slightly faster TFP growth.

Table 4.5 Labour productivity growth and its sources, 1850–2020 (annual average logarithmic rates %)

				Income-based		Education-based	
	GDP/hour worked	Land input/hour	Capital input/hour	Labour quality	TFP	Labour quality	TFP
1850–2020	1.9	0.0	1.0	0.2	0.6	0.3	0.6
1850–1872	1.1	0.0	0.5	0.1	0.5	0.1	0.5
1873–1892	1.2	0.0	0.6	0.0	0.6	0.2	0.4
1893–1913	0.6	0.0	0.6	0.1	−0.1	0.0	0.0
1914–1919	0.1	0.0	0.6	0.1	−0.6	−0.1	−0.4
1920–1929	3.5	0.0	1.2	0.4	1.9	0.1	2.2
1930–1935	−1.6	−0.1	0.5	0.7	−2.7	0.3	−2.3
1936–1939	−5.9	0.0	−0.2	−0.9	−4.7	−0.1	−5.5
1940–1945	2.1	0.0	0.1	−0.2	2.2	−0.2	2.2
1946–1953	2.1	0.0	0.4	0.1	1.7	0.6	1.3
1954–1958	4.9	−0.1	1.2	0.7	3.1	0.4	3.4
1959–1975	6.2	0.0	2.5	0.8	2.9	0.5	3.3
1976–1985	5.6	0.0	2.8	0.7	2.0	0.8	2.0
1986–2007	1.0	−0.1	1.0	0.1	0.0	0.6	−0.5
2008–2013	1.7	0.0	2.4	0.2	−0.9	0.3	−1.1
2014–2020	0.4	0.0	0.6	0.1	−0.3	0.8	−1.0

Sources: See the text

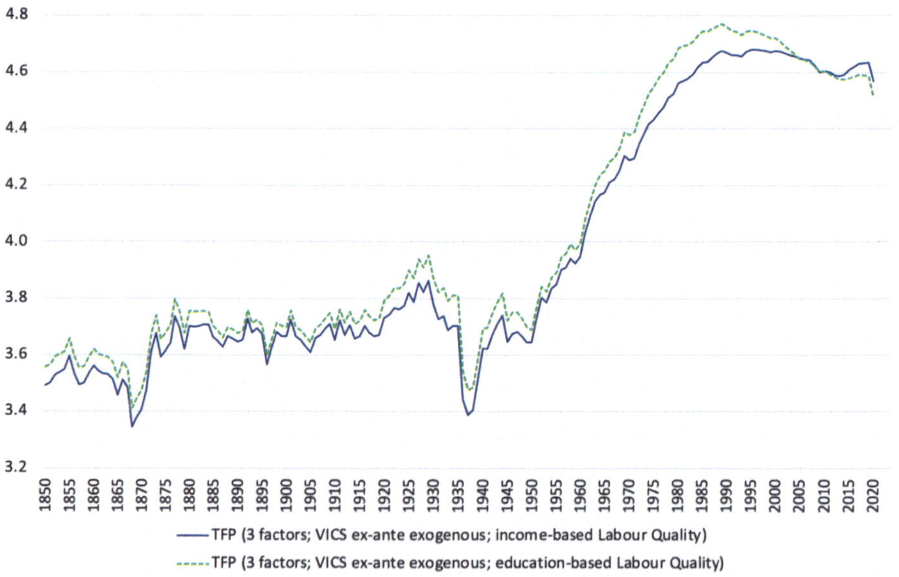

Fig. 4.5 Total factor productivity: alternatively estimated with income- and education-based labour quality (2010=100) (logs)

The 1920s witnessed a vigorous performance of labour productivity, trebling its pre-1890 growth. Capital deepening doubled its pace and contributed about one-third of labour productivity growth. However, TFP was the main driver, with its contribution ranging from over half to nearly two-thirds of labour productivity growth (depending on whether it is derived with income- or education-based labour quality). During the 1930s, TFP collapse accounted almost exclusively for the decline in labour productivity growth. TFP made also the largest contribution to its post-Civil War recovery.

Output per hour worked grew exceptionally fast from 1954 to 1985 (5.8%), a period that encompasses the Golden Age and the 'transition to democracy' decade. Efficiency gains contributed half of its growth and physical capital accounted for another two-fifths, with the rest attributable to labour quality. A closer look reveals that during the Golden Age (1954–1975) TFP contributed over half labour productivity growth, and over one-third in the 'transition to democracy' decade, while the contribution of capital deepening rose from over one-third in the Golden Age to half in the 'transition' years.

Then, between Spain's accession to the EU (1985) and the eve of the Global Financial Crisis (2007), labour productivity growth shrank to less than one-fifth compared to 1954–1985, becoming largely extensive, rather than intensive. Capital deepening accounted for the sluggish output per hour growth and TFP did not contribute at all. Sluggish labour productivity growth played, thus, a secondary role in a long phase of robust (absolute and per capita) GDP growth (3.5% and 2.8%) that was driven by the increase in hours worked per person resulting from higher employment (Table 4.1).

The Great Recession (2008–2013) was another episode in which capital drove the mild acceleration in labour productivity growth, while TFP growth was negative. In the post-Global Financial Crisis years, capital deepening prevented negative labour productivity growth. When only the education-based labour quality is considered, human capital made a contribution that cancelled negative TFP growth.

As human capital is a major factor in narratives of economic growth, the role of labour quality in Spain's long run growth merits some comments. If we follow the education-based approach, labour quality added to labour productivity growth from the mid-twentieth century onwards, and has made a significant contribution since Spain's accession to the European Union (1985), second only to capital deepening. Such an optimistic outcome needs to be set against reservations with regard to educational attainment as a measure of human capital; in particular, the demand for said attainment as a high-income elastic consumption good. The income-based approach, although upwards biased as it assumes perfect competition, suggests, instead, that labour quality contributed to labour productivity growth during the Golden Age and the 'transition to democracy' decade, but not thereafter, which sounds a more persuasive narrative.

We have replicated the growth accounting exercise using only two factors of production, as is conventionally the case (assuming that the share of capital is 1 less the share of labour), in order to provide a robustness test for our results. Figure 4.6 presents the evolution of TFP that results from growth accounting exercises with two

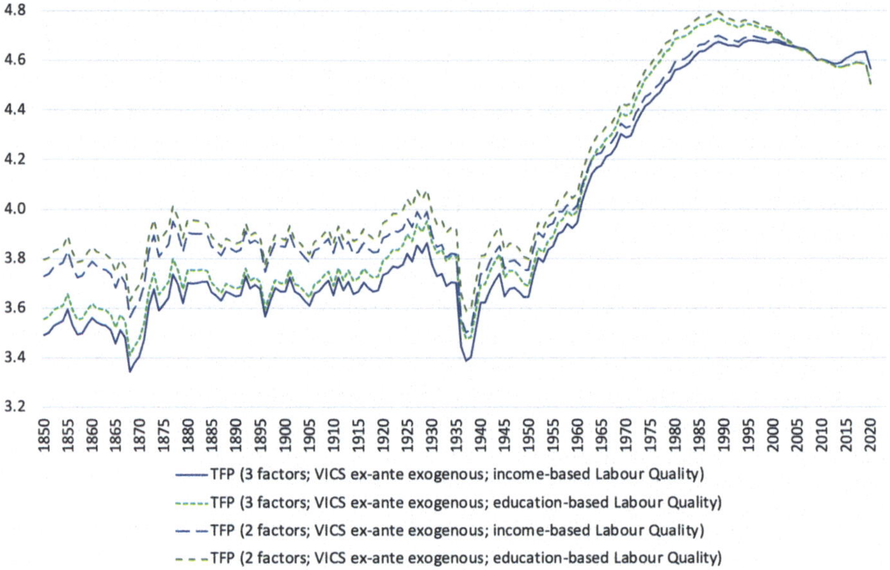

Fig. 4.6 Total factor productivity: estimated with three and two factors of production and income- and education-based labour quality (2010=100) (logs)

and three factors of production for both estimates with income- and education-based labour quality. Both sets of estimates follow the same pattern, but the two-factor estimates present a higher level relative to 2010, the benchmark year. This implies slightly slower TFP growth, which results from the fact that capital input, which grows much faster than land input, receives a larger weight (as it includes the land share in GDP) in the growth accounting exercise (Table 4.6). An implication of this comparison is that growth accounting exercises for developing economies that neglect the land input tend to over-exaggerate the share of capital and, hence, underestimate TFP growth.

How do our results for the evolution of the TFP compare with earlier studies? Figure 4.7 compares our new estimates, derived with both the income- and education-based labour quality with those by Prados de la Escosura and Rosés (2009) for 1850–2000, derived with income-based labour quality, and Bergeaud et al. (2016), updated estimates, using 2000 as reference. These two series present a close evolution until the last quarter of the twentieth century, as they rely on the same sources.[21] When compared to our new estimates, a similar evolution is observed but both earlier estimates grow faster during the 1960s and early 1970s and, in the case

[21] Bergeaud et al. (2016, updated) use GDP from the Maddison Project Dataset (which comes from Prados de la Escosura, 2017), investment (up to 1980) and employment (up to 1950) from Prados de la Escosura (2017), and hours worked from Prados de la Escosura and Rosés (2010). For the rest of the years, they seem to rely on OECD statistics. They provide no sources and procedures for estimating human capital.

Table 4.6 Labour productivity growth and its sources, 1850–2020: two factors of production (annual average logarithmic rates %)

	GDP per hour worked	Capital input/ hour	Income-based		Education-based	
			Labour quality	TFP	Labour quality	TFP
1850–2020	1.9	1.1	0.2	0.5	0.3	0.4
1850–1872	1.1	0.5	0.1	0.5	0.1	0.4
1873–1892	1.2	0.8	0.0	0.4	0.2	0.2
1893–1913	0.6	0.7	0.1	−0.2	0.0	−0.1
1914–1919	0.1	0.8	0.1	−0.7	−0.1	−0.5
1920–1929	3.5	1.5	0.4	1.6	0.1	1.9
1930–1935	−1.6	0.6	0.7	−2.9	0.3	−2.5
1936–1939	−5.9	−0.3	−0.9	−4.7	−0.1	−5.6
1940–1945	2.1	0.2	−0.2	2.2	−0.2	2.2
1946–1953	2.1	0.5	0.1	1.6	0.6	1.1
1954–1958	4.9	1.6	0.7	2.6	0.4	2.9
1959–1975	6.2	2.7	0.8	2.6	0.5	3.0
1976–1985	5.6	2.9	0.7	2.0	0.8	1.9
1986–2007	1.0	1.0	0.1	−0.1	0.6	−0.6
2008–2013	1.7	2.5	0.2	−1.0	0.3	−1.1
2014–2020	0.4	0.6	0.1	−0.3	0.8	−1.0

Sources: See the text

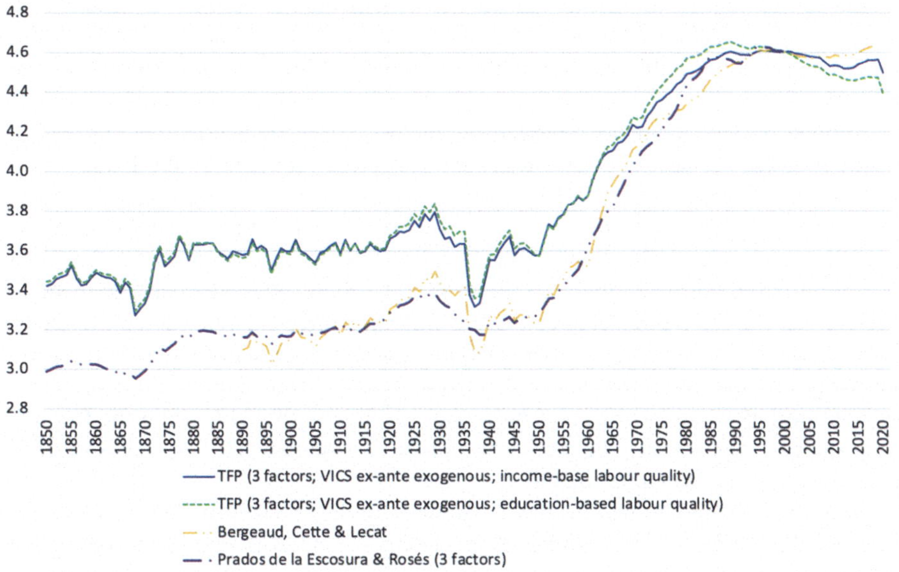

Fig. 4.7 Long run trends in total factor productivity: comparative estimates (2000=100) (logs). Note: New estimates derived with income- and education-based labour quality

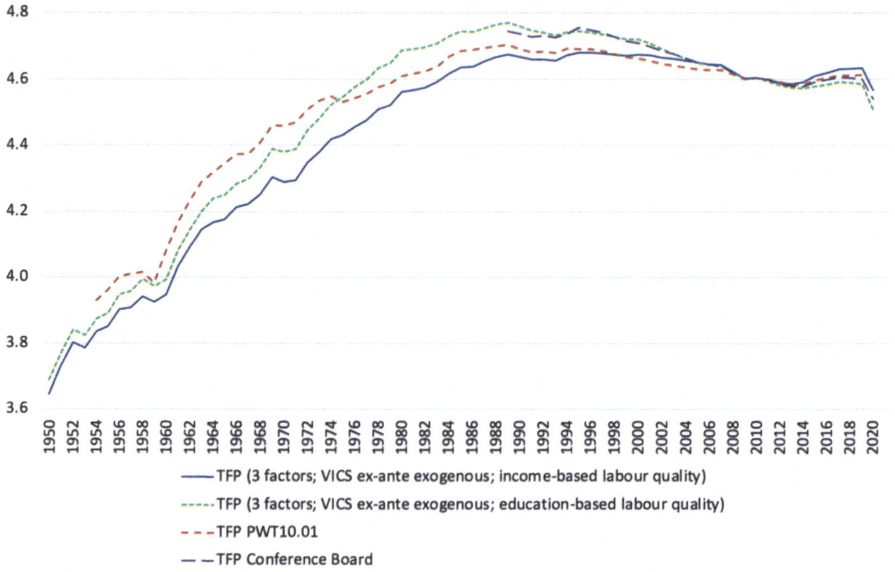

Fig. 4.8 Total factor productivity since 1950: alternative estimates (2010=100) (logs). Note: New estimates derived with income- and education-based labour quality

of Prados de la Escosura and Rosés (2009) the growth differential with our new estimates continues during the 'transition to democracy' years. It is also worth mentioning that Bergeaud et al. series present a sharp deceleration after 1986 but still some progress, unlike the stagnation or negative TFP growth in the rest of the estimates.

Another possible comparison regarding the post-1950 era is provided in Fig. 4.8, which presents the new estimates together with those provided by the Penn World Tables 10.0 (Feenstra et al., 2015, updated) for the post-1954 era, and the Conference Board (2022) from 1990 onwards, in which TFP is derived using education-based labour quality. The Conference Board's TFP series closely match our own education-based estimates, while the Penn World Tables series adopt an intermediate position between two new set of estimates. Although there are noticeable differences in the pace of growth, these trends largely coincide, with the PWT10.01 series showing, like the new estimates with income-based labour quality, sustained TFP growth until 1989 and, then, mild but steady decline until 2013, while the Conference Board series stresses the post-1990 fall, as do the new TFP estimates derived with education-based labour quality.

How does Spain compare to other countries during phases of TFP acceleration such as the 1920s or the Golden Age (1950–1973)? Although methodological differences may bias the results, a face value comparison provides some informative results.[22] In the 1920s, when contrasted with other Peripheral European countries, TFP growth appears more intense in Spain than Portugal and Turkey, but less than in Italy. Portugal's yearly growth was below 1% and Turkey's was negative, while in Italy and Spain growth reached 2.5% and 1.9–2.2% (depending on the use of income- or education-based labour quality), respectively.[23] Moreover, TFP grew faster in Spain than in the U.K. and the U.S. However, from 1850 to 1890, the previous phase of TFP acceleration, Spain's TFP growth was lower than in the U.K. but higher than in the U.S. and Italy.[24]

In the Golden Age, the yearly rate of growth in Spain (2.9–3.2% from 1954 to 1975) was, again, above those of Portugal (1.5%) and Turkey (0.8%), but below Italy's (4.0%), although Spain TFP's behaved better than Italy's in the late 1970s and 1980s.[25] Spain also exhibited faster TFP growth than the leading socialist countries of Central and Eastern Europe—Czechoslovakia, Hungary, and Poland—, which grew at 1.3%, 2.1%, and 1.9%, respectively, from 1950 to 1970 (Vonyó and Klein, 2019: 335). If we extend the comparison to South East Asia, where TFP acceleration started after 1960, we observe that Spain's rate of growth (2.4–2.6% in the years 1959–1985) was higher than in Hong-Kong, South Korea, and Taiwan, 2.3%, 1.7%, and 2.1%, respectively, from 1966 to 1991 (Young, 1995: 672). Lastly, if the contrast is carried out with the advanced economies, it emerges that TFP grew faster in Spain than in the U.S. (2.1%) and the U.K. (1.9%), similarly to Germany and Japan (3.3% and 3.2%), but slower than in France (3.6%).[26]

It can therefore be concluded that Spain compared to the best performers during phases of generalised TFP growth acceleration such the 1920s and the years 1950–1975.

If we now turn to the long phase of TFP deceleration since 1986, what explains the shift from efficiency gains to capital deepening as labour productivity's main driver? The fact that TFP growth halted helps explain the shift, but why did this happen to TFP? A convergence hypothesis can be considered. As TFP grew sharply over three decades (Fig. 4.8), Spain moved closer to the technological frontier and achieving further efficiency gains became more difficult. Furthermore, once-and-for-

[22] Methodological differences extend to the way capital and labour inputs are computed, the number of factors considered, and the use of fixed or variable factor shares. Whenever possible, the TFP estimates obtained with the closer methodology (i.e. those that take into account capital and labour quality) have been chosen. The comparison is restricted to historical estimates carried out for individual countries.

[23] Data come from Lains (2003: 277), for Portugal, 1910–1934 (0.7%); Altug et al. (2008: 409) for Turkey, 1914–1929: and Giordano and Zollino (2021) for Italy, 1919–1929.

[24] Data for the U.K. come from Crafts (2021: Tables 2 and 3) for 1924–1937 and 1856–1889; for the U.S., from Crafts and Woltjer (2021: Table 6) for 1919–1929, and Abramovitz and David (2001), for 1855–1890, and Giordano and Zollino (2021) for Italy, 1861–1896.

[25] Data come from Lains (2003: 277), for Portugal, 1947–1973; Altug et al. (2008: 409) for Turkey, 1950–1979: and Giordano and Zollino (2021) for Italy, 1951–1973 and 1974–1993.

[26] Data come from Crafts (2021) for the U.K. 1950–1973; Crafts and Woltjer (2021) for Germany and France, 1950–1974 (Table 1) and the U.S. 1948–1973 (Table 6); and Fukao et al. (2021) for Japan, 1950–1970 (Table 1).

Table 4.7 Labour productivity in 1990 (2019 EKS US$) and TFP growth 1990–2019 (%)

	Output per hour worked	TFP growth (%)	
	1990	1990–2007	1990–2019
Norway	59	0.7	−0.1
Belgium	58	0.0	−0.3
Switzerland	57	−0.2	−0.3
Netherlands	57	0.3	0.0
Denmark	56	0.2	0.0
France	53	0.2	−0.1
Italy	51	0.1	−0.2
Germany	48	0.4	0.2
United States	48	0.7	0.5
Austria	46	0.2	−0.1
Spain	45	−0.7	−0.5
Sweden	43	0.5	0.1
Canada	42	0.0	−0.1
Finland	40	1.4	0.5
Australia	39	−0.2	−0.3
United Kingdom	39	0.8	0.4
Ireland	36	1.3	0.6
Israel	35	−0.2	−0.2
Singapore	34	0.3	−0.3
New Zealand	34	0.2	0.1
Japan	31	−0.5	−0.3
Greece	31	0.3	−0.5
Portugal	27	−0.1	−0.3
Czech Republic	24	0.3	0.1
Hungary	21	0.8	0.4
Taiwan	18	2.3	1.8
Slovak Republic	17	0.5	0.4
Poland	16	1.0	1.0
South Korea	12	2.3	1.7

Sources: Conference Board (2022)

all structural change associated with the shift of resources from sectors of low or slow growing productivity to those of high, or fast growing productivity (i.e. labour moving from agriculture into manufacturing) had already taken place by the time Spain joined the EU. Thus, Spain's potential for catching up would have been exhausted, and TFP growth slowed down, adjusting to its pace in advanced economies.

Table 4.7 compares levels of output per hour worked in 1990 (expressed in 2019 EKS US dollars) in OECD countries (ranked from top to bottom) with their TFP growth rates since 1990 using the Conference Board (2022) dataset. In both periods considered, that of expansion, 1990–2007, and 1990–2019, Spain had the poorest

TFP performance, and all countries with higher initial levels of output per hour worked than Spain in 1990 exhibit faster TFP growth in both periods. Such results refute, therefore, the convergence hypothesis.[27]

Alternative explanations have been put forward to explain why during the last three decades labour productivity growth has slowed down in Spain and become extensive rather than intensive. It has been hypothesised that, as resources were re-allocated towards sectors that attracted less innovation (from traded to non-traded sectors, i.e. low skill services and construction), aggregate efficiency declined. Specifically, Díaz and Franjo (2016) blamed investment in residential structures, stimulated by favourable relative prices and subsidies, together with low investment specific technical change (ISTC), for the TFP slowdown. Pérez and Benages (2017) stressed the low investment in intangibles and the excess capacity and limited use of their capital by predominantly small firms. The picture was completed by Cuadrado et al. (2020) who pointed to the limited exploitation of new technologies because of workers' low skills. The recovery of the share of structures in net capital stock and its substantial contribution to total value of capital services in the early twenty-first century support these assertions (Chap. 2). Moreover, the low ISTC is consistent with the deceleration of capital 'quality' since 1990 (Fig. 4.5).

García-Santana et al. (2020) offered a nuanced view of the TFP slowdown in which it is allocative inefficiency across firms, rather than across sectors, that accounts for the deceleration.[28] Moreover, they found that government regulation (cronyism) is its ultimate determinant. Looking at the context in which this misallocation has taken place, Gopinath et al. (2015) argued that, by lowering interest rates and encouraging an inflow of capital, the adoption of the Euro may have been partly responsible for the allocation of capital to less productive firms and, hence, for the low TFP growth.

Furthermore, companies' low expenditure on research and development and low investment in intangible capital, which hampers TFP (Corrado et al., 2013), are associated with regulatory restrictions on competition in product and factor markets (Alonso-Borrego, 2010). Specifically, retail trade regulation, the costs of company creation, lack of flexibility in the labour market, bankruptcy legislation and judicial procedures all militate against competition (Mora-Sanguinetti and Fuentes, 2012).

[27] TFP growth rates for Spain computed by the Conference Board are close to our estimates using the education-based approach to obtain labour quality (which is the approach employed by the Conference Board), −0.7% and −0.6% for 1990–2007 and 1990–2019, respectively. Nonetheless, TFP growth derived with income-based labour quality is −0.1% for each of these periods.

[28] Moral Benito (2018) finds that companies' high capital deepening during the Great Recession and low capital deepening thereafter underlies the TFP contraction during the Great Recession and its rise during the economic recovery.

4.5 Concluding Remarks

The current productivity slowdown has stimulated research on the causes of growth. This chapter has explored long-term growth and its proximate sources in Spain. Labour productivity dominated GDP long-run growth. Half the increase in labour productivity came from capital deepening and one-third from efficiency gains. In phases of labour productivity acceleration, total factor productivity was its driving force and a complementarity existed between capital deepening and efficiency gains. Moreover, Spain was among the best performers during phases of generalised TFP acceleration such as the 1920s and the Golden Age.

Since the mid-1970s, the Spanish economy has been unable to combine employment creation with labour productivity growth and capital deepening, a finding consistent with the fact that expanding sectors that created more jobs experienced slower output per hour growth, as they were less successful in attracting investment and technological innovation. During the 'transition to democracy' decade (1976–1985), labour productivity continued to thrive, since deep structural change and industrial re-structuring eliminated sheltered low-productivity industries.

Labour productivity slowdown only began after Spain's accession to the European Union, associated with deceleration in capital deepening and TFP stagnation. GDP growth became extensive, largely depending on the increase in hours worked per person as employment grew until the Global Financial Crisis. Capital misallocation, low investment in intangibles and ISTC negatively affecting capital deepening and TFP growth resulted from obstacles to competition in product and factor markets, subsidies, and cronyism.

So do restrictions to economic freedom, regulation and worsening property rights, in particular, help explain the poor labour productivity performance during the last three decades? Furthermore, does economic freedom constitute an ultimate determinant of capital deepening and TFP growth over the long run? Answering these questions require further research.

Appendix

See Tables 4.8, 4.9, 4.10, 4.11 and 4.12.

See Figs. 4.9 and 4.10.

Table 4.8 Real GDP and its composition, 1850–2020 (2010=100)

	GDP	Population	GDP/hour	Hours/person
1850	2.0	31.7	4.6	139.6
1851	2.1	31.9	4.6	139.5
1852	2.2	32.2	4.7	141.2
1853	2.2	32.4	4.8	139.0
1854	2.2	32.6	4.9	138.7
1855	2.3	32.6	5.1	138.2
1856	2.2	32.8	4.8	140.6
1857	2.2	33.1	4.6	141.6
1858	2.2	33.2	4.7	142.2
1859	2.3	33.4	4.9	142.1
1860	2.4	33.6	5.1	141.6
1861	2.5	33.8	5.1	142.8
1862	2.5	34.1	5.1	142.0
1863	2.5	34.4	5.1	142.9
1864	2.5	34.6	5.1	142.8
1865	2.4	34.7	4.9	143.3
1866	2.6	34.8	5.2	142.8
1867	2.6	35.0	5.1	143.8
1868	2.2	35.1	4.4	143.6
1869	2.3	35.1	4.6	143.9
1870	2.4	35.1	4.7	143.6
1871	2.6	35.2	5.0	145.1
1872	3.0	35.3	5.8	145.1
1873	3.2	35.4	6.2	147.2
1874	2.9	35.4	5.7	145.6
1875	3.0	35.5	5.9	145.6
1876	3.1	35.6	6.1	145.1
1877	3.5	35.7	6.7	146.1
1878	3.4	35.9	6.5	144.6
1879	3.1	36.2	6.1	143.6
1880	3.4	36.4	6.6	143.3
1881	3.5	36.7	6.6	143.5
1882	3.5	36.9	6.7	142.6
1883	3.6	37.1	6.8	141.7
1884	3.6	37.2	7.0	139.5
1885	3.5	37.3	6.7	138.7
1886	3.4	37.4	6.7	136.3
1887	3.4	37.6	6.6	135.5
1888	3.5	37.7	6.9	135.3
1889	3.5	37.8	6.8	136.0
1890	3.5	37.8	6.8	136.2
1891	3.6	37.8	6.9	137.1
1892	3.9	37.9	7.4	137.2

(continued)

Table 4.8 (continued)

	GDP	Population	GDP/hour	Hours/person
1893	3.7	38.1	7.1	137.5
1894	3.8	38.2	7.2	136.7
1895	3.7	38.3	7.1	136.5
1896	3.4	38.5	6.4	136.8
1897	3.6	38.8	6.9	134.9
1898	3.9	39.2	7.2	136.4
1899	3.9	39.6	7.2	137.9
1900	4.0	39.9	7.3	137.8
1901	4.3	40.2	7.8	137.9
1902	4.2	40.6	7.5	137.8
1903	4.2	41.0	7.4	137.6
1904	4.1	41.4	7.3	137.4
1905	4.1	41.6	7.1	137.6
1906	4.4	41.8	7.6	137.1
1907	4.5	42.0	7.7	136.9
1908	4.6	42.3	8.0	136.7
1909	4.8	42.6	8.2	136.6
1910	4.5	42.8	7.8	136.3
1911	4.9	43.0	8.4	134.8
1912	4.7	43.3	8.1	135.2
1913	5.0	43.5	8.5	135.3
1914	4.9	44.0	8.2	135.9
1915	5.0	44.6	8.3	135.0
1916	5.2	45.1	8.6	134.5
1917	5.1	45.4	8.4	134.1
1918	5.1	45.5	8.4	132.5
1919	5.2	45.6	8.6	132.2
1920	5.6	45.9	9.2	132.0
1921	5.8	46.3	9.5	131.6
1922	6.0	46.7	9.8	131.0
1923	6.1	47.1	9.9	130.5
1924	6.3	47.5	10.2	130.0
1925	6.7	47.9	10.8	129.6
1926	6.6	48.4	10.6	129.2
1927	7.3	48.9	11.5	128.8
1928	7.2	49.5	11.4	128.5
1929	7.8	50.0	12.2	128.3
1930	7.5	50.6	11.5	128.1
1931	7.3	51.5	11.1	128.1
1932	7.6	52.4	11.3	128.1
1933	7.4	53.2	10.8	128.2
1934	7.7	54.1	11.1	128.3
1935	7.8	54.9	11.1	128.5

(continued)

Table 4.8 (continued)

	GDP	Population	GDP/hour	Hours/person
1936	6.0	55.6	8.5	126.2
1937	5.6	55.9	8.0	125.0
1938	5.5	56.1	8.0	124.0
1939	6.0	55.7	8.8	123.2
1940	6.6	55.2	9.7	122.7
1941	6.6	55.1	9.7	123.3
1942	7.0	55.1	10.3	124.1
1943	7.4	55.4	10.7	124.8
1944	7.7	55.9	11.0	125.6
1945	7.1	56.5	10.0	126.4
1946	7.4	57.0	10.2	127.2
1947	7.6	57.6	10.3	128.1
1948	7.6	58.5	10.1	128.9
1949	7.7	59.5	9.9	129.8
1950	7.8	60.1	9.9	130.7
1951	8.6	60.5	10.9	130.1
1952	9.4	60.9	11.9	129.5
1953	9.4	61.4	11.8	129.0
1954	10.0	61.9	12.6	129.1
1955	10.4	62.3	13.0	128.6
1956	11.2	62.8	13.9	128.5
1957	11.6	63.4	14.3	128.3
1958	12.4	64.0	15.1	128.5
1959	12.2	64.6	15.1	124.7
1960	12.5	65.4	15.8	121.1
1961	14.0	66.1	17.6	120.8
1962	15.4	66.7	19.1	120.9
1963	16.8	67.3	20.6	121.1
1964	17.8	67.9	22.0	119.6
1965	19.1	68.6	22.7	122.6
1966	20.5	69.5	24.3	121.4
1967	21.8	70.4	25.5	121.4
1968	23.2	71.3	27.4	118.6
1969	25.4	72.1	30.1	117.0
1970	26.2	72.8	30.8	116.9
1971	27.7	73.5	31.9	118.0
1972	30.5	74.3	34.8	118.0
1973	33.2	75.1	37.0	119.2
1974	35.7	75.9	40.2	116.9
1975	36.8	76.8	43.3	110.8
1976	38.5	77.6	46.3	107.2
1977	40.1	78.4	49.0	104.5
1978	41.4	79.2	52.9	99.0

(continued)

Table 4.8 (continued)

	GDP	Population	GDP/hour	Hours/person
1979	42.1	79.9	55.6	94.7
1980	43.5	80.5	60.2	89.7
1981	43.6	81.1	62.9	85.5
1982	44.3	81.6	65.2	83.3
1983	45.3	82.0	68.1	81.3
1984	46.0	82.3	72.3	77.3
1985	47.3	82.6	75.5	75.8
1986	48.9	82.8	76.6	77.0
1987	51.9	83.1	78.1	80.1
1988	55.0	83.3	80.0	82.5
1989	58.0	83.4	82.0	84.8
1990	60.5	83.5	82.4	88.0
1991	62.3	83.6	83.3	89.4
1992	63.1	84.1	85.8	87.5
1993	62.5	84.5	87.7	84.4
1994	64.2	84.9	90.3	83.7
1995	66.4	85.3	91.6	84.9
1996	68.1	85.7	92.7	85.8
1997	70.7	86.0	92.5	88.8
1998	73.8	86.4	92.1	92.8
1999	77.1	86.7	91.7	96.9
2000	81.1	87.1	92.2	101.0
2001	84.3	87.6	92.3	104.3
2002	86.6	89.0	92.5	105.3
2003	89.2	90.6	92.7	106.1
2004	92.0	92.0	93.0	107.4
2005	95.3	93.8	93.4	108.9
2006	99.3	95.3	93.9	110.9
2007	102.8	97.2	95.0	111.4
2008	103.7	98.8	95.2	110.3
2009	99.8	99.6	97.5	102.8
2010	100.0	100.0	100.0	100.0
2011	99.2	100.4	101.5	97.4
2012	96.3	100.4	103.4	92.6
2013	94.9	100.1	105.0	90.4
2014	96.2	99.8	105.3	91.6
2015	99.9	99.7	106.1	94.5
2016	103.0	99.8	106.6	96.8
2017	106.0	99.9	107.5	98.6
2018	108.4	100.4	107.3	100.7
2019	110.6	101.2	107.9	101.3
2020	98.2	101.7	107.7	89.7

Sources: Prados de la Escosura (2017), updated data accessible at https://frdelpino.es/investigacion/en/category/01_social-sciences/01_spanish-economy/02_historical-perspective-spanish-economy/

Table 4.9 Hours worked per person and its composition, 1850–2020 (2010=100)

	Hours per head	Hours/FTE worker	FTE worker/WAN	WAN/population
1850	139.6	150.2	103.3	90.0
1851	139.5	150.0	103.3	90.1
1852	141.2	151.7	103.3	90.1
1853	139.0	149.2	103.3	90.2
1854	138.7	148.7	103.3	90.3
1855	138.2	148.1	103.3	90.4
1856	140.6	150.5	103.3	90.4
1857	141.6	151.4	103.3	90.6
1858	142.2	151.9	101.6	92.2
1859	142.1	151.3	101.5	92.5
1860	141.6	150.4	101.4	92.8
1861	142.8	151.4	101.7	92.7
1862	142.0	150.2	102.1	92.7
1863	142.9	150.7	102.4	92.6
1864	142.8	150.2	102.8	92.5
1865	143.3	150.3	103.1	92.4
1866	142.8	149.4	103.5	92.4
1867	143.8	150.0	103.8	92.3
1868	143.6	149.5	104.2	92.2
1869	143.9	149.3	104.5	92.2
1870	143.6	148.7	104.9	92.1
1871	145.1	149.8	105.3	92.0
1872	145.1	149.5	105.6	91.9
1873	147.2	151.3	106.0	91.9
1874	145.6	149.2	106.3	91.8
1875	145.6	148.8	106.7	91.7
1876	145.1	147.9	107.1	91.6
1877	146.1	148.5	107.4	91.6
1878	144.6	147.8	107.0	91.4
1879	143.6	147.8	106.4	91.3
1880	143.3	148.4	105.9	91.2
1881	143.5	149.6	105.3	91.1
1882	142.6	149.6	104.8	90.9
1883	141.7	149.7	104.3	90.8
1884	139.5	148.3	103.7	90.7
1885	138.7	148.4	103.2	90.6
1886	136.3	146.8	102.7	90.4
1887	135.5	146.8	102.2	90.3
1888	135.3	146.5	102.3	90.3
1889	136.0	147.1	102.3	90.3
1890	136.2	147.2	102.4	90.3
1891	137.1	148.0	102.5	90.3
1892	137.2	148.0	102.6	90.3

(continued)

Table 4.9 (continued)

	Hours per head	Hours/FTE worker	FTE worker/WAN	WAN/population
1893	137.5	148.2	102.7	90.3
1894	136.7	147.2	102.8	90.3
1895	136.5	146.8	102.9	90.3
1896	136.8	147.0	103.0	90.3
1897	134.9	144.8	103.1	90.3
1898	136.4	146.2	103.2	90.3
1899	137.9	147.7	103.3	90.3
1900	137.8	147.5	103.5	90.3
1901	137.9	147.3	103.8	90.2
1902	137.8	147.2	103.9	90.1
1903	137.6	147.0	104.0	90.0
1904	137.4	146.8	104.2	89.8
1905	137.6	146.7	104.6	89.7
1906	137.1	146.5	104.4	89.6
1907	136.9	146.3	104.6	89.5
1908	136.7	146.1	104.7	89.3
1909	136.6	146.0	104.9	89.2
1910	136.3	145.6	105.0	89.1
1911	134.8	144.4	104.7	89.2
1912	135.2	145.0	104.4	89.4
1913	135.3	145.3	104.0	89.5
1914	135.9	146.2	103.7	89.6
1915	135.0	145.4	103.4	89.7
1916	134.5	145.0	103.2	89.9
1917	134.1	144.8	102.9	90.0
1918	132.5	143.2	102.6	90.1
1919	132.2	143.1	102.4	90.3
1920	132.0	143.0	102.1	90.4
1921	131.6	142.4	102.2	90.5
1922	131.0	141.7	102.1	90.6
1923	130.5	141.1	102.0	90.6
1924	130.0	140.4	102.0	90.7
1925	129.6	139.8	102.0	90.8
1926	129.2	139.1	102.1	90.9
1927	128.8	138.5	102.2	91.0
1928	128.5	137.9	102.3	91.1
1929	128.3	137.3	102.5	91.2
1930	128.1	136.6	102.7	91.3
1931	128.1	136.2	102.8	91.5
1932	128.1	135.6	103.1	91.7
1933	128.2	135.1	103.3	91.9
1934	128.3	134.5	103.6	92.1
1935	128.5	133.9	104.0	92.3

(continued)

Table 4.9 (continued)

	Hours per head	Hours/FTE worker	FTE worker/WAN	WAN/population
1936	126.2	133.2	102.4	92.5
1937	125.0	133.5	101.1	92.7
1938	124.0	133.7	99.9	92.9
1939	123.2	134.0	98.8	93.1
1940	122.7	134.3	97.9	93.3
1941	123.3	134.3	98.0	93.7
1942	124.1	134.3	98.1	94.2
1943	124.8	134.2	98.3	94.6
1944	125.6	134.2	98.5	95.0
1945	126.4	134.2	98.7	95.5
1946	127.2	134.2	98.9	95.9
1947	128.1	134.2	99.1	96.4
1948	128.9	134.2	99.3	96.8
1949	129.8	134.1	99.5	97.2
1950	130.7	134.1	99.8	97.7
1951	130.1	133.8	99.9	97.3
1952	129.5	133.5	100.0	97.0
1953	129.0	133.3	100.2	96.7
1954	129.1	133.5	100.4	96.3
1955	128.6	132.4	101.2	96.0
1956	128.5	131.3	102.3	95.7
1957	128.3	130.2	103.3	95.3
1958	128.5	129.2	104.6	95.0
1959	124.7	128.2	102.7	94.7
1960	121.1	127.3	100.4	94.7
1961	120.8	126.4	101.2	94.4
1962	120.9	125.5	102.3	94.1
1963	121.1	124.6	103.6	93.8
1964	119.6	123.4	104.2	93.1
1965	122.6	122.9	107.6	92.8
1966	121.4	123.0	106.8	92.4
1967	121.4	123.5	106.9	91.9
1968	118.6	121.2	106.9	91.5
1969	117.0	120.7	106.1	91.3
1970	116.9	121.2	105.9	91.2
1971	118.0	121.8	105.5	91.8
1972	118.0	120.7	106.6	91.7
1973	119.2	120.0	108.4	91.7
1974	116.9	118.6	107.6	91.6
1975	110.8	116.6	103.8	91.6
1976	107.2	114.5	102.2	91.6
1977	104.5	112.6	101.3	91.6
1978	99.0	110.4	97.8	91.7

(continued)

Table 4.9 (continued)

	Hours per head	Hours/FTE worker	FTE worker/WAN	WAN/population
1979	94.7	108.3	95.1	92.0
1980	89.7	107.3	90.5	92.4
1981	85.5	105.6	87.2	92.8
1982	83.3	104.4	85.5	93.4
1983	81.3	102.6	84.3	94.0
1984	77.3	100.3	81.5	94.5
1985	75.8	99.7	80.0	95.1
1986	77.0	99.2	81.2	95.6
1987	80.1	98.6	84.6	96.1
1988	82.5	98.3	87.0	96.6
1989	84.8	97.4	89.6	97.1
1990	88.0	97.4	92.5	97.7
1991	89.4	97.8	93.0	98.3
1992	87.5	97.4	90.8	98.9
1993	84.4	97.1	87.4	99.4
1994	83.7	97.1	86.3	99.9
1995	84.9	96.9	87.4	100.3
1996	85.8	97.2	87.9	100.5
1997	88.8	97.5	90.4	100.7
1998	92.8	98.1	93.8	100.8
1999	96.9	98.3	97.7	100.9
2000	101.0	98.2	102.0	100.8
2001	104.3	98.7	105.0	100.6
2002	105.3	99.0	105.6	100.7
2003	106.1	99.1	106.2	100.8
2004	107.4	99.3	107.0	101.1
2005	108.9	99.1	108.4	101.3
2006	110.9	99.1	110.6	101.1
2007	111.4	98.6	111.7	101.3
2008	110.3	99.2	110.0	101.1
2009	102.8	99.5	102.7	100.6
2010	100.0	100.0	100.0	100.0
2011	97.4	100.5	97.4	99.4
2012	92.6	100.7	93.0	98.9
2013	90.4	101.2	90.8	98.3
2014	91.6	101.3	92.5	97.7
2015	94.5	101.2	95.9	97.3
2016	96.8	101.0	98.8	97.0
2017	98.6	100.2	101.7	96.8
2018	100.7	100.5	103.6	96.7
2019	101.3	98.7	106.2	96.8
2020	89.7	93.9	98.6	96.9

Sources: Prados de la Escosura (2017), updated data accessible at https://frdelpino.es/investigacion/en/category/01_social-sciences/01_spanish-economy/02_historical-perspective-spanish-economy/
Notes: *FTE* full time equivalent, *WAN* working age population (15–64)

Table 4.10 Labour input and its composition, 1850–2020 (2010=100)

		Income-based		Education-based	
	Labour quantity	Labour quality	Labour input	Labour quality	Labour input
1850	44.2	55.7	24.6	49.9	22.1
1851	44.5	55.7	24.8	49.9	22.2
1852	45.4	55.7	25.3	50.0	22.7
1853	45.0	55.7	25.1	50.1	22.5
1854	45.2	55.8	25.2	50.1	22.7
1855	45.0	55.8	25.1	50.2	22.6
1856	46.1	55.8	25.7	50.3	23.2
1857	46.9	55.8	26.2	50.3	23.6
1858	47.2	55.8	26.3	50.4	23.8
1859	47.4	55.8	26.4	50.5	23.9
1860	47.5	55.9	26.5	50.6	24.0
1861	48.3	56.0	27.0	50.6	24.5
1862	48.5	56.2	27.3	50.7	24.6
1863	49.1	56.3	27.7	50.8	24.9
1864	49.4	56.5	27.9	50.8	25.1
1865	49.7	56.6	28.1	50.9	25.3
1866	49.7	56.7	28.2	51.0	25.3
1867	50.4	56.9	28.7	51.0	25.7
1868	50.4	57.1	28.8	51.1	25.8
1869	50.5	57.2	28.9	51.2	25.8
1870	50.4	57.4	28.9	51.2	25.8
1871	51.1	57.4	29.3	51.3	26.2
1872	51.2	57.6	29.5	51.7	26.5
1873	52.1	57.7	30.0	51.8	27.0
1874	51.6	57.8	29.8	51.9	26.8
1875	51.7	57.9	30.0	52.0	26.9
1876	51.7	58.2	30.0	52.1	26.9
1877	52.2	58.2	30.4	52.5	27.4
1878	52.0	58.1	30.2	52.6	27.3
1879	52.0	58.1	30.2	52.8	27.4
1880	52.2	58.2	30.4	53.0	27.7
1881	52.7	58.3	30.7	53.2	28.0
1882	52.7	58.3	30.7	53.4	28.1
1883	52.6	58.3	30.6	53.7	28.2
1884	51.9	58.0	30.1	53.9	28.0
1885	51.8	58.0	30.0	54.1	28.0
1886	51.0	57.9	29.5	54.3	27.7
1887	51.0	57.8	29.5	54.5	27.8
1888	51.0	57.8	29.5	54.7	27.9
1889	51.4	58.0	29.8	54.8	28.2
1890	51.5	58.1	29.9	55.0	28.3
1891	51.8	58.3	30.2	55.1	28.6
1892	52.0	58.3	30.4	55.2	28.7

(continued)

Table 4.10 (continued)

		Income-based		Education-based	
	Labour quantity	Labour quality	Labour input	Labour quality	Labour input
1893	52.3	58.5	30.6	55.3	29.0
1894	52.2	58.4	30.5	55.4	28.9
1895	52.3	58.5	30.6	55.4	29.0
1896	52.7	58.6	30.9	55.5	29.2
1897	52.4	58.5	30.6	55.5	29.1
1898	53.5	58.8	31.4	55.6	29.7
1899	54.6	59.1	32.3	55.6	30.3
1900	55.0	58.7	32.3	55.6	30.6
1901	55.4	58.8	32.6	55.6	30.8
1902	55.9	58.9	32.9	55.7	31.1
1903	56.4	59.1	33.3	55.7	31.4
1904	56.9	59.2	33.6	55.7	31.7
1905	57.3	59.3	34.0	55.7	31.9
1906	57.3	59.4	34.0	55.7	32.0
1907	57.6	59.5	34.2	55.8	32.1
1908	57.8	59.6	34.5	55.8	32.3
1909	58.1	59.7	34.7	55.8	32.4
1910	58.4	59.7	34.8	55.8	32.6
1911	58.0	59.6	34.6	55.8	32.4
1912	58.5	60.1	35.2	55.8	32.6
1913	58.9	60.5	35.6	55.7	32.8
1914	59.8	61.2	36.6	55.6	33.3
1915	60.1	61.2	36.8	55.6	33.4
1916	60.6	61.3	37.1	55.5	33.6
1917	60.9	61.4	37.4	55.4	33.7
1918	60.3	61.3	36.9	55.3	33.4
1919	60.3	61.2	36.9	55.2	33.3
1920	60.6	61.4	37.2	55.2	33.4
1921	60.9	61.9	37.7	55.2	33.6
1922	61.2	62.4	38.2	55.2	33.8
1923	61.5	62.8	38.6	55.2	34.0
1924	61.7	63.3	39.1	55.3	34.1
1925	62.0	63.8	39.6	55.5	34.4
1926	62.5	64.3	40.2	55.6	34.7
1927	63.0	64.7	40.8	55.8	35.2
1928	63.6	65.2	41.4	56.0	35.6
1929	64.1	65.7	42.1	56.2	36.0
1930	64.9	66.1	42.9	56.4	36.6
1931	65.9	66.8	44.0	56.6	37.3
1932	67.1	67.5	45.3	56.9	38.1
1933	68.3	68.2	46.6	57.2	39.0
1934	69.4	69.0	47.9	57.5	39.9
1935	70.5	69.7	49.1	57.9	40.8

(continued)

Table 4.10 (continued)

		Income-based		Education-based	
	Labour quantity	Labour quality	Labour input	Labour quality	Labour input
1936	70.1	69.0	48.4	58.1	40.8
1937	69.9	68.1	47.6	58.2	40.7
1938	69.6	67.3	46.8	58.0	40.4
1939	68.6	66.4	45.6	57.7	39.6
1940	67.7	65.5	44.4	57.3	38.8
1941	68.0	65.4	44.5	56.9	38.7
1942	68.3	65.4	44.6	56.7	38.7
1943	69.2	65.3	45.1	56.5	39.1
1944	70.3	65.2	45.8	56.5	39.7
1945	71.4	65.1	46.5	56.4	40.3
1946	72.6	65.0	47.2	56.6	41.1
1947	73.8	64.9	47.9	56.9	42.0
1948	75.5	64.8	48.9	57.4	43.3
1949	77.3	64.8	50.0	58.1	44.9
1950	78.6	64.7	50.8	58.8	46.2
1951	78.7	64.8	51.0	59.4	46.8
1952	78.8	65.3	51.5	59.9	47.3
1953	79.2	65.8	52.1	60.4	47.8
1954	79.9	66.3	52.9	60.7	48.5
1955	80.2	66.8	53.6	61.1	49.0
1956	80.8	67.7	54.6	61.5	49.6
1957	81.3	68.4	55.6	61.8	50.3
1958	82.2	69.1	56.8	62.2	51.1
1959	80.6	69.2	55.8	62.6	50.5
1960	79.1	69.5	55.0	63.0	49.9
1961	79.9	70.3	56.1	63.5	50.7
1962	80.6	71.2	57.4	63.9	51.5
1963	81.5	72.0	58.7	64.3	52.4
1964	81.2	74.1	60.2	64.8	52.6
1965	84.2	75.1	63.2	65.2	54.9
1966	84.4	75.2	63.5	65.7	55.4
1967	85.5	76.3	65.3	66.2	56.6
1968	84.6	77.4	65.4	66.7	56.4
1969	84.3	78.4	66.1	67.1	56.6
1970	85.1	79.5	67.6	67.6	57.5
1971	86.7	80.5	69.8	68.1	59.0
1972	87.7	81.7	71.6	68.4	60.0
1973	89.6	82.6	74.0	68.9	61.7
1974	88.8	83.7	74.3	69.3	61.6
1975	85.0	85.5	72.7	69.8	59.4
1976	83.1	86.9	72.3	70.4	58.5
1977	81.9	88.2	72.2	71.0	58.2
1978	78.4	89.1	69.8	71.7	56.2

(continued)

Table 4.10 (continued)

		Income-based		Education-based	
	Labour quantity	Labour quality	Labour input	Labour quality	Labour input
1979	75.7	90.2	68.2	72.5	54.9
1980	72.2	91.1	65.8	73.4	53.0
1981	69.4	92.2	63.9	74.3	51.6
1982	68.0	93.0	63.2	75.4	51.2
1983	66.6	93.7	62.4	76.4	50.9
1984	63.6	94.4	60.1	77.5	49.3
1985	62.6	95.2	59.6	78.6	49.2
1986	63.8	96.0	61.3	79.7	50.8
1987	66.5	96.2	64.0	80.7	53.7
1988	68.7	96.5	66.3	81.5	56.0
1989	70.7	97.2	68.7	82.3	58.2
1990	73.4	97.7	71.7	83.2	61.1
1991	74.7	98.2	73.4	84.2	62.9
1992	73.5	98.4	72.4	85.2	62.7
1993	71.3	98.4	70.1	85.9	61.3
1994	71.1	98.4	69.9	86.7	61.6
1995	72.4	98.5	71.3	87.5	63.4
1996	73.5	98.5	72.5	88.3	65.0
1997	76.4	98.8	75.5	89.2	68.1
1998	80.1	98.8	79.2	89.8	72.0
1999	84.0	99.0	83.2	90.5	76.0
2000	88.0	98.9	87.0	91.1	80.2
2001	91.3	98.6	90.0	92.6	84.5
2002	93.7	98.6	92.3	94.1	88.2
2003	96.2	98.5	94.7	95.7	92.0
2004	98.9	98.6	97.4	97.4	96.3
2005	102.1	98.7	100.8	99.1	101.1
2006	105.7	98.9	104.5	99.3	104.9
2007	108.3	98.7	106.9	99.4	107.7
2008	108.9	99.1	108.0	99.6	108.5
2009	102.4	99.8	102.2	99.8	102.2
2010	100.0	100.0	100.0	100.0	100.0
2011	97.7	100.2	98.0	101.2	98.9
2012	93.1	100.3	93.4	101.5	94.4
2013	90.4	100.3	90.7	102.5	92.7
2014	91.4	100.2	91.6	103.6	94.7
2015	94.2	99.9	94.1	105.5	99.3
2016	96.6	99.9	96.5	106.5	102.9
2017	98.6	99.8	98.4	107.2	105.7
2018	101.1	99.8	100.8	107.9	109.1
2019	102.5	99.9	102.4	109.1	111.8
2020	91.2	101.5	92.6	113.0	103.0

Sources: See the text

Table 4.11 Factor shares (% GDP), 1850–2020 (current prices)

	Capital share	Labour share	Land share
1850	0.20	0.73	0.07
1851	0.19	0.73	0.07
1852	0.19	0.75	0.06
1853	0.20	0.74	0.06
1854	0.20	0.73	0.07
1855	0.22	0.68	0.10
1856	0.20	0.73	0.07
1857	0.22	0.75	0.03
1858	0.23	0.75	0.02
1859	0.23	0.75	0.02
1860	0.23	0.75	0.02
1861	0.22	0.75	0.03
1862	0.23	0.75	0.02
1863	0.24	0.73	0.02
1864	0.24	0.74	0.02
1865	0.24	0.75	0.01
1866	0.24	0.72	0.04
1867	0.23	0.69	0.08
1868	0.24	0.75	0.01
1869	0.23	0.75	0.02
1870	0.22	0.75	0.03
1871	0.21	0.72	0.07
1872	0.23	0.67	0.10
1873	0.26	0.66	0.08
1874	0.25	0.67	0.08
1875	0.25	0.74	0.01
1876	0.23	0.73	0.04
1877	0.24	0.67	0.09
1878	0.24	0.66	0.10
1879	0.25	0.67	0.09
1880	0.27	0.66	0.07
1881	0.29	0.64	0.08
1882	0.30	0.60	0.10
1883	0.33	0.57	0.10
1884	0.30	0.60	0.10
1885	0.30	0.60	0.10
1886	0.32	0.58	0.10
1887	0.32	0.64	0.05
1888	0.32	0.59	0.09
1889	0.32	0.64	0.04
1890	0.32	0.64	0.03
1891	0.32	0.63	0.05
1892	0.32	0.64	0.04

(continued)

Table 4.11 (continued)

	Capital share	Labour share	Land share
1893	0.33	0.62	0.05
1894	0.32	0.65	0.04
1895	0.30	0.67	0.03
1896	0.24	0.72	0.04
1897	0.29	0.66	0.06
1898	0.32	0.63	0.05
1899	0.34	0.63	0.03
1900	0.37	0.60	0.03
1901	0.35	0.57	0.08
1902	0.33	0.62	0.05
1903	0.34	0.59	0.07
1904	0.37	0.53	0.10
1905	0.35	0.56	0.09
1906	0.35	0.57	0.08
1907	0.34	0.56	0.10
1908	0.35	0.58	0.07
1909	0.31	0.61	0.08
1910	0.34	0.63	0.03
1911	0.35	0.55	0.10
1912	0.38	0.57	0.05
1913	0.38	0.52	0.10
1914	0.37	0.55	0.08
1915	0.34	0.56	0.10
1916	0.43	0.47	0.10
1917	0.38	0.52	0.10
1918	0.40	0.50	0.10
1919	0.35	0.56	0.09
1920	0.35	0.55	0.10
1921	0.32	0.61	0.07
1922	0.30	0.63	0.07
1923	0.31	0.65	0.04
1924	0.33	0.60	0.07
1925	0.35	0.55	0.10
1926	0.35	0.58	0.07
1927	0.34	0.56	0.10
1928	0.35	0.59	0.06
1929	0.33	0.57	0.10
1930	0.35	0.58	0.07
1931	0.29	0.64	0.07
1932	0.24	0.68	0.09
1933	0.22	0.75	0.03
1934	0.22	0.71	0.07
1935	0.22	0.72	0.06

(continued)

Table 4.11 (continued)

	Capital share	Labour share	Land share
1936	0.21	0.75	0.04
1937	0.24	0.75	0.01
1938	0.22	0.75	0.03
1939	0.23	0.73	0.04
1940	0.25	0.71	0.04
1941	0.28	0.70	0.01
1942	0.33	0.61	0.06
1943	0.33	0.62	0.05
1944	0.31	0.59	0.10
1945	0.31	0.64	0.05
1946	0.31	0.647	0.05
1947	0.28	0.700	0.02
1948	0.27	0.690	0.04
1949	0.26	0.690	0.05
1950	0.24	0.695	0.07
1951	0.29	0.605	0.10
1952	0.31	0.586	0.10
1953	0.34	0.563	0.10
1954	0.20	0.73	0.07
1955	0.20	0.72	0.08
1956	0.21	0.71	0.07
1957	0.22	0.70	0.08
1958	0.23	0.69	0.08
1959	0.24	0.69	0.07
1960	0.25	0.69	0.06
1961	0.27	0.67	0.06
1962	0.29	0.66	0.06
1963	0.29	0.66	0.06
1964	0.33	0.65	0.03
1965	0.32	0.65	0.03
1966	0.30	0.67	0.03
1967	0.29	0.69	0.02
1968	0.31	0.67	0.02
1969	0.32	0.66	0.02
1970	0.34	0.66	0.01
1971	0.34	0.64	0.02
1972	0.33	0.66	0.01
1973	0.32	0.66	0.01
1974	0.33	0.66	0.01
1975	0.33	0.66	0.01
1976	0.32	0.67	0.01
1977	0.32	0.67	0.01
1978	0.32	0.67	0.02

(continued)

Table 4.11 (continued)

	Capital share	Labour share	Land share
1979	0.32	0.67	0.01
1980	0.33	0.65	0.02
1981	0.33	0.66	0.01
1982	0.34	0.64	0.02
1983	0.35	0.64	0.01
1984	0.38	0.61	0.02
1985	0.38	0.60	0.02
1986	0.40	0.58	0.02
1987	0.40	0.58	0.02
1988	0.40	0.58	0.02
1989	0.40	0.57	0.02
1990	0.39	0.58	0.03
1991	0.38	0.59	0.02
1992	0.38	0.60	0.02
1993	0.37	0.60	0.02
1994	0.39	0.58	0.02
1995	0.40	0.58	0.02
1996	0.40	0.57	0.03
1997	0.40	0.57	0.03
1998	0.40	0.58	0.03
1999	0.40	0.58	0.03
2000	0.40	0.57	0.03
2001	0.41	0.56	0.03
2002	0.42	0.56	0.02
2003	0.42	0.55	0.02
2004	0.43	0.55	0.02
2005	0.43	0.55	0.02
2006	0.44	0.55	0.02
2007	0.43	0.55	0.02
2008	0.41	0.57	0.02
2009	0.41	0.58	0.01
2010	0.41	0.57	0.02
2011	0.42	0.56	0.02
2012	0.43	0.55	0.02
2013	0.44	0.55	0.02
2014	0.43	0.55	0.02
2015	0.44	0.54	0.02
2016	0.44	0.54	0.02
2017	0.45	0.53	0.02
2018	0.44	0.54	0.02
2019	0.43	0.55	0.02
2020	0.39	0.59	0.02

Sources: See the text

Table 4.12 GDP per hour worked and its proximate determinants, 1850–2020 (2010=100)

				Income-based		Education-based	
	GDP/ hour	Capital input/hour	Land input/hour	Labour quality	TFP (income)	Labour quality	TFP (education)
1850	4.6	0.6	171.3	55.7	32.9	49.9	35.1
1851	4.6	0.6	170.6	55.7	33.2	49.9	35.4
1852	4.7	0.6	167.8	55.7	34.1	50.0	36.4
1853	4.8	0.6	169.7	55.7	34.4	50.1	36.7
1854	4.9	0.6	169.4	55.8	34.8	50.1	37.0
1855	5.1	0.7	170.7	55.8	36.4	50.2	38.8
1856	4.8	0.6	167.2	55.8	34.2	50.3	36.4
1857	4.6	0.6	164.7	55.8	32.9	50.3	35.0
1858	4.7	0.7	164.2	55.8	33.1	50.4	35.1
1859	4.9	0.7	164.0	55.8	34.3	50.5	36.4
1860	5.1	0.8	164.1	55.9	35.2	50.6	37.3
1861	5.1	0.8	160.9	56.0	34.6	50.6	36.7
1862	5.1	0.8	160.0	56.2	34.2	50.7	36.4
1863	5.1	0.9	157.5	56.3	34.1	50.8	36.3
1864	5.1	0.9	156.4	56.5	33.5	50.8	35.7
1865	4.9	0.9	155.0	56.6	31.8	50.9	33.8
1866	5.2	0.9	154.5	56.7	33.5	51.0	35.7
1867	5.1	1.0	152.2	56.9	32.6	51.0	34.7
1868	4.4	1.0	151.7	57.1	28.3	51.1	30.3
1869	4.6	1.0	151.1	57.2	29.3	51.2	31.4
1870	4.7	1.0	150.9	57.4	30.1	51.2	32.3
1871	5.0	1.0	148.6	57.4	32.2	51.3	34.5
1872	5.8	1.0	147.8	57.6	37.0	51.7	39.5
1873	6.2	0.9	145.0	57.7	39.5	51.8	42.2
1874	5.7	1.0	146.0	57.8	36.3	51.9	38.7
1875	5.9	1.0	145.4	57.9	37.2	52.0	39.7
1876	6.1	1.0	145.1	58.2	38.2	52.1	40.8
1877	6.7	1.0	143.3	58.2	41.9	52.5	44.6
1878	6.5	1.0	143.6	58.1	40.3	52.6	42.7
1879	6.1	1.1	143.2	58.1	37.4	52.8	39.5
1880	6.6	1.1	142.2	58.2	40.5	53.0	42.8
1881	6.6	1.1	140.6	58.3	40.5	53.2	42.7
1882	6.7	1.2	140.3	58.3	40.5	53.4	42.7
1883	6.8	1.2	140.2	58.3	40.8	53.7	42.8
1884	7.0	1.3	141.6	58.0	40.8	53.9	42.6
1885	6.7	1.3	141.7	58.0	39.0	54.1	40.6
1886	6.7	1.4	143.4	57.9	38.4	54.3	39.9
1887	6.6	1.4	143.2	57.8	37.7	54.5	39.0
1888	6.9	1.4	142.6	57.8	39.1	54.7	40.4
1889	6.8	1.4	141.4	58.0	38.8	54.8	40.0

(continued)

Table 4.12 (continued)

	GDP/ hour	Capital input/hour	Land input/hour	Income-based Labour quality	Income-based TFP (income)	Education-based Labour quality	Education-based TFP (education)
1890	6.8	1.4	140.8	58.1	38.4	55.0	39.6
1891	6.9	1.4	142.9	58.3	38.6	55.1	39.9
1892	7.4	1.5	147.5	58.3	41.6	55.2	43.0
1893	7.1	1.5	146.7	58.5	39.6	55.3	40.9
1894	7.2	1.5	146.9	58.4	40.2	55.4	41.5
1895	7.1	1.5	145.2	58.5	39.5	55.4	40.7
1896	6.4	1.5	146.7	58.6	35.4	55.5	36.5
1897	6.9	1.5	157.1	58.5	37.8	55.5	38.9
1898	7.2	1.5	156.1	58.8	39.7	55.6	41.0
1899	7.2	1.5	151.9	59.1	39.2	55.6	40.6
1900	7.3	1.6	150.5	58.7	39.1	55.6	40.4
1901	7.8	1.7	150.5	58.8	41.5	55.6	42.8
1902	7.5	1.7	151.8	58.9	39.1	55.7	40.5
1903	7.4	1.7	150.8	59.1	38.7	55.7	40.0
1904	7.3	1.8	150.5	59.2	37.8	55.7	39.1
1905	7.1	1.8	150.7	59.3	37.0	55.7	38.3
1906	7.6	1.8	154.6	59.4	38.9	55.7	40.3
1907	7.7	1.9	154.8	59.5	39.3	55.8	40.8
1908	8.0	1.9	155.9	59.6	40.2	55.8	41.8
1909	8.2	1.9	156.5	59.7	40.9	55.8	42.5
1910	7.8	2.0	156.1	59.7	38.6	55.8	40.1
1911	8.4	2.0	158.1	59.6	41.4	55.8	43.1
1912	8.1	2.1	155.8	60.1	39.3	55.8	41.1
1913	8.5	2.1	156.2	60.5	40.7	55.7	42.7
1914	8.2	2.2	152.9	61.2	38.8	55.6	40.9
1915	8.3	2.2	154.1	61.2	39.1	55.6	41.3
1916	8.6	2.2	153.9	61.3	40.6	55.5	43.0
1917	8.4	2.2	154.1	61.4	39.7	55.4	42.1
1918	8.4	2.3	157.2	61.3	39.1	55.3	41.4
1919	8.6	2.3	158.3	61.2	39.3	55.2	41.7
1920	9.2	2.4	157.7	61.4	41.8	55.2	44.4
1921	9.5	2.5	157.9	61.9	42.3	55.2	45.1
1922	9.8	2.6	155.0	62.4	43.3	55.2	46.4
1923	9.9	2.6	156.7	62.8	43.1	55.2	46.3
1924	10.2	2.7	156.1	63.3	43.7	55.3	47.2
1925	10.8	2.8	157.3	63.8	45.6	55.5	49.5
1926	10.6	2.9	157.1	64.3	44.2	55.6	48.0
1927	11.5	3.0	156.9	64.7	47.2	55.8	51.4
1928	11.4	3.1	155.6	65.2	45.7	56.0	49.9
1929	12.2	3.3	155.3	65.7	47.6	56.2	52.1

(continued)

Table 4.12 (continued)

	GDP/ hour	Capital input/hour	Land input/hour	Income-based Labour quality	Income-based TFP (income)	Education-based Labour quality	Education-based TFP (education)
1930	11.5	3.5	156.3	66.1	43.8	56.4	48.0
1931	11.1	3.7	155.4	66.8	41.6	56.6	45.8
1932	11.3	3.7	152.5	67.5	42.1	56.9	46.5
1933	10.8	3.7	149.1	68.2	40.0	57.2	44.3
1934	11.1	3.7	148.0	69.0	40.6	57.5	45.2
1935	11.1	3.7	145.2	69.7	40.6	57.9	45.3
1936	8.5	3.7	143.6	69.0	31.4	58.1	34.6
1937	8.0	3.7	141.8	68.1	29.6	58.2	32.4
1938	8.0	3.6	140.6	67.3	30.1	58.0	32.7
1939	8.8	3.5	140.7	66.4	33.6	57.7	36.2
1940	9.7	3.5	145.8	65.5	37.5	57.3	40.2
1941	9.7	3.5	148.1	65.4	37.4	56.9	40.3
1942	10.3	3.6	147.5	65.4	39.4	56.7	42.5
1943	10.7	3.6	144.2	65.3	40.9	56.5	44.2
1944	11.0	3.6	143.4	65.2	42.1	56.5	45.5
1945	10.0	3.6	140.7	65.1	38.4	56.4	41.4
1946	10.2	3.6	139.8	65.0	39.5	56.6	42.6
1947	10.3	3.6	138.1	64.9	39.7	56.9	42.6
1948	10.1	3.6	136.2	64.8	39.1	57.4	41.6
1949	9.9	3.7	134.2	64.8	38.3	58.1	40.4
1950	9.9	3.7	132.6	64.7	38.3	58.8	40.0
1951	10.9	3.8	133.6	64.8	41.7	59.4	43.4
1952	11.9	3.9	133.7	65.3	44.9	59.9	46.6
1953	11.8	4.0	132.4	65.8	44.1	60.4	45.8
1954	12.6	4.1	130.7	66.3	46.3	60.7	48.2
1955	13.0	4.3	130.1	66.8	47.1	61.1	49.0
1956	13.9	4.6	129.5	67.7	49.5	61.5	51.8
1957	14.3	4.9	128.6	68.4	49.8	61.8	52.4
1958	15.1	5.2	127.5	69.1	51.5	62.2	54.3
1959	15.1	5.7	128.9	69.2	50.6	62.6	53.1
1960	15.8	6.1	131.1	69.5	51.8	63.0	54.3
1961	17.6	6.3	130.7	70.3	56.4	63.5	59.3
1962	19.1	6.7	129.7	71.2	59.8	63.9	63.1
1963	20.6	7.1	128.6	72.0	63.0	64.3	66.7
1964	22.0	7.6	127.3	74.1	64.6	64.8	69.3
1965	22.7	8.1	122.3	75.1	65.1	65.2	70.1
1966	24.3	8.9	121.3	75.2	67.5	65.7	72.5
1967	25.5	9.8	119.2	76.3	68.2	66.2	73.5
1968	27.4	11.0	120.2	77.4	70.3	66.7	76.2
1969	30.1	12.2	120.3	78.4	74.0	67.1	80.6

(continued)

Table 4.12 (continued)

	GDP/ hour	Capital input/hour	Land input/hour	Income-based		Education-based	
				Labour quality	TFP (income)	Labour quality	TFP (education)
1970	30.8	13.3	120.1	79.5	72.9	67.6	79.7
1971	31.9	14.2	123.0	80.5	73.4	68.1	80.5
1972	34.8	15.2	121.9	81.7	77.3	68.4	85.3
1973	37.0	16.3	118.7	82.6	79.8	68.9	88.4
1974	40.2	18.2	119.5	83.7	82.9	69.3	92.2
1975	43.3	20.9	124.7	85.5	84.1	69.8	94.4
1976	46.3	23.1	126.3	86.9	86.2	70.4	97.3
1977	49.0	25.1	128.6	88.2	87.8	71.0	99.5
1978	52.9	27.9	134.3	89.1	90.9	71.7	103.0
1979	55.6	30.6	139.2	90.2	92.1	72.5	104.5
1980	60.2	33.7	145.8	91.1	95.8	73.4	108.6
1981	62.9	36.9	151.9	92.2	96.3	74.3	109.1
1982	65.2	39.4	155.8	93.0	97.2	75.4	109.7
1983	68.1	41.9	158.9	93.7	98.7	76.4	111.0
1984	72.3	45.6	167.0	94.4	101.2	77.5	113.4
1985	75.5	47.9	169.1	95.2	103.1	78.6	115.1
1986	76.6	48.9	166.2	96.0	103.3	79.7	115.0
1987	78.1	49.1	159.6	96.2	105.1	80.7	116.2
1988	80.0	50.2	154.6	96.5	106.6	81.5	117.4
1989	82.0	52.1	150.4	97.2	107.4	82.3	118.0
1990	82.4	53.5	143.8	97.7	106.6	83.2	116.7
1991	83.3	55.9	139.9	98.2	105.6	84.2	115.3
1992	85.8	59.9	141.6	98.4	105.7	85.2	114.7
1993	87.7	64.3	144.5	98.4	105.3	85.9	113.7
1994	90.3	66.6	140.8	98.4	107.1	86.7	114.9
1995	91.6	67.8	139.8	98.5	107.8	87.5	115.2
1996	92.7	69.4	139.0	98.5	107.9	88.3	114.7
1997	92.5	69.6	132.9	98.8	107.6	89.2	114.0
1998	92.1	69.4	126.3	98.8	107.4	89.8	113.2
1999	91.7	69.5	120.1	99.0	106.9	90.5	112.4
2000	92.2	70.0	114.9	98.9	107.3	91.1	112.3
2001	92.3	71.1	110.4	98.6	107.1	92.6	110.9
2002	92.5	72.8	107.2	98.6	106.3	94.1	109.1
2003	92.7	74.4	103.5	98.5	105.8	95.7	107.5
2004	93.0	76.0	99.6	98.6	105.2	97.4	105.9
2005	93.4	77.6	96.8	98.7	104.7	99.1	104.5
2006	93.9	79.4	93.7	98.9	104.2	99.3	104.0
2007	95.0	82.1	92.5	98.7	103.9	99.4	103.5
2008	95.2	86.2	92.6	99.1	101.9	99.6	101.6
2009	97.5	95.2	98.1	99.8	99.6	99.8	99.6

(continued)

Table 4.12 (continued)

	GDP/ hour	Capital input/hour	Land input/hour	Income-based		Education-based	
				Labour quality	TFP (income)	Labour quality	TFP (education)
2010	100.0	100.0	100.0	100.0	100.0	100.0	100.0
2011	101.5	104.5	102.9	100.2	99.5	101.2	98.9
2012	103.4	111.4	108.0	100.3	98.5	101.5	97.9
2013	105.0	115.8	111.4	100.3	98.2	102.5	97.1
2014	105.3	115.7	110.5	100.2	98.7	103.6	96.9
2015	106.1	113.6	107.6	99.9	100.5	105.5	97.5
2016	106.6	112.3	105.3	99.9	101.5	106.5	98.0
2017	107.5	111.7	104.3	99.8	102.7	107.2	98.7
2018	107.3	111.0	102.6	99.8	102.8	107.9	98.5
2019	107.9	111.7	101.5	99.9	103.0	109.1	98.2
2020	107.7	127.5	114.1	101.5	96.3	113.0	90.8

Sources: See the text

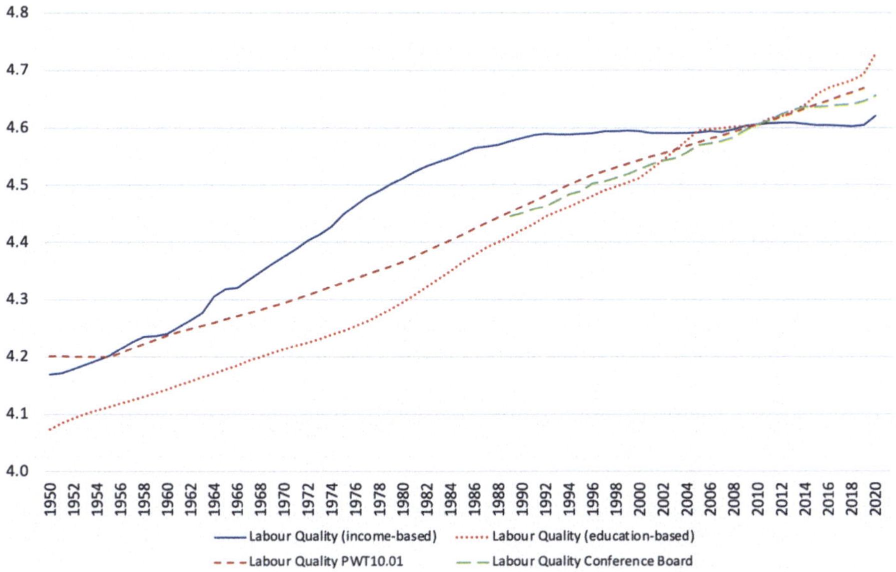

Fig. 4.9 Labour quality: new income- and education-based estimates compared to PWT10.01 and conference board education-based estimates (2010=100) (logs)

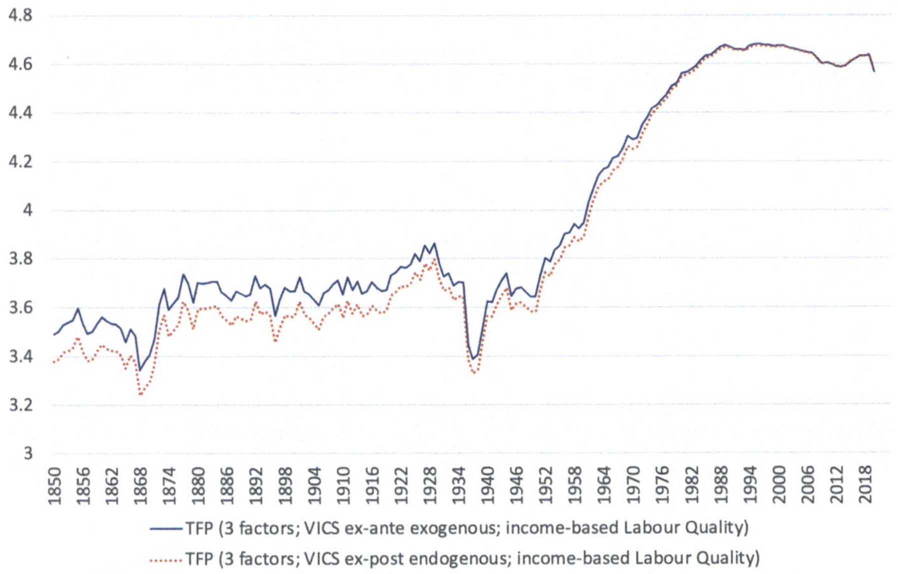

Fig. 4.10 Total factor productivity: alternatively estimated with VICS ex-ante exogenous and ex-post endogenous and income-based labour quality (2010=100) (logs)

References

Abramovitz, M. and P. David (2001), "Two Centuries of American Macroeconomic Growth from Exploitation of Resource Abundance to Knowledge-Driven Development." SIEPR Discussion Paper No. 01-05.

Alonso Borrego, C. (2010), Firm behavior, Market Deregulation and Productivity in Spain. Banco de España Documento de Trabajo 1035.

Altug, S., A. Filiztekin, and S. Pamuk (2008), "Sources of Long-Term Economic Growth for Turkey, 1880-2005", *European Review of Economic History* 12: 393-430.

Antràs, P. H.J. Voth (2003), "Factor Prices and Productivity Growth during the British Industrial Revolution." *Explorations in Economic History* 40(1): 52-77.

Barro, R. and J.-W. Lee (2013), "A New Data Set of Educational Attainment in the World, 1950–2010", *Journal of Development Economics* 104:184-198, Dataset accessible at http://www.barrolee.com/

Bergeaud, A., G. Cette, and R. Lecat (2016) "Productivity Trends in Advanced Countries between 1890 and 2012", *Review of Income and Wealth* 62(3): 420–444. Updated dataset 10/10/2019 http://www.longtermproductivity.com/

Bosworth, B.P., and Collins, S.M. (2003), *The Empirics of Growth: An Update*, Brookings Papers in Economic Activity 34(2), 113-179.

Bosworth, B.P. and S. M. Collins (2007), Accounting for Growth: Comparing China and India, NBER Working Paper No. 12943.

Conference Board (2017), Total Economy Database A Detailed Guide to its Sources and Methods, https://conference-board.org/

Conference Board (2022), Total Economy Database. Growth Accounting and Total Factor Productivity, 1990–2022, dataset accessible at https://www.conference-board.org/data/economydatabase/total-economy-database-productivity

Corrado, C., J. Haskel, C. Jona_lasinio, and M. Iommi (2013), Innovation and Intangible Investment in Europe, Japan and the US, Imperial College Business School, Discussion Paper 2013/1.

Crafts, N. (2018), *Forging Ahead, Falling Behind and Fighting Back. British Economic Growth from the Industrial Revolution to the Financial Crisis*, Cambridge: Cambridge University Press.
Crafts, N. (2021), "The Sources of British Economic Growth since the Industrial Revolution: Not the Same Old Story", *Journal of Economic Surveys* 35(3): 697-709.
Crafts, N. and Woltjer (2021), "Growth Accounting in Economic History: Findings, Lessons, and New Directions", *Journal of Economic Surveys* 35(3): 670-696.
Cuadrado, P., E. Moral-Benito, and I. Solera (2020), Sectoral Anatomy of the Spanish Productivity Puzzle, Banco de España Documentos Ocasionales 2006.
Díaz, A. and L. Franjo (2016), "Capital Goods, Measured TFP and Growth: The Case of Spain", *European Economic Review* 83(1): 19-39.
Encuesta de Precios de la Tierra (2023) https://www.mapa.gob.es/es/estadistica/temas/estadisticas-agrarias/economia/encuesta-precios-tierra/
Encuesta sobre superficies y rendimientos de cultivos en España, (ESYRCE) (2023) https://www.mapa.gob.es/es/estadistica/temas/estadisticas-agrarias/agricultura/esyrce/
Feenstra, R. C., R. Inklaar and M.P. Timmer (2015), "The Next Generation of the Penn World Table", *American Economic Review* 105(10): 3150-3182, Updated dataset at www.ggdc.net/pwt
Fraumeni, B.M. (2015), Choosing a Human Capital Measure: Educational Attainment Gaps and Rankings, NBER Working Paper 21283.
Fukao, K., T. Makino, and T. Settu (2021), "Human Capital and Economic Growth in Japan: 1885–2015", *Journal of Economic Surveys* 35(3): 710-740.
García-Santana, M., E. Moral-Benito, J. Pijoan-Mas, and R. Ramos (2020), "Growing Like Spain: 1995–2007", *International Economic Review* 61(1): 383-416.
Giordano, C. and F. Zollino (2021), " Long-run Factor Accumulation and Productivity Trends in Italy", *Journal of Economic Surveys* 35(3): 741-803.
Gopinath, G., S. Kalemli-Ozcan, L. Karabarbounis, and C. Villegas-Sanchez (2015), Capital Allocation and Productivity in South Europe, NBER Working Paper No 21453.
Izquierdo, M., J.F. Jimeno, and A. Lacuesta (2015), Spain: from Immigration to Emigration?, Banco de España Documentos de Trabajo no. 1503.
Jorgenson, D.J. (1990), "Productivity and Economic Growth", in E.R. Berndt and J.E. Tripplett (eds.), *Fifty Years of Economic Measurement. The Jubilee of the Conference on Research in Income and Wealth*, Chicago: University of Chicago Press NBER Studies in Income and Wealth, vol. 54, pp. 19-118.
Kaldor, N. (1957), "A Model of Economic Growth", *Economic Journal* 67 (268): 591–624
Kuznets, S. (1966), *Modern Economic Growth: Rate, Structure, and Spread*, New Haven: Yale University Press.
Lains, P. (2003), "Catching Up to the European Core: Portuguese Economic Growth, 1910–1990", *Explorations in Economic History* 40: 369-86.
Le, T., J. Gibson, and L. Oxley (2003), "Cost- and Income-based Measures of Human Capital", *Journal of Economic Surveys* 17 (3): 271-307.
Lee and Lee (2016), "Human Capital in the long Run", *Journal of Development Economics* 122 (1): 147–169.
Liu, G. and B.M. Fraumeni (2020), A Brief Introduction to Human Capital Measures, NBER Working Paper 27561.
Mincer, J. (1958), "Investment in Human Capital and Personal Income Distribution", *Journal of Political Economy* 66 (4), 281–302.
Montenegro, C.E. and H.A. Patrinos (2014), Comparable Estimates of Returns to Schooling Around the World, World Bank Policy Research Working Papers 7020.
Mora-Sanguinetti, J.S. and A. Fuentes (2012), An analysis of productivity performance in Spain before and during the crisis: Exploring the role of institutions, OECD Economics Department Working Paper 973.
Moral-Benito, E. (2018), The Evolution of Spanish Total Factor Productivity since the Global Financial Crisis, Banco de España Documentos Ocasionales 1808.

Mulligan, C. B. and Sala-i-Martin, X. (1997), "A Labor Income-based Measure of the Value of Human Capital: An Application to the States of the United States, Japan and the World Economy", 9 (2): 159–191.

Núñez, C.E. (2005), "Educación", in A.Carreras and X. Tafunell (eds.), *Estadísticas Históricas de España, siglos XIX y XX*, Bilbao: Fundación BBBV, vol. I, pp. 155-244

OECD (2009), *Measuring Capital: OECD Manual*, Paris: OECD Publishing.

OECD (2019), *OECD Compendium of Productivity Indicators 2019*, Paris: OECD Publishing https://doi.org/10.1787/b2774f97-en

Oxley, L., J. Gibson, and T. Le (2008), "Measuring Human Capital: Alternative methods and International Evidence", *Korean Economic Review* 24 (2): 283-344.

Pérez, F. and E. Benages (2017), "The Role of Capital Accumulation in the Evolution of Total Factor Productivity in Spain", *International Productivity Monitor* 33: 24-50.

Prados de la Escosura, L. (2016), "Mismeasuring Long Run Growth. The Bias from Spliced National Accounts: The Case of Spain", *Cliometrica* 10 (3): 251-275

Prados de la Escosura, L. (2017), *Spanish Economic Growth, 1850-2015*, London: Palgrave Macmillan. https://www.palgrave.com/la/book/9783319580418

Prados de la Escosura, L., and J.R. Rosés (2009), "The Sources of Long-run Growth in Spain, 1850-2000", *Journal of Economic History* 69 (4), 1062-1090.

Prados de la Escosura, L., and J.R. Rosés, (2010), "Human Capital and Economic Growth in Spain, 1850-2000", *Explorations in Economic History* 47(4): 520–532

Psacharopoulos, G. and H.A. Patrinos (2004), "Returns to Investment in Education: A Further Update", *Education Economics* 12 (2): 111-134.

Rosés, J.R. (1998), "Measuring the Contribution of Human Capital to the Development of the Catalan Factory System (1830-61)", *European Review of Economic History* 2(1): 25-48.

Vonyó, T. and A. Klein (2019), "Why Did Socialist Economies Fail? The Role of Factor Inputs Reconsidered", *Economic History Review* 72(1): 317-345.

Wössmann, L. (2003), "Specifying Human Capital", *Journal of Economic Surveys* 17 (3): 239-270.

Young, A. (1995), "The Tyranny of Numbers: Confronting the Statistical Realities of the East Asian Growth Experience", *Quarterly Journal of Economics* 90 (2): 641-680.

Chapter 5
Inequality and Poverty

> [S]peculation is an effective way of presenting a broad view of the field; and so long as it is recognized as a collection of hunches calling for further investigation rather than a set of fully tested conclusions, little harm and much good may result (Simon Kuznets, 1955: 26)

5.1 Introduction

This chapter aims to assess long-run inequality and the joint impact of growth and inequality on absolute poverty. Modern Spain provides a good case study, as this is a mid-size country that experienced a long and painful transition from the Ancien Régime to a liberal society during the nineteenth century, broken by revolutions and civil strife; a short and convulsive democratic experience, followed by a bloody civil war (1936–1939); and long-lasting autocracy under General Franco (1939–1975) until the emergence of a liberal-democratic society.

Since the mid-nineteenth century, Spain has seen irreversible modern economic growth. Real Net National Disposable Income per person multiplied by 13.5 over 170 years, which represents an average growth rate of 1.5% per year (Fig. 5.1). But how much of this growth percolated through to reach the lower deciles of the income distribution and had an impact on absolute poverty reduction? This is the question addressed in this chapter, which consists of five sections. Lack of direct income distribution estimates based on microeconomic evidence prior to 1973 led me to resort to an indirect macroeconomic approach to appraising inequality (Sect. 5.2), and on the basis of the available information, to reconstruct the Gini coefficient and provide an aggregate picture of the evolution of inequality since the mid-nineteenth

An earlier version was published as L. Prados de la Escosura (2008), "Inequality, Poverty, and the Kuznets Curve in Spain, 1850–2000", *European Review of Economic History* 12(3): 287–324. This chapter draws on it but includes a deep revision and extension of the estimates covering the post-2000 period and a full re-working of the text.

L. Prados de la Escosura, *A Millennial View of Spain's Development*, Frontiers in Economic History, https://doi.org/10.1007/978-3-031-60792-9_5

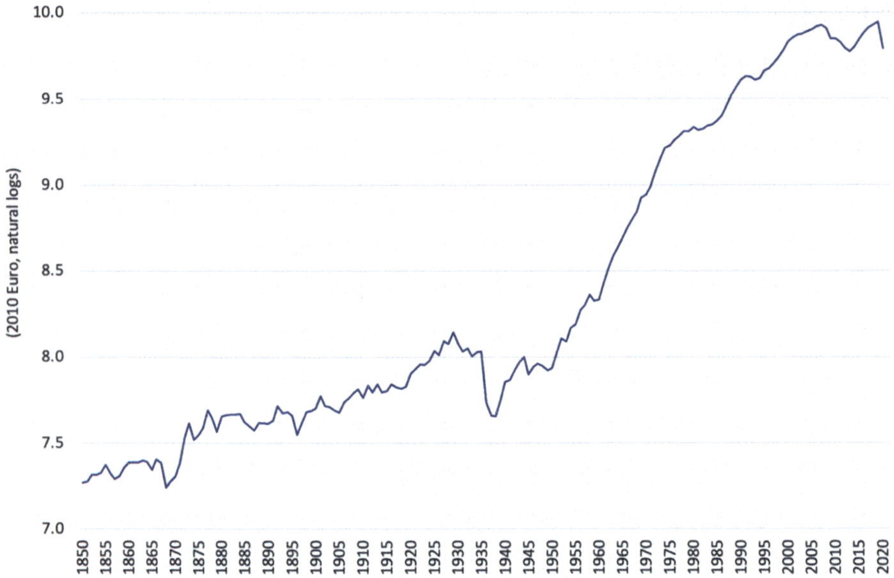

Fig. 5.1 Real per capita net national disposable income, 1850–2020 (2010 Euro, natural logs) (Prados de la Escosura, 2017, updated)

century (Sect. 5.3). Section 5.4 offers some explanatory hypotheses for inequality trends. And Sect. 5.5 attempts to calibrate the impact of growth and inequality on absolute poverty. The chapter closes with some hypotheses for further research.

The main findings are as follows. The evolution of income inequality resembles a wide inverted U with a peak in 1916, and when the Gini coefficient is plotted against real per capita income, a single Kuznets curve results. Economic rather than political forces appear to have driven long-run trends in Spanish income distribution. Stolper-Samuelson forces only partially explain inequality trends. World and civil wars affected inequality but lacked permanent effects, and progressive taxation had no impact until the 1980s. Economic growth, together with a decline in inequality during the interwar years and between the mid-1950s and the early 1970s, led to a long-run reduction in absolute poverty. The fall in inequality since the mid-1950s and the eradication of absolute poverty by the early 1970s represented major departures with respect to Latin America's patterns and matched those followed by OECD countries.

The chapter's results provide some hypotheses for further research. The Civil War (1936–1939) occurred after one and a half decades of declining inequality and an alleviation of poverty, offering an interesting paradox. There was an 'overshooting' of inequality, possibly as a consequence of the Civil War, during the early years of Franco's dictatorship, in which an association between isolation, sluggish growth, and inequality resulted in high levels of absolute poverty. The late Francoist period appears as a benign phase of economic development in which growth and structural change contributed significantly to alleviating inequality and eradicating absolute poverty.

5.2 Assessing Long-Run Inequality

In the absence of direct estimates of income distribution (household budget surveys) prior to 1973, an alternative approach is needed.[1] 1999Historical evidence on income distribution in Spain in the 'pre-statistical era' (i.e. before 1973) is as unsatisfactory as is often the case for present day developing countries.[2] Any attempt to provide orders of magnitude for personal income distribution over such a long time span is perhaps too audacious, but could be justified in so far it provides hypotheses for future researchers to test.

The scattered and asymmetric time coverage (mostly post-1960) of conventional inequality datasets across countries has prompted attempts to construct alternative inequality measures on the basis of miscellaneous information (factor incomes, salary differences across professions, tax returns, etc.). My approach here is an eclectic one, in which choosing between wage and salary dispersion and property income's share in total income is avoided, and all are used to depict trends in aggregate inequality.[3] Thus, for example, the association between the functional and the personal distribution of income is explored.[4]

I will begin with the simplest case in which only two social groups, property owners (who do not receive returns for their labour) and workers (who do not own property) exist. In order to ascertain the evolution of income inequality, we need to know the gap between the average income of the two groups, as well as the dispersion of income within each group. Classical economists stressed the breach between average returns to proprietors and to workers. As David Ricardo (1817) asserted,

> The produce of earth—all that is derived from its surface by the united application of labour, machinery, and capital, is divided among three classes of the community, namely, the proprietor of the land, the owner of the stock or capital necessary for its cultivation, and

---

[1]For a discussion of available household budget data and its treatment for the case of Spain, cf. Alcaide (1999) and Goerlich and Mas (2001, 2004). Unfortunately, the microdata from the 1958 and 1964/1965 household budget surveys are currently missing.

[2]Cf. Morrisson and Snyder (2000) for a similar picture on nineteenth-century France.

[3]On such a dichotomy, cf. Williamson (1982) and Dumke (1988, 1991).

[4]Changes in the distribution of income between workers and proprietors should not be neglected if we want to retain the political dimension in the study of inequality. Dumke (1988), for example, stresses that given restricted franchise, income inequality implied political inequality in nineteenth-century Germany. This is also true of many other countries in Europe, including Spain (Cabrera and del Rey, 2002: 72), where universal male suffrage was only introduced in the late nineteenth or early twentieth century.

the labourers by whose industry it is cultivated. To determine the laws which regulate this distribution is the principal problem in Political Economy.

The classical economists' focus on the functional distribution of income was grounded on the implicit assumption that, as the overwhelming majority of workers were unskilled (and lived near subsistence), the variance of labour incomes was very low. Later, as the economy developed and physical and human capital deepened, skilled workers increased their share within the labour force and, hence, the dispersion of labour returns rose (Kuznets, 1955). Thus, the implied conjecture is that, in early stages of development, income inequality is driven by the gap between average returns of proprietors and workers and only later, as economic progress takes place, is personal income distribution driven by dispersion of factor returns (labour, in particular). If confirmed, this interpretation would help to explain why societies are more sensitive to different types of inequality over time.

Thus, in order to ascertain long-run trends in personal income distribution, we need to assess both between- and within-group inequality. However, historians and social scientists often focus on only one of these at a time. Thus, while the Williamson index, the property (capital and land) share in national income, and, it could be added, the top income shares approach are examples of between-group inequality measures, the skill premium, skilled-unskilled wage gaps, and wage dispersion illustrate the emphasis on within-group inequality. Let us briefly examine some of these approaches for the Spanish case.

A major endeavour to derive yearly series of top income (and wealth) shares in national income for a growing sample of countries in the twentieth century was undertaken by Atkinson, Piketty, Saez and their associates on the basis of income tax statistics. This appealing approach, rooted in Kuznets (1953) classical work[5] has, nonetheless, important shortcomings: only a very small fraction of the population was subjected to individual income taxation in many countries prior to the late-twentieth century, while fraud and tax evasion challenge the reliability of fiscal records as we move back in time or focus on countries with low quality-institutions. The historical case of Spain seems to fit this picture. High levels of fiscal evasion characterized the Spanish economy until the late twentieth century. Lack of political will to enforce taxation implied that no actual means (statistical records, bureaucracy) were available to fight evasion and fraud until the 1980s.[6] In fact, income tax only became widespread from 1979 onwards, after a fiscal reform took place, and its share of total tax receipts went up from less than 2% over 1940–1978 to 30% in the

[5]The sample initially included OECD countries but has been gradually widened to cover developing countries (Atkinson and Piketty, 2007; Alvaredo et al. 2013; Atkinson et al., 2011; https://wid.world/income-comparator/). There are precedents of assessing inequality on the basis of the shares of national income accruing to the top of the distribution (cf. Brenner et al., 1991) but only recently has such an approach been applied extensively and to a recent period.

[6]Tax evasion was estimated in 40% of tax receipts by the late 1970s (Comín, 1996). However, Alvaredo and Saez (2009) claim that, among top income earners, fraud and evasion prior to 1980 was much lower than usually assumed, and not significantly higher than in France and the U.S.

early 1980s (Comín, 1996).[7] Alvaredo and Saez (2009) applied this approach to Spain since the early 1930s. One of their main findings is that income concentration was much higher in the 1930s than at the end of the twentieth century. Their figures for the top 0.01% income share show a dramatic decline between 1935 and 1961,[8] especially marked throughout the 1940s, and suggest stability between 1961 and 1981.[9] Top income shares increased in the last two decades, as the joint outcome of top salary increases and capital gains.[10]

An alternative measure of inequality has been put forward by Jeffrey Williamson (1997), who proposed an 'inequality index' defined as the ratio between GDP per worker and the unskilled wage (*y/wus*), which has the advantage of being easily computable for most countries over long time spans.[11] The rationale for *y/wus* is that while the numerator reflects returns to all factors of production, the denominator only encapsulates returns to raw labour, so it compares the middle to the bottom of income distribution. Nonetheless, it is worth stressing that as societies develop and broad capital deepening takes place, the proportion of unskilled workers within the labour force dwindles. In this scenario, comparisons over time tend to be inconsistent and inequality measured by *y/wus* tends to be over exaggerated (upward biased). An alternative is to use the average returns to all labour (w), including both skilled and unskilled workers, as the denominator in the inequality index.[12] This alternative measure (y/w) is similar to the inverse of share of labour compensation in national income[13] under the assumption that the return per head of self-employed workers

[7] In practice, in today's Spain, income tax represents a tax on salaried incomes as 70% of evasion occurs among high incomes (Comín, 2006). The huge tax debt uncovered by tax inspection between 1979 and 1994 suggests a significant increase in the Government's commitment to fight fiscal evasion (Pan-Montojo, 2007).

[8] Alvaredo and Saez (2009) alert readers to the fact that tax avoidance could be behind this striking inequality decline. It is worth mentioning that the income tax introduced in 1932, as part of the reforms implemented by the II Republic (1931–1936), was widely evaded. The generalization of tax evasion and fraud was confirmed when at the time of the 1957 and 1964 fiscal reforms the Government was still unable to assess incomes rigorously or to enforce tax collection (Comín, 1996).

[9] Actually, Alvaredo and Saez (2009) only have evidence for three single years (1961, 1971, 1981) to compute top income shares over 1962–1980. Furthermore, a break in the income tax series prevents a rigorous comparison with their inequality computations for 1981–2002.

[10] The finding that increases in top income shares at the end of the twentieth century are associated to labour income concentration—top wage earners—is consistent with the results for the English-speaking countries obtained by Piketty, Saez, and their associates.

[11] Ideally, each component should be normalized by the amount of hours worked and expressed in nominal terms, that is, the nominal GDP per hour divided by the nominal unskilled wage per hour. Using nominal instead of real GDP and wage avoids the use of deflators that may follow different trends, as their composition is rather different.

[12] In such a case, the inequality index would be defined as the ratio, in nominal terms, of GDP per hour worked to average wage per hour.

[13] That is, the labour share, wE/GDP, where w is the average wage and E, total employment, equals w/y.

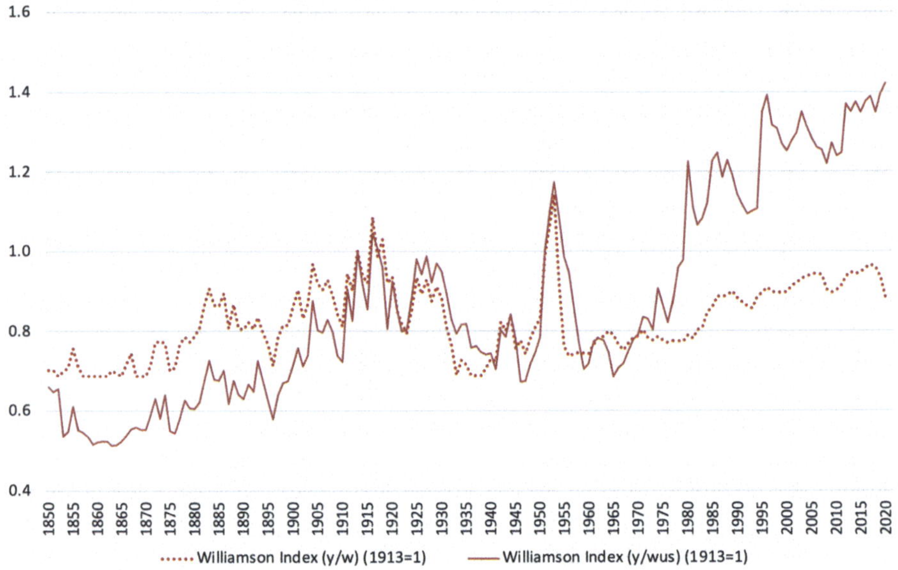

Fig. 5.2 Alternative Williamson indices, 1850–2020 (1913=100). Source: See text

matches the average compensation of employees in their corresponding industry.[14] In other words, this approach identifies the functional with the personal distribution of income.

As returns to unskilled workers represented most of labour compensation in national income until the second half of the twentieth century, inequality indices computed with either unskilled (*y/wus*) or average wages (*y/w*) might be expected scarcely to differ up to the 1950s. Thereafter, as skilled labour increased its share in national income, large disparities between these alternative indices can be anticipated.[15] The two short-cut measures are opposed in Fig. 5.2 and, as predicted, no major discrepancy between their trends is observed, except for the lower level of *y/w* in the nineteenth century, until 1970, when a widening gap between the two inequality indices steadily opened up and the Williamson index y/wus experienced a sustained and dramatic increase.[16] Thus, as the unskilled labour share in the workforce declines, the significance of *y/wus* as a measure of inequality fades away.

---

[14] This assumption is made to compute factor shares in the case of Spain (Chap. 4). The functional distribution of income has been used to measure inequality trends in Britain during the Industrial Revolution (Allen, 2009) and Germany over 1850–1950 (Dumke, 1988, 1991), and for a sample of (mostly) the twentieth-century Western European countries (Flora, 1983).

[15] An increase in labour returns inequality between skilled and unskilled workers could be expected in the presence of capital-skill complementarity in production (Katz and Autor, 1999).

[16] See Appendix for a description of the sources and procedures used in their construction. It is worth noting that similar results are obtained for Germany, 1850–1913 by Dumke (1988: 20). Dumke interpreted the fact that skilled and unskilled labour shares did progress as contrary to the

The *y/w* provides a measure of inequality only in so far as the dispersion within labour and property compensation does not change significantly.[17] The assumption of stability in wage dispersion as the proportion of skilled workers within total employment increases is, however, entirely unrealistic (Kuznets, 1955). In fact, within-group inequality measures such as wage inequality or wage gaps have often been used as a short-cut for the evolution of personal income distribution.[18] The bottom line of this assessment of alternative inequality measures is that no conclusion can be reached about trends in total inequality unless different components, namely, the gap between property and labour returns and the dispersion within both property and labour, are simultaneously considered. This this suggests the need for a historical reconstruction of total (between- and within-group) inequality.

5.3 A Reconstruction of Aggregate Inequality: The Gini

Income inequality over the long run can only be estimated on the basis of scattered and miscellaneous information. One possibility is to start with the breakdown of an inequality index and to build this by estimating each of its components and adding them up. Branko Milanovic (2005: 20–2) proposed a decomposition of the Gini coefficient as follows,

$$Gini = \sum G_i n_i \pi_i + \sum \left(\left(y_p - y_w \right) / y_l \right) \pi_w n_p + L \qquad (5.1)$$

Where the first part of the right hand term, $\sum G_i \, n_i \, \pi_i$ (*Gini A*, hereafter) is a weighted sum of within-group inequality, G being the Gini coefficient for each group ($_i$) and n_i and π_i the group's shares in population and national income, respectively. In this case, I have only distinguished two groups, workers and proprietors.

The second element, $\sum ((y_p - y_w)/ y_w) \, \pi_w \, n_p$ (*Gini B*, henceforth), corresponds to between-group inequality. Groups are ranked according to their mean income, so property owners (y_p) appear above those getting labour returns (y_w) and their relative distance ($(y_p - y_w)/ y_w$) is weighted by the product of the labour returns' share in

view that human (and physical) capital is a substitute for unskilled labour. The Spanish experience suggests, however, that the parallel evolution of *y/wus* and *y/w* is the outcome of the relatively small share of skilled labour in total labour force prior 1970.

[17] According to Piketty (2003), in many countries, long-run wage inequality has been very stable, so trends in income inequality have depended on income distribution changes between property and labour.

[18] Cf. Williamson (1982), and Williamson and Lindert (1980). It is also customary to rely on the gap between skilled and unskilled wages to draw wage inequality trends. Cf. Brenner et al. (1991) and Morrisson and Snyder (2000). Wage gaps or skill premia and wage dispersion can, however, evolve in opposite directions, as the fall in wage inequality is not precluded by the rise in the skill premium as the proportion of skilled workers within the labour force increases.

national income (π_w) and the property owners' share in population (n_p).[19] Average incomes of proprietors and workers have been obtained as follows,

$$y_p = \pi_p \, \text{GDP}/n_p N \tag{5.2}$$

$$y_w = \pi_w \, \text{GDP}/n_w N \tag{5.3}$$

where N is total population.

Finally, L is the overlapping, or residual component, and it accounts for the fact that someone who is a property owner may still have a lower income than someone who is a worker and only gets labour returns.

How can the different components of the Gini, *Gini A* and *Gini B*, be estimated? Since GDP and population are available (Prados de la Escosura, 2017, updated), all we require is the Gini of earnings within each group, proprietors and workers, and the shares of labour (w) and property (p) in national income (π_w and π_p) and in population (n_w and n_p).

In the case of labour returns, inequality has been proxied by the dispersion of average annual nominal wage earnings across industries (1850–1900, 19 sectors; 1900–1954, 21; 1954–1985, 24; 1985–1995, 53; and 1995–2021, 63). Subsequently, the resulting inequality measures for each of these five periods have been spliced into a single one using their ratios in overlapping years. Thus,

$$\text{Gw}_\text{i}' = \left(\text{Gw}_\text{o}'/\text{Gw}_\text{o}\right)\text{Gw}_\text{i} \tag{5.4}$$

Where Gw_i' represents the wage Gini series closer to the present (and with wider coverage of industries) and Gw_i, the more remote one (with narrower coverage), while Gw'_o/ Gw_o represents their ratio in the year they overlap (Fig. 5.3) (see Appendix, A.1 Sources).

In the case of returns accruing to property, lack of direct evidence has forced me to assume that their dispersion was higher but evolved with that of wages. Property ownership of capital and land has been highly concentrated in Spain (Martin, 1990; Simpson and Carmona, 2020: 157) and the distribution of property has usually been considered to be more uneven than that of labour incomes (Pigou, 1920, cited in Dumke, 1988: 12). Since the highest wage inequality corresponds to 1850, I allocated an arbitrary value of 0.8, twice the peak for wage dispersion, to that year and moved it through time with the rate of variation of wage dispersion.[20]

---

[19] It should be borne in mind, that, by construction, those who obtain returns from property (labour) do not receive any from labour (property).

[20] As an alternative, we could assume that property income inequality was high and constant over time. The extension of home ownership and the relatively lower concentration of wealth at the top of the distribution in the late twentieth century Alvaredo and Artola Blanco (2016) suggest, however, that a high fixed level of proprietors' inequality is unlikely. The comparison between the aggregate Gini resulting from assuming a variable and a fixed level of inequality among property returns shows practically identical values until 1960 but divergence thereafter (Fig. 5.12).

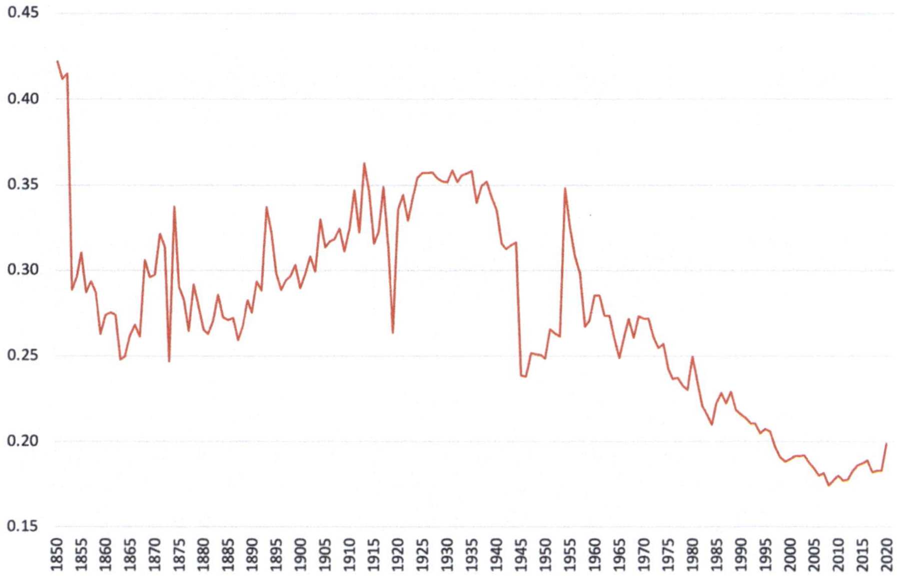

Fig. 5.3 Spliced Wage Gini, 1850–2020. Source: See text

Comparing the wage dispersion with the top income shares in national income provides a crude test for my proposition, as the latter could be largely seen as a historical proxy for the concentration of proprietors' earnings.[21] It appears that, except for the early 1950s and from the late 1990s onwards, their tendencies are largely coincidental (Fig. 5.4).

The next step is to ascertain the shares in national income and in population of those who get returns *exclusively* from either labour or property. For the period 1850–1954, I obtained the amount of labour compensation by multiplying daily wage rates by the number of days worked in each industry, and adding them up. For the post-1954 period, modern national accounts distinguish two income components: compensation of employees (wages and salaries) and gross mixed income, which includes incomes accruing to proprietors and to the self-employed. Income components from different rounds of official national accounts were spliced through linear interpolation to obtain a consistent series for the entire period (see Prados de la Escosura, 2017: 173–174).

But what proportion of gross mixed income corresponds to returns to labour? Colin Clark (1957) and Simon Kuznets (1966) favoured the approach of attributing to entrepreneurs and self-employed workers an average labour income equal to the

[21] It can be argued that top income earners have mainly been receivers of property incomes, rather than labour incomes, until recent decades (Atkinson et al., 2011).

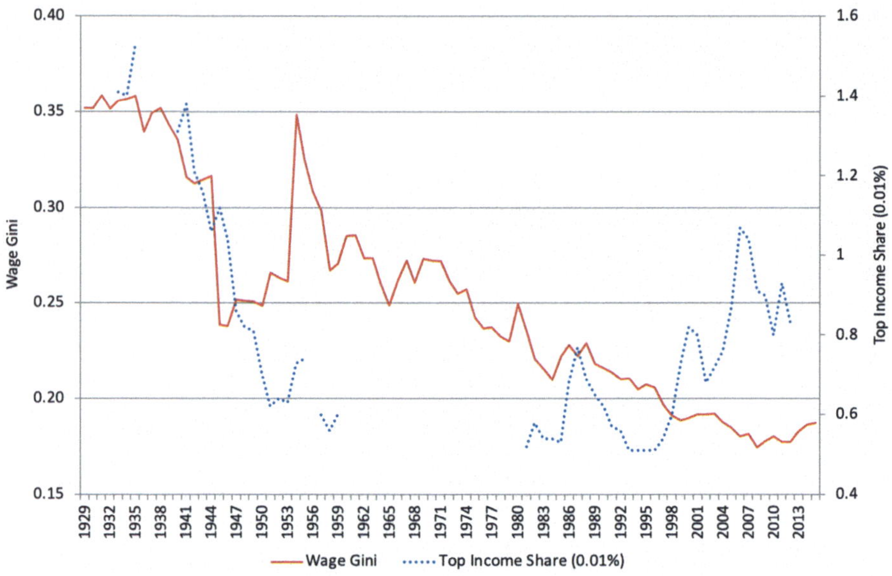

Fig. 5.4 Wage Gini and top income share (0.01%), 1929–2015. Sources: Wage Gini, text; Top income share, Alvaredo and Saez (2009, updated)

average employee compensation.[22] I have, therefore, assumed an average return for non-wage labour identical to that of wage earners in each industry, and derived the income accruing to labour by dividing the amount of wages and salaries by the share of wage earners in the labour force. Then, the labour income share (π_w) was obtained by dividing total labour compensation by GDP at market prices (Chap. 4).[23]

The two labour income share series (1850–1954 and 1954–2021) overlap in 1954 but their respective levels do not match. As compromise solution, I have distributed the gap between the two series in the overlapping year T (1954) at a constant rate over 1945–1954.

$$\pi_{wt} = \pi^n{}_{wt} * \left[\left(\pi^n{}_{wT} / \pi^o{}_{wT} \right)^{1/n} \right]^t \qquad \text{for } 0 \leq t \leq T \tag{5.5}$$

π_w being the linearly *interpolated* new series, $\pi^n{}_w$ and $\pi^o{}_w$ the values pertaining to the labour share according to the 1850–1954 and 1954–2021 series, respectively; t, the year considered; T, the overlapping year (1954) between the two series; and n, the number of years in between the initial (0) (1945), and the final (T) (1954), dates

[22] That is, according to the principle of opportunity cost, the return to their labour would be equal to that of the average worker in each industry.

[23] Computing the labour share in terms of GDP at market prices implies that net taxes on products and imports (taxes minus subsidies) are attributed to capital income. This procedure is also employed by the Conference Board (2022: 32).

considered. Then, the property income share (π_p) was derived as a residual ($\pi_p = 1 - \pi_w$).[24]

The breakdown of the population into the 'equivalents' of those whose income exclusively accrues from property and from labour, while avoiding any overlapping between these two groups, provides a further challenge and only a crude and arbitrary procedure has been possible in its estimation. As for the first 100 years considered, population censuses only provide figures of proprietors for 3 years, 1860, 1920, and 1950. I computed the share of proprietors in working age population (15–64) for these 3 years plus 1960 and linearly interpolated the resulting figures to derive a crude annual series. As regards the post-1954 era, I firstly computed the proportion of property income in gross mixed income and, then, applied this ratio to the share of non-occupied population in working age population in order to obtain a rough proportion of 'equivalent' property owners (that is, the share of economically active population whose income derives exclusively from property).[25] However, a possible objection to the estimate is that the average proprietor was probably richer than the average person earning non-wage income, so their actual number would be lower. Moreover, the estimate may include the self-employed and, hence, overstate the number of proprietors. In order to allow for this objection, I have assumed that the income of the average proprietor was twice that of the average self-employed person, and proportionally reduced the number of proprietors previously estimated. Interestingly, the share of proprietors in working age population (n_p) for the late 1950s obtained this way matches closely that derived through interpolation for the pre-1960 period. Then, the pre-1954 series were re-scaled with the average ratio between the two estimates for the overlapping years 1954–1960 (1.038). Lastly, I obtained the share of the 'equivalent' population whose returns derived exclusively from labour as a residual ($n_w = 1 - n_p$) for the entire time span considered, 1850–2020.

As regards the overlapping *L* component, since it cannot be computed directly, an indirect procedure has been used. Household expenditure Gini on the basis of household surveys are available for 1973/1974, 1980/1981, and 1990/1991 (Goerlich and Mas, 2001) and from 1993 onwards (National Statistical Institute [INE]).[26] I have computed the annual ratio between the directly computed Gini and the 'historical' Gini estimate (that is, *Gini A* + *Gini B*) over 1973–2000. The average ratio can be employed to correct the 'historical' Gini over 1850–1972. For the missing years (1975–1979, 1982–1989, and 1994), the Gini was interpolated by projecting back and forth the closest available direct Gini with the "historical Gini" and, then, computing a variable weighted geometric average in which the closest

[24] Hoffmann et al. (1965: 506–9) and Matthews et al. (1982: 164–72) used similar procedures for the cases of Germany and the United Kingdom, respectively.

[25] This is a very crude procedure, as the unemployed are also part of the non-occupied working age population.

[26] Actually homogenous estimates are only available from 1995 onwards. I spliced them with data for 1993–1995 derived from the European Union Household Panel (EUHP) that was kindly supplied by Luis Ayala.

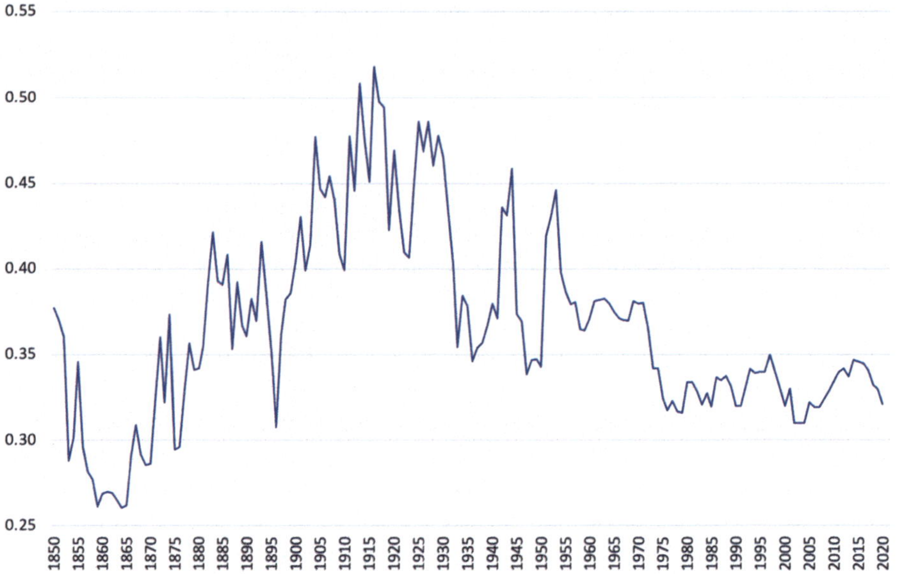

Fig. 5.5 Income inequality in Spain, 1850–2020: Gini coefficient. Source: See text

benchmark receives a larger weight. The overlapping component *L* results from the difference between the aggregate Gini and the 'historical' Gini (Gini A + Gini B). It is worth noting, however, that resulting overlapping component *L* not only captures the fact that someone who is a property owner may still have a lower income than someone receiving labour returns, but also any measurement errors in the computation of *Gini A* and *B*.[27]

Trends in aggregate inequality, measured by the Gini coefficient, are presented in Fig. 5.5. Needless to say, they merely represent a set of explicit hypotheses about income distribution in modern Spain. The evolution of inequality presents the shape of a wide inverted U between 1880 and 1976 with a peak in 1916.

Different long swings can be observed in the evolution of inequality. A long-term rise is noticeable during the early phase of globalization that peaked by World War I. The interwar period shows a marked reduction in inequality in two phases, up to 1923 and in the early 1930s, stabilised during the Civil War (1936–1939) and sharply reversed during the autarchy years, with peaks in 1944 and 1953. After a

[27] An alternative estimate of the overlapping component *L* can be obtained by assuming that the lower the gap between average returns to labour and property, the larger the relative importance of *L*, so the problem is reduced to establishing its size. A possibility is to derive the size of *L* as a residual by deducing the sum of *Gini A* and *B* estimates from official direct computations of the Gini at benchmark years (1973–1974, 1980–1981, 1990–1991, and 1993–2000). The average *L* obtained for can be projected backwards to 1850, with the gap between returns per proprietor and returns per worker (π_w / π_p). The Gini would be reached by adding up the Gini A and B plus the L component. It is worth noting that the resulting Gini from these two alternative procedures largely coincide.

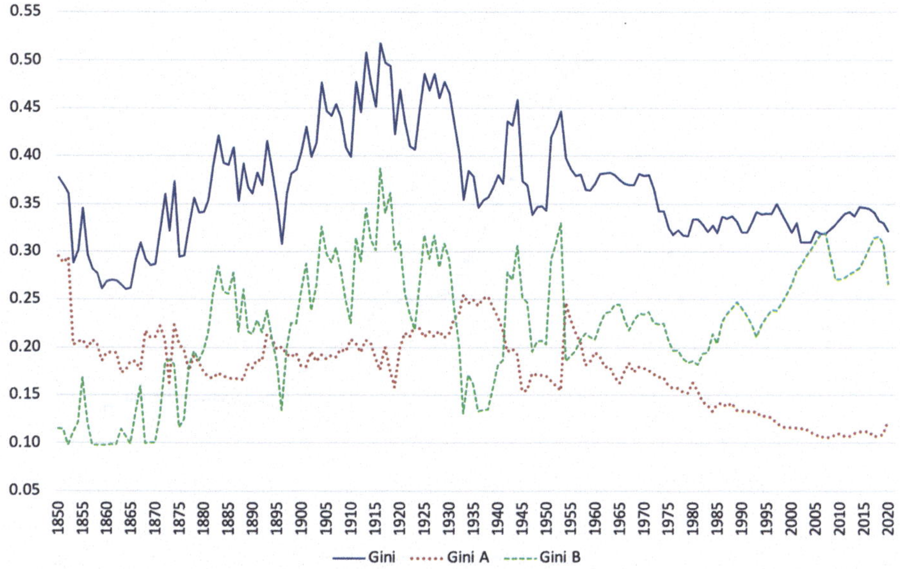

Fig. 5.6 The Gini and its Gini A and Gini B components, 1850–2020. Source: See text

dramatic fall during the second half of the 1950s, inequality stabilised, before exhibiting a steady contraction in the early 1970s. From the mid-1970s to the present, the Gini has fluctuated within a narrow range (0.31–0.35), with peaks in 1997 and 2014.

If we now look at the composition of the Gini, two distinctive phases emerge (Fig. 5.6). From 1850 to 1950s, *Gini B*, i.e. between-group inequality, dominated personal income distribution. The reason is that, as unskilled labour represented the overwhelming majority of employment, the gap between property and labour returns drove aggregate inequality. Then, from the mid-1950s onwards, as the economy initiated a process of accelerated growth and structural change, skilled labour increased its share of employment and the dispersion of labour returns rose; thus, *Gini A*, or within-group inequality, became the main driver of personal income distribution.

The fact that differences between returns to property and to labour dominated inequality trends during the first century of modern economic growth in Spain confirms that functional distribution of income is an appropriate proxy for personal income distribution in early stages of development.

Does the evolution of personal income distribution fit a Kuznets curve? In the historical literature, there have been challenges to this venerable hypothesis (Lindert, 2000; Rossi et al., 2001). The Kuznets hypothesis associates the evolution of inequality with economic growth (Kuznets, 1955). Thus, the relevant test is to compare levels of inequality and per capita income. In Fig. 5.7, the Gini Hodrick-

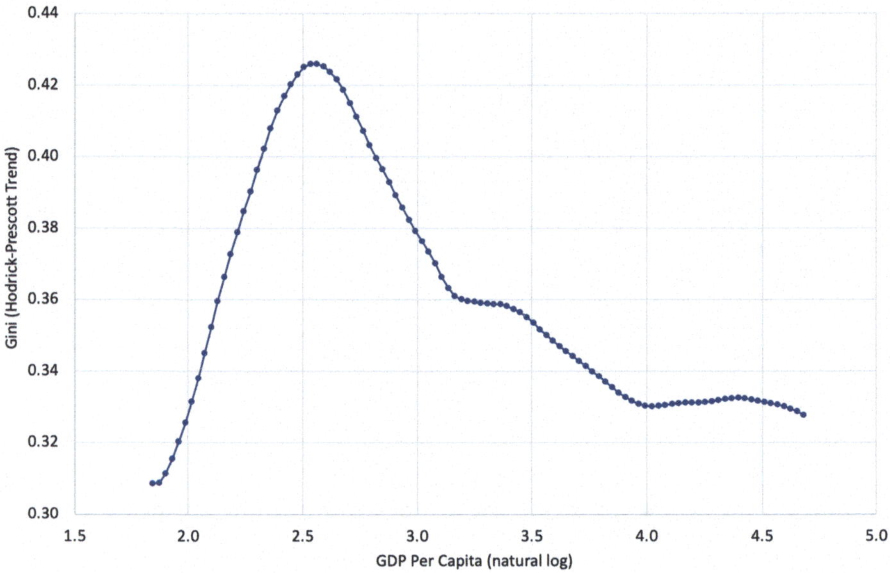

Fig. 5.7 The Kuznets curve (Kernel Fit, Epanechnikov, h=0.4042). Source: See text

Prescott trend is plotted against the natural logarithm of real GDP per head, and a single Kuznets curve emerges.[28]

5.4 Interpreting Inequality

How can these inequality trends be interpreted? Different hypotheses have been put forward in the literature. Alvaredo et al. (2013) have underlined external shocks and progressive income tax as major determinants of inequality trends. Specifically, World Wars and the Great Depression negatively affected the top incomes share in national income (in particular, capital income concentration) while progressive taxation did not allow its recovery. Significant changes, not always coincidental with those taking place in Western Europe, occurred in Spain during the period 1914–1950. Besides, the potential impact of progressive taxation was reduced by its delayed introduction in Spain (1979).

World War I represented a major shock for Spain: relative prices changed so dramatically that they may have affected income distribution (Prados de la Escosura, 2017; Rosés and Sánchez-Alonso, 2004). The increase in inequality observed in

[28] The log of per capita GDP and the Hodrick-Prescott filter for the Gini coefficient are introduced to highlight their relationship. The Hodrick-Prescott filter used a parameter $\lambda = 100$. The Gini HP trend was plotted against the log of per capita income using a Kernel Fit Epanechnikov, with h=0.4042. Real GDP series come from Prados de la Escosura (2017, updated).

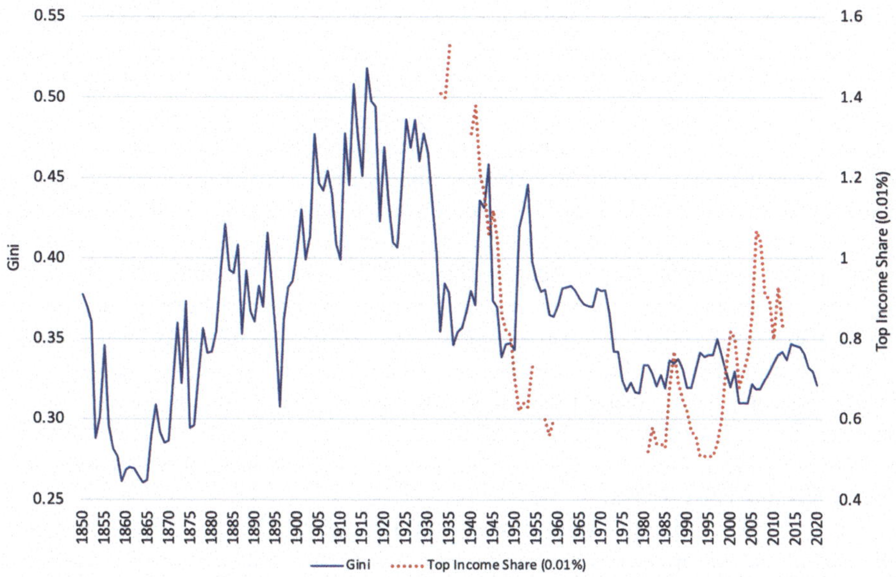

Fig. 5.8 The Gini and top income share (0.01%), 1850–2020. Sources: Gini, see text; Top income share (0.01%), Alvaredo and Saez (2009, updated)

Spain during World War I has also been identified in other neutral countries (Denmark and the Netherlands) as profits rose due to increases in foreign demand and import substitution, while wages did not keep up with rising prices (Morrisson, 2000: 249). This evolution is at odds with that of belligerent countries during World War I. Moreover, the fall in income inequality resulting from 'destruction, inflation, bankruptcies, and fiscal shocks for financing wars' (Atkinson et al., 2011; Alvaredo et al., 2013) that occurred in France, Japan, or the U.S. is missing in Spain (a non-belligerent country during World War II), where the decline in inequality in the early 1930s was more than offset by the re-distribution of income towards property owners after the Civil War.

Alvaredo and Saez (2009) suggest a dramatic fall in top income shares inequality during the first two decades of Francoism. However, the behaviour of top income shares does not explain the evolution of the Gini in post-World War II Spain (Fig. 5.8). It could be argued that, in fact, the rise in total inequality was not determined by changes in the concentration of capital income—that would have fallen, according to the decline in top income shares (Alvaredo and Saez 2009)—, but by an increase in the share of property income within total income (Fig. 5.6). Thus, the distinction between Spain, where the Civil War had a divisive effect in the society, and most Western European countries, where World Wars tended to increase social cohesion, may be relevant to understand their post-war differences.

How can we explain changes in the functional distribution of income? A clue is provided by Christian Morrisson's (2000: 251) remark that the institutional design historically guaranteed rents to proprietors but not to unskilled workers. Tariff protectionism, for example, could be interpreted in this light and the Stolper-Samuelson model used to provide explicit hypotheses about inequality trends (Williamson, 2002). Does this model apply satisfactorily to the case of Spain?

The fall in inequality during phases of opening up to international competition (the late 1850s and early 1860s, the late 1880s) and the rise in inequality (from the late 1890s to the end of World War I) coinciding with a return to strict protectionism, could be predicted within a Stolper-Samuelson (1941) framework that posits that protectionism favours the scarce factors (land and capital, in this case) while it penalizes the abundant one (labour). In Spain, at the turn of the nineteenth century, redistribution towards the owners of scarce factors would have been reinforced by the fact that tariff protection did not drive out workers as in other protectionist European countries (i.e. Italy and Sweden). The depreciation of the peseta in the 1890s and early 1900s made the decision to migrate more difficult, as the cost of passage increased dramatically (Sánchez-Alonso, 2000, 2007). The Stolper-Samuelson model fails, however, to explain the rise in inequality between the mid-1860s and early 1880s.[29]

The reduction in inequality during in both the early 1920s and 1930s, within a phase of globalization backlash, would not be consistent within a Stolper-Samuelson framework.[30] Other major forces conditioned the evolution of inequality. Accelerated growth and structural change all helped to reduce total inequality in the 1920s. Wage inequality rose with rural-urban migration and urbanization, given that urban wages were higher than rural wages, but the gap between returns to property and labour declined.[31] Institutional reforms that included new social legislation, especially the reduction in the number of working hours per day, and the increasing voice of trade unions, contributed to a rise in wages relative to property incomes (Cabrera and del Rey, 2002; Comín, 2002).

The fall in inequality during the early 1930s, at the time of increasing restrictions to commodity and factor mobility, is, again, at odds with the Stolper-Samuelson view. Forces pushing for re-distribution were in place in Spain. On the whole, a reduction in the gap between returns to property and labour more than offset the rise in wage inequality (See the behaviour of Gini B and Gini A in Fig. 5.6). The Great Depression may have had a negative impact on top income shares by reducing property income concentration, as Piketty and Saez would expect.[32] Wages (nominal and real) certainly rose in a context of increasing bargaining power of the trade

[29] A possible hypothesis is that the rise in capital and land returns relative to wages associated with the railroads construction and with the exploitation of the mining resources after its liberalization and to the agricultural export boom (exacerbated by French imports of wine after the phylloxera plague) accounted for this.

[30] Conventionally, the 1920s are depicted as years of intense isolation. However, this is no longer the prevailing view, as trade protectionism in the twenties was paralleled by substantial foreign capital inflows that broke the close link between investment and saving (Prados de la Escosura, 2017).

[31] On rural-urban wage gaps and migration, see Rosés and Sánchez-Alonso (2004) and Silvestre (2005). Urbanization figures are provided in Tafunell (2005).

unions and labour unrest. In the early 1930s, new legislation that tended to increase labour costs, threats to land ownership, and attempts at factory control by workers created insecurity among proprietors, leading to a severe investment collapse and polarization in Spanish society (Comín, 2002: 294–295, Cabrera and del Rey, 2002: 221–235; Simpson and Carmona, 2020: 201–204).[33]

How can the evolution of inequality during the post-Civil War, autarchic years (1939–1953) be interpreted? After the inequality reduction resulting from the war itself and from the pro-labour policies of the II Republic, Franco's victory reversed the inequality decline. Wage compression resulted from the re-ruralisation of Spanish economy (the share of agriculture increased in both output and employment) and the ban on trade unions. Simultaneously, there was a parallel decline in the 0.01% top income shares during the 1940s. Thus, while inequality was falling within both labour and capital returns, the gap between property and labour widened, leading to a rise in total inequality. The autarchy years provide, hence, a mirror image of the early 1930s. International isolation, resulting from autarchic policies, would intensify these trends, with inequality rising as scarce factors, land and capital, were favoured at the expense of the abundant and more evenly distributed factor, labour.

A dramatic decline in inequality occurred during the 1950s, that is, prior to the conventional phase of liberalization and opening up that followed the 1959 reforms (Chap. 8). A possible hypothesis is that this was triggered by economic agents' increasing confidence in the viability of Franco's dictatorship after the U.S.-Spanish cooperation agreements (Calvo-González, 2007) that led to imports of new vintage equipment and to an increase in the investment rate. Between 1953 and 1958, a spurt of economic growth led to improvements in living standards (private consumption grew parallel to per capita GDP), urbanization, and an increase in the labour share within national income (Prados de la Escosura, 2017). Furthermore, the populist policies of Franco's Minister of Labour led to a substantial pay rise across the board in 1956 (Barciela, 2002).

It appears, then, that international economy forces were not alone in playing a role in reducing inequality during the second half of the twentieth century. Growth and structural change played a not inconsiderable role. The rise in savings, helped by the financial development that accompanied economic growth (Comín, 2007; Martín-Aceña and Pons, 2005), facilitated access to housing ownership which, in turn, helped reduce the concentration of property incomes. The diffusion of education (Núñez, 2005) certainly played a role in the decline of inequality by reducing the concentration of human capital. Furthermore, the decrease in regional disparities, conditioned by technological catch-up, the generalization of basic education, and the spatial redistribution of employment (de la Fuente, 2002; Martínez-Galarraga et al., 2015; Díez-Minguela et al., 2018), must also have impacted income distribution.

[32] Alvaredo and Saez (2009) observe in Spain, however, an increase in top income shares for 1933–1935. Was this a post-crash recovery?

[33] Between 1929 and 1936, gross domestic capital formation was cut by half in real terms (and shrank to one-quarter in the case of investment in dwellings), while its share in nominal GDP fell from 16.9% in 1929 to 11.6% in 1936 (Prados de la Escosura, 2017, updated).

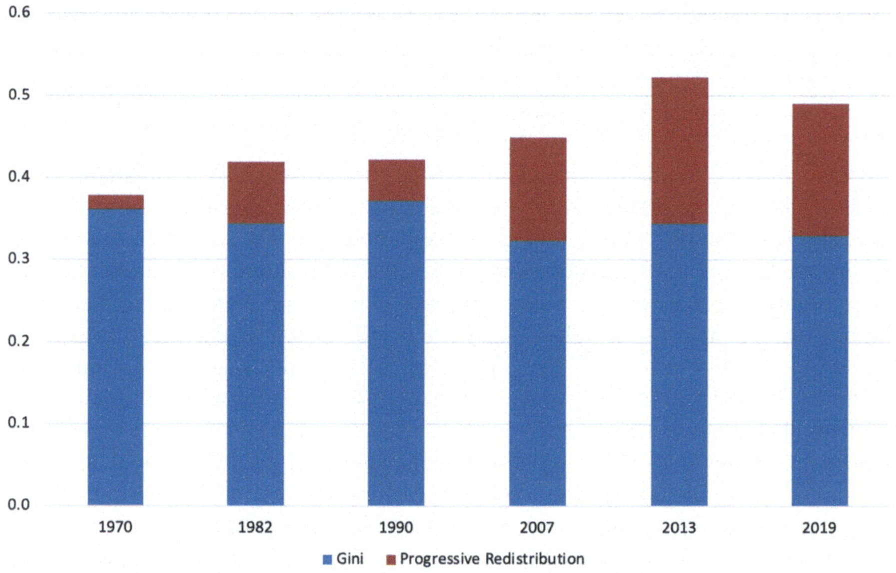

Fig. 5.9 Inequality before and after taxes and transfers, 1970–2019: Post-fisc Gini and progressive redistribution. Sources: 1970–1990, Torregrosa Hetland (2015); 2007–2019, OECD

The coincidence between the social policies of the late Francoism and the cautious opening up of the economy could perhaps be interpreted in terms of an association between exposure to international trade and the weight of the government sector (Rodrik, 1997). Even though the modern welfare state was not fully introduced in Spain until the transition to democracy, social expenditures had already increased during late Francoism and must have had an effect on reducing inequality.[34] The share of social spending in GDP went up from 3.9% in 1958 to 12.1% in 1974, representing limited catching up with Western Europe's share (Espuelas, 2012: 214).[35]

Increasing political participation after democracy was reinstated in 1977 led to a progressive fiscal reform and to substantial increases in public expenditure on social transfers (unemployment, pensions, education, and health) that had a substantial redistributive impact, as observed when inequality before and after taxes and social transfers are compared (Fig. 5.9). However, the Gini of disposable income has remained trendless, fluctuating within a 0.31–0.35 Gini range since 1973. It clearly emerges that progressive redistribution accounts for the stability of disposable income distribution, while the market or pre-fisc Gini (that is, prior to taxes and transfers) has increased to levels comparable to the 1916 peak (or, by the same token,

[34] As Sergio Espuelas (2022: 563) finds, 'after 1967, social spending started to increase in parallel with growing trade openness (. . .) suggesting that trade openness and social spending could be positively correlated'.

[35] Spain was still far behind Ireland (20.2%) and Italy (26.5%) in 1974 (Espuelas, 2012: 214).

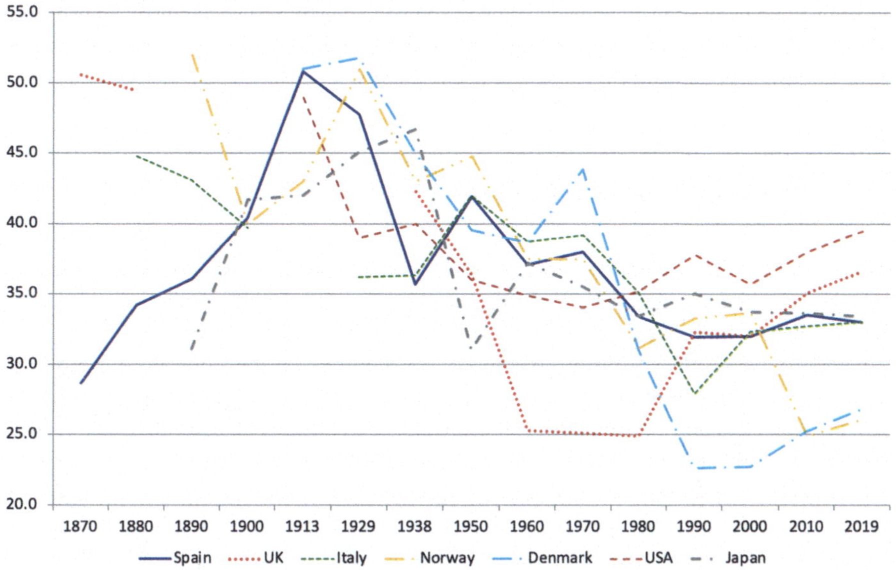

Fig. 5.10 Inequality in OECD countries, 1870–2019. Source: See text, fn. 37

to present day Brazilian levels). However, the stability of the post-fisc Gini poses the question of why the inequality of disposable income has not fallen since the instauration of democracy in Spain (Torregrosa-Hetland, 2015).

How does the case of Spain compare to other historical experiences? Estimates for aggregate income inequality over the long run are only available for a few OECD countries. Denmark, Norway, Italy, and the U.K. have Gini estimates dating back to the late nineteenth century, as do Japan and the U.S. Some crude historical estimates of inequality for Latin America are also available (Prados de la Escosura, 2007). However, comparability problems between Gini estimates constructed using different kind of data have led to a focus on trends rather than on levels (Gottschalk and Smeeding, 2000: 285). Hence, the historical evidence on Gini estimates I am presenting for a handful of countries should be taken with a grain of salt. Figure 5.10 indicates that Spain matched the behaviour of OECD countries except for the autarchic period that followed the Civil War.[36] Interestingly, the comparison with Italy in the twentieth century depicts the latter as a case of more benign development. The contrast with the case of Latin America is illuminating (Prados de la Escosura, 2007). Contrary to the usual assumption of high and enduring inequality in Latin America since colonial times, an upward trend until the 1960s brought inequality to

[36]Data on Gini coefficients for OECD countries come from WIDER (2022) and Deininger and Squire (1996, updated) completed with Flora (1983) and Morrisson (2000) for Denmark and Norway, Rossi et al. (2001) for Italy, Lindert (2000) for the U.S.A., Lindert (2000) and Williamson (1985) adjusted to Lindert's revision (http://www.econ.ucdavis.edu/faculty/fzlinder/Massie1759rev.htm) for the U.K.

the high plateau, where it stabilized for the rest of the twentieth century. Spain and Latin America followed similar patterns until the mid-1950s, when Spain shifted away to converge towards OECD inequality levels.

5.5 Trends in Absolute Poverty

How do trends in inequality and economic growth impinge on poverty reduction over the last century and a half? In this section, I will calibrate trends in absolute poverty from which hypotheses for further research could be derived.

I will focus on the absolute growth of the incomes of the poor (Ravallion and Chen, 2003) rather than on whether these experienced a relatively disproportionate growth (Kakwani and Pernia, 2000); therefore, the evolution of absolute poverty will be defined with reference to a fixed international poverty line.

If a fixed poverty line (PL) is defined at $2.10 (1990 purchasing-power adjusted international dollars) per person and day,[37] it was not until 1880 that Spanish average incomes (real net national disposable income per capita) doubled the poverty line and until 1930 that the latter was trebled. If we bear in mind the results from empirical research in developing countries (for example, Bourguignon, 2002; Klasen, 2004; López, 2004; Ravallion, 1997, 2004) such a low level of development probably hampered the impact of growth on poverty reduction (Deininger and Squire, 1998). In the ongoing debate on pro-poor growth, few views are shared. One of them is that the higher the initial level of inequality, the lower the reduction in poverty for a given rate of growth in GDP per head. Thus, poverty reduction would depend on the initial level of average income and its subsequent growth, on the initial income distribution and its evolution over time, and on how sensitive poverty is to growth and inequality changes (Bourguignon, 2002; Ravaillon, 2004; López and Servén, 2006).

How much impact would average incomes growth and distribution changes have had, then, on absolute poverty in the case of Spain? During the nineteenth century and up to World War I, low per capita income and increasing inequality may have drastically reduced the impact of economic growth on poverty. High initial inequality would have also mitigated the effect on poverty of the acceleration in economic activity during the 1920s, as would have been the case during the 1953–1958 growth recovery. Moreover, faltering growth in the early 1930s would have weakened the effect of falling inequality on poverty reduction. The unprecedented growth of the 1959–1974 years suggests, however, that as the low initial income constraint was removed, the impact on poverty intensified.

Can these hypotheses be put to the test? Alas, no microeconomic data are available on Spain's household expenditures to compute poverty levels and trends

[37] Equivalent to $2 a day/person expressed in 1985 dollars, and $4.30 in international (GEKS) 2017 dollars. This represents twice the conventional World Bank poverty line of 1985 $1 per day/person.

before the late twentieth century. In these circumstances, François Bourguignon and Morrisson's (2002) assumption that income distribution remained unaltered in Spain from the early nineteenth to the mid-twentieth century has much in its favour. In such a case, it would suffice to know the growth rate of GDP per head to assess the evolution of absolute poverty over time. In fact, some researchers suggest that a large proportion of long-run changes in poverty are accounted for by the growth in averages incomes (Kraay, 2006), and, consequently, emphasize the protection of property rights, stable macroeconomic policies, and openness to international trade as simultaneous means to achieve growth and suppress absolute poverty (Klasen, 2004). Assuming a one-for-one reduction in poverty with per capita GDP growth seems to be, however, a gross misrepresentation,[38] and I have therefore preferred to rely on the available macroeconomic evidence on growth and changes in income distribution to propose conjectures about historical trends in absolute poverty.

I have calibrated the impact of growth and inequality changes on absolute poverty (those living below G-K 1990 \$2.10) for the case of Spain on the basis of López and Servén (2006), who, drawing on a large micro database for a wide sample of developing and developed countries over the last four decades and using a parametric approach, found that the observed distribution of income is consistent with the hypothesis of log-normality. Under log-normality, the contribution of growth and inequality changes to poverty reduction only depends on the poverty line/average incomes ratio, and on a measure of inequality (the Gini coefficient). The poverty headcount, P_o, that is, the share of population below the poverty line, is derived as,

$$P_o = \Phi(\log(z/\nu)/\sigma + \sigma/2), \tag{5.6}$$

$$\text{where } \sigma = \sqrt{2}\,\Phi^{-1}((1 + G)/2) \tag{5.7}$$

in which Φ, is a cumulative normal distribution; ν, the average per capita income; z, the poverty line; σ, the standard deviation of the distribution; and G, the Gini coefficient. Thus, all I need to calibrate the poverty headcount is the poverty line/average income ratio and the Gini coefficient.

A long-run decline in absolute poverty is observed in Fig. 5.11 (continuous line). Poverty reduction occurred, nonetheless, at differing speeds over time—a result that supports the view that the impact of growth on poverty is weakened in the presence of rising inequality and low initial levels of development—, while once the initial income constraint is released, its effect heightens. A major contraction took place between 1850 and 1880, which reverted its trend and peaked at the beginning of the twentieth century. Growth underlies the fall in absolute poverty over the third quarter of the nineteenth century, as inequality did not change substantially. Sluggish growth and rising inequality explain the increase in absolute poverty from the

[38] Ravallion (2004) proposed associating poverty changes with economic growth using the expression: *Rate of poverty reduction* = [*Constant* × (*1* − *Inequality index*)$^{\theta}$] × *growth rate*. In which the constant is negative (−9.3 in Ravaillon's example) and the aversion coefficient θ is not less than one (Ravaillon suggests $\theta = 3$).

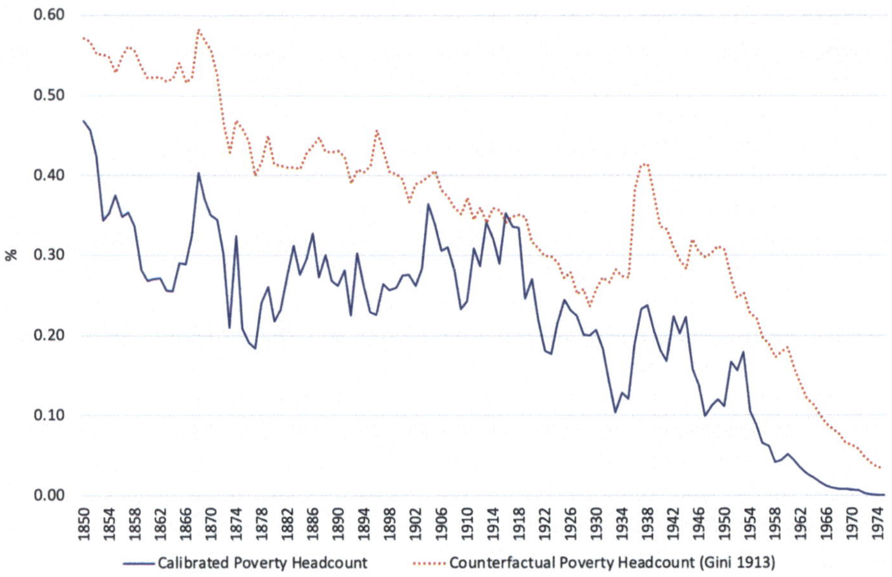

Fig. 5.11 Calibrated and counterfactual* poverty headcount (Poverty Line 1990 G-K $2.10 day/person). *Assuming a fixed 1913 Gini. Source: See text and Table 5.2

1880s to the end of World War I. The sharp decline in absolute poverty during the interwar years (1919–1935) was the combined outcome of a sustained fall in inequality in the early 1920s and 1930s and the fast growth of the 1920s. This constitutes a counterintuitive result, as an association between staggering inequality and extreme poverty and the break-up of the Civil War has often been hinted at, though never proved, in the historical literature (cf. Pérez Ledesma, 1990, and Payne, 1993). During the early years of Francoism (1939–1953), rising inequality and poor economic performance brought the share of those below the poverty line back to late 1920 levels. Conversely, the late phase of Franco's dictatorship appears as an epoch of falling inequality and increasing per capita income, factors that jointly eradicated absolute poverty by the early 1970s.

A glance at Fig. 5.5 might suggest, however, that given the similar level of inequality in the mid-nineteenth and in the late twentieth century, growth alone would explain the eradication of absolute poverty. Was this the case? I have carried out a counterfactual exercise in which I computed the poverty headcount under the assumption that inequality remained unchanged at a high level (that of 1913) over time. The results for the counterfactual and the calibrated poverty headcounts are shown in Fig. 5.11 (dotted line). It turns out that although economic growth was the main force behind the long-run fall in absolute poverty, during episodes of intense poverty decline, a significant contribution came from the rapid decline in inequality (such as the late 1920s-early 1930s, and from the late 1950s to the early 1970s).

The case of Spain presents interesting similarities to and differences from Latin America. Spain shadowed the evolution of Latin American poverty until the 1950s, when inequality levels in Spain departed from those prevailing in Latin America and initiated a fast convergence towards OECD patterns.[39] Thus, the growth of per capita income had a higher payoff in terms of absolute poverty suppression in Spain than in Latin America, where the poverty headcount still remained at the end of the twentieth century.[40]

5.6 Conclusions

In Spain, inequality rose during the late nineteenth century and up to World War I, reversed during the interwar years, witnessed an upsurge in the post-Civil War autarchy, and fell between the mid-1950s and the early 1970s, stabilising thereafter. During the first 100 years considered, the gap between property and labour returns drove aggregate inequality. Then, from the mid-1950s onwards, as growth and structural change accelerated, skilled labour increased its share of employment and the dispersion of labour returns became the main determinant of personal income distribution.

The contrast between Spain and Latin America offers a parallel long-run evolution up to the mid-twentieth century, when Spain deviated to converge towards OECD levels. World and Civil Wars affected inequality—although they did not have permanent effects—, and progressive taxation only had an impact as of 1980.

In modern Spain, no trade-off between inequality and growth is observed. In its most dynamic phases, inequality declined—the 1920s, the Golden Age (1954–1973)—but also increased (1850–1883), while in years of sluggish performance, inequality deepened (1880s-1920, the post-Civil War autarchy) though it shrank too (during the II Republic, 1931–1936). Furthermore, economic growth and declining inequality had dramatically different outcomes during the world crisis of the 1930s and 1970s, with political and social strife leading to civil war in the former period, and democratic stability and social consensus in the latter.

Absolute poverty experienced a long run decline. Growth prevailed over falling inequality as the main cause of poverty reduction, but a more egalitarian income distribution played a significant part in crucial phases of absolute poverty decline. The contrast with Latin America reveals that thanks to a lower degree of initial

---

[39] I have carried out a provisional calibration, similar to the one I conducted for Spain, for the sample of OECD countries included in Fig. 5.10, which suggests that absolute poverty had been suppressed (that is, represented less than 1% of the population) in the U.S., the U.K., Denmark, and Norway by 1950 and in Italy and Japan by 1960 and 1965, respectively.

[40] According to my calculations (Prados de la Escosura, 2007) using the same approach, those living on 1990 $2.10 or less represented, by 1990, 17% of the population in Colombia, 15% in Brazil, 11% in Chile, and the numbers had only been reduced to zero in Uruguay. Meanwhile the poverty headcount ranged between one-third and half the population in most Central America and Bolivia. My estimates are significantly lower, though, than Székely's (2001) direct computations.

inequality, Spanish economic growth in the third quarter of the twentieth century had a much larger payoff in terms of absolute poverty alleviation.

From this preliminary assessment of modern Spain's experience, some hypotheses about the connections between growth, inequality, and social conflict emerge. Attempts to introduce institutional and social reforms during the II Republic (1931–1936) were accompanied by increasing social turmoil and political unrest that led to General Franco's uprising and to the Civil War (1936–1939). Were there economic reasons for this conflict? Was there a war of attrition on income and wealth distribution at the roots of the Spanish Civil War (Boix 2004)? The fact that it broke out after one and a half decades of inequality decline and poverty alleviation demands new explanatory hypotheses. Unfulfilled hopes of sharing share increases in wealth on the part of those at the bottom of the distribution may have contributed to the social unrest that preceded the Civil War. Furthermore, the shrinking gap between returns to property and to labour in a context of social unrest, including threats to property, during the early 1930s, provides a potential explanation for the support lent by a not inconsiderable sector of Spanish society to the military coup d'état that triggered the Civil War.

The outcome of the Civil War, Franco's long-lasting dictatorship (1939–1975), encompassed two distinctive phases: autarchy and sluggish growth, in the former; in the latter, cautious liberalization and fast economic progress. My estimates suggest that a dramatic increase in inequality, possibly a consequence of the Civil War, together with sluggish growth, resulted in striking poverty, with one out of four Spaniards below the poverty line by the early 1950s. A benevolent picture emerges, however, from the mid-1950s onwards, since, as income distribution became more egalitarian and growth accelerated, absolute poverty was practically suppressed by the early 1970s. Did the successful transition to democracy in the last quarter of the twentieth century have its roots in the late Francoism?

Appendix

A.1 Sources

Nominal GDP derives from Prados de la Escosura (2017, updated). Data available at https://frdelpino.es/investigacion/en/category/01_social-sciences/01_spanish-economy/02_historical-perspective-spanish-economy/

Nominal unskilled wage correspond to that for agriculture over 1850–1954. From 1954 onwards, the weighted average unskilled wage rate per hour (weights are the number of hours worked in each branch of economic activity).

Nominal average wage is the nominal weighted average wage rate per hour (weights are the number of hours worked in each of branch of economic activity).

Employment

Only the latest series of national accounts (CNE15, CNE10) provide full-time equivalent (FTE) workers and its distribution by industry from 1995 to 2020.

However, the 1995-based quarterly national accounts (CNTR95) present data on FTE workers for 1980–1995. I have, then, spliced the two sets of FTE workers through linear interpolation to get consistent estimates over 1980–2020.[41]

For the pre-1980 years, García Perea and Gómez (1994) provide estimates of employment back to 1964 that can be pushed further back to 1954 with the rate of variation of employment provided in earlier national accounts (CNE64) (Instituto de Estudios Fiscales, 1969: 33–34). I have assumed that the number of FTE workers evolved alongside employment and projected its 1980 level backwards to 1954 with the employment rate of variation in order to derive FTE employment series for the period 1954–2020.

Linking the post-1954 series with the historical evidence back to 1850 represents a challenge. On the basis of population censuses I constructed yearly employment estimates for 1850–1954 for the four main sectors: agriculture, forestry, and fishing; industry, mining, and utilities; construction; and services. Major shortcomings appear in Spanish census data: working population is only available at benchmark years and refers to the economically active population [EAN, thereafter], with no regard of involuntary unemployment.[42] Moreover, censuses tend to only record one activity per person, that which individuals consider being their principal activity (farmer usually). However, in a developing society the division of labour is low and a single person might undertake various work tasks over the course of a year.[43] Henceforth, activities corresponding to the industrial and, particularly, service sectors end up being underestimated in population censuses.[44] In addition, figures for female EAN in agriculture seem to be inconsistent over time.[45] Therefore, I have

---

[41]The CN10/CNTR95 ratio in the overlapping year, 1995, is 1.02 for total FTE workers and 0.99, 0.93, 1.00, and 1.04 for full-time equivalent workers employed in agriculture, industry, construction, and services, respectively. See Prados de la Escosura (2017) for the linear interpolation procedure used.

[42]Nevertheless, in a predominantly agricultural economy such as that of Spain up to the 1950s, modern unemployment in the modern sense of the word was quite reduced, save during exceptional crises. Still, there was a lot of seasonal as well as hidden unemployment in the agricultural sector (labour hoarding) (Pérez Moreda, 1999: 57).

[43]Moreover, as the opportunity cost of allocating agricultural labour to alternative occupations during the slack season was minimal, peasants carried out additional non-agricultural activities, such as producing their own implements, clothing and providing services such as transportation and storing, and working in construction industry.

[44]The time of year in which census data was collected will also affect the very definition of one's occupation. If, for example, a census is conducted during the harvest season, results for agricultural employment include all those persons temporarily employed in agriculture, despite the fact that their principal occupation during the rest of the year may be in a separate sector.

[45]Female labour was not included in agricultural EAN in the 1797 and 1860 population censuses and represented a small and declining proportion of male labour, thereafter. Thus, female/male ratios in agricultural EAN were, according to population censuses around 0.2 over 1877–1900 and ranged between 0.05 and 0.1 during the first half of twentieth century (Nicolau, 2005).

been forced to make some choices. For example, in order to derive consistent figures over time for EAN in agriculture, I excluded the census figures for female population, while assumed that female labour represented a stable proportion of male labour force in agriculture and, hence, increased the number of days assigned to each male worker (see below).[46] Moreover, as the share of EAN in agriculture is suspiciously stable over 1797–1910, in spite of industrialization and urbanization, I corrected it by assuming that the agricultural share of EAN moved along, and could not exceed, the proportion of rural population (living in towns with less than 5000 inhabitants) in total population.[47] Thus, I adjusted downwards the percentage of EAN employed in agriculture between 1887 and 1920 by redistributing 'excess' agricultural workers proportionally between industry, construction, and services.[48] The next step was to obtain yearly EAN figures through log-linear interpolation of benchmark observations. Since the resulting estimates do not capture yearly fluctuations in economically active population, a partial solution has been, firstly, to compute EAN share in working age population (WAN) and WAN share in total population (N), being WAN and N computed through linear interpolation (i) between population censuses.[49] Then, these ratios have been multiplied by the yearly population estimates (N) (Prados de la Escosura, 2017) to derive annual figures of economically active population (EAP). Thus,

[46] The exclusion of females working in agriculture from the total working population is usual in Spanish historical literature (Nicolau, 2005; Erdozáin and Mikelarena, 1999; Pérez Moreda, 1999: 55). Carré et al. (1976: 89) followed a similar strategy to one proposed here for the French case.

[47] Pre-1930 figures for rural population come from Gómez Mendoza and Luna Rodrigo (1986) and EAN from Pérez Moreda (1999), for 1860 and 1877, and Nicolau (2005), thereafter. Not everyone living in rural districts worked in agriculture, as some proportion, however small it might be, must have been employed in the provision of services and processed goods. It is often alleged that, at least in the south of the Iberian peninsula, there were agglomerations of fairly expansive populations that had no urban characteristics until the mid-1900s, as their inhabitants continued to carry out agricultural tasks. However, in these population centres a significant portion of the working population provided services and non-agricultural goods to the rest of the inhabitants. Thus, I have made the reasonable conjecture that those persons employed in agriculture but living in urban centres would tend to balance out with the population of industrial and service-sector workers living in rural population centres. Moreover, as income levels increase, both the rural population and the overall population of agricultural workers will decrease, although the latter does so at a faster rate, as there always exists some part of the population that opts to live in the countryside despite not being employed primarily in either agriculture or the raising of livestock (Prados de la Escosura, 2017).

[48] Thus, the percentage share of agriculture in EAN for 1887 (65.3), 1900 (66.3), 1910 (66.0) and 1920 (57.2) became 62.7% 60.75%, 58.0%, and 54.5%, respectively. Original shares come from Nicolau (2005).

[49] Yearly estimates of population aged 15–64 for 1858–1960 were derived through interpolation between age cohorts at census benchmarks by David Reher, who kindly supply them to me. I extended the estimates back to 1850.

$$EAP = (EAP^i/WAN^i)(WAN^i/N^i)N \tag{5.8}$$

Later, in order to adjust for differences in labour intensity across main economic sectors and obtain a crude measure of full-time equivalent worker by industry, the data on EAP was converted into days worked per year. I assumed that each full-time worker was employed 270 days per annum in industry, construction, and services. Such figure results from deducting Sundays and religious holidays plus an allowance for illness. This assumption is in line with contemporary testimonies and supported by the available evidence.[50] In agriculture, however, contemporary and historians' estimates point to a lower figure for the working days per occupied, as full employment among peasants only occurred during the summer and, consequently, workers were idle for up to 4 months every year. It can be assumed that the working load per year for the average male worker in agriculture would range, at most, between 210 and 240 days.[51] However, in order to make for the exclusion of female employment in agriculture (due to the absence of consistent data), I increased the number of days assigned to male workers employed in agriculture to match the figure used for the rest of economic sectors (270).[52]

Lastly, full-time equivalent employment figures by economic sector for 1850–1953 were derived by assuming that their yearly changes mirrored those in economically active population and, thus, FTE employment estimates for 1954 were backwards projected with those for economically active population (EAN). It is worth noting that, in 1954, the ratio between FTE employment and EAN for each economic sector is 1.003 (agriculture), 0.872 (industry), 1.095 (construction), and 1.069 (services), and 1.000, for the aggregate. The implication, in the case of agriculture, is that, the upper bound figure for male employment (resulting from an attempt to make for missing female labour figures) matches that of full-time equivalent total employment (including female work).

---

[50] Soto Carmona (1989: 608) pointed out that, on average, the number of days worked per occupied up to 1919 ranged between 240 and 270. Vandellós (1925) reckoned that, in 1914, the average number of days worked per year in mining was 250. Domènech (2007: 472), in turn, provides a figure of 291 days per year for textile industry workers in the early twentieth century.

[51] Gómez Mendoza (1982: 101) emphasized the seasonal nature of late nineteenth century employment and estimated that, on average, a farm labourer worked 210 days out of 275–300 working days per year. This figure is not far from Bairoch (1965) estimate of 196 days for nineteenth-century Europe. Simpson (1992) obtained even a lower figure (108–130 days per worker-year) from labour requirements in Andalusia's agriculture between 1886 and 1930. García Sanz (1979–1980: 63) provided a higher figure, 242 days per year, for day labourers in mid-nineteenth century Spain.

[52] The implication is that the assumed female/male ratio, in equivalent work effort, would range between 0.125 and 0.286, depending on whether male employees in agriculture are assumed to work 240 or 210 days per year, respectively. However, the ratio would reach 0.378 if Bairoch's days worked were accepted, while women would be on pair with men were Simpson's number of working days accepted.

Wages:

The quality and availability of wage data necessary to construct these estimates vary enormously through time. Different periods can be distinguished:

1850–1908: Agricultural wages come from Bringas (2000). Wages in construction and services from Reher and Ballesteros (1993) were re-scaled to the national levels provided by Rosés and Sánchez-Alonso (2004). Wages for mining are from Chastagneret (2000) and Escudero (1998). Levels of manufacturing wages in all industry and services sectors at different dates (1850, 1880, 1905) were obtained, respectively, from Cerdá (1867), the U.S. Department of Labor (1900), and Anuario Estadístico de Barcelona (1905). Benchmark wage levels were interpolated with Fisher indices constructed with yearly data from Camps (1995), Llonch (2004), and Soler Becerro (1997) for consumer industries, and Escudero (1998) and Pérez Castroviejo (1992), for the rest.

1908–1920: the detailed wage enquires conducted by the Instituto de Reformas Sociales (various issues) with information by gender on minimum, maximum and average wages for 20 branches of industry (kindly supplied by Javier Silvestre) were used. Wages in agriculture and services were taken from Bringas (2000) and Reher and Ballesteros (1993), respectively.

1920–1954: Wage levels from a detailed survey for 1914, 1920, 1925 and 1930 (Ministerio de Trabajo, 1931) were interpolated with wage variation rates provided in Anuario Estadístico de España [AEE] (various issues) (only 9 occupations up to 1925, 15 thereafter) to derive nominal wage series, classified by industry, for the period 1920–1936. For 1936–1954, wage levels for 1930 and 1955 were projected back and forth with wages' rates of variation taken from data in AEE and Vilar (2004) and the resulting series were combined as Fisher index to obtain yearly wage levels.

1954–1985: Unit labour costs by sectors of economic activity from Fundación BBV (1999).

1985–1995: Unit labour costs for 53 Industries come from National Accounts (CNE86).

1995–2021: Unit labour costs for 63 Industries come from National Accounts (CNE2010, CNE2015).

See Tables 5.1 and 5.2.

See Fig. 5.12.

Table 5.1 Gini and its components, 1850–2020

	Gini	Gini A	Gini B	L
1850	0.38	0.29	0.12	−0.03
1851	0.37	0.29	0.11	−0.03
1852	0.36	0.29	0.10	−0.03
1853	0.29	0.20	0.11	−0.03
1854	0.30	0.21	0.12	−0.03
1855	0.35	0.21	0.17	−0.03
1856	0.30	0.20	0.12	−0.03
1857	0.28	0.21	0.10	−0.02
1858	0.28	0.20	0.10	−0.02
1859	0.26	0.19	0.10	−0.02
1860	0.27	0.19	0.10	−0.02
1861	0.27	0.20	0.10	−0.02
1862	0.27	0.19	0.10	−0.02
1863	0.26	0.17	0.11	−0.02
1864	0.26	0.18	0.11	−0.02
1865	0.26	0.19	0.10	−0.02
1866	0.29	0.19	0.13	−0.03
1867	0.31	0.18	0.16	−0.03
1868	0.29	0.22	0.10	−0.03
1869	0.29	0.21	0.10	−0.02
1870	0.29	0.21	0.10	−0.02
1871	0.32	0.22	0.13	−0.03
1872	0.36	0.21	0.18	−0.03
1873	0.32	0.16	0.19	−0.03
1874	0.37	0.22	0.18	−0.03
1875	0.29	0.20	0.12	−0.03
1876	0.30	0.20	0.12	−0.03
1877	0.33	0.18	0.18	−0.03
1878	0.36	0.19	0.20	−0.03
1879	0.34	0.18	0.19	−0.03
1880	0.34	0.17	0.20	−0.03
1881	0.35	0.17	0.22	−0.03
1882	0.39	0.17	0.26	−0.03
1883	0.42	0.17	0.29	−0.04
1884	0.39	0.17	0.26	−0.03
1885	0.39	0.17	0.26	−0.03
1886	0.41	0.17	0.28	−0.04
1887	0.35	0.17	0.22	−0.03
1888	0.39	0.17	0.26	−0.03
1889	0.37	0.18	0.22	−0.03
1890	0.36	0.18	0.21	−0.03
1891	0.38	0.19	0.23	−0.03
1892	0.37	0.19	0.22	−0.03

(continued)

Table 5.1 (continued)

	Gini	Gini A	Gini B	L
1893	0.42	0.21	0.24	−0.04
1894	0.39	0.21	0.21	−0.03
1895	0.35	0.20	0.18	−0.03
1896	0.31	0.20	0.13	−0.03
1897	0.36	0.19	0.20	−0.03
1898	0.38	0.19	0.23	−0.03
1899	0.39	0.19	0.23	−0.03
1900	0.40	0.18	0.26	−0.04
1901	0.43	0.18	0.29	−0.04
1902	0.40	0.20	0.24	−0.03
1903	0.41	0.19	0.26	−0.04
1904	0.48	0.19	0.33	−0.04
1905	0.45	0.19	0.30	−0.04
1906	0.44	0.19	0.29	−0.04
1907	0.45	0.19	0.30	−0.04
1908	0.44	0.20	0.28	−0.04
1909	0.41	0.20	0.25	−0.04
1910	0.40	0.21	0.23	−0.03
1911	0.48	0.20	0.31	−0.04
1912	0.45	0.19	0.29	−0.04
1913	0.51	0.21	0.35	−0.04
1914	0.48	0.20	0.31	−0.04
1915	0.45	0.19	0.30	−0.04
1916	0.52	0.18	0.39	−0.05
1917	0.50	0.20	0.34	−0.04
1918	0.49	0.18	0.36	−0.04
1919	0.42	0.16	0.30	−0.04
1920	0.47	0.20	0.31	−0.04
1921	0.43	0.22	0.26	−0.04
1922	0.41	0.21	0.23	−0.04
1923	0.41	0.22	0.22	−0.04
1924	0.45	0.22	0.26	−0.04
1925	0.49	0.21	0.32	−0.04
1926	0.47	0.22	0.29	−0.04
1927	0.49	0.21	0.32	−0.04
1928	0.46	0.22	0.28	−0.04
1929	0.48	0.21	0.31	−0.04
1930	0.47	0.21	0.29	−0.04
1931	0.43	0.23	0.24	−0.04
1932	0.40	0.23	0.20	−0.04
1933	0.35	0.25	0.13	−0.03
1934	0.38	0.25	0.17	−0.03
1935	0.38	0.25	0.16	−0.03

(continued)

Table 5.1 (continued)

	Gini	Gini A	Gini B	L
1936	0.35	0.24	0.13	−0.03
1937	0.35	0.25	0.13	−0.03
1938	0.36	0.25	0.14	−0.03
1939	0.37	0.24	0.16	−0.03
1940	0.38	0.23	0.18	−0.03
1941	0.37	0.22	0.19	−0.03
1942	0.44	0.20	0.28	−0.04
1943	0.43	0.20	0.27	−0.04
1944	0.46	0.19	0.31	−0.04
1945	0.37	0.15	0.25	−0.03
1946	0.37	0.15	0.25	−0.03
1947	0.34	0.17	0.20	−0.03
1948	0.35	0.17	0.21	−0.03
1949	0.35	0.17	0.21	−0.03
1950	0.34	0.17	0.20	−0.03
1951	0.42	0.16	0.29	−0.04
1952	0.43	0.16	0.31	−0.04
1953	0.45	0.15	0.33	−0.04
1954	0.40	0.25	0.19	−0.03
1955	0.39	0.23	0.19	−0.03
1956	0.38	0.22	0.20	−0.03
1957	0.38	0.21	0.21	−0.03
1958	0.36	0.18	0.21	−0.03
1959	0.36	0.18	0.21	−0.03
1960	0.37	0.19	0.21	−0.03
1961	0.38	0.19	0.22	−0.03
1962	0.38	0.18	0.24	−0.03
1963	0.38	0.18	0.24	−0.03
1964	0.38	0.17	0.24	−0.03
1965	0.37	0.16	0.24	−0.03
1966	0.37	0.17	0.23	−0.03
1967	0.37	0.18	0.22	−0.03
1968	0.37	0.17	0.23	−0.03
1969	0.38	0.18	0.23	−0.03
1970	0.38	0.18	0.23	−0.03
1971	0.38	0.18	0.24	−0.03
1972	0.37	0.17	0.23	−0.03
1973	0.34	0.17	0.22	−0.05
1974	0.34	0.17	0.23	−0.05
1975	0.32	0.16	0.21	−0.04
1976	0.32	0.16	0.20	−0.04
1977	0.32	0.16	0.20	−0.03
1978	0.32	0.15	0.19	−0.03

(continued)

Table 5.1 (continued)

	Gini	Gini A	Gini B	L
1979	0.32	0.15	0.18	−0.02
1980	0.33	0.16	0.19	−0.02
1981	0.33	0.15	0.18	0.00
1982	0.33	0.14	0.19	−0.01
1983	0.32	0.14	0.19	−0.01
1984	0.33	0.13	0.21	−0.02
1985	0.32	0.14	0.20	−0.02
1986	0.34	0.14	0.23	−0.03
1987	0.33	0.14	0.24	−0.04
1988	0.34	0.14	0.24	−0.05
1989	0.33	0.13	0.25	−0.05
1990	0.32	0.13	0.24	−0.06
1991	0.32	0.13	0.23	−0.05
1992	0.33	0.13	0.22	−0.02
1993	0.34	0.13	0.21	0.00
1994	0.34	0.13	0.22	−0.01
1995	0.34	0.13	0.23	−0.02
1996	0.34	0.13	0.24	−0.03
1997	0.35	0.12	0.24	−0.01
1998	0.34	0.12	0.25	−0.02
1999	0.33	0.12	0.26	−0.04
2000	0.32	0.12	0.27	−0.06
2001	0.33	0.12	0.28	−0.07
2002	0.31	0.12	0.29	−0.09
2003	0.31	0.11	0.30	−0.10
2004	0.31	0.11	0.30	−0.10
2005	0.32	0.11	0.31	−0.10
2006	0.32	0.11	0.32	−0.11
2007	0.32	0.11	0.32	−0.11
2008	0.32	0.11	0.30	−0.08
2009	0.33	0.11	0.27	−0.05
2010	0.34	0.11	0.27	−0.05
2011	0.34	0.11	0.27	−0.04
2012	0.34	0.11	0.28	−0.04
2013	0.34	0.11	0.28	−0.05
2014	0.35	0.11	0.28	−0.05
2015	0.35	0.11	0.29	−0.06
2016	0.35	0.11	0.30	−0.07
2017	0.34	0.11	0.31	−0.08
2018	0.33	0.11	0.32	−0.09
2019	0.33	0.11	0.31	−0.08
2020	0.32	0.12	0.26	−0.06

Sources: See the text

Note: *Gini A*, within-group inequality; *Gini B*, between-group inequality; *L*, overlapping component

Table 5.2 Poverty headcount, 1850–1975: calibrated and counterfactual

	Calibrated poverty headcount	Counterfactual poverty headcount (Gini 1913)
1850	0.47	0.57
1851	0.46	0.57
1852	0.42	0.55
1853	0.34	0.55
1854	0.35	0.55
1855	0.38	0.53
1856	0.35	0.55
1857	0.35	0.56
1858	0.34	0.56
1859	0.28	0.54
1860	0.27	0.52
1861	0.27	0.52
1862	0.27	0.52
1863	0.26	0.52
1864	0.26	0.52
1865	0.29	0.54
1866	0.29	0.52
1867	0.32	0.52
1868	0.40	0.58
1869	0.37	0.57
1870	0.35	0.56
1871	0.34	0.53
1872	0.30	0.46
1873	0.21	0.43
1874	0.33	0.47
1875	0.21	0.46
1876	0.19	0.44
1877	0.18	0.40
1878	0.24	0.42
1879	0.26	0.45
1880	0.22	0.41
1881	0.23	0.41
1882	0.28	0.41
1883	0.31	0.41
1884	0.28	0.41
1885	0.30	0.43
1886	0.33	0.44
1887	0.27	0.45
1888	0.30	0.43
1889	0.27	0.43
1890	0.26	0.43
1891	0.28	0.42
1892	0.23	0.39

(continued)

Table 5.2 (continued)

	Calibrated poverty headcount	Counterfactual poverty headcount (Gini 1913)
1893	0.30	0.41
1894	0.26	0.40
1895	0.23	0.41
1896	0.23	0.46
1897	0.26	0.43
1898	0.26	0.40
1899	0.26	0.40
1900	0.27	0.40
1901	0.28	0.37
1902	0.26	0.39
1903	0.28	0.39
1904	0.37	0.40
1905	0.34	0.41
1906	0.31	0.38
1907	0.31	0.37
1908	0.28	0.36
1909	0.23	0.35
1910	0.24	0.37
1911	0.31	0.35
1912	0.29	0.36
1913	0.34	0.34
1914	0.32	0.36
1915	0.29	0.36
1916	0.35	0.34
1917	0.34	0.35
1918	0.33	0.35
1919	0.25	0.35
1920	0.27	0.32
1921	0.22	0.31
1922	0.18	0.30
1923	0.18	0.30
1924	0.22	0.29
1925	0.24	0.27
1926	0.23	0.28
1927	0.22	0.25
1928	0.20	0.26
1929	0.20	0.24
1930	0.21	0.26
1931	0.18	0.27
1932	0.14	0.27
1933	0.10	0.28
1934	0.13	0.27
1935	0.12	0.27

(continued)

Table 5.2 (continued)

	Calibrated poverty headcount	Counterfactual poverty headcount (Gini 1913)
1936	0.19	0.38
1937	0.23	0.41
1938	0.24	0.41
1939	0.21	0.38
1940	0.18	0.34
1941	0.17	0.33
1942	0.22	0.31
1943	0.20	0.29
1944	0.22	0.28
1945	0.16	0.32
1946	0.14	0.30
1947	0.10	0.30
1948	0.11	0.30
1949	0.12	0.31
1950	0.11	0.31
1951	0.17	0.27
1952	0.16	0.25
1953	0.18	0.25
1954	0.10	0.23
1955	0.09	0.22
1956	0.07	0.20
1957	0.06	0.19
1958	0.04	0.17
1959	0.04	0.18
1960	0.05	0.18
1961	0.04	0.16
1962	0.03	0.14
1963	0.03	0.12
1964	0.02	0.11
1965	0.02	0.10
1966	0.01	0.09
1967	0.01	0.08
1968	0.01	0.08
1969	0.01	0.07
1970	0.01	0.06
1971	0.01	0.06
1972	0.00	0.05
1973	0.00	0.04
1974	0.00	0.04
1975	0.00	0.03

Sources: See text

Note: Calibrated and counterfactual* poverty headcount (Poverty Line 1990 G-K $2.10 day/person). *Assuming a fixed 1913 Gini

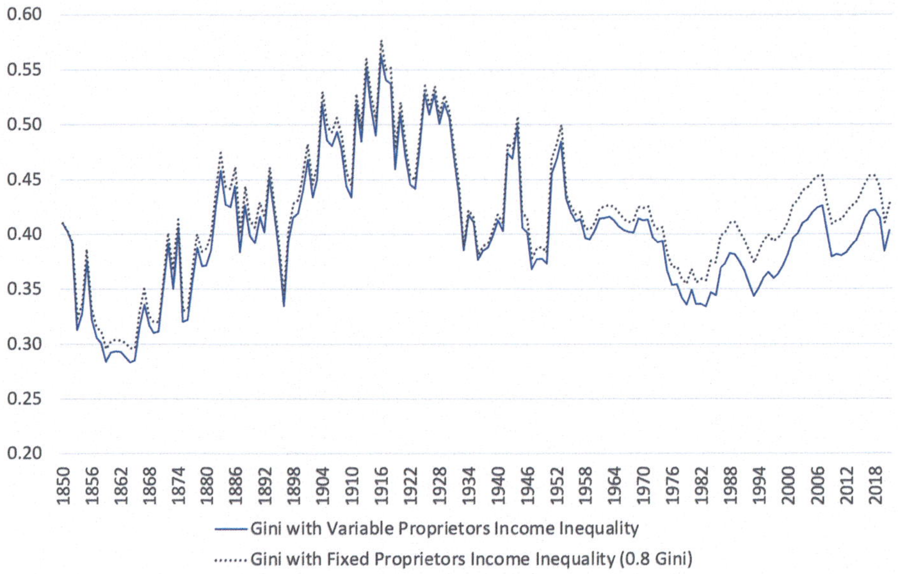

Fig. 5.12 Unadjusted Gini with fixed and variable proprietors income inequality

References

Alcaide Inchausti, J. (1999), "Distribución sectorial, factorial y personal de la renta", in J.L. García Delgado (ed.), *España, Economía: Ante el siglo XXI*. Madrid: Espasa, pp. 457-481.

Allen, R.C. (2009), "Engels' Pause: Technical Change, Capital Accumulation, and Inequality in the British Industrial Revolution", *Explorations in Economic History* 46: 418–435.

Alvaredo, F. and E. Saez (2009), "Income and Wealth Concentration in Spain from a Historical and Fiscal Perspective", *Journal of the European Economic Association* 7(5): 1140-1167.

Alvaredo, F., A.B. Atkinson, T. Piketty, and E. Saez (2013), "The Top 1 Percent in International and Historical Perspective", *Journal of Economic Perspectives* 27(3): 3-20.

Alvaredo, F. and M. Artola Blanco (2016), Wealth Concentration in Spain in the European Context, 1900-2010 Local versus Global Forces, Unpublished ms.

Anuario Estadístico de Barcelona (1905). Barcelona: Ayuntamiento de Barcelona.

Anuario Estadístico de España, (various issues).

Atkinson, A.B. and T. Piketty (2007), *Top Incomes over the Twentieth Century*. Oxford: Oxford University Press.

Atkinson, A. B., T. Piketty, and E. Saez (2011), "Top Incomes in the Long Run of History", *Journal of Economic Literature* 49(1): 3-71.

Bairoch, P. (1965), "Niveaux de développement économique de 1810 à 1910", *Annales ESC* 20: 1091–1117.

Barciela, C. (2002), "Guerra Civil y primer franquismo", i F.n Comín, E. Llopis, and M. Hernández (eds). *Historia Económica de España. Siglos X-XX*. Barcelona: Crítica, pp. 331-367.

Brenner, Y. S., H. Kaelble, and M. Thomas (eds.) (1991), *Income Distribution in Historical Perspective*, Cambridge: Cambridge University Press

Boix, C. (2004), Spain: Development, Democracy and Equity, IBRD World Development Report 2006 Background Paper.

Bourguignon, F. (2002), The Growth Elasticity of Poverty Reduction: Explaining Heterogeneity Across Countries and Time Periods, Delta Working Papers 2002-03.

Bourguignon, F. and C. Morrisson (2002), "Inequality among World Citizens: 1820-1992", *American Economic Review* 92(4): 727-744.

Bringas Gutiérrez, M.A (2000), *La productividad de los factores en la agricultura española (1752-1935)*, Madrid: Banco de España Estudios de Historia Económica 39.

Cabrera, M. and F. del Rey Reguillo (2002), *El poder de los empresarios. Política y economía en la España contemporánea (1875-2000)*, Madrid: Taurus.

Calvo-González, O. (2007), "American Military Interests and Economic Confidence in Spain under Franco Dictatorship", *Journal of Economic History* 67: 740-767.

Camps, E. (1995), *La formación del mercado de trabajo industrial en la Cataluña del siglo XIX*, Madrid: Ministerio de Trabajo y Seguridad Social.

Carré, J.J., P. Dubois, and E. Malinvaud (1976), *French Economic Growth*, Stanford, CA: Stanford University Press.

Cerdá, I. (1867), *Teoría General de la Urbanización y aplicación de sus principios y doctrinas a la reforma y ensanche de Barcelona*. Barcelona: Imprenta Española.

Chastagnaret, G. (2000). *L'Espagne, puissance minière dans l'Europe du XIXe siècle*. Madrid: Casa de Velásquez.

Clark, C. (1957), *The Conditions of Economic Progress*, 3rd ed. London: Macmillan.

Comín, F. (1996), *Historia de la Hacienda pública*, II *España (1808-1995)*, Barcelona: Crítica.

Comín, F. (2002), "El periodo de entreguerras (1919-1935)", in F. Comín, E. Llopis, and M. Hernández (eds.), *Historia Económica de España. Siglos X-XX*, Barcelona: Crítica, pp. 285-329.

Comín, F. (2006), Reaching a Political Consensus for Tax Reform in Spain: The Moncloa Pacts, Joining the European Union and the Best of the Journey, Georgia State University, Andrew Young School of Policy Studies, International Studies Program Working Paper 06-01.

Comín, F. (2007), "The Spanish Savings Banks And The Competitive Cooperation Model (1928-2002)", *Revista de Historia Económica / Journal of Iberian and Latin American Economic History* 25(2): 199-229.

Conference Board (2022),Total Economy Database A Detailed Guide to its Sources and Methods https://www.conference-board.org/retrievefile.cfm?filename=TED_SMDetailed_apr2022.pdf&type=subsite

Deininger, K., Squire, L. (1996, updated), "A New Data Set Measuring Income Inequality", *World Bank Economic Review* 10: 565-591.

Deininger, K., Squire, L. (1998). New ways of looking at old issues: inequality and growth. *Journal of Development Economics* 57, pp. 257-85.

Diez-Minguela, A., J. Martínez-Galarraga, D.A. Tirado (2018), *Regional Inequality in Spain 1860-2015*, London: Palgrave Macmillan.

Domènech, J. (2007), "Working Hours in the European Periphery. The Length of the Working Day in Spain, 1880-1920", *Explorations in Economic History* 44: 469-486.

Dumke, R. (1988), "Income Inequality and Industrialization In Germany, 1850-1913: Images, Trends and Causes of Historical Inequality", *Research in Economic History* 11: 1-47.

Dumke, R. (1991), "Income Inequality and Industrialization in Germany, 1850-1913: the Kuznets Hypothesis Re-visited", in Y.S. Brenner, H. Kaelble, and M. Thomas, (eds.), *Income Distribution in Historical Perspective*, Cambridge: Cambridge University Press, pp. 117-148.

Erdozáin Azpilicueta, P. y F. Mikelarena Peña (1999), "Las cifras de activos agrarios de los censos de población española del período 1877-1991. Un análisis crático", *Boletín de la Asociación de Demografía Histórica* XVII (1): 89-113.

Escudero, A. (1998), *Minería e industrialización de Vizcaya*, Barcelona: Crítica.

Espuelas, S. (2012), "Are Dictatorships Less Redistributive? A Comparative Analysis of Social Spending in Europe, 1950-1980", *European Review of Economic History* 16: 211-232.

Espuelas, S. (2022), "Trade Globalization and Social Spending in Spain, 1850–2000", *European Review of Economic History* 26: 555–578.

Flora, P. (1983)., *State, Economy and Society in Western Europe, 1815-1975*, Frankfurt: Campus. 2 vols.

Fuente, A. de la (2002), "On the Sources of Convergence: A Close Look at Spanish Regions", *European Economic Review* 46: 569-599.
Fundación BBV (1999), *Renta nacional de España y su distribución provincial: serie homogénea años 1955 a 1993 y avances 1994 a 1998*, Bilbao: Fundación BBV.
García Perea, P. y R. Gómez (1994), Elaboración de series históricas de empleo a partir de la encuesta de población activa (1964–1992), Banco de España, Servicio de Estudios, Documento de Trabajo 9409.
García Sanz, A. (1979/80), "Jornales agrícolas y presupuesto familiar campesino en España a mediados del siglo XIX", *Anales del CUNEF* 49–71.
Goerlich, F.J. and M. Mas (2001), "Inequality in Spain 1973-91: Contribution to a Regional Database", *Review of Income and Wealth* 47: 361-378.
Goerlich, F.J. and M. Mas (2004), "Distribución personal de la renta en España. 1973-2001", *Papeles de Economía Española* 100: 50-58.
Gómez Mendoza, A. (1982), *Ferrocarriles y cambio económico en España*, 1855-1913, Madrid: Alianza.
Gómez Mendoza, A. y G. Luna (1986), "El desarrollo urbano en España, 1860-1930", *Boletín de la Asociación de Demografía Histórica* IV(2): 3-22.
Gottschalk, P. and T.M. Smeeding (2000), "Empirical Evidence On Income Inequality In Industrialized Countries", in A.B. Atkinson and F. Bourguignon (eds.), *Handbook of Income Distribution*, Amsterdam: Elsevier, I, pp. 261-307.
Hoffmann, W.G., F. Grumbach, and H. Hesse (1965). *Das Wachstum der Deutschen Wirtschaft seit der Mitte des 19. Jahrunderts*, Berlin: Springer.
Instituto de Estudios Fiscales (1969), *La Contabilidad Nacional de España. Años 1954 a 1964*, Madrid: Ministerio de Hacienda.
Instituto de Reformas Sociales (various issues), *Memorias Generales de la Inspección de Trabajo*, Madrid: Instituto de Reformas Sociales.
Kakwani, N. and E. Pernia (2000), "What Is Pro-poor Growth?", *Asian Development Review* 18: 1–16.
Katz, L. and D. Autor (1999), "Changes in the Wage Structure and Earnings Inequality", in O.C. Ashenfelter and D. Card (eds.), *Handbook of Labor Economics*, vol. 3A. Amsterdam: Elsevier, pp. 1463-1555.
Klasen, S. (2004), "In Search of the Holy Grail: How to Achieve Pro-Poor Growth?", in B. Tungodden, N. Stern, and I. Kolstad (eds.), *Toward Pro-Poor Policies. Aid, Institutions, Globalization*, New York: Oxford University Press, pp. 63-93.
Kraay, A. (2006), "When Is Growth Pro-Poor? Evidence from a Panel of Countries", *Journal of Development Economics* 80: 198-227.
Kuznets, S. (1953), *Shares of Upper Income Groups in Income and Savings*. New York: N.B.E.R.
Kuznets, S. (1955), "Economic Growth and Income Inequality", *American Economic Review* 45(1): 1-28.
Kuznets, S. (1966), *Modern Economic Growth: Rate, Structure, and Spread*. New Haven: Yale University Press.
Lindert, P.H. (2000), "Three Centuries of Inequality in Britain and America", in A.B. Atkinson and F. Bourguignon (eds.), *Handbook of Income Distribution*, Amsterdam: Elsevier, I, pp. 167-216.
Lopez, J. H. (2004), Pro-Poor-Pro-Growth: Is there a Trade Off?, World Bank Policy Research Working Paper 3378.
López, J.H. and L. Servén (2006), A Normal Relationship? Poverty, Growth, and Inequality, World Bank Policy Research Working Paper 3814.
Llonch, M. (2004), "Jornada, salarios y costes laborales en el sector textil catalán", *Revista de Historia Industrial* 26: 101-140.
Martin, B. (1990), *The Agony of Modernization. Labor and Industrialization in Spain*, Ithaca, N.Y.: ILR Press.

Martín-Aceña, P. And M.A. Pons (2005), "Sistema monetario y financiero", in A. Carreras and X. Tafunell (eds.), *Estadísticas históricas de España*, Madrid: Fundación BBVA, II, pp. 647-706.

Martínez-Galarraga, J., J.R. Rosés, D.A. Tirado (2015), "The Long-Term Patterns of Regional Income Inequality in Spain, 1860–2000", *Regional Studies* 49(4) 502-517.

Matthews, R.C.O., C.H. Feinstein, and J.C. Odling-Smee (1982), *British Economic Growth 1856-1973*, Oxford: Clarendon Press.

Milanovic, B. (2005). *Worlds Apart. Measuring International and Global Inequality*. Princeton: Princeton University Press.

Ministerio de Trabajo (1931), *Estadística de salarios y jornadas de trabajo: 1914-1930. Resultados globales en toda la Nación,* Madrid: Ministerio de Trabajo.

Morrisson, C. (2000), "Historical Perspectives on Income Distribution: The Case of Europe", in A.B. Atkinson and F. Bourguignon (eds.), *Handbook of Income Distribution*, Amsterdam: Elsevier, I, pp. 217-260.

Morrisson, C. and W. Snyder (2000), "The Income Inequality of France in Historical Perspective", *European Review of Economic History* 4: 59-83.

Nicolau, R. (2005), "Población, salud y actividad", en A. Carreras y X. Tafunell, eds.,*Estadísticas Históricas de España. Siglos XIX-XX*, Bilbao: Fundación BBVA, 3 vols., I, eds., 77–154.

Núñez, C.E. (2005), "Educación", in A. Carreras and X. Tafunell (eds.), *Estadísticas históricas de España*, Madrid: Fundación BBVA, I, pp. 155-244.

Pan-Montojo, J. (ed.) (2007), *Los inspectores de Hacienda en España: una mirada histórica*, Madrid: Centro de Estudios Financieros-APIFE.

Payne, S.G. (1993), *Spain's First Democracy. The Second Republic, 1931-1936*. Maddison: University of Wisconsin Press.

Pérez Castroviejo, P.M. (1992), *Clase obrera y niveles de vida en las primeras fases de la industrialización vizcaina,* Madrid: Ministerio de Trabajo y Seguridad Social.

Pérez Ledesma, M. (1990), *Estabilidad y conflicto social. España, de los iberos al 14-D*. Madrid: Nerea.

Pérez Moreda, V. (1999), "Población y economía en la España de los siglos XIX y XX", en G. Anes, ed.,*Historia Económica de España. Siglos XIX y XX*. Barcelona: Galaxia Gutemberg/ Círculo de Lectores, pp. 7-62.

Pigou, A.C. (1920), *The Economics of Welfare*, London: Macmillan.

Piketty, T. (2003), "Income Inequality in France, 1901-1998", *Journal of Political Economy* 111(5): 1004-1042.

Prados De La Escosura, L. (2007), "Inequality and Poverty in Latin America: a Long-run Exploration", in T.J. Hatton, K.H. O'Rourke, and A.M. Taylor (eds.), *New Comparative Economic History*. Cambridge, M.A.: M.I.T. Press, pp. 291-315.

Prados de la Escosura, L. (2017), *Spanish Economic Growth, 1850-2015*, London: Palgrave Macmillan. https://www.palgrave.com/la/book/9783319580418

Ravallion, M. (1997), "Can High Inequality Development Countries Escape Absolute Poverty?", *Economics Letters* 56: 51-57.

Ravallion, M. and S. Chen (2003), "Measuring Pro-poor Growth". *Economics Letters* 78: 93–99.

Ravallion, M. (2004), Pro-poor Growth: A Primer. World Bank Policy Research Working Paper no. 3242.

Reher, D.S. and E. Ballesteros (1993), "Precios y salarios en Castilla la Nueva: la construcción de un índice de salarios reales, 1509-1991", *Revista de Historia Económica* 11(1): 101-151.

Ricardo, D. (1817), *Principles of Political Economy and Taxation*, London: John Murray

Rodrik, D. (1997), Trade, Social Insurance, and the Limits to Globalization, NBER Working Paper 5905.

Rossi, N., G. Toniolo, and G. Vecchi (2001), "Is the Kuznets Curve Still Alive? Evidence from Italian Household Budgets, 1881-1961", *Journal of Economic History* 61(4): 904-925.

Rosés, J.R. and B. Sánchez-Alonso (2004), "Regional Wage Convergence in Spain, 1850-1930", *Explorations in Economic History* 41: 404-425.

Sánchez-Alonso, B. (2000), "European Emigration In The Late Nineteenth Century: The Paradoxical Case of Spain", *Economic History Review* 53: 309-330.

Sánchez-Alonso, B. (2007), "The Other Europeans: Immigration into Latin America and the International Labour Market, 1870-1930", *Revista de Historia Económica/ Journal of Iberian and Latin American Economic History* 25(3): 395-426.

Silvestre, J. (2005), "Internal Migrations in Spain, 1877-1930", *European Review of Economic History* 9: 233-265.

Simpson, J. (1992), "Technical Change, Labor Absorption, and Living Standards in Andalucia 1886–1936", *Agricultural History* 66 (3): 1–24.

Simpson, J. y J. Carmona (2020), *Why Democracy Failed. The Agrarian Origins of the Spanish Civil War*, Cambridge: Cambridge University Press

Soler Becerro, R. (1997), "La evolución del salario en una empresa textil algodonera. La fábrica de La Rambla de Vilanova i la Geltrú (1891-1925)", *Revista de Historia Económica* 15(2): 399-411.

Soto Carmona, A. (1989), *El trabajo industrial en la España contemporánea: (1874-1936)*, Barcelona: Anthropos.

Stolper, W. and P. Samuelson (1941), "Protection and Real Wages", *Review of Economic Studies* 9: 58-73.

Székely, M. (2001), The 1990s in Latin America: Another Decade of Persistent Inequality, But with Somewhat Lower Poverty, Inter-American Development Bank Working Paper Series 454.

Tafunell, X. (2005), "Construcción y vivienda", in A. Carreras and X. Tafunell (eds.), *Estadísticas históricas de España*, Madrid: Fundación BBVA, I, pp. 455-499.

Torregrosa Hetland, S. (2015), "Did Democracy Bring Redistribution? Insights from the Spanish Tax System, 1960-90", *European Review of Economic History* 19 (3): 294-315.

U.S. Department Of Labor (1900), *Fifteenth Annual Report of the Commissioner of Labor: Wages in Commercial Countries*, Washington DC: GPO.

Vandellós (1925), "La richesse et le revenu de la Péninsule Ibérique", *Metron* V(4): 151-186.

Vilar, M. (2004), "La ruptura posbélica a través del comportamiento de los salarios industriales: nueva evidencia cuantitativa (1908-1963)", *Revista de Historia Industrial* 45: 81-126.

WIDER (2022), *World Income Database*, Helsinki: UNO/WIDER/UNDP. https://www.wider.unu.edu/database/world-income-inequality-database-wiid

Williamson, J.G. (1982), "The Structure of Pay in Britain, 1710-1911", *Research in Economic History* 7: 1-54.

Williamson, J.G. (1985), *Did British Capitalism Breed Inequality?*, London: Allen and Unwin.

Williamson, J.G. (1997), "Globalization and Inequality, Past and Present" *World Bank Research Observer* 12(2): 117–135.

Williamson, J.G. (2002), "Land, Labor, and Globalization in the Third World, 1870–1940", *Journal of Economic History* 62(1): 55-85.

Williamson, J.G. and P.H. Lindert (1980), *American Inequality. A Macroeconomic History.* New York: Academic Press.

Part II
Spain in the Global Economy

Chapter 6
The Loss of the American Empire

6.1 Introduction

The repercussions on the Spanish economy and society of the emancipation of the colonies on the American continent are a common reference for historians seeking to explain Spain's backwardness in the European context during the nineteenth century, as well as for those addressing the political and institutional transition from the Ancien Régime to liberal society. Historians agree that the political and economic rupture between Spain and its American possessions was an influential element in Spain's path towards modernisation. The wars with France and Great Britain, the Napoleonic invasion of the Peninsula, and the loss of most of the empire, are events that coincided in time and, consequently, it is extremely difficult to disentangle the impact that each of them had on Spanish society. However, in the context of Western Europe, the transition to the liberal regime appears longer and more costly in Spain than in other societies. Thus, in the early nineteenth century, historians have detected a discontinuity in the expansionary process that had begun in the final decades of the eighteenth century (Tedde de Lorca, 1988). The available evidence tends to support this view and suggests that, while at the end of the eighteenth century living standards were behind, but at a moderate distance from, countries such as France and even Great Britain, by the mid-nineteenth century the Spanish position had deteriorated sharply (Chap. 2, Fig. 2.14).

Attempts to explain Spain's inability to develop along the lines of north-western European nations usually distinguish between endogenous and exogenous causal factors (Prados de la Escosura, 1988; Tortella, 1994). Most historians, however, have emphasised the role of external forces in Spain's backwardness (Nadal, 1975).

An earlier version appeared as L. Prados de la Escosura (1993), "La pérdida del imperio y sus consecuencias económicas", in L. Prados de la Escosura and S. Amaral, eds., *La independencia americana: consecuencias económicas*, Madrid: Alianza, pp. 253–300. A full revision of the estimates and the main text has been carried out.

L. Prados de la Escosura, *A Millennial View of Spain's Development*, Frontiers in Economic History, https://doi.org/10.1007/978-3-031-60792-9_6

The loss of empire as a result of the Napoleonic Wars and the subsequent reorientation towards Europe, as well as the gradual integration into the Western European economy, have been judged detrimental to Spanish economic development. The emancipation of the colonies constituted a serious setback for Spanish economic modernisation, and those regions closely linked to colonial trade saw their modern development frustrated.[1] For decades, this line of argument has been reiterated by historians who, nonetheless, have failed to provide conclusive evidence in support of their interpretation.[2]

This chapter pursues this objective by providing new quantitative evidence on the annual evolution of the foreign sector between 1778 and 1820, and incorporating series of Treasury revenues (Merino, 1987). These data allow us to qualify previous results but do not by any means settle the debate. The effects of colonial emancipation on the accumulation and allocation of resources need to be investigated in detail, at both sectoral and regional level. Furthermore, the loss of the colonies needs to be placed in the context of the slow and complex emergence of liberal society, which defined new property rights and institutions.

Among the main findings, the following can be highlighted. The loss of the mainland colonies in the Americas impacted negatively upon the metropolis, especially in the short run, with a contraction of international trade, domestic investment and the Monarchy's revenues. However, the aggregate effects on the economy were narrower and less deep than conventionally assumed by historians and may have contributed to the demise of the Ancien Régime that paved the way to the liberal society.

Several sections comprise the chapter. Sections 6.2 and 6.3 draw on new quantitative evidence to assess the effects of the loss of empire on public finances and the foreign sector, respectively. Section 6.4 offers an attempt to establish the direct impact of American independence on the Spanish economy by contrasting it with population and economic activity. Section 6.5 outlines some hypotheses regarding the indirect effects of colonial emancipation on the allocation of resources. Finally, by way of conclusion, some reflections on the regional and sectoral impact of American independence are offered.

---

[1] Cf. Vicens Vives, 1959: 13, 555; Parry, 1966: 361; Crouzet, 1964: 574; Broder et al., 1985: 86; Berend and Ranki, 1982: 154; Milward and Saul, 1977: 220–221; Pollard, 1982: 244; Fontana, 1970, 1991.

[2] An important exception is the research carried out by Cuenca Esteban (1981b, 1982, 1984, 1987, 1989, 1991). Cuenca (1981b: 414) hazards the conjecture that if Spain had not been affected simultaneously by the French invasion and the colonial rebellion, the erosion of its commercial monopoly would have been less and more gradual.

6.2 The Impact of Independence on the Treasury

Historians' revisionist work on economic policies during the second half of the eighteenth century has cast doubt on the 'developmentalist' intentions of Charles III's governments.[3] The argument put forward is that financial policy was guided by the criteria of sustaining the absolute monarchy, which entailed strengthening military power, with unbalancing consequences for the budget, leading to progressive indebtedness. The origin of the resources of the Old Regime Treasury aggravated the situation: faced with the inflexibility of ordinary revenues from internal sources, the State's external revenues constituted a solid support that could be increased, while at the same time allowing the tax burden on peninsular subjects to be reduced (Barbier and Klein, 1981; Fontana, 1991). The role of tax revenues of colonial origin—customs revenue, in part, and the so-called remittances from the Indies—became particularly important (Cuenca Esteban, 1981a; Merino, 1987). The Ancien Régime thus depended on this fiscal system, at the risk of endangering its institutional stability. Therefore, supporters of this interpretation argue that a priority objective of state expenditure was the maintenance of the colonial status quo, which entailed a considerable defensive effort with its consequent repercussions on the expenditure composition (Barbier, 1980, 1984; Barbier and Klein, 1985). A dissenting opinion is held by Tedde de Lorca (1987a, 1990), who distinguishes between the financial situation of the reign of Charles III and the early years of Charles IV, in which a balanced budget prevailed and economic policy favoured economic progress in a framework of openness to the international economy, and that which corresponds to the late eighteenth century, when the monarchy, faced with the distressing situation of the Treasury due to the wars, would have had to resort to the issue of royal vouchers (*vales reales*) and the confiscation of ecclesiastical property in order to finance growing defence expenditure. Tedde de Lorca (1990) also points out that the Spanish fiscal structure was not antagonistic to that of successful economic countries such as Great Britain (see also García-Cuenca, 1991). Thus, it is of great interest to contrast the composition of revenues and expenditures in both countries. The available evidence corroborates this hypothesis and suggests that, contrary to the revisionist interpretation, there is a certain similarity between the two treasuries: the structure of public expenditure in wartime (1776–1783) shows that, in both Spain and Britain, defence accounted for just over 60% of expenditure, while debt servicing amounted to 30% in the British case and barely half of this percentage in the Spanish case (O'Brien, 1988; Tedde de Lorca,

[3] A clear exposition is given in Fontana (1991: 310), who points out the overvaluation of the empire by the Enlightenment rulers, which resulted in 'a large part of the resources of the State being allocated to its conservation, renouncing to invest them for the benefit of Spanish economic growth'.

1990).[4] In peacetime (1784–1792), however, the discrepancies were more marked: while in the British case, defence expenditure did not reach a third of the total, in Spain it remained close to wartime levels.[5] This feature of the Spanish expenditure structure would, however, tend to support Barbier and Klein's interpretation, although the lower weight of debt interest would have allowed Spain more room for manoeuvre in civil administration expenditure. The similarity between the spending structure of the Spanish and British states highlights the mercantilist conception that presided over the economic decisions of both monarchies and allows us to reconcile the developmentalist aspects with a strategy (inevitable in the international context) of military and political power: military spending could be considered as a prerequisite for economic progress (O'Brien, 1991). Foreign markets, essential for the achievement of economic progress, had to be conquered at the expense of enemy powers, and their protection required a heavy investment in naval power. Thus, the increasing military expenditure was intended to guarantee the exclusive right to trade with the Indies. At the same time, foreign trade provided the monarchy with a flexible source of taxation to sustain the empire.[6]

If, alternatively, revenues are considered, we detect the not inconsiderable role of those coming from abroad in Spain and Great Britain, whose structure, once again, was not so different. The idea of economic progress in a context of financial stability and high public spending, as shown by Tedde Lorca for the reign of Charles III, is fully consistent with the mercantilist context outlined. Therefore, the wars against England and, later, France, must have constituted an external shock on the basis of the information on the Spanish financial structure, a shock that did not seem to have been anticipated by the economic agents but which, nevertheless, would unbalance this structure due to the sharp fall in colonial revenues.

With the interruption of economic relations with the colonies, the absolutist state saw its revenues seriously affected (Fig. 6.1). Thus, while total revenue rose slightly (by 9% between 1794/1796 and 1815/1820), external revenue, which represented just over a quarter on the eve of the Napoleonic Wars, fell to a third of its volume (i.e. at a cumulative annual rate of −4% at constant prices) and, after the war, accounted for less than 10% of total revenue. Part of the decline can be attributed to the disappearance of the so-called *Remesas de Indias*, the silver surplus of the colonial treasuries which, after deducting administrative expenses, were sent to Spain (Canga-Argüelles, 1833–1834: ii; Artola, 1978: 204; Fontana, 1971. 57–67).

---

[4]In wartime, the percentages for defence expenditure, debt interest payments and civil administration expenditure are, respectively, as follows: Britain, 62%, 30%, and 8% (O'Brien, 1988: 2); Spain, 62%, 21% and 17% (Tedde de Lorca, 1990: 143).

[5]In peacetime, the percentages of defence, debt and civil administration expenditure are, in the British case, 31%, 56%, and 13%; in Spain, 57%, 20%, and 23%, respectively.

[6]As Tedde de Lorca (1990: 215) noted, with reference to Spain's participation in the war of emancipation in the Thirteen North American Colonies, 'if liberalising legislation for American trade was expected to lead to increased exports and higher tax revenues ... a prior investment of a military nature was logical in order to clear British threats'.

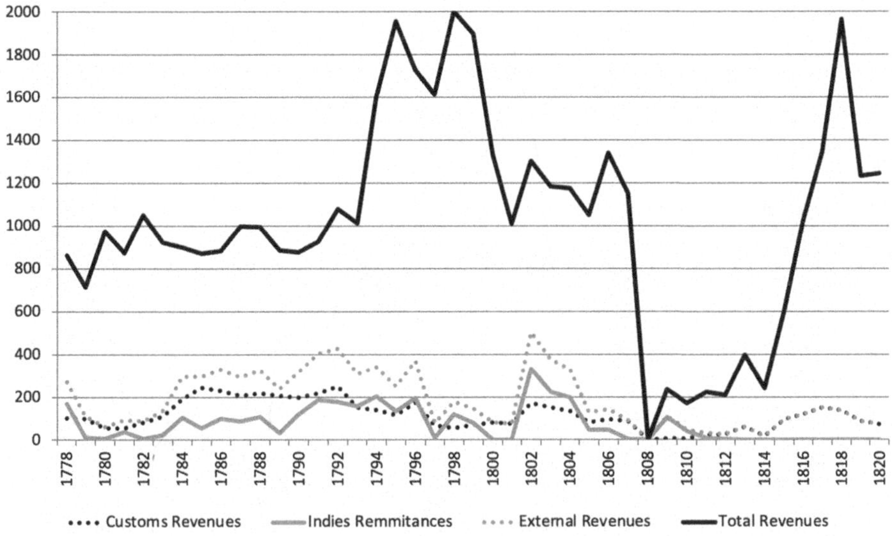

Fig. 6.1 Total revenues and its composition, 1778–1820 (1808 Reales). Sources: Table 6.2

Indies Remittances came to represent 20% of the state's overall revenue in 1791.[7] The rest of the fall in external revenues was due to the contraction of customs revenues to about half their volume (at −2% per annum), and they fell from 17% of total revenues in 1784/1792 to 9% in 1815/1820. Expenditure, on the other hand, increased during the wars and did not return to pre-war levels after the restoration of peace. The relative impact on the Spanish economy can be observed in Fig. 6.2. Comparison with the British case again shows analogies such as customs revenue, which in Britain amounted to between a fifth and a quarter of crown revenues on the eve of the Napoleonic wars, while the differentiating feature was the impossibility for Spain to maintain the same proportion in wartime.[8]

6.3 The Impact of Independence on the External Sector

The contribution of foreign trade, and especially colonial trade, to economic growth during the eighteenth century has been a source of controversy in European historiography. The reason is the opposition between the Ricardian theory of comparative advantage, in which, under conditions of full employment, the role of trade depends on the differential remuneration between productive factors employed in production for the domestic or international market, and the Smithian doctrine, which

[7] Cuenca Esteban (1981a: 194) assigns this maximum to 1792.

[8] In the British case, customs revenue amounted to 22% of total revenue to the Exchequer in 1786–1795 (Beckett and Turner, 1990: 389–391). See also O'Brien (1989).

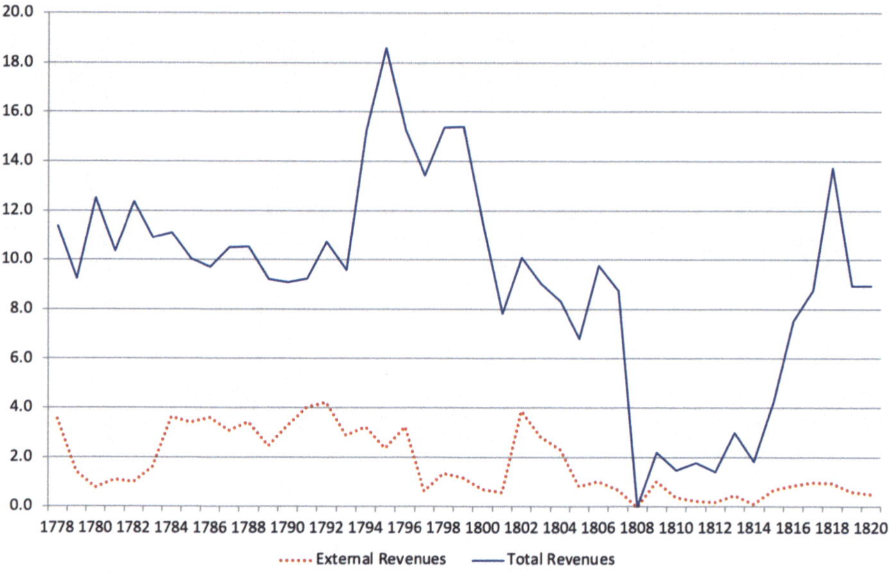

Fig. 6.2 Total and external revenues, 1778–1820 (% GDP) (current prices). Sources: Table 6.3

establishes a long-term relationship between growth and trade in which exports provide a 'vent for surplus' for resources for which there is no demand at home.[9]

In his evaluation of financial and trade policies under Charles III, Tedde de Lorca (1990: 207) formulated a positive interpretation of the role played by foreign trade in the Spanish economy during the late eighteenth century: the boom in trade favoured a productivity increase of the Spanish economy between 1778 and 1790 through an increase in production—thanks to the use of idle or underemployed resources—and a rise in marginal efficiency in some sectors and regions as a consequence of greater specialisation.[10] Fontana's (1991: 305–309) assessment coincides in underlining the importance of colonial trade for the Spanish economy, derived, in part, from contemporaries' perception of the vital nature of the colonies for the metropolis as a reserved market for its manufactures and a means of supplying raw materials and foodstuffs.[11]

In Spain, the historical debate on the role of colonial trade in growth has focused on the controversy surrounding the economic effects of so-called 'Free Trade' between the ports of the metropolis and those of the colonies (and between the

---

[9]Cf. Myint (1977) for a discussion from the perspective of economic thought. For its application to the context of the Industrial Revolution, see O'Brien and Engerman (1991) and Thomas and McCloskey (1981).

[10]For the moderate positive impact of the colonial market on Spanish agriculture, see Anes (1983).

[11]Fontana (1991), however, acknowledged the negative economic effects of the post-Latin American independence attempts at reconquest, which stemmed from the contemporary perception of the colonies as vital to the Spanish economy, as it delayed their adaptation to the new circumstances.

colonies themselves), which became particularly noticeable after the end of the American War of Independence. The 'Free Trade Regulations' were aimed at increasing colonial trade, with the consequent repercussions on customs revenues. The interpretation of the 'free trade' decrees is divided into two positions: those who see an increase in the volume of exports, both of national and foreign products, which was, however, exceeded by the increase in imports of colonial products; and those who see the Bourbon measures as a wasted opportunity to promote the export of domestic products—overestimated, as foreign goods were re-exported under their guise—by giving priority to tax revenue rather than economic development.[12] It is therefore appropriate to examine the level and structure of foreign trade at the end of the eighteenth century and to assess the changes this trade underwent as a result of colonial emancipation.

The lack of complete annual statistics, such as those available for Great Britain, France or the United States, is not an insurmountable obstacle to the study of the effects on the foreign sector of the independence of the colonies on the American continent. The statistical reconstruction of colonial trade, together with the reworking of the American, French and British series for Spain's trade with these countries, permits an attempt to reconstruct an annual series of Spanish foreign trade between 1778 and 1820. Naturally, the use of the new series must be cautious, for while it seems adequate in order to trace the long-term evolution of trade, its reliability is more doubtful for short-term analysis. Appendix describes the sources and procedures used to derive the trade series.

The evolution of total exports of Spanish products shows a decline, in real terms, of almost 25% (i.e. a cumulative annual rate of −1%) between 1784/1796 and 1815/1820, mostly attributable to colonial trade (Fig. 6.3). The moderate decline in demand for Spanish products in Western Europe (less than 10% between 1784/1796 and 1815/1820) reduced the impact on the total volume exported of the sharp contraction in colonial markets—the level in 1815/1820 fell to 40% of that in 1784/1796, at an average annual rate of −3.2%—. The consequence was an appreciable alteration in the geographical composition of trade, which broke a secular balance between exports to Europe and the Indies (64% and 36%, respectively, by 1784/1796) in favour of exports abroad, which came to account for about four-fifths after the end of the Napoleonic Wars (Table 6.1). The new balance would persist throughout the nineteenth century.

The total volume of net imports (i.e. retained for domestic consumption) did not experience any decline, since, as the weight of colonial products was a minority (23% in 1786/1796), the fall in colonial imports destined for the Spanish market after the Napoleonic Wars—up to 53% of the 1784/1796 level—was offset by the rise in imports from the rest of the world (Fig. 6.4). After the Napoleonic wars, the share of products of colonial origin in net imports fell to around 15% in 1815/1820, a

[12] Cf. Martínez Shaw (1974) and Delgado Ribas (1986, 1987), as examples of competing assessments of the effects of free trade. For an assessment of the controversy, see Tedde de Lorca (1990: 199–215).

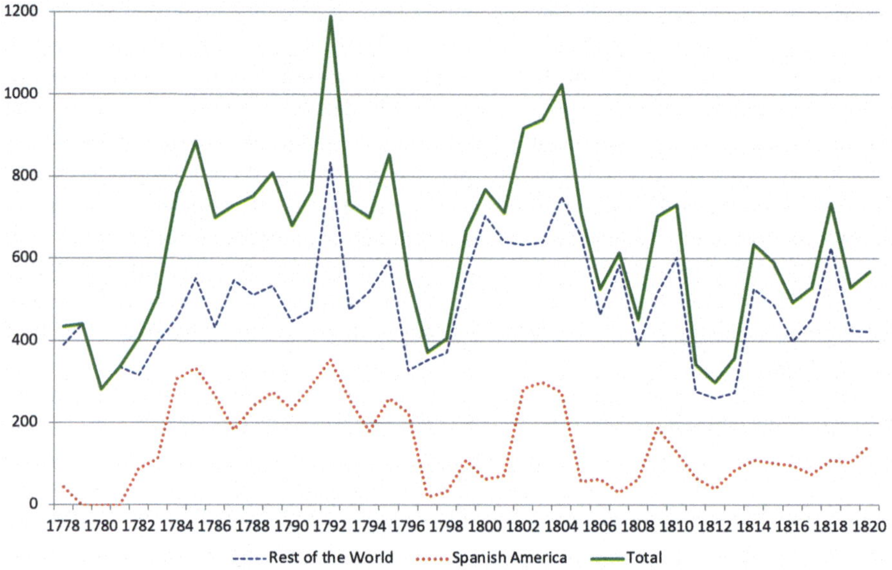

Fig. 6.3 Real exports and its composition, 1778–1820 (1808 Reales). Sources: Table 6.6

Table 6.1 International trade composition, 1792–1827 (%) (1778 prices for 1792 and current prices for 1827)

	Domestic exports			Net imports		
	Foodstuffs	Raw materials	Manufactures	Foodstuffs	Raw materials	Manufactures
Colonies						
1792	31.0	0.1	68.9	93.5	6.5	0.0
1827	71.0	0.1	28.9	85.3	14.7	0.0
Rest of the World						
1792	27.7	67.4	4.9	31.1	12.2	56.7
1827	39.4	50.6	10.0	13.2	13.6	73.2
Total						
1792	29.1	39.9	31.0	43.0	12.4	44.6
1827	44.5	42.5	13.0	26.9	13.8	59.3

Sources: Balanza(s) del comercio, 1792 (1803) and 1827 (1831)

proportion that changed little until the independence of Cuba and Puerto Rico in 1898 (Prados de la Escosura, 1982b: 48).

The decline of Spanish trade with Latin America following independence also involved the collapse of the financial, transport and maritime insurance services that constituted a not inconsiderable part of the profits of the colonial system. Thus, the fall in total re-exports, at an annual rate of −3.4% in real terms, is indicative of the decline in services performed by Spaniards, which, in 1815/1820, accounted for

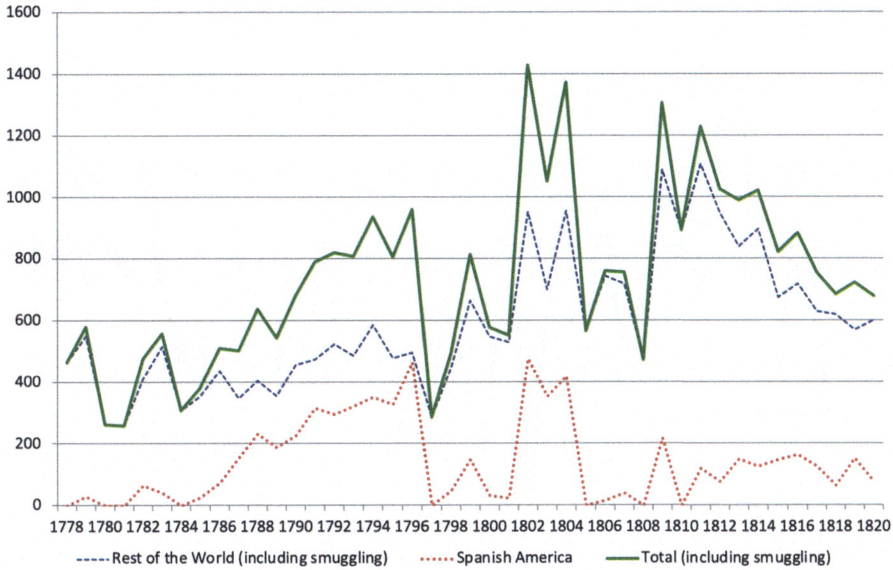

Fig. 6.4 Real imports and its composition, 1778–1820 (1808 Reales). Sources: Table 6.6

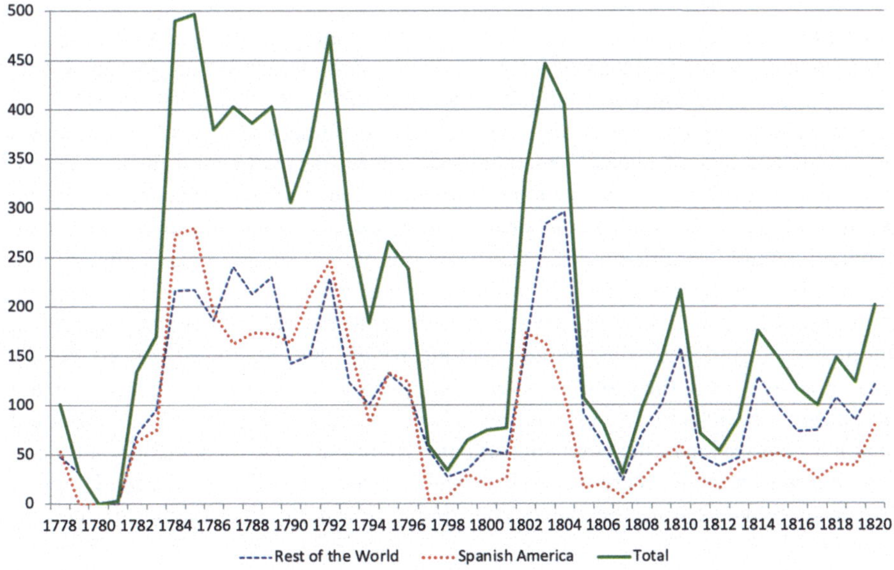

Fig. 6.5 Real re-exports and its composition, 1778–1820 (1808 Reales). Sources: Table 6.6

39% of the level reached in 1784/1796 (Fig. 6.5). The collapse of re-exports of European products to the colonies was even more pronounced, as after the Napoleonic wars they accounted for only 25% of the pre-war level. Moreover, as colonial

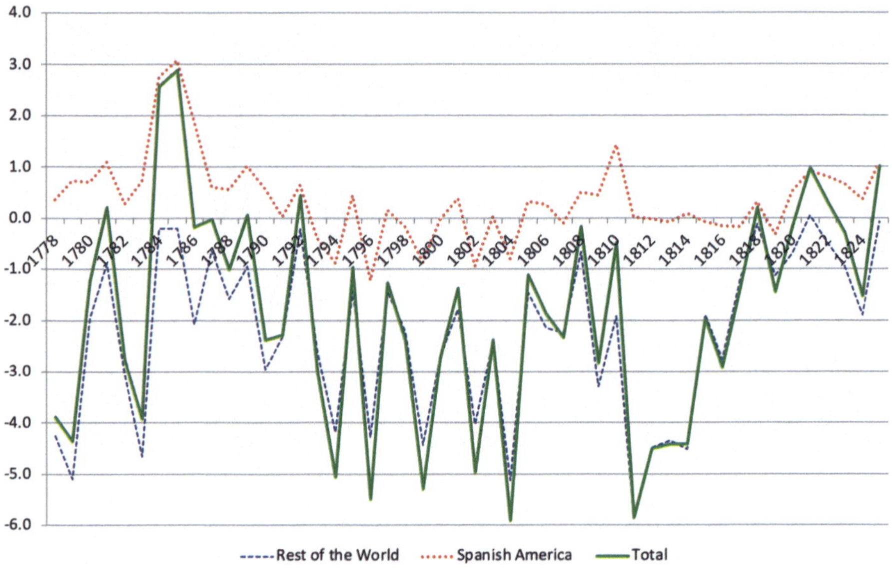

Fig. 6.6 Trade balance and its composition, 1778–1820 (% GDP) (current prices). Sources: Table 6.5

legislation, which excluded traffic on non-Spanish flagged ships, ceased to apply, shipping and maritime insurance services were contracted out to foreign agents offering more advantageous conditions (Ashton, 1955: 134; Izard, 1974: 303).

The balance of trade was also affected by the independence of the colonies (Fig. 6.6). The loss of overseas markets led to a drastic contraction of the colonial merchandise surplus and a consequent deepening of the Spanish trade deficit. Private remittances from the Indies, i.e. private shipments of gold and silver to Spain, provide valuable additional information about the balance of payments of the metropolis with the colonies.[13] In addition to the difference between total imports and exports (i.e. including re-exports of European and colonial products), private shipments of gold and silver would include freight and insurance carried out by Spaniards, as well as the profits derived from the commercialisation of exported and re-exported products in the colonial markets (Cuenca, 1981b: 423–424).[14] After the Napoleonic invasion of the peninsula and the beginning of the emancipation process, private remittances of precious metals probably also included repatriation of capital. Private remittances from the Indies contributed decisively to financing the current

[13]The evidence comes from Fisher (1985: 52) for private shipments of gold and silver arriving in Cadiz and Barcelona (undoubtedly the vast majority thereof) between 1782 and 1796, and from Cuenca (1981b: 410) for precious metals sent by private individuals between 1792 and 1820.

[14]Cuenca (1981b) stresses the wide trade margins charged by Spanish traders on the original prices of imported products, which would reflect the 'monopolistic' profits of Spanish trade. See also Fontana (1991: 312, n. 6).

account deficit of the Spanish balance of payments (generated by trade with foreign countries). Indeed, despite the precariousness of the quantitative information available on Spain's balance of services and unilateral transfers abroad, it is possible to carry out some arithmetic exercises to verify the plausibility of this hypothesis. Thus, for example, in the period 1784/1796, American silver outgoing from Spain to foreign countries, including smuggling, amounted to 321.5 million Reales (Tedde de Lorca, 1990: 210–214).[15] In the same period, private shipments of precious metals from the colonies averaged 355.1 million Reales a year. Thus, both items tended to balance out with a slight surplus for Spain (33.6 million).[16] On the other hand, if one notes that the balance of the Spanish balance of goods in these years was −125.8 million, and compares this figure with the 321.5 million silver sent abroad, one could conjecture that there was also a negative balance in terms of services and unilateral transfers. In the years 1815/1820, private silver remittances amounted to 134.4 million for the period 1815/1820, while the deficit of the Spanish balance of merchandise amounted to 179.4 million, which shows that, after the Napoleonic wars, the mechanism of financing the current account deficits of the Spanish balance of payments that had prevailed in the colonial period was broken, with foreseeable deflationary consequences (Cuenca, 1981b: 424; Fontana, 1970).

The favourable trend in the terms of trade, i.e. the relative prices of exports in terms of imports, prevented a further deterioration in the international position of the Spanish economy (Fig. 6.7). This was because the deterioration in the terms of trade between Spain and the Indies (which fell by 15% between 1784/1796 and 1815/1820) was offset by the improvement with foreign countries (by 61% in these years), resulting in a 20% increase in purchasing power per unit exported.

After emancipation, trade between Spain and the new republics virtually disappeared. The image is somewhat exaggerated, as the Spanish Antilles maintained their role as a distribution centre in Spanish America for goods from the Spanish mainland.[17] However, trade links with the new republics would take a long time to be resumed, unlike the immediate re-establishment of economic relations that took place between Britain and its thirteen former colonies in North America (Shepherd and Walton, 1976). From the outbreak of war with Britain in October 1796, regular contacts were virtually interrupted for two decades. The war conflict was to be compounded by the refusal of successive Spanish governments to accept the sovereignty of the new nations, which included plans for reconquest (Parry, 1966: 362; Cuenca Esteban, 1982: 447–448).

[15] Tedde de Lorca (1990) estimates that smuggling amounts to 60% of legal outlets.

[16] A similar exercise can be carried out for the period 1782–1807, during which private shipments of precious metals amounted to an annual average of 250 million Reales, while silver outflows (assuming 60% smuggling) represented 189 million annually. In these years, the Spanish merchandise balance deficit averaged 223 million Reales a year.

[17] Moreau de Jonnés (1835: 254) estimates that 11% of Cuban imports from Spain were re-exported by 1829–1830, and that re-exports constituted 10% of Cuba's total exports.

Fig. 6.7 Terms of trade, 1778–1820 (1808=100). Sources: Table 6.7

6.4 The Direct Impact on the Economy

So far, we have examined the repercussions on those sectors most immediately and directly affected by the emancipation of the colonies. It would be of interest to find out what the impact was on the level of economic activity and the material well-being of the Spanish population.

The decline in economic activity in Spain as a result of the independence of the American colonies could be calculated as the decline in trade with the Indies, weighted by the relative importance of colonial trade in the economy. Thus, the decline in the volume of Spanish exports between 1784/1796 and 1815/1820, multiplied by the ratio of exports to gross domestic product in 1784/1796, would give a measure of the direct impact of the loss of empire. However, the contribution of a given sector to the growth of the economy is measured by the difference its contribution makes at the margin (O'Brien, 1982: 17). In this case, the importance of colonial trade for the Spanish economy should be measured as the difference between the remuneration received for the factors of production embodied in the exported goods and services, and the hypothetical remuneration that would be derived if the same resources had been allocated to other productive activities.[18] Consequently, only when there was no alternative use for the factors devoted to the production of exportables, i.e. when exports allowed for the employment of

[18] For a discussion of the Ricardian and Smithian positions in the British case, see O'Brien and Engerman (1991: 199–206).

resources that would otherwise remain idle, could it be deduced that the loss to the economy would be equal to the amount of the fall suffered by colonial trade (Myint, 1958, 1977).

In Spain at the end of the Ancien Régime, the opportunity cost of allocating factors of production to the foreign sector must have been low, especially in the case of labour, which was probably underemployed.[19] In the short term, the transfer of productive resources to the rest of the economy from the sectors that produced for the colonial markets would be slow and painful, and not without political costs for the Ancien Régime, while the remuneration per unit of factors of production (capital, labour, natural resources) would decrease. The alternative assumption would imply accepting that, without colonial trade, full employment and productivity levels would have been maintained. It is difficult to accept, however, that the investment opportunities and incentives for technical and organisational innovation generated by colonial trade in the eighteenth century would have remained unchanged in its absence (Myint, 1977; O'Brien and Engerman, 1991).[20] Consequently, without colonial trade, national income would predictably be lower. In the long run, however, there would tend to be an adjustment in the distribution of productive resources, and the factors of production previously allocated to the export sector would have been re-employed in production to supply domestic or foreign demand.[21]

It is impossible to measure precisely the cost to Spain of the loss of the empire. However, a tentative calculation can be made by systematically biasing estimates in favour of the generally accepted hypothesis that the independence of the colonies constituted a serious setback for the Spanish economy (Coelho, 1972–1973: 254). Thus, if the per capita cost of Spanish-American emancipation were small, it could be argued that, in reality, the true cost was even lower.

First, I will assume that the productive resources embodied in the Spanish goods exported to the colonies would not have found alternative employment outside the foreign sector. In other words, the fall in exports of Spanish products, as a result of American independence, could only be compensated for by increasing trade with other regions of the world. Exports of national goods to the colonies contracted by 59.7%, or 124.9 million Reales, at 1784/1796 prices, between these years and 1815/1820.

The reduction of Spanish maritime transport services used in commercial traffic between the metropolis and its colonies represents the second cost to be considered. In contrast to trade with the rest of the world, which was almost entirely carried out by non-Spanish ships, trade with the Indies, under colonial legislation, was reserved

[19] Cf. García Sanz (1979–1980), on peasant employment in the mid-nineteenth century. It is foreseeable that a similar situation would have arisen a few decades earlier.

[20] Shifting resources from the export sector to the domestic sector would have depressive effects on investment and innovation, as prices decline as a result of falling demand.

[21] Cf. Fontana (1991: 306) on the internal market, and Prados de la Escosura (1982a) on the reorientation towards European markets after the loss of the American colonies.

for national ships. The decline of trade with Spanish America, following its independence, meant a contraction of the transport services provided by Spaniards. I will assume, therefore, that the financial and transport services (freight and insurance) provided by Spaniards in the colonial trade would decline in parallel with the contraction of the colonial merchandise trade. This decline would not be compensated to any extent by the hypothetical increase in trade with the rest of the world, which would be carried out by ships and companies from other countries. Thus, the productive resources allocated to the provision of maritime transport services would not find alternative employment in the Spanish economy. In order to estimate this cost, the procedure followed consists of calculating the percentage of the value of trade that freight, insurance and mercantile commissions may constitute, and applying it to the contraction experienced by colonial trade. Between 1784/1796 and 1815/1820, the fall in trade with the Indies can be estimated at 56.8%, i.e. 417.4 million Reales in 1784/1796, and 30% of this sum, 125.2 million Reales, corresponds to transport services.[22]

Finally, it would be necessary to consider the profits obtained in the commercialisation of products exported and re-exported to America, and subsequently repatriated to the metropolis, which would disappear with the reduction of trade after American independence. Exports, both of Spanish and foreign products, contracted by 65.8% between 1784/1796 and 1815/1820, that is, by 291.5 million at 1784/1796 prices; if we accept a trade margin in their distribution and sale of 80%, the total sum that Spanish merchants ceased to receive would amount to 233.2 million Reales, at 1784/1796 prices.[23] If 50% of this amount, 116.6 million Reales, represented profits remitted to the peninsula, this would give an upper limit to the amount that would cease to be sent to Spain as a result of the loss of the empire.[24]

[22] AHN, Estado, leg. 3188[1]. O'Brien (1982: 6) provides a similar percentage for the British case in 1784/1786. Fontana (1991: 312) underlines the strong variations in freight, insurance, etc., between times of war and peace and provides information on transport and marketing costs which, in peacetime, would stand at 4% for insurance (1802) and 10% for the commercial interest rate (1787).

[23] The assumption of a trade margin of 80% is based on Fontana (1991: 312, n. 6) who cites evidence of silk handkerchiefs which, with a price on arrival in the West Indies of 12.5 Catalan pounds, would sell for 22.5 pounds. However, the assumption of freight, insurance and merchant commission costs of 4% is exaggeratedly low even in peacetime. Thomas Sothuel, in 1785, calculated that insurance alone amounted to 4% of the value of the goods exported to the Indies, while together with freight costs, it amounted to 29–33% of the value of the merchandise put on the ship (or f.o.b.), while including duties and taxes, which would have to be paid on arrival in the Indies, would amount to 40% of the f.o.b. value (AHN, Estado, leg. 3188[1]). In this case, the 11.3 Catalan pounds of the f.o.b. price would have to be increased to 15.8 pounds before the first sale. If the selling price was 22.5 pounds, this would mean a commercial margin of 42.2%. In this case, the amount that the merchants would lose would be 123.1 million Reales. Ortiz de la Tabla (1978: 309) calculates freight rates for Argentinean hides as 26.7% between Montevideo and La Coruña in 1788.

[24] A repatriated profit rate of 50% is probably an exaggeration. If one were to accept the more realistic assumption about trade margins expressed in the previous note, the amount would be reduced to 61.5 million. Thomas (1968: 39) admits 40% as the highest rate of profit in shipping for the British West Indies.

If we add up the three previous items, corresponding to the trade in goods and services and their commercialisation, we reach a figure of 366.7 million, which corresponds approximately to that of private remittances from the Indies or shipments of gold and silver made by individuals, 355.1 million.[25]

The losses to the Treasury caused by the disappearance of the remittances of precious metals received from the colonial administrations (*caudales de Indias*) and by the reduction in general and customs revenues as a result of colonial independence, represent a cost to the Spanish economy that must also be evaluated. The *caudales de Indias* amounted to an annual average of 114.1 million Reales in the period 1784/1796, and became insignificant in the wake of the Napoleonic Wars, before finally disappearing with the final emancipation of the colonies. This decline could be identified as the loss resulting from the end of silver shipments to the Royal Treasury, assuming they were all retained in Spain.[26]

Finally, the decline in revenue from customs duties levied on exports and re-exports to the Indies and products of colonial origin that Spain re-exported abroad must be assessed. It should be stressed that, from the point of view of Spanish welfare, only taxes levied on exports and re-exports with price-inelastic demand should be taken into account, since otherwise, the volume of exports and re-exports would tend to be reduced. On the other hand, customs duties on imports destined for the Spanish market should not be included in the computation of the costs of the loss of the colonies, as they burdened domestic consumers and reduced their purchasing power (to a lesser extent if the demand was price-elastic). In estimating the cost of the fall in customs revenue, I have accepted the assumption that both colonial demand for imports and European demand for colonial products were perfectly price inelastic. This is, therefore, an upward estimate of the impact of the loss of empire on the Spanish economy.

In this estimate, as in the estimate of remittances from the Indies, I have assumed that the Treasury's use of its colonial revenues was fully productive and entirely carried out on the mainland. Thus, the decline in the revenues of the Treasury would have had a negative effect on welfare in Spain. Since it is doubtful that all the state revenue of the Ancien Régime was used productively, the estimates given here represent an upper limit.

---

[25] This coincidence would corroborate the interpretation by Cuenca (1981b: 423–424), for whom private remittances from the Indies represented, in addition to the balance of the balance of merchandise, the transport and insurance paid for by Spaniards and the profits derived from the commercialisation in colonial markets of products from the peninsula.

[26] This assumption clearly constitutes an upward bias in the estimate as shown by Barbier (1984: 179–187), who establishes a connection between remittances from the Indies and Spanish naval power and states: 'it is a cliché to stress that the Spanish state, unlike the British or the French, was able to drain funds directly from its colonies; that, for the peninsular Treasury, the benefits of colonialism were direct rather than indirect. This generalisation is perhaps appropriate when applied to the late Habsburgs or early Bourbons, but not to the reign of Charles III'. A contrary view to Barbier's is held by Marichal and Souto (1994).

To obtain the customs revenues derived from colonial trade in the periods 1784/1796 and 1815/1820, I calculated the percentage of Spain's foreign trade represented by total re-exports and exports to the colonies (35%), and applied it to the total value of general and customs revenues. Between 1784/1796 and 1815/1820, the drop in customs revenue caused by American independence would have been 60.6%, or 35.2 million Reales (1784/1796 prices).

The total direct costs of independence under restrictions that bias them upwards would therefore amount to some 516 million Reales, expressed at average prices for the period 1784/1796.

In order to make economic sense of this figure, it is necessary to relate it to some indicator of Spanish productive activity. It could also be compared with the taxes levied on the population: for example, the impact of American independence would be equivalent to five times the volume of provincial revenues or consumption taxes (Merino, 1987).[27]

An alternative way would be to relate the per capita burden of colonial emancipation to wages. Thus, the per capita impact of American independence would represent an amount comparable to that of 10 days' wages for a rural labourer, or 7 days' wages for a bricklayer.[28] If we assume that a *bracero* worked 170 days a year, this would represent a 6% income drop.[29]

If we compare the total direct costs of colonial independence to population, this gives a figure of 46.5 Reales per head (at 1784/1796 prices).[30] This represents a 5.3% loss in terms of per capita GDP (881 Reales at 1784/1796 prices).

The various estimates offered of the direct impact of the loss of empire on the Spanish economy are subject to very restrictive assumptions that bias them upwards, such as accepting that the productive resources allocated to the production of goods and services for the colonial market would be unemployed in the absence of the colonies. This means that the magnitude of the fall in per capita income is only an upper limit to what actually took place. If the estimates obtained in this tentative arithmetical exercise are compared with the dominant view among historians, a marked discrepancy becomes apparent. Can American independence still be

[27] As is well known, provincial revenues were the generic term for a set of taxes levied on consumption (*alcabalas*, *cientos*, *millones*, etc.). Similarly, the impact of independence would be equivalent to five times the tax revenue from tobacco.

[28] Calculated with the average wages in Castilla la Nueva and Catalonia provided by Hamilton (1947: 270–271) and Felíu (1991, ii: 106–109, 122–126), respectively.

[29] The Ensenada Cadastre provides an average of 168 days for the economically active population and 120 for day labourers (Álvarez-Nogal and Prados de la Escosura, 2013: 7). The proportion would be 4% in the case of a bricklayer. The number of working days for a *bracero* in the nineteenth century would be 210 days (Gómez Mendoza, 1982a: 99–104). If we adopt this figure, the proportion of a labourer's income would be of 5% and of 3% for a bricklayer.

[30] Compared with the new annual population estimates (Table 2.3). If, alternatively, The Spanish population, according to the 1787 and 1797 censuses, is used, it would represent 49 Reales per capita, that is, 5.6% of per capita income.

described as a 'brutal event, a 'disaster', or a 'serious economic and financial disruption'?

6.5 The Impact on Resource Allocation

The use of average measures such as those employed so far could be objected to. Expressing the value of any economic activity as a percentage of national income tends to create a false impression of insignificance (O'Brien and Engerman, 1991: 178). It may conceal its impact on the structural transformations accompanying economic growth. Moreover, the disparate regional effects of the contraction of colonial trade would challenge the conclusions drawn from national aggregates (Fontana, 1991: 313–316).[31] The task of pinpointing the externalities of colonial trade on the Spanish economy is beyond the scope of this chapter. Nevertheless, in the following paragraphs, I have attempted to sketch the most immediate implications of the loss of empire for the modernisation of the Spanish economy.

It is therefore worth examining the gains from specialisation induced by colonial trade. The composition of colonial imports, primary products, mostly foodstuffs (sugar and cocoa amounted to 61.4% of imports retained for domestic consumption in 1792) shows that the possibility of increasing Spanish production through a reallocation of resources towards industry would have been small, and that most of the gains must have come from improved consumption patterns. It can be argued, however, that the tasks of refining and processing these raw materials would increase industrial value added.[32] However, colonial products could be purchased on the international market and, consequently, the gains from trade with the Indies would only occur if, under the colonial system, Spain obtained the same goods at lower prices.[33] In the case of sugar, moreover, there were no alterations in the colonial relationship, as it came from Cuba. The recovery of cocoa imports, on the other hand, was already a fact in the 1830s (Prados de la Escosura, 1982a: 238, 246).

On the other hand, the colonies' dependence on the Spanish industry for supplies was small (cotton, indigo and dye sticks together accounted for 4.1% of imports retained in 1792). In the case of Catalan cotton manufactures, one of the most

[31] According to Fontana (1991), the impact on the hinterlands of Cadiz and other Andalusian and Cantabrian coastal cities may not have been compensated by "the restructuring of the internal market" and the reorientation towards foreign markets.

[32] An approximate idea of the contribution of sugar and cocoa derivatives to industrial value added in the mid-nineteenth century is provided by Nadal (1987: 35), based on the industrial contribution in 1856. The chocolate industry would contribute 2.3% of the manufacturing industry, in fiscal terms. Sugar, included together with the distillation of grapes and grains, constituted 6.5% of the industrial contribution.

[33] Considering that Spain's entry into the international market as a buyer of primary products would not alter prices significantly implies defining Spain as a small country and, therefore, as a price taker.

dynamic industries at the end of the eighteenth century, the imports of yarns, of European origin, had a much greater weight than those of raw cotton of colonial origin (2.9% and 0.2% of total retained imports in 1792, respectively), which, in turn, reveals the weakness of spinning in Catalonia (Prados de la Escosura, 1982a: 86, 238; Vilar, 1968, ii: 131, 138; Nadal, 1975: 189–190).

Manufactured exports to the colonies must have stimulated industrial development in Spain, as they were concentrated in a few sectors: two-thirds were textiles (36.8%), iron and steel (3.2%), paper (4.4%) and foodstuffs (22.3%).[34] Some of these industries represented advanced manufacturing sectors, with important external economies and frequent regional development effects, such as the cotton and silk textile industry. On the other hand, colonial legislation made Spanish manufactures artificially competitive in the Spanish-American market.[35] Even so, the lack of competitiveness of Spanish manufactures at the end of the eighteenth century is highlighted by the volume of manufactures re-exported to the colonies, despite the high taxes levied on them when they entered Spain and when they were re-shipped to the colonies.[36] One consequence of this lack of competitiveness was reflected in the export of manufactured products in which the Spanish contribution to their added value was only in the finishing stage, as in the case of Catalan prints.[37] The loss of Latin American markets for the Spanish industry seems, however, to date back to earlier times. Thus, for example, after the establishment of free ports in the British West Indies in 1766, traffic between Britain and the Spanish colonies expanded without the mediation of the metropolis.[38] On the other hand, it has been argued that the increasing fiscal pressure on colonial trade between 1792 and 1820, in order to counteract the rising budget deficit, constituted an additional obstacle to the competitiveness of Spanish manufactures (Cuenca Esteban, 1982: 393).

It is therefore appropriate, in view of the evidence presented, to try to compare the contraction of manufacturing exports with indicators of industrial activity. However, one question that remains after this examination is whether or not the externalities derived for the economy from industrial exports are underestimated by their share in the value added of the manufacturing sector or their contribution to employment. In

[34] Cf. Prados de la Escosura, (1988: 92) for exports of national products in 1792 (at 1778 prices). The food industry includes exported wine and brandy, flour and olive oil.

[35] Evidence presented to the Real Sociedad Económica Matritense de Amigos del País in 1778 (RSEM, 1778, III) on the comparative costs of foreign and Spanish wool manufactures corroborates this.

[36] Cf. Fisher (1981: 23, 33) on the differential between taxes on foreign and Spanish goods sent from the metropolis to the Indies. Also Delgado Ribas (1986: 73).

[37] More optimistic interpretations of this fact could be made, such as, for example, that the Catalan textile industry had acquired a comparative advantage in finishing operations as opposed to weaving. On the other hand, in England, the penetration of Asian fabrics, under the temporary acquiescence of the authorities, seems to have had a delayed stimulating effect on British industry by creating a market for these products and encouraging specialisation in dyeing and printing (O'Brien, 1990: 167; O'Brien et al., 1991: 410, 412–414).

[38] On 'free ports', cf. Jones (1934), Goebel (1938), Horsfall (1948), and Armytage (1953).

the years 1784/1796, 144.1 million Spanish manufactured goods were exported to the colonies.[39] It is not easy to calculate the share of manufactured goods in exports to America in 1815/1820 unless one accepts a percentage analogous to that of 1827. In this case, the contraction of manufactured exports would amount to 119.7 million, at 1784/1796 prices.[40] If we subtract from this figure the amount of raw material inputs used in manufacturing production, we obtain a crude estimate of the fall in the value added exported, 47.9 million Reales (40% of the value of the final product), which is equivalent to the impact of the loss of the empire on the industry.[41] Its relative importance depends on the employment that this sum could generate or the proportion it represents of the industrial product.

The industrial sector employed nearly half a million men in 1797, 15.2% of the male labour force (Pérez Moreda, 1982).[42] To these should be added, in addition to the female population employed full-time in industry, an undetermined but not negligible proportion of the working population whose main occupation was agriculture but who supplemented their income with occasional work in industry.[43] The

---

[39] I accept as manufactures of Spanish manufacture those thus registered without distinguishing those that were only finished on the peninsula, so that the figure obtained tends to be exaggerated.

[40] This figure, which would be equivalent to 95.8% of the contraction in total Spanish exports, is perhaps excessive if one considers that Cuba and Puerto Rico were still under colonial rule. A lower limit could be obtained by assuming that the fall in Spanish exports of goods was divided between primary and manufactured goods according to their percentage share of total exports in peacetime (1784–1796). Thus, the reduction of the volume of exported manufactures would be 86 million Reales (0.689 × 124.9). Since I am trying to obtain an upward estimate of the impact of colonial emancipation, I have opted for the upper limit.

[41] No information is available on the value added/value of production ratio for Spanish industry at this time. It is possible, however, to make reasonable assumptions on the basis of partial information or for later periods. Thus, Deane (1957: 220) estimates value added at 60% of the value of the final product for the English wool industry in 1799. Deane and Cole (1967: 185–210) provide the following ratios for the textile industry at the end of the eighteenth century: cotton (0.69); wool (0.57); linen (0.60); silk (0.66). Markovitch (1965) presents much lower ratios for French industry in 1781–1790: food industry (0.18); textile (0.17); paper (0.35); iron (0.52). The difference lies in the fact that, in the British case, it is the value added to the main raw material and, therefore, it is an upper limit. In the Spanish case, Gómez Mendoza (1982b) gives a ratio of 0.59 for the cotton industry in 1831–1835. My own estimates (Prados de la Escosura, 1983) for silk and linen fabrics give value-added ratios to the main raw material/final product around 1787–1799 of 0.41 and 0.55, respectively. I have chosen to retain the ratios of Markovitch (1965), for the food, paper and steel industries, while for cotton and wool I have accepted those of Deane and Cole (1967), and have preferred my own estimates for silk and linen. The result for the ratio value added/final value, weighted by the share of exports to America, is 0.3884, which, for the sake of simplicity, I rounded it up to 0.4.

[42] Pérez Moreda (1982) evaluates the 1797 census figures for the male labour force and proposes some rectifications of the census values that slightly reduce the original percentage for industry (17.1%).

[43] Pérez Moreda (1982) considers lowering the figure of 450,709 which he initially proposed in order to eliminate the active population engaged in part-time work in industry. I have kept it in order to compensate as far as possible for the underestimation of industrial employment (and the over exaggeration of agricultural employment) which is usual in the population censuses of underdeveloped countries.

impact of the loss of the American continental market on industrial employment could be approximated by calculating the number of full-time male workers who could have been recruited from a sum analogous to the fall in exported industrial value added under the generous and unrealistic assumption that all this value added accrued to labour and none to capital. Thus, with a wage equivalent to that of a bricklayer and a working year of 250 days, the volume of employment destroyed would amount to 27,000 workers, representing a maximum of 7% of the industrial workforce.[44] If, more realistically, we adjust this figure by attributing one-quarter of the value added reduction to capital returns, the contraction in industrial employment would be about 5%.

It is more difficult to estimate the contribution of the secondary sector to gross domestic product. However, a lower limit could be inferred from the information collected by the Ensenada Cadastre for the Crown of Castile around 1752 (12.3%).[45] The industrial share of gross value added could be about 13%.[46] If we compare the loss in industrial value added, 47.9 million Reales (at 1784/1796) resulting from the contraction in industrial exports, with the industry share in gross value added (13% times GDP at constant 1784/1796 prices), we obtain a crude approximation to the impact of the loss of colonial markets on industry, about 4%, of its industrial value added.[47] It can be concluded, therefore, that, taken as a whole, the stimulus of the

[44] This is an upward biased calculation for several reasons: the wage, average of that of New Castile (Hamilton (1947) and Catalonia (Felíu, 1991), corresponds to unskilled labour (a carpenter would receive 70% more); the number of days is also a lower limit of a working year which could reach 300 days (this would reduce to 5.9% of the volume of employment generated by the external sector); the lowest level of industrial employment proposed by Pérez Moreda (1982), 389,462 males, which excludes those who might simultaneously have another occupation, has been chosen (had I taken the figure initially accepted by this author, 450,709, the volume of employment would fall to 6%).

[45] Cf. Group 75 (1977: 169, 186–187). In addition to being from an earlier period and only for the Crown of Castile, which excludes regions such as Catalonia or Valencia, whose secondary sector occupied considerably higher proportions of the active population. Thus, Pérez Moreda (1982) shows that, in 1797, 25.1% and 19.1% of the male labour force in Catalonia and Valencia came from the industrial sector as opposed to the 14.4% in the Crown of Castile, which it would represent 9.7% in 1752 (Group 75, 1977: 75, 132).

[46] The 13% results from applying to the contribution of industry to the GDP of the Crown of Castile, the ratio of industrial employment in Spain and in the Crown of Castile ((15.24/14.44) × 12.36 = 13.04). I assume that the industrial output per male worker was identical in the Crown of Castile and in Spain (the latter would probably be somewhat higher). Prados de la Escosura (1988: 59) estimates suggest a similar percentage, 13.8% for the industrial sector's contribution to GDP in 1800. It is also worth noting that industry contributed 13.6% of gross value added in 1850 (Prados de la Escosura, 2017, updated).

[47] If, like O'Brien and Engerman (1991), a value added/value of final product ratio of 0.5 is adopted, the decline would be about 5%. The Census of Fruits and Manufactures of 1799 provides a figure of 1156 million Reales for industrial product, which yields a figure of 931 million at 1784/1796 prices (Hamilton, 1947: 172–173, price index of non-agricultural products), which is below the 13% share of industry in gross value added adopted here (1237 million Reales expressed at 1784/1796 prices). Accepting the Census figure, the impact of the loss of colonial markets would represent a contract of 5% of industrial value added.

colonies to reallocate factors of production towards industry was weak, as can be seen from the impact of American emancipation on both industrial production and employment.

The loss of the colonies would be felt most severely in some branches of industry such as textiles and iron and steel, and in regions such as Andalusia and Catalonia (Fontana, 1982).[48] It is difficult to quantify the regional or sectoral impact of independence, although it is possible to point out that of the industrial sectors most closely linked to the colonies, cotton and silk, in the textile sector, and paper and distillates, suffered the greatest impact. However, the evolution of the different industries from 1820 onwards shows that the medium and long-term consequences of the loss of the colonies depended on the flexibility and dynamism of supply. Thus, for example, the Basque iron and steel industry would have experienced a loss of competitiveness from 1770 onwards and Spanish-American demand had to compensate, in part, for the decline in European demand, absorbing more than a third of production towards the end of the eighteenth century (Bilbao and Fernández de Pinedo, 1982; Uriarte, 1988). A similar situation appears in the case of the Valencian silk industry, as revealed by the fact that, between the 1790s and the 1820s, exports of raw silk increased at the same time that net imports of fabrics rose (Martínez-Santos, 1981). The experience of the Catalan shipping industry is that of another sector that expanded under the protection of the reserved market of the colonies (Delgado Ribas, 1979, 1983).

Despite the role that colonial demand played in its origins, the cotton industry expanded in Catalonia on the basis of the domestic market, which absorbed four-fifths of its production (Martínez Shaw, 1974; García Baquero, 1974; Fontana, 1974, 1982; Nadal, 1975: 190–191). In contrast to the previous examples, the rise and maturity of the cotton industry took place after Spanish-American independence (Maluquer de Motes, 1987; Nadal, 1975: 194–209). Catalan textile production, on the other hand, did not develop on the exclusive basis of import substitution, as its period of expansion coincided with the irruption into the Spanish market of British cotton manufactures, illegally introduced from Gibraltar and Portugal (Prados de la Escosura, 1978, 1984). The rise in demand for cotton fabrics, partly due to the substitution of traditional fibres (wool and, above all, linen), as well as the lack of integration of the Spanish market, are plausible hypotheses to explain the simultaneous expansion of national production and smuggling (Prados de la Escosura, 1983).

The profits from colonial trade also helped to finance investment in the Spanish economy. It could be argued that they did so to a considerable extent and that the loss of the empire meant the disappearance of a decisive flow of capital in the process of

[48] On the impact in Andalusia, see Sánchez-Albornoz (1966) and García-Baquero (1972: 215–254), but also, Tedde de Lorca (1987b: 302–305). On the effects in Catalonia, cf. Maluquer de Motes (1984: 271–273).

accumulation necessary to cope with the modernisation of the Spanish economy. Private remittances (shipments of gold and silver made by individuals) from the colonies to the metropolis can be estimated at 355.1 million Reales. Although the composition of private remittances from the Indies is not entirely clear, it seems that in the years prior to the Napoleonic Wars, they represented profits from colonial trade, both in merchandise and in financial and mercantile services, and after independence, they may have incorporated repatriated capital (Cuenca Esteban, 1981b: 424).

If the proportion of profits of colonial origin reinvested in the Spanish economy were known, and an overall estimate of domestic investment in Spain was available, it would be possible to guess the colonial contribution to capital accumulation in Spain. In the absence of the necessary information, one has to resort to indirect procedures and introduce systematic upward biases in the calculations to obtain, at least, an upper limit to it. O'Brien (1982: 7) has suggested that in Britain in the 1780s, the upper limit for reinvestment of profits from the colonies would be 30%. This extreme frugality does not seem to have been common in the Spanish case, and it would therefore be appropriate to accept a somewhat lower percentage (20%) for colonial profits reinvested productively in Spain, which would still constitute an upper limit (71 million Reales at 1784/1796 prices).[49] The level of investment is also unknown. The closer estimates for the investment rate start in 1850 (Prados de la Escosura, 2017). If we accept the average for 1850/1854 (5.8%), the value of domestic investment would reach 567 million Reales in 1784/1796 (i.e. the investment rate times GDP), so the fall in profits resulting from colonial emancipation would represent as much as 13% of Spain's capital accumulation. After independence, capital remitted to the metropolis, and invested in Spain, would partly compensate for the fall in investment caused by the disappearance of private colonial remittances.[50]

6.6 Concluding Remarks

Colonial emancipation certainly had a negative impact on the Spanish economy, particularly in the short term. International trade in goods and services and investment declined significantly. The domestic industry lost a reserved market. The Monarchy's financial difficulties worsened as a result of falling external revenues

[49] This results from 0.2 times 355.1 million Reales, the volume of private remittances. The percentage accepted by O'Brien for Great Britain seems exaggerated for the Spanish case in the light of the evidence on the behaviour of Cadiz colonial traders (García-Baquero, 1972).

[50] Cf. González Gordon (1970: 197) for an account of capital investment in the Jerez region after Spanish-American independence.

and an ossified tax system. Nevertheless, it is in the inherent difficulties of the manufacturing industry and the inadequacies of a treasury with a weak fiscal base that the key to the delicate situation of the post-imperial Spanish economy must be sought.

The most flexible and competitive sectors, however, managed to adapt to the new circumstances (cf. Fradera, 1987, on the Catalan case). This is the case of commercialised agriculture, which reoriented its supply towards the expanding markets of Western Europe (Prados de la Escosura, 1988). The quantitative evidence and controlled conjectures offered in this chapter also allow us to suggest that, for the Spanish economy, the loss of the colonies had, in global terms, a less broad and profound impact than historians have suggested.

The institutional implications of the emancipation of the colonies should be investigated. Fontana (1991: 316) pointed to the existence of a direct link between Spanish-American independence and the fall of the Ancien Régime and the Liberal Revolution in Spain. If this hypothesis is correct, the loss of the empire would have made a significant contribution to Spain's economic and social modernisation. Exploring these connections requires further and more detailed research.

Appendix

A.1 An Annual Series of Spanish International Trade, 1778–1820

The sources used for the reconstruction of an annual series of Spanish foreign trade between 1778 and 1820 have consisted of the series available for Spanish trade with Spanish America, France, Great Britain and the United States and the trade balances of 1792 and 1827. These provide the geographical composition of Spanish foreign trade and, consequently, allow us to assign weights to the different regional series of Spanish trade. These include, firstly, the annual series at 1778 prices of trade between Spain and the American colonies constructed by John Fisher for 1778–1796 and by Javier Cuenca based on the tax of the avería for 1792–1820. In a later study, Cuenca applies the prices of products traded in Cadiz to the quantities exported during the period 1782–1820 both for exports of Spanish products and for re-exports of European products to the colonies. In the case of imports, for the period 1782–1791, as well as for the year 1778, I have resorted to the import data collected by Fisher (1981). I have had to exclude precious metals and tobacco sent directly to the Treasury in order to make the series homogeneous with that of Cuenca. Since it only offers detailed information that allows this adjustment to be made for the cases of trade through the ports of Barcelona and Cadiz, I have assumed that the proportion of imports through Cadiz and Barcelona within total imports was identical with and without precious metals and tobacco. The series obtained is calculated at constant prices between 1778 and 1790, so I have refracted it using an index constructed by Cuenca from the prices provided by Hamilton.

For Spanish trade with foreign countries, I have been able to use the series corresponding to the USA (from 1791 to 1820), France (1787–1789, 1797–1820, to which I have added 1792, 1795–1796) and Great Britain (1778–1812, 1814–1820). I have reworked the series so that exports are f.o.b. and imports are c.i.f. In the case of the USA, I have been able to use the freight and insurance series constructed by Cuenca. In the case of France, I have adopted the same series that I used in the British case (Prados de la Escosura, 1984). I have converted the values of trade with foreign countries into Reales with the exchange rates provided by Cuenca (1987) for the years 1787–1821, which I have supplemented with my own estimates from the same sources as Cuenca (Castaign) for the preceding years.

The lack of coverage of the period considered by the statistics of the four regions and countries has made it necessary to carry out estimates with smaller coverage which has subsequently been reconciled with the estimates for the full sample. This has been done by means of regressions between the full sample and the partial samples. In all cases, both the R^2 and the *t-statistics* were significant. In order to obtain the percentage share of the countries in the sample in total trade, we have used the official Spanish trade statistics available for 1792 and 1827. The proportions for 1792 have been used for the period 1778–1807, while those for 1827 have been used for the years 1808–1820.

The statistics used distinguish between exports of Spanish and foreign products, on the one hand, and total imports, on the other. I have made the assumption that re-exports abroad were always of colonial products so that I have been able to obtain net imports from abroad by subtracting re-exports from Spain to Latin America from total imports from abroad. In the case of net imports from the colonies, I have assumed that the difference between total re-exports and those destined for America were those destined abroad and, therefore, are those that had to be subtracted from total imports from America.

The series obtained at current prices have been deflated and expressed in Reales of 1808. The procedure has been analogous to the calculation of the values at current prices of exports and imports, as well as the sources used.

See Tables 6.2, 6.3, 6.4, 6.5, 6.6 and 6.7.

Table 6.2 Public revenues at current and 1808 prices, 1778–1820 (million Reales)

	Public revenues (current prices)				Public revenues (1808 prices)			
	Customs Revenues	Indies Remittances	External Revenues	Total Revenues	Customs Revenues	Indies Remittances	External Revenues	Total Revenues
1778	74	124	198	630	101	169	270	861
1779	81	10	91	593	98	12	110	714
1780	49	5	54	854	56	6	62	974
1781	48	33	81	760	55	38	93	872
1782	64	5	69	836	81	6	87	1050
1783	88	19	107	730	111	24	135	924
1784	145	80	225	685	190	105	295	900
1785	197	44	241	707	243	54	297	872
1786	177	77	254	684	228	99	327	881
1787	156	67	223	758	205	88	293	998
1788	176	85	261	799	218	106	324	994
1789	163	25	188	702	206	31	238	886
1790	168	101	269	745	198	119	316	876
1791	188	161	349	800	217	187	403	926
1792	183	130	313	793	248	177	426	1078
1793	138	142	279	924	151	155	306	1013
1794	133	196	329	1547	138	203	341	1602
1795	120	139	258	2025	116	134	250	1956
1796	212	237	449	2107	174	195	368	1731
1797	89	12	101	2099	68	9	78	1612
1798	62	132	194	2198	56	120	177	2003
1799	79	91	170	2210	68	78	146	1899
1800	91	1	93	1501	81	1	82	1331

(continued)

Table 6.2 (continued)

	Public revenues (current prices)				Public revenues (1808 prices)			
	Customs Revenues	Indies Remittances	External Revenues	Total Revenues	Customs Revenues	Indies Remittances	External Revenues	Total Revenues
1801	82	0	82	1085	76	0	77	1008
1802	181	350	531	1375	171	332	503	1302
1803	161	240	402	1274	150	223	373	1183
1804	144	214	358	1280	132	197	329	1175
1805	84	50	134	1100	80	48	128	1049
1806	86	41	127	1197	97	46	142	1340
1807	88	3	90	1170	86	3	89	1152
1808	1	0	1	0	1	0	1	0
1809	6	118	124	260	6	106	111	234
1810	6	41	47	173	6	40	46	170
1811	21	7	28	195	24	7	32	224
1812	22	2	25	187	25	2	27	208
1813	53	0	53	347	61	0	61	399
1814	16	0	16	236	16	0	16	240
1815	90	0	90	567	95	0	95	604
1816	113	0	113	985	118	0	118	1024
1817	140	0	140	1242	152	0	152	1346
1818	114	0	114	1648	136	0	136	1966
1819	74	0	74	1059	86	0	86	1234
1820	66	0	66	1121	73	0	73	1245

Sources: Merino (1987) and see the text

Table 6.3 Public revenues (% Trade and GDP), 1778–1820 (current prices)

	External revenues (% Trade)			Public revenues (% GDP)	
	Customs revenues	Indies remittances	External revenues	External revenues	Total revenues
1778	9.1	15.3	24.4	3.6	11.4
1779	8.6	1.1	9.7	1.4	9.2
1780	9.7	1.1	10.8	0.8	12.5
1781	7.6	5.3	13.0	1.1	10.4
1782	6.9	0.5	7.4	1.0	12.4
1783	7.8	1.7	9.5	1.6	10.9
1784	9.3	5.1	14.5	3.6	11.1
1785	11.6	2.6	14.2	3.4	10.0
1786	11.9	5.2	17.1	3.6	9.7
1787	12.0	5.2	17.2	3.1	10.5
1788	11.7	5.7	17.4	3.4	10.5
1789	11.4	1.7	13.2	2.5	9.2
1790	11.2	6.7	17.9	3.3	9.1
1791	11.1	9.5	20.6	4.0	9.2
1792	9.7	6.9	16.5	4.2	10.7
1793	7.8	8.1	15.9	2.9	9.6
1794	7.2	10.5	17.7	3.2	15.2
1795	6.1	7.1	13.2	2.4	18.6
1796	10.2	11.4	21.6	3.2	15.2
1797	8.1	1.1	9.2	0.6	13.4
1798	5.9	12.5	18.3	1.4	15.4
1799	4.6	5.2	9.8	1.2	15.4
1800	6.5	0.1	6.6	0.7	11.4
1801	5.6	0.0	5.6	0.6	7.8
1802	6.4	12.4	18.8	3.9	10.1
1803	6.3	9.4	15.7	2.9	9.1
1804	4.8	7.2	12.0	2.3	8.3
1805	5.4	3.2	8.7	0.8	6.8
1806	6.6	3.1	9.7	1.0	9.8
1807	6.0	0.2	6.2	0.7	8.8
1808	0.1	0.0	0.1	0.0	0.0
1809	0.3	4.8	5.1	1.0	2.2
1810	0.3	2.0	2.3	0.4	1.5
1811	1.4	0.4	1.8	0.3	1.8
1812	1.7	0.2	1.9	0.2	1.4
1813	4.1	0.0	4.1	0.5	3.0
1814	0.9	0.0	0.9	0.1	1.8
1815	6.1	0.0	6.1	0.7	4.3
1816	7.9	0.0	7.9	0.9	7.5
1817	11.1	0.0	11.1	1.0	8.8
1818	8.8	0.0	8.8	1.0	13.7
1819	6.3	0.0	6.3	0.6	9.0
1820	5.1	0.0	5.1	0.5	9.0

Sources: Table 6.2 and see the text

Table 6.4 Spain's international trade, 1778–1820 (million current Reales)

	Domestic exports			Net imports[a]			Re-exports		
	Rest of the World	Hispanic America	Total	Rest of the World[b]	Hispanic America	Total	Rest of the World	Hispanic America	Total
1778	187	28	215	509	0	509	43	46	89
1779	218	73	291	611	16	627	28	0	28
1780	147	56	202	298	0	298	0	0	0
1781	227	93	320	302	0	302	0	3	3
1782	208	62	271	468	38	506	63	93	156
1783	224	83	307	618	21	639	85	93	178
1784	345	224	570	362	0	362	191	432	623
1785	417	279	696	434	10	445	192	367	559
1786	326	201	527	513	30	543	165	251	416
1787	341	133	473	401	74	475	141	207	348
1788	351	172	524	500	119	619	137	219	356
1789	351	197	548	442	99	542	125	213	337
1790	327	163	490	611	108	719	127	171	298
1791	346	201	547	578	198	776	135	239	374
1792	442	276	718	463	211	674	207	295	502
1793	364	199	563	639	240	879	112	202	313
1794	421	147	568	861	239	1100	91	102	193
1795	488	288	776	637	241	879	120	178	298
1796	353	239	592	839	375	1214	104	165	269
1797	421	20	441	593	0	593	55	7	62
1798	328	29	357	616	51	667	25	7	32
1799	407	99	506	953	205	1158	41	27	69
1800	457	53	511	773	56	829	51	19	70
1801	546	71	618	774	20	794	40	26	67
1802	683	280	963	1201	401	1602	93	172	265
1803	659	293	952	976	288	1263	169	179	348
1804	645	266	911	1365	378	1743	198	129	326
1805	593	52	644	816	0	816	72	17	89
1806	439	51	490	734	13	747	60	17	77
1807	535	28	563	830	40	870	21	6	28
1808	389	63	452	472	0	472	72	26	97
1809	771	208	978	1121	159	1280	123	47	169
1810	669	166	835	890	0	890	204	66	270
1811	262	79	341	1000	76	1076	60	23	83
1812	237	47	284	906	47	954	54	15	69
1813	211	93	304	791	102	894	59	36	95
1814	395	130	525	984	117	1102	113	40	153
1815	409	114	523	675	125	799	93	45	138
1816	350	115	465	725	137	861	72	35	107
1817	400	84	484	585	109	694	66	20	86
1818	510	99	609	527	53	580	74	35	110
1819	348	89	437	503	132	636	64	33	96
1820	414	135	549	511	63	574	108	56	164

Sources: See Appendix, A.1 An Annual Series of Spanish International Trade, 1778–1820
Notes: [a]For domestic consumption, [b]Includes smuggling

Table 6.5 Spain's openness (% Trade/GDP), 1778–1820 (current prices)

	Domestic exports			Net imports[a]			Re-exports	Trade balance (domestic exports – net imports)		
	Rest of the World	Hispanic America	Total	Rest of the World[b]	Hispanic America	Total	Total	Rest of the World	Hispanic America	Total
1778	2.5	0.4	2.8	6.7	0.0	6.7	1.2	−4.3	0.4	−3.9
1779	2.8	0.9	3.8	7.9	0.2	8.1	0.4	−5.1	0.7	−4.4
1780	1.9	0.7	2.6	3.8	0.0	3.8	0.0	−1.9	0.7	−1.2
1781	2.7	1.1	3.8	3.6	0.0	3.6	0.0	−0.9	1.1	0.2
1782	2.5	0.7	3.2	5.5	0.4	6.0	1.8	−3.1	0.3	−2.8
1783	2.7	1.0	3.6	7.3	0.3	7.6	2.1	−4.6	0.7	−3.9
1784	4.3	2.8	7.0	4.5	0.0	4.5	7.7	−0.2	2.8	2.6
1785	4.8	3.2	8.0	5.0	0.1	5.1	6.4	−0.2	3.1	2.9
1786	3.6	2.2	5.8	5.7	0.3	6.0	4.6	−2.1	1.9	−0.2
1787	3.6	1.4	5.0	4.2	0.8	5.0	3.7	−0.6	0.6	0.0
1788	3.7	1.8	5.5	5.3	1.3	6.6	3.8	−1.6	0.6	−1.0
1789	3.7	2.0	5.7	4.6	1.0	5.6	3.5	−1.0	1.0	0.1
1790	3.4	1.7	5.1	6.3	1.1	7.5	3.1	−3.0	0.6	−2.4
1791	3.5	2.0	5.5	5.8	2.0	7.7	3.7	−2.3	0.0	−2.3
1792	4.4	2.7	7.1	4.6	2.1	6.7	5.0	−0.2	0.7	0.4
1793	3.5	1.9	5.3	6.1	2.3	8.3	3.0	−2.6	−0.4	−3.0
1794	4.0	1.4	5.4	8.2	2.3	10.4	1.8	−4.2	−0.9	−5.1
1795	4.6	2.7	7.4	6.1	2.3	8.4	2.8	−1.4	0.4	−1.0
1796	3.1	2.1	5.2	7.4	3.3	10.7	2.4	−4.3	−1.2	−5.5
1797	3.5	0.2	3.7	4.9	0.0	4.9	0.5	−1.4	0.2	−1.3
1798	2.5	0.2	2.7	4.7	0.4	5.1	0.2	−2.2	−0.2	−2.4
1799	3.3	0.8	4.1	7.7	1.7	9.4	0.6	−4.4	−0.9	−5.3
1800	3.9	0.5	4.4	6.6	0.5	7.1	0.6	−2.7	0.0	−2.7

(continued)

Table 6.5 (continued)

	Domestic exports			Net imports[a]			Re-exports	Trade balance (domestic exports – net imports)		
	Rest of the World	Hispanic America	Total	Rest of the World[b]	Hispanic America	Total	Total	Rest of the World	Hispanic America	Total
1801	4.2	0.6	4.8	6.0	0.2	6.2	0.5	_1.8	0.4	_1.4
1802	5.3	2.2	7.5	9.3	3.1	12.4	2.1	_4.0	_0.9	_5.0
1803	5.0	2.2	7.3	7.5	2.2	9.7	2.7	_2.4	0.0	_2.4
1804	4.6	1.9	6.5	9.7	2.7	12.4	2.3	_5.1	_0.8	_5.9
1805	3.8	0.3	4.2	5.3	0.0	5.3	0.6	_1.5	0.3	_1.1
1806	3.2	0.4	3.6	5.3	0.1	5.4	0.6	_2.1	0.3	_1.9
1807	4.1	0.2	4.3	6.3	0.3	6.6	0.2	_2.2	_0.1	_2.3
1808	3.1	0.5	3.6	3.8	0.0	3.8	0.8	_0.7	0.5	_0.2
1809	7.2	2.0	9.2	10.5	1.5	12.0	1.6	_3.3	0.5	_2.8
1810	5.8	1.4	7.3	7.7	0.0	7.7	2.3	_1.9	1.4	_0.5
1811	2.1	0.6	2.7	8.0	0.6	8.6	0.7	_5.9	0.0	_5.9
1812	1.6	0.3	1.9	6.1	0.3	6.4	0.5	_4.5	0.0	_4.5
1813	1.6	0.7	2.3	5.9	0.8	6.7	0.7	_4.3	_0.1	_4.4
1814	3.0	1.0	4.0	7.5	0.9	8.4	1.2	_4.5	0.1	_4.4
1815	2.9	0.8	3.7	4.8	0.9	5.7	1.0	_1.9	_0.1	_2.0
1816	2.6	0.8	3.4	5.3	1.0	6.3	0.8	_2.8	_0.2	_2.9
1817	2.6	0.5	3.2	3.8	0.7	4.5	0.6	_1.2	_0.2	_1.4
1818	3.6	0.7	4.3	3.7	0.4	4.1	0.8	_0.1	0.3	0.2
1819	2.5	0.6	3.2	3.7	1.0	4.6	0.7	_1.1	_0.3	_1.4
1820	3.0	1.0	3.9	3.7	0.5	4.1	1.2	_0.7	0.5	_0.2

Sources: See Appendix, A.1 An Annual Series of Spanish International Trade, 1778–1820
Notes: [a]For domestic consumption, [b]Includes smuggling

Table 6.6 Spain's international trade, 1778–1820 (million 1808 Reales)

	Real domestic exports			Real net imports[a]			Real re-exports		
	Rest of the World	Hispanic America	Total	Rest of the World[b]	Hispanic America	Total	Rest of the World	Hispanic America	Total
1778	389	44	434	465	0	465	48	53	101
1779	440	0	440	549	30	579	32	0	32
1780	280	0	280	261	0	261	0	0	0
1781	337	0	337	257	0	257	0	3	3
1782	316	90	405	410	65	475	70	64	134
1783	395	112	507	515	42	557	95	75	170
1784	453	307	760	306	0	306	216	273	490
1785	551	334	885	354	26	379	217	280	497
1786	433	267	700	437	73	510	186	193	379
1787	547	183	730	346	155	501	240	162	403
1788	511	241	752	405	231	636	213	174	386
1789	534	275	809	355	188	543	230	173	403
1790	448	234	682	455	226	681	142	163	306
1791	475	290	764	474	316	789	150	212	363
1792	835	355	1191	523	295	818	229	246	475
1793	477	257	734	486	320	807	123	164	287
1794	521	180	701	586	351	936	101	82	183
1795	595	260	855	477	327	805	133	133	266
1796	329	225	554	496	464	959	114	124	238
1797	353	20	373	284	0	284	55	5	60
1798	372	33	405	447	46	493	27	7	34
1799	558	109	668	665	149	814	35	30	65
1800	706	63	769	547	31	578	55	19	74
1801	641	72	713	529	22	551	50	26	77
1802	633	284	918	953	476	1428	158	173	331
1803	639	299	938	699	352	1051	284	163	446
1804	751	275	1025	956	417	1373	296	109	405
1805	654	57	711	564	0	564	92	16	108
1806	463	64	527	743	16	759	60	20	80
1807	584	31	615	717	40	757	24	7	31
1808	389	63	452	472	0	472	72	26	97
1809	516	188	704	1089	217	1306	101	46	146
1810	603	129	731	894	0	894	157	59	217
1811	277	67	344	1108	121	1228	47	24	71
1812	259	40	299	948	77	1025	37	16	53
1813	274	85	358	840	151	991	46	40	86
1814	526	110	635	896	126	1022	128	47	175
1815	488	102	590	674	147	822	97	51	148
1816	399	96	495	718	165	883	73	44	117
1817	453	76	529	628	126	754	74	26	100
1818	626	109	735	618	65	684	108	40	148
1819	425	104	530	570	152	722	84	39	123
1820	422	146	568	600	78	678	121	80	201

Sources: See Appendix, A.1 An Annual Series of Spanish International Trade, 1778–1820
Notes: [a]For domestic consumption, [b]Includes smuggling

Table 6.7 Spain's terms of trade, 1778–1820 (1808=100)

	Rest of the World	Hispanic America	Total
1778	43.9	129.2	45.3
1779	44.5		61.0
1780	45.9		63.3
1781	57.4		80.9
1782	57.9	120.1	62.8
1783	47.4	145.3	52.8
1784	64.5	182.6	63.5
1785	61.6	203.8	67.0
1786	64.0	181.6	70.6
1787	53.8	151.1	68.4
1788	55.7	139.4	71.6
1789	52.7	135.7	67.9
1790	54.4	145.3	68.0
1791	59.6	111.0	72.8
1792	59.8	108.9	73.3
1793	58.1	103.2	70.4
1794	55.0	119.7	69.0
1795	61.4	150.6	83.2
1796	63.4	131.1	84.4
1797	57.1	122.3	56.6
1798	63.8	80.2	65.0
1799	50.8	65.9	53.3
1800	45.8	46.8	46.3
1801	58.3	109.7	60.1
1802	85.5	117.0	93.6
1803	73.9	119.9	84.4
1804	60.1	107.1	70.0
1805	62.6	102.9	62.6
1806	96.0	95.4	94.4
1807	79.2	90.4	79.7
1808	100.0	100.0	100.0
1809	145.2	150.5	141.8
1810	111.5	190.2	114.6
1811	105.1	186.1	113.2
1812	95.6	191.6	101.9
1813	81.8	161.3	93.9
1814	68.4	127.7	76.7
1815	83.7	132.7	91.1
1816	87.0	145.0	96.4
1817	94.8	128.1	99.4
1818	95.6	111.7	97.6
1819	92.7	97.3	93.6
1820	115.2	114.9	114.3

Sources: See the text

References

Álvarez-Nogal, C. and L. Prados de la Escosura (2013), "The Rise and Decline of Spain, 1270-1850", *Economic History Review* 66 (1): 1-37.

Anes, G. (1983), "La agricultura española y el mercado americano", in G. Anes, A. Rojo, and P. Tedde (eds.) *Historia económica y pensamiento social. Ensayos en homenaje a Diego Mateo del Peral*, Madrid: Alianza, pp. 193-204.

Armytage F. (1953), *The Free Port System in the British West Indies. A Study in Commercial Policy, 1766-1822*, London: Royal Empire Society.

Artola, M. (1978), *Antiguo Régimen y revolución liberal*, Barcelona: Ariel.

Ashton, T.S. (1955), *An Economic History of England: The 18th Century*, London: Methuen.

Barbier, J.A. (1980), "Peninsular Finances and Colonial Trade: the Dilemma of Charles IV's Spain", *Journal of Latin American Studies* 12(1): 21-37.

Barbier, J.A. (1984), "Indies Revenues and Naval Spending: the Cost of Colonialism for the Spanish Bourbons, 1763-1805", *Jahrbuch für Gescheite von Staat, Wirtschaft und Gesellschaft Lateinamerikas* 21: 171-188.

Barbier, J.A. and H. Klein (1981), "Revolution Wars and Public Finance : the Madrid Treasury, 1784-1808", *Journal of Economic History* 41(2): 315-339.

Barbier, J.A. and H. Klein (1985), "Las prioridades de un monarca ilustrado: el gasto público bajo el reinado de Carlos III", *Revista de Historia Económica* 3(3): 473-495.

Beckett, J.V. and M. Turner (1990), "Taxation and Economic Growth in Eighteenth Century England", *Economic History Review* 43(3): 377-403.

Berend, I.T. and G. Ranki (1982), *The European Periphery and Industrialization, 1780-1914*, Cambridge, Cambridge University Press

Bilbao, L.M. and E. Fernández de Pinedo (1982), "Auge y crisis de la siderometalurgia tradicional en el País Vasco (1700-1850)", in G. Anes, M. Artola J. Fontana, and P. Tedde (eds.), *La economía española al final del Antiguo Régimen*, 4 vols., Madrid: Alianza, II, pp. 133-228.

Broder, A. G. Chastagnaret, and E. Témime (1985), "Capital y crecimiento en la España del siglo XIX", in B. Benassar (ed.), *Orígenes del atraso económico español*, Barcelona: Ariel, pp. 83-105.

Canga-Argüelles, J. (1833-34, 1968), *Diccionario de Hacienda*, 2 vols., Madrid, Imprenta de Calero y Portocarrero, reprinted by Instituto de Estudios Fiscales.

Coelho, P.R.P. (1972-73), "The Profitability of Imperialism: the British Experience in the West Indies, 1768-1972", *Explorations in Economic History* 10: 253-280.

Crouzet, T. (1964), "Wars, Blockage and Economic Change in Europe, 1792-1815", *Journal of Economic History* 24: 567-590

Cuenca Esteban, J. (1981a), "Ingresos netos del Estado español, 1788-1820", *Hacienda Pública Española* 69: 183-208.

Cuenca Esteban, J. (1981b), "Statistics of Spain's Colonial Trade, 1792-1820: Consular Duties, Cargo Inventories and Balances of Trade", *Hispanic American Historical Review* 61(3): 381-428.

Cuenca Esteban, J. (1982): "Comercio y Hacienda en la caída del Imperio español, 1778-1820", in G. Anes, M. Artola J. Fontana, and P. Tedde (eds.), *La economía española al final del Antiguo Régimen*, 4 vols., Madrid: Alianza, III, pp. 389-453.

Cuenca Esteban, J. (1984), "Trends and Cycles in U.S. Trade with Spain and the Spanish Empire, 1790-1819", *Journal of Economic History* 44(2): 251-543.

Cuenca Esteban, J. (1987): "Fundamentos para una interpretación de las estadísticas comerciales francesas de 1787-1821 con referencia especial al comercio franco-español!", *Hacienda Pública Española* 108/109: 221-251.

Cuenca Esteban, J. (1989), "The Markets for Latin American Exports, 1790-1820: A Comparative Analysis of International Prices", in L. L. Johnson and E. Tandeter (eds.), *Growth and Integration in the Atlantic Economy*, Alburquerque, University of New Mexico Press.

Cuenca Esteban, J. (1991), "Precios y cantidades en el comercio español con Francia y Gran Bretaña, 1797-1807: Coyuntura internacional y opciones imperiales", *Revista de Historia Económica* 9: 127-163.
Deane, P. (1957), "The Output of the British Woolen Industry in the Eighteenth Century", *Journal of Economic History* 27: 207-223.
Deane, P. and W.A. Cole (1967), *British Economic Growth, 1688-1959*, Cambridge: Cambridge University Press, 2nd edition.
Delgado Ribas, J.M. (1979), "Auge y decadencia de la marina colonial catalana (1729-1821)", *Boletín Americanista* 21: 31-64.
Delgado Ribas, J.M. (1983) "La construcció i la industria naval a Catalunya (1710-1820)", *Recerques* 13: 45-64.
Delgado Ribas, J.M. (1986), "Libre comercio: mito y realidad», in T. Martínez Vara (ed.), *Mercado y desarrollo económico en la España contemporánea*, Madrid: Siglo XXI, pp. 69-83.
Delgado Ribas, J.M. (1987), "Conseqüències econòmiques deis decrets de comerç lliure (1765-1820)", *Revista Económica de Catalunya* 4: 48-56.
Feliu, G. (1991), *Precios y salarios en la Cataluña moderna*, 2 vols., Madrid: Banco de España.
Fisher, J. (1981), "Imperial 'Free Trade' and the Hispanic Economy, 1778-1796", *Journal of Latin American Studies* 13(1): 21-56.
Fisher, J. (1985) "The Imperial Response to 'Free Trade': Spanish Imports from Spanish America, 1778-1796", *Journal of Latin American Studies* 17(1): 35-78.
Fontana, J. (1970), "Colapso y transformación del comercio exterior español entre 1792 y 1827. Un aspecto de la crisis de la economía del Antiguo Régimen en España", *Moneda y Crédito* 115: 3-23.
Fontana, J. (1971), *La quiebra de la monarquía absoluta, 1814-1820*, Barcelona: Ariel.
Fontana, J. (1982), "Comercio colonial y crecimiento económico: revisiones e hipótesis», in G. Anes, M. Artola, J. Fontana, and P. Tedde (eds.), *La economía española al final del Antiguo Régimen*, 4 vols., Madrid: Alianza, III, pp. xi-xxxiv.
Fontana, J. (1991), "La crisis colonial en la crisis del Antiguo Régimen español», in H. Bonilla (ed.), *El sistema colonial en la América española*, Barcelona: Crítica, pp. 305-320.
Fontana, J. (1974), "Comercio colonial e industrialización: Una reflexión sobre los orínes de la industria moderna en Cataluña", in J. Nadal and G. Tortella (eds.), Agricultura, comercio colonial y crecimiento económico en la España contemporánea, Barcelona: Ariel, pp. 358-365.
Fradera, J.M. (1987), *Indústria i mercat. Les bases comercials de la industria catalana moderna (1814-1845)*, Barcelona: Crítica.
García-Baquero, A. (1972), *Comercio colonial y guerras revolucionarias: La decadencia económica de Cádiz a raíz de la emancipación americana*, Sevilla: CSIC, Escuela de Estudios Hispanoamericanos.
García Baquero, A. (1974), "Comercio colonial y producción industrial en Cataluña a fines del siglo XVIII", in J. Nadal and G. Tortella (eds.), *Agricultura, comercio colonial y crecimiento económico en la España contemporánea*, Barcelona: Ariel, pp. 268-294.
García-Cuenca, T. (1991), "El sistema impositivo y las rentas generales o de aduanas en España en el siglo XVIII", *Hacienda Pública Española*, monografías, I, pp. 59-74.
García Sanz, A. (1979-1980), "Jornales agrícolas y presupuesto familiar campesino en España a mediados del siglo XIX", *Anales del CUNEF*: 49-71
Goebel, D.B. (1938), "British Trade to the Spanish Colonies, 1796-1823", *American Historical Review* 43: 288-320.
Gómez Mendoza, A. (1982a), *Ferrocarriles y cambio económico en España, 1855-1913*, Madrid: Alianza.
Gómez Mendoza, A. (1982b), La industria algodonera, 1816-1913, Banco de España Unpublished Research Report.
González Gordon, M. (1970), *Jerez-Xeres-Sherry*, Jerez de la Frontera: Gráficas del Exportador.
Grupo '75 (1977), *La economía del Antiguo Régimen. La 'renta nacional' de la Corona de Castilla*, Madrid: Universidad Autónoma de Madrid.

Hamilton, E.J. (1947), *War and Prices in Spain, 1651-1800*, Cambridge, Mass.: Harvard University Press.

Horsfall, L.F. (1948), "The West Indian Trade», in C.N. Parkinson (ed.), *Trade Winds. A Study of British Overseas Trade During the French Wars 1793-1815*, London: George Allen & Unwin, pp. 157-194.

Izard, M. (1974), "Comercio libre, guerras coloniales y mercado americano", in J. Nadal and G. Tortella (eds.), *Agricultura, comercio colonial y crecimiento económico en la España contemporánea*, Barcelona: Ariel, pp. 295-321.

Jones, J.S. (1934), Historical Study of Anglo-South American Trade, with Special Reference to the Period 1807-1825, London University Unpublished Ph.D. Dissertation.

Maluquer de Motes, J. (1984), "La Historia económica de Cataluña", *Papeles de Economía Española* 20: 268-280

Maluquer de Motes, J. (1987), "The Industrial Revolution in Catalonia", in N. Sánchez-Albornoz (ed.), *The Economic Modernization of Spain, 1830-1930*, New York: New York University Press, pp. 169-190.

Marichal, C. and M. Souto (1994), "Silver and Situados: New Spain and the Financing of the Spanish Empire in the Caribbean in the Eighteenth Century", *Hispanic American Historical Review* 74(4): 587-613.

Markovitch, T. J. (1965): "L'industrie française de 1789 á 1964. Sources et méthodes", *Cahiers de l'ISEA* AF 4.

Martínez-Santos Isern, V. (1981), *Cara y cruz de la sedería valenciana. Siglos XVIII-XIX*, Valencia: Institució Alfons el Magnànim.

Martínez Shaw, C. (1974), "Los orígenes de la industria algodonera catalana y el comercio colonial", in J. Nadal and G. Tortella (eds.), *Agricultura, comercio colonial y crecimiento económico en la España contemporánea*, Barcelona: Ariel, pp. 343-267.

Merino, J.P. (1987), *Las cuentas de la Administración Central española, 1750-1820*, Instituto de Estudios Fiscales, monografía 50.

Milward, A. and S.B. Saul (1977), *The Development of the Economies of Continental Europe, 1850-1914*, London: George Allen & Unwin.

Moreau de Jonnés, A. (1835), *Estadística de España*, Barcelona: Imprenta de M. Rivadeneyra y Cía. Translation by P. Madoz.

Myint, H. (1958), "The 'Classical' Theory of International Trade and the Underdeveloped Countries", *Economic Journal* 68: 317-337.

Myint, H. (1977), "Adam Smith's Theory of International Trade in the Perspective of Economic Development", *Economica* 44: 231-248.

Nadal, J. (1975), *El fracaso de la revolución industrial de España*, Barcelona: Ariel.

Nadal, J. (1987), "La industria fabril española en 1900. Una aproximación", in J. Nadal, A. Carreras, and C. Sudriá (eds.), *La economía española en el siglo XX. Una perspectiva histórica*, Barcelona: Ariel, pp. 23-61.

O'Brien, P.K. (1982), "European Economic Development: The Contribution of the Periphery", *Economic History Review* 35(1): 1-18.

O'Brien, P.K. (1988), "The Polítical Economy of British Taxation, 1660-1815", Economic History Review 41(1): 1-32.

O'Brien, P.K. (1989), "The Impact of the Revolutionary and Napoleonic Wars, 1793-1815, on the Long-Run Growth of the British Economy", Review 12: 335-395.

O'Brien, P.K. (1990), "European Industrialization: from the Voyages of Discovery to the Industrial Revolution», in H. Pohl (ed.), *The European Discovery of the World and lts Economic Effects on Re-Industrial Society, 1500-1800*, VSWG 98, Stüttgart: Franz Steiner, pp. 155-177.

O'Brien, P.K. (1991), Power with Profit: the State and the Economy, 1688-1815, Inaugural lecture, University of London.

O'Brien, P.K. and S.L. Engerman (1991), "Exports and the Growth of the British Economy from the Glorious Revolution to the Peace of Amiens", in Barbara L. Solow (ed.), *Slavery and the Rise of the Atlantic System*, Cambridge: Cambridge University Press, pp. 177-209.

O'Brien, P.K., T. Griffiths, and P. Hunt (1991), "Polítical Components of the Industrial Revolution: Parliament and the English Cotton Textile Industry, 1660-1774", *Economic History Review* 44(3): 395-423.

Ortiz de la Tabla Ducasse, J. (1978), *Comercio exterior de Veracruz, 1778-1821. Crisis de dependencia*, Sevilla: Escuela de Estudios Hispanoamericanos.

Parry, J.H. (1966), *The Spanish Seaborne Empire*, London: Hutchinson.

Pérez Moreda, V. (1982), La población activa española y su distribución sectorial de fines del siglo XVIII a 1877, Banco de España Unpublished Research Report.

Pollard, S. (1982), *Peaceful Conquest. The Industrialization of Europe, 1760-1970*, Oxford: Oxford University Press.

Prados de la Escosura, L. (1978), "El comercio exterior de España, 1790-1830: una reconsideración", *Hacienda Pública Española* 55: 339-349.

Prados de la Escosura, L. (1982a), "Comercio exterior y cambio económico en España (1792 1849)", in G. Anes, M. Artola J. Fontana, and P. Tedde (eds.), *La economía española al final del Antiguo Régimen*, 4 vols., Madrid: Alianza, III, pp. 171-249.

Prados de la Escosura, L. (1982b), *Comercio exterior y crecimiento económico en España, 1826-1913: Tendencias a largo plazo*, Madrid: Banco de España.

Prados de la Escosura, L. (1983), "Producción y consumo de tejidos en España, 1800-1913: primeros resultados", in G. Anes, L.A. Rojo and P. Tedde (eds.), *Historia económica y pensamiento social, Ensayos en homenaje a Diego Mateo del Peral*, Madrid: Alianza, pp. 455-471.

Prados de la Escosura, L. (1984), "El comercio hispano-británico durante los siglos XVIII y XIX. (I) Reconstrucción", *Revista de Historia Económica* 2(2): 113-162.

Prados de la Escosura, L. (1988), *De imperio a nación. Crecimiento y atraso económico en España (1780-1930)*, Madrid: Alianza.

Prados de la Escosura, L. (2017), *Spanish Economic Growth, 1850-2015*, London: Palgrave Macmillan.

Sánchez-Albornoz, N. (1966), "Cádiz bajo la ocupación francesa en 1825", *Mélanges à la mémoire de Jean Sarrailh*, 2 vols., Paris: Centre de Recherches de l'Institut d'Études Hispaniques, II, pp. 345-353.

Shepherd, J.F. and G.M. Walton (1976), "Economic Change after the American Revolution: Pre- and Post-War Comparisons of Maritime Shipping and Trade", *Explorations in Economic History* 13: 397-422.

Tedde de Lorca, P. (1987a), "Crisis del Estado y Deuda Pública a comienzos del siglo XIX", *Hacienda Pública Española* 108/109: 169-195.

Tedde de Lorca, P. (1987b), "On the Historical Origins of Andalusian Underdevelopment", in N. Sánchez-Albornoz (ed.), *The Economic Modernization of Spain, 1830-1930*, New York: New York University Press, pp. 251-267.

Tedde de Lorca, P. (1988). *El Banco de San Carlos*, Madrid: Alianza/Banco de España.

Tedde de Lorca, P. (1990), "Política financiera y política comercial en el reinado de Carlos III", in Actas del Congreso Internacional sobre Carlos III y la Ilustración, 3 vols., Madrid: Siglo XXI, II, pp. 129-217.

Thomas, R.P. (1968), "The Sugar Colonies of the Old Empire: Profit or Loss for Great Britain", *Economic History Review* 21(1): 30-45.

Thomas, R.P. and D N. McCloskey (1981), "Overseas Trade and Empire 1700-1860", in R. Floud and D.N. McCloskey (eds.), *The Economic History of Britain since 1700*, Cambridge: Cambridge University Press, 2 vols., I, pp. 87-101.

Tortella, G. (1994), "Patterns of Economic Retardation and Recovery in South-Western Europe in the Nineteenth and Twentieth Centuries", *Economic History Review* 47(1): 1-21.

Uriarte Ayo, R. (1988), *Estructura, desarrollo y crisis de la siderurgia tradicional vizcaína (1700-1840)*, Bilbao: Universidad del País Vasco.

Vicens Vives, J. (1959), *Manual de Historia Económica de España*, Barcelona: Teide.

Vilar, P. (1968), *Catalunya dins l'Espanya moderna. Recerques sobre els fonaments económics de les estructures nacionals*, 4 vols., Barcelona: Edicions 62.

Chapter 7
The Terms of Trade Between Spain and Britain and the Industrial Revolution

7.1 Introduction

The terms of trade between industrialized nations and primary producers have been the subject of considerable debate since Ricardo's (1817) and Torrens's (1821) early writings. For more than a century, British economists from J. S. Mill to Marshall and Keynes interpreted secular trends in terms of trade as unfavourable to industrializing countries, reflecting the law of diminishing returns in agriculture and extractive industries, in contrast to constant or increasing returns in manufacturing industries (Rostow, 1950b; Spraos, 1980; Diakosavvas and Scandizzo, 1991).

After World War II, the terms of trade became one of the main concerns of development economists. Empirical studies carried out by the Statistical Department of the League of Nations under the supervision of Folke Hilgerdt (1945), and by Raul Prebisch (1949) at the Economic Commission for Latin America at the United Nations, suggested that there had been a deterioration in the net barter terms of trade of primary producers vis-á-vis industrialized countries between 1870 and 1938. This gave rise to a widely accepted Prebisch interpretation which suggests that, in the long run, the terms of trade between countries specialized in the production of raw materials and foodstuffs and industrial nations tend to deteriorate to the disadvantage of the former (Prebisch, 1949, 1950, 1959, 1963).[1] Furthermore, Hans Singer (1950, 1974–1975) stressed that favourable terms of trade would result in a sub-optimal resource allocation, favouring primary production and leading to de-industrialization.

[1] For a discussion of Prebisch's work, cf. Flanders (1964), Södersten (1970), Hadass and Williamson (2003). Also, early contributions by Lewis (1952), Kindleberger (1956, 1958), Meier (1963), Lipsey (1963), and Ellsworth (1956).

L. Prados de la Escosura, *A Millennial View of Spain's Development*, Frontiers in Economic History, https://doi.org/10.1007/978-3-031-60792-9_7

The controversy about the secular trends in terms of trade of primary products percolated throughout economic history.[2] Ivan Berend and Giorgy Ranki (1980: 550) observed an improvement in Scandinavia's and Hungary's net barter terms of trade through the nineteenth century, but noted that 'the situation was quite different in the case of the countries of the Iberian Peninsula'. In Spain, Nicolás Sánchez-Albornoz (1968: 145) asserted, `if the terms of trade circumstantially evolved in [its] favour, the historical trend shows that they did not last very long', and Jordi Nadal (1975: 53) suggested that the net barter terms of trade deteriorated in the last quarter of the nineteenth century, while Joaquim Nadal Farreras (1978) claimed that the terms of trade between Spain and Britain provided a measure of Spanish dependency.

More recently, research has shifted from debating whether and why the terms of trade for primary vis-á-vis industrial producers (or primary vs. industrial goods) deteriorated, to investigating the shocks caused by the terms of trade and the impact of their volatility on developing countries (Hadass and Williamson, 2003; Blattman et al., 2007; Williamson, 2008) as well as analysing the statistical properties of long series of the terms of trade (Bleaney and Greenaway, 1993; Zanias, 2005; Ocampo and Parra-Lancourt, 2003, 2010). Nonetheless, some monographs investigate the Prebisch hypothesis of the terms of trade deterioration and its causes (Appleyard, 2006; Frankema et al., 2018).

This chapter investigates the long-run terms of trade between Spain and Britain over 200 years, encompassing the Industrial Revolution and Spain's reorientation towards north-western Europe in the wake of Spanish American emancipation. It assesses whether the purchasing power of Spanish exports deteriorated vis-á-vis Britain and, more decisively, which country benefitted more from Spanish-British bilateral trade.

Different types of indices are proposed to analyse long swings in terms of trade. The net barter terms of trade (*NBTT*), that is, the relative price of exports in terms of imports, measures the purchasing power per unit of exports in terms of imports. However, if a change in the *NBTT* were endogenous, it would have no clear welfare significance, as it could be simply a consequence of an increase in the efficiency of exports production, or in job opportunities. That is why the purchasing power per unit of labour embodied in exported goods using the single factorial terms of trade (*SFTT*) requires consideration.

Both the *NBTT* and *SFTT* measure absolute differences between countries that result from patterns of trade and specialization. However, relative differences in per capita income between countries have been stressed as much as absolute gains in a country's per capita income. Traditional patterns of trade between developing and developed countries (Periphery and Core), that is, primary goods in exchange for manufactured goods, it has been argued, have had an asymmetric impact on Core and Periphery, increasing international inequality. The income gap between

[2]Cf. Bairoch (1975), and Bhatia (1969) on India, Sideri (1970) on Portugal, Glazier et al. (1972, 1975) on Italy, and Peláez (1976) on Brazil.

developed and developing countries would have widened as trade reinforced the Periphery's comparative advantage in primary produce (Hadass and Williamson, 2003).[3] The double factorial terms of trade (*DFFT*) provide a measure of countries' relative gains from trade.

2023The chapter shows that the *NBTT* improved remarkably in the hundred years prior to 1880, but became unfavourable between 1880 and 1913. Moreover, their impact on absolute and relative welfare was positive until 1900, as the (employment corrected weighted) single and double factorial terms of trade (*ECWSFTT* and *ECWDFTT*), show long-term gains, due to employment opportunities and productivity gains opened by an expanding trade sector. Thus, the view of a secular deterioration of the terms of trade between Spain and Britain throughout the eighteenth and nineteenth centuries is not supported by the evidence.

The chapter is organized as follows. Section 7.2 discusses the meaning and assessment of the net barter terms of trade, and Sects. 7.3 and 7.4 consider the trends of the NBTT and their immediate determinants, export and import prices. The impact on absolute and relative welfare stemming from international trade and specialization is examined in Sect. 7.5. Some closing remarks are offered in Sect. 7.6.

7.2 The Net Barter Terms of Trade: Concept and Measurement

The net barter terms of trade (*NBTT*) can be represented as:

$$NBTT = P_X : P_M \tag{7.1}$$

where P_X and P_M are index numbers of export and import prices, respectively. An increase in the *NBTT* means, on the basis of the price relationship alone, that a greater volume of imports can be obtained per unit of exports. In principle, an increase in the *NBTT* implies that the real income of a country grows faster than its output due to the growth of purchasing power per unit of its exports. There are, however, some important qualifications to be made before a deterioration in the terms of trade can be accepted as a reduction in a country's real income. Only under classical assumptions of constant supply of resources, no technological change, full employment, and free competition do changes in the net barter terms of trade imply changes in real income (Baldwin, 1955: 263).

Nevertheless, movements in terms of trade are interesting for historians to analyse (Rostow, 1950a; Haberler, 1961). For instance, why do the terms of trade change?

[3]Moreover, the volatility of the terms of trade would have reduced growth in the Periphery (Blattman et al., 2007; Williamson, 2008). This view has, nonetheless, been challenged. See Chilosi et al. (2023) for a recent example. However, I will not address the volatility of the terms of trade here.

Have foreign or domestic supply curves shifted? Are changes in the terms of trade accompanied by changes in the export volume? Do changes in the net barter terms of trade relate to productivity changes in export industries?

I have constructed index numbers for both import and export prices. These index numbers do not reflect quality changes in the commodities traded and become less reliable over the long run. Even if base years are changed to cover segments of the time series, splicing becomes necessary to provide a long-term view. Still, these index numbers can only provide rough orders of magnitude for changes over long periods (Hansen, 1977). Among the different types of indices available, the Laspeyres index, in which the prices of each commodity are weighted with their base period quantities, has the advantage of reflecting only price variations. The Paasche index, weighted annually with the quantities traded, has the advantage of taking into consideration annual changes in the composition of trade, although it does not only reflect price changes over time. The Fisher index, the geometric mean of the Laspeyres and Paasche indices, is a compromise on which the discussion will focus (Kindleberger, 1956: 318–321; Allen, 1975; Hansen, 1977).

If P and Q represent price and quantity indices for each commodity exported $_X$ and imported $_M$ and the subindices i = 1,2,3 ... and o indicate the current year and base year respectively, the net barter terms of trade can be defined as

$$NBTT_{\text{Lapeyres}} = (P_{\text{Xi}}Q_{\text{Xo}}/P_{\text{Xo}}Q_{\text{Xo}}) : (P_{\text{Mi}}Q_{\text{Mo}}/P_{\text{Mo}}Q_{\text{Mo}}) \quad (7.2)$$

$$NBTT_{\text{Paasche}} = (P_{\text{Xi}}Q_{\text{Xi}}/P_{\text{Xo}}Q_{\text{Xi}}) : (P_{\text{Mi}}Q_{\text{Mi}}/P_{\text{Mo}}Q_{\text{Mi}}) \quad (7.3)$$

$$NBTT_{\text{Fisher}} = (NBTT_{\text{Laspeyres}} \cdot NBTT_{\text{Paasche}})^{1/2} \quad (7.4)$$

An important distinction to be made is that, whereas prices for exports (1714–1869) and for imports (1714–1812) are price quotations for specific commodities, prices for exports (1870–1913) and for imports (1814–1913) are unit values.[4] Unit values not only reflect changes in price quotations for specific kinds of goods, but also changes in the composition of commodity groups, including changes in type and quality.[5] I have used f.o.b. prices for Spanish domestic exports, and f.o.b. and c.i.f. prices for imports of British goods in order to show how transport costs affected prices paid in Spain for imports, but since most trade was carried in British ships, c.i.f. prices are most relevant for computing shifts in Spain's net barter terms of trade.

To make some allowance for changes in the structure of relative prices over time, each index has been constructed in nine distinct sub-periods, using the end year as the base year. These nine sub-periods have been chosen because there were no significant changes in the commodity composition of trade during each time span.

---

[4]For a discussion of unit values, see Kindleberger (1956: 317–318), Allen (1975: 186–211), and Silver (2009).

[5]For each commodity, unit values are Paasche indices. This fact does not affect, however, the general price index.

Table 7.1 Construction of export and import prices

Periods	Link year	Base year	Coverage in the base year (%)	
			Exports	Imports
1714–1750		1750	88.5	90.3
	1750			
1750–1778		1778	89.0	94.7
	1778			
1770–1796		1796	85.0	77.5
	1796			
1796–1814		1814	88.7	68.6
	1814			
1814–1827[a]		1827[a]	86.6	88.9[b]
	1827[a]			
1827–1854[c]		1654	72.6	78.7
	1854			
1854–1873		1873	72.4	69.8
	1873			
1873–1896		1896	87.9	50.1
	1896			
1896–1913		1913	89.8	60.6

Sources: Appendix, Tables 7.2 and 7.3. See the text
Notes: [a]For imports, the period covers 1814–1832, with 1832 as the base year. The link year with the next period, 1832–1854, is also 1832
[b]Percentage for 1832
[c]For imports, the period covers 1832–1854

These intervals have been linked at the overlapping years to obtain indices covering the whole period, and 1854 has been adopted as the final base year. The commodities involved in the construction of export and import price indices are shown in the Appendix, Tables 7.2 and 7.3. The chosen periods, link years, and base years for building the indices, together with the coverage of goods included in the price indices over total trade in the base years, are shown in Table 7.1.

The lack of quantitative data for some commodities, and the fact that the value of other products make up a negligible percentage of total trade, renders a 70% coverage acceptable. The lower coverage for imported commodities during the second half of the nineteenth century stems from the fact that for a high percentage information is only available for values, not quantities. I have adopted the accepted convention of assuming that changes in the prices of commodities not included in the prices indices will be of similar amplitude and move in the same direction as those that make up the indices (Allen, 1975: 199–202).

7.3 Trends in the Net Barter Terms of Trade

The evolution of the Fisher net barter terms of trade reveals distinctive phases (Fig. 7.1).[6] From 1714 to the early 1770s, the *NBTT* show no clear trend, but for a decline between the mid-1720s and -1740s and a subsequent recovery until the early 1750s, so the import capacity per unit of output exported remained practically unchanged. An expansionary phase encompassed from the late 1770s to the mid-1840s, during which time the import capacity per unit of exports quadrupled. War interrupted the expansion. The *NBTT* stalled in the 1790s, during the early stages of the Revolutionary and Napoleonic Wars and slowed down during the Peninsular War (1808–1814) and the first Carlist War (1833–1840). The long-run improvement in the *NBTT* was followed by stagnation from the mid-1840s to the late 1850s and, subsequently, decline until the late 1860s, at the time of financial and political crises. A swift recovery in the 1870s led to a historical a peak in the early 1880s (in which import capacity per unit of exports quintupled the level of the early eighteenth century). The *NBTT* then experienced a sustained deterioration until the eve of World War I, shrinking by one-third. Thus, by 1913, the import capacity per unit of output exported had fallen to the mid-1820s level, but the substantial increase in the purchasing power in terms of imports per unit of exports achieved during the Industrial Revolution was still preserved.

Thus, on the basis of price effects alone, the import capacity of a given volume of exports by 1913 was three and a half times greater than in 1714. The favourable long-run trend of Spain's terms of trade with Britain meant that the number of British goods that could be obtained in exchange for £1 of Spanish goods in 1714 could be acquired for less than £0.3 by 1913.

After 1880, productivity gains in shipping were reflected in falling freight rates (North, 1965; Cairncross, 1953: 176). Because of the low percentage of transport costs in c.i.f. import values, as British manufactures had a very high value to bulk ratio, differences between f.o.b. and c.i.f. import prices were negligible for most of the 200 years considered. However, after 1880, coal imports from Britain became extremely important for Spain (Prados de la Escosura, 1988). Hence, the decline in freight rates partially offset the rise in prices for British commodities imported into Spain and, from 1884 to 1913, Spanish import capacity per unit of exports improved by 8% due to improvements in the efficiency of British shipping.[7]

[6] Laspeyres and Paasche indices for the NBTT are provided in the Appendix, Fig. 7.5 and in Tables 7.4 and 7.5.

[7] The gains from falling freight rates transferred to Spanish consumers can be estimated by comparing the net barter terms of trade estimated with f.o.b. and c.i.f. price indices for Spanish imports, which amounts to measuring shifts in the terms of trade with constant and actual (falling) freight rates (see Tables 7.4 and 7.5).

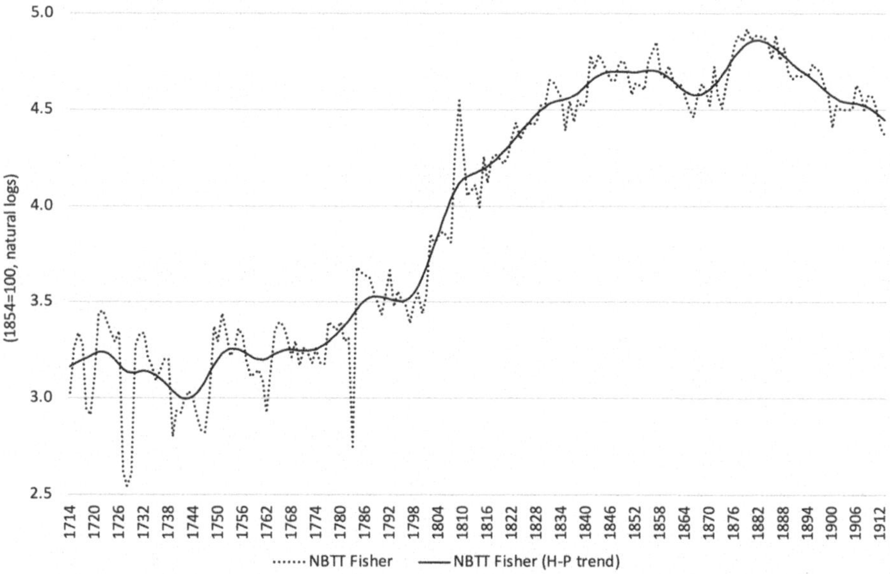

Fig. 7.1 Net barter terms of trade, 1714–1913: Fisher Index (1854=100, natural logs) (f.o.b. exports and c.i.f. imports). Note: Hodrick-Prescott trend, smoothing parameter set at $\lambda = 100$. Sources: Table 7.5

7.4 Terms of Trade Drivers: Trends in Export and Import Prices

A series representing the terms of trade is a moving ratio between price indices which reflects the forces operating on the economy (Rostow, 1950a). Price indices for exports and imports followed a similar path, albeit with different intensities, in synchrony with the international economy (Bordo and Schwartz, 1981).

Distinctive phases can be discerned for Fisher export and import prices (Fig. 7.2).[8] First, a phase in which prices declined, from 1714 until the mid-1740s for exports, and up to the mid-1750s, but at a slower pace, for imports. A second phase of price recovery spanned from the mid-eighteenth century to the Peninsular War, slower until the early 1790s for exports, and faster, up to the mid-1780s, for imports; and, then, prices accelerated to the 1800s, faster now in the case of exports, and peaking earlier for imports (1802) than for exports (1810), coinciding with major events of the Revolutionary and Napoleonic Wars: the Peace of Amiens (1802) and the Peninsular War (1808–1814), respectively.

Two phases can be also observed between the Napoleonic Wars and the First World War. In the first one, a remarkable price decline took place until 1830, deeper

[8]Laspeyres and Paasche indices for export and import prices are provided in Figs. 7.6 and 7.7 and in Tables 7.4 and 7.5 of Appendix.

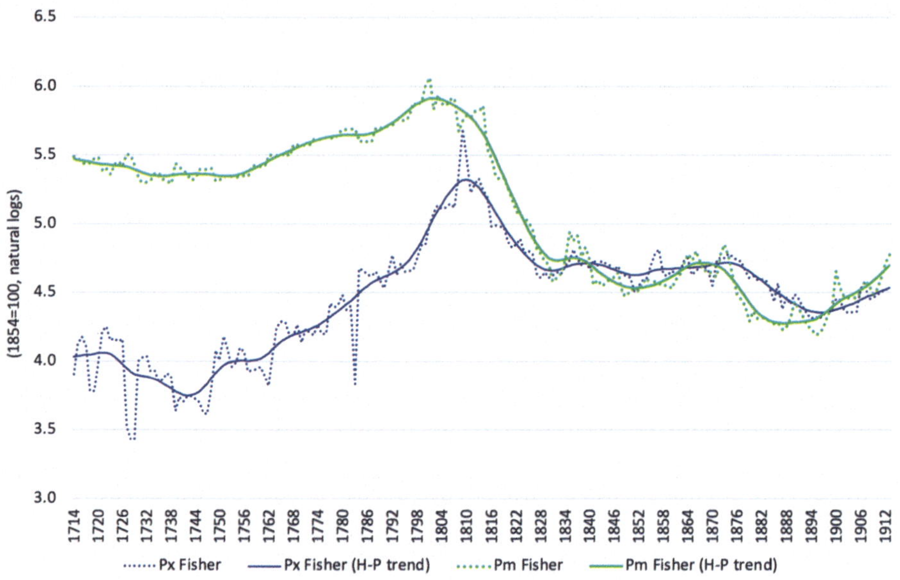

Fig. 7.2 Export and import prices, 1714–1913: Fisher Index (1854=100, natural logs) (f.o.b. exports and c.i.f. imports). Note: Hodrick-Prescott trend, smoothing parameter set at $\lambda = 100$. Sources: Table 7.5

for import prices, which fell to 30% of their peak level, while export prices shrank by a half. In the second phase up to World War I, prices exhibited fluctuations around a flat long-run trend. However, an episode of substantial price contraction took place in the late nineteenth century, with a 30% drop for exports from the mid-1870s to the late 1890s, and a fall of 35% for imports between the late 1860s and 1880s. A recovery followed, but only partially in the case of exports.

Rising British demand for primary goods, which composed most of Spanish exports—for which supply was relatively inelastic—, and increasing efficiency in the production of British (primarily manufactured) goods passed on as lower prices, explain the higher growth of Spanish export prices than import prices between the late eighteenth century and the Napoleonic Wars, and a slower decline from the end of the Napoleonic Wars up to the middle of the nineteenth century. This helps explain the long-run increase in the purchasing power per unit of Spanish exports. Shifts in the British offer curve largely accounted for the improvements in Spain's net barter terms of trade with Britain during British industrialization. The growth of total factor productivity in British export industries supports this interpretation.[9]

The episode of declining purchasing power per unit of exports from the late 1850s to the late 1860s derives, to a large extent, from the rise in import prices. Growth in

[9]In Britain, between 1780 and 1860, total factor productivity, growing at 1.15% in the 'modernized' sectors that dominated exports (Crafts, 2021: 318) evolved inversely to export prices, shrinking at –1.3% (Imlah, 1958: 94–98).

international demand for British goods, together with rising prices for raw cotton during the American Civil War, reflected in the prices of cotton manufactures, account for this increase. In addition, Spanish imports of British goods rose substantially in the late 1850s and early 1860s when railway construction started in Spain and required considerable quantities of technical equipment and fuel, leading to the single period of persistent trade deficit (1856–1865) with Britain between the Napoleonic Wars and the First World War.[10] This situation, common to other areas of the world, helps explain the rise in prices for British manufacturers. Besides, coal shortages also occurred during these years, affecting not only the price of British coal—in great demand because of the spread of the railway and modern industry in Western Europe and other parts of the world—, but also the prices of steel and engineering goods, for which foreign demand was also rising very fast. The recovery of Spain's *NBTT* in the 1870s is again connected with import prices. Coal shortages were eventually resolved and prices for British coal and those manufactures which used it as an input in their production fell sharply (Rostow, 1978: 93).

The deterioration of Spanish *NBTT* from 1880 to 1913 was partly due to the faster decline of export prices up to 1896, and their subsequent slower recovery. Furthermore, slackening productivity growth in British industry, coupled with strong demand for British manufactures from areas of recent settlement, driven by British investment, contributed to the post-1896 rise in import prices.[11] A shortage of coal in the late 1890s and early 1900s was also behind the rise in import prices for coal and steel and engineering manufactures (Rostow, 1978: 94).[12]

A partial explanatory element of the unfavourable trend in the *NBTT* in the 1890s and early 1900s is the lagged currency depreciation after Spain abandoned the convertibility of its currency, the Peseta, into gold in 1883. In the hypothetical absence of depreciation of Spanish currency, NBTT would have deteriorated only mildly until 1904 but would then have fallen more sharply (Fig. 7.8).

7.5 The Factorial Terms of Trade

Exogenous changes in the *NBTT* imply a gain or a loss of welfare, but the significance in terms of welfare is ambiguous when these changes are endogenous. *NBTT* may deteriorate as a result of increases in productivity, or in job opportunities in a

---

[10] For the trade balance between Spain and Britain, see Prados de la Escosura (1984: 157–159). For the derived demand for equipment and fuel from railway construction, see Gómez Mendoza (1982, Ch. 4–5).

[11] In the late nineteenth century, British total factor productivity decelerated from 1.34% in 1856–1873 to 0.68% in 1873–1913 (Crafts, 2021: 701). For the patterns and pace of British overseas investment, see Edelstein (1982).

[12] Productivity in coal mining was declining in Britain in the years 1890–1913 (Cf. Lewis, 1978: 95, 132). For the economy as a whole, TFP growth stalled from 1899 to 1907 (Crafts, 2021: 702).

context of unemployment. The factorial terms of trade broaden the scope and take productivity and employment on board.

Spanish terms of trade with Britain were affected by changes in either productivity or employment. Agriculture and mining provided most of Spain's exports to Britain from 1880 to 1913. The exploitation of mineral resources with modem techniques, often by foreign investors, increased productivity, which was passed on to the international consumer in the form of lower export prices. Estimates of output per worker in the production of major ores and metals exported show clear improvements, with a 61% increase in average labour productivity.[13] Export-oriented agriculture also experienced a labour productivity increase over the same period (Ayuda and Pinilla, 2021).

In nineteenth-century Spain, as in other Mediterranean economies, unemployment and underemployment were defining features of the labour markets (Toniolo, 1983). Day labourers (*jornaleros*) were out of work for one-quarter of the year in the 1850s (Garcia Sanz, 1979–1980: 63). Seasonal employment prevailed in the late nineteenth century: 210 days for the average *bracero* or farm labourer, out of a possible 300 days a year working (275 days as a lower bound) (Gómez Mendoza, 1982: 99–104). While Vandellós (1925: 119) suggested 250 days per worker/year estimated for 1913, close to García Sanz's 242 days, and James Simpson's (1992, 1995) detailed computations for Andalusia and Catalonia offer even fewer days worked per day labourer. Full employment occurred only during the summer months and peasants were idle for 3 or 4 months every year. Therefore, the opportunity cost of allocating agricultural labour to alternative occupations during the dead season was minimal.

The exploitation of minerals to cater for foreign demand provided more jobs, although the numbers involved were small and the mining industry never represented above 2% of the total hours worked in the Spanish economy (Prados de la Escosura, 2017). Internal migration and shifts within occupations from subsistence into more labour-intensive trade-oriented agriculture and mining was also stimulated by export growth.

7.5.1 Single Factorial Terms of Trade

To allow for changes in productivity in the export sector, economists examine the single factorial terms of trade (*SFTT*). This index measures a country's absolute

[13]Estimated metric tons of minerals and metals per man over 18 years old, from iron ore, lead, quicksilver, copper metal (*Estadística minera* data kindly supplied by José Ramón Castillo); for copper ore and pyrites, Harvey (1981: 128–332). On this basis, I constructed a Laspeyres index of output per male worker in two segments using 1896 and 1913 as base years, and 1895–1899 as the link years. The weights used are the shares of each mineral in the total value of mineral exports (Prados de la Escosura, 1982). For the extractive industry as a whole, output per hour worked increased by 52% over 1880–1913 (Prados de la Escosura, 2017, updated).

welfare resulting from international trade and specialization. The *SFTT* adds labour productivity in exportable production to the *NBTT* already weighted by the share of imports in home consumption.[14]

$$SFTT = WSFTT = NBTT^{\omega} O/L \tag{7.5}$$

where ω is the share of imports in home consumption and *O*/*L* stands for labour productivity in the home country's exportable output.

If there were chronic unemployment or underemployment, as in the case of nineteenth-century Spain, an increase in employment derived from export expansion would have the same effect on absolute real income as an increase in labour productivity. In this case, an 'employment-corrected' (EC) index is appropriate:

$$ECWSFTT = NBTT^{\omega} O/LN \tag{7.6}$$

where *N* stands for an index of the volume of labour used in exportable production.

Given that $NBTT = P_X/P_M$ and $P_X O/L\ N = V$, where *V* stands for the value of exportable output, *ECWSFTT* can be written as follows,

$$ECWSFTT = \left(P_X{}^{\omega-1} V\right)/P_M{}^{\omega} \tag{7.7}$$

In the case of Spanish-British trade, the value of exportable output (V) may be proxied by the value of exports (Prados de la Escosura, 1984). Minerals accounted for half the value of exports from the late 1870s to 1913, and most of this output was exported. A significant part of the production of commercial agriculture along the Mediterranean coast (almonds, oranges, raisins, as well as cork and Sherry wine), found its way to Britain (Prados de la Escosura, 1982, 1984). As for the share of imports in home consumption for the post-1778 period, it has been proxied by the ratio of total Spanish c.i.f. imports to GDP.[15]

Figure 7.3 presents estimates for employment-corrected weighted single factorial terms of trade (ECWSFTT) from 1778 to 1913. After an intense recovery from a war scenario in the 1780s, a phase of sustained improvement, but for the Peninsular War years, covered from 1790 to 1850 (at 1.5% trend growth rate). This long phase gave way to another of acceleration until the early 1900s (3.7%). However, the decade up to the First World War witnessed a deterioration (−1.1%). Over the entire period considered, however, the *ECWSFTT* multiplied by 40, which implies a trend growth of 2.9% per year.

[14] Labour productivity has been suggested as the relevant productivity measure in *SFTT* estimates, since it is an indicator of changes in welfare, i.e. changes in real per capita income, abstracting from distribution (Spraos, 1983: 70–80).

[15] Import c.i.f. values come from Chap. 6 (1778–1820) and Prados de la Escosura (1988). GDP at current prices from Table 2.3 (1778–1849) and Prados de la Escosura (2017, updated) (1850–1913).

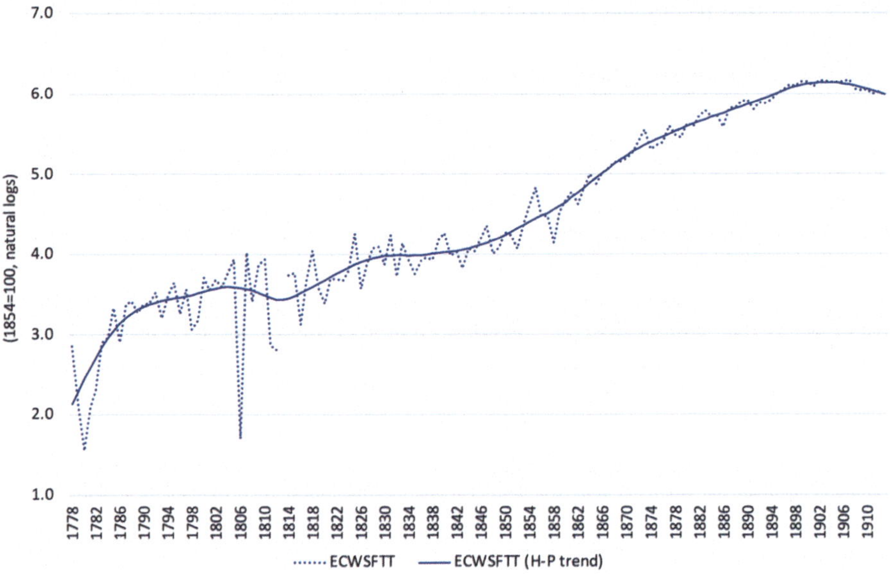

Fig. 7.3 Employment corrected weighted single factorial terms of trade, 1778–1913 Fisher Index (1854=100, natural logs) (f.o.b. exports and c.i.f. imports). Note: Hodrick-Prescott trend, smoothing parameter set at $\lambda = 100$. Sources: Table 7.6

Thus, the deterioration of the *NBTT* from 1880 to 1913 (−1.2%) was more than offset by improvements in employment opportunities and in labour productivity in the exportable sector, with the *ECWSFTT* trend growth reaching 1.2%. It was only during the first decade of the twentieth century (1903–1913) that the single factorial terms of trade deteriorated.

We may conclude that *immiserizing* growth, that is, allocating an increasing amount of resources to the production of exportables for which the *SFTT* deteriorate, did not occur in the economic relations between Spain, a primary producer, and Britain, the first industrial nation, from the late eighteenth to the twentieth century.

So far, only changes in absolute welfare stemming from international trade and specialization have been considered. We have seen, however, the apparent paradox of nineteenth-century Spain raising its income per head and simultaneously worsening its position vis-à-vis the core countries of north-west Europe (Figs. 1.5 and 1.11). Thus, it is theoretically possible for patterns of trade and specialization to increase absolute welfare for Spain as measured by the *ECWSFTT* but, at the same time, to decrease the country's income relative to Britain.

7.5.2 Double Factorial Terms of Trade

Double factorial terms of trade (*DFTT*) are designed to assess the impact of patterns of trade on relative welfare. More specifically, the *DFTT* represent 'the number of man-hours needed on average to produce foreign exportables of a value equal to 1 hour's production of home exportables' (Spraos, 1983: 76). When weighted by the import share of each country involved, to take into account the relative importance trade commodities in each country's consumption basket, the *DFTT* can be written:

$$WDFTT = (NBTT^{\omega+\omega*} O/L) : O^*/L^*) \tag{7.8}$$

where * stands for the foreign country, in this case, Britain.

Employment correction appears necessary where unemployment and underemployment were persistent, as in the case of Spain, but not for Britain (Matthews et al., 1982: 81–95; Williamson, 1985: 20–22).[16] An appropriate index in which relative welfare is accounted for with allowances for changes in employment can be expressed as

$$ECWDFTT = (NBTT^{\omega+\omega*} O/LN) : (O^*/L^*) \tag{7.9}$$

and, as in (7.7), it may be transformed into

$$ECWDFTT = \left(\mathrm{P_X}^{\omega+\omega*\,-1} V\right) : (\mathrm{P_M}^{\omega+\omega*} O^*/L^*). \tag{7.10}$$

Figure 7.4 presents the findings for relative welfare stemming from Ricardian patterns of trade and specialization, which reveal an initial phase, in which after a post-war strong recovery until 1790, a mild improvement took place between 1790 and 1850 (1.0% trend growth rate), punctuated by episodes of acceleration (up to 1790, 1814–1830) as well as of stagnation or decline. A second, steadier phase extended up to 1900 in which the trend growth rose to 2.6%. A third phase of negative trend growth (−1.9%) lasted until the First World War. Over the entire time span considered (1778–1913), the relative welfare derived from patterns of trade and specialization, measured by the *ECWDFTT* multiplied 14-fold, at a 2.1% trend growth rate.[17]

These results imply that, together with the evolution of the *NBTT*, the increase in employment and labour productivity provided by trade specialization more than offset the rise in British labour productivity from 1778 to 1900. Specifically, the deterioration of the *NBTT* after 1880 was more than offset, as shown by the evolution

[16]For Britain, the value of c.i.f. imports comes from Cuenca Esteban (2001), for 1778–1820 and Imlah (1958) for 1820–1913 in Bank of England (2018), series A.36. GDP at current prices and labour productivity (output per worker) from Broadberry et al. (2015) and Feinstein (1972), also in Bank of England (2018), series A9, Nominal GDP(A) 1700–2014 and series A56, labour productivity.

[17]It is worth noting that when most of the exportable output in the primary producer is sent to the industrial, developed country, the latter in exchange, only exports a small proportion of its output, so $\omega + \omega^*$ tends to approach 1 (Spraos, 1983: 75). This scenario is not far from the observed patterns of trade between Spain and Britain as the comparison between the weighted and unweighted *ECSFTT* and *ECDFTT* show (Appendix, Figs. 7.8 and 7.9).

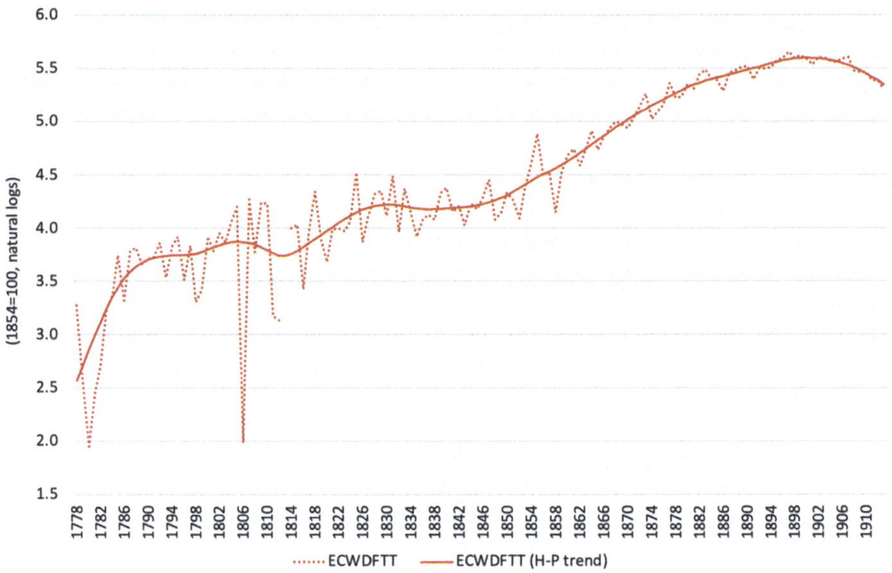

Fig. 7.4 Employment corrected weighted double factorial terms of trade, 1778–1913: Fisher Index (1854=100, natural logs) (f.o.b. exports and c.i.f. imports). Note: Hodrick-Prescott (H-P) trend, smoothing parameter set at $\lambda = 100$. Sources: Table 7.6

of both the *ECWSFTT* and *ECWDFTT*, thereby precluding inequalising trade between Spain and Britain. It was only during the decade prior to the First World War that Spanish-British terms of trade provoked immiserizing growth and trade had an inequalising effect.

Furthermore, both single and factorial terms of trade exhibited a positive trend until 1900, satisfying the welfare-neutral requirement to prevent a deterioration of welfare when exports which include natural resources, are exchanged for reproducible goods (Spraos, 1983: 78–79).

7.6 Conclusions

After the loss of the American mainland empire, Spain reoriented towards Western Europe's markets, increasing its share of trade with the early industrial nations. It has been often argued that this led to an unequal exchange that, albeit favourable to some interest groups was, on the whole, negative for the Spanish economy, as it pushed it towards a sub-optimal path of development. This sub-optimal path resulted from following Spain's comparative advantage in primary produce, with the implicit opportunity cost of failing to develop along the lines traced by the pioneers of the Industrial Revolution. This chapter has addressed the issue by looking at the evolution of the terms of trade between Spain and Britain, the cradle of the Industrial Revolution.

The *NBTT* improved remarkably over 1780–1880, though it fell from 1880 to 1913. Changes in the *NBTT* have, however, different implications for a country's welfare, depending on whether they derive from endogenous or exogenous sources. In fact, what really matters is not the purchasing power per unit of export—what *NBTT* measure—but the purchasing power per unit of labour embodied in export goods—what the factorial terms of trade measure. Estimates for the (employment-corrected weighted) single factorial terms of trade (*ECWSFTT*) show long-term gains due to employment opportunities and productivity gains resulting from opening up. This implies that absolute welfare for those employed in sectors linked to international trade improved until the twentieth century. Furthermore, double factorial terms of trade (adjusted for unemployment) [*ECWDFTT*] also exhibit sustained gains throughout the late eighteenth and nineteenth centuries. Rising employment in the exportable sector and improvements in labour productivity more than offset labour productivity gains achieved by the British economy. Hence, Spain's incomes from trade and specialisation evolved favourably relative to Britain's until 1900.

All this suggests that the negative assessment of Spain's reorientation towards north-western Europe is unwarranted. Falling behind Western European levels cannot be blamed on economic specialization along lines of comparative advantage. On the contrary, throughout the late eighteenth and nineteenth century the Spanish economy took full advantage of British industrialization. The sectors most closely associated with international patterns of specialisation did not share the inequalising experience that the Spanish economy as a whole suffered over the century. The explanation for the growing gap in living standards between Spain and Britain (and, by extension, the Core countries of Western Europe) must be sought outside the export sector.

Appendix

See Tables 7.2, 7.3, 7.4, 7.5 and 7.6.

See Figs. 7.5, 7.6, 7.7, 7.8, 7.9 and 7.10.

Table 7.2 Annual series for export and import price indices

Commodities included in the Export Price Indices
1714–1750, Almonds, Barilla, Iron bars, Olive oil, Raisins, Salt, Silk, Sherry and Wool
1750–1778, Almonds, Barilla, Iron bars, Olive oil, Raisins, Salt, Silk, Sherry and Wool
1778–1796, Almonds, Barilla, Iron bars, Olive oil, Raisins, Sherry and Wool
1796–1814, Almonds, Barilla, Olive oil, Quicksilver, Raisins, Sherry and Wool
1814–1827, Almonds, Barilla, Brandy, Olive oil, Quicksilver, Raisins, Sherry and Wool
1827–1854, Barilla, Lead bars, Olive Oil, Quicksilver, Raisins, Sherry and Wool
1854–1873, Almonds, Copper(metal), Copper(ore), Cork, Corks, Lead bars, Oranges, Olive oil, Oxen, Quicksilver, Raisins, Common wine, Sherry and Wool
1873–1896, Almonds, Copper(ore), Copper(regulus), Pyrites, Cork, Corks, Iron ore, Lead bars, Oranges, Olive oil, Quicksilver, Raisins, Common wine, Sherry and Wool
1896–1913, Almonds, Copper(ore), Copper(regulus), Pyrites, Cork, Corks, Esparto grass, Grapes, Iron ore, Lead bars, Oranges, Olive oil, Onions, Quicksilver, Raisins, Common wine Sherry and Wool
Commodities included in the Import Price Indices
1714–1778, Brass & Copper manufactures, Coal, Fish, Flour, Hats, Iron & Steel manufactures, Lead, Leather manufactures, Linen manufactures, Tin, Wheat, Woollen manufactures
1750–1778, Brass & Copper manufactures, Coal, Fish, Flour, Hats, Iron & Steel manufactures, Lead, Leather manufactures, Linen manufactures, Tin, Wheat, Woollen manufactures
1778–1796, Brass & Copper manufactures, Coal, Fish, Flour, Hats, Iron & Steel manufactures, Lead, Leather manufactures, Linen manufactures, Tin, Woollen manufactures
1796–1814, Brass & Copper manufactures, Coal, Fish, Hats, Iron & Steel manufactures, Lead, Leather manufactures, Tin, Woollen manufactures
1814–1827, Brass & Copper manufactures, Coal, Cotton manufactures, Cotton yarn, Hats, Hardware & Cutlery, Iron & Steel manufactures, Lead, Linen manufactures, Tin, Woollen manufactures
1827–1854, Brass & Copper manufactures, Coal, Cotton manufactures, Cotton yarn, Hardware & Cutlery, Iron & Steel manufactures, Linen manufactures, Linen yarn, Tin, Woollen manufactures, Woollen yarn
1854–1873, Brass & Copper manufactures, Alkali, Coal, Cotton manufactures, Cotton yarn, Iron & Steel manufactures, Linen manufactures, Linen yarn, Linseed oil, Tin, Woollen manufactures
1873–1896, Brass & Copper manufactures, Alkali, Coal, Cotton manufactures, Cotton yarn, Iron & Steel manufactures, Jute yam, Line manufactures, Linen yarn, Linseed oil, Tin, Woollen manufactures
1896–1913, Brass & Copper manufactures, Alkali, Coal, Cotton manufactures, Cotton yarn, Iron & Steel manufactures, Jute yarn, Linen manufactures, Linen yarn, Linseed oil, Manure Tin Woollen manufactures

Sources: Table 7.3

Table 7.3 Price series and their sources

British goods imported into Spain (1714–1812)
Iron Manufactures, Beveridge (1939), 1714–1781 (nails); Tooke & Newmarch (1838), 1782–1789 (pig iron); Gayer et al. (1953), 1790–1812 (pig iron).
Copper & Brass Manufactures, Beveridge (1939), 1714–1781; Tooke (1823), 1782–1789; Gayer et al. (1953), 1790–1812.
Tin, Posthumus (1946), 1714–1781 (English tin); Tooke (1823), 1782–1789; Gayer et al. (1953), 1790–1812.
Lead, Posthumus (1946), 1714–1781 (English lead); Tooke (1823), 1782–1789; Gayer et al. (1953), 1790–1812
Coal, Beveridge (1939), 1714–1787 (Westminster); Mitchell (1988), 1788–1812.
Leather Manufactures, Beveridge (1939), 1714–1789 (leather backs); Gayer et al. (1953), 1790–1812 (leather boots)
Hats, Beveridge (1939), 1714–1812
Linens, Mitchell (1988), 1728–1812 (A.Warden)
Fish, Beveridge (1939), 1714–1812 (salmon & cod)
Wheat, Beveridge (1939), 1714–1771 (Winchester) Mitchell (1988), 1771–1812 (average English price, London Gazette)
Flour & Wheatmeal, Beveridge (1939), 1714–1812 (London & Greenwich)
Cotton Manufactures, Only relevant from the late eighteenth century. Since official values are close to market values (cf. Davis (1979: 84), they have been accepted as current prices for the years before 1793. For 1793–1812, it has been assumed that prices were similar to those in 1814 and official values for 1793–1812 were revalued with the ratio between declared and official values in 1814.
Woollen & Worsted Manufactures, Beveridge (1939) provides a series for men's stockings (Greenwich Hospital) and perpets & serges (Lord Chamberlain's Department). Bvereidge also provides price series for different kinds of cloth which, surprisingly, do not show any major increase at the end of the eighteenth century, in contrast to the evidence provided by Mann (1971) and Deane and Cole (1967). Beveridge (1939: 172) believed that behind such price rigidity were quality changes. Deane and Cole (1967: 84) provide a 5-year price index for broadcloth exported by the East India Company, and their index has been used here instead of Beveridge's for revaluing the official values of woollen and worsted manufactures, other than men's stockings and perpets and serges, for which Beveridge's prices are used.
Non-British goods imported into Spain from Britain (1714–1853)
Cocoa, Posthumus (1946), 1714–1789; Gayer et al. (1953), 1790–1850; The Economist, 1851–1853
Black Pepper, Posthumus (1946), 1714–1781; Tooke & Newmarch (1838), 1782–1789; Gayer et al. (1953), 1790–1850; The Economist, 1851–1853
Carolina Rice, Thorold Rogers (1866), 1714–1781; Tooke & Newmarch (1838), 1782–1850; The Economist, 1851–1853
Jamaica Rum, Tooke & Newmarch (1838), 1782–1850; The Economist, 1851–1853
Virginia Tobacco, Posthumus (1946), 1714–1781; Tooke & Newmarch (1838), 1782–1789; Gayer et al. (1953), 1790–1850; The Economist, 1851–1853
Muscovado Sugar, Sheridan (1974), 1714–1775; Ragatz (1928), 1776–1781; Tooke & Newmarch (1838), 1782–1789; Gayer et al. (1953), 1790–1850; The Economist, 1851–1853
Ceylon Cinnamon, Tooke & Newmarch (1838), 1782–1789; Gayer et al. (1953), 1790–1850; The Economist, 1851–1853
Indian Cotton Goods, Marshall (1833), 1799–1831;

(continued)

Table 7.3 (continued)

German Linens, Beveridge (1939), 1714–1820
Spanish Goods exported to Britain (1714–1853)
Olive Oil, Posthumus (1946), 1714–1781; Tooke & Newmarch (1838), 1782–1789; Gayer, et al. (1953), 1790–1850; London Price Currents, 1851–1853
Brandy, London Price Currents, 1783–1853
Almonds, Posthumus (1946), 1714–1778 (Valencia); London Price Currents, 1779–1853 (Valencia)
Barilla, Posthumus (1946), 1714–1778 (Alicante); London Price Currents, 1779–1789; Gayer et al. (1953), 1790–1850; London Price Currents, 1851–1853
Flour, Board of Trade, 1827–1853
Iron Bars, Posthumus (1946), 1714–1778; London Price Currents, 1779–1782
Wool, Posthumus (1946), 1714–1778 (Leonesa, Segovia, Soria & Sevilla); London Price Currents, 1779–1853 (Leonesa, Segovia, Soria & Sevilla)
Quicksilver, Gayer et al. (1953), 1790–1850; The Economist, 1851–1853
Raisins, Posthumus (1946), 1714–1778; London Price Currents, 1779–1853
Lead in Bars, London Price Currents, 1825–1853
Silk, Tooke & Newmarch (1838), 1782–1850; London Price Currents, 1851–1853
Wheat, Mitchell, 1817–1853 (London Gazette)
Lead in Bars, London Price Currents, 1825–1853
Silk, Tooke & Newmarch (1838), 1782–1850; London Price Currents, 1851–1853
Wheat, Mitchell, 1817–1853 (London Gazzette)
Wine, Posthumus (1946), 1714–1778 (Sherry); 1778–1853, London Price Currents, (Sherry, common red)
Spanish re-exports of colonial goods to Britain (1714–1853)
Raw Cotton, Posthumus (1946), 1714–1781; Tooke & Newmarch (1838), 1782–1789; Gayer, 1790–1850; London Price Currents, 1851–1853
Indigo, Posthumus (1946), 1714–1781 (Guatemala Indigo); London Price Currents, 1782–1853
Cochineal, Posthumus (1946), 1714–1778; London Price Currents, 1779–1853
Bark, London Price Currents, 1779–1853
Logwood, Tooke & Newmarch (1838), 1782–1789; Gayer et al. (1953), 1790–1850; London Price Currents, 1851–1853

Table 7.4 Net barter terms of trade between Spain and Britain, (1714–1913) (f.o.b. export and import prices)

	Export price indices			Import price indices			Net barter terms of trade		
	Laspeyres	Paasche	Fischer	Laspeyres	Paasche	Fischer	Laspeyres	Paasche	Fischer
1714	36.0	68.5	49.7	233.3	232.4	232.8	15.4	29.5	21.3
1715	44.2	86.8	61.9	260.1	227.5	243.3	17.0	38.1	25.5
1716	50.1	84.5	65.1	247.4	225.7	236.3	20.3	37.5	27.6
1717	43.7	83.7	60.5	239.3	226.2	232.7	18.3	37.0	26.0
1718	32.3	59.5	43.9	218.1	224.4	221.3	14.8	26.5	19.8
1719	32.4	59.2	43.8	233.4	225.5	229.4	13.9	26.3	19.1
1720	38.9	71.9	52.9	234.1	229.0	231.6	16.6	31.4	22.8
1721	47.9	96.7	67.9	219.9	225.0	222.4	21.8	43.0	30.5
1722	48.4	101.0	69.9	228.6	231.3	229.9	21.2	43.7	30.4
1723	45.2	89.1	63.5	222.2	212.9	271.5	20.3	41.9	29.2
1724	46.1	89.7	64.3	243.1	226.4	234.6	19.0	39.6	27.4
1725	45.2	87.4	62.9	248.3	230.9	239.4	18.2	37.9	26.3
1726	45.5	89.8	63.9	228.3	228.6	228.4	19.9	39.3	28.0
1727	25.2	45.4	33.8	259.0	214.5	235.7	9.7	21.2	14.4
1728	23.5	40.9	31.0	255.5	211.8	232.6	9.2	19.3	13.3
1729	23.3	40.8	30.9	221.8	221.2	217.0	10.5	19.2	14.2
1730	39.2	75.8	54.5	213.8	208.8	211.3	18.3	36.3	25.8
1731	39.9	78.7	56.0	203.3	205.3	204.3	19.6	38.3	27.4
1732	40.5	79.1	56.6	204.0	206.4	205.2	19.8	38.3	27.6
1733	36.6	70.2	50.6	209.5	207.8	208.7	17.5	33.8	24.3
1734	37.0	69.3	50.7	223.9	215.8	219.8	16.5	32.1	23.1
1735	34.5	64.1	47.0	228.2	210.7	219.2	15.1	30.4	21.4
1736	35.0	65.0	47.7	213.2	206.8	210.0	16.4	31.4	22.7
1737	36.6	67.7	49.8	211.2	203.4	207.3	17.3	33.3	24.0

(continued)

Table 7.4 (continued)

	Export price indices			Import price indices			Net barter terms of trade		
	Laspeyres	Paasche	Fischer	Laspeyres	Paasche	Fischer	Laspeyres	Paasche	Fischer
1738	35.9	66.9	49.0	207.2	199.8	203.5	17.3	33.5	24.1
1739	26.7	53.8	37.9	230.3	208.1	218.9	11.6	25.9	17.3
1740	30.7	57.3	41.9	209.9	213.8	221.9	14.6	26.8	19.8
1741	29.9	55.9	40.7	206.8	208.0	207.4	14.3	26.9	19.6
1742	31.6	56.1	42.1	193.5	204.6	199.0	16.3	27.4	21.2
1743	33.2	53.9	42.3	184.6	197.1	190.8	18.0	27.3	22.2
1744	31.3	54.4	41.3	191.3	198.4	194.8	16.4	27.4	21.2
1745	31.3	52.2	40.4	213.0	204.0	208.5	14.7	25.6	19.4
1746	28.7	48.4	37.3	214.1	203.5	208.7	13.4	23.8	17.9
1747	26.7	51.6	37.1	213.3	204.0	208.6	12.5	25.3	17.8
1748	34.5	58.5	45.0	215.9	205.5	210.6	16.0	28.5	21.3
1749	42.8	81.9	59.2	221.7	204.2	208.0	20.2	40.1	28.5
1750	40.1	75.4	55.0	213.8	204.7	209.2	18.7	36.8	26.3
1751	47.1	91.2	65.5	214.2	219.6	216.9	22.0	41.5	30.2
1752	43.4	82.5	59.9	214.3	219.0	216.7	20.3	37.7	27.6
1753	38.9	70.7	52.4	216.3	216.2	216.3	18.0	32.7	24.2
1754	38.1	76.9	54.2	215.7	215.0	215.4	17.7	35.8	25.2
1755	43.7	82.4	60.1	215.6	215.3	215.5	20.3	38.3	27.9
1756	42.7	80.0	58.5	218.0	211.9	214.9	19.6	37.8	27.2
1757	37.0	70.0	50.9	215.6	212.1	213.8	17.1	33.0	23.8
1758	37.5	69.6	51.1	235.4	233.2	234.3	15.9	29.9	21.8
1759	38.2	69.6	51.6	235.5	229.2	232.3	16.2	30.4	22.2
1760	38.6	71.0	52.3	235.2	228.5	231.8	16.4	31.1	22.6
1761	34.8	68.9	49.0	235.2	227.5	231.3	14.8	30.3	21.2

1762	33.4	62.0	45.5	235.2	236.6	235.9	14.2	26.2	19.3
1763	41.7	81.1	58.2	254.9	252.6	253.7	16.4	32.1	22.9
1764	52.1	93.5	69.8	255.1	250.4	252.7	20.4	37.4	27.6
1765	54.7	96.8	72.8	255.0	249.4	252.1	21.5	38.8	28.9
1766	52.7	100.4	72.7	257.1	257.9	257.5	20.5	38.9	28.2
1767	47.0	94.5	66.7	257.1	246.3	251.6	18.3	38.4	26.5
1768	49.5	87.2	65.7	277.4	269.9	273.6	17.9	32.3	24.0
1769	51.2	99.0	71.2	277.1	268.1	272.6	18.5	36.9	26.1
1770	45.7	85.7	62.6	277.1	267.7	272.4	16.5	32.0	23.0
1771	52.2	91.2	69.0	277.1	269.0	273.0	18.8	33.9	25.3
1772	52.6	86.1	67.3	277.2	269.9	273.5	19.0	31.9	24.6
1773	50.9	85.8	66.1	288.3	279.9	284.1	17.7	30.7	23.3
1774	53.9	94.0	71.2	288.1	278.7	283.3	18.7	33.7	25.1
1775	51.1	87.3	66.8	288.8	280.4	284.5	17.7	31.1	23.5
1776	50.3	88.5	66.7	288.9	280.4	284.6	17.4	31.6	23.5
1777	61.7	112.2	83.2	290.0	281.6	285.8	21.3	39.8	29.1
1778	62.2	104.9	80.8	286.8	279.1	282.9	21.7	37.6	28.6
1779	61.7	109.5	82.2	287.9	279.0	283.4	21.4	39.3	29.0
1780	70.3	110.8	88.3	299.2	289.9	294.5	23.5	38.2	30.0
1781	64.3	98.2	79.5	296.3	287.2	291.7	21.7	34.2	27.2
1782	63.8	104.6	81.6	299.2	289.9	294.5	21.3	36.1	27.7
1783	36.7	58.3	46.3	300.2	290.3	295.2	12.2	20.1	15.7
1784	84.7	134.9	106.9	290.8	284.3	287.6	29.1	47.4	37.2
1785	81.6	137.0	105.7	299.4	285.4	292.3	27.3	48.0	36.2
1786	82.6	126.6	102.3	290.4	284.4	287.4	28.4	44.5	35.6
1787	80.4	128.5	101.6	289.0	285.2	287.1	27.8	45.1	35.4
1788	80.2	136.2	104.5	319.9	319.8	319.9	25.1	42.6	32.7

(continued)

Table 7.4 (continued)

	Export price indices			Import price indices			Net barter terms of trade		
	Laspeyres	Paasche	Fischer	Laspeyres	Paasche	Fischer	Laspeyres	Paasche	Fischer
1789	77.3	126.0	98.7	320.3	318.0	319.2	24.1	39.6	30.9
1790	74.4	115.8	92.8	324.5	317.8	321.1	22.9	36.5	28.9
1791	82.4	130.1	103.5	326.4	321.9	324.1	25.2	40.4	31.9
1792	90.7	154.3	118.3	327.6	323.5	325.5	27.7	47.7	36.3
1793	83.2	125.2	102.1	335.7	332.3	334.0	24.8	37.7	30.6
1794	84.1	146.0	110.8	336.8	333.7	335.2	25.0	43.8	33.1
1795	80.8	135.8	104.7	328.2	328.8	332.0	24.1	41.3	31.5
1796	81.0	137.1	105.4	342.4	338.7	340.5	23.7	40.5	30.9
1797	87.1	128.8	106.2	298.0	456.1	368.7	29.4	28.2	28.8
1798	85.6	154.2	114.9	296.2	439.9	361.0	28.9	35.1	31.8
1799	98.2	163.6	126.7	354.5	400.9	377.0	27.7	40.8	33.6
1800	102.5	158.5	127.5	463.0	391.4	452.7	22.1	40.5	29.9
1801	120.7	177.1	146.2	485.9	417.5	450.4	24.9	42.4	32.5
1802	132.5	195.2	160.8	355.9	371.9	363.8	37.2	52.5	44.2
1803	138.2	208.2	169.6	391.3	430.4	410.4	35.3	48.4	41.3
1804	136.5	202.1	166.0	356.7	371.6	364.1	38.3	54.4	45.6
1805	136.4	205.9	167.6	355.0	360.9	357.9	38.4	57.1	46.8
1806	140.3	209.7	171.6	359.6	401.8	380.1	39.0	52.2	45.1
1807	137.9	203.8	167.7	358.8	410.7	383.9	38.4	49.6	43.7
1808	166.4	258.3	207.3	281.0	296.3	288.6	59.2	87.1	71.9
1809	307.8	284.4	295.8	299.4	330.1	314.4	102.8	86.1	94.1
1810	192.9	283.8	234.0	298.8	365.5	330.5	64.6	77.6	70.8
1811	153.7	225.8	186.3	290.4	364.2	325.2	52.9	62.0	57.3
1812	164.9	241.4	199.6	335.2	347.6	341.4	49.2	69.4	58.5

1813	171.0	248.2	206.0	336.9	349.5	343.2	50.8	71.0	60.0
1814	157.6	228.8	189.9	354.4	363.4	358.9	44.5	63.0	52.9
1815	149.5	217.1	180.1	271.5	243.0	256.8	55.1	89.3	70.2
1816	129.8	164.1	146.0	246.5	233.5	239.9	52.7	70.3	60.9
1817	125.9	171.2	146.8	224.3	196.4	209.9	56.1	87.1	69.9
1818	126.3	168.8	146.0	222.2	188.4	204.6	56.9	89.6	71.4
1819	126.4	166.1	144.9	219.8	204.3	211.9	57.5	81.3	68.4
1820	124.2	137.4	130.6	200.6	194.0	197.3	61.9	70.8	66.2
1821	116.8	133.1	124.7	185.1	179.2	182.1	63.1	74.3	68.5
1822	116.8	139.6	127.7	168.1	163.1	165.8	69.5	85.4	77.1
1823	126.3	140.7	133.3	163.8	159.2	161.5	77.1	88.3	82.5
1824	112.8	126.7	119.6	163.1	153.4	158.1	69.2	82.6	75.6
1825	110.7	134.7	122.1	157.0	149.6	153.2	70.5	90.0	79.7
1826	110.0	129.0	119.1	147.1	141.8	144.4	74.8	90.9	82.5
1827	99.2	106.7	102.8	127.4	120.9	124.1	77.9	88.2	82.9
1828	97.4	102.8	100.0	123.0	116.1	119.5	79.2	88.5	83.7
1829	102.8	105.7	104.2	115.6	108.9	112.2	88.9	97.1	92.9
1830	97.5	103.2	100.3	113.5	107.7	110.6	85.9	95.9	90.8
1831	99.2	104.9	102.0	99.8	92.6	96.1	99.5	113.3	106.2
1832	98.9	109.7	104.1	102.8	96.2	99.4	96.2	114.0	104.7
1833	98.9	107.3	103.0	120.8	91.7	105.2	81.9	117.0	97.9
1834	106.0	112.3	109.1	115.6	117.3	116.5	91.7	95.7	93.7
1835	109.5	116.7	113.0	163.2	129.6	145.4	67.1	90.0	77.7
1836	122.3	124.0	123.2	150.3	120.1	134.3	81.4	103.3	91.7
1837	111.2	118.1	114.9	154.1	125.9	139.3	72.6	93.8	82.5
1838	108.8	111.2	110.0	117.7	114.3	116.0	92.4	97.2	94.8
1839	111.4	117.4	114.4	137.4	117.3	127.0	81.1	100.0	90.1

(continued)

Table 7.4 (continued)

	Export price indices			Import price indices			Net barter terms of trade		
	Laspeyres	Paasche	Fischer	Laspeyres	Paasche	Fischer	Laspeyres	Paasche	Fischer
1840	105.5	107.3	106.4	122.4	102.8	112.2	86.3	104.4	94.9
1841	112.5	115.0	113.7	97.1	95.5	96.3	115.8	120.4	118.1
1842	107.9	111.5	109.7	97.9	103.0	100.4	110.3	108.3	109.3
1843	108.0	118.1	112.9	92.5	95.9	94.2	116.7	123.1	119.9
1844	109.7	112.1	110.9	99.6	95.9	97.7	110.1	116.9	113.4
1845	107.0	111.8	109.4	100.3	101.2	100.8	106.7	110.5	108.6
1846	105.7	106.0	105.8	101.0	100.9	101.0	104.6	105.0	104.8
1847	106.1	111.6	108.8	102.7	102.5	102.6	103.4	108.9	106.1
1848	102.3	102.5	102.4	92.2	89.7	91.0	110.9	114.3	112.6
1849	98.6	104.5	101.5	89.6	89.8	89.7	110.1	116.3	113.2
1850	104.4	96.1	100.2	95.5	95.4	95.4	109.3	100.8	105.0
1851	89.8	90.5	90.2	95.7	96.6	96.2	93.8	93.7	93.7
1852	95.0	93.4	94.2	93.3	92.1	92.7	101.8	101.3	101.6
1853	98.7	97.8	98.3	96.6	96.2	96.4	102.2	101.7	102.0
1854	100.0	100.0	100.0	100.0	100.0	100.0	100.0	100.0	100.0
1855	105.2	113.8	109.4	96.9	95.9	96.4	108.6	118.7	113.5
1856	113.8	125.5	119.5	101.1	97.2	99.1	112.7	129.2	120.6
1857	116.0	130.0	122.8	102.9	94.3	98.5	112.7	137.9	124.6
1858	99.0	106.8	102.8	100.7	92.4	96.5	98.3	115.6	106.6
1859	100.2	103.1	101.7	103.6	91.5	97.3	96.8	112.8	104.5
1860	105.5	104.4	104.9	96.0	88.5	92.2	109.8	118.0	113.9
1861	101.4	106.7	104.0	101.9	89.0	95.3	99.4	119.9	109.2
1862	102.7	103.8	103.2	111.8	94.6	102.9	91.8	109.7	100.4
1863	113.3	113.0	113.1	126.9	103.6	114.6	89.3	109.1	98.7

1864	116.0	114.8	115.4	136.6	115.1	125.4	84.9	99.7	92.0
1865	100.6	104.7	102.6	127.0	111.1	118.8	79.2	94.2	86.4
1866	106.6	103.7	105.1	132.5	122.4	127.3	80.5	84.7	82.6
1867	109.1	108.0	108.6	121.0	111.2	116.0	90.2	97.2	93.6
1868	111.5	106.5	109.0	111.9	103.2	107.4	99.7	103.2	101.5
1869	105.0	106.5	105.8	113.7	105.3	109.5	92.3	101.1	96.6
1870	94.1	94.5	94.3	110.5	100.4	105.3	85.2	94.1	89.5
1871	110.4	116.9	113.6	107.1	100.4	103.7	103.2	116.4	109.6
1872	111.2	120.7	115.9	129.2	118.5	123.7	86.1	101.9	93.7
1873	110.6	120.9	115.6	139.0	127.5	133.1	79.6	94.8	86.9
1874	115.5	122.6	119.0	122.3	119.0	120.6	94.4	103.1	98.7
1875	107.7	125.6	116.3	101.7	109.6	105.5	106.0	114.6	110.2
1876	107.0	120.1	113.4	86.8	99.4	92.9	123.3	120.8	122.1
1877	106.8	119.8	113.1	82.7	94.6	88.5	129.1	126.6	127.9
1878	99.1	111.7	105.2	78.4	89.8	83.9	126.4	124.4	125.4
1879	93.6	107.1	100.1	70.9	79.3	75.0	131.9	135.1	133.5
1880	95.6	107.7	101.5	75.0	84.2	79.5	127.5	127.9	127.7
1881	92.1	105.6	98.6	72.2	79.9	76.0	127.5	132.1	129.8
1882	92.8	105.5	98.9	73.9	81.5	77.6	125.7	129.4	127.5
1883	93.0	103.7	98.2	75.0	80.6	77.7	124.0	128.7	126.3
1884	87.9	98.7	93.1	72.8	80.5	76.5	120.8	122.6	121.7
1885	78.7	90.1	84.2	71.3	81.1	76.0	110.4	111.1	110.7
1886	91.4	100.9	96.0	72.4	81.6	76.9	126.2	123.6	124.9
1887	74.8	85.4	79.9	67.8	77.7	72.6	110.4	109.8	110.0
1888	79.6	94.5	86.7	68.9	78.2	73.4	115.6	120.8	118.1
1889	76.5	89.4	82.7	74.5	83.3	78.7	102.7	107.4	105.0
1890	82.5	95.8	88.9	86.4	92.8	89.6	95.4	103.3	99.3

(continued)

Table 7.4 (continued)

	Export price indices			Import price indices			Net barter terms of trade		
	Laspeyres	Paasche	Fischer	Laspeyres	Paasche	Fischer	Laspeyres	Paasche	Fischer
1891	80.2	92.4	86.1	81.6	88.5	85.0	98.2	104.4	101.3
1892	75.7	87.2	81.2	76.4	85.8	80.9	99.0	101.7	100.4
1893	71.6	82.5	76.9	71.2	80.4	75.6	100.6	102.7	101.6
1894	69.3	80.3	74.6	70.1	79.4	74.6	99.0	101.1	100.0
1895	70.1	81.2	75.5	66.1	76.5	71.1	106.1	106.2	106.2
1896	68.8	80.1	74.2	66.5	77.5	71.8	103.5	103.2	103.4
1897	70.6	83.5	76.8	69.6	82.1	75.6	101.5	101.7	101.6
1898	72.1	83.9	77.8	76.2	89.6	82.6	94.7	93.6	94.1
1899	72.5	86.7	79.3	82.7	91.3	86.9	87.7	95.0	91.3
1900	74.3	99.2	85.9	111.6	115.1	113.3	66.6	86.2	75.8
1901	73.5	98.9	85.3	97.0	105.3	101.1	75.8	93.9	84.4
1902	69.2	90.4	79.1	90.1	100.7	95.3	76.8	89.7	83.0
1903	67.3	89.8	77.8	88.5	100.2	94.1	76.1	89.7	82.6
1904	67.8	89.8	78.0	87.0	103.2	94.7	78.0	87.0	82.4
1905	68.2	89.9	78.3	86.9	103.6	94.9	78.6	86.8	82.6
1906	78.9	108.2	92.4	90.7	107.9	98.6	87.0	100.9	93.7
1907	82.1	113.9	96.7	99.1	114.4	106.5	82.9	99.6	90.8
1908	73.7	99.3	85.5	96.2	111.1	103.0	76.6	89.3	82.7
1909	74.8	99.6	86.3	89.6	105.1	97.1	83.4	94.8	89.0
1910	76.5	102.2	88.5	92.9	107.8	100.1	82.4	94.8	88.4
1911	78.6	105.1	90.9	102.6	116.2	109.2	76.6	90.4	83.2
1912	78.5	105.8	91.1	110.7	129.5	119.7	70.9	81.7	76.1
1913	81.3	108.6	93.9	119.6	139.7	129.2	68.0	77.8	72.7

Sources: See text and Tables 7.2 and 7.3

Table 7.5 Net barter terms of trade between Spain and Britain, (1714–1913) (f.o.b. export and c.i.f. import prices)

	Export price indices			Import price indices			Net barter terms of trade		
	Laspeyres	Paasche	Fischer	Laspeyres	Paasche	Fischer	Laspeyres	Paasche	Fischer
1714	36.0	68.5	49.7	236.4	246.6	241.4	15.2	27.8	20.6
1715	44.2	86.8	61.9	255.4	222.2	238.2	17.3	39.0	26.0
1716	50.1	84.5	65.1	243.3	220.4	231.6	20.6	38.4	28.1
1717	43.7	83.7	60.5	235.5	220.9	228.1	18.5	37.9	26.5
1718	32.3	59.5	43.9	221.9	240.2	230.9	14.6	24.8	19.0
1719	32.4	59.2	43.8	236.5	240.8	238.7	13.7	24.6	18.3
1720	38.9	71.9	52.9	237.2	243.8	240.5	16.4	29.5	22.0
1721	47.9	96.7	67.9	215.1	219.3	217.2	22.3	44.1	31.3
1722	48.4	101.0	69.9	223.4	219.9	221.6	21.7	45.9	31.5
1723	45.2	89.1	63.5	217.3	207.5	212.3	20.8	43.0	29.9
1724	46.1	89.7	64.3	237.3	220.3	228.6	19.5	40.7	28.1
1725	45.2	87.4	62.9	242.3	224.7	233.3	18.7	38.9	27.0
1726	45.5	89.8	63.9	223.1	226.7	224.9	20.4	39.6	28.4
1727	25.2	45.4	33.8	260.9	232.3	246.2	9.7	19.6	13.7
1728	23.5	40.9	31.0	257.7	230.2	243.5	9.1	17.8	12.7
1729	23.3	40.8	30.9	225.4	230.4	227.9	10.3	17.7	13.5
1730	39.2	75.8	54.5	209.2	203.6	206.4	18.7	37.3	26.4
1731	39.9	78.7	56.0	199.3	200.1	199.7	20.0	39.3	28.1
1732	40.5	79.1	56.6	199.9	201.3	200.6	20.2	39.3	28.2
1733	36.6	70.2	50.6	205.1	202.6	203.9	17.8	34.6	24.8
1734	37.0	69.3	50.7	219.0	210.1	214.5	16.9	33.0	23.6
1735	34.5	64.1	47.0	223.1	205.1	213.9	15.5	31.3	22.0
1736	35.0	65.0	47.7	208.7	201.3	205.0	16.8	32.3	23.3
1737	36.6	67.7	49.8	206.8	198.1	202.4	17.7	34.2	24.6

(continued)

Table 7.5 (continued)

	Export price indices			Import price indices			Net barter terms of trade		
	Laspeyres	Paasche	Fischer	Laspeyres	Paasche	Fischer	Laspeyres	Paasche	Fischer
1738	35.9	66.9	49.0	203.0	194.9	198.9	17.7	34.3	24.6
1739	26.7	53.8	37.9	233.5	227.8	230.6	11.5	23.6	16.5
1740	30.7	57.3	41.9	214.0	232.4	223.0	14.3	24.7	18.8
1741	29.9	55.9	40.7	211.0	226.9	218.8	14.0	24.6	18.6
1742	31.6	56.1	42.1	198.3	224.1	210.8	15.9	25.1	20.0
1743	33.2	53.9	42.3	189.8	218.6	203.7	17.5	24.7	20.8
1744	31.3	54.4	41.3	196.2	220.0	207.8	15.9	24.7	19.9
1745	31.3	52.2	40.4	217.0	224.4	220.7	14.4	23.3	18.3
1746	28.7	48.4	37.3	218.0	223.3	220.6	13.2	21.7	17.0
1747	26.7	51.6	37.1	217.3	224.2	220.7	12.3	23.0	16.8
1748	34.5	58.5	45.0	219.8	224.9	222.3	15.7	26.0	20.2
1749	42.8	81.9	59.2	206.3	199.3	202.8	20.8	41.1	29.2
1750	40.1	75.4	55.0	208.3	199.6	203.9	19.2	37.8	26.9
1751	47.1	91.2	65.5	206.1	213.6	209.8	22.8	42.7	31.2
1752	43.4	82.5	59.9	206.2	213.2	209.7	21.1	38.7	28.6
1753	38.9	70.7	52.4	208.1	210.4	209.3	18.7	33.6	25.1
1754	38.1	76.9	54.2	207.6	209.3	208.4	18.4	36.8	26.0
1755	43.7	82.4	60.1	207.4	209.7	208.5	21.1	39.3	28.8
1756	42.7	80.0	58.5	215.2	205.4	210.2	19.9	39.0	27.8
1757	37.0	70.0	50.9	213.0	205.7	209.3	17.4	34.0	24.3
1758	37.5	69.6	51.1	231.5	223.3	227.4	16.2	31.2	22.5
1759	38.2	69.6	51.6	231.5	220.0	225.7	16.5	31.6	22.9
1760	38.6	71.0	52.3	231.3	219.5	225.3	16.7	32.3	23.2
1761	34.8	68.9	49.0	231.3	218.5	224.8	15.1	31.6	21.8

1762	33.4	62.0	45.5	239.6	250.2	244.8	14.0	24.8	18.6
1763	41.7	81.1	58.2	249.7	239.5	244.5	16.7	33.9	23.8
1764	52.1	93.5	69.8	245.1	243.5	244.3	21.3	38.4	28.6
1765	54.7	96.8	72.8	245.0	242.7	243.9	22.3	39.9	29.8
1766	52.7	100.4	72.7	247.0	250.8	248.9	21.3	40.0	29.2
1767	47.0	94.5	66.7	247.0	239.5	243.2	19.0	39.5	27.4
1768	49.5	87.2	65.7	266.0	262.0	264.0	18.6	33.3	24.9
1769	51.2	99.0	71.2	265.7	260.4	263.1	19.3	38.0	27.1
1770	45.7	85.7	62.6	265.7	260.0	262.8	17.2	33.0	23.8
1771	52.2	91.2	69.0	265.7	261.4	263.5	19.6	34.9	26.2
1772	52.6	86.1	67.3	265.8	262.5	264.2	19.8	32.8	25.5
1773	50.9	85.8	66.1	276.2	272.0	274.1	18.4	31.6	24.1
1774	53.9	94.0	71.2	276.0	270.7	273.3	16.5	34.7	26.0
1775	51.1	87.3	66.8	281.5	273.0	277.2	18.1	32.0	24.1
1776	50.3	88.5	66.7	281.5	273.4	277.5	17.9	32.4	24.0
1777	61.7	112.2	83.2	282.6	274.4	278.5	21.8	40.9	29.9
1778	62.2	104.9	80.8	279.6	272.4	276.0	22.3	38.5	29.3
1779	61.7	109.5	82.2	290.5	283.7	287.1	21.2	38.6	28.6
1780	70.3	110.8	88.3	300.0	292.8	296.4	23.4	37.8	29.8
1781	64.3	98.2	79.5	297.7	290.6	294.1	21.6	33.8	27.0
1782	63.8	104.6	81.6	300.0	292.5	296.2	21.3	35.8	27.6
1783	36.7	58.3	46.3	300.9	291.5	296.2	12.2	20.0	15.6
1784	84.7	134.9	106.9	262.0	276.9	269.3	32.3	48.7	39.7
1785	81.6	137.0	105.7	269.2	277.8	273.5	30.3	49.3	38.7
1786	82.6	126.6	102.3	261.6	276.6	269.0	31.6	45.8	38.0
1787	80.4	128.5	101.6	260.5	277.4	268.8	30.9	46.3	37.8
1788	80.2	136.2	104.5	286.5	311.0	298.5	28.0	43.8	35.0

(continued)

Table 7.5 (continued)

	Export price indices			Import price indices			Net barter terms of trade		
	Laspeyres	Paasche	Fischer	Laspeyres	Paasche	Fischer	Laspeyres	Paasche	Fischer
1789	77.3	126.0	98.7	286.8	309.1	297.8	27.0	40.8	33.2
1790	74.4	115.8	92.8	290.3	309.0	299.5	25.6	37.5	31.0
1791	82.4	130.1	103.5	291.9	312.8	302.2	28.2	41.6	34.3
1792	90.7	154.3	118.3	292.9	314.5	303.5	31.0	49.1	39.0
1793	83.2	125.2	102.1	317.0	314.5	315.7	26.3	39.8	32.3
1794	84.1	146.0	110.8	317.9	315.8	316.8	26.5	46.3	35.0
1795	80.8	135.8	104.7	316.5	311.6	314.1	25.5	43.6	33.3
1796	81.0	137.1	105.4	326.1	323.0	324.5	24.8	42.5	32.5
1797	87.1	128.8	106.2	298.8	428.4	357.8	29.1	30.1	29.7
1798	85.6	154.2	114.9	297.3	414.6	351.1	28.8	37.2	32.7
1799	98.2	163.6	126.7	348.8	384.3	366.1	28.2	42.6	34.6
1800	102.5	158.5	127.5	444.8	375.8	408.8	23.0	42.2	31.2
1801	120.7	177.1	146.2	465.1	397.2	429.8	26.0	44.6	34.0
1802	132.5	195.2	160.8	337.5	344.0	340.7	39.3	56.8	47.2
1803	138.2	208.2	169.6	368.8	392.9	380.7	37.5	53.0	44.6
1804	136.5	202.1	166.0	350.8	359.7	355.2	38.9	56.2	46.7
1805	136.4	205.9	167.6	349.2	350.9	350.1	39.1	58.7	47.9
1806	140.3	209.7	171.6	353.3	384.4	368.5	39.7	54.6	46.6
1807	137.9	203.8	167.7	352.6	391.7	371.7	39.1	52.0	45.1
1808	166.4	258.3	207.3	283.8	297.4	290.5	58.7	86.9	71.4
1809	307.8	284.4	295.8	300.0	327.1	313.2	102.6	87.0	94.4
1810	192.9	283.8	234.0	299.5	358.1	327.5	64.4	79.2	71.4
1811	153.7	225.8	186.3	292.1	357.1	323.0	52.6	63.2	57.6
1812	164.9	241.4	199.6	331.7	341.7	336.7	49.7	70.7	59.3

1813	171.0	248.2	206.0	333.3	343.3	338.2	51.3	72.3	60.9
1814	157.6	228.8	189.9	346.2	354.2	350.2	45.5	64.6	54.2
1815	149.5	217.1	180.1	269.0	242.7	255.5	55.6	89.5	70.5
1816	129.8	164.1	146.0	243.4	231.4	237.3	53.4	70.9	61.5
1817	125.9	171.2	146.8	223.0	197.2	209.7	56.5	86.8	70.0
1818	126.3	168.8	146.0	221.0	189.8	204.8	57.2	89.0	71.3
1819	126.4	166.1	144.9	214.5	201.1	207.7	58.9	82.6	69.7
1820	124.2	137.4	130.6	194.3	190.2	192.2	63.9	72.3	68.0
1821	116.8	133.1	124.7	177.5	175.3	176.4	65.8	75.9	70.7
1822	116.8	139.6	127.7	164.4	160.8	162.6	71.1	86.8	78.6
1823	126.3	140.7	133.3	160.4	156.6	158.5	78.7	89.8	84.1
1824	112.8	126.7	119.6	159.3	151.0	155.1	70.8	83.9	77.1
1825	110.7	134.7	122.1	153.6	147.6	150.6	72.0	91.2	81.1
1826	110.0	129.0	119.1	142.8	139.2	140.9	77.1	92.7	84.5
1827	99.2	106.7	102.8	126.9	120.9	123.8	78.2	88.2	83.0
1828	97.4	102.8	100.0	121.9	115.6	118.7	79.9	88.9	84.3
1829	102.8	105.7	104.2	116.0	109.7	112.8	88.6	96.4	92.4
1830	97.5	103.2	100.3	113.2	107.7	110.4	86.2	95.8	90.9
1831	99.2	104.9	102.0	100.5	93.7	97.1	98.8	111.9	105.1
1832	98.9	109.7	104.1	103.2	97.2	100.2	95.8	112.8	103.9
1833	98.9	107.3	103.0	117.0	91.4	103.4	84.5	117.4	99.6
1834	106.0	112.3	109.1	112.4	115.6	114.0	94.3	97.2	95.7
1835	109.5	116.7	113.0	154.6	127.1	140.2	70.8	91.8	80.6
1836	122.3	124.0	123.2	144.5	118.8	131.0	84.6	104.4	94.0
1837	111.2	118.1	114.9	149.2	124.7	136.4	75.0	94.7	84.3
1838	108.8	111.2	110.0	118.2	115.0	116.6	92.0	96.6	94.3
1839	111.4	117.4	114.4	134.0	116.6	125.0	83.2	100.7	91.5

(continued)

Table 7.5 (continued)

	Export price indices			Import price indices			Net barter terms of trade		
	Laspeyres	Paasche	Fischer	Laspeyres	Paasche	Fischer	Laspeyres	Paasche	Fischer
1840	105.5	107.3	106.4	123.6	105.6	114.3	85.4	101.6	93.1
1841	112.5	115.0	113.7	95.5	94.7	95.1	117.8	121.4	119.6
1842	107.9	111.5	109.7	96.0	100.8	98.4	112.4	110.6	111.5
1843	108.0	118.1	112.9	92.8	95.8	94.3	116.3	123.2	119.7
1844	109.7	112.1	110.9	98.0	94.9	96.5	111.9	118.1	114.9
1845	107.0	111.8	109.4	99.2	100.1	99.7	107.9	111.7	109.8
1846	105.7	106.0	105.8	100.6	100.6	100.6	105.1	105.4	105.2
1847	106.1	111.6	108.8	104.1	103.9	104.0	101.9	107.4	104.6
1848	102.3	102.5	102.4	90.1	88.1	89.1	113.5	116.3	114.9
1849	98.6	104.5	101.5	87.2	87.8	87.5	113.1	119.0	116.0
1850	104.4	96.1	100.2	91.1	92.0	91.6	114.5	104.5	109.4
1851	89.8	90.5	90.2	91.7	93.6	92.6	98.0	96.7	97.3
1852	95.0	93.4	94.2	91.3	90.7	91.0	104.1	103.0	103.5
1853	98.7	97.8	98.3	96.2	95.8	96.0	102.6	102.1	102.3
1854	100.0	100.0	100.0	100.0	100.0	100.0	100.0	100.0	100.0
1855	105.2	113.8	109.4	95.0	93.9	94.4	110.8	121.2	115.9
1856	113.8	125.5	119.5	99.6	96.0	97.8	114.3	130.8	122.2
1857	116.0	130.0	122.8	99.7	92.1	95.8	116.4	141.1	128.1
1858	99.0	106.8	102.8	98.2	90.7	94.4	100.8	117.8	109.0
1859	100.2	103.1	101.7	101.1	89.6	95.2	99.2	115.1	106.8
1860	105.5	104.4	104.9	96.0	89.4	92.6	109.8	116.8	113.3
1861	101.4	106.7	104.0	103.8	93.6	98.6	97.7	114.0	105.5
1862	102.7	103.8	103.2	110.2	94.4	102.0	93.2	109.9	101.2
1863	113.3	113.0	113.1	121.3	100.6	110.5	93.4	112.3	102.4

1864	116.0	114.8	115.4	127.7	111.2	119.1	90.8	103.3	96.9
1865	100.6	104.7	102.6	121.5	106.6	113.8	82.8	98.2	90.2
1866	106.6	103.7	105.1	127.0	116.4	121.6	84.0	89.1	86.5
1867	109.1	108.0	108.6	117.1	107.2	112.1	93.2	100.8	96.9
1868	111.5	106.5	109.0	109.8	101.2	105.5	101.5	105.2	103.3
1869	105.0	106.5	105.8	110.7	101.7	106.1	94.9	104.7	99.7
1870	94.1	94.5	94.3	108.0	97.6	102.7	87.2	96.8	91.9
1871	110.4	116.9	113.6	104.1	97.5	100.8	106.1	119.9	112.8
1872	111.2	120.7	115.9	124.6	114.1	119.2	89.3	105.9	97.2
1873	110.6	120.9	115.6	133.5	122.4	127.8	82.8	98.8	90.5
1874	115.5	122.6	119.0	116.2	115.1	115.7	99.4	106.5	102.9
1875	107.7	125.6	116.3	98.1	105.5	101.7	109.8	119.1	114.3
1876	107.0	120.1	113.4	82.8	95.7	89.0	129.3	125.6	127.4
1877	106.8	119.8	113.1	80.1	91.2	85.5	133.4	131.4	132.4
1878	99.1	111.7	105.2	76.8	87.0	81.7	129.0	128.4	128.7
1879	93.6	107.1	100.1	69.6	76.8	73.1	134.4	139.4	136.9
1880	95.6	107.7	101.5	74.6	82.5	78.5	128.2	130.5	129.3
1881	92.1	105.6	98.6	71.3	78.0	74.5	129.3	135.4	132.3
1882	92.8	105.5	98.9	71.7	78.4	75.0	129.4	134.5	131.9
1883	93.0	103.7	98.2	72.3	77.3	74.7	128.6	134.2	131.4
1884	87.9	98.7	93.1	69.4	76.4	72.8	126.7	129.2	127.9
1885	78.7	90.1	84.2	67.8	76.0	71.8	116.1	118.5	117.3
1886	91.4	100.9	96.0	68.7	76.2	72.4	133.0	132.5	132.7
1887	74.8	85.4	79.9	64.5	73.1	68.6	115.9	116.9	116.4
1888	79.6	94.5	86.7	66.2	73.9	69.9	120.2	127.9	124.0
1889	76.5	89.4	82.7	71.4	78.8	75.0	107.1	113.5	110.3
1890	82.5	95.8	88.9	81.2	87.5	84.3	101.5	109.6	105.5

(continued)

Table 7.5 (continued)

	Export price indices			Import price indices			Net barter terms of trade		
	Laspeyres	Paasche	Fischer	Laspeyres	Paasche	Fischer	Laspeyres	Paasche	Fischer
1891	80.2	92.4	86.1	76.6	83.4	79.9	104.6	110.8	107.7
1892	75.7	87.2	81.2	71.8	80.7	76.1	105.4	108.1	106.7
1893	71.6	82.5	76.9	66.6	75.0	70.7	107.5	110.0	108.7
1894	69.3	80.3	74.6	64.9	74.2	69.4	106.8	108.1	107.5
1895	70.1	81.2	75.5	61.5	71.2	66.2	114.1	114.1	114.1
1896	68.8	80.1	74.2	62.1	71.7	66.7	110.8	111.7	111.2
1897	70.6	83.5	76.8	64.9	75.4	69.9	108.9	110.8	109.8
1898	72.1	83.9	77.8	71.3	82.2	76.5	101.2	102.0	101.6
1899	72.5	86.7	79.3	77.1	85.2	81.1	93.9	101.8	97.8
1900	74.3	99.2	85.9	103.1	106.5	104.8	72.1	93.1	81.9
1901	73.5	98.9	85.3	88.6	97.0	92.7	83.0	102.0	92.0
1902	69.2	90.4	79.1	82.1	93.2	87.5	84.3	97.0	90.4
1903	67.3	89.8	77.8	80.8	92.5	86.4	83.3	97.2	90.0
1904	67.8	89.8	78.0	79.3	94.6	86.6	85.5	94.9	90.1
1905	68.2	89.9	78.3	79.6	94.5	86.7	85.7	95.2	90.3
1906	78.9	108.2	92.4	83.3	97.7	90.2	94.7	110.8	102.4
1907	82.1	113.9	96.7	91.1	105.3	97.9	90.1	108.2	98.7
1908	73.7	99.3	85.5	88.1	102.7	95.1	83.7	96.6	89.9
1909	74.8	99.6	86.3	82.3	96.3	89.0	90.9	103.4	97.0
1910	76.5	102.2	88.5	85.3	99.2	92.0	89.8	103.0	96.2
1911	78.6	105.1	90.9	95.1	106.2	100.5	82.6	99.0	90.4
1912	78.5	105.8	91.1	104.1	118.5	111.0	75.4	89.3	82.1
1913	81.3	108.6	93.9	110.3	127.4	118.6	73.7	85.0	79.1

Sources: See text and Tables 7.2 and 7.3

Table 7.6 Single and double factorial terms of trade between Spain and Britain, (1778–1913) (f.o.b. export and c.i.f. import prices)

	ECWSFTT	*ECSFTT*	*ECWDFTT*	*ECDFTT*
1778	17.4	5.5	26.5	9.8
1779	8.4	2.7	13.0	4.7
1780	4.8	1.5	7.1	2.5
1781	8.1	2.3	11.7	3.8
1782	10.1	3.0	15.0	5.1
1783	18.2	3.3	25.5	5.6
1784	19.4	8.0	29.2	13.7
1785	28.0	11.4	42.4	19.7
1786	18.2	7.4	27.7	12.7
1787	29.2	11.6	44.1	20.3
1788	30.4	11.4	45.6	20.1
1789	26.3	9.3	38.9	16.2
1790	29.3	9.9	41.1	16.5
1791	29.6	11.0	41.6	18.4
1792	34.0	14.1	47.7	23.0
1793	24.7	8.8	34.4	14.4
1794	32.6	12.7	45.9	21.2
1795	38.4	14.0	50.6	21.9
1796	26.0	9.5	33.6	14.8
1797	35.2	11.1	46.4	17.4
1798	21.4	7.4	27.4	11.7
1799	23.8	9.1	30.6	14.1
1800	40.8	13.9	50.4	20.8
1801	34.9	12.7	43.7	19.0
1802	39.9	20.8	52.4	30.7
1803	36.2	17.5	47.6	26.2
1804	43.0	22.2	57.4	33.3
1805	51.2	25.5	67.0	37.2
1806	5.5	2.7	7.3	3.9
1807	55.7	26.5	71.7	38.0
1808	30.2	21.8	43.4	32.7
1809	47.9	45.5	69.7	66.8
1810	51.4	37.7	69.0	53.4
1811	17.6	10.6	23.9	15.2
1812	16.6	10.2	23.0	15.0
1813				
1814	41.9	24.0	54.7	34.4
1815	43.2	31.1	56.6	42.8
1816	22.8	14.5	30.8	20.7
1817	39.0	27.7	52.7	39.3
1818	57.3	41.4	77.2	59.1
1819	35.7	25.3	49.3	36.5

(continued)

Table 7.6 (continued)

	ECWSFTT	*ECSFTT*	*ECWDFTT*	*ECDFTT*
1820	29.6	20.5	39.6	28.6
1821	40.2	28.7	54.1	40.2
1822	40.3	31.9	54.8	44.6
1823	39.2	33.2	53.2	46.0
1824	44.4	34.6	58.1	46.7
1825	70.9	58.0	92.0	77.6
1826	35.4	30.1	47.9	41.5
1827	47.5	39.7	61.2	52.4
1828	58.7	49.7	75.4	65.3
1829	59.8	55.4	77.7	72.7
1830	48.0	43.7	61.3	56.5
1831	69.4	72.8	89.4	93.1
1832	41.5	43.1	52.7	54.5
1833	62.4	62.2	79.3	79.0
1834	51.0	48.9	63.7	61.4
1835	42.8	34.8	50.4	42.2
1836	50.1	47.2	59.7	56.8
1837	52.4	44.4	61.9	53.7
1838	50.8	48.0	59.2	56.4
1839	65.8	60.4	76.5	71.2
1840	71.1	66.4	80.0	75.6
1841	53.6	63.7	64.0	73.8
1842	56.4	62.6	67.4	73.6
1843	45.8	54.5	56.2	65.2
1844	58.5	66.9	68.7	77.0
1845	56.8	62.1	65.2	70.3
1846	65.8	69.0	72.8	75.8
1847	78.1	81.6	86.2	89.3
1848	54.9	62.7	59.4	66.5
1849	59.1	68.3	63.5	71.4
1850	71.9	78.3	76.2	81.6
1851	69.3	67.5	71.3	69.8
1852	58.2	60.2	59.9	61.5
1853	77.5	79.3	79.9	81.3
1854	100.0	100.0	100.0	100.0
1855	125.6	144.6	132.5	148.1
1856	87.8	106.0	90.2	104.1
1857	88.0	110.8	92.6	109.5
1858	63.1	68.3	63.6	67.5
1859	92.5	98.5	91.2	95.5
1860	107.8	121.1	108.1	117.5
1861	118.7	124.7	114.7	118.8

(continued)

Table 7.6 (continued)

	ECWSFTT	*ECSFTT*	*ECWDFTT*	*ECDFTT*
1862	102.6	103.7	98.0	98.8
1863	123.6	126.3	113.9	115.7
1864	149.1	144.8	136.2	133.5
1865	131.7	119.7	114.4	107.1
1866	149.3	130.4	127.3	116.1
1867	159.1	154.4	139.4	136.5
1868	171.4	176.7	148.2	151.3
1869	172.8	172.3	145.2	144.9
1870	180.3	166.5	139.6	132.0
1871	194.9	217.9	154.3	166.7
1872	221.5	215.8	170.5	167.5
1873	257.8	234.4	194.0	181.6
1874	202.4	207.9	152.2	155.0
1875	212.7	241.2	163.8	178.4
1876	220.3	276.3	174.3	203.0
1877	269.6	351.4	213.8	254.3
1878	240.5	305.3	185.8	218.1
1879	234.4	314.7	188.3	228.9
1880	279.3	354.8	211.6	246.6
1881	268.3	348.9	202.8	241.3
1882	305.5	395.3	230.8	273.1
1883	326.3	419.2	241.8	283.8
1884	302.6	380.3	222.4	258.9
1885	306.7	355.6	219.8	242.9
1886	266.0	345.7	197.6	237.1
1887	336.3	386.9	235.2	259.4
1888	341.1	416.5	241.1	276.6
1889	366.1	399.9	248.4	263.5
1890	372.7	391.1	250.3	258.6
1891	332.5	355.8	220.4	230.6
1892	362.5	385.0	244.8	254.9
1893	358.8	387.8	245.3	258.9
1894	376.5	402.1	247.6	259.3
1895	404.0	456.1	263.9	287.3
1896	425.7	468.7	270.7	289.2
1897	449.8	489.3	286.2	303.3
1898	445.0	451.5	269.9	272.7
1899	470.6	461.3	277.0	273.1
1900	470.6	393.7	268.2	237.3
1901	440.6	408.9	253.0	240.3
1902	477.4	436.1	270.5	254.2
1903	473.3	430.6	271.1	254.4

(continued)

Table 7.6 (continued)

	ECWSFTT	*ECSFTT*	*ECWDFTT*	*ECDFTT*
1904	465.0	423.2	261.7	245.7
1905	467.0	426.5	258.8	243.5
1906	468.3	478.7	268.9	272.8
1907	480.0	474.5	272.1	270.0
1908	427.1	387.6	239.9	224.7
1909	422.3	410.6	237.1	232.8
1910	423.3	408.6	237.1	231.8
1911	403.7	368.6	219.0	206.4
1912	415.9	348.5	218.8	195.6
1913	397.4	323.4	200.7	176.2

Note:
ECWSFTT Employment Corrected Weighted Single Factorial Terms of Trade
ECSFTT Employment Corrected Single Factorial Terms of Trade (Unweighted)
ECWDFTT Employment Corrected Weighted Double Factorial Terms of Trade
ECDFTT Employment Corrected Double Factorial Terms of Trade (Unweighted)
Sources: Table 7.5
Also, Spain, exports to Britain at current prices, Prados de la Escosura (1984); Spain's c.i.f. imports at current prices, Table 6.4, for 1778–1820, and Prados de la Escosura (1988), 1821–1913; nominal GDP, Chap. 2, Table 2.3, 1778–1849, and Prados de la Escosura (2017, updated)
Britain, of c.i.f. imports at current prices, Cuenca Esteban (2001), 1778–1820, and Imlah (1958) 1820–1913, reproduced in Bank of England (2018), series A.36. GDP at current prices and labour productivity Broadberry et al. (2015) and Feinstein (1972), also in Bank of England (2018), series A9, Nominal GDP(A) 1700–2014 and series A56, labour productivity

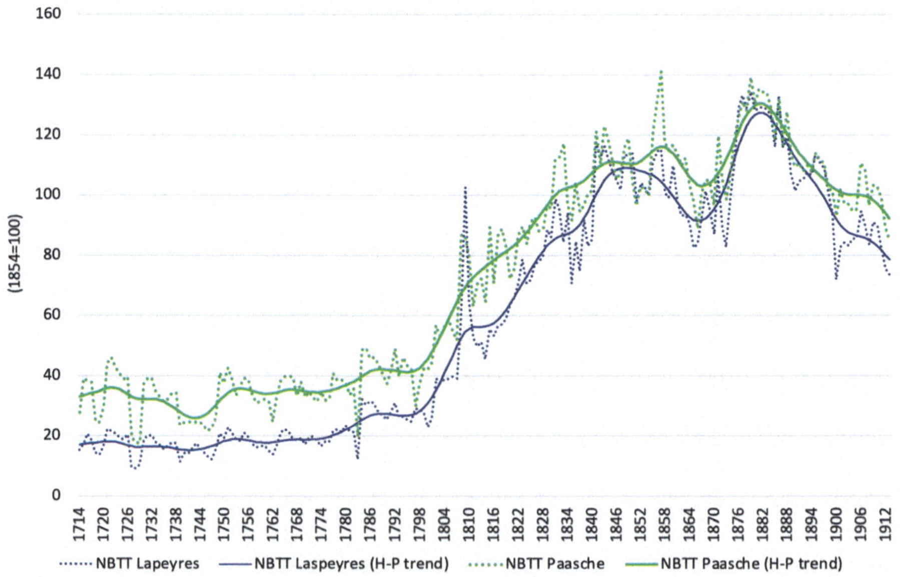

Fig. 7.5 Net barter terms of trade, 1714–1913: Laspeyres and Paasche Indices (1854=100) (f.o.b. exports and c.i.f. imports). Note: Hodrick-Prescott (H-P) trend, smoothing parameter set at $\lambda = 100$. Sources: Table 7.5

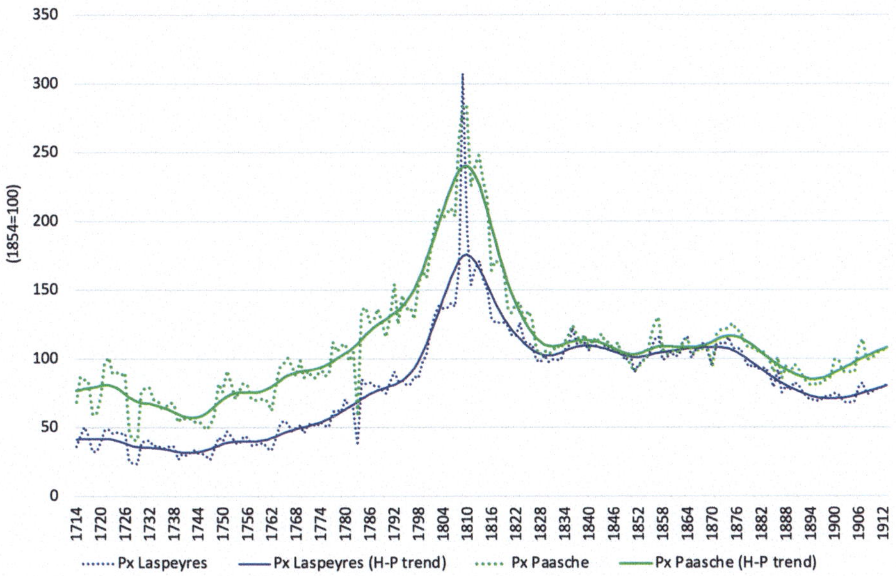

Fig. 7.6 Export f.o.b. prices, 1714–1913: Laspeyres and Paasche Indices (1854=100). Note: Hodrick-Prescott (H-P) trend, smoothing parameter set at $\lambda = 100$. Sources: Table 7.5

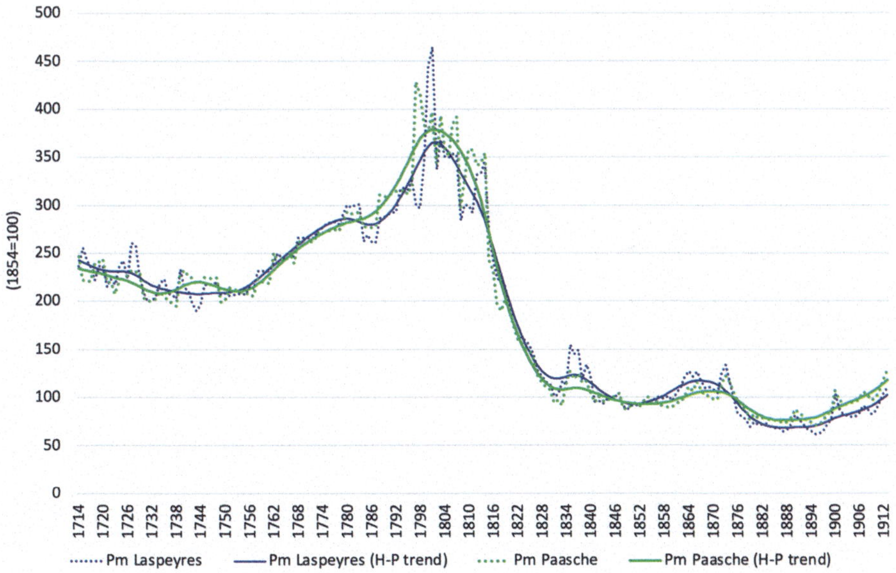

Fig. 7.7 Import c.i.f. prices, 1714–1913: Laspeyres and Paasche Indices (1854=100). Note: Hodrick-Prescott (H-P) trend, smoothing parameter set at $\lambda = 100$. Sources: Table 7.5

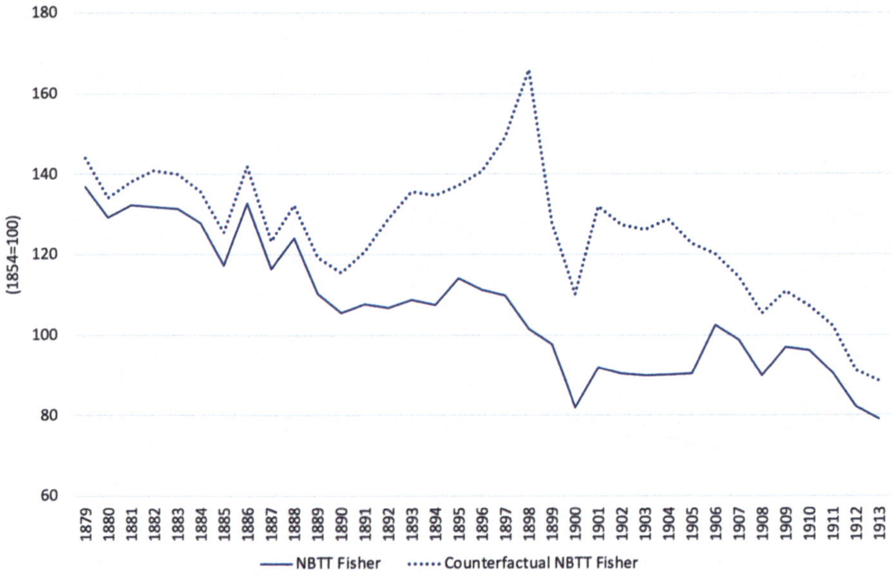

Fig. 7.8 Actual and counterfactual* NBTT, 1879–1913: Fisher Index (1854=100). *In the counterfactual of the absence of Peseta's depreciation

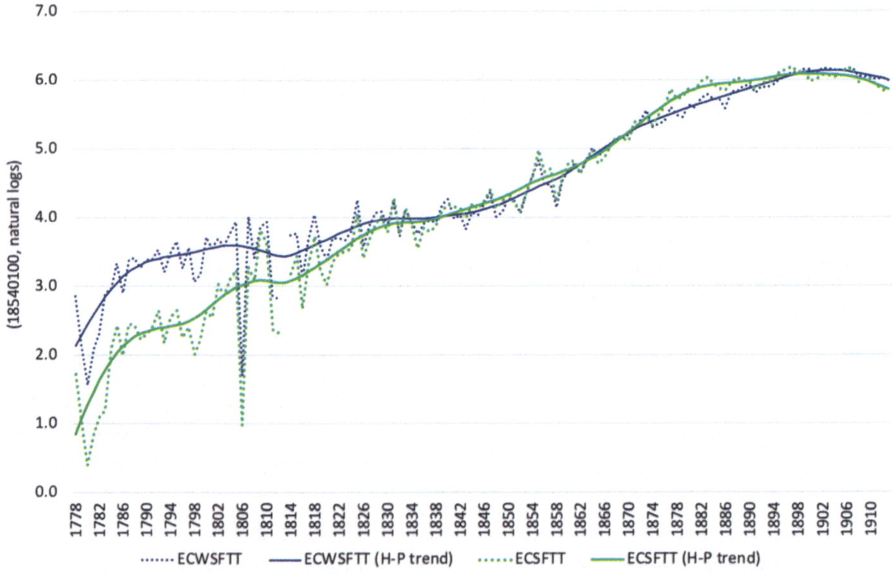

Fig. 7.9 Employment corrected weighted and unweighted single factorial terms of trade, 1778–1913: Fisher Index (1854=100, natural logs) (f.o.b. exports, c.i.f. imports). Note: Hodrick-Prescott trend, smoothing parameter set at $\lambda = 100$. Sources: Table 7.6

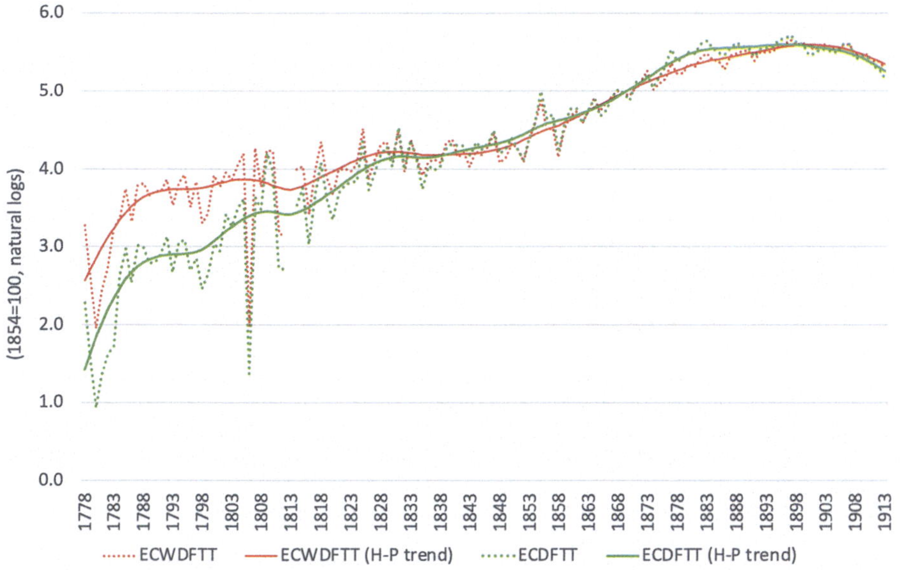

Fig. 7.10 Employment corrected weighted and unweighted double factorial terms of trade, 1778–1913: Fisher Index (1854=100, natural logs) (f.o.b. exports, c.i.f. imports). Note: Hodrick-Prescott (H-P) trend, smoothing parameter set at $\lambda = 100$. Sources: Table 7.6

References

Allen, R.G.D. (1975), *Index Numbers in Theory and Practice*, London: Macmillan.

Appleyard, D.R. (2006), "The Terms of Trade between the United Kingdom and British India, 1858–1947", *Economic Development and Cultural Change*: 635–654.

Ayuda, M.I. and V. Pinilla (2021), "Agricultural Exports and Economic Development in Spain during the First Wave of Globalisation", *Scandinavian Economic History Review* 69(3): 199-216.

Bairoch, P. (1975), *The Economic Development of the Third World*, London: Methuen.

Baldwin, R.E. (1955), "Secular Movements in the Terms of Trade", *American Economic Review* 45: 259-269.

Bank of England (2018), A Millennium of Macroeconomic Data for the UK. The Bank of England's Collection of Historical Macroeconomic and Financial Statistics. Version 3.1 https://www.bankofengland.co.uk/statistics/research-datasets

Berend, I.T. and G. Ranki (1980), "Foreign Trade and Industrialization of the European Periphery in the XIXth century", *Journal of European Economic History* 9(3): 539-584.

Beveridge, W. (1939), *Prices and Wages in England from the Twelfth to the Nineteenth Century*, I. *Price Tables: Mercantile Era*, London: Frank Cass.

Bhatia, B.M. (1969), "The Terms of Trade and Economic Development: A Case Study of India, 1861-1939", Indian Economic Journal. 16(4-5): 414-433.

Blattman, C., J. Hwang, and J.G. Williamson (2007), "Winners and Losers in the Commodity Lottery: The Impact of Terms of Trade, Growth and Volatility in the Periphery, 1870–1939", *Journal of Development Economics* 82(1): 156–179.

Bleaney, M. and D. Greenaway (1993), "Long-Run Trends in the Relative Price of Primary Commodities and in the Terms of Trade of Developing Countries", *Oxford Economic Papers* 45(3): 349-363.

Bordo, M.D. and A. J. Schwartz (1981), "Money and Prices in the 19th Century: Was Thomas Tooke right?", *Explorations in Economic History* 18: 97 127.
Broadberry, S., B.M.S. Campbell, A. Klein, M. Overton, and B. van Leeuwen (2015), *British Economic Growth, 1270-1870*, Cambridge: Cambridge University Press.
Cairncross, A.K. (1953), *Home and Foreign Investment, 1870-1913: Studies in Capital Accumulation*, Cambridge: Cambridge University Press.
Chilosi, D., G. Federico, and A. Tena-Junguito (2023), "Terms of Trade during the First Globalization: New Evidence, New Results", *European Review of Economic History* 27: 91-122.
Crafts, N. (2021), "Understanding Productivity Growth in the Industrial Revolution", *Economic History Review* 74(2): 309-339.
Cuenca Esteban, J. (2001), "The British Balance of Payments 1772-1820: India Transfers and War Finance", *Economic History Review* 54(1): 58-86.
Davis, R. (1979), *The Industrial Revolution and British Overseas Trade*, Leicester: Leicester University Press.
Deane, P. and W.A. Cole (1967), *British Economic Growth 1688-1959. Trends and Structure*, 2nd edition, Cambridge: Cambridge University Press.
Diakosavvas, D. and P.L. Scandizzo (1991), "Trends in the Terms of Trade of Primary Commodities, 1900-1982: The Controversy and Its Origins", *Economic Development and Cultural Change* 39(2): 231-264.
Edelstein, M. (1982), *Overseas British Investment in the Age of High Imperialism. 1850-1914*, New York: Columbia University Press.
Ellsworth, P.T. (1956), "The terms of Trade between Primary Producing and Industrial Countries", *Inter American Economic Affairs* 10: 47-65.
Feinstein, C.H. (1972), *National income, Output, and Expenditure of the United Kingdom, 1855-1965*, Cambridge: Cambridge University Press.
Flanders, J.J: (1964), "Prebisch on Protectionism: An Evaluation", *Economic Journal* 74: 305-326.
Frankema, E., J. Williamson, and P. Woltjer (2018), "An Economic Rationale for the West African Scramble? The Commercial Transition and the Commodity Price Boom of 1835–1885", *Journal of Economic History* 78(1): 231-267.
García Sanz, A. (1979/1780), "Jornales agrícolas y presupuesto familiar campesino en España a mediados del siglo XIX", *Anales del CUNEF* 51-71.
Gayer, D., W. W. Rostow & A. J. Schwartz (1953), *The Growth and Fluctuations of the British Economy, 1790-1850*, Oxford: Oxford University Press, 2 vols. and statistical microfilm supplement.
Glazier, I.A. and V. N. Bandera (1972), "Terms of Trade between South Italy and the United Kingdom 1817-1869", *Journal of European Economic History* 1(1): 7-36.
Glazier, I.A., V. N. Bandera and R. B. Brenner, (1975), "Terms of Trade between Italy and the United Kingdom 1815-1913", *Journal of European Economic History* 4(1): 5-48.
Gómez Mendoza, A. (1982), *Ferrocarriles y cambio económico en España 1855-1913*, Madrid: Alianza.
Haberler, G. (1961), "Terms of Trade and Economic Development", in H. S. Ellis and H. C. Wallich (eds.), *Economic Development in Latin America*, New York: , pp. 257-297.
Haddas, Y.S. and J.G. Williamson (2003), "Terms of Trade Shocks and Economic Performance 1870–1940: Prebisch and Singer Revisited", *Economic Development and Cultural Change* 51(3): 629–656.
Hansen, B. (1977), "On the Biases in Foreign Trade Indices", *Review of Income and Wealth* 23: 397-404.
Harvey, C.E. (1981), *The Rio Tinto Company. An Economic History of a Leading International Mining Concern 1873-1954*, Penzance:
Hilgerdt, F. (1945), Industrialization and Foreign Trade, Geneva: League of Nations.
Imlah, A.H. (1958), *Economic Elements in the Pax Britannica. Studies in British Foreign Trade in the Nineteenth Century*, Cambridge, MA: Harvard University Press.

Kindleberger (1956), *The Terms of Trade: A European Case Study*, New York: MIT and John Wiley & Sons..

Kindleberger, C.P. (1958), "The Terms of Trade and Economic Development", *Review of Economics and Statistics* 40 (supplement) (1, pt. 2): 72-90.

Lewis, W.A. (1952), "World Production, Prices and Trade, 1870-1960", *Manchester School of Economic and Social Studies* 20(2): 105-138

Lewis, W.A. (1978), *Growth and Fluctuations, 1870-1914*, London: Allen and Unwin.

Lipsey, R.E. (1963), *Price and Quantity Trends in the Foreign Trade of the United States*, Princeton, N.J.: Princeton University Press.

Mann, J. de L. (1971), *The Cloth Industry in the West of England from 1640 to 1880*, Oxford: Oxford University Press..

Marshall, J. (1833), *A Digest of all Accounts*, London: J.Haddon.

Matthews, R.C.O., C.H. Feinstein and J.C. Odling-Smee (1982), *British Economic Growth, 1856-1973*, Oxford: Clarendon Press.

Meier, G.M. (1963), *Trade and Development*, New York: Harper & Row.

Mitchell B.R (1988), *British Historical Statistics*, Cambridge: Cambridge University Press.

Nadal Farreras, J. (1978), *Comercio exterior y subdesarrollo. España y Gran Bretaña de 1772 a 1914: política económica y relaciones comerciales*, Madrid: Instituto de Estudios Fiscales.

Nadal, J. (1975), *El fracaso de la Revolución industrial en España, 1814-1913*, Barcelona: Ariel.

North, D.C. (1965), "The Role of Transportation in the Economic Development of North America", in J. Heers (ed.), *Les grandes voles maritimes dans le monde XV-XIX siècles*, Paris: Ëditions Jean Touzot/S.E.V.P.E.N., pp. 209-246.

Ocampo, J.A. and M.A. Parra-Lancourt (2003), "The Terms of Trade for Commodities in the Twentieth Century", *CEPAL Review* 79: 7-35

Ocampo, J.A. and M. Parra-Lacourt (2010), "The Terms of Trade for Commodities since the mid-19th Century", *Revista de Historia Económica/Journal of lberian and Latin American Economic History* 10: 1-33.

Peláez, C.M. (1976), "The Theory and Reality of Imperialism in the Coffee Economy of Nineteenth-Century Brazil", *Economic History Review* 29: 276-290.

Posthumus, N.W. (1946), *The History of Prices in Holland*, Leiden: Brill.

Prados de la Escosura, L. (1982), *Comercio exterior y crecimiento económico en España, 1826-1913: Tendencias a largo plazo*, Madrid: Banco de España.

Prados de la Escosura, L. (1984), "El comercio hispano-británico en los siglos XVIII y XIX. I. Reconstrucción", *Revista de Historia Económica* 2(2): 113-162.

Prados de la Escosura, L. (1988), *De imperio a nación. Crecimiento y atraso económico en España (1780-1930)*, Madrid: Alianza.

Prados de la Escosura, L. (2017), *Spanish Economic Growth, 1850-2015*, London: Palgrave Macmillan.

Prebisch, R. (1949), *Relative Prices of Exports and Imports of Under-developed Countries*, Lake Success, NY: United Nations.

Prebisch, R. (1950), *The Economic Development of Latin America and its Principal Problems*, Lake Success, NY: United Nations.

Prebisch, R. (1959), "Commercial Policy in Underdeveloped Countries", *American Economic Review* (Papers and Proceedings) 49: 251-273.

Prebisch, R. (1963), *Towards a Dynamic Development Policy in Latin America*, Lake Success, NY: United Nations.

Ragatz, L.J. (1928), *Statistics for the Study of the British Caribbean Economic History, 1763-1833*, London: Bryan Edwards Press.

Ricardo, D. (1817), *Principles of Political Economy and Taxation*, London: John Murray.

Rostow, W.W. (1950a), "The Historical Analysis of the Terms of trade", *Economic History Review* 4: 53-76.

Rostow, W.W. (1950b), "The Terms of Trade in Theory and Practice", *Economic History Review* 3(1): 1-20.

Rostow, W.W. (1978), *The World Economy: History and Prospects*, London: Macmillan.
S. Sideri, (1970), *Trade and Power, Informal Colonialism in Anglo-Portuguese Relations*, Rotterdam:
Sánchez-Albornoz, N. (1968), *España hace un siglo: una economía dual*, Barcelona: Península.
Sheridan, R.B. (1974), *Sugar and Slavery. An Economic History of the British West Indies, 1623-1775*, Aylesbury, Bucks.: Ginn and Company.
Silver, M. (2009), Do Unit Value Export, Import, and Terms of Trade Indices Misrepresent Price Indices?, *IMF Staff Papers* 56(2): 297-322.
Simpson, J. (1992), "Technical Change, Labor Absorption and Living Standards in Rural Andalucia, 1886-1936", *Agricultural History* 66(3): 1-24
Simpson, J. (1995), *Spanish Agriculture: The Long Siesta, 1765-1965*, Cambridge: Cambridge University Press.
Singer, H.W. (1950), "The distribution of Gains between Investing and Borrowing Countries", *American Economic Review* (Papers and Proceedings) 11(2): 473-485.
Singer, H.W. (1974–1975), "The distribution of Gains from Trade and Investment Revisited", *Journal of Development Studies* 11: 376-382.
Södersten, B. (1970), *International Economics*, London: Macmillan.
Spraos, J. (1980), "The Statistical Debate on the Net Barter Terms of Trade Between Primary Commodities and Manufactures", *Economic Journal* 90(357): 107-128.
Spraos, J. (1983), *Inequalising Trade? A Study of Traditional North/South Specialisation in the Context of Terms of Trade Concepts*, Oxford: Clarendon Press.
Thorold Rogers, J. (1866-1902), *A History of Agriculture and Prices in England*, Oxford: Clarendon Press, 7 vols.
Toniolo, G. (1983), "Railways and Economic Growth in Mediterranean Countries: Some Methodological Remarks", in P. O'Brien (ed.), *Railways and Economic Development of Western Europe 1830-1914*, London: Macmillan, pp. 227-36.
Tooke, T. (1823), *Thoughts and Details on the High and Low Prices on the Last Thirty Years*, London: John Murray.
Tooke, T. and W. Newmarch (1838-1857), *A History of Prices, 1793-1856*, 6 vols., London: Longman, Orme, Brown, Green, and Longmans.
Torrens, R. (1821), *An Essay on the Production of Wealth*, London: Longman, Hurst, Rees, Orme, and Brown.
Vandellós, J.A. (1925), "La richesse et le revenu de la Péninsule Ibérique", *Metron* 5(4): 151-186.
Williamson, J.G. (1985), *Did British Capitalism Breed Inequality?*, London: George Allen and Unwin.
Williamson, J.G. (2008), "Globalization and the Great Divergence: Terms of Trade Booms, Volatility and the Poor Periphery, 1782–1913", *European Review of Economic History* 12: 355-391.
Zanias, G.P. (2005), "Testing for Trends in the Terms of Trade between Primary Commodities and Manufactured Goods", *Journal of Development Economics* 78: 49-59.

Primary Sources

Manuscript

British Library
– London Price Current 1787-1799 and 1822-1842 (Newspapers Library)
Guildhall Library
– London Price Current 1799-1785

Weekly publication on imported and exported commodity prices in London. Available under slightly different names in the Guildhall Library (1779-1785), the British Library (1787-1799), the Public Record Office (1797-1821), and the Newspapers Library (1822-1853). From 1843, price quotations for the main commodities are shown in The Economist.
Public Record Office
– London Price Current 1797-1821
British Customs Ledgers, Kew: The National Archives.
– Ledgers of Imports and Exports, Customs 3, 1697-1780
– States of Commerce, Navigation and Revenue, Customs 17, 1772-1808
– Ledgers of Imports under Countries, Customs 4, 1809-1853
– Ledgers of Exports of British Merchandise under Articles, Customs 9, 1809-1853
– Ledgers of exports of Foreign and Colonial Merchandise under Articles, Customs 11, 1809-1853

Printed

Board of Trade (1855–1913), *Annual Statement of the Trade and Navigation of the United Kingdom with Foreign Countries and British Possession*, London: Eyre and Spottiswoode.

Board of Trade (1903), *Report on Wholesale and Retail Prices in the United Kingdom in 1902 with Comparative Statistical Tables for a Series of Years*, London: Eyre and Spottiswoode.

Chapter 8
Spain's Financial Position in the First Globalization

8.1 Introduction

After the loss of the American empire, the integration into international commodity and factor markets led to a persistent deficit on current account that slowed down Spanish economic growth and deepened the country's backwardness throughout the nineteenth and early twentieth century.

This thought-provoking but unfounded assertion offers stimulating hypotheses for research. This chapter tests the view that Spain's international integration hindered growth on the basis of a reconstruction of the balance of payments on current account, and complements the discussion provided in Chap. 7. The main outcome is that the sustained deficit on current account over 1850–1890 highlights the fact that a net inflow of foreign capital made possible to meet the demand for domestic investment and, thus, boosted Spanish economic performance; conversely, current account reversals help explain the economic slowdown at the turn of the century.

The chapter is organized as follows: Sect. 8.2 presents current assessments of Spain's international financial position. The reconstruction of the balance of payments on current account is discussed in Sect. 8.3, and Sect. 8.4 presents the balance of payments' main trends and determinants from a "sudden stop" perspective.[1]

This Chapter draws partially on my earlier work, published as L. Prados de la Escosura (2020), "Foreign Capital in 19th Century Spain's Investment Boom", European Review of Economic History 24(2): 314–331, and L. Prados de la Escosura (2010), "Spain's International Position, 1850–1913", Revista de Historia Económica / Journal of Iberian and Latin American Economic History 28(1): 1–43, but represents a full revision of the methodology and estimates and a full rewriting of the text.

[1] A 'sudden stop' represents an unexpected and significant reduction in a country's net capital inflow.

L. Prados de la Escosura, *A Millennial View of Spain's Development*, Frontiers in Economic History, https://doi.org/10.1007/978-3-031-60792-9_8

Section 8.5 discusses the implications for growth of Spain's financial position. Section 8.6 concludes.

8.2 Assessing Spain's International Financial Position

The conventional view of Spain's position in the international economy until World War I is one of chronic deficit on current account.[2] This diagnosis stems from the official trade figures (*Estadística del comercio exterior*), which show a sustained negative commodity trade balance, and from the scattered evidence about the gross inflow of foreign capital into Spain.[3]

Spain's trade balance experienced, according to Sardá Dexeus (1948: 277), a sustained deficit for long periods, while Tortella (1974: 122) asserted that the trade balance was negative throughout the late nineteenth century. The persistent deficit represented, in Vicens Vives's view (1959: 631), a heavy burden that contributed to the economic failure of the Restoration (1876–1923).

This chronic deficit hindered economic growth, according to most historical accounts. Allegedly, the current account deficit historians inferred from the commodity trade deficit set a limit on the growth of demand to which supply had to adjust, slowing down growth.[4] The acceptance of an external constraint on growth caused by a structural balance of payments deficit has major economic policy implications, as it would require protective measures in order to limit imports, plus a floating exchange rate. Herranz-Loncán and Tirado (1996: 24) observed that the values of income elasticities for imports and exports point to the existence of a constraint on Spain's economic growth resulting from the trade balance.[5] Serrano

[2]Cf. Tortella (1994), Herranz-Loncán and Tirado (1996), Serrano Sanz (1997), Gutiérrez et al. (1998), and Cubel et al. (1998).

[3]Since Sardá Dexeus's classical study (1948), the only estimate of the total volume of foreign capital invested in Spain during the nineteenth century is that of Broder (1976). Foreign investment in railways and mining have been estimated by Tedde (1978) and Harvey and Taylor (1987) respectively. Stone (1999) has published figures for British portfolio investment in Spain between 1865 and 1914.

[4]In the 'external constraint to growth' argument proposed by Thirlwall (1979), under the assumptions of international stability of relative prices and the absence of capital flows, the potential growth—that is, the one compatible with balance of payments equilibrium—, is defined by the ratio of the growth rate of real exports to the income elasticity of imports.

[5]It should be noted, however, that the elasticities estimated by Herranz-Loncán and Tirado (1996) are seriously questionable, due to the fact that, in line with Tena (1989), they use the volume indices for imports and exports obtained from the official trade figures (Prados de la Escosura, 1982) instead of deflating the series at current prices (revised both for the under-registration of quantities, including smuggled goods, and for errors in the official unit values) in Prados de la Escosura (1986, 1988). These authors also use Tena's (1989) foreign trade price indices, which were obtained by dividing the corrected current values in index form (Prados de la Escosura 1986) by the volume indices for imports and exports derived from the official trade statistics (Prados de la Escosura 1982). Thus, the implicit price (unit value) indices used are meaningless (especially in the case of

Sanz (1997) estimated the theoretical growth rate for the Spanish economy, which was compatible with the current account equilibrium.[6] As long as the theoretical rate were above the actual one, there would be no problem. This would have been the case of Spain from 1869 to 1891. However, if the theoretical rate were below the actual rate, as apparently occurred during 1892–1935, the external sector would have hindered long run growth.[7] In a long-run view of Spain's external sector, Bajo-Rubio (2010: 115) reached a rather different conclusion: the foreign sector did not represent a constraint on Spain's long-run growth and only under exceptionally fast growth would an external restriction, resulting from a potentially unsustainable trade deficit, emerge.

Thirlwall's (1979) 'external constraint on growth' is, however, predicated under the assumption that the terms of trade are stable and international capital flows negligible. In the context of the first globalization (1850–1913), such an assumption is far-fetched. Intense international commodity and factor flows took place, while the terms of trade suffered dramatic changes (O'Rourke and Williamson, 1999; Obstfeld and Taylor, 2004; Blattman, Hwang and Williamson, 2007). In fact, the proponents of the 'external constraint on growth' view accept that, in the presence of a sustained current account deficit financed through capital inflows, their prediction of the long-term growth rate is inadequate and it would be the pace and magnitude of foreign investment that would set the limit on growth (Thirlwall and Hussain 1982: 501). Thus, before jumping to conclusions about a potential external constraint on growth, it seems necessary to investigate the evolution of the current account over time.

One issue to be considered is the quality of Spain's trade statistics. Maluquer de Motes (1999: 110–11, 189) argued that exports to the remaining Spanish colonies, Cuba and the Philippines, in particular, were over-exaggerated during the years 1895–1898, as they included supplies for the Spanish troops (military equipment but also foodstuffs, clothing, etc.) that did not involve a commercial transaction.[8] Were this the case, military supplies should be removed from exports and considered

imports), as they include adjustments in the quantities traded in the numerator but not in the denominator.

[6]Serrano Sanz (1997) departs from Thirlwall as he takes the evolution of relative prices into account. If, alternatively, Herranz-Loncán and Tirado (1996) elasticities are used in Serrano Sanz estimates, the results are not very different. It should be noted that since Serrano Sanz (1997) employed the same data set as Herranz-Loncán and Tirado (1996), his results are as questionable as theirs.

[7]This would be the case because, in Serrano Sanz's view (1997: 320), the alternative option of financing the deficit through a surplus in other, smaller and more volatile components of the balance of payments, such as services or unilateral transfers, was unlikely.

[8]Maluquer de Motes (1999) accepts the argument put forward by a distinguished representative of the protectionist Basque lobby, Pablo de Alzola y Minondo (1903: 34–35, 89), who claimed that the commodity trade surplus over 1896–1898 was fictitious and pointed out that, in 1897, 130 million Pesetas in specie and substantial quantities of foodstuffs, clothing, and weaponry sent to supply colonial troops during the Cuban War of Independence, were included as exports. Unfortunately, the author does not provide any evidence to prove his assertion. In any case, it should be noted that specie flows are excluded from my estimates of the commodity trade balance (see next section).

as current Government transfers.[9] Previously, however, one should prove that no commercial transaction had taken place and that military supplies were sent to the colonies by the Government. If, alternatively, supplies for troops were provided by private firms, they would represent exports. Furthermore, it could be simply the case that, as a result of the increasing number of Spanish troops in the colonies, the demand for foodstuffs and clothing increased. Another important reason behind the increase in exports to the colonies (and to the rest of the world) during the late 1890s is the (real effective) depreciation of the Peseta, which improved the competitiveness of Spanish exports. In fact, the estimated values of export price elasticity suggest that, other things being equal, the depreciation would have triggered a significant rise in the volume of exports.[10] Moreover, an examination of the official trade statistics for 1897 indicates that there were no separate "State trade" records for exports.[11] Therefore, I decided not to correct the official exports figures to allow for the hypothetical inclusion of Government supplies to colonial troops.

Tortella (1994) raised objections to the revised figures for nineteenth-century Spanish foreign trade.[12] He noted a contradiction between the corrected trade balance figures—which reduce the commodity trade deficit in the 1850s and 1860s and provide a surplus after 1870—and the inflow of foreign capital.[13] Tortella (1994: 132) argues that with a positive inflow of capital and emigrant remittances at the end of the nineteenth century, it would be hard to explain the peseta's depreciation if there had been a trade surplus. This assertion, which seems logical at first sight, is, however, the result of identifying the commodity trade balance with the current account balance, in other words, with the overall balance for goods, services (which includes net income from abroad) and current transfers (including emigrant remittances). Such identification would be only warranted if the balances of services and current transfers were close to equilibrium, or if they cancelled each other out. In the case of the balance of services, such an assumption is inconsistent with the size of both external public debt and foreign investment in the private sector, which

[9] In a private communication, Francisco Comín informs me that it is highly unlikely that they were Government transfers, since the cost of military supplies was assumed by Cuba's colonial public budget. As previously, during the Ten Years' War (1868–1878), the Cuban War of Independence was not financed by Spain's Government budget, but by Cuba's colonial budget. Only after the Treaty of Paris (1898) was Spain forced to assume the cost of colonial debts. (Cf. Comín, 2004).

[10] The value of own price elasticity of demand ranged between −1.1 and −1.3 according to Herranz-Loncán and Tirado (1996: 23–4), and Serrano Sanz (1997: 123). A detailed analysis of trade between Spain and Cuba over 1878–1898 can be found in Piqueras Arenas (1998) in which the increase in Spanish exports is attributed to their competitiveness, and only partly would result from the depreciation of the currency.

[11] In fact, strictly military supplies (weapons and ammunition) represent a small share of 'general' exports. For example, fire arms only amounted to 3.5 million Pesetas in 1897.

[12] Cf. Prados de la Escosura (1986) for the revision of foreign trade figures between 1850 and 1913 in which official valuation of goods were corrected by using market prices and under-registration of imports was revised upwards to allow for smuggling.

[13] Tortella (1994) combines the official figures for the commodity trade balance with Broder's (1976) estimates for gross foreign investment in order to assess the current account balance.

involved large interest and dividend payments. Moreover, the identification of *gross* foreign investment with the (negative of the) current account balance is unjustified, as the latter only records *net* foreign investment into Spain. Furthermore, migrant remittances, the main component of the balance of current transfers, only became significant at the very end of the period under consideration, as Spanish mass emigration was a comparatively late phenomenon in a European perspective (Sánchez-Alonso, 2000).

Tortella's argument raises interesting questions. When did emigrant remittances become significant? Why did the depreciation not take place in 1883, as soon as the convertibility of the peseta was suspended? What were the causes behind the delayed, post-1891, depreciation of the peseta? Sardá Dexeus (1948: 219) offered an early diagnosis: 'the economic causes of this depreciation may be linked to the possible existence of domestic inflation caused by the increase in the quantity of silver and bank notes, with repercussions on prices and the trade balance', adding, then, 'it is better to seek the immediate cause in the evolution of the balance of payments'. But it is only the second part of Sardá's second part of the argument that has enjoyed support in the literature (Gutiérrez et al., 1998; Cubel et al., 1998; Catalan, Sudrià and Tirado, 2001).

Alternative interpretations to Sardá's have been offered, however. Martín-Aceña (1993: 140–1) underlined the association between macroeconomic stability and a stable exchange rate of the peseta, and Tortella (1981: 131–48) identified Government financial problems as the main cause of the nominal depreciation of the Spanish currency between 1891 and 1905. Later, Sabaté et al. (2006) argued that the Treasury financing needs led to money creation and, hence, to sacrificing a fixed exchange rate.

Unfortunately, the debate is seriously constrained by the lack of quantitative evidence vis-à-vis Spain's international position. The reconstruction of the balance of payments on current account therefore appears to be an urgent task. The next section of the chapter is devoted to this.

8.3 A Reconstruction of the Balance of Payments on Current Account

The balance of payments systematically summarizes the economic transactions of an economy with the rest of the world. These are the transactions involving goods, services, and income; financial claims on, and liabilities to, the rest of the world; and transfers (IMF, 1993: 6). I have estimated every item of the balance of payments on current account (commodity and service trade and current transfers). The procedure and sources used in the reconstruction of the main components of balance of payments on current account are summarily discussed in this section, although enough detail is provided for the reader who wants to replicate the computations. Needless to say, these computations are highly tentative and only further research will eliminate the potential errors of my estimates.

8.3.1 Commodity Trade Balance

Exports and imports of goods
Free on board (f.o.b.) value of goods exported and imported needs to be computed. Estimates on the basis of Spanish official trade statistics and corrected for quantity underestimation, including an estimate of smuggling through Gibraltar and Portugal, and for price biases by Prados de la Escosura (1986) have been used.[14] Cost, insurance, and freight (c.i.f.) imports were converted into f.o.b. imports to comply with balance of payments conventions.

Gold and silver
Quantities of gold and silver recorded in Spanish trade statistics (coins, bars and paste) are considered as monetary gold and silver and, therefore, not included in the estimates of net exports of goods and services.[15]

8.3.2 Service Trade Balance

Three main categories are considered under this label: a) freight and insurance services, b) tourism, emigrants' funds, passenger services and other services, and c) net income from abroad.

Freight and insurance
Freight income received for exports carried in Spanish ships less freight expenses paid for imports transported in foreign vessels constitutes the first item to be computed under this label. Following North and Heston (1960), the freight-value method, or freight factor, was preferred to the earnings per ton method.[16] Total freight revenues on exports and imports were first computed by applying freight factors to the f.o.b. value of exports and imports and, then, in order to ascertain the freight income on exports (a credit for Spain) the share of tonnage exported carried under Spanish flag was used, while the share of imported tonnage in foreign ships

[14] Official imports for 1850–1913 have now been corrected with a coefficient derived from a sample of Spain's main trading partners instead of with coefficients obtained from commodity and country samples for primary products and manufactures, respectively, as in Prados de la Escosura (1986). This change has been introduced to maintain consistency with Tena (1992) and Martínez Ruiz (2003, 2006) estimates for 1914–1958. The new results are, nonetheless, very close to the earlier ones.

[15] There are serious doubts about the way in which gold and silver exports and imports were recorded in official trade statistics (Tortella, 1974: 121–122). It could be argued that, since Spain never was part of the Gold Standard, trade in gold and silver should be treated as non-monetary. The fact that Spanish monetary authorities often shadowed the gold parity has led me to consider gold and silver exports and imports as monetary.

[16] Cf. also Simon (1960), whom I tried to follow as closely as the data permitted. Freight factor is the ratio of freight costs to the current value of traded commodities.

was employed to compute freight expenses on imports.[17] In addition, freight income from carrying trade between foreign ports was assumed, following North (1960) and Simon (1960), to represent a percentage of freight earnings, and a 10% of freight income on exports was accepted.[18] Port outlays by Spanish ships in foreign ports and by foreign ships in Spain's harbours as payments for port dues, loading and unloading expenses and coal are assumed to represent a fixed share of shipping earnings and expenses.[19] Foreign ships transported more tonnage than Spanish vessels, as they had a more efficient transport capacity ratio.[20] I assumed that more fully loaded vessels made smaller outlays per ship and, hence, port outlays by Spanish ships abroad (a debit) were established at 30% of the freight income on exports, while port outlays by foreign ships in Spain (a credit) were fixed at 20% of freight expenses on imports.[21] Finally, marine insurance income and expenses were computed under the widely shared assumption that underwriting follows the flag and exports in Spanish ships were, therefore, usually insured by Spanish companies, while imports in foreign vessels were insured by foreign companies.[22] I arbitrarily assumed that insurance rates were identical by Spanish and foreign companies and accepted those used by Prados de la Escosura (1986), to which I added an extra 2% to include shipping commissions and brokerage.

Tourism, emigrants' funds, passenger services and other services

Yearly income from tourist services was derived on the basis of expenses per visitor (net of Spanish tourist expenses abroad) calculated for 1931 by Jáinaga (1932), times the annual number of tourists and, then, reflated with a cost of living index to obtain current price estimates.[23] Unfortunately, the total number of tourists is only known since 1929 and was backward projected to 1882 with the rate of variation of

[17] Freight factors are taken from Prados de la Escosura (1986). The distribution of tons exported and imported between Spanish and foreign ships comes from Valdaliso (1991).

[18] North (1960) and Simon (1960) both assumed a 20%. Given the less efficient Spanish merchant shipping, I discretionally adopted a 10% rate.

[19] For similar assumptions for the U.S. and the Netherlands, cf. Simon (1960) and Smits et al. (2000).

[20] Cf. Valdaliso (1991: 71).

[21] The idea that more fully loaded ships made smaller outlays is taken from Simon (1960). These figures roughly correspond to those accepted by Smits et al. (2000).

[22] This assumption is borrowed from Simon (1960). It could, however, over-exaggerate Spain's earnings from marine insurance, as it was rather common for Spanish ships to be underwritten by foreign companies (Lloyd's, for example).

[23] The implicit assumption here is that real expenses per tourist remained constant over time. The cost of living index has resulted from splicing Ojeda's (1988) index for 1909–1913 with Reher and Ballesteros (1993) for the previous years. The alternative use of Maluquer de Motes's (2006) consumer price index does not change the results significantly.

passengers arriving by sea, while no tourism was assumed to exist during the period 1850–1881.[24]

Spain was a net emigration country over the late nineteenth and early twentieth century (Sánchez-Alonso (1995). Emigrants carried small sums with them to cover their arrival expenses. It can be estimated that, by 1931, emigrant funds to America represented, on average, 200 gold pesetas, that is, 400 current pesetas, including the fare and small amounts to cover arrival expenses (Jáinaga, 1932). If the fare represented around 340 current pesetas, 60 pesetas would correspond to emigrant's funds.[25] However, Jáinaga only added 'a small amount for unavoidable expenses', to the cost of the passage, and this sum is most likely an underestimate.[26] Therefore, I accepted a higher estimate, 100 pesetas for those emigrating to America, and one-tenth, 10 pesetas, for those to Algeria (and to France) for the eve of World War I.[27] These average sums times the number of emigrants to America, Algeria and France cast a yearly series of emigrants' funds that was reflated with Reher and Ballesteros (1993) unskilled wage index.

In addition, revenues and expenses from passenger transport have to be taken into account. Fares paid by tourists carried by Spanish ships and by returning immigrants returning in Spanish vessels are included on the credit side, while fares paid by emigrants to foreign shipping companies represented a debit. The number of migrants provided by Sánchez-Alonso (1995) for 1882–1913 has been completed with an estimate of migrants from 1850 to 1881 on the basis of scattered foreign evidence.[28] The share of arrivals and departures in Spanish and foreign ships is provided by official migration statistics from 1911 onwards and shows a stable

[24]For passengers arriving by ship, cf. Nicolau (2005: 139). The low numbers in the early 1880s allows for the presumption that tourism was not economically significant until the late nineteenth century.

[25]Vázquez (1988) provides third class fares to Cuba (325 pesetas), Argentina and Brazil (356 pesetas) in 1930 that yield an average of 340 pesetas.

[26]This figure, 60 pesetas, corresponds to a lower bound estimate of the average funds brought by Italian immigrants into the U.S.A. in 1892, according to Simon (1960: 676–677).

[27]The 1 to 10 ratio was derived by comparing fares to America (Vázquez (1988) with those to Algeria (Inspección General de Emigración , 1935) in 1934. These are roughly similar to the lower bound figures produced by Marolla and Roccas (1992: 252), for Italian emigrants to America and Europe in 1911. Llordén (1988: 62) provides a larger sum for Spanish emigrants' funds in the 1860s, 125–200 pesetas, once the fare is deducted.

[28]For 1850–1881, figures of Spanish immigration in Argentina, Uruguay, Brazil and the U.S.A., provided by the recipient countries' official statistics were completed with emigration to Cuba in 1860–1861 from *Anuario(s) Estadístico(s)* that was assumed to remain constant over the period. Emigration to Algeria was derived from Spanish arrivals in Alger and Oran for the years 1872–1881, while the figures for 1850–1871 were estimated under the arbitrary assumption that the share of emigrants who remained in Algeria after 1 year of residence was similar to the one over the period 1872–1881 (25%). Estimates for returned migration were computed by assuming that the average returns from America for 1869–1873 were acceptable for 1850–1868, while 92% of emigrants to Algeria returned home within the first year. A consistency check of the yearly migration data was performed using the migration balances from population censuses along the lines described in Sánchez-Alonso (1995). Data for returned migration from America, 1869–1881,

pattern; roughly one third of emigrants returned home under a Spanish flag and three-fourths left in foreign ships.[29] These shares were accepted for the nineteenth and early twentieth century. The fares for trips to Argentina, Cuba and Algeria are derived from Vázquez (1988), Llordén (1988), and official emigration statistics.[30]

Lastly, Government transactions (credits and debits) taken from official sources were added up (Díaz García, 1976).

8.3.3 Net Income from Abroad

Due to a dearth of data, only crude estimates of foreign capital incomes, on the debit side, and of Spanish labour returns abroad (wages and salaries), on the credit side, have been carried out. These are assumed to be the main components of net income from abroad, as neither Spanish investments abroad nor foreign labour in Spain were significant during the period considered.

Foreign capital income

Ascertaining the amount of and the returns to each type of capital asset invested abroad and foreign capital invested at home is fraught with difficulties and becomes an all but impossible task in historical terms. Investment, whether domestic or foreign, results from microeconomic decisions of multiple agents, and no statistics exist to register all of them, particularly as we move back in time. Even in nineteenth century Britain, 'investment was a private matter and the income from abroad was not subject to distinctive report until late in the century, and then only for certain classes of such income' (Imlah, 1952: 222).

The realization of this intractable problem led Imlah (1952) and Brezis (1995), North (1960) and Simon (1960), Hartland (1960), Lévy-Leboyer (1977), and Gregory (1979), to construct indirect 'residual' measures of the capital account balance for the United Kingdom, the United States, Canada, France, and Russia, respectively.

---

was taken from Yáñez (1994: 120). Data on migration to Algeria over 1850–1881 comes from Vilar (1989).

[29]The Consejo Superior de Emigración (1916) provides evidence for 1911–1915. The actual percentages used were 0.354 for returned migration under Spanish flag and 0.764 for emigrants in foreign ships.

[30]Llordén (1988) provides fares to Havana from 1862 to 1876; Vázquez (1988) provides the lowest fares to Cuba, Brazil and Argentina from 1880 to 1913 at 1913 prices, that I have reflated to obtain current price fares using the same Sardá Dexeus (1948) wholesale price index he employed to derive constant price fares. Missing years were interpolated (1862 fares to Cuba were accepted for 1850–1861; fares to Argentina prior 1880 were assumed to move together fares to Cuba). I assumed that fares to Algeria fluctuated in line with the fares to America and that the fares ratio Algeria/ Argentina in 1934 (Inspección General de Emigración 1935) was stable over the considered period. I also assumed that tourist fares from Europe changed in line with with migrants' fares.

In the indirect, 'residual' approach, the net payments to capital from abroad is computed indirectly by applying a rate of interest to the country's international indebtedness at the beginning of the considered period, which is yearly updated with the net inflow of capital. It requires, then, a benchmark level of international indebtedness plus a representative rate of interest. Unfortunately, this implies arbitrary assumptions (Simon, 1960: 694). The initial amount of a country's international indebtedness is not accurately computed and 'informed guesses' have frequently been used in historical studies (Imlah, 1952: 227; North, 1960: 587). Moreover, the rate of return applied hardly captures the average returns of a wide and changing variety of capital assets and even less with yearly precision (Imlah, 1952: 222). Furthermore, any alteration in either the interest rate applied or the initial estimate of international indebtedness results in far from negligible differences in the current account balance over the long run (North 1960: 574–5).

I have carried out both direct and indirect estimates of the net foreign capital income from abroad, although I find the indirect approach preferable and the discussion will focus on its results.

Direct approach

Due to the dearth of data only a few major sectors can considered, and returns from banking are, for example, neglected. It can therefore be conjectured that, most probably, the estimates provide a lower bound of the actual returns to foreign capital.

I have distinguished three main items: the external debt service; dividends and interests paid to foreign owned railway shares and debentures; and returns to foreign factors in mining. These three items together represented four-fifths of British portfolio investment in Spain over 1865–1913 (Stone, 1999).[31]

Service payments on the external debt have been computed by applying specific interest rates to each class of Government bonds.[32] Some caveats about the volume of external public debt in foreign hands are needed. After the sovereign debt re-scheduling in 1882, which exchanged existing foreign debt for new bonds (at 43.75% of its nominal value), and simultaneously with the abandonment of gold convertibility of Spanish currency in 1883, debt repatriation started as Spaniards found it more secure to invest in bonds serviced in gold pesetas as a shelter against currency depreciation.[33] As of 1891, when the peseta started depreciating, Spanish citizens purchased external debt bonds, while foreign bondholders tried to get rid of them. The Government reacted by introducing the so called 'affidavit' in 1898, which implied that only non-resident bondholders would continue receiving

[31] According to Stone (1999: 251), public debt, railways, and mining represented, on average, 24.3%, 25.3%, and 31.2%, respectively, of total British portfolio investment in Spain over 1865–1913.

[32] External debt figures and the interest rates applied are provided in Fernández Acha (1976).

[33] This appears to be a case of 'original sin', to use Eichengreen and Hausmann (1999) expression to describe external debt denominated in gold or in foreign currency. For this paragraph I draw on Sardá Dexeus (1948) who provides a detailed evaluation of Spain's external public debt in the late nineteenth and early twentieth century.

their interest payments in gold pesetas (or in French francs), while the rest would be paid in current pesetas (and given the opportunity to convert their external debt bonds into internal debt). As a result, the external public debt fell, in 1903, to 52.7% of its volume in 1898, which implies that Spanish residents had purchased almost half Spain's external public debt between 1891 and 1898. Hence, only half of the interests paid (52.7%) on external debt should be computed as payments to foreign capital invested in external debt over 1891–1898. I have, then, assumed that the interest payments effectively paid to foreign bondholders from 1891 to 1902 should be computed on the volume of external debt in existence in 1903.[34] Moreover, in so far as external debt was serviced in gold pesetas, the amount of interests paid (obtained by applying the interest rate to foreign debt in non-residents' hands) has to be increased by the depreciation rate of the current peseta with respect to the gold peseta from 1891 to 1914.[35]

Railway companies were highly concentrated, and the detailed research by Tedde de Lorca (1978, 1980) provides enough evidence to estimate dividends on share capital and interests on debentures paid to non-residents.[36] Dividends paid to shareholders and interest payments on debentures issued by the three major railway companies are available from the mid-nineteenth century onwards.[37] Both the percentage represented by the three main companies in the total capital invested in railways and the proportion of railways capital in foreign hands have to be ascertained in order to compute the returns to foreign capital invested in Spanish railways. Tedde de Lorca provides total capital shares and bonds held by the three major companies and their proportion in total investment, and, on the basis of Broder's research, also the participation of French capital in total capital invested in 1867, at the time of network construction and through the nineteenth century.[38]

[34] An alternative hypothesis is to assume that the external public debt gradually passed into Spanish hands. The results of this alternative computation, although they provide higher interest payments, do not change the trend of the estimates used here.

[35] This is often the result of the so called 'original sin'. The depreciation rate of the peseta against the French franc provided by Martín-Aceña and Pons (2005) has been used.

[36] Cf. Tedde de Lorca (1978, 1980) for research on Norte, MZA and Andaluces, the three main railway companies. Evidence on foreign investment in railways has been gathered in Broder (1976, 1981).

[37] Tedde de Lorca (1978), Appendices IV-9 and IV-18, provides the data on dividends and interests paid by Norte and MZA companies, while Tedde de Lorca (1980: 44–45), presents the same evidence for Andaluces company.

[38] Cf. Tedde de Lorca (1978: 243–4, 248–51, 256–7; 1980: 37, 40). Thus, I have estimated, firstly, the dividend and interest payments corresponding to French citizens by applying the share of French capital in total capital for the three big railway companies. Then, I have re-scaled the resulting sum by the share of French capital invested in these three companies over total French investment in Spanish railways. The latter share is only available for the years 1867 and 1890 so I have used that one for 1867 for the pre-1867 years, and the 1890 share for the post-1890 period, while I interpolated log-linearly 1867 and 1890 shares over 1868–1889.

Broder's estimates of foreign investment in railways made it possible, in turn, to re-scale French railways capital to cover all foreign capital.[39]

Foreign capital in mining was mainly British. On the basis of effective capital invested by British companies and cumulated total foreign investment in mining, it can be suggested that, from 1870 to 1913, more than half of all foreign capital in Spanish mining came from the U.K.[40] Decadal averages of dividend and interest payments to British companies provided by Harvey and Taylor (1987) were re-scaled to include all payments to foreign capital in Spanish mining for 1851–1913, assuming similar rates of return in non-British foreign investment, and using the estimated British participation in total foreign capital.[41] Estimates of foreign capital returns in mining derived through this procedure were then distributed annually with an index of non-retained value in Spanish mineral exports.[42]

Indirect approach

The first challenge has been selecting a stock representative of Spain's international indebtedness at the beginning of 1850. Since private foreign investment in early nineteenth century Spain has been considered negligible (Sardá, 1948: 262), a sensible assumption would be to consider the level of international indebtedness

---

[39] I re-scaled interest and dividend payments to French capital by its share in total foreign capital invested in Spanish railways using the decennial shares provided for 1850–1913 by Broder (1976: 62).

[40] Cf. Harvey and Taylor (1987: 197) for British capital (effective share capital and debentures and mortgage bonds). Cumulated total foreign investment (excluding railways) and cumulated French investment in mining were derived from Broder (1976, 1981). When only French and British capital in mining are considered (the large majority of it), the British share ranged from 63% to 73% from 1870 to 1900, the mining boom years (and only in 22–41% range in the earlier period 1851–1870). If, alternatively, Broder's estimates of non-railway investment from other countries are cumulated, British capital represented from 52% to 61% from 1870 to 1900 (22–31% in 1851–1870). Evidence in Muñoz et al. (1976) indicates that British capital was above 50% in the years 1900–1913 (53% average for 1900 and 1912).

[41] Unfortunately, Chastagnaret (2000) does not carry out a similar estimate to that of Harvey and Taylor (1987) for the British capital invested in mining, which would have precluded this crude estimate. Thus, British participation in total foreign capital was assumed to be 30% in 1850–1870, 60% in 1870–1890, and 50% in 1890–1913 (see the previous footnote).

[42] Non-retained exports represent the value of exports receipts that accrued to foreign productive factors used in mining production and, therefore, were not kept in Spain. Non-retained values over total mineral export proceeds represent 0.35 for iron ore, 0.40 for lead, 0.49 and 0.625 for copper pyrites (before and after 1896), 0.54 for mercury, according to Prados de la Escosura (1988) who took them from González Portilla (1981), Broder (1981), Harvey (1981) and Nadal (1975), respectively. The revisionist work by Escudero (1996) suggests that these shares should be revised upwards and Témime et al. (1982) pointed out that 70–75% of export proceeds were not retained in Spain. Escudero (1998) has estimated that the share of foreign returns in Basque iron ore mining represented 39.5% (204 million pesetas) of its total over 1876–1913, to which should be added the differential between market prices and much lower preferential prices (that foreign mining companies charged their matrix firms abroad) times the quantities sold at preferential prices, approximately 200 million pesetas, so the share of non-retained exports would be over half of total export proceeds. I have used, then, upgraded non-retained shares of 0.55 for iron ore, 0.90 for lead, and 0.73 for pyrites.

equivalent to the value of external public debt. The nominal value of the external debt by January 1, 1850 can be estimated at 1504.8 million Pesetas (Comín, 1996: 131).[43] It is widely acknowledged in the historical literature that that external debt was never traded above half its nominal value in nineteenth-century Spain (Sardá, 1948: 257).[44] However, interests were paid on the nominal debt, so it is the nominal value of the investment that should be considered when computing interest payments (Tedde, 2015: 174).

As regards the rate of return, a weighted average of specific interest rates paid to each class of external debt bonds may provide a reasonable measure.[45] The use of the interest rate on nominal external debt may be considered to represent, however, a lower bound for the rate of return on all foreign investment.[46] Nonetheless, it is worth noting that the higher the interest rate applied to the stock of international indebtedness, the larger the resulting amount of net payments to foreign capital and, hence, the current account deficit.[47] As this exercise aims to test whether the net capital inflow derived from the direct approach results in an underestimate, biasing the indirect estimates against the hypothesis seems advisable.

Net payments to foreign capital for 1850 can thus be computed by applying the weighted nominal interest rate on external debt on that year to the nominal value of the external debt on January 1st, 1504.8 million pesetas. For subsequent years, the level of international indebtedness has been updated with the net inflow of capital.

Spanish labour returns from abroad

Assessing returns to Spanish labour employed abroad is a complex task, as labour incomes (wages and salaries), which belong to the balance of services, have to be distinguished from emigrants' remittances, which belong to the balance of unilateral transfers. Actually, the distinction can only be made since 1917 and I accepted that only 5% of those emigrating to America and 60% of those migrating to Algeria returned within the year from 1850 to 1913.[48] The next step was to assess the amount

---

[43] Sardá (1948: 257) provides a slightly higher figure of nominal external debt, 1623 million Pesetas.

[44] The acquisition value might have been even lower. Broder (1976: 45) and Tedde (2015: 173) suggest a lower ratio of the effective to nominal external debt. According to Broder, the effective external debt would reach 293 million French Francs (255 million Pesetas).

[45] External debt figures and the interest rates applied are taken from Fernández Acha (1976).

[46] Imlah (1952: 223–224/225) warns against using too high an interest rate as not all capital was productively invested and defaults were frequent in the nineteenth century.

[47] An alternative rate of return would result from a weighted average of specific interest rates paid to each class of external debt bonds and to railways bonds and shares, which were the most frequent assets held by foreign investors in Spain at the time. I have replicated the computations with this alternative rate and the results hardly differ.

[48] Evidence on transatlantic emigrants returned after less than a year abroad is presented in Yáñez (1994) for 1917–1921 and 1925–1930 and in Inspección General de Emigración (1935: 14), for 1926–1934. It represents between 3.5 and 6.2% of total emigration to America, averaging 5%, so I have accepted 5% for 1850–1913. For the share of emigrants to Algeria returning within a year, Bonmatí (1989: 135) points to 59% of total emigrants.

that, on average, was brought home by Spanish workers returning after 1 year, or less, away from home. I computed an average sum that was taken home by the temporary emigrant or sent annually by the long-term emigrant to their relatives and friends. Estimates of total sums sent home by emigrants have been gathered in recent historical research for the early twentieth century.[49] García López (1992) presents the most comprehensive estimates for the years prior World War I, 250–300 million pesetas as an annual average over 1906–1910, which amounts to around 340–400 pesetas per emigrant (either returning home or sending remittances). I accepted 400 pesetas per emigrant as a benchmark that was then projected backwards and forwards with a nominal wage index constructed for the destination countries, and adjusted for the exchange rate between the peseta and each destination country's currency over 1850–1913.[50] Finally, returns to Spanish labour abroad were obtained by multiplying the annual sum per head by the number of emigrants returning home within their first year abroad.

Once net payments to foreign capital were obtained, they were added to net payments to domestic labour to derive the balance on payments to foreign factors.

8.3.4 Current Transfers Balance

Emigrants' remittances constituted the main historical component in Spain prior to 1913. Not all emigrants sent money home while abroad. In historical estimates, it is usually accepted that most of those who established themselves abroad stopped sending money after 5 or 6 years, either because they had already paid for their debts or because they planned to invest in the receiving country. I discretionally assumed that emigrants only sent money home within their first 5 years, and computed emigrants' remittances by multiplying the estimated average sum per emigrant by the cumulative figure of emigrants arrived in the last 5 years, after deducting those migrants who returned home within 1 year.[51]

---

[49] Unfortunately, no distinction can be made between short- and long-term migrants. Contemporary estimates are collected in Chamorro (1976), for 1899, 1900 and 1904; Vázquez (1988) for 1906, 1908–1913 and 1920–1922; and García López (1992), for 1906–1910 and 1920–1921 averages.

[50] Nominal wages for Argentina are collected in Williamson (1995). Zanetti and García (1977) provide nominal wages for Cuba from 1903 onwards. French nominal wages from Williamson (1995) are used for emigrants to France and Algeria. The trading exchange rates of the peseta against the peso, the French franc and the US dollar are computed on the basis of Cortés Conde (1979), della Paolera (1988), and Martín-Aceña (1989).

[51] As explained in the previous section, due to lack of data, no distinction has been made between the sum brought back home by the emigrant who returned home within his/her first year abroad and the average remittances sent during the five first years abroad by the rest of emigrants. Following Simon (1960) I have attributed double weight to the latter on of each 5-year period considered.

8.3.5 The Balance of Payments on Current Account and the Net Inflow of Capital

Adding up the balances of goods, services—including net payments to foreign factors—, and current transfers, the balance of payments on current account is obtained.

The capital account balance is obtained by subtracting the current account balance from the net change in reserves. The estimates of net changes in reserves result from adding the net imports of gold and silver to the annually minted figures.[52]

8.4 Trends in Spain's International Financial Position

Let us begin by looking at the commodity trade balance. Two clearly defined periods can be distinguished: one of deficit, from 1850 to the 1866 crisis, except for 3 years, 1854–1856, followed by one of surplus up to the eve of World War I, except for 1876 (Fig. 8.1). If we now turn to the balance of services, a persistent deficit is

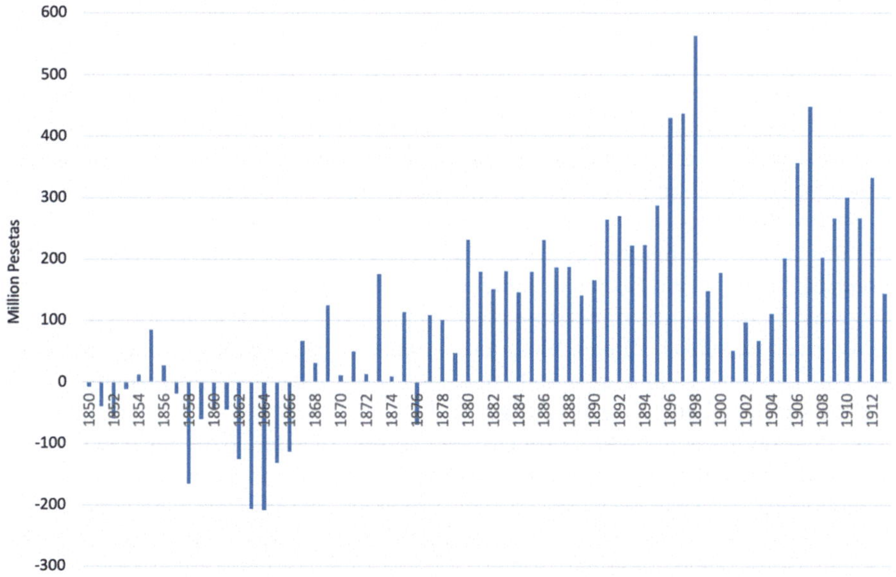

Fig. 8.1 Commodity trade balance (million Pesetas). Sources: See text and Table 8.1

[52]The official estimates (option A) used here are more conservative than the estimates obtained with the revised figures of specie net imports (option B) because imports are nil for 1850–1874. See Appendix, A.1 The Metallic Stock.

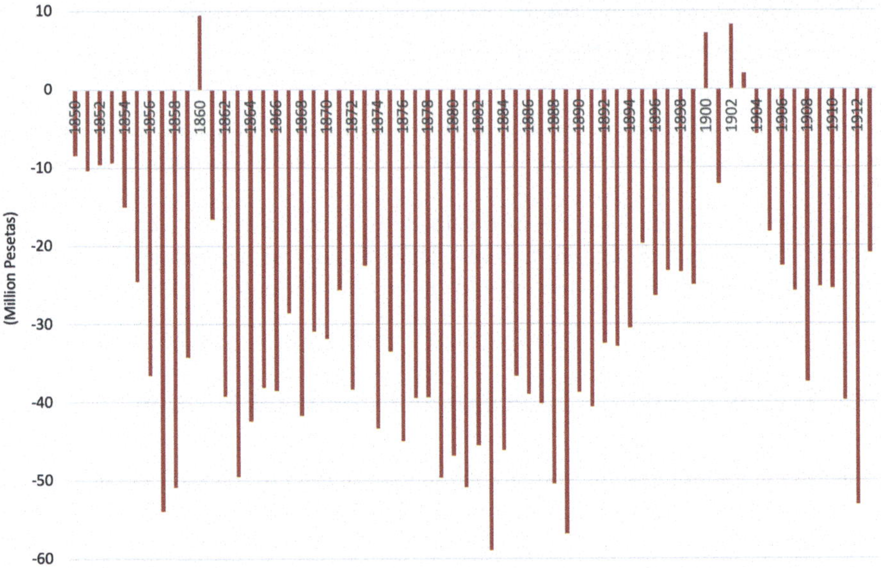

Fig. 8.2 Services trade balance (excluding net income from abroad) (million Pesetas). Sources: See text and Table 8.1

observed. Transport, tourism and intergovernmental transactions show a negative sign (Fig. 8.2) and, more importantly, the balance of services main item, the net income from abroad, too (Fig. 8.3).[53] The service of the public debt dominated net income from abroad until the beginning of the Restoration (1876). After the sovereign debt re-scheduling (1882) and, especially, from 1890 onwards, this situation changed with net returns to foreign capital in railways and mining gaining weight. The results confirm that the direct computation of net payments to foreign capital produces lower levels than the indirect approach. Such a difference derives, as suggested in the historical literature (Goldsmith, 1955), from its incomplete coverage of investment from abroad. Emigrant remittances became increasingly important from the late 1880s and increased dramatically from 1904 onwards, partially offsetting the net payments to foreign factors (Fig. 8.4).

Adding up the commodity, services, and current transfers balances provides the current account balance. Two distinctive phases, with 1891 as a turning point, can be distinguished. A sustained current account deficit was in place throughout the period 1850–1890. Then, from 1891 up to World War I, a surplus prevailed, with the exception from 1899–1904 (Fig. 8.5).[54]

[53] For the direct estimate of the net income from abroad, see Fig. 8.17.

[54] The finding of a current account surplus from 1891 onwards confirms contemporary quantitative assessments of Spain's International position (see Prados de la Escosura, 1988: 196). For the direct estimate of the current account balance, see Fig. 8.18.

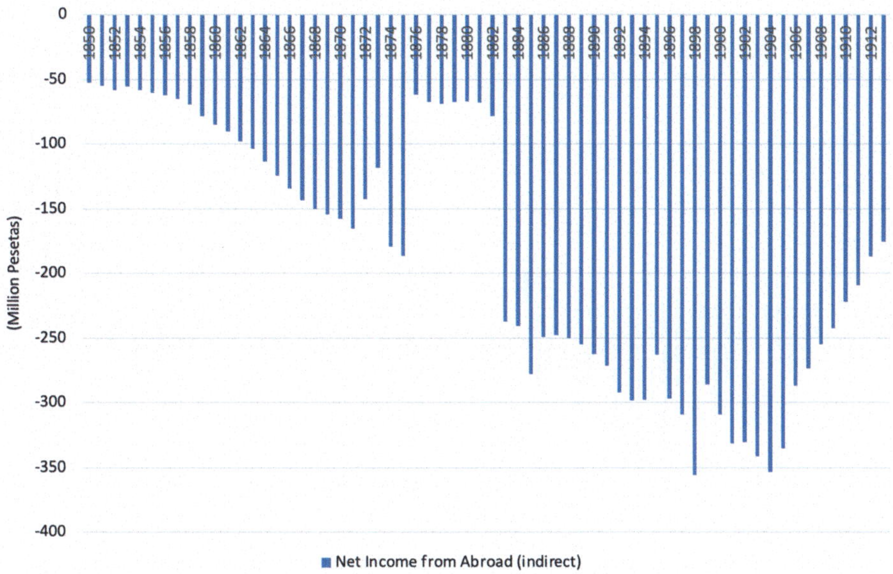

Fig. 8.3 Services trade balance: net income from abroad (million Pesetas). Indirect estimates. Sources: See text and Table 8.1

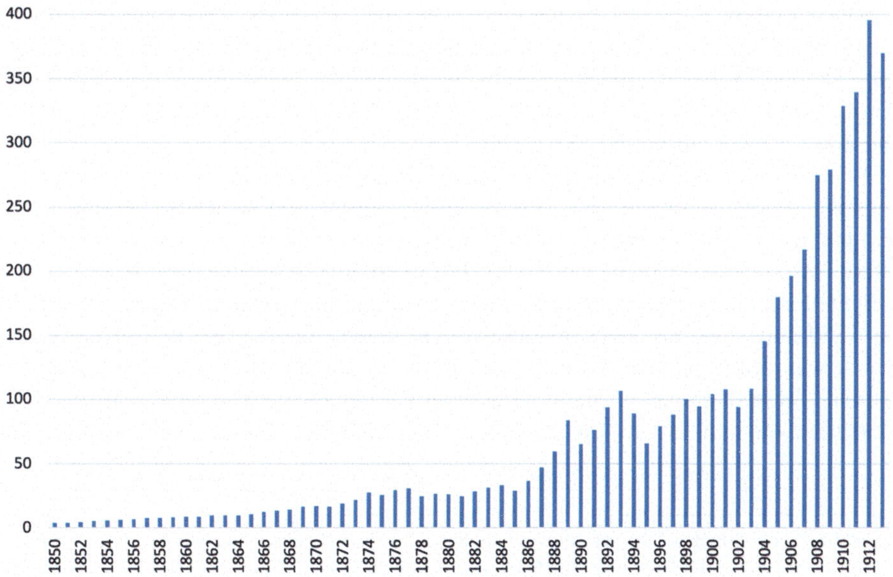

Fig. 8.4 Current transfers balance (million Pesetas). Sources: See text and Table 8.1

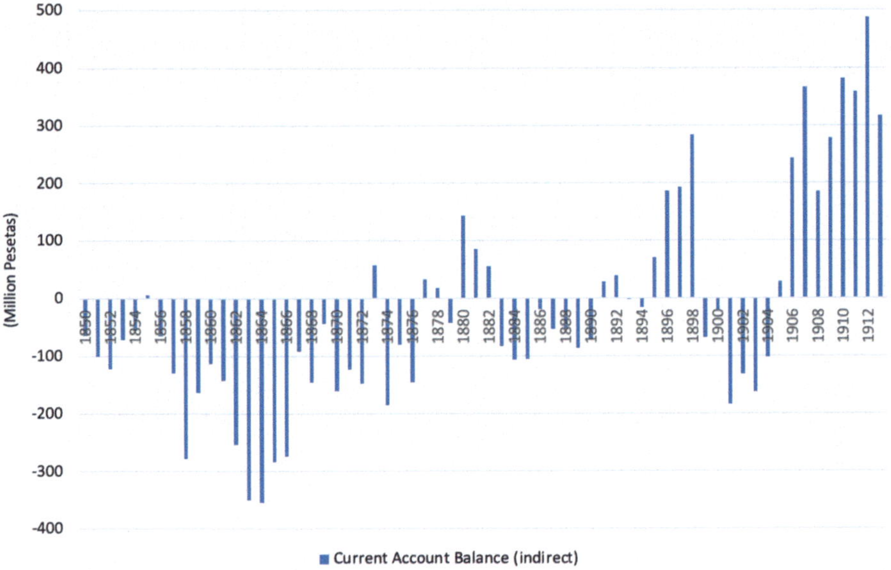

Fig. 8.5 Current account balance: indirect estimates (million Pesetas). Sources: See text and Table 8.1

The net inflow of capital, higher when computed indirectly,[55] provides the mirror image of the current account balance, although it presents a higher absolute level from 1859 to 1874 and, especially, in the wake of Cuba's (and Puerto Rico's and the Philippines') independence (1898), when capital repatriation presumably took place, and a lower level during the 1880s (Fig. 8.6).

Finally, crude estimates of the annual balance of Spain's international indebtedness are presented in Fig. 8.7.[56] A previous clarification is needed though. The nominal level of public debt at the beginning of the period under study (1st January 1850) was assumed to represent the level of international indebtedness to which the weighted nominal interest rate was applied to obtain net payments to foreign capital for 1850 and, thus, the level of international indebtedness at the end of the year, which was yearly updated with the net inflow of capital. However, if we want to estimate the actual level of Spain's international indebtedness, a more realistic way to achieve this is to accept the effective, rather than the nominal, value of Spain's

[55] For the direct estimate of the net inflow of capital, see Fig. 8.19. Direct estimates of the net inflow of capital not only suffer from incomplete coverage, but also from being valued at different years as significant fluctuations in the value of investment occurred over time. The comparison produces similar results to Goldsmith's (1955) dual (direct and indirect) reconstruction of the U.S. capital account balance in the early twentieth century, in which substantially lower levels of net capital inflow were obtained when derived through the direct approach, as it did not 'exhaust total capital movements due to the paucity of capital flows data' (Williamson, 1964: 235).

[56] For the direct estimate of international indebtedness, see Fig. 8.20.

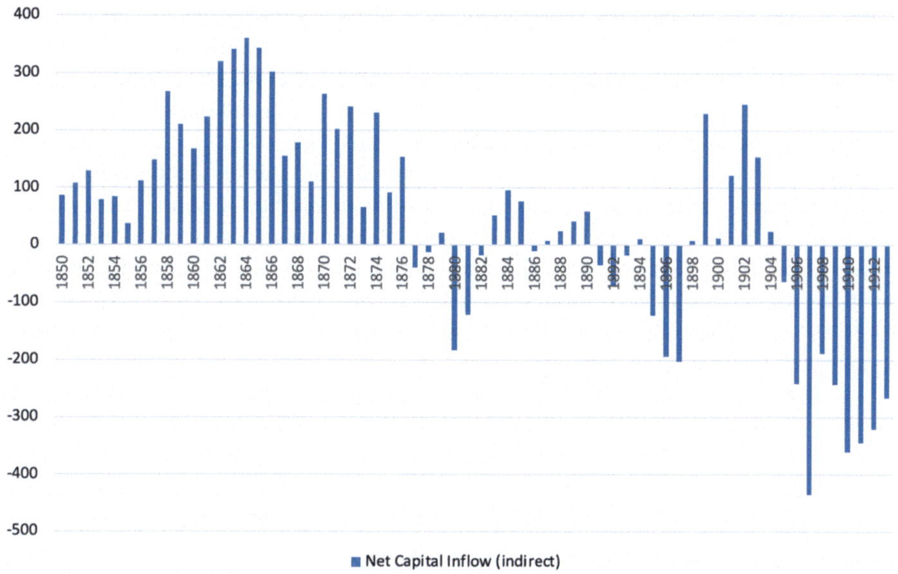

Fig. 8.6 Net capital inflow: indirect estimates (million Pesetas). Sources: See text and Table 8.1

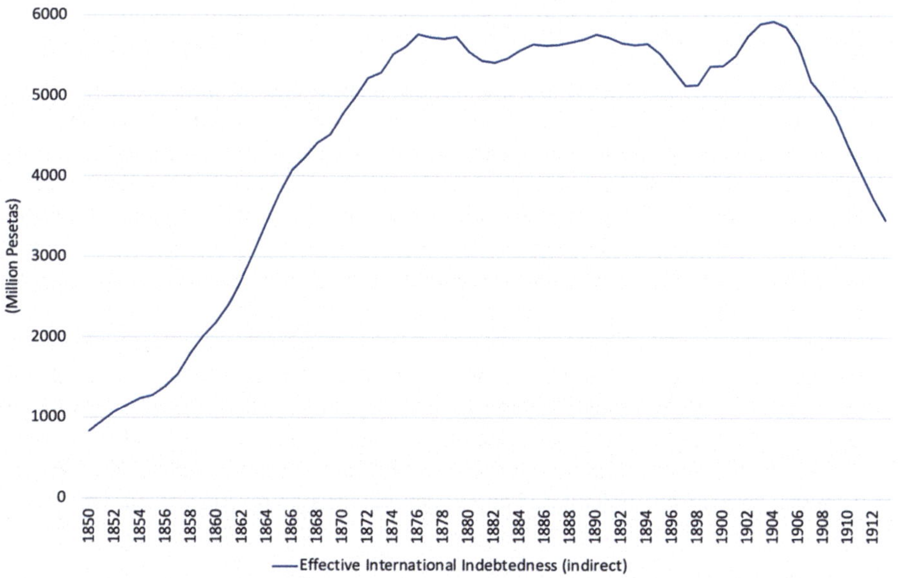

Fig. 8.7 Effective international indebtedness: indirect estimates (million Pesetas). Sources: See text and Table 8.1

external debt on 1st January 1850, about 50% of its nominal value, 752.4 million, and then updating it with the yearly estimates of the net capital inflow. It appears that international indebtedness grew up to the mid-1870s, before stabilizing until the mid-1900s, except for episodes of decline in the early 1880s and during Cuba's War of Independence (1895–1898), and declined steadily thereafter.

A sharp contrast results between the commodity and current account balances. The commodity trade balance is positive in 49 out of the 64 years, with deficit concentrated in the years 1857–1866—in which large imports associated to railways construction took place—; meanwhile the current account was in deficit for most of the time except for three episodes of rising levels, 1880–1882, 1895–1898, and 1906–1913.[57] These three periods and 1857–1866 are the only ones in which the signs of the two balances coincide.

The divergent evolution of the various components of the balance of payments enables us to reconcile the positions of those who maintained that, from 1870 onwards, the commodity trade deficit resulting from the official figures was implausible (Prados de la Escosura, 1986) and those who stressed that Spain's international position was one of deficit (Sardá Dexeus, 1948; Tortella, 1994). The explanation for the apparent contradiction between the two balances is to be found in the growing role played by net income from abroad that was not counter-balanced by current transfers, as emigrant remittances only became significant from 1904 onwards. Thus, the current account deficit appears to be associated with the costs of investing in new infrastructures and exploiting natural resources.

How could the current account surplus for the years 1895–1898 and 1906–1913 be explained? The reasons behind the change from a current account deficit to a surplus can be explored in the light of 'sudden stops'. Edwards (2004: 19) has defined a 'sudden stop' episode as 'an abrupt and major reduction in capital inflow to a country that up to that time had been receiving large volumes of foreign capital'. Sudden stops are, thus, sharp reversals in capital inflows which constrict domestic consumption smoothing.[58] During the first wave of financial globalization that took place in the late nineteenth and early twentieth century, the main effects associated with sudden stops are drops in the exchange rate and deceleration of economic activity.[59]

Exogenous forces conditioned sudden stops. Monetary tightening in advanced countries (rise in central bank discount rates, for example) represented a significant exogenous element in the reversal of capital inflows. In addition, international crisis irradiating from capital importer countries, such as Argentina during the Baring crisis in the early 1890s, constituted an exogenous force to be considered. However,

[57] 1891–1898 and 1905–1913 in the case of the direct estimates (Fig. 8.18).

[58] Interestingly, this approach has been neglected in the Spanish historical literature. This is, perhaps, attributable to the isolated consideration of Spain's experience.

[59] The contraction in external financing implies that the current account has to improve through currency depreciation and GDP contraction unless international reserves absorb the shock. Cf. Catão (2007) excellent study on which I draw for the next paragraphs. Also, Bordo et al. (2010).

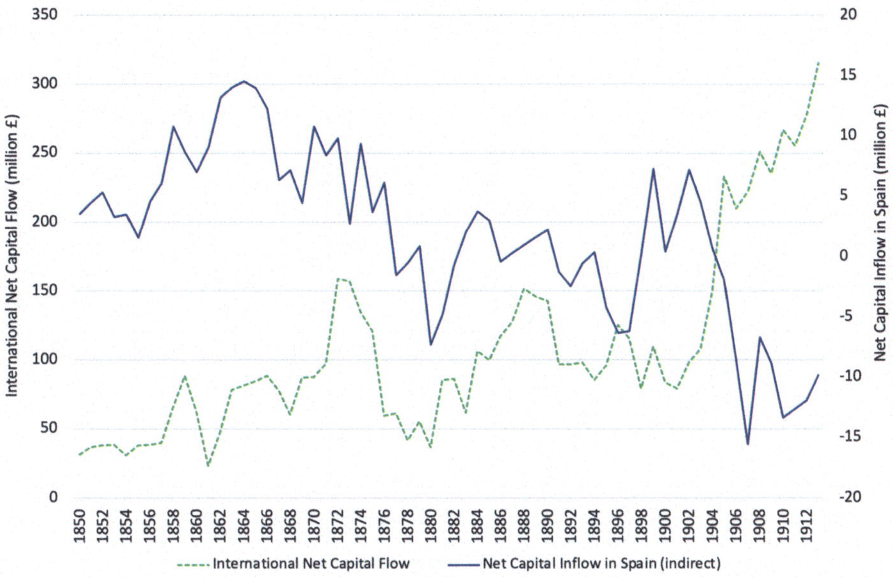

Fig. 8.8 International net capital flow and Spain's net capital inflow (indirect estimates) (million £). Sources: See text and Table 8.1, and Jones and Obstfeld (1997)

the fact that not all capital importers suffered a given sudden stop to the same extent suggests that endogenous factors also mattered.

Let us examine the Spanish experience in the light of sudden stops (*SS*, hereafter). In Fig. 8.8, international capital flows, proxied by British, French and German aggregated current account (excluding all gold flows), are confronted with the net capital inflow in Spain, both expressed in Sterling.[60] Several slowdown episodes in international capital flows are observed, starting in 1860, 1866, 1873, 1890, and 1896, of which those of 1873 and 1890 appear to have special intensity. In Spain, sudden stops can be observed in 1866–1869, 1876–1880, 1890–1896, and 1904–1907, with particular intensity in the last two episodes. Interestingly, the last sudden stop, at odds with the previous ones, occurred during the expansion of international capital exports prior to World War I.

Which of the predicted effects of the *SS* are observed in the Spanish experience? To begin with, currency crashes occurred during 1891–1893 and 1896–1898, but not in earlier *SS*, or in 1904–1907, when the opposite happened and the peseta returned to its position in 1891 (Fig. 8.9).[61] Why such an uneven response to different *SS*?

[60] Data for net capital exports from the U.K., France, and Germany come from Jones and Obstfeld (1997). For a comparison with the direct estimate of Spain's net capital inflow, see Fig. 8.21.

[61] The 1890s sudden stops conform with Calvo et al. (2003) model in which an abrupt interruption of foreign capital inflow leads to a deep current account reversal and a substantial depreciation of the real exchange rate (measured as domestic currency per unit of foreign currency). The multilateral nominal effective exchange rate has been computed using Spain's bilateral trade weights for

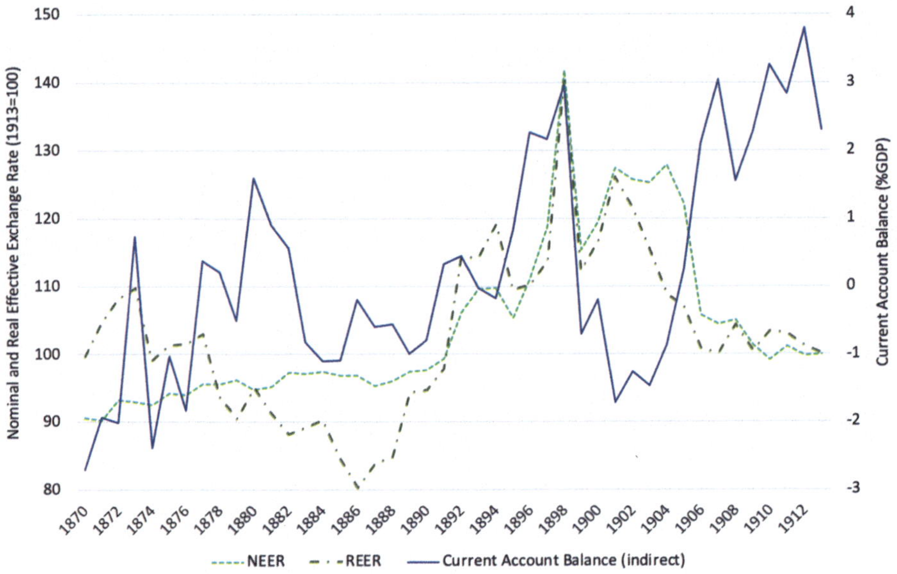

Fig. 8.9 Spain's current account balance indirect estimates (% GDP) and nominal and real effective exchange rate (1913=100), 1870–1913. Sources: See the text and Table 8.2

The consequences of two exogenous events, the Baring crisis (1890) and the Cuban War of Independence (1896–1898) are, no doubt, part of the explanation. According to Catão (2007: 266–9), during the first wave of financial globalization, countries that experienced rapid monetary expansion and had a lax fiscal behaviour were more prone to currency crashes.[62] In fact, money supply (M2) appears to have grown faster than GDP in Spain during the cyclical upswings 1885–1889 and 1896–1898 (Fig. 8.10). Meanwhile, the public debt/GDP ratio, sharply reduced as a result of the 1882 sovereign debt re-scheduling, experienced a sustained increase over 1893–1896 and went up further in the aftermath of the Cuban War of Independence (1899–1903) (Fig. 8.11).[63]

most of its trading partners (Prados de la Escosura and Tena, 1994). The real effective exchange rate is a multilateral rate index calculated using CPIs for the main trading partners and the private consumption deflator for Spain (Prados de la Escosura, 2017). For a comparison with the direct estimate of the current account balance (% GDP), see Fig. 8.22.

[62] In addition, Edwards (2004: 33) points out that the probability of experiencing a current account reversal is higher for a country with a large current account deficit, a high external debt ratio, and a rapid rate of growth of domestic credit.

[63] Interestingly, while the Cuban War of independence (1896–1898) does not seem to have had a major direct negative effect on Spain's economy, the macroeconomic instability brought about by the financing of the military conflict was to have significant effects on Spain's position of international isolation (Fraile Balbín and Escribano, 1998). On the financing of the war, cf. Maluquer de Motes (1996) and Tedde de Lorca (1999).

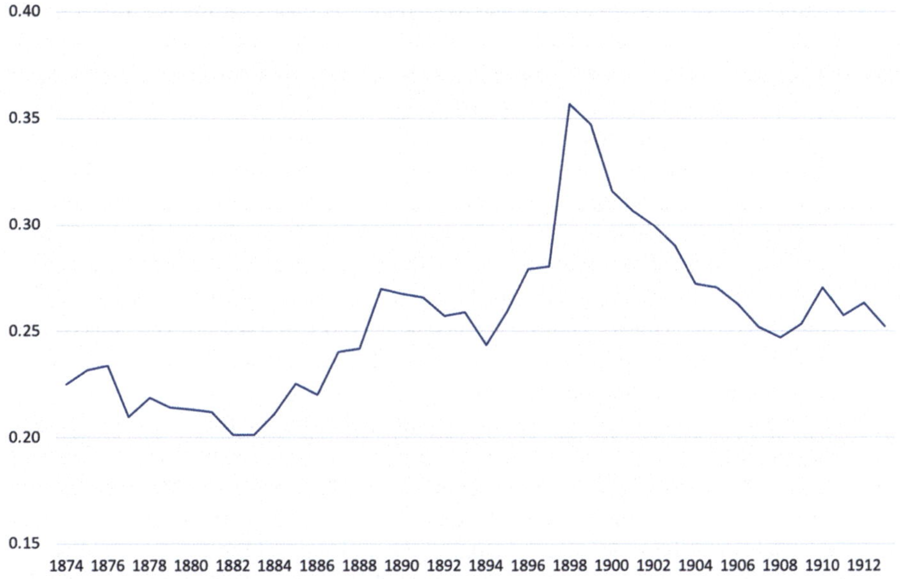

Fig. 8.10 Ratio M2/GDP (1874–1913). Sources: M2, Martín-Aceña and Pons (2005); GDP, Prados de la Escosura (2017)

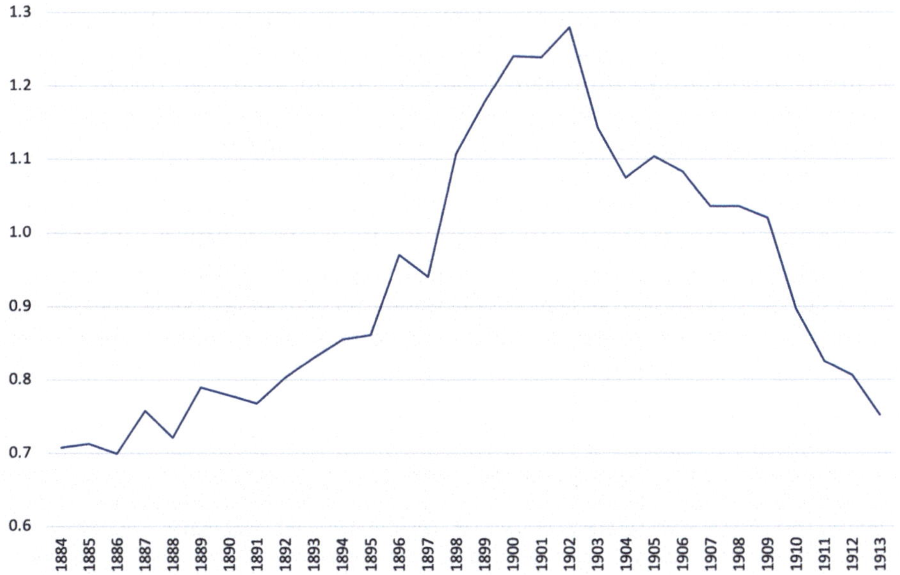

Fig. 8.11 Public Debt/GDP (1884–1913). Sources: Public Debt, Comín and Díaz Fuentes (2005); GDP, Prados de la Escosura (2017)

The simultaneity of sudden stops and exchange rate drops during the 1890s tends to downplay the suspension of the gold convertibility of the peseta (1883) suggesting that, during the 1880s, as long as an inflow of foreign capital continued, the Spanish currency remained stable, regardless of whether the exchange rate floated (Fig. 8.9).

This result has implications for the debate between those who emphasise the advantages of a floating exchange rate for a developing economy, due to the high opportunity cost of maintaining gold reserves, as well as the shock absorber role of the exchange rate (Sardá Dexeus, 1948; Tortella, 1974: Flandreau and Zumer, 2004), and those who stress that belonging to the Gold Standard sent the right signal of compliance with orthodox financial practice to capital markets (Martín-Aceña, 1993; Bordo and Rockoff, 1996). To the extent that it could be factored out, macroeconomic stability rather than belonging to the Gold Standard seems to have been the relevant signal for international investors.

When macroeconomic discipline was abandoned at the time of the Baring crisis and, then, again, by the need to finance the Cuban War of Independence, the control mechanism which stopped the peseta from falling disappeared.[64] Macroeconomic instability, especially inflation, which soared over 1895–1904 (Fig. 8.12), had negative effects on the reputation of Spain's economy, making it less attractive to international capital, as suggested by the spread between the discount rate of the Bank of Spain and those of the central banks in the main capital investing countries during the 1890s (Fig. 8.13).[65]

After the independence of Cuba, Puerto Rico and the Philippines, a current account deficit reappeared between 1899 and 1904, which could be associated with the repatriation of capital from the former colonies in the sound economic environment provided by Fernández-Villaverde's stabilization plan (Comín, 1999).

Why, then, the sudden stop of 1904–1907, at the time of an international expansion of capital flows, and why was the current account reversal accompanied by an improvement in the exchange rate of the peseta? There are good reasons to explain why the exchange rate did not drop. The fact that, for most of the period up to World War I, inflation remained moderate and the public debt/GDP and M2/GDP ratios continued to fall, as opposed to what had happened in the 1890s, helps explain why a currency crash was avoided. Furthermore, no exogenous events such as the Cuban War of Independence took place, while emigrant remittances played an important offsetting role in the current account balance (Fig. 8.4). However, why

[64] For those who favour the importance of being part of the Gold Standard, the argument would be that, as long as the belief in the authorities' commitment to restoring convertibility at the pre-1883 parity existed in the markets, the peseta would remain unaltered. Then, when macroeconomic instability occurred, economic agents realized that the suspension of convertibility was not a temporary measure and that the authorities had no intention of restoring convertibility. This situation led to an outflow of capital which dragged the peseta down (Cf. Bordo and Kydland, 1995). Martín-Aceña (1993: 140–145) notes that the hopes of a rapid return to the parity of 1883, together with the government's restrictive policies, would have contributed to the peseta's stability.

[65] Cf. Martín-Aceña (1993: 155) and Broder (1976: 62). Bordo and Rockoff (1996: 414) claim that Spain had a 3% risk premium as a non-gold standard country is confirmed by Fig. 8.13.

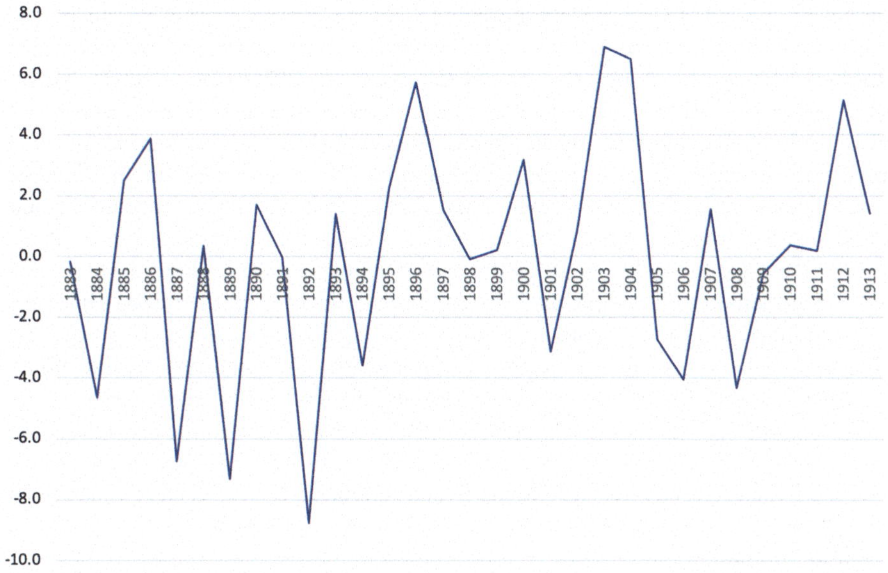

Fig. 8.12 Rate of Inflation (%) (1883–1913). Sources: GDP deflator from Prados de la Escosura (2017)

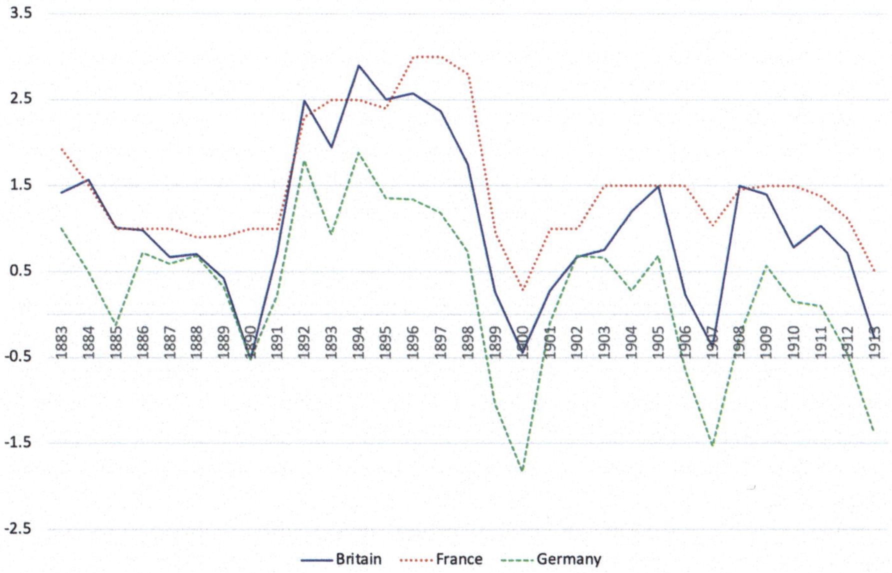

Fig. 8.13 Spain's interest rate spread with Britain, France, and Germany (1884–1913). Sources: Central banks discount rates, Spain, Martín-Aceña and Pons (2005); Britain, France, and Germany, Homer and Sylla (1991)

was Spain omitted from the international wave of investment prior to World War I? It is noteworthy that the Italian and Portuguese current account balances also experienced a surplus during this period (Bordo et al., 2010; Catão, 2007). Meanwhile Argentina, Brazil, Canada, and Russia became the main capital importers. Why were south-western European countries excluded? Was it because investment opportunities had dried up, or because the opportunity cost was too high? It would be worth investigating the extent to which the decline in a sustainable current account deficit results from a reduction in foreigners' demand of an emerging country's assets (Edwards, 2004). In Spain, by the end of the nineteenth century, those sectors that had attracted most foreign capital were already developed: the railway network was completed and mining resources fully exploited. Perhaps this fact helps explain why, in the absence of new investment opportunities, international capital inflow into Spain slowed down.[66] This is, no doubt, an avenue for further research.

To sum up, the idea that the suspension of the convertibility of the peseta in 1883 and its delayed effect in terms of a currency crash in the 1890s was the result of endemic balance of payment problems is not supported by the evidence presented here. In fact, it is the sudden stops, in a context of domestic financial imperfections, that were to blame.

8.5 Did International Integration Hold Back Growth?

The traditional view among Spanish economic historians, reinforced by those who argue in terms of the 'external constraint on growth' approach, associates a current account deficit with a deterioration of the economic situation or to a threat to growth. Conversely, a current account reversal—that is, a surplus on current account—will imply, according to the sudden stop literature, a decline in investment and, thus, in economic growth that tends to intensify if the country is less open (Edwards, 2004; Bordo et al., 2010).

No consensus has been reached with regard to the importance for growth of a large and resilient current account deficit. The optimistic view emphasizes the intertemporal nature of the current account, arguing that insofar as they reflect a rise in investment, there is no reason for concern (Sachs, 1981; Corden, 1994). The opposite, pessimistic view, epitomized in Thirlwall's approach (1979), has a more recent expression in Fischer (1988), for whom the first sign of a crisis is the current account deficit. In this context of uncertainty, historical research can make a useful contribution.

How did the interruption of foreign capital inflow affect economic growth in Spain?

[66] As from the beginning of the twentieth century, investments in public utilities (electricity, gas) and, later, financial investments (Sardá Dexeus, 1948: 268) were to become more significant. For the British investments in these sectors for the period up to 1914 (Stone, 1999).

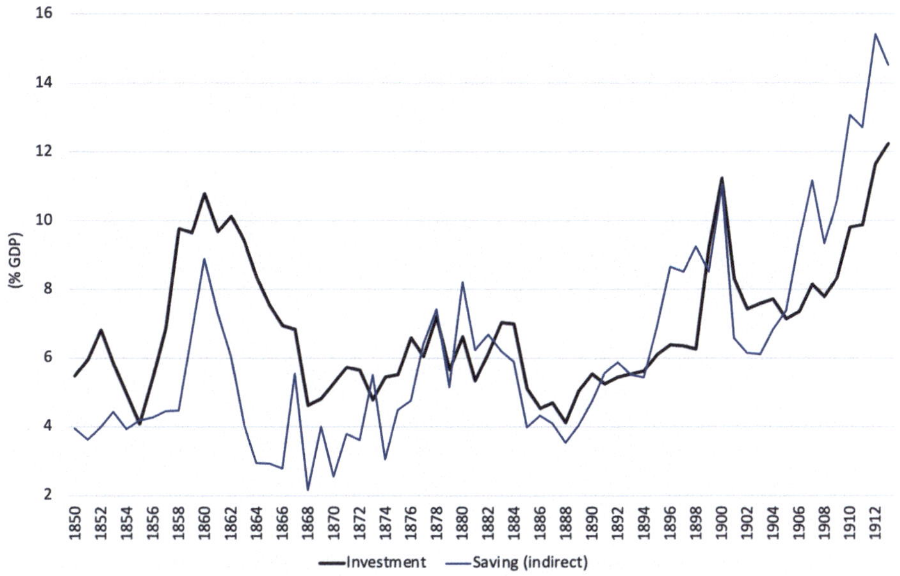

Fig. 8.14 Gross investment and saving (indirect estimates) (% GDP). Sources: Investment, Prados de la Escosura (2017); Saving, see the text and Table 8.2

Let us begin with the current account identity:

$$CAB = X–M + NCT + NY = S–I \tag{8.1}$$

Where *CAB* is the current account balance; *X* and *M* are exports and imports of goods and services, respectively; *NCT*, net current transfers; and *NY*, net income from abroad; while *CAB* equals the difference between gross domestic saving (*S*) and investment (*I*).[67] Here we can normalize with respect to GDP (*Y*), to provide an idea of the relative size of each item,

$$CAB/Y = S/Y–I/Y \tag{8.2}$$

Two distinctive phases can be observed in the relationship between investment and saving, with 1890 as the turning point (Fig. 8.14).[68] Domestic investment was above saving between 1850 and 1890 (except for 1880–1882), which means that foreign capital supplemented domestic saving to meet investment demand. The gap between

[67] If we start from the basic national account identity, $GDP = C + G + I + X–M$, where *C* and *G* are private and Government consumption; *I*, gross domestic investment, and *X* and *M* are exports and import of goods and services, respectively. We, then, define the current account balance (*CAB*) as, $CAB = X - M + NCT + NY$, and the Gross National Product as $GNP = C + G + I + CAB$. We can derive gross domestic saving as $S = GNP - C - G$. Thus, $S = I + CAB$, so $CAB = S - I$.

[68] For a comparison with the direct estimate of savings (% GDP), see Fig. 8.23.

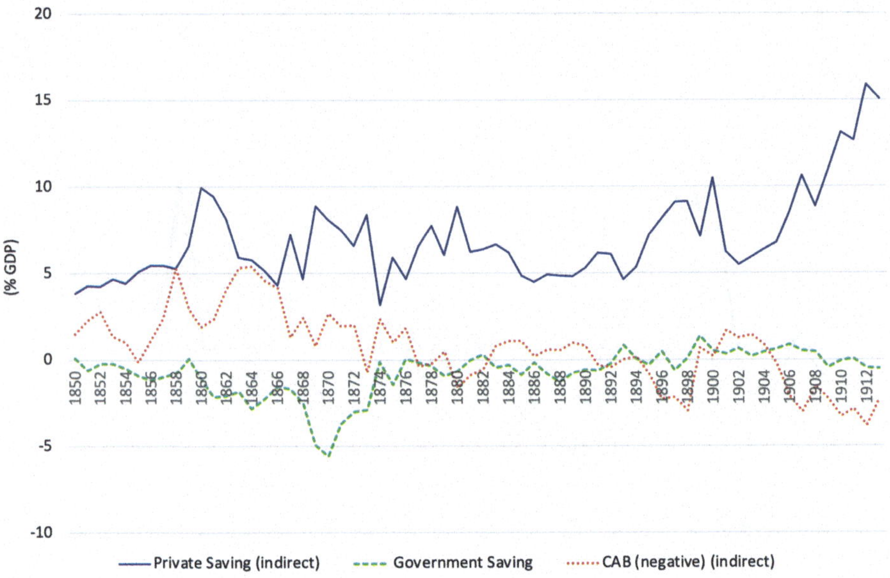

Fig. 8.15 Decomposing gross investment: private and government saving and the (negative of the) current account balance (indirect estimates) (% GDP). Sources: Government Saving, Comín and Díaz Fuentes (2005); for the rest, see the text and Table 8.2

investment and saving was particularly noticeable from 1850 to 1866. This upsurge of investment, which reached 10% of GDP in the early 1860s, was associated with the construction of the railway network, in which foreign capital played a significant role. From 1890 to World War I, investment depended almost exclusively on domestic saving, as a current account surplus prevailed (exception made of the years 1899–1904). All in all, investment and saving followed the same trend, with investment remaining below 8% of GDP up to 1898, except for the years of the railway construction boom.

The small size of investment and saving, in terms of GDP, conceals the relative importance of foreign investment in Spain's gross domestic capital formation. Starting from expression (8.2) we can decompose gross domestic investment into gross domestic saving (private, Sp/Y, and Government, Sg/Y, saving) and the (negative of the) current account balance (Fig. 8.15).[69]

$$I/Y = S/Y\text{–}CAB/Y = Sp/Y + Sg/Y\text{–}CAB/Y \tag{8.3}$$

Government saving was negative up to 1892, especially between 1861 and 1873, and was not offset by a rise in private saving but by a current account deficit financed through a net inflow of foreign capital. This way, the decrease in government saving

[69] For a comparison with the direct estimate of private and government savings (% GDP), see Fig. 8.24.

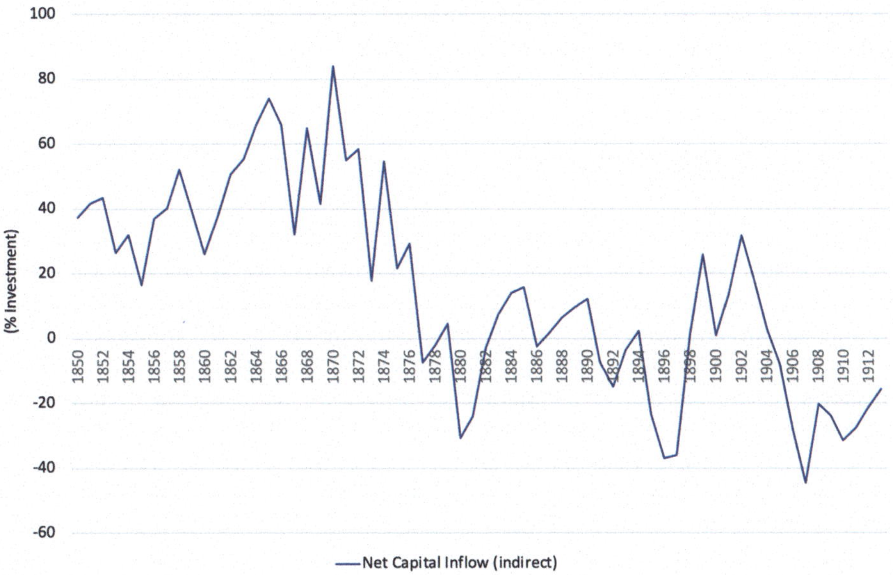

Fig. 8.16 Net capital inflow as a proportion of gross investment (indirect estimates) (%). Sources: See the text and Table 8.2

did not imply a constraint on the investment ratio. This finding implies that the view of a decline of investment derived from a decrease in government saving—the crowding out hypothesis occasionally discussed in the literature—, is not confirmed by the evidence.

The relative importance of the net capital inflow contribution to capital formation is reflected by its share of gross investment (Fig. 8.16).[70] Between 1850 and 1890, foreign capital financed nearly 30% of domestic investment, rising to almost a half during the third quarter of the nineteenth century. Conversely, in the years 1891–1913, the net *outflow* of capital implied a contraction of domestic investment (11%), which reached 15% over the period 1891–1897, but experienced a reversal episode over 1899–1903, in which the net inflow of foreign capital represented more than 15% of gross capital formation.

Thus, it can be suggested that, during the late nineteenth century, as foreign capital complemented domestic saving to meet a growing investment demand, economic growth intensified and, although difficult to quantify, improvements in the quality of capital and embodied technology in new capital goods, whose acquisition was funded by foreign capital, most probably made the economy more efficient. Conversely, the sudden stops at the turn of the century slowed down growth, as the increase in capital accumulation decelerated, and, presumably, the efficiency of the economy declined. Hence, sudden stops, by causing current account

[70] For a comparison with the direct estimate of net capital inflow (% investment), see Fig. 8.25.

reversals and currency drops in a context of domestic macroeconomic imperfections, had a clearly negative effect on Spain's long-run growth.

8.6 Concluding Remarks

Between 1850 and 1890, economic expansion coincided with a significant current account deficit, while between 1891 and 1913, growth slowed down at a time of positive current account balances. This inverse correlation between the current account surplus and economic growth casts serious doubts on the widespread view of an external restriction to Spain's growth during the nineteenth century. This chapter's results suggest an alternative interpretation: the balance of payments reacted to changes in the equilibrium between saving and investment. Thus, the current account deficit resulted from an inflow of capital which allowed the rate of investment to rise and, in turn, to contribute to more rapid growth. Only when isolation from the international economy increased since 1891, did investment demand have to rely on domestic saving. In the context of globalization that characterized the classical gold standard era, there was no reason why an open economy should not enjoy sustained access to international capital markets and break the link between investment and domestic saving. From this perspective, the persistence of the current account deficit between 1850 and 1890 is better understood.

At the turn of the century, domestic macroeconomic imperfections exacerbated the current account reversals that had been provoked by sudden stops, undermining the confidence of foreign investors in the Spanish economy and encouraging the flight of foreign capital. Furthermore, as Sánchez-Alonso (2000) has shown, the migration push of the 1891 protectionist tariff was largely offset by the microeconomic consequences of the currency crash, preventing individuals from migrating for one and a half decades.

The view that Spanish integration in international markets contributed to a slowing down of economic growth appears to be incorrect. One might suggest that without the current account deficit—that is, without an inflow of foreign capital—Spain would have grown at a slower speed during the second half the nineteenth century. As the inflow of capital dried up, investment had to rely exclusively on domestic savings, slowing down capital accumulation and economic growth.

Appendix

A.1 The Metallic Stock

In the construction of the metallic stock, setting its initial level represents the first step. Tortella (1981: 124) provides an estimate for 1865. Then, its annual level from

1866 onwards would result from adding to the initial level the yearly gold and silver coinage (newly minted, less re-minted, plus illegal coinage) and the net imports (legal and illegal or unregistered) of gold and silver coin, and subtracting gold and silver coin hoarded, lost or destroyed.

Alas, re-minting is an unknown, as are illegal minting and gold and silver hoarded or lost, even though re-minting was a very small proportion of total coinage in the late 1860s (when data are available) (Anes, 1974: 111; Tortella, 1974: 120).

In addition, the available data on the net imports of gold and silver also raise objections. Trade in gold and silver is poorly covered in most countries' historical statistics. Spanish official gold and silver trade statistics have been deemed incomplete due to underreporting (Tortella 1974: 121–122; Moro et al., 2015, suppl. 2). Specifically, official statistics do not record any imports of gold and silver between 1850 and 1882.

Fortunately, however, trade statistics of Spain's main trading partners offer an alternative source. The U.K. trade statistics provide gold and silver trade (imports from Spain only since 1858) between the United Kingdom and Spain and Gibraltar (the latter as a proxy for smuggling), and the United States trade statistics supply the value of gold and silver exported to and imported from Spain. Moreover, Tedde (2015: 181) presents the Bank of Spain's imports of gold and silver, mainly from France but also from Britain, during 1859–1874. Tedde (2015) also provides smaller purchases of silver during 1849–1855 that I have assumed came from France too and distributed them evenly through 1850–1855. All this information allowed me to revise, at least partially, the official figures. The revised series of gold and silver trade result from replacing official figures of exports and imports by those from the statistics of Spain's main trading partners but only for those years in which the latter exceeded the former. It is worth stressing that most of the correction of the official figures of gold and silver trade corresponds to imports.

Thus, crude estimates of the metallic stock for 1866 and successive years would be derived by adding the annually minted gold and silver and the net imports of gold and silver coin to the stock in the previous year (being 1865 the initial year). For 1850–1864 the stock would be obtained by deducting the annually minted gold and silver and the net imports of gold and silver coin from the stock in 1865.

The annual change in metallic stock provides a measure of the change in reserves, with two options available, one in which the net imports of gold and silver coin derive from the official series (option A) and another that derive from the revised estimates (option B).

See Tables 8.1, 8.2, 8.3 and 8.4.

Direct Estimates

See Figs. 8.17, 8.18, 8.19, 8.20, 8.21, 8.22, 8.23, 8.24 and 8.25.

Table 8.1 The balance of payments on current account, net capital inflow, and international indebtedness, 1850–1913 (million Pesetas): indirect 'residual' estimates

	Exports goods fob	Exports services[a]	Payments domestic labour	Current transfers	Imports goods fob	Imports services[a]	Payments to foreign capital	Commodity balance	Balance of services[a]	Net income from abroad	Net current transfers	Current account balance	Variation in reserves	Net capital inflow	Effective international indebtedness
1850	161.9	8.2	0.2	4.2	169.5	16.6	52.6	−7.6	−8.4	−52.4	4.2	−64.1	22.5	86.6	839.0
1851	142.8	8.4	0.2	4.2	182.1	18.8	55.1	−39.3	−10.3	−54.9	4.2	−100.4	7.3	107.7	946.7
1852	134.6	8.8	0.2	4.3	194.1	18.3	58.6	−59.5	−9.5	−58.3	4.3	−123.1	6.0	129.1	1075.8
1853	185.9	12.8	0.3	5.3	198.0	22.1	55.8	−12.1	−9.3	−55.5	5.3	−71.6	7.7	79.3	1155.1
1854	229.5	16.4	0.3	6.1	217.5	31.4	58.4	12.0	−15.0	−58.1	6.1	−55.0	29.1	84.0	1239.2
1855	322.0	16.4	0.3	6.4	237.0	40.9	61.1	85.0	−24.5	−60.7	6.4	6.2	44.2	38.0	1277.2
1856	319.4	20.4	0.4	7.1	291.9	57.0	63.1	27.5	−36.6	−62.7	7.1	−64.8	47.8	112.5	1389.7
1857	318.1	22.5	0.5	8.0	337.0	76.5	65.8	−19.0	−53.9	−65.4	8.0	−130.3	18.2	148.5	1538.2
1858	179.9	18.9	0.5	8.0	345.4	69.8	70.3	−165.5	−50.9	−69.8	8.0	−278.2	−10.6	267.6	1805.8
1859	236.9	15.3	0.5	8.4	297.0	49.5	79.3	−60.1	−34.2	−78.8	8.4	−164.6	45.4	209.9	2015.7
1860	262.9	61.7	0.5	8.6	308.5	52.2	85.7	−45.7	9.4	−85.2	8.6	−112.8	54.5	167.3	2183.1
1861	281.0	35.1	0.5	8.6	325.8	51.7	91.1	−44.8	−16.5	−90.6	8.6	−143.4	79.7	223.0	2406.1
1862	235.0	20.0	0.8	9.9	360.9	59.2	99.0	−125.9	−39.2	−98.2	9.9	−253.4	66.7	320.1	2726.2
1863	236.9	21.9	0.7	9.5	443.0	71.3	104.5	−206.1	−49.5	−103.7	9.5	−349.8	−7.8	342.0	3068.1
1864	219.9	33.1	0.8	9.8	427.9	75.4	114.6	−208.0	−42.4	−113.9	9.8	−354.5	6.6	361.1	3429.2
1865	250.2	22.4	0.8	10.5	381.5	60.5	125.6	−131.3	−38.1	−124.8	10.5	−283.8	60.3	344.1	3773.3
1866	267.0	21.1	0.9	12.7	380.3	59.6	135.6	−113.4	−38.5	−134.7	12.7	−273.9	28.1	302.0	4075.3
1867	367.4	19.9	1.0	13.4	299.9	48.5	144.7	67.5	−28.6	−143.8	13.4	−91.5	63.7	155.1	4230.4
1868	374.4	23.7	1.0	14.6	343.3	65.4	151.1	31.1	−41.7	−150.1	14.6	−146.1	32.3	178.3	4408.8
1869	429.3	21.9	1.2	16.9	304.5	52.8	155.8	124.8	−30.9	−154.6	16.9	−43.8	65.8	109.6	4518.3
1870	334.2	21.1	1.2	17.3	322.7	53.0	159.1	11.5	−31.9	−157.9	17.3	−160.9	102.4	263.3	4781.7
1871	433.1	32.3	1.1	16.9	382.8	57.9	166.7	50.3	−25.6	−165.6	16.9	−124.0	77.6	201.5	4983.2
1872	493.2	29.8	1.7	19.4	479.5	68.1	144.4	13.7	−38.4	−142.7	19.4	−147.9	93.6	241.5	5224.8
1873	582.5	33.4	2.1	22.1	406.5	55.9	120.6	176.0	−22.5	−118.6	22.1	57.1	123.8	66.7	5291.5
1874	506.7	28.6	2.6	28.0	497.5	71.8	182.0	9.2	−43.3	−179.4	28.0	−185.5	45.5	231.0	5522.5
1875	537.9	26.6	2.4	25.9	423.4	60.0	189.0	114.6	−33.4	−186.6	25.9	−79.5	12.6	92.1	5614.6

1876	451.7	28.2	3.4	29.8	521.2	73.1	65.2	−69.5	−44.9	−61.9	29.8	−146.5	7.5	154.0	5768.6
1877	566.4	29.5	3.5	31.0	457.5	68.9	71.0	109.0	−39.4	−67.5	31.0	33.0	−5.8	−38.8	5729.8
1878	534.2	29.6	1.6	25.1	433.1	69.0	70.6	101.1	−39.3	−69.0	25.1	17.8	4.9	−12.9	5716.8
1879	540.7	31.6	2.9	26.9	493.1	81.2	70.8	47.6	−49.6	−67.9	26.9	−43.0	−21.2	21.8	5738.6
1880	734.5	39.5	3.1	26.3	502.9	86.3	70.5	231.6	−46.8	−67.4	26.3	143.7	−39.5	−183.2	5555.4
1881	755.6	42.8	1.7	24.7	575.9	93.7	69.9	179.7	−50.9	−68.1	24.7	85.4	−35.8	−121.2	5434.2
1882	764.0	47.1	2.9	28.7	613.1	92.6	81.3	150.9	−45.5	−78.4	28.7	55.7	38.1	−17.6	5416.6
1883	831.1	31.7	2.8	31.8	650.2	90.6	240.3	181.0	−58.9	−237.5	31.8	−83.7	−31.5	52.2	5468.8
1884	718.4	32.3	2.7	33.3	572.1	78.5	243.2	146.3	−46.1	−240.5	33.3	−107.0	−10.8	96.2	5565.0
1885	760.0	35.6	3.1	29.3	579.6	72.2	281.5	180.4	−36.6	−278.4	29.3	−105.3	−27.9	77.4	5642.4
1886	817.9	41.1	4.9	36.6	586.0	80.0	254.2	232.0	−39.0	−249.3	36.6	−19.7	−30.2	−10.5	5631.9
1887	753.2	44.1	5.0	47.5	565.9	84.2	252.8	187.2	−40.1	−247.8	47.5	−53.2	−46.0	7.2	5639.1
1888	810.1	49.2	5.4	59.5	621.7	99.6	255.6	188.4	−50.4	−250.2	59.5	−52.7	−27.8	24.9	5664.0
1889	834.3	57.0	5.9	84.1	693.0	113.8	261.1	141.2	−56.8	−255.2	84.1	−86.6	−45.1	41.5	5705.5
1890	867.2	53.5	3.5	65.2	701.3	92.2	266.1	166.0	−38.7	−262.7	65.2	−70.2	−11.0	59.2	5764.8
1891	933.7	50.6	4.6	76.3	669.0	91.2	276.0	264.8	−40.6	−271.4	76.3	29.1	−6.1	−35.2	5729.6
1892	931.9	51.7	5.2	93.7	661.1	84.1	297.7	270.8	−32.4	−292.5	93.7	39.6	−32.7	−72.3	5657.3
1893	881.3	52.5	5.3	106.6	658.9	85.3	304.0	222.5	−32.8	−298.7	106.6	−2.4	−19.9	−17.5	5639.8
1894	899.0	55.0	7.2	89.2	675.5	85.5	305.0	223.5	−30.5	−297.9	89.2	−15.7	−4.9	10.8	5650.6
1895	861.8	47.8	3.9	65.7	574.3	67.5	267.1	287.4	−19.7	−263.2	65.7	70.3	−52.6	−122.9	5527.7
1896	1067.7	63.0	5.4	79.1	637.1	89.4	302.3	430.6	−26.4	−296.9	79.1	186.4	−7.6	−194.0	5333.7
1897	1127.0	72.4	5.2	88.1	689.4	95.6	314.6	437.6	−23.2	−309.4	88.1	193.1	−9.8	−202.9	5130.8
1898	1272.3	69.2	5.6	100.4	709.2	92.5	361.7	563.2	−23.4	−356.1	100.4	284.1	291.8	7.7	5138.5
1899	1058.3	89.9	6.4	94.7	910.0	114.9	292.7	148.2	−25.0	−286.3	94.7	−68.4	161.5	229.9	5368.3
1900	1181.1	129.4	6.9	104.2	1003.2	122.3	316.1	177.9	7.1	−309.3	104.2	−20.1	−8.1	12.0	5380.3
1901	1104.5	87.5	6.6	108.2	1053.6	99.6	338.3	50.9	−12.1	−331.7	108.2	−184.8	−63.5	121.3	5501.6
1902	1103.5	97.0	7.4	94.1	1006.7	88.7	338.3	96.7	8.2	−330.9	94.1	−131.7	113.8	245.5	5747.1
1903	1152.0	103.9	8.0	108.7	1084.3	101.9	349.8	67.6	2.0	−341.8	108.7	−163.5	−9.5	154.0	5901.1
1904	1202.0	104.7	11.2	145.7	1090.6	110.5	364.8	111.4	−5.8	−353.5	145.7	−102.2	−78.2	24.0	5925.1
1905	1318.5	125.1	12.5	180.0	1116.1	143.4	347.9	202.4	−18.2	−335.4	180.0	28.7	−35.3	−64.0	5861.1

(continued)

Table 8.1 (continued)

	Exports goods fob	Exports services[a]	Payments domestic labour	Current transfers	Imports goods fob	Imports services[a]	Payments to foreign capital	Commodity balance	Balance of services[a]	Net income from abroad	Net current transfers	Current account balance	Variation in reserves	Net capital inflow	Effective international indebtedness
1906	1323.5	94.7	9.9	196.5	967.0	117.3	297.3	356.5	−22.6	−287.3	196.5	243.0	1.3	−241.7	5619.4
1907	1405.1	86.7	9.3	217.2	956.2	112.5	283.1	448.9	−25.8	−273.8	217.2	366.5	−68.7	−435.2	5184.1
1908	1140.6	77.8	11.8	275.0	937.5	115.3	266.8	203.1	−37.4	−255.0	275.0	185.7	−3.2	−188.9	4995.3
1909	1120.8	78.2	9.7	279.2	854.5	103.4	252.2	266.3	−25.2	−242.5	279.2	277.8	34.8	−243.0	4752.3
1910	1237.6	97.7	12.8	328.8	936.8	123.1	234.9	300.8	−25.5	−222.1	328.8	382.0	22.1	−359.9	4392.4
1911	1377.8	104.4	12.7	339.9	1110.6	144.1	222.0	267.1	−39.8	−209.3	339.9	357.9	14.0	−343.9	4048.5
1912	1490.7	129.3	17.2	395.8	1158.5	182.4	204.6	332.2	−53.1	−187.4	395.8	487.5	167.3	−320.2	3728.2
1913	1524.3	135.4	15.9	370.3	1380.6	156.4	191.8	143.7	−21.0	−175.9	370.3	317.2	50.9	−266.3	3462.0

[a]Excluding factor payments

Sources: See text

Table 8.2 Investment and saving, 1850–1913 (million Pesetas and % GDP): indirect estimates

	(million Pesetas)						(% GDP)						(% Gross investment)	
	Gross investment	Current account balance	Gross saving	Government saving	Private saving	Net capital inflow	Gross investment	Current account balance	Gross saving	Government saving	Private saving	Net capital inflow	Current account balance (negative)	Net capital inflow
1850	232.3	−64.1	168.1	4.0	164.1	86.6	5.5	−1.5	4.0	0.1	3.9	2.0	27.6	37.3
1851	258.3	−100.4	157.9	−27.0	184.9	107.7	5.9	−2.3	3.6	−0.6	4.3	2.5	38.9	41.7
1852	297.7	−123.1	174.7	−10.0	184.7	129.1	6.8	−2.8	4.0	−0.2	4.2	3.0	41.3	43.4
1853	300.8	−71.6	229.2	−11.0	240.2	79.3	5.8	−1.4	4.4	−0.2	4.7	1.5	23.8	26.4
1854	264.3	−55.0	209.4	−27.0	236.4	84.0	5.0	−1.0	3.9	−0.5	4.4	1.6	20.8	31.8
1855	230.4	6.2	236.6	−52.0	288.6	38.0	4.1	0.1	4.2	−0.9	5.1	0.7	−2.7	16.5
1856	304.3	−64.8	239.5	−66.0	305.5	112.5	5.4	−1.2	4.3	−1.2	5.5	2.0	21.3	37.0
1857	370.1	−130.3	239.8	−54.0	293.8	148.5	6.9	−2.4	4.4	−1.0	5.4	2.8	35.2	40.1
1858	513.2	−278.2	235.0	−42.0	277.0	267.6	9.8	−5.3	4.5	−0.8	5.3	5.1	54.2	52.1
1859	539.9	−164.6	375.3	6.0	369.3	209.9	9.6	−2.9	6.7	0.1	6.6	3.7	30.5	38.9
1860	642.2	−112.8	529.4	−65.0	594.4	167.3	10.8	−1.9	8.9	−1.1	10.0	2.8	17.6	26.1
1861	588.0	−143.4	444.7	−131.0	575.7	223.0	9.7	−2.4	7.3	−2.2	9.5	3.7	24.4	37.9
1862	632.1	−253.4	378.8	−130.0	508.8	320.1	10.1	−4.1	6.1	−2.1	8.1	5.1	40.1	50.6
1863	617.4	−349.8	267.6	−121.0	388.6	342.0	9.4	−5.3	4.1	−1.8	5.9	5.2	56.7	55.4
1864	548.2	−354.5	193.6	−186.0	379.6	361.1	8.3	−5.4	2.9	−2.8	5.8	5.5	64.7	65.9
1865	464.9	−283.8	181.1	−139.0	320.1	344.1	7.5	−4.6	2.9	−2.2	5.2	5.6	61.0	74.0
1866	458.9	−273.9	185.0	−101.0	286.0	302.0	6.9	−4.1	2.8	−1.5	4.3	4.6	59.7	65.8
1867	482.6	−91.5	391.2	−118.0	509.2	155.1	6.8	−1.3	5.5	−1.7	7.2	2.2	19.0	32.1
1868	275.1	−146.1	129.0	−149.0	278.0	178.3	4.6	−2.4	2.2	−2.5	4.7	3.0	53.1	64.8
1869	264.0	−43.8	220.3	−270.0	490.3	109.6	4.8	−0.8	4.0	−4.9	8.9	2.0	16.6	41.5
1870	313.4	−160.9	152.5	−331.0	483.5	263.3	5.2	−2.7	2.6	−5.5	8.1	4.4	51.3	84.0
1871	367.1	−124.0	243.1	−238.0	481.1	201.5	5.7	−1.9	3.8	−3.7	7.5	3.1	33.8	54.9

(continued)

Table 8.2 (continued)

	(million Pesetas)						(% GDP)						(% Gross investment)	
	Gross investment	Current account balance	Gross saving	Government saving	Private saving	Net capital inflow	Gross investment	Current account balance	Gross saving	Government saving	Private saving	Net capital inflow	Current account balance (negative)	Net capital inflow
1872	413.4	−147.9	265.4	−219.0	484.4	241.5	5.6	−2.0	3.6	−3.0	6.6	3.3	35.8	58.4
1873	374.3	57.1	431.4	−227.0	658.4	66.7	4.8	0.7	5.5	−2.9	8.4	0.9	−15.3	17.8
1874	423.2	−185.5	237.7	−10.0	247.7	231.0	5.4	−2.4	3.1	−0.1	3.2	3.0	43.8	54.6
1875	424.6	−79.5	345.1	−111.0	456.1	92.1	5.5	−1.0	4.5	−1.4	5.9	1.2	18.7	21.7
1876	526.2	−146.5	379.7	6.0	373.7	154.0	6.6	−1.8	4.7	0.1	4.7	1.9	27.8	29.3
1877	532.0	33.0	565.0	−13.0	578.0	−38.8	6.0	0.4	6.4	−0.1	6.6	−0.4	−6.2	−7.3
1878	628.4	17.8	646.2	−30.0	676.2	−12.9	7.2	0.2	7.4	−0.3	7.8	−0.1	−2.8	−2.1
1879	479.9	−43.0	436.9	−78.0	514.9	21.8	5.6	−0.5	5.1	−0.9	6.1	0.3	9.0	4.5
1880	595.2	143.7	738.9	−58.0	796.9	−183.2	6.6	1.6	8.2	−0.6	8.8	−2.0	−24.1	−30.8
1881	503.7	85.4	589.1	−1.0	590.1	−121.2	5.3	0.9	6.2	0.0	6.2	−1.3	−17.0	−24.1
1882	612.7	55.7	668.4	31.0	637.4	−17.6	6.1	0.6	6.7	0.3	6.4	−0.2	−9.1	−2.9
1883	712.9	−83.7	629.2	−45.0	674.2	52.2	7.0	−0.8	6.2	−0.4	6.6	0.5	11.7	7.3
1884	682.0	−107.0	575.0	−28.0	603.0	96.2	7.0	−1.1	5.9	−0.3	6.2	1.0	15.7	14.1
1885	490.5	−105.3	385.2	−82.0	467.2	77.4	5.1	−1.1	4.0	−0.9	4.8	0.8	21.5	15.8
1886	444.2	−19.7	424.5	−15.0	439.5	−10.5	4.5	−0.2	4.3	−0.2	4.5	−0.1	4.4	−2.4
1887	420.8	−53.2	367.7	−73.0	440.7	7.2	4.7	−0.6	4.1	−0.8	4.9	0.1	12.6	1.7
1888	386.0	−52.7	333.3	−122.0	455.3	24.9	4.1	−0.6	3.5	−1.3	4.8	0.3	13.6	6.4
1889	438.4	−86.6	351.8	−67.0	418.8	41.5	5.0	−1.0	4.0	−0.8	4.8	0.5	19.8	9.5
1890	488.8	−70.2	418.6	−50.0	468.6	59.2	5.5	−0.8	4.7	−0.6	5.3	0.7	14.4	12.1
1891	472.6	29.1	501.7	−54.0	555.7	−35.2	5.2	0.3	5.6	−0.6	6.2	−0.4	−6.2	−7.4
1892	485.7	39.6	525.3	−19.0	544.3	−72.3	5.4	0.4	5.9	−0.2	6.1	−0.8	−8.1	−14.9
1893	481.3	−2.4	478.8	75.0	403.8	−17.5	5.5	0.0	5.5	0.9	4.6	−0.2	0.5	−3.6

1894	477.9	−15.7	462.2	6.0	456.2	10.8	5.6	−0.2	5.4	0.1	5.4	0.1	3.3	2.3
1895	523.9	70.3	594.2	−26.0	620.2	−122.9	6.1	0.8	6.9	−0.3	7.2	−1.4	−13.4	−23.5
1896	524.3	186.4	710.7	40.0	670.7	−194.0	6.4	2.3	8.6	0.5	8.2	−2.4	−35.6	−37.0
1897	564.5	193.1	757.6	−54.0	811.6	−202.9	6.3	2.2	8.5	−0.6	9.1	−2.3	−34.2	−35.9
1898	599.4	284.1	883.5	8.0	875.5	7.7	6.3	3.0	9.2	0.1	9.1	0.1	−47.4	1.3
1899	894.1	−68.4	825.8	134.0	691.8	229.9	9.2	−0.7	8.5	1.4	7.1	2.4	7.6	25.7
1900	1150.2	−20.1	1130.2	52.0	1078.2	12.0	11.2	−0.2	11.0	0.5	10.5	0.1	1.7	1.0
1901	893.5	−184.8	708.7	38.0	670.7	121.3	8.3	−1.7	6.6	0.4	6.2	1.1	20.7	13.6
1902	773.1	−131.7	641.4	71.0	570.4	245.5	7.4	−1.3	6.2	0.7	5.5	2.4	17.0	31.8
1903	844.3	−163.5	680.8	23.0	657.8	154.0	7.6	−1.5	6.1	0.2	5.9	1.4	19.4	18.2
1904	905.9	−102.2	803.6	54.0	749.6	24.0	7.7	−0.9	6.8	0.5	6.4	0.2	11.3	2.7
1905	808.4	28.7	837.1	72.0	765.1	−64.0	7.1	0.3	7.4	0.6	6.7	−0.6	−3.6	−7.9
1906	849.4	243.0	1092.5	103.0	989.5	−241.7	7.3	2.1	9.4	0.9	8.6	−2.1	−28.6	−28.5
1907	978.8	366.5	1345.3	65.0	1280.3	−435.2	8.1	3.0	11.2	0.5	10.6	−3.6	−37.4	−44.5
1908	929.3	185.7	1114.9	56.0	1058.9	−188.9	7.8	1.6	9.3	0.5	8.9	−1.6	−20.0	−20.3
1909	1015.9	277.8	1293.7	−51.0	1344.7	−243.0	8.3	2.3	10.6	−0.4	11.0	−2.0	−27.3	−23.9
1910	1145.1	382.0	1527.1	−6.0	1533.1	−359.9	9.8	3.3	13.1	−0.1	13.1	−3.1	−33.4	−31.4
1911	1245.7	357.9	1603.6	6.0	1597.6	−343.9	9.9	2.8	12.7	0.0	12.7	−2.7	−28.7	−27.6
1912	1493.7	487.5	1981.3	−62.0	2043.3	−320.2	11.6	3.8	15.4	−0.5	15.9	−2.5	−32.6	−21.4
1913	1685.0	317.2	2002.1	−71.0	2073.1	−266.3	12.2	2.3	14.5	−0.5	15.0	−1.9	−18.8	−15.8

Sources: See the text and Table 8.1. GDP and Investment, Prados de la Escosura (2017); Public Saving, Comín and Díaz Fuentes (2005)

Table 8.3 The balance of payments on current account, net capital inflow, and international indebtedness, 1850–1913 (million Pesetas): direct 'residual' estimates

	Exports goods fob	Exports services[a]	Payments domestic labour	Current transfers	Imports goods fob	Imports services[a]	Payments to foreign capital	Commodity balance	Balance of services[a]	Net income from abroad	Net current transfers	Current account balance	Variation in reserves	Net capital inflow	Effective international indebtedness
1850	161.9	8.2	0.2	4.2	169.5	16.6	55.9	−7.6	−8.4	−55.7	4.2	−67.4	22.5	89.9	842.3
1851	142.8	8.4	0.2	4.2	182.1	18.8	49.2	−39.3	−10.3	−49.0	4.2	−94.5	7.3	101.8	944.1
1852	134.6	8.8	0.2	4.3	194.1	18.3	51.3	−59.5	−9.5	−51.0	4.3	−115.8	6.0	121.8	1065.9
1853	185.9	12.8	0.3	5.3	198.0	22.1	47.7	−12.1	−9.3	−47.4	5.3	−63.6	7.7	71.3	1137.2
1854	229.5	16.4	0.3	6.1	217.5	31.4	47.8	12.0	−15.0	−47.5	6.1	−44.4	29.1	73.4	1210.6
1855	322.0	16.4	0.3	6.4	237.0	40.9	43.3	85.0	−24.5	−43.0	6.4	24.0	44.2	20.3	1230.9
1856	319.4	20.4	0.4	7.1	291.9	57.0	42.2	27.5	−36.6	−41.8	7.1	−43.9	47.8	91.6	1322.5
1857	318.1	22.5	0.5	8.0	337.0	76.5	40.7	−19.0	−53.9	−40.2	8.0	−105.2	18.2	123.3	1445.9
1858	179.9	18.9	0.5	8.0	345.4	69.8	43.9	−165.5	−50.9	−43.4	8.0	−251.8	−10.6	241.2	1687.1
1859	236.9	15.3	0.5	8.4	297.0	49.5	45.8	−60.1	−34.2	−45.3	8.4	−131.1	45.4	176.5	1863.6
1860	262.9	61.7	0.5	8.6	308.5	52.2	51.6	−45.7	9.4	−51.1	8.6	−78.8	54.5	133.3	1996.9
1861	281.0	35.1	0.5	8.6	325.8	51.7	50.1	−44.8	−16.5	−49.6	8.6	−102.4	79.7	182.0	2178.9
1862	235.0	20.0	0.8	9.9	360.9	59.2	55.9	−125.9	−39.2	−55.1	9.9	−210.3	66.7	277.0	2455.9
1863	236.9	21.9	0.7	9.5	443.0	71.3	51.2	−206.1	−49.5	−50.4	9.5	−296.5	−7.8	288.6	2744.5
1864	219.9	33.1	0.8	9.8	427.9	75.4	72.8	−208.0	−42.4	−72.1	9.8	−312.7	6.6	319.3	3063.8
1865	250.2	22.4	0.8	10.5	381.5	60.5	51.8	−131.3	−38.1	−51.0	10.5	−210.0	60.3	270.3	3334.1
1866	267.0	21.1	0.9	12.7	380.3	59.6	67.9	−113.4	−38.5	−66.9	12.7	−206.1	28.1	234.2	3568.3
1867	367.4	19.9	1.0	13.4	299.9	48.5	66.4	67.5	−28.6	−65.4	13.4	−13.1	63.7	76.8	3645.1
1868	374.4	23.7	1.0	14.6	343.3	65.4	83.3	31.1	−41.7	−82.3	14.6	−78.3	32.3	110.6	3755.7
1869	429.3	21.9	1.2	16.9	304.5	52.8	113.5	124.8	−30.9	−112.3	16.9	−1.4	65.8	67.2	3822.9
1870	334.2	21.1	1.2	17.3	322.7	53.0	113.2	11.5	−31.9	−112.1	17.3	−115.1	102.4	217.5	4040.4
1871	433.1	32.3	1.1	16.9	382.8	57.9	126.6	50.3	−25.6	−125.5	16.9	−83.9	77.6	161.5	4201.9
1872	493.2	29.8	1.7	19.4	479.5	68.1	137.6	13.7	−38.4	−135.9	19.4	−141.1	93.6	234.7	4436.6

1873	582.5	33.4	2.1	22.1	406.5	55.9	140.1	176.0	−22.5	−138.0	22.1	37.7	123.8	86.1	4522.7
1874	506.7	28.6	2.6	28.0	497.5	71.8	193.9	9.2	−43.3	−191.3	28.0	−197.3	45.5	242.9	4765.6
1875	537.9	26.6	2.4	25.9	423.4	60.0	191.9	114.6	−33.4	−189.5	25.9	−82.4	12.6	95.0	4860.6
1876	451.7	28.2	3.4	29.8	521.2	73.1	112.9	−69.5	−44.9	−109.5	29.8	−194.2	7.5	201.7	5062.3
1877	566.4	29.5	3.5	31.0	457.5	68.9	123.7	109.0	−39.4	−120.2	31.0	−19.7	−5.8	13.9	5076.2
1878	534.2	29.6	1.6	25.1	433.1	69.0	126.4	101.1	−39.3	−124.8	25.1	−37.9	4.9	42.8	5119.0
1879	540.7	31.6	2.9	26.9	493.1	81.2	123.8	47.6	−49.6	−120.9	26.9	−96.0	−21.2	74.8	5193.7
1880	734.5	39.5	3.1	26.3	502.9	86.3	136.2	231.6	−46.8	−133.1	26.3	78.0	−39.5	−117.5	5076.2
1881	755.6	42.8	1.7	24.7	575.9	93.7	173.0	179.7	−50.9	−171.3	24.7	−17.8	−35.8	−18.0	5058.2
1882	764.0	47.1	2.9	28.7	613.1	92.6	187.5	150.9	−45.5	−184.6	28.7	−50.5	38.1	88.6	5146.8
1883	831.1	31.7	2.8	31.8	650.2	90.6	208.7	181.0	−58.9	−205.9	31.8	−52.0	−31.5	20.5	5167.3
1884	718.4	32.3	2.7	33.3	572.1	78.5	192.6	146.3	−46.1	−189.9	33.3	−56.4	−10.8	45.6	5212.9
1885	760.0	35.6	3.1	29.3	579.6	72.2	199.2	180.4	−36.6	−196.1	29.3	−23.0	−27.9	−4.9	5208.0
1886	817.9	41.1	4.9	36.6	586.0	80.0	203.1	232.0	−39.0	−198.2	36.6	31.4	−30.2	−61.6	5146.4
1887	753.2	44.1	5.0	47.5	565.9	84.2	193.1	187.2	−40.1	−188.1	47.5	6.5	−46.0	−52.5	5093.9
1888	810.1	49.2	5.4	59.5	621.7	99.6	218.0	188.4	−50.4	−212.7	59.5	−15.2	−27.8	−12.6	5081.3
1889	834.3	57.0	5.9	84.1	693.0	113.8	217.3	141.2	−56.8	−211.3	84.1	−42.8	−45.1	−2.3	5079.0
1890	867.2	53.5	3.5	65.2	701.3	92.2	224.2	166.0	−38.7	−220.8	65.2	−28.3	−11.0	17.3	5096.3
1891	933.7	50.6	4.6	76.3	669.0	91.2	214.0	264.8	−40.6	−209.4	76.3	91.1	−6.1	−97.2	4999.2
1892	931.9	51.7	5.2	93.7	661.1	84.1	198.9	270.8	−32.4	−193.7	93.7	138.4	−32.7	−171.1	4828.1
1893	881.3	52.5	5.3	106.6	658.9	85.3	201.3	222.5	−32.8	−196.0	106.6	100.3	−19.9	−120.2	4707.9
1894	899.0	55.0	7.2	89.2	675.5	85.5	199.3	223.5	−30.5	−192.1	89.2	90.1	−4.9	−95.0	4613.0
1895	861.8	47.8	3.9	65.7	574.3	67.5	191.9	287.4	−19.7	−188.0	65.7	145.4	−52.6	−198.0	4414.9
1896	1067.7	63.0	5.4	79.1	637.1	89.4	218.2	430.6	−26.4	−212.8	79.1	270.5	−7.6	−278.1	4136.8
1897	1127.0	72.4	5.2	88.1	689.4	95.6	246.2	437.6	−23.2	−241.0	88.1	261.5	−9.8	−271.3	3865.5
1898	1272.3	69.2	5.6	100.4	709.2	92.5	298.0	563.2	−23.4	−292.4	100.4	347.8	291.8	−56.0	3809.5
1899	1058.3	89.9	6.4	94.7	910.0	114.9	342.2	148.2	−25.0	−335.8	94.7	−117.9	161.5	279.4	4088.9

(continued)

Table 8.3 (continued)

	Exports goods fob	Exports services[a]	Payments domestic labour	Current transfers	Imports goods fob	Imports services[a]	Payments to foreign capital	Commodity balance	Balance of services[a]	Net income from abroad	Net current transfers	Current account balance	Variation in reserves	Net capital inflow	Effective international indebtedness
1900	1181.1	129.4	6.9	104.2	1003.2	122.3	348.3	177.9	7.1	−341.4	104.2	−52.2	−8.1	44.1	4133.0
1901	1104.5	87.5	6.6	108.2	1053.6	99.6	291.7	50.9	−12.1	−285.1	108.2	−138.2	−63.5	74.7	4207.6
1902	1103.5	97.0	7.4	94.1	1006.7	88.7	295.1	96.7	8.2	−287.7	94.1	−88.5	113.8	202.3	4410.0
1903	1152.0	103.9	8.0	108.7	1084.3	101.9	302.7	67.6	2.0	−294.7	108.7	−116.4	−9.5	106.9	4516.8
1904	1202.0	104.7	11.2	145.7	1090.6	110.5	315.8	111.4	−5.8	−304.6	145.7	−53.3	−78.2	−24.9	4491.9
1905	1318.5	125.1	12.5	180.0	1116.1	143.4	320.1	202.4	−18.2	−307.6	180.0	56.5	−35.3	−91.8	4400.1
1906	1323.5	94.7	9.9	196.5	967.0	117.3	371.2	356.5	−22.6	−361.2	196.5	169.2	1.3	−167.9	4232.3
1907	1405.1	86.7	9.3	217.2	956.2	112.5	412.4	448.9	−25.8	−403.1	217.2	237.2	−68.7	−305.9	3926.3
1908	1140.6	77.8	11.8	275.0	937.5	115.3	317.8	203.1	−37.4	−306.0	275.0	134.7	−3.2	−137.9	3788.5
1909	1120.8	78.2	9.7	279.2	854.5	103.4	324.9	266.3	−25.2	−315.3	279.2	205.0	34.8	−170.2	3618.3
1910	1237.6	97.7	12.8	328.8	936.8	123.1	321.4	300.8	−25.5	−308.6	328.8	295.5	22.1	−273.4	3344.8
1911	1377.8	104.4	12.7	339.9	1110.6	144.1	285.2	267.1	−39.8	−272.4	339.9	294.8	14.0	−280.8	3064.0
1912	1490.7	129.3	17.2	395.8	1158.5	182.4	322.6	332.2	−53.1	−305.4	395.8	369.5	167.3	−202.2	2861.8
1913	1524.3	135.4	15.9	370.3	1380.6	156.4	383.8	143.7	−21.0	−367.9	370.3	125.1	50.9	−74.2	2787.6

[a]Excluding factor payments

Sources: See text

Table 8.4 Investment and saving, 1850–1913 (million Pesetas and % GDP): direct estimates

	(million Pesetas)						(% GDP)						(% Gross investment)	
	Gross investment	Current account balance	Gross saving	Government saving	Private saving	Net capital inflow	Gross investment	Current account balance	Gross saving	Government saving	Private saving	Net capital inflow	Current account balance (negative)	Net capital inflow
1850	232.3	−67.4	164.8	4.0	160.8	89.9	5.5	−1.6	3.9	0.1	3.8	2.1	29.0	38.7
1851	258.3	−94.5	163.8	−27.0	190.8	101.8	5.9	−2.2	3.8	−0.6	4.4	2.3	36.6	39.4
1852	297.7	−115.8	181.9	−10.0	191.9	121.8	6.8	−2.6	4.2	−0.2	4.4	2.8	38.9	40.9
1853	300.8	−63.6	237.2	−11.0	248.2	71.3	5.8	−1.2	4.6	−0.2	4.8	1.4	21.1	23.7
1854	264.3	−44.4	220.0	−27.0	247.0	73.4	5.0	−0.8	4.1	−0.5	4.6	1.4	16.8	27.8
1855	230.4	24.0	254.4	−52.0	306.4	20.3	4.1	0.4	4.5	−0.9	5.4	0.4	−10.4	8.8
1856	304.3	−43.9	260.4	−66.0	326.4	91.6	5.4	−0.8	4.7	−1.2	5.8	1.6	14.4	30.1
1857	370.1	−105.2	264.9	−54.0	318.9	123.3	6.9	−1.9	4.9	−1.0	5.9	2.3	28.4	33.3
1858	513.2	−251.8	261.4	−42.0	303.4	241.2	9.8	−4.8	5.0	−0.8	5.8	4.6	49.1	47.0
1859	539.9	−131.1	408.8	6.0	402.8	176.5	9.6	−2.3	7.3	0.1	7.2	3.1	24.3	32.7
1860	642.2	−78.8	563.4	−65.0	628.4	133.3	10.8	−1.3	9.5	−1.1	10.5	2.2	12.3	20.8
1861	588.0	−102.4	485.7	−131.0	616.7	182.0	9.7	−1.7	8.0	−2.2	10.1	3.0	17.4	31.0
1862	632.1	−210.3	421.8	−130.0	551.8	277.0	10.1	−3.4	6.7	−2.1	8.8	4.4	33.3	43.8
1863	617.4	−296.5	320.9	−121.0	441.9	288.6	9.4	−4.5	4.9	−1.8	6.7	4.4	48.0	46.8
1864	548.2	−312.7	235.5	−186.0	421.5	319.3	8.3	−4.8	3.6	−2.8	6.4	4.9	57.0	58.2
1865	464.9	−210.0	255.0	−139.0	394.0	270.3	7.5	−3.4	4.1	−2.2	6.4	4.4	45.2	58.1
1866	458.9	−206.1	252.8	−101.0	353.8	234.2	6.9	−3.1	3.8	−1.5	5.3	3.5	44.9	51.0
1867	482.6	−13.1	469.5	−118.0	587.5	76.8	6.8	−0.2	6.6	−1.7	8.3	1.1	2.7	15.9
1868	275.1	−78.3	196.8	−149.0	345.8	110.6	4.6	−1.3	3.3	−2.5	5.8	1.9	28.5	40.2
1869	264.0	−1.4	262.6	−270.0	532.6	67.2	4.8	0.0	4.8	−4.9	9.7	1.2	0.5	25.5
1870	313.4	−115.1	198.3	−331.0	529.3	217.5	5.2	−1.9	3.3	−5.5	8.9	3.6	36.7	69.4
1871	367.1	−83.9	283.2	−238.0	521.2	161.5	5.7	−1.3	4.4	−3.7	8.1	2.5	22.9	44.0

(continued)

Table 8.4 (continued)

	(million Pesetas)						(% GDP)						(% Gross investment)	
	Gross investment	Current account balance	Gross saving	Government saving	Private saving	Net capital inflow	Gross investment	Current account balance	Gross saving	Government saving	Private saving	Net capital inflow	Current account balance (negative)	Net capital inflow
1872	413.4	−141.1	272.3	−219.0	491.3	234.7	5.6	−1.9	3.7	−3.0	6.7	3.2	34.1	56.8
1873	374.3	37.7	411.9	−227.0	638.9	86.1	4.8	0.5	5.3	−2.9	8.2	1.1	−10.1	23.0
1874	423.2	−197.3	225.9	−10.0	235.9	242.9	5.4	−2.5	2.9	−0.1	3.0	3.1	46.6	57.4
1875	424.6	−82.4	342.2	−111.0	453.2	95.0	5.5	−1.1	4.4	−1.4	5.9	1.2	19.4	22.4
1876	526.2	−194.2	332.0	6.0	326.0	201.7	6.6	−2.4	4.1	0.1	4.1	2.5	36.9	38.3
1877	532.0	−19.7	512.3	−13.0	525.3	13.9	6.0	−0.2	5.8	−0.1	6.0	0.2	3.7	2.6
1878	628.4	−37.9	590.5	−30.0	620.5	42.8	7.2	−0.4	6.8	−0.3	7.1	0.5	6.0	6.8
1879	479.9	−96.0	383.9	−78.0	461.9	74.8	5.6	−1.1	4.5	−0.9	5.4	0.9	20.0	15.6
1880	595.2	78.0	673.2	−58.0	731.2	−117.5	6.6	0.9	7.5	−0.6	8.1	−1.3	−13.1	−19.7
1881	503.7	−17.8	486.0	−1.0	487.0	−18.0	5.3	−0.2	5.1	0.0	5.2	−0.2	3.5	−3.6
1882	612.7	−50.5	562.1	31.0	531.1	88.6	6.1	−0.5	5.6	0.3	5.3	0.9	8.2	14.5
1883	712.9	−52.0	660.8	−45.0	705.8	20.5	7.0	−0.5	6.5	−0.4	6.9	0.2	7.3	2.9
1884	682.0	−56.4	625.7	−28.0	653.7	45.6	7.0	−0.6	6.4	−0.3	6.7	0.5	8.3	6.7
1885	490.5	−23.0	467.5	−82.0	549.5	−4.9	5.1	−0.2	4.8	−0.9	5.7	−0.1	4.7	−1.0
1886	444.2	31.4	475.6	−15.0	490.6	−61.6	4.5	0.3	4.8	−0.2	5.0	−0.6	−7.1	−13.9
1887	420.8	6.5	427.3	−73.0	500.3	−52.5	4.7	0.1	4.8	−0.8	5.6	−0.6	−1.5	−12.5
1888	386.0	−15.2	370.8	−122.0	492.8	−12.6	4.1	−0.2	3.9	−1.3	5.2	−0.1	3.9	−3.3
1889	438.4	−42.8	395.6	−67.0	462.6	−2.3	5.0	−0.5	4.5	−0.8	5.3	0.0	9.8	−0.5
1890	488.8	−28.3	460.5	−50.0	510.5	17.3	5.5	−0.3	5.2	−0.6	5.8	0.2	5.8	3.5
1891	472.6	91.1	563.7	−54.0	617.7	−97.2	5.2	1.0	6.3	−0.6	6.9	−1.1	−19.3	−20.6
1892	485.7	138.4	624.1	−19.0	643.1	−171.1	5.4	1.5	7.0	−0.2	7.2	−1.9	−28.5	−35.2
1893	481.3	100.3	581.5	75.0	506.5	−120.2	5.5	1.2	6.7	0.9	5.8	−1.4	−20.8	−25.0

1894	477.9	90.1	567.9	6.0	561.9	−95.0	5.6	1.1	6.7	0.1	6.6	−1.1	−18.8	−19.9
1895	523.9	145.4	669.3	−26.0	695.3	−198.0	6.1	1.7	7.8	−0.3	8.1	−2.3	−27.8	−37.8
1896	524.3	270.5	794.8	40.0	754.8	−278.1	6.4	3.3	9.7	0.5	9.2	−3.4	−51.6	−53.0
1897	564.5	261.5	826.0	−54.0	880.0	−271.3	6.3	2.9	9.3	−0.6	9.9	−3.0	−46.3	−48.1
1898	599.4	347.8	947.2	8.0	939.2	−56.0	6.3	3.6	9.9	0.1	9.8	−0.6	−58.0	−9.3
1899	894.1	−117.9	776.2	134.0	642.2	279.4	9.2	−1.2	8.0	1.4	6.6	2.9	13.2	31.2
1900	1150.2	−52.2	1098.0	52.0	1046.0	44.1	11.2	−0.5	10.7	0.5	10.2	0.4	4.5	3.8
1901	893.5	−138.2	755.3	38.0	717.3	74.7	8.3	−1.3	7.0	0.4	6.7	0.7	15.5	8.4
1902	773.1	−88.5	684.6	71.0	613.6	202.3	7.4	−0.8	6.6	0.7	5.9	1.9	11.5	26.2
1903	844.3	−116.4	728.0	23.0	705.0	106.9	7.6	−1.0	6.5	0.2	6.3	1.0	13.8	12.7
1904	905.9	−53.3	852.6	54.0	798.6	−24.9	7.7	−0.5	7.3	0.5	6.8	−0.2	5.9	−2.7
1905	808.4	56.5	864.9	72.0	792.9	−91.8	7.1	0.5	7.6	0.6	7.0	−0.8	−7.0	−11.4
1906	849.4	169.2	1018.6	103.0	915.6	−167.9	7.3	1.5	8.8	0.9	7.9	−1.5	−19.9	−19.8
1907	978.8	237.2	1216.0	65.0	1151.0	−305.9	8.1	2.0	10.1	0.5	9.6	−2.5	−24.2	−31.3
1908	929.3	134.7	1063.9	56.0	1007.9	−137.9	7.8	1.1	8.9	0.5	8.4	−1.2	−14.5	−14.8
1909	1015.9	205.0	1220.9	−51.0	1271.9	−170.2	8.3	1.7	10.0	−0.4	10.4	−1.4	−20.2	−16.8
1910	1145.1	295.5	1440.7	−6.0	1446.7	−273.4	9.8	2.5	12.3	−0.1	12.4	−2.3	−25.8	−23.9
1911	1245.7	294.8	1540.5	6.0	1534.5	−280.8	9.9	2.3	12.2	0.0	12.2	−2.2	−23.7	−22.5
1912	1493.7	369.5	1863.2	−62.0	1925.2	−202.2	11.6	2.9	14.5	−0.5	15.0	−1.6	−24.7	−13.5
1913	1685.0	125.1	1810.1	−71.0	1881.1	−74.2	12.2	0.9	13.1	−0.5	13.6	−0.5	−7.4	−4.4

Sources: See the text and Table 8.1. GDP and Investment, Prados de la Escosura (2017); Public Saving, Comín and Díaz Fuentes (2005)

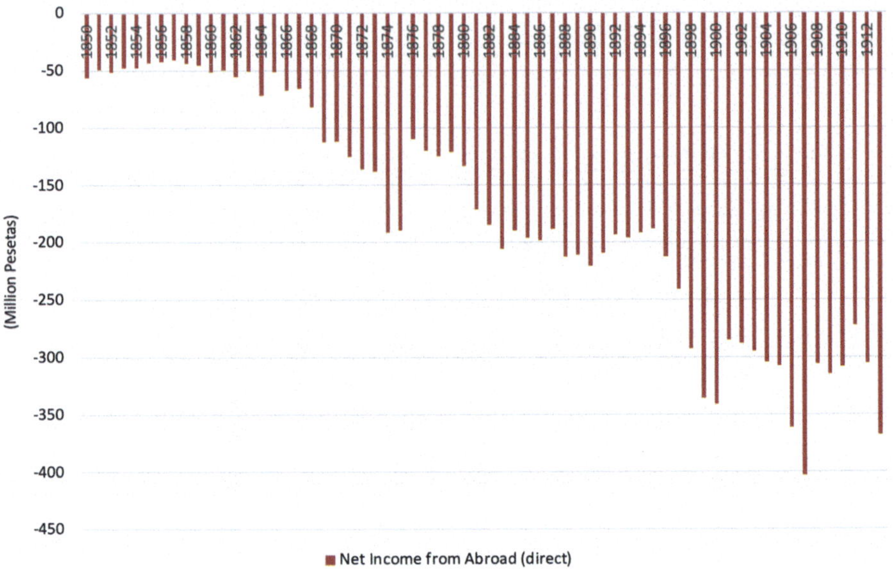

Fig. 8.17 Services trade balance: net income from abroad (million Pesetas). Direct estimates. Sources: See text and Table 8.3

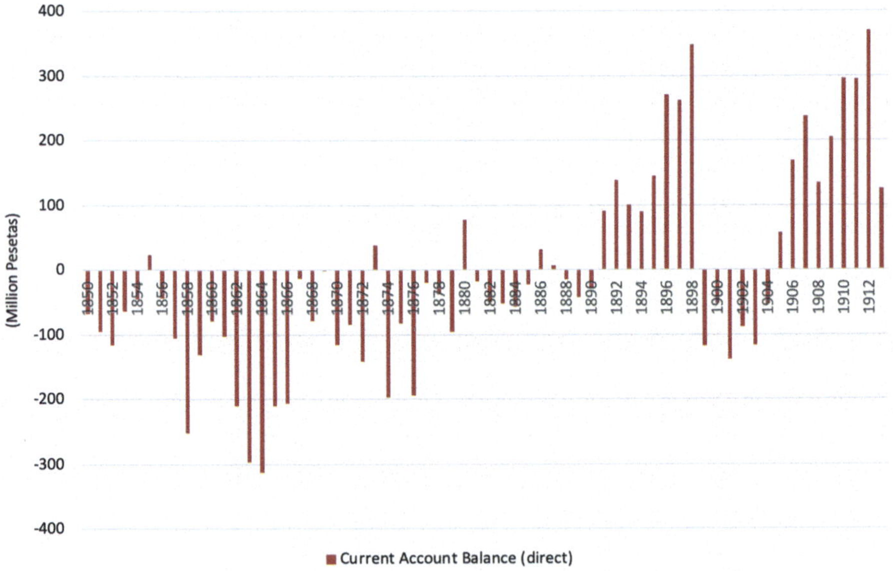

Fig. 8.18 Current account balance: direct estimates (million Pesetas). Sources: See text and Table 8.3

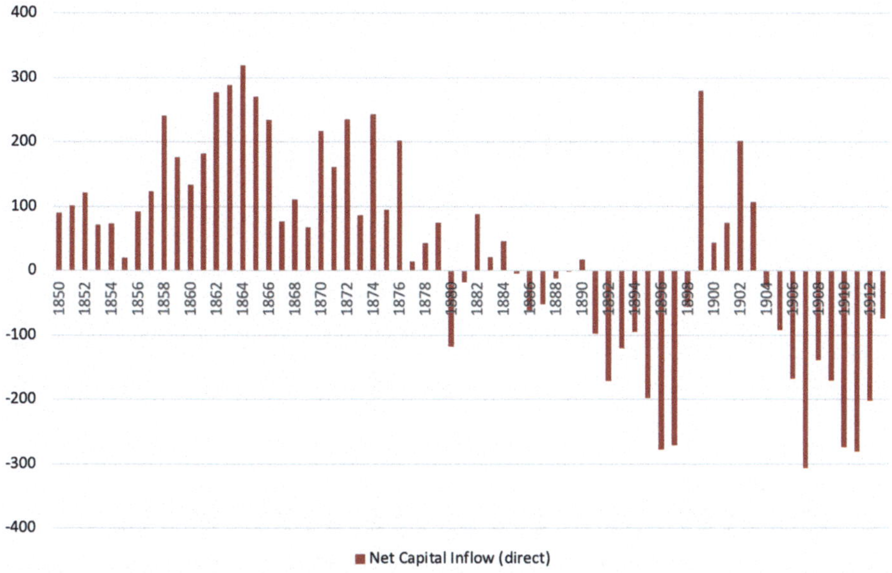

Fig. 8.19 Net capital inflow: direct estimates (million Pesetas). Sources: See text and Table 8.3

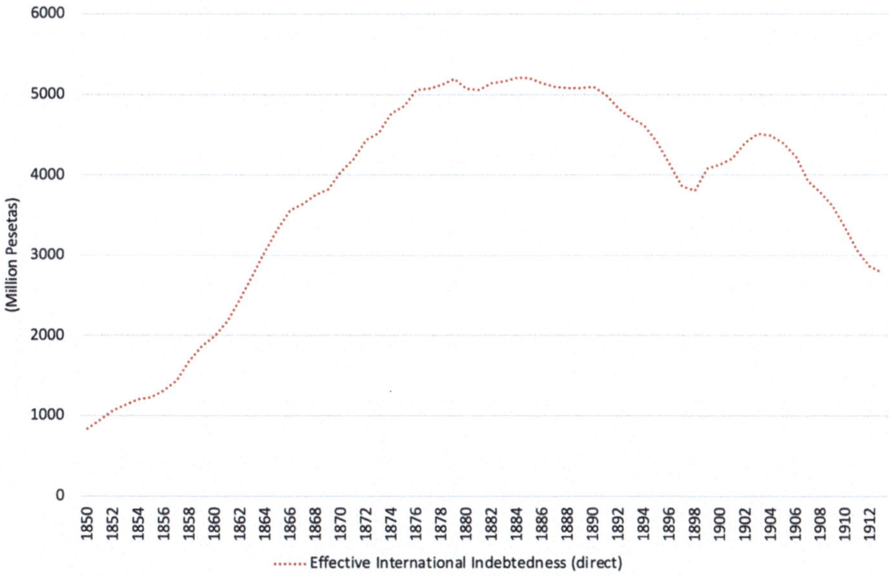

Fig. 8.20 Effective international indebtedness: direct estimates (million Pesetas). Sources: See text and Table 8.3

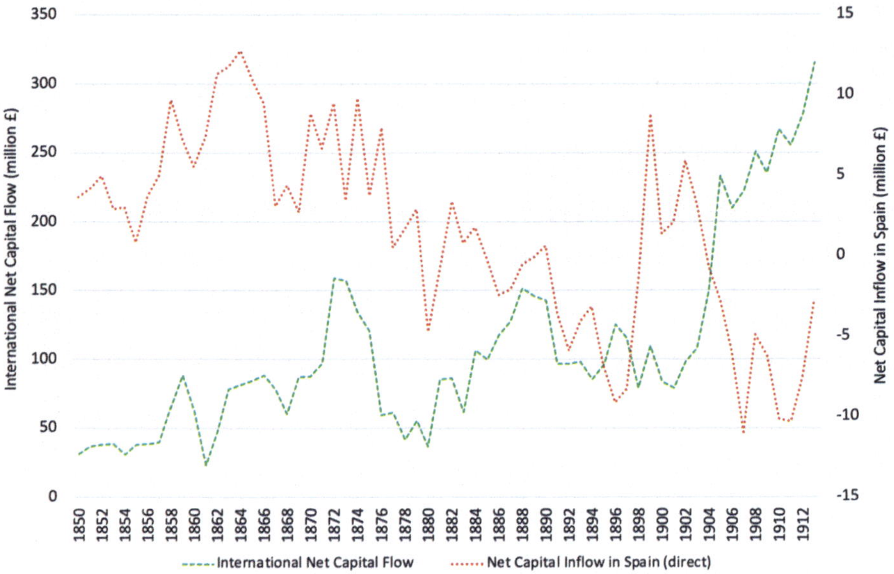

Fig. 8.21 International net capital flow and Spain's net capital inflow (direct estimates) (million £). Sources: See text, Table 8.3, and Jones and Obstfeld (1997)

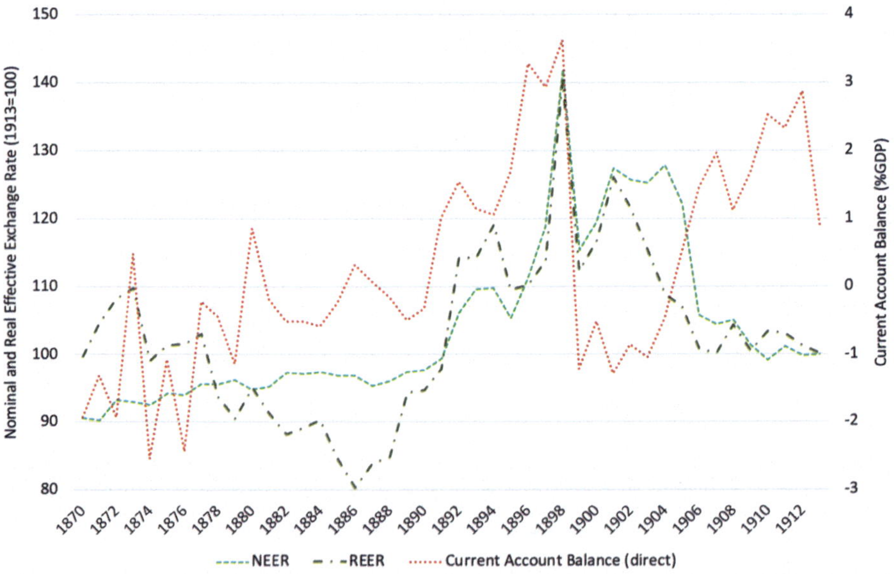

Fig. 8.22 Spain's current account balance (direct estimates) (% GDP) and nominal and real effective exchange rate (1913=100), 1870–1913. Sources: See the text and Table 8.4

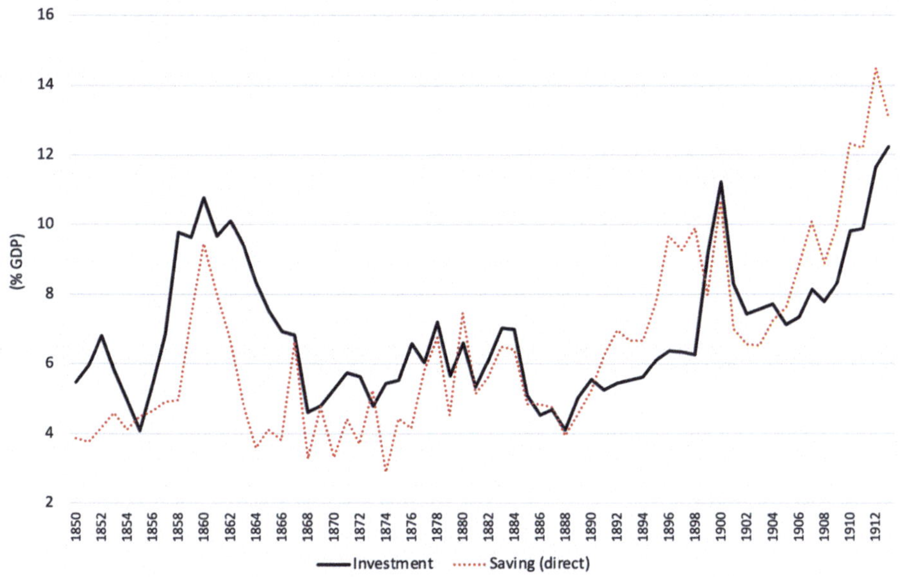

Fig. 8.23 Gross investment and saving (direct estimates) (% GDP). Sources: Investment, Prados de la Escosura (2017); Saving, see the text and Table 8.4

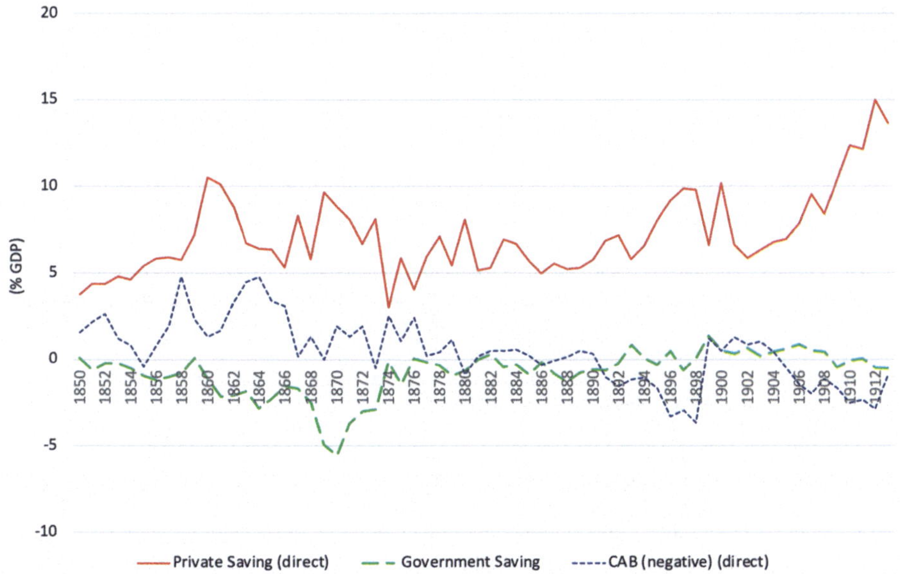

Fig. 8.24 Decomposing gross investment: private and government saving and the (negative of the) current account balance (direct estimates) (% GDP). Sources: Government Saving, Comín and Díaz Fuentes (2005); for the rest, see the text and Table 8.4

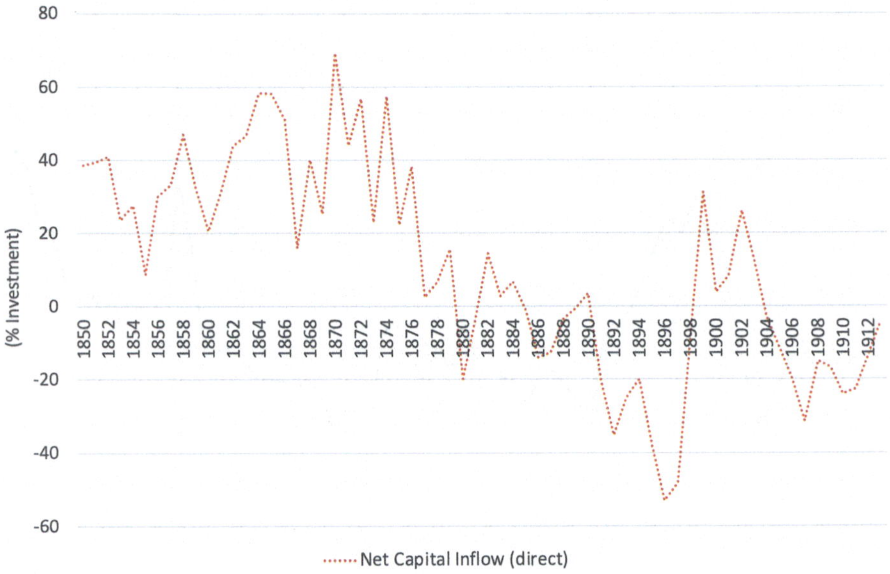

Fig. 8.25 Net capital inflow as a proportion of gross investment (direct estimates) (%). Sources: See the text and Table 8.4

References

Anuario(s) Estadístico(s) de España (varios años), Madrid: INE.

Alzola Y Minondo, P. De (1903), *Informes relativos a tratados de comercio, mejora de los cambios y ley de huelgas*, Bilbao: Liga vizcaína de productores, Imprenta de la Casa de Misericordia.

Anes, R. (1974), "Estimación de la moneda de plata existente en España entre 1874 y 1915", in G. Tortella and P. Schwartz (eds.), *La banca española en la Restauración*. 2 Vols., Madrid: Tecnos, II, pp. 99-116.

Bajo-Rubio, O. (2010), "The Balance-of-Payments Constraint on Economic Growth in a Long-Term Perspective: Spain, 1850-2000", *Explorations In Economic History* 49(1): 105-117.

Blattman, C., J. Hwang, and J.G. Williamson (2007), "Winners and Losers in the Commodity Lottery: The Impact of Terms of Trade Growth and Volatility in the Periphery 1870–1939", *Journal of Development Economics* 82: 156-179.

Bonmatí Antón, J. F. (1989), *La emigración alicantina a Argelia (Siglo XIX Y primer tercio del Siglo XX)*, Alicante: Universidad de Alicante.

Bordo, M.D. and F.E. Kydland (1995), "The Gold Standard as a Rule: An Essay in Exploration", *Explorations In Economic History* 32(4): 423-464.

Bordo, M.D. and H. Rockoff (1996), "The Gold Standard as a 'Good Housekeeping Seal of Approval'", *Journal of Economic History* 56(2): 389-428.

Bordo, M.D., A.F. Cavallo, and C.M. Meissner (2010), "Sudden Stops: Determinants and Output Effects in the First Era of Globalization, 1880-1913", *Journal of Development Economics* 91(1): 227-241.

Brezis, E. S. (1995), "Foreign Capital Flows in the Century of Britain's Industrial Revolution: New Estimates, Controlled Conjectures", *Economic History Review* 48(1): 46-67.

Broder, A. (1976), « Les investissements étrangers en Espagne au XIx^{e} siècle: méthodologie et quantification », *Revue d'Histoire Économique et Sociale* 54(1): 29-63.

Broder, A. (1981), "Le rôle des intérêts étrangers dans la croissance de l'Espagne (1767-1923", Université de Paris IV-Sorbonne, Unpublished Ph.D. Diss.

Calvo, G.A., A. Izquierdo, and E. Talvi (2003), Sudden Stops, the Real Exchange Rate, and Fiscal Sustainability: Argentina's Lessons, N.B.E.R. Working Paper 9828, Cambridge, Ma: National Bureau of Economic Research.

Catalan, J., C. Sudrià, and D. A. Tirado (2001), "Peseta y protección: el debate historiográfico", In C. Sudrià and D. Tirado (eds.), *Peseta y protección. comercio exterior, moneda y crecimiento económico en la España de la restauración*, Barcelona: Editions de la Universitat de Barcelona, pp. 11-42.

Catao, L. (2007), "Sudden Stops and Currency Drops: A Historical Look", in S. Edwards, G. Esquivel, And G. Márquez (eds.), *The Decline of Latin American Economies. Growth, Institutions, and Crisis*. Chicago: Chicago University Press and N.B.E.R., pp. 243-289.

Chamorro, S. (1976), "Bosquejo histórico de la balanza de pagos de España", *Información Comercial Española* 517: 151-159.

Chastagnaret, G. (2000), *L'Espagne, puissance minière dans l'Europe du XIXe siècle*, Madrid: Casa de Velázquez.

Consejo Superior de la Emigración Española (1916), *La Emigración Española Transoceánica, 1911-1915*, Madrid: Hijos de T. Minuesa de los Ríos.

Corden, W. M. (1994), *Economic Policy, Exchange Rates, and the International System*, Chicago: University of Chicago Press.

Cortés Conde, R. (1979), *El progreso argentino 1880-1914*, Buenos Aires: Editorial Sudamericana.

Comín, F. (1996), *Historia de la Hacienda Pública.* II *España (1808-1995)*, Barcelona: Crítica.

Comín, F. (1999), "La reforma en la Hacienda de Fernández Villaverde", in Tedde de Lorca (ed.) (1999), *Economía y colonias en la España del 98*, Madrid: Síntesis, pp. 235-260.

Comín, F. (2004), "El gasto y la industria de defensa en la España contemporánea", *Cuadernos Aragoneses de Economía* 14(2): 297-320.

Comín, F. and D. Díaz Fuentes (2005), "Sector público administrativo y estado del bienestar", in A. Carreras and X. Tafunell (eds.), *Estadísticas Históricas de España. Siglos XIX-XX*, Bilbao: Fundación BBVA, 3 Vols., II, pp. 873-964.

Cubel, A., J. Palafox and C. Sudrià (1998), "Public Deficit, Debt, Monetary Policy and External Equilibrium. Spain, 1880-1930", in V. Bovykine, A. Broder, and R. Maranhao (eds.), *Public Debt, Public Finance, Money and Balance of Payments in Debtor Countries, 1890-1932/33*, Madrid: 12th International Economic History Congress, pp. 73-88.

Díaz García, R. (1976), "Clasificación económica de los gastos e ingresos del Estado (1850-1957), in Instituto De Estudios Fiscales (ed.), *Datos Básicos para la Historia Financiera ee España (1850-1975)*, Madrid: Instituto de Estudios Fiscales, 2 vols., I, pp. 19-627.

Edwards, S. (2004), "Thirty Years of Current Account Imbalances, Current Account Reversals, and Sudden Stops", *IMF Staff Papers*, 51: 1-49.

Eichengreen, B. and R. Hausmann (1999), Exchange Rate Regimes and Financial Fragility, NBER Working Paper 7418.

Escudero, A. (1996), "Pesimistas Y Optimistas Ante El 'Boom' Minero", *Revista de Historia Industrial* 10: 69-91.

Escudero, A. (1998), *Minería e industrialización en Vizcaya*, Barcelona: Crítica Universidad De Alicante.

Fernández Acha, (1976), "La Deuda Pública", in Instituto de Estudios Fiscales (dd.), *Datos básicos para la Historia Financiera de España, 1850-1975*, Madrid: Imprenta De La Fábrica De La Moneda Y Timbre. II.

Fischer, S. (1988), "Real Balances, the Exchange Rate, and Indexation: Real Variables in Disinflation", *Quarterly Journal Of Economics* 103(1): 27–49.

Flandreau, M. and F. Zumer (2004), *The Making of Global Finance 1880-1913*, Paris: OECD.

Fraile Balbín, P. and A. Escribano (1998), "The Spanish 1898 Disaster: The Drift Towards National-Protectionism", in P.K. O'Brien and L. Prados de la Escosura (eds.), The Costs and

Benefits of European Imperialism, special issue of *Revista de Historia Económica* 16(1): 265-290.

García López, J. R. (1992), *Las remesas de emigrantes españoles en América. Siglos XIX y XX*, Colombres: Ediciones Júcar.

González Portilla, M. (1981), *La formación de la sociedad capitalista en el País Vasco (1876-1913)*, 2 Vols. San Sebastián: Haramburu.

Goldsmith, R.W (1955), *A Study of Saving in the United States*, Princeton: Princeton University Press.

Gregory, P.R. (1979), "The Russian Balance of Payments, The Gold Standard, and Monetary Policy: A Historical Example of Foreign Capital Movements", *Journal of Economic History* 39 (2): 379-399.

Gutiérrez, M., A. Herranz, and D. Tirado (1998), "Economic Integration, Growth Potentialities and Balance of Payments Constraints In Some European Peripheral Economies: Spain, Sweden, And Italy, 1870-1913", in G. Federico, J. Ljungberg, K.G. Persson, and L. Schön (eds.), *Integration of Commodity Markets in History*, Madrid: 12th International Economic History Congress, pp. 147-160.

Hartland, P. (1960), "Canadian Balance of Payments since 1868", in W.N. Parker (ed.),*Trends in the American Economy in the Nineteenth Century*, Studies in Income and Wealth, vol. 24, Princeton: Princeton University Press, pp. 717-753.

Harvey, C.E. (1981), *The Rio Tinto Company. An Economic History of a Leading International Mining Concern, 1873-1954*. Penzance: Alison Hodge.

Harvey, C.E. and P. Taylor (1987), "Mineral Wealth and Economic Development: Foreign Direct Investment in Spain, 1815-1913", *Economic History Review* 11(2): 185-207.

Herranz-Loncán, A. and D. Tirado (1996), "La restricción exterior al crecimiento económico español (1870-1913)", *Revista de Historia Económica* 14(1): 11-49.

Homer, S. And R. Sylla (1991), *A History of Interest Rates*. Rutgers, N.J.: Rutgers University Press.

Imlah, A.H. (1952), "The British Balance of Payments and Export of Capital, 1816-1913",*Economic History Review* 5(1): 208-239.

International Monetary Fund [IMF] (1993), *Balance of Payments Manual*, Washington D.C.: International Monetary Fund.

Inspección General De Emigración (1934, 1935): *Estadística general de la emigración española en el año de 1932*, Madrid: Ministerio de Trabajo y Previsión.

Jáinaga, F. (1932), *Balance de pagos internacionales. Año 1931*. Madrid: Gráficas Reunidas. Reprinted in *Revista De Economía Política* 8(2): 586-605.

Jones, M.T. and M. Obstfeld (1997) Saving, Investment, and Gold: A Reassessment of Historical. Current Account Data, N.B.E.R. Working Paper 6103. Database available at http://www.nber.org.strauss.uc3m.es:8080/databases/jones-obstfeld/

Lévy-Leboyer, M. (1977), "La balance des paiements et l'exportation des capitaux français", in M. Lévy-Leboyer (ed.), *La position internationale de la France. Aspects économiques et financiers XIXe-XXe siècles*, Paris: École des Hautes Études en Sciences Sociales, pp. 75-142.

Llordén, M. (1988), "Los inicios de la emigración asturiana a América, 1858-1870", in N. Sánchez-Albornoz (ed.), *Españoles hacia América. La emigración en masa, 1880-1930*, Madrid: Alianza, pp. 53-65.

Maluquer de Motes, J. (1996): "La financiación de la guerra de Cuba y sus consecuencias sobre la economía española. La Deuda Pública", in C. Naranjo, M. A. Puig-Samper, and L. M. García Mora (eds.), *La Nación Soñada: Cuba, Puerto Rico Y Filipinas*, Madrid: Doce Calles, pp. 317-329.

Maluquer de Motes, J. (1999), *España en la crisis de 1898. De la gran depresión a la modernización económica del siglo XX*, Barcelona: Península.

Maluquer de Motes, J. (2006), "La paradisíaca estabilidad de la anteguerra. elaboración de un índice de precios de consumo de España, 1830-1936", *Revista de Historia Económica/Journal of Iberian and Latin American Economic History* 24(2): 333-382.

Martín Aceña, P. (1989), (1989), "Sector financiero", in A. Carreras (ed.), Estadísticas Históricas de España. Siglos XIX-XX, Madrid: Fundación Banco Exterior, pp. 363-394.

Marolla, M. and M. Roccas (1992), "La ricostruzione della bilancia internazionale dei servizi i trasferimenti unilaterali dell'anno 1911", in G. Rey (ed.), *I conti economici dell'Italia.* II. *Una stima del valore aggiunto per il 1911*, Roma: Laterza, pp. 241-282.

Martín-Aceña, P. (1993), "Spain during the Classical Gold Standard Years, 1880-1914", in M.D. Bordo and F. Capie (eds.), *Monetary Regimes in Transition*, Cambridge: Cambridge University Press, pp. 135-172.

Martín-Aceña, P. and M. A. Pons (2005), "Sistema Monetario Financiero", in A. Carreras and X. Tafunell (eds.), *Estadísticas Históricas De España. Siglos XIX-XX*, Bilbao: Fundación BBVA, 3 Vols., II, pp. 645-706.

Martínez Ruiz, E. (2003), *El sector exterior durante la Autarquía. Una reconstrucción de las balanzas de pagos de España (1940-1958)*, Madrid: Banco de España, Estudios De Historia Económica 43.

Martínez Ruiz, E. (2006), *Guerra Civil, comercio y capital extranjero. El sector exterior de la economía española (1936-1939)*, Madrid: Banco de España, Estudios de Historia Económica 49.

Mitchell, B.R. (1988), *British Historical Statistics*, Cambridge: Cambridge University Press.

Moro, A., G. Nuño, P. Tedde (2015), "A Twin Crisis with Multiple Banks of Issue: Spain in the 1860s"*European Review of Economic History* 19: 171-194.

Muñoz, J., S. Roldán, and A. Serrano (1976), "Minería y capital extranjero", *Información Comercial Española* 514: 59-89.

Muñoz, J., S. Roldán, and A. Serrano (1978), "La involución nacionalista y la vertebración del capitalismo español", *Cuadernos Económicos de ICE* 5: 13-221.

Nadal, J. (1975), *El fracaso de la revolución industrial en España, 1814-1913*. Barcelona: Ariel.

Nicolau, R. (2005): "Población, salud y actividad", in A. Carreras and X. Tafunell (eds.), *Estadísticas Históricas de España. Siglos XIX-XX*. Bilbao: Fundación BBVA, 3 Vols., I, pp. 77-154.

North, D.C. (1960), "The United States Balance of Payments, 1790-1860", in W.N. Parker (ed.), *Trends in the American Economy in the Nineteenth Century*, Studies in Income and Wealth, Vol. 24, Princeton: Princeton University Press, pp. 573-627.

North, D.C. and A. Heston (1960), "The Estimation of Shipping Earnings in Historical Studies of the Balance of Payments", *Canadian Journal of Economics and Political Science* 26: 265-276.

Obstfeld, M. and A.M. Taylor (2004), *Global Capital Markets: Integration, Crisis and Growth,* Cambridge: Cambridge University Press.

Ojeda, A. de (1988), *Índices de precios en España en el período 1913-1987*, Madrid: Banco de España. Estudios de Historia Económica 17.

O'Rourke, K.H. and J.G. Williamson (1999), *Globalization and History. The Evolution of a Nineteenth Century Atlantic Economy*, Cambridge: MIT Press.

Paolera, G. della (1988), How the Argentine Economy Performed during the International Gold Standard: A Re-Examination, University Of Chicago, Unpublished Ph.D. Dissertation.

Piqueras Arenas, J. A. (1998), "Mercados protegidos y consumo desigual. Cuba y el capitalismo español entre 1878 y 1898", *Revista de Historia Económica* 16(1): 747-779.

Prados De La Escosura, L. (1982), *comercio exterior y crecimiento económico en España, 1826-1913: Tendencias a largo `lazo*, Madrid: Banco e España, Estudios de Historia Económica 7.

Prados De La Escosura, L. (1986), "Una serie anual del comercio exterior español (1821-1913)", *Revista de Historia Económica* 4(1): 103-150.

Prados De La Escosura, L. (1988), *De Imperio a Nación. Crecimiento y atraso económico en España (1780-1930)*, Madrid: Alianza.

Prados De La Escosura, L. y A. Tena (1994), "Protectionism in Spain, 1869-1930", in P.H. Lindert, J.V. Nye, and J.M. Chevet (eds.), *Political Economy of Protectionism and Commerce, 18th-20th Centuries*. Milano: Bocconi, pp. 63-76.

Prados de la Escosura, L. (2017), *Spanish Economic Growth*, 1850-2015, London: Palgrave Macmillan. https://www.palgrave.com/la/book/9783319580418
Reher, D. S. and E. Ballesteros (1993): "Precios y salarios en Castilla La Nueva: La construcción de un índice de salarios reales, 1501-1991", *Revista de Historia Económica* 11(1): 101-151.
Sabaté Sort, M., M.D. Gadea and R. Escario (2006), "Does Fiscal Policy Influence Monetary Policy? The Case of Spain, 1874–1935", *Explorations In Economic History* 43: 309–331.
Sánchez-Alonso, B. (1995), *Las causas de la emigración española, 1880-1930*, Madrid: Alianza.
Sánchez-Alonso, B. (2000), "European Emigration in the Late Nineteenth Century: The Paradoxical Case of Spain", *Economic History Review* 53(2): 309-330.
Sachs, J. (1981), "The Current Account and Macroeconomic Adjustment in the 1970s", Brookings Papers on Economic Activity 1: 201-282.
Sardá Dexeus, J. (1948), *La política monetaria y las fluctuaciones de la economía española en el siglo XIX,* Madrid: Instituto Sancho de Moncada, CSIC.
Serrano Sanz, J.M. (1997), "Sector exterior y desarrollo en la economía española contemporánea", *Papeles ee Economía Española* 73: 308-339.
Simon, M. (1960), "The United States Balance Of Payments, 1861-1900", in W.N. Parker (ed.), *Trends in the American Economy in the Nineteenth Century*, Studies in Income and Wealth, Vol. 24, Princeton: Princeton University Press, pp. 629-715.
Smits, J.P., E. Horlings and J.L. Van Zanden (2000): *The Measurement of Gross National Product and its Components*, Groningen: Growth and Development Centre.
Stone, I. (1999), *The Global Export of Capital from Great Britain, 1865-1914. A Statistical Survey*, London: Macmillan.
Tedde De Lorca, P. (1978), "Las compañías ferroviarias en España, 1855-1935", in M. Artola (ed.) *Los Ferrocarriles en España, 1844-1943*, 2 vols., Madrid: Tecnos, II, pp. 9-354.
Tedde De Lorca, P. (1980), "La Compañía de los Ferrocarriles Andaluces (1878-1920): una empresa de transportes en la España de la restauración", *Investigaciones Económicas* 12: 27-76.
Tedde, P. (1999), "La economía española entorno al 98", in P. Tedde (ed.),*Economía y colonias en la España del 98*, Madrid: Síntesis, pp. 73-98.
Tedde, P. (2015), *El Banco de España y el Estado Liberal (1847-1874)*, Madrid: Gadir.
Temine, E., A. Broder, and G. Chastagnaret (1982), *Historia de la España contemporánea. Desde 1808 hasta nuestrosdDías.* Barcelona: Ariel.
Tena Junguito, A. (1989), "Comercio Exterior", in A. Carreras (ed.), *Estadísticas Históricas de España. Siglos XIX-XX*, Madrid: Fundación Banco Exterior, pp. 329-359.
Tena Junguito, A. (1992), *Las estadísticas históricas del comercio internacional: fiabilidad y comparabilidad*, Madrid: Banco de España. Estudios de Historia Económica 24.
Thirlwall, A.P. (1979), "The Balance of Payments Constraint as an Explanation of International Growth Rate Differences", *Banca Nazionale Del Lavoro Quarterly Review* 128: 44-53.
Thirlwall, A.P. and M.N. Hussain (1982), "The Balance of Payments Constraint, Capital Flows and Growth Rate Differences Between Developing Countries", *Oxford Economic Papers* 34(3): 498-509.
Tortella, G. (1974), "Estimación del 'stock' de oro En España (1874-1914)", in G. Tortella and P. Schwartz (eds.), *La banca española en la Restauración.* 2 Vols., Madrid: Tecnos, II, pp. 117-139.
Tortella, G. (1981), "La economía española, 1830-1900", in M. Tuñón de Lara (ed.),*Historia de España*. VIII. *Revolución burguesa, oligarquía y constitucionalismo (1834-1923),* Barcelona: Labor, pp. 11-167.
Tortella, G. (1994), *El desarrollo de la España contemporánea. Historia económica de los siglos XIX y XX*, Madrid: Alianza.
Valdaliso, J.M. (1991), *Los navieros vascos y la marina mercante en España, 1860-1935. Una historia económica*, Bilbao: Instituto Vasco de Administración Pública.
Vázquez, A. (1988), "La emigración gallega. Migrantes, transporte y remesas", in N. Sánchez-Albornoz (ed.), *Españoles hacia América. La emigración en masa, 1880-1930*, Madrid: Alianza, pp. 80-104.

Vicens Vives, J. (1959):,*Manual de historia económica de España*, Barcelona: Teide.
Vilar, J. B. (1989), *Los españoles en la Argelia francesa (1840-1914)*. Murcia: C.S.I.C. / Universidad De Murcia.
Williamson, J.G. (1964), *American Growth and the Balance of Payments, 1820-1913*, Chapel Hill: University of North Carolina Press.
Williamson, J.G. (1995), "The Evolution of Global Labor Markets Since 1830: Background Evidence and Hypotheses", *Explorations In Economic History* 32: 141-196.
Yáñez Gallardo, C. (1994), *La emigración española a América (Siglos XIX y XX). Dimensión y características cuantitativas*, Colombres: Fundación Archivo de Indianos.
Zanetti, O. y A. García (1977), *United Fruit Company: Un caso de dominio imperialista en Cuba*, La Habana: Ediciones de Ciencias Sociales.

SPRINGER NATURE

GPSR Compliance

The European Union's (EU) General Product Safety Regulation (GPSR) is a set of rules that requires consumer products to be safe and our obligations to ensure this.

If you have any concerns about our products, you can contact us on ProductSafety@springernature.com

In case Publisher is established outside the EU, the EU authorized representative is:

Springer Nature Customer Service Center GmbH
Europaplatz 3
69115 Heidelberg, Germany

The manufacturer's authorised representative in the EU is Springer Nature Customer Service Centre GmbH, Europaplatz 3, 69115 Heidelberg, Germany. If you have any concerns regarding our products, please contact ProductSafety@springernature.com

Printed and bound by CPI Group (UK) Ltd, Croydon, CR0 4YY
01/10/2026
02225852-0017